POLICY STUDIES REVIEW ANNUAL
Volume 6

EDITORIAL ADVISORY BOARD

Clark C. Abt, *Abt Associates, Cambridge, Massachusetts*
Robert F. Boruch, *Department of Psychology, Northwestern University*
Eleanor Chelimsky, *Institute for Program Evaluation, General Accounting Office*
John P. Crecine, *College of Humanities and Social Sciences, Carnegie-Mellon University*
Lois-ellin Datta, *National Institute of Education, Washington, D.C.*
Bleddyn Davies, *Personal Social Services Research Unit, University of Kent at Canterbury, England*
Yehezkel Dror, *Faculty of Social Sciences, Hebrew University of Jerusalem, Israel*
Carroll L. Estes, *Department of Social and Behavioral Sciences, University of California, San Francisco*
Amitai Etzioni, *Center for Policy Research, Washington, D.C.*
Howard E. Freeman, *Institute for Social Science Research, University of California, Los Angeles*
Robert W. Haley, *Bureau of Epidemiology, Center for Disease Control, Atlanta, Georgia*
Robert Haveman, *Department of Economics, University of Wisconsin—Madison*
Harold Hodgkinson, *National Training Laboratories, Arlington, Virginia*
Irving Louis Horowitz, *Department of Sociology, Livingston College, Rutgers University*
Dorothy James, *Department of Political Science, Virginia Polytechnic Institute and State University*
Charles O. Jones, *Department of Political Science, University of Pittsburgh*
Michael W. Kirst, *School of Education, Stanford University*
Robert Lampman, *Department of Economics, University of Wisconsin—Madison*
Katharine C. Lyall, *Center for Metropolitan Planning and Research, Johns Hopkins University*
Laurence E. Lynn, Jr., *Public Policy Program, Kennedy School of Government, Harvard University*
Julius Margolis, *School of Social Sciences, University of California, Irvine*
Theodore R. Marmor, *Center for Health Studies, Yale University*
Arnold J. Meltsner, *Graduate School of Public Policy, University of California, Berkeley*
Melvin Mister, *National Conference of Mayors, Washington, D.C.*
Stuart S. Nagel, *Policy Studies Organization, University of Illinois—Urbana-Champaign*
John H. Noble, Jr., *Office of Social Services Policy, Department of Health and Human Services*
Mancur Olson, *Department of Economics, University of Maryland*
Albert Pepitone, *Department of Psychology, University of Pennsylvania*
Bertram H. Raven, *Department of Psychology, University of California, Los Angeles*
Rodney J. Reed, *School of Education, University of California, Berkeley*
Martin Rein, *School of Social and Urban Studies, Massachusetts Institute of Technology and Harvard University*
John Rex, *Research Unit on Ethnic Relations, University of Aston in Birmingham, England*
Robert F. Rich, *Woodrow Wilson School of Public and International Affairs, Princeton University*
Ezra Stotland, *Society and Justice Program, University of Washington, Seattle*
Robert Taggart, *National Council on Employment Policy, Washington, D.C.*
Gordon Tullock, *Center for the Study of Public Choice, Virginia Polytechnic Institute and State University*
Carol H. Weiss, *Graduate School of Education, Harvard University*
Charles Wolf, *The Rand Corporation, Santa Monica, California*
Jerome M. Ziegler, *New York State College of Human Ecology, Cornell University*

POLICY STUDIES REVIEW ANNUAL

1982   Volume 6

Edited by
Ray C. Rist

Routledge
Taylor & Francis Group

LONDON AND NEW YORK

First published 1982 by Transaction Publishers

Published 2017 by Routledge
2 Park Square, Milton Park, Abingdon, Oxon OX14 4RN
711 Third Avenue, New York, NY 10017, USA

First issued in paperback 2018

Routledge is an imprint of the Taylor & Francis Group, an informa business

Copyright © 1982 by Taylor & Francis.

All rights reserved. No part of this book may be reprinted or reproduced or utilised in any form or by any electronic, mechanical, or other means, now known or hereafter invented, including photocopying and recording, or in any information storage or retrieval system, without permission in writing from the publishers.

Notice:
Product or corporate names may be trademarks or registered trademarks, and are used only for identification and explanation without intent to infringe.

Library of Congress Catalog Card No. 77-72938

International Standard Series Number 0163-108X

ISBN 13: 978-1-138-51321-1 (pbk)
ISBN 13: 978-0-8039-1875-7 (hbk)

CONTENTS

Introduction
    RAY C. RIST   13

PART I. POLICY RESEARCH IN PERSPECTIVE   17

1. Policy Research in the Context of Diffuse Decision Making
   CAROL H. WEISS   19

2. Social Science Analysis and the Formulation of Public Policy: Illustrations of What the President "Knows" and How He Comes to "Know" It
   ERNST W. STROMSDORFER   37

3. Applied Social Research? The Use and Non-Use of Empirical Social Inquiry by British and American Governmental Commissions
   MARTIN BULMER   55

4. Policy Analysis and Policy Politics
   ROBERT D. BEHN   83

5. Social Science and the Reagan Administration
   IRVING LOUIS HOROWITZ   111

PART II. POLICY ISSUES AND POLICY STUDIES   115

INCOME SUPPORT POLICY   117

6. Retrenchment or Reorientation: Options for Income Support Policy
   SHELDON DANZIGER, ROBERT HAVEMAN, and ROBERT PLOTNICK   119

7. The Net Impact of the Social Security System on the Poor
   RICHARD V. BURKHAUSER and TIMOTHY M. SMEEDING   137

8. Prices and Incomes Policy Options: Problems Arising from the British Experience
   EAMONN BUTLER   157

9. Forecasting the Effects of a Negative Income Tax Program
   TERRY R. JOHNSON and JOHN H. PENCAVEL   177

THE BLOCK GRANT MECHANISM   191

10. The Concept of Block Grants
    THE ADVISORY COMMISSION ON INTERGOVERNMENTAL RELATIONS   193

11. Block Grants and State Discretion: A Study
    of the Implementation of the Partnership
    for Health Act in Three States
    GEORGE D. GREENBERG 204
12. "Reforming" the Federal Grant-in-Aid System
    for States and Localities
    RICHARD P. NATHAN 233
13. Block Grants for the Needy: The Case of AFDC
    HOWARD CHERNICK 239
14. Making Block Grants Accountable
    ELEANOR CHELIMSKY 253

TARGETING FEDERAL FUNDS 285

15. The Targeting of Federal Aid:
    Continued Ambivalence
    PAUL G. FARNHAM 287
16. UDAG: Targeting Urban Economic Development
    JERRY A. WEBMAN 305
17. Federal Authority and Grass-Roots Accountability:
    The Case of CETA
    ERWIN C. HARGROVE and GILLIAN DEAN 324

HEALTH CARE POLICY 347

18. Competitive and Health Cost Containment:
    Cautions and Conjectures
    LAWRENCE D. BROWN 348
19. Some Dilemmas in Health Care Policy
    DAVID MECHANIC 393
20. Policy Shifts and Their Impact on Health
    Care for Elderly Persons
    CARROLL L. ESTES and PHILIP R. LEE 408
21. Future Research and Policy Directions
    in Physician Reimbursement
    PETER McMENAMIN 416
22. Health Insurance and Health Policy
    in the Federal Republic of Germany
    UWE E. REINHARDT 431

YOUTH UNEMPLOYMENT AND TRAINING 445

23. Youth Unemployment and Its Educational Consequences
    HENRY M. LEVIN 447

24. Vocational Education: Federal Policies
    for the 1980s
    PAUL E. BARTON   471
25. Mandating Collaboration Through Federal Legislation:
    YEDPA and the CETA-School Linkage
    RAY C. RIST   491
26. Inequality and Youth Unemployment:
    Can Work Programs Work?
    STEPHEN F. HAMILTON and JOHN F. CLAUS   511

SOCIAL WELFARE POLICY   535
27. Profits and Policy: Child Care in America
    MONCRIEFF COCHRAN   537
28. Housing Vouchers for the Poor
    JILL KHADDURI and RAYMOND J. STRUYK   550
29. Work Tests for Welfare Recipients: The Gap
    Between the Goal and the Reality
    CHARLES S. RODGERS   563
30. Public Policy and Black Economic Polarization
    STEVEN P. ERIE   576

EDUCATION AND EQUITY: POLICY CONSIDERATIONS   589
31. Evaluating Education Programs for Federal
    Policymakers: Lessons from the NIE
    Compensatory Education Study
    PAUL T. HILL   591
32. Measuring the Equity of School Finance Policies:
    A Conceptual and Empirical Analysis
    ROBERT BERNE and LEANNA STIEFEL   620
33. Public Schools, Private Schools,
    and the Public Interest
    JAMES COLEMAN   643

URBAN HOUSING POLICY   655
34. Redlining: An Assessment of the Evidence
    of Disinvestment in Metropolitan Boston
    HARRIETT TEE TAGGART and KEVIN W. SMITH   657
35. Private Neighborhood Redevelopment and Displacement:
    The Case of Washington, D.C.
    DAVID R. GOLDFIELD   674

36. Price Increases Caused by Housing Assistance Programs
    C. PETER RYDELL, JOHN E. MULFORD,
    and LAWRENCE HELBERS   690

37. Entrepreneurship and Government Policy:
    The Case of the Housing Market
    MARY K. FARMER and RAY BARRELL   709

ENERGY POLICY   735

38. Managing Nuclear Waste
    TODD R. LA PORTE   737

39. Approaches to Nuclear Fuel Assurance: Balancing
    Nonproliferation with Energy Security?
    RANDY J. RYDELL   746

40. Energy Conservation and Public Policy:
    If It's Such a Good Idea, Why Don't We
    Do More of It?
    DAVID MORELL   753

About the Editor   776

*For Irving Louis Horowitz—
teacher, mentor, and friend*

POLICY STUDIES REVIEW ANNUAL
Volume 6

INTRODUCTION

Ray C. Rist

Policy studies came of age during a period of broad reforms in American society. The 1960s and 1970s saw the impact of reforms in many areas, including education, housing, political participation, access to legal and social services, employment opportunities, and health care. The policy studies conducted during this reform period were premised on achieving social change through programmatic initiatives. The studies were predicated on a number of political assumptions about how the United States ought to distribute its resources, structure its forms of political participation, and address past inequities and injustices. The policy analysts conducting these studies thought themselves part of a progressive and enlightened effort to improve society.

As the United States enters the 1980s, the political agenda and ideological assumptions are quite different. It is a period of counterreform. It is a time of stressing the conservation of social institutions instead of their change, of the delegation and decentralization of political power away from the federal government to state and local governments, and of shifting social responsibilities from the public to the private sector. Issues previously thought to be matters of justice are now interpreted as matters of charity—and charity is to come from the voluntary actions of persons, not from the structured programs of government. It is a time when the "politics of scarcity" prevails over the "politics of plenty."

This volume of *Policy Studies Review Annual (PSRA)* is thus quite different in content and tone from the five that have preceded it. It seeks to reflect the changes that are under way within the policy studies community. Changes in the basic assumptions about the role of the federal government and the criteria by which people would qualify for federal assistance have rendered superfluous many of the previous efforts in the policy studies community. This is a period when the focus is not on the further expansion of federally controlled categorical programs, but on the decentralization of fiscal responsibility and decision making through the block grant mechanism. Likewise, this is not a time of developing strategies for increasing the population of persons to be covered by programs, but to target resources to fewer persons through tighter eligibility requirements. Many of the chapters in this volume allude to this shift and its implications for the future of policy studies.

The shift in focus for this volume is not an endorsement of the ideological rationale that has generated these changes. It seeks, rather, to alert those in the policy studies community that persevering during the 1980s with strategies and assumptions operant in the 1970s is to guarantee anonymity. There is a role for policy studies in a counterreform period. The form and content of that role find expression in numerous pieces in this volume. This shift ought also to serve as a warning to policy analysts that the vitality and credibility of their craft hinge on the ability to transcend association with a single political party or a single strategy for social change, i.e., federal intervention.

Not only does the policy studies community confront a change in the definition of problems facing the nation, it also confronts considerable skepticism among those currently in policymaking positions. This skepticism is, as it were, the price to be paid for the large amount of mediocre work produced during the 1970s. The "quick and dirty" or "hit and run" work that abounded during that time has more than justified the present disdain. The critique, however, is not limited simply to a matter of methods. It is also the case that the analyses so plentiful during the reform period were little more than a stream of polemics that justified the continued throwing of programs at problems. The basic contradictions and tensions in the system were not addressed; they were glossed over by attempting to offer something to everyone. The lack of evenhandedness has come home with a vengeance.

What has exacerbated the difficulties of policy analysts attuned to reform is that the conflicting pressures and demands on the resources of the society are difficult to resolve during a period of prolonged economic stagnation and monetary inflation. The field of policy studies grew during a period when the emphasis was on the potential growth in the system, growth that would fund the demand for federal support from countless hundreds of special interest groups. Policy analysts and politicians alike have been trapped by a lack of understanding of what this long period of little or no growth now means for the 1980s. Cynically, one might argue that the people themselves understood it intuitively far sooner than did those in the policy arena. Proposition 13 in California and other such initiatives across the entire nation have spoken to limits and constraints much sooner than has the policy community. In this one instance, the policy apparatus is running to catch up, rather than leading.

But all is not doom and gloom for the policy studies community. Admittedly, a considerable readjustment is necessary and some considerable skepticism must be overcome. Yet the selections in this volume of *PSRA* reflect a vitality and level of insight into current issues that bodes well for the field. They also reflect an understanding of the changes now under way in the society and the implications of these demands on those in decision-making positions. One theme that finds a dominant place in the articles is that the intellectual challenges confronting policy analysts in the 1980s will be far greater and far more taxing than those that guided work in previous years. It is in rising to meet these challenges that the policy studies community may well mature in unanticipated yet welcome ways.

The discontinuities between this and the previous volumes of *PSRA* have been noted. There are, however, continuities as well. These are manifest in several ways. First, there continues to be a strong emphasis on cross-cultural work. Such an emphasis reinforces the view of previous editors in this series that the context for policy analysis is not exclusively defined by work under way in the United States. In this volume, studies from Australia, the Federal Republic of Germany, and Great Britain are included. They attest to the commonality of policy issues and questions that confront all industrial societies. Hospital care and health insurance in Germany, youth unemployment programs in Australia, and low-income housing in England have all been studied in ways that can inform the work in these areas in the United States.

Second, there continues with this volume a presentation of varying analytic and methodological strategies employed in the policy analysis field. The absence of a unified theoretical or methodological approach is lamented by some, but the diversity of strategies evident here is persuasive in suggesting that a pursuit of orthodoxy is not what is needed in the field. So long as the approaches in policy analysis are driven by the information needs of policymakers working in real time, a repertoire of approaches will be necessary to best match problem formulation to methods and modes of analysis.

A third continuity, and this appears to be something of a ritual among the editors of the different volumes, is the acknowledgment of the diversity of sources from which the articles in the volume are drawn. There has emerged something of a glut of published material in the past few years that claims to be policy analysis or policy-relevant research. Sifting through the literally hundreds of articles, monographs, books, interim and final reports, position papers, occasional papers, and papers-in-draft had for me two quite opposite impacts. I frequently became numb working through paper after paper, finding many that were mundane at best and a waste of paper at worst. Alternatively, there were a sizable number (far more than could be included here) of high-quality papers that caught my interest and indicated a solid and substantial capability to conduct policy studies in several areas. If this book were to make no other contribution, I would be content to know that readers thought this a meaningful selection from the avalanche of printed material falling on us all.

What gives a special intensity to policy analysis is the belief that knowledge has an important role in the affairs of people. Whether on the global scale of dealing with nutrition and energy or on the very local level of providing viable child care, the thrust of policy analysis is that people and plans can make the difference. I trust that the present volume does justice to this belief.

PART I

POLICY RESEARCH IN PERSPECTIVE

An important shift is under way in the field of policy studies. This shift involves a dramatic reorientation and reformulation of the paradigm governing the presumed linkages between knowledge and decision making. What makes this change noteworthy is that it holds important implications for our understanding of the policy studies endeavor, of the decision-making process, and of the linkage between these two. In short, both the components of the linkage and the linkage itself are being viewed in a new and different way.

To take the policy studies area first, the conventional approach is to portray the area as intellectually tight and methodologically crisp. Indeed, elaborate methodological techniques and displays of multivariate analysis have been used to show rigor in the area and to demonstrate the powerful analytic tools available to those toiling in the field. What has been obscured or ignored in this rush to methodological nirvana is that there is little agreement regarding when one methodology or another is more appropriate to policy analysis. The several disciplines most closely associated with policy studies have each offered theoretical approaches. But again, which approach is most useful or powerful in the analysis of policy-related data is not clear. As a result, policy studies has no unified theory, method, or strategy. In short, a presumption of coherence and uniformity is giving way to a recognition of diversity.

The same processes are at work in our understanding of decision making in the policy arena. The conventional approach has been to portray decision making as a logical and rational process whereby the decision maker integrates various discrete forms of information, analyzes them, and deduces the appropriate decision. Decision making has been seen as a linear and sequential process. More recent interpretations and descriptions of decision making suggest an alternative approach. Rather than linear and deductive, the process may be seen as disjointed, incremental, often obtuse, and frequently not even understood as decision making in the traditional sense. Decision making is complex, multidimensional, and sometimes irrational.

It is this reinterpretation of both policy analysis and decision making that is necessarily forcing a new understanding of the linkage between the two. Whereas both were previously described as linear and driven by the logical application of principles akin to those found in engineering, this revisionist approach suggests that there is no one-to-one match between knowledge and decision making. Stated differently, it is not possible to instigate or sustain a linear linkage between the essentially disjointed and internally diverse processes.

The beneficial consequences of this reinterpretation, for both the policy studies field and the decision makers, are several. First, the continuing promises that policy analysts make and cannot keep regarding the fruits of policy analysis need no longer be made. Second, the decision makers need no longer wait for that perfect policy study promising to provide the tight answers to tough questions. Third, the presumptions about the link between knowledge and decision making can be revised to reflect more clearly the diversity inherent in the system. This should result in more carefully conscribed studies and more circumspect promises of information on any given topic. It should also provide the basis for modes of analysis that recognize the system for what it is, not as some hope it to be. Analysis predicated on an incorrect understanding of decision making is doomed to be viewed as irrelevant. This misperception has seriously handicapped those working in policy studies in developing strategies of research and analysis that reflect the actual milieu in which knowledge is both developed and applied. The emerging reorientation promises to reinvigorate the field as a more appropriate meld between knowledge and decision making is made.

The articles in this section speak to this shift in the paradigm of policy studies. Weiss and Stromsdorfer, in particular, detail the dynamics of the decision-making process and the role that policy analysis might play. Their conclusions and recommendations suggest a direction for the field quite different from that dominant through the 1970s. The articles by Bulmer and Behn also speak to this shift, but from a different vantage. The point driven home in these pieces is that policy analysis takes place in a political context, not a vacuum. Thus if the analysis is to be utilized, analysts must not only conduct the research, but must also be sensitive to and even suggest means for its application and implementation. Ignoring the political context is to diminish the opportunity for involvement and influence. Finally, the article by Horowitz speaks to the changed political climate in the 1980s and what this portends for the relation of social science research to the centers of power. A growing emphasis on applied instead of theoretical work, on agendas being driven by private-sector market needs, and on the shifting of resources from the federal to state and local jurisdictions suggests a decade for policy studies quite different from that in which it began to come of age.

1

POLICY RESEARCH IN THE CONTEXT OF DIFFUSE DECISION MAKING

Carol H. Weiss

A distinctive characteristic of educational policies in the United States in the past 15 years has been the mandate for evaluation that has accompanied them. Most major policy initiatives of education, as in health and social services, have been attended by formal, systematic evaluation of the effects of the policy for its intended beneficiaries. Over all, the federal government has been spending hundreds of millions of dollars annually to learn how well human service policies are achieving the ends for which they were designed.

The upsurge in evaluation activity and expenditures has a rational cast. The presumed purpose of all this analysis is to improve the effectiveness of policy. Evaluation, the rhetoric goes, will identify the programs and policies that are working well so that they can be expanded, and will locate the programs and policies that are working poorly so that they can be terminated or modified. Evaluations that analyze the effects of component strategies of intervention—that indicate which components of policies are successful for which types of clientele under which conditions—will provide the basis for modifying policies and attuning them to the needs and life conditions of the participants. The enterprise, in short, is meant to use the methods and techniques of social science in the service of rational allocation of resources and the improvement of welfare policy.

American social scientists by the thousands have been attracted to evaluation and associated policy studies. Not only do they find research funds available for the study of important and interesting social and economic phenomena, but the social consequences of the work also look attractive: Evaluation results will be put to work to improve the lot of the needy. Despite reservations among a few social scientists about becoming technicians for the bureaucratic welfare state (Gouldner, 1970; Dye, 1972), policy studies look like an ideal opportunity to combine research practice with social conscience. Researchers are able to do good while they are doing well.

AUTHOR'S NOTE: This is a revised version of a paper presented at the Workshop on Educational Research and Public Policy Making, sponsored by the Foundation for Educational Research in the Netherlands, The Hague, May 20-22, 1981.

From Carol H. Weiss, "Policy Research in the Context of Diffuse Decision Making." Reprinted by permission of the author.

THE USES OF EVALUATION AND POLICY RESEARCH

By the early 1970s, after about five or six years of relatively large-scale evaluation and policy studies, it was becoming obvious that study results were not having visible impacts on policy decisions. Programs that evaluators had found relatively ineffective, such as the Head Start preschool program, were continued —and even expanded. Programs that evaluators had found effective, such as direct federal loans to low-income college students, were cut back. And much of the detailed advice contained in the "recommendations" sections of policy study reports simply went unheeded. Social scientists who had expected their work to shape future government policy became disillusioned. Not only were they not counselors to the prince, they were not even influential advisors to the bureau of vocational education. Given their general tendency to turn their experiences into "findings," they began to contribute articles to scholarly journals about the nonuse and abuse of policy studies. During the 1970s there was a persistent recitation of the nonutilization tale—the resistance of self-serving government agencies to the lessons from research, the ignorance or inattention of legislators, the waste of social science wisdom, the triumph of bureaucratic routine and special-interest politics.

Recent investigations, however, provide a different interpretation of events. True, cases of immediate and direct influence of research findings on specific policy decisions are not frequent. Examples can be found, and may even be increasing, but they remain relatively uncommon. But to acknowledge this is not the same as saying that research findings have little influence on policy. On the contrary, evidence suggests that evaluation and policy studies have had significant consequences, but not necessarily on discrete provisions nor in the linear sequence that social scientists expected (Weiss, 1980b).

Rarely does research supply an "answer" that policy actors employ to solve a policy problem. Rather, research provides a background of data, empirical generalizations, and ideas that affect the way that policy makers think about problems. It influences their conceptualization of the issues with which they deal; it affects which facets of the issue they consider inevitable and unchangeable and which they perceive as amenable to policy action; it widens the range of options that they consider; it challenges some taken-for-granted assumptions about appropriate goals and appropriate activities. Often, it helps them make sense of what they have been doing after the fact, so that they come to understand which courses of action have gone by default. Sometimes it makes them aware of the over-optimistic grandiosity of their objectives in light of the meagerness of program resources. At times it helps them reconsider entire strategies of action for achieving wanted ends (for example, investment in compensatory education as a means for altering the distribution of income). In sum, policy studies—and social science research more generally—have made significant contributions by altering the terms of policy discussion.

This kind of indirect conceptual contribution is not easy to see. It is not visible to the naked eye. Sometimes it is manifested only over lengthy periods of time and after numbers of studies have yielded convergent results. For example, scores of evaluations were done of rehabilitation programs for prison inmates, most of which concluded that counseling, education, and associated services had little effect in reducing subsequent recidivism. Correctional authorities paid little attention, and efforts at in-prison rehabilitation went on relatively unchanged for a long while. However, the research results percolated through relevant bureaus, agencies, and legislative chambers, and in the past few years significant changes have been made. Not only correctional practice but also sentencing codes and judicial acts have been affected.

The State of California, for example, used to view correctional institutions as agencies of rehabilitation. Judges sentenced convicted offenders to indeterminate terms of imprisonment, leaving the date of a prisoner's release up to the decision of prison authorities on the basis of the prisoner's progress toward rehabilitation. In 1976, the California legislature officially gave up on rehabilitation. It changed the indeterminate sentencing law, and provided instead for relatively fixed terms of sentence. The new law began with a statement of change of goals. The preamble, in a marked shift, stated that the purpose of imprisonment is punishment. Prison programs aiming at rehabilitation continue, although more and more on a voluntary rather than compulsory basis (Lipson and Peterson, 1980), but the state has absorbed the lessons of evaluation: It has scaled down its expectations of rehabilitation and shifted to a different rationale for incarceration. Research results played a large part in the change (Knott and Wildavsky, 1980).[1]

In similar ways, social science results and social science concepts have had effects in many fields. It is not usually a single finding or the recommendation derived from a single study that is adopted in executive or legislative action (although this occasionally happens). More often, it is the ideas and general notions coming from research that have had an impact. Nor is it usually the particular "decision maker" for whom the study was done who uses the findings. Since few decisions in government are made by a single decision maker or even a small group of decision makers, and almost no decisions are made of sufficient scope to qualify for the category of policy, this is not the usual route to influence. Instead, what seems to happen is that generalizations and ideas from numbers of studies come into currency indirectly—through articles in academic journals and journals of opinion, stories in the media, the advice of consultants, lobbying by special interest groups, conversation of colleagues, attendance at conferences or training programs, and other uncatalogued sources. Ideas from research are picked up in diverse ways and percolate through to office holders in many offices who deal with the issues.

As the ideas from research filter through, officials test them against the standards of their own knowledge and judgment. They do not uncritically accept every set of conclusions they hear about, even if the conclusions bear the imprimatur of social science. They have many sources of information other than social science, ranging from their own firsthand experience to systematic and unsystematic reports from the field. The extent to which they accept a research idea, or give it at least provisional hearing, depends on the degree to which it resonates with their prior knowledge. If it "makes sense," if it helps to organize and make sense of their earlier knowledge and impressions, they tend to incorporate it into their stock of knowledge (Weiss and Bucuvalas, 1980).

This prevalent process of merging research results with other sources of information and ideas has two curious consequences. First, the merger often gives research results extra leverage as they shape officials' understanding of issues. Because research provides powerful labels for previously inchoate and unorganized experience, it helps to mold officials' thinking into categories derived from social science. Think of the policy effects of such category labels as externalities, aptitude test scores, deinstitutionalization, white flight, or intergenerational dependency.

Second, because social science is merged with other knowledge, officials are largely unaware of when and how they use research. An investigator going out to study the uses of policy research quickly finds out that respondents have great difficulty disentangling the lessons they have learned from research from their whole configuration of knowledge. They do not catalog research separately; they do not remember sources and citations. With the best will in the world, all they can usually say is that in the course of their work they hear about a great deal of research and they're sure it affects what they think and do. They can't give specific illustrations of their use of a specific study, because that is not how they work (Caplan et al., 1975; Weiss, 1980a).

So, if recent investigations of the consequences of research for policy leave us with greater respect for the influence of research, the influence appears to lie in affecting the shape and content of policy discourse rather than concrete choices. The nature of the effect has been called "enlightenment" (Janowitz, 1970; Crawford and Biderman, 1969): Research modifies the definition of problems that policymakers address, how they think about them, which options they discard and which they pursue, and how they conceptualize their purposes. For those who had hoped for greater direct influence on policy, it is a limited victory.

Elsewhere I have noted that even in the provisionally optimistic imagery of enlightenment, there lurk some dangers. For one thing, the research that policy actors hear about and come to accept is not necessarily the best, most comprehensive, or most up-to-date research. Sometimes they become aware of shoddy studies, outmoded ideas, and biased findings. No quality-control mechanisms screen the good and relevant from the partial and sensational. The phenomenon that has been discussed as enlightenment may turn out to be, in fact, endarkenment (Weiss 1980b).

Another limitation is that for all the potential power of shifts in policymakers' awareness and attention, thinking differently is not the same as acting differently.

While changed discourse is likely to result—eventually—in new modes of action, the process may be agonizingly slow and inexact. The policy action that finally emerges cannot be expected to correspond closely with the preferred state envisioned by the social scientist.

So much is prologue. The question to which I would like to turn is why the use of evaluation and other social science research goes through such tortuous process. Why isn't there more immediate and direct use of research results in the making of policy? Given the fact that government agencies responsible for particular policies sponsor studies with the avowed intent of improving those policies, how come they don't put the results to use directly?

Obviously the answers to this question are multiple and complex. Some of them have to do with the inconclusiveness of the research. Many, probably most, studies are fragile guides to action, because of limitation in the research, or the ambiguous nature of the findings, or—often most serious—the problematic relationship between the findings and any clear-cut policy recommendations. To move from data about what *is* to recommendations about what *should be* (and how to get there) usually requires an extensive leap. Researchers who have done a painfully careful evaluation study have been known to throw caution to the winds when they come to drawing implications for action and leap to unanalyzed, untested, and perhaps unworkable recommendations. Other reasons for the lack of immediate adoption have to do with the nature of government agencies (for example, their limited repertoire of available policy responses) and the imperative of policy decisions (for example, the overriding need to reconcile diverse interests as well as reach "right" decisions). But one important reason has received little attention, and it is this reason that I want to discuss—the nature of political decision-making processes.

THE NATURE OF POLICY DECISION MAKING

Both the popular and the academic literature picture decision making as an event; a group of authorized decision makers assemble at particular times and places, review a problem (or opportunity), consider a number of alternative courses of action with more or less explicit calculation of the advantages and disadvantages of each option, weigh the alternatives against their goals or preferences, and then select an alternative that seems well suited for achieving their purposes. The result is a decision.[2]

There are five major constructs in this imagery of decision making. The first is *boundedness*. Decision making is, in effect, set off from the ongoing stream of organizational activity. It involves a discrete set of *actors* who occupy authoritative positions, people who are officially responsible for, and empowered to make, decisions for the organization. Decision making is bounded in *time*, taking place over a relatively short period. It is usually bounded in *location*, with the relevant actors in contact with each other, or able to be in contact with each other, to negotiate the decision. The customary conceptualization of decision making thus has much in common with the three unities of Greek drama.

A second construct is *purposiveness*. It is commonly assumed that decision makers have relatively clear goals in view; they want to bring about a desired end-state or avoid an undesired state. Since Simon's (1947) seminal work, it has become accepted that decision makers do not try to optimize decisions, but rather satisfice, that is, settle for something "good enough." Nevertheless, they are expected to have overt criteria for what is good enough and to seek a decision that promises progress toward attaining their purposes.

The third construct is *calculation*. Decision makers are expected to generate (or have generated for them) a set of alternatives. In the past decades, scholars have recognized that no comprehensive set of alternatives is developed; limits on human abilities of cognitive processing preclude a complete canvass of options. But in the going imagery, decision makers consider the costs and benefits of a variety of responses. Their calculation will often be informal and intuitive rather than systematic, as they proceed on the basis of experience, informed judgment, or gut feeling. Their goals need not represent only properly respectable public objectives, but will usually include such unexpressed aims as bureaucratic advantage, career interests, and the furtherance of electoral chances. But however mixed the objectives and however informal the assessment procedures may be, it is assumed that decision makers weigh the relative advantages of several alternatives against their goals and their formulation of desired end-states. The alternative that registers an acceptable balance of costs and benefits will be selected. Scholars have lowered their expectations for the rationality of the calculus employed, and they have tempered their assumptions of systematic and methodological assessment of trade-offs, but they retain belief that a process of calculation takes place.

Fourth, implicit in the concept of decision making is a construct of *perceived significance*. A decision marks a step of some moment. People who make the decision perceive the act as consequential, that is, having consequences. When the decision involves "policy," whichever of the many meanings are invested in that term (Heclo 1972), the connotations of far-reaching importance are underscored, and a "policy decision" is doubly endowed with intimations of significance. People who make a policy decision are viewed as self-consciously aware of registering a decisive commitment to an important course of action. Scholars have noted that some decisions involve a choice to do nothing, to leave the situation unchanged (for example, see Bachrach and Baratz, 1963). Yet even when this is the case, the choice is expected to represent a matter of consequence to those who make the decision.

Finally, there is an assumption of *sequential order*. The sequence is regarded as beginning with recognition of a problem. It proceeds to the development and consideration of alternative means for coping with the problem,[3] goes next to assessment of the relative advantages of the alternatives, and ends with selection of a decision.

These five constructs—boundedness, purposiveness, calculation, perceived significance, and sequential order—underlie most images of decision making. And they capture essential elements of much of the decision making that goes on at bureau, division, and department levels, in executive agencies and legislatures, in private and public organizations. Allison's (1971) account of the "essence of decision" by President Kennedy and his small group of advisers considering the American response to the Cuban missile crisis is an archetypical decision of this kind. Similarly, a university deciding whether or not to construct a new building, the U.S. Congress debating passage of tax-cutting legislation, an executive agency developing proposals for change in eligibility requirements for federal aid —all go through a process that may be well represented by these constructs.

Yet many policy decisions emerge through processes that bear little relationship to these descriptors. Much decision making differs from the traditional model because one or more of the five characteristics is low, or even absent. Policies, even policies of fateful magnitude, often take shape by jumbled and diffuse processes that differ in vital ways from the conventional imagery.

Government is a continuous bustle of activity, with people in many offices bumping up against problems, new conditions, discrepant rules, unprecedented requests for service, and the promulgations of other offices. In coping with their daily work, people in many places take small steps, without conscious awareness that their actions are pushing policy down certain paths and foreclosing other responses. They do not necessarily perceive themselves as making—or even influencing—policy, but their many small steps (writing position papers, drafting regulations, answering inquiries, making plans, releasing news bulletins) may fuse, coalesce, and harden. Over time, the congeries of small acts can set the direction, and the limits, of government policy. Only in retrospect do people become aware that policy was made.

While the people who engage in incremental adaptations are not necessarily conscious of participating in policymaking, officials at the top echelon may be equally convinced that they are not making decisions. From the top, it often looks as though they are presented with a fait accompli. Accommodations have been reached and a decision negotiated by people in the warren of offices below, and they have little option but to accept it. Only rarely, and with the expenditure of a considerable amount of their political capital, can they change or reject the advice they are offered. To them, the job often looks like rubber-stamping decisions already made.

Even in legislatures, the quintessential locus of decision making, individual legislators have limited options. In the United States, committees receive drafts of complex legislative bills from the executive agencies. Committee staffs may identify controversial points in the light of legislators' general preferences and work out accommodations with agency staffs. From time to time, particularly interested and influential legislators get particular provisions added, amended, or deleted. But when the lengthy bills come up for vote, no individual legislator can be familiar with more than a handful of provisions. By and large, he or she must either vote against the entire bill or accept it. To the participants, their own influence on policy often looks marginal.

Given the fragmentation of authority across multiple bureaus, departments, and legislative committees, and the disjointed stages by which actions coalesce into decisions, the traditional model of decision making is a highly stylized rendition of reality. Identification of any clear-cut group of decision makers can be difficult. (Sometimes a middle-level bureaucrat has taken the key action, although he or she may be unaware that his or her action was going to be—or was—decisive.) The goals of policy are often equally diffuse, except in terms of "taking care of" some undesirable situation. Which options are considered, and what sets of advantages and disadvantages are assessed, may be impossible to tell in the interactive, multiparticipative, diffuse processes of formulating policy. The complexity of government policymaking often defies neat compartmentalization.

ALTERNATIVE ROUTES TO POLICY

Yet policies do get made. If government often proceeds to decisions without bounded, purposeful, sequential acts of perceived significance, how do decisions emerge? Some of the undirected strategies appear to be these:

(a) Reliance on custom and implicit rules. Officials do what the agency has traditionally done. Even if a situation is unprecedented, officials may interpret it to fall within customary procedures. In doing so, they in effect make new policy by subsuming the novel contingency within a familiar rubric.

(b) Improvisation. Another tactic is to improvise. Confronted with an unanticipated situation, officials may exercise their ingenuity, stretching a point here, combining a few tried-and-true procedures there, adding a dash of novelty, much like a chef concocting a new recipe. Through impromptu accommodation, an agency may begin to fashion new policy.

(c) Mutual adjustment. As Lindblom (1965) has indicated, officeholders who lack any sense of common purpose ("partisans," in his term) may reach decisions by simply adapting to decisions made around them. If one office has invoked convention or made improvisations, other offices can adjust their actions to accommodate to the situation.

(d) Accretion. Once officials have extemporized under the press of events, or adapted to actions taken in other offices, they may repeat the procedures when similar—or even not so similar—situations recur. The first responses provide a precedent and, if they seem to work, they will be followed again. Over time, when numbers of cases have been handled in like fashion, or when several different contingencies have been adopted to deal with an array of exceptional circumstances, they may coalesce and rigidify. Like skeletons of millions of tiny sea creatures building up into giant coral reefs, the result can become fixed.

(e) Negotiation. When authority is fragmented and agencies have overlapping and discrepant mandates, overt conflicts may arise. Many are settled by direct negotiation among the interested units. Threats and promises, discussion and debate on the issues, trade-offs of advantage and obligation—these are the currency of bargaining. The aim is less to reach a rational decision in the usual sense than to work out an arrangement that will at least minimally satisfy the key interests of each of the parties. Through processes long familiar in the Congress (logrolling, horse trading), a bargain is arranged.

(f) Move and countermove. If bargaining breaks down, an agency may take a unilateral move to advance its position. Other affected agencies counter with moves of their own. This kind of antagonistic adjustment is particularly likely when present policies leave some new policy territory unclaimed (for instance, the agencies' scramble to move into the turf of "children's policy" during the Carter administration). The series of competitive moves may continue until mutual adjustment reaches stalemate, or until resolution is shifted up to higher levels. Move and countermove is an accustomed mode of decision in international relations.

(g) A window for solutions. Not infrequently, the solution precedes the identification of the problem. In fact, it can be argued that unless a plausible solution is envisioned, the issue will not be identified as a problem. It will be considered a "condition" that has to be endured, like death, the weather, and (for many centuries) poverty. Officials often become wedded to pet remedies and they seek opportunities to implement these remedies. One group may want to install a computer system and engage in a search for places and occasions that would justify its introduction. Another group may be wedded to the idea of deregulation as an all-purpose panacea and scour the federal system for areas amenable to regulatory rollback. These are cases in which the solution is in hand, and partisans actively seek a "window" that will provide an opening for their ready-made nostrum.

(h) Indirection. Another route by which policy emerges is as a by-product of other decisions. In this case, policy outcomes are unintended, but because of decisions made to achieve other desired ends, they nevertheless come about. Federal guarantees of home mortgages, undertaken after World War II to help families purchase their own homes, led to an exodus from central cities and massive growth of suburbs. Federal aid to education designed to improve the quality of education particularly for disadvantaged and low-achieving students, has led to some shift of authority over educational practice from local to state and federal education agencies. No decisions were consciously made to create such shifts, but they emerged by indirection.

This list of nondecisional processes that produce policy outcomes is probably not exhaustive. Nevertheless, it indicates a variety of ways in which major outputs can issue from government without considered review or rational assessment. In time, ad hoc actions may have to be formalized by legislation. But often the early response is decisive, and legislative action merely ratifies the decisions that have already emerged. At some periods and in some areas, it is only a slight exaggeration to say that ratification of the status quo, and allocation of funds to support it, is a main function of legislation.

THE PLACE OF RESEARCH

If government policy can "happen" without the set piece of formal decision making, how does policy research get a hearing? When decisions take shape over long periods of time, through the incremental actions of multiple actors, and often without participants' awareness that they are shaping decisions, the opportunity for formal consideration of research information looks distinctly limited. In such situations, research data on constituents' needs, the benefits and costs of policies, or effectiveness and shortcomings of programs seem to have little chance for impact.

Yet one of the interesting facets of the situation, verified repeatedly in empirical investigation and borne out by the record, is that U.S. officials value social science research. They say that it is important and useful, and they sponsor large numbers of studies. If opportunities to use research results as a guide to policy are limited by the diffuse processes of government decision making, there must be other purposes that research serves. It seems important to identify them.

One possible reason for officials' allegiance to research, we can conjecture, is that research serves as a device of control. In a federal system, federal agencies set policy and allocate resources but local agencies deliver direct services. With day-to-day control of education, health services, and welfare in local hands, there can be a wide gap between federal intent and local performance. Only when the federal agency has good information about what local services are doing—their structure, the processes of service delivery, and the outcomes for clients—can it begin to exercise the authority that rule making and resource allocation allow. Evaluation and policy studies can become the mechanism by which federal agencies stay informed.

Federal education officials, intent on ensuring compliance with federal purpose, can find out whether local school districts are actually spending funds provided under Title I of the Elementary and Secondary Education Act to enrich educational opportunities for low-income and low-achieving students. Federal health officials can find out the extent to which neighborhood health centers improve the health status of low-income clienteles. If local agencies are found to be performing poorly, the federal agency can institute stricter controls over recipient agencies, tightening up rules and even terminating particular local grants. Research results may become the basis for control, and the mere decision to undertake research can serve as an implicit threat that stricter control is impending. The U.S. Congress sometimes seems to write evaluation provisions into legislation for just this kind of purpose—to serve notice on agencies that it will have the capability to review the effectiveness of their operations—even if it never does.

Another possible purpose that policy research can serve is to provide support and vindication for current policies. Federal officials often expect research to justify at least some of their claims—that large numbers of people are in need of their services, that programs do some good, that constituents like the attention and want services to continue. Even an evaluation showing little direct benefit to clients will often yield some positive evidence of this kind. The agency can use findings selectively to buttress its case for legislative reauthorization and additional funding.

A third possibility is that decision makers support research because the use of objective information is one of the hallmarks of rationality. They go through the motions of commissioning studies and searching for evidence in order to lay claim to the mantle of intelligent choice. In effect, they seek to demonstrate the quality of their decisions, in situations where criteria for "quality" are highly ambiguous, by appropriate performance of the rituals of information processing. As Feldman and March (1981: 177-178) note:

> Command of information and information sources enhances perceived competence and inspires confidence. . . . A good decision maker is one who makes decisions in the way a good decision maker does, and decision makers and organizations establish their legitimacy by their use of information.

There may be high symbolic value in requesting research and justifying decisions on evidential grounds. Even when the actual linkage between research input and policy output is weak, political actors can signal their commitment to the ideology of rational choice by taking an appropriate posture regarding research. In this way, they seek to bolster their reputation for intelligent and unbiased decision making.

If these reasons for continued sponsorship of policy research seem unduly skeptical, a fourth basis can be advanced. It is possible that federal officials support research because they recognize that every agency, even the most progressive, tends to grow musty and stale. It settles into a rut, taking old assumptions for granted, substituting routine for thought, tinkering at best with policy minutiae rather than venturing in new directions. To overcome hardening of organizational arteries, they may welcome the fresh insights and critical perspectives that good research brings. By subjecting conventional practice to evaluation, they may seek to help the agency renew its sense of mission and adapt to changing conditions.

One may hope that some part of the reason for high levels of research support comes from motives of this sort. But even if the thrust for evaluation and policy studies springs from less high-minded sources, even if it is the resultant of adversarial forces (department heads checking up on the performance of bureaus, the Congress checking up on departments, agencies seeking legitimation for their programs), even if it represents only rhetorical commitment to the norms of accountability and rational procedure, even then it has consequences. The regularized practice of evaluation and analysis has become embedded in government structures. Offices of research and evaluation exist at bureau, division, and department levels in many federal agencies. Their professional staffs do what evaluation and analysis staffs know how to do—continue and expand the flow of research information to the agency. Even the U.S. General Accounting Office, which used to serve the Congress only as financial auditor, now has its Institute of Program Evaluation. As procedures develop to transmit the results of policy studies routinely to officials through government, an important mechanism for learning becomes institutionalized.

The importance of the inclusion of evaluation and analysis units in departmental structures should not be underestimated. They are institutionalized mechanisms for collecting, sponsoring, synthesizing, and disseminating research and evaluation information. The informational function that they represent is embedded not only in the agency's table of organization, but also in procedures, the flow of paper, and the division and coordination of work. Members of evaluation and analysis units sit on agency committees that discuss present programs and future policy; they prepare position papers and option statements, marshaling the evidence for and against specific proposals; their reports and analyses circulate to key officials and are discussed in meetings; their comments—and in some cases, their approval and sign-off—are built into the processes of agency work.

In many ways, the incorporation of evaluation and analysis units into agency structures represents an organizational commitment to the use of information. The knowledge that they provide goes beyond the level of *individual* learning. It is not only individuals here and there in the agency who become enlightened by the results of evaluation studies. The evaluation process is embedded in the procedures and routines, in the *dailiness,* of agency work. It represents a mechanism for organizational learning.

THE VIEW FROM OUTSIDE

Outside researchers who engage in policy-oriented studies under government sponsorship are often disillusioned by their experience. They rarely see the slow and indirect uses of their research that I have been describing, or the learnings that accrue to government agencies as research findings wend their way through bureaucratic channels. They are much more aware of the *absence* of dramatic response in the short term. This is probably particularly true for researchers in universities who undertake evaluation and policy studies with the expectation of making an immediate contribution to policymaking—and the university administrators who encourage contract research in their institutions not only for the fiscal attractiveness of overhead-cost recovery but also with the aim of rendering "public service." They see that the research is done and then nothing much seems to change.

The message of this article is: Don't leap to the conclusion that research is ignored. The expectation of direct and immediate policy effects from research is frequently unrealistic. Since policy decisions often accrete through multiple disjointed steps (and for other reasons as well), looking for blockbuster impact from research results represents a misreading of the nature of policymaking. If you stay around long enough—and close enough to the decision apparatus—you are better able to gauge the real consequences. It may still turn out that research leaves few ripples behind, but it is premature to make that judgment without a long-term and close-up view of the issue-arena.

Are there some things that researchers can do to facilitate the use of their research? After all, shouldn't the policy process, however diffuse, accommodate the more accurate description of conditions and incisive analysis of events that research at its best provides? Those of us who hanker for rationality look for strategems that will enhance the power of research as a basis for policy decisions.

In the local case, there are undoubtedly acts that can lead participants in decision making to pay greater attention to research results. The literature is replete with admonitions: locate the potential users of research in advance, understand which policy variables they have the authority to change, concentrate the study on the feasible (manipulable) variables, involve the potential users in the research process, establish a relationship of trust, demonstrate awareness of the constraints that limit the users' options, report promptly, provide practical recommendations, write results clearly and simply, communicate results in person. All of these prescriptions are directed at influencing one decision maker, or a small group of decision makers, to use research in making a direct, concrete, immediate choice.

While one or another of these precepts, or all of them combined, may indeed pay off in increased consideration of research conclusions, they provide no guarantee that, even in a small hierarchical organization, research will carry the day. Officials are not blank pages to which research transfers truth. Officials have their own body of information, their career interests at stake, their patterned assumptions and ideological positions growing out of the sum of their life experience. While they can usually be induced—through the nurturance of good relationships and the logic of scientifically reputable analysis—to attend to the evidence that research producers, they will not automatically cast aside all other influences and embrace the researchers' conclusions.

Nor do researchers always want to abide by the restrictions embedded in the traditional prescriptions for influence. To accept officials' formulation of the problem or to limit the study to alternatives that are politically and organizationally feasible often represents undue constraint on the scope and focus of investigation. Studies too tightly tied to current operating "realities" rapidly become obsolete. If they lose their one shot at immediate application, they have little left to say.

Finally, it is well to acknowledge the limits of social science research. Policy studies address a small subset of the issues involved in any decision of moment. They inevitably omit a variety of factors that responsible officials have to take into account, such as the reaction of constituency groups, budgetary implications, contests over program turf. Policy studies, too, are shaped by implicit value assumptions. They do not represent mirror images of some reality "out there"; as Merton (1968) has noted, data are not "given" but created. Which variables are considered, how they are conceptualized and measured, the completeness of the explanatory model, all influence the nature of the results.

Moreover, different investigators studying the same phenomena often come up with divergent—even conflicting—conclusions, and even well-accepted research generalizations can be undermined over time as the sweep of contemporary events overtakes and discredits them. The claims of social science studies to the status of eternal truth are tenuous indeed. Participants in decision making view study results critically not only because they are self-seeking or poorly informed or prey to pressure groups (although they may sometimes be all these things), but also because careful scrutiny is a responsible act.

DECISION ACCRETION AND KNOWLEDGE CREEP

If all of these factors can limit the influence of policy studies in a small localized agency, the distractions are far greater at more rarified levels of policymaking. A significant feature of the policy process, as we have noted, is the diffuse manner in which decisions often accrete. When policy seems to "happen" without synoptic review and rational choice, few occasions exist for careful review of relevant policy research. Officials respond to situations by hunch and experience, drawing on whatever mix of knowledge—and of course much else besides knowledge—they have on hand.

But there are ways other than formal review of study reports by which research gets a hearing. Officials absorb a great deal of research knowledge through informal routes. They read widely, go to meetings, listen to people, discuss with colleagues—all without necessarily having a particular decision in mind. Research information and ideas filter into their awareness, whether or not they label it research as they absorb it. This diffuse process of "enlightenment" contributes to their stock of knowledge. When they engage in the stream of activities that aggregate into policy, they draw upon the knowledge that they have gathered from a variety of sources, including research, and apply it to their work.

The diffuse process of research use that we are calling "enlightenment" is highly compatible with the diffuse processes of policymaking. It informs the work of many policy actors in many locations as they perform their bits and pieces of policy work. Unlike the usual notion of a single research sponsor who acquires a directed set of findings for a particular decisional purpose, it does not suggest a monopoly on research knowledge by the bureaucrat who funds the study. Many different people with different interests and ideologies, inside and outside government, can be enlightened by research, and they can exercise their knowledge at many points, cooperatively or adversarially, as policy takes shape.

Of course, the enlightenment image represents no ideal model. When research comes to people's attention haphazardly, the process is unorganized, slow, wasteful, and sloppy. Some policy actors may fail to hear about relevant research; others may fail to take the research they hear about seriously. Some people may become enchanted with catchy, faddish, irrelevant, obsolete, partial, or invalid findings, or latch on to only the subset of findings that supports their predispositions and policy interests. The whole process reeks of oversimplification. People tend to forget the complexities and qualifications and remember the slogans ("the poverty program failed," "a guaranteed income leads to little reduction in work effort"). Diffuse enlightenment is no substitute for careful, directed analysis of the policy implications of research. Ways still have to be found—and used—to improve targeted applications of targeted research as well.

Nevertheless, the fit between the diffuse processes of policymaking and officials' diffuse absorption of research is noteworthy. It seems to represent one of the most important contributions that social science research makes to public policy. The ideas derived from research provide organizing perspectives that help people make sense of experience. These ideas offer frameworks within which problems are interpreted and policy actions considered. Retrospectively, they help people understand what government has been doing and what the consequences have been. Prospectively, they help raise the possibility of alternative courses of action.

Perhaps most valuable of all, research can be a medium of criticism. Subjecting old assumptions to empirical test and introducing alternative perspectives are vital contributions. Even when officials have themselves suspected policy shortcomings or negative side effects, research crystallizes the suspicions and makes them visible to others; the review of research results provides an occasion for mapping new responses. Of course, specific findings may be questioned, and the implications that researchers single out for attention may not be accepted. Research cannot be expected to prevail over all contending influences. Yet even in cases where officials dispute the particulars, they often find themselves using the concepts and frameworks of the research to reconsider accustomed practice.

To the extent that such contributions to the public arena are important, they suggest different lessons to policy researchers from those associated with direct research application. Concern about pleasing—or, at least, satisfying—the immediate client is secondary when dozens of other actors will affect the shape of policy. Being practical and timely and keeping the study within feasible boundaries may be unimportant, or even counterproductive. If the research is not completed in time for this year's budget cycle, it is probably no great loss. The same issues, if they are important, will come up again and again. Keeping the study within the accepted constraints of one set of actors will often imply irrelevance to the concerns of other sets of policy actors. In the enlightenment tradition, the researcher is well advised to broaden the scope of the question and take time to do first-quality research.

Other scholars have noted that research contributes to the policy process in ways far different from the traditional "rational" image, and they have urged that its realistic potential for influence should be exploited. Lindblom (1968: 117) wrote years ago about the use of policy analysis in government:

> Policy is analyzed not in an unrealistic attempt to reach conclusive determinations of correct policy, but simply to persuade.

More recently, Cronbach and his associates (1980: 47) wrote about program evaluations:

> Instead of promoting single definitive studies that promise unquestionable guidance on a narrow issue of policy, evaluations should be contributing to the slow, continuous, cumulative understanding of a problem or an intervention.

And further:

> What is needed is information that will facilitate negotiation of a compromise rather than information that can be cranked into a decision rule [Cronbach et al., 1980: 116].

In fact, this lesson may be the most important implication from the recent studies of the uses of social science research in decision making. Researchers need to be aware that the work they do, no matter how applied in intent and how practical in orientation, is not likely to have major influence on the policy decision at which it is purportedly directed—at least not if policy actors' interests and ideologies are engaged. Adherence to all the traditional strictures— acceptance of decision makers' constraints, focus on manipulable variables, timeliness, jargon-free communication, and the like—seems to increase the actual application of research results only marginally. Of course, improvement at the margin can sometimes be significant. But when competing with other powerful factors, such as officials' concern with political or bureaucratic advantage, one limited study (and all studies are limited in some way) is likely to have limited impact.

On the other hand, the stream of social science research has consequences. The generalizations, the *ideas,* that emerge from social science research help to shape the assumptions on which policy is based. Ill-conceived and slipshod research will yield conclusions of questionable value; quick-and-dirty ad hoc studies, which cut methodological corners in order to meet an arbitrary deadline or satisfy an impatient client, are more likely to muddy than to clarify the issues. To serve the longer-term policy needs of officials, research should be grounded in relevant theory and existing knowledge; it should look at issues comprehensively in all their multivariate complexity; it should be done with the greatest methodological skill that advances in research and analytic techniques have made possible.

This is not a call for retreat to the ivory tower. Researchers need to be sophisticated about the shape and contour of policy issues if their work is to be relevant to current debates. They need to recognize that decision makers cannot wait for certainty and authoritativeness (which social science may in fact never be able to provide), but must proceed on the basis of the best knowledge available at the time. But as social scientists, their responsibility is to convince government agencies to allow them the opportunity to do the best social science of which they are capable.

The critical ingredients will be independence of thought, conceptual sophistication, methodological rigor, and, when the research has produced something worth saying, serious efforts through many channels to get its message heard by the multiple participants in policymaking.

NOTES

1. Social scientists continue to debate whether the evaluation studies that provide much of the impetus for the change were valid enough to support the conclusion that in prison programs "nothing works."

2. There was a time when the characterization of decision making was considerably crisper than this. In what is commonly referred to as the rational model, several additional assumptions were made, for example, explicit goals consensually weighted, generation of all possible alternatives, explicit calculation of all costs and benefits for each option, selection of the optimal option. Scholars from the several disciplines engaged with decision making have been chipping away at the formulation for over a generation in light of actual organizational behavior. The statement given here is what generally remains.

3. Despite the ubiquity of the phrase "problem solving," most people understand that current-day government problems are rarely "solved" once and for all, or even for long periods of time. Any solution is temporary, as likely to generate new problems as to remove the condition that it is intended to solve. And many problems, such as poverty or insufficient oil resources, are so deep-rooted and intractable that government action can at best make modest inroads. Therefore, I have selected the word "coping" rather than "solving" to characterize the kinds of alternatives that officials consider.

REFERENCES

ALLISON, G. T. (1971) Essence of Decision: Explaining the Cuban Missile Crisis. Boston: Little, Brown.
BACHRACH, P. and M. S. BARATZ (1963) "Decisions and nondecisions: an analytic framework." American Political Science Review 57.

CAPLAN, N., A. MORRISON, and R. J. STAMBAUGH (1975) The Use of Social Science Knowledge in Policy Decisions at the National Level. Ann Arbor: Institute for Social Research, University of Michigan.
CRAWFORD, E. T. and A. D. BIDERMAN [eds.] (1969) Social Scientists and International Affairs. New York: John Wiley.
CRONBACH, L. J. and Associates (1980) Toward Reform of Program Evaluation: Aims, Methods, and Institutional Arrangements. San Francisco: Jossey-Bass.
DYE, T. R. (1972) "Policy analysis and political science: some problems at the interface." Policy Studies Journal 1, 2.
FELDMAN, M. S. and J. G. MARCH (1981) "Information in organizations as signal and symbol." Administrative Science Quarterly 26: 171-186.
GOULDNER, A. W. (1970) The Coming Crisis in Western Sociology. New York: Basic Books.
HECLO, H. H. (1972) "Review article: policy analysis." British Journal of Political Science 2: 83-108.
JANOWITZ, M. (1970) "Sociological models and social policy," pp. 243-259 in M. Janowitz, Political Conflict: Essays in Political Sociology. Chicago: Quadrangle.
KNOTT, J. and A. WILDAVSKY (1980) "If dissemination is the solution, what is the problem?" Knowledge: Creation, Diffusion, Utilization 1, 4: 537-578.
LINDBLOM, C. E. (1968) The Policy-Making Process. Englewood Cliffs, NJ: Prentice-Hall.
——— (1965) The Intelligence of Democracy. New York: Macmillan.
LIPSON, A. and M. PETERSON (1980) California Justice Under Determinate Sentencing: A Review and Agenda for Research. Santa Monica, CA: Rand Corporation.
MERTON, R. K. (1968) Social Theory and Social Structure. New York: Macmillan.
SCHICK, A. (1971) "From analysis to evaluation." Annals of the American Academy of Political and Social Science 394: 57-71.
SIMON, H. A. (1947) Administrative Behavior. New York: Macmillan.
WEISS, C. H. (1980a) "Knowledge creep and decision accretion." Knowledge: Creation, Diffusion, Utilization 1 (March).
——— (1980b) Social Science Research and Decision-Making. New York: Columbia University Press. (with M. J. Bucuvalas)
——— and M. J. BUCUVALAS (1980) "Truth tests and utility tests: decision makers' frames of reference for social science research." American Sociological Review 45 (April).

2

SOCIAL SCIENCE ANALYSIS AND THE FORMULATION OF PUBLIC POLICY
Illustrations of What the President "Knows" and How He Comes to "Know" it

Ernst W. Stromsdorfer

All projects and programs are of course evaluated, with more or less accuracy and effectiveness, as decisions are made to continue, terminate, or redirect various activities. . . . How best to do the evaluation, what skills are needed by the evaluators, and what specific questions need to be answered for local, State and Federal purposes—these are problems that have not been fully resolved, and to which differing views and experience combine to give quite different answers [U.S. Department of Health, Education and Welfare, Office of Education, 1971: 34].

This study analyzes the manner in which social science analysis is developed and utilized by legislators and policymakers to formulate social policy. The initial charge for this study was to determine whether information about social and economic behavior was more likely to be used in policy development if developed from a classical experimental as distinct from a quasi-experimental method of analysis. Based on the way policymakers behave, this charge proved to be too narrow a focus. While it is certainly true that data on behavior derived from properly designed social experiments are more believable and do allow unambiguous assertions of cause and effect, it requires more than random assignment to a treatment and control group to make experimental data *usable* and *reliable*. This is borne out by the discussion of Dennis Aigner on residential electricity time-of-use pricing experiments and by experiments such as the National Supported Work Demonstration, which, while yielding positive employment results for welfare women, still has a variety of methodological problems that reduce the reliability of the results and constrain its application (Masters, 1980).

Next, on reading commentary on the policy development process and inspecting policy and budgetary documents and evaluations of actual social programs, it has become obvious that policymakers, while not totally subjective and nonrational, will use whatever data are at hand to support their case, regardless of the

---

AUTHOR'S NOTE: I would like to express my thanks for the helpful criticism of Henry Aaron, Robert Boruch, Laurence Lynn, Fred Siskind, and David Whitman. Errors of fact and misguided opinion are clearly my responsibility.

From Ernst W. Stomsdorfer, "Social Science Analysis and the Formulation of Public Policy: Illustrations of What the President 'Knows' and How He Comes to 'Know' It," original manuscript. Copyright © 1982 by Sage Publications, Inc.

methodological purity with which it has been developed. Canons of scientific evidence are not ignored but are applied selectively. Taste or preferences for certain methods, such as the case study approach, are as much determinants of what data are used as is any perceived methodological purity or rigor. Furthermore, the same person or agency, when evaluating two programs whose, say, economic effect on state and local governments is the same, is capable of using evidence quite selectively to support one program and reject another. As pointed out below, the cases of Public Service Employment (PSE) and educational block grants to state and local governments are an example of this interesting bit of policy rationalization. The phenomena of substitution and displacement are used to reject the former program while they are not mentioned for the latter, where they also operate fully.

As a result, the initial question posed for this chapter is probably not as interesting as the general question of analyzing how information is generated and used. Thus I shall instead discuss the following types of questions:

- To what extent does information lead to policy formulation or change?
- What is the context of the application of research to policy?
- Does analysis precede or follow development of policy?
- Does analysis ever account for the variance or change in policy formulation and application?
- How are research methods and the resulting information constrained by the political process?
- Under what conditions do research and analysis appear to have no impact?

The analysis of social policies and programs will always receive a weight of less than unity in policy development, given the complex nature of the political development of a program. Also, the results of analysis will sometimes be used in ways and for purposes that are not entirely consistent with the original objectives of the analysis. Furthermore, the political process will often dictate that some kinds of analysis simply cannot be performed, or, if performed, the research must be carried out in a fashion that is inconsistent with the most appropriate scientific method. In fact, I would argue that the above phenomena are the rule rather than the exception in the conduct and application of social research. And, finally, research based on a range of methods varying in their appropriateness to the specific problem at hand will be found to exist side by side in a given agency charged to provide information to policymakers.

I do not really intend to paint a pessimistic and cynical picture of this process. Some information, if founded on an understanding of the policy in question, is better than none at all. And if one route of analysis, such as a benefit-cost analysis, is cut off, it is often possible to use alternative routes, such as an analytic treatment of program process and service delivery. Indeed, although we might prefer to think otherwise, a complex or expensive analysis of a program or policy is not always needed, especially if there is little or no conceptual development to guide the execution of such work. It has been the case that simple cross-tabulations of salient program data have been sufficient to effect major changes in programs. The Public Service Employment component of the Comprehensive Employment and Training Act (CETA) was significantly revised using such simple data. At the same time, it is depressing to recognize that occasionally the U.S. Congress will expressly prohibit the use of public funds to carry out certain types of analysis. For example, Section III(b) of CETA prohibits use of CETA funds to conduct research on the subminimum wage. Classical experiments are also illegal with respect to analyzing the Employment Service and the Unemployment Insurance program—at least as of 1977.

However, this same adversary relationship, given the existence of our open government and the canons of scientific evidence to which our system subscribes, forces or induces the execution of research that is politically unpopular. The case discussed below of substitution and displacement within the PSE program is instructive of this. Highlighted by the work of George Johnson, this issue generated an incredibly heated and sometimes acrimonious debate within the Department of Labor throughout the late 1970s (Johnson and Tomola, 1977). Nevertheless, the Department of Labor did fund a demand-side study in the Employment Opportunity Pilot Projects to study this phenomenon in the private, private nonprofit, and public sectors.

Plan of the Chapter

Before moving into the main body of the discussion, it is useful first to discuss the production of knowledge as it is generated by and for government and the general ways in which it is utilized by government.

Following this, the study will discuss examples of social research projects that have had an impact on public policy and others that have not. For both types I will describe cases in which the research was on the cutting edge, initiating debate, and other cases in which the research followed debate.

THE PRODUCTION AND USE OF INFORMATION

Analysis of this issue requires that the process of translation of analytical results into social policy be broken down into two broad components:

(1) How is knowledge produced?
(2) How is knowledge utilized?

Each of these two questions requires further breakdown.

Knowledge Production

The production of knowledge occurs through at least three processes:

(1) The production of management information system (MIS) data. Such MIS data can be classified into three general types:

(a) *MIS data developed within a behavioral context:* data on program inputs that can be related to program outputs. Such MIS data are generally rare, mainly because it appears to be beyond the capacity of bureaucracies to produce it.

(b) *MIS data not developed within a behavioral context:* situations in which measures of inputs or outputs only are collected and cannot be related to their respective outputs or inputs. Most commonly, measures of inputs only are collected. When such data are used in policy development, outputs are assumed to be equivalent to inputs. Educational policy data often are of this type, for example, more teachers imply better education.

(c) *MIS data that measure neither inputs nor outputs directly:* for instance, simple counts of people receiving a broad, undifferentiated program treatment, such as the number of people covered by a new law. Program data on the federal minimum wage come directly to mind. Depending on whether one is an opponent or proponent of minimum wage legislation, legislation that implies wider coverage is worse or better.

The conditions under b and c above tend to arise out of two general contexts. First, the most common, most programs are not designed with the purpose of discovering whether or not they are effective. They are generally passed by Congress on the consensual assumption that they work. A major example is Title I of the Elementary and Secondary Education Act of 1965 (ESEA) or the (extinct) Neighborhood Youth Corps (NYC; Rivlin, 1971: 80). Second, it is intended that the program not be analyzed in terms of its behavioral impact. This was the case until most recently with the Unemployment Insurance program, which was not analyzed behaviorally until the early 1970s, while over the parallel time period, the Manpower Development and Training Act (MDTA) and CETA both had an evaluation component built directly into them. In fact, the MDTA was the major catalyst for modern evaluation of social programs in the U.S. Department of Labor.

In general, the more political support there is for a program, the more limited will be the available systematic information on that program. The old National Alliance of Businessmen JOBS program is a case in point. In contrast, a relatively unpopular program, such as Job Corps during the Nixon administration, was required regularly to report very detailed *cost* data, though the first relatively valid study of Job Corps *benefits* did not occur *until 1977* (Mallar et al., 1978).

(2) The production of knowledge through natural or quasi-experiments. Here, two general approaches are discernible:

    (a) Natural or quasi-experiments that attempt to model an existing program's process and estimate its effect through econometric or other means. All evaluations of the federal minimum wage program and the Unemployment Insurance System are of this class.

    (b) Natural or quasi-experiments in the form of (more or less) carefully designed demonstration projects. Dozens of examples exist here, such as the Youth Incentive Entitlement Pilot Projects (YIEPP) or the Minnesota Work Equity Project, both of which are subsidized employment and training/education programs, the former for disadvantaged youth and the latter for welfare clients. Following Rivlin (1971), this form of analysis can be through either systematic development or through more or less unfocused innovation. The Youth Act of 1977, with a $1.1 billion combined research and program component, had both systematic development—the Youth Incentive Entitlement Pilot Projects—and unfocused innovation—the bulk of the Act and its resources.

(3) The production of knowledge through classical experiments wherein there is random assignment to treatment and nontreatment groups, thus allowing assertions of cause and effect to be made. Examples are the National Supported Work Demonstration, the Seattle and Denver Income Maintenance Experiments (SIME/DIME), and the Housing Allowance Demand Experiment.

Finally, there is possible a fourth form of knowledge production: knowledge that arises in the form of untested but testable hypotheses through independent theoretical development. The human capital revolution, and its extensive application in the War on Poverty, is in part an expression of this phenomenon.

Knowledge Utilization

Not only are there diverse forms and qualities of information production, but decisions based on such knowledge are also diverse. Given the political drive to develop a given policy, it is the general case that any data that is at hand and supports the case will be used. Policy decisions are made on the basis of:

(1) No data or information at all, but rather faith, bias, or political desire. Someone wants something and has enough votes to get it. The decentralization of CETA is a straightforward example. This is discussed further below.

(2) Hypotheses suggested by impressions of regularities in data associated with a social program. Title I of the ESEA had this characteristic. Consider the following:

    (a) Educated people are less likely to be poor—a datum.
    (b) Children from poor families tend to perform badly in school—a datum.

(c) Therefore, provide poor children with compensatory education and you will break the cycle of poverty—a hypothesis to be tested. However, as Rivlin (1971) points out, ESEA was not set up to test the hypothesis.

The Neighborhood Youth Corps was developed at about the same time and in a similar way. Consider the following:

(a) Rich kids are less likely to drop out of school than poor kids—a datum.
(b) The dropout rate of poor kids is directly related to the business cycle—a datum.
(c) Therefore, give poor kids a job while they are in school and they will be less likely to drop out due to the opportunity costs of staying in school—a hypothesis to be tested. However, the program designers assumed the hypothesis was not rejected and proceeded to set up the NYC. Subsequent tests showed no effect on schooling retention (Somers and Stromsdorfer, 1970).

(3) Hypotheses tested by data from natural experiments. The Public Service Employment components, Titles II-D and VI of CETA, have been under attack for several years in Congress and are currently scheduled for elimination, largely due to the econometric analysis performed to measure substitution and displacement. The argument that substitution reduces PSE effectiveness is directly employed both by the Congressional Budget Office (1981) and the OMB (1981) in suggesting budget cuts for the FY82 federal budget. For instance, the OMB (1981) argues:

> Charges that PSE is primarily a subsidy supporting State and local services are based on experience in the rapid 1977-78 build-up of Title VI and may not be as true today as then. . . . Independent estimates of the proportion of PSE jobs that are substituted for regular State and local jobs range from a high of 90% (after three years) to a low of 20%.

Two observations are in order here. First, although substitution undoubtedly exists and is probably pretty high—consensus seems to fall in a range from 40 percent to 60 percent at this time—neither of the studies from which the above numbers are apparently taken are reliable (Johnson and Tomola, 1977, for the "90%" and Nathan et al., 1979, for the "20%"; see Borus and Hamermesh, 1978, for a critique of these results). Next, the Reagan administration, while objectively rejecting PSE due to the substitution phenomenon, does not mention the fact that the noncategorical block grants proposed for education are almost pure revenue sharing and should therefore result in 100 percent substitution (OMB, 1981). Thus one begins to wonder about the basis upon which research and analysis results are applied. The persons in question apparently also engage in this selective use of analysis in good faith and apparently are unaware of (or uninterested in) the inconsistency in their thinking and practice.

(4) Hypotheses tested by data from classical experiments. Classical experiments are relatively new to the scene as well as rare in the area of social and

economic behavior. With one or two exceptions, there are no classical experiments of *existing* Department of Labor (DOL) programs. In fact, as noted above, for the "old" DOL programs, they are illegal. Thus *all* of the policy development in the DOL has been based on quasi-experiments as well as intuitive or impressionistic methods.

Also, where experiments have been conducted, we have had to undergo a considerable learning process. Experiments are not simple to design. Aigner (forthcoming) rejects five of the fifteen residential electricity time-of-use pricing experiments as not of use. With respect to the negative income tax (NIT) experiments, only SIME/DIME appears to be highly reliable and usable. The Rural NIT Experiment appears to be useless. The National Supported Work Experiment's (Masters, 1980) positive results for subsidized employment for welfare women are encouraging, but are qualified since, in particular, substitution and displacement are not netted out of final program impact.

The National Supported Work Demonstration employs a random assignment to an experimental/control group. Through closely supervised work experience in a supportive peer group environment, the program seeks to improve job skills per se and to change personal behavior such as work habits and motivation. AFDC women, drug addicts, ex-offenders and disadvantaged youth represent the four treatment groups. The treatment period is constrained variously to 12 to 18 months. The AFDC women had to *volunteer* for the program. Thus this study group represented less than 18 percent of the AFDC population. Masters (1980) reports positive results on employment, though unsubsidized private-sector effects were not as large as hoped. The study is strongly indicative but not conclusive that such a program can reduce welfare dependency. The positive results are concentrated in just a few sites, there is apparent interaction between treatment and site effects, and, as noted above, there is an undetermined amount of displacement and substitution (Masters, 1980). Supported Work represents our only *experiment* of subsidized public sector employment. It is not clear that the Reagan administration even knew of its results before it moved against PSE. And, had the administration known, it is not clear that such knowledge would have made any difference in its desire to eliminate PSE, since the evidence, while positive, is limited in scope.

Finally, the Housing Allowance Demand Experiments show a minor impact of housing allowance on increased consumption of housing, yet there is no attack on this program in the OMB (1981) budget document nor does the CBO (1981) budget document discuss this program. In short, a variety of experimental data exist, but they are of uneven quality and they are not used consistently.

We turn now to a more detailed discussion of the use of research with respect to specific social programs.

RESEARCH WITH AN IMPACT: INITIATING DEBATE

Within the past few years policy research has initiated debate and forced the consideration of issues that would otherwise have received less attention by

Congress and the several administrations. Examples of such issues are welfare reform, unemployment insurance, and Social Security.

Welfare Reform

The reform of welfare is a perennial policy issue. The basic concern with welfare services has been the presence of too many and too complex categorical aid programs, the eligibility requirements and cumulative tax rates of which have led to considerable horizontal inequity (unequal treatment of equals) and reduction in the work incentive. Milton Friedman, James Tobin, and others proposed substituting a negative income tax for the existing set of categorical aid programs. This idea was timely and struck a responsive chord among academics, government administrators, and policy formulators. As a result of this interest, a set of classical experiments was developed to test the impact on labor market and other social and psychological behaviors of differently structured income maintenance programs. Experiments were conducted in New Jersey and Pennsylvania; Gary, Indiana; Seattle, Washington; Denver, Colorado; and rural counties in Iowa and North Carolina.

Since the concern over the work disincentive effects of welfare was high, initial analysis of the data from these experiments centered on estimating individual and family labor supply behavior. Results based on 3 years of experimental treatment indicate that the labor supply of married white males with wives present in the household may be reduced by as much as 5 percent in response to a modest income maintenance program. For white females with husbands present in the household, labor supply may be reduced by over 20 percent (Journal of Human Resources, 1980). The income and substitution elasticities of this study have been used in developing recent welfare reform proposals to estimate the demand for low-wage PSE jobs and structured job search.

The five-year treatment shows larger labor supply reductions and will most certainly solidify resistance to an NIT among those in the new administration (as well as others), though at present the administration's rejection of an NIT seems to be due less to the work disincentive effects than to the dilemma posed by the interdependence of the welfare tax rate, the minimum income guarantee, and the income cut-off, and the resulting budgetary cost implications (Anderson, 1978, 1980; Socioeconomic Newsletter, 1981).

However, a propos the way in which experimental (and other) data are *interpreted*, we should note that, based on the results from the New Jersey Experiment, the following policy implications were initially proffered:

> First, public opposition to coverage of all intact families by an income-related case transfer program—to the extent that such opposition is based on fear of large reductions in work effort—should decrease. Second, the concern of policy makers about the disincentive effects of particular tax rates and guarantee levels should diminish. . . . Third, the case for a work test in an income-related case transfer program covering intact families is weakened [Barth et al., 1975].

For a time, these attitudes probably did prevail. However, with the hearings held by Senator Moynihan in 1978, the previously "low" rates of labor supply reduction were now seen to be "high" (Lynn et al., 1979: Sequel, 15-16). And the focus on a work test is paramount in the Reagan administration, whether one is discussing food stamps, AFDC, or Unemployment Insurance.

Workfare, in several forms and emphases, has been the polar alternative to the NIT. Versions of a strong work test and provision of PSE jobs were incorporated in the Family Assistance Program under President Nixon as well as in proposals in discussion during the Ford and Carter administrations. Rejecting the subsidized employment component of past workfare proposals, the Reagan administration is strongly fostering work tests for AFDC, food stamps, and the Unemployment Insurance programs (OMB, 1981; Boston Globe, 1981), without being fully aware that this particular institution is observed in the breach and that significant enforcement of a work test has nontrivial budgetary costs. (The OMB document does note that projected cost savings do not net out enforcement costs.)

Currently, the Department of Labor is testing workfare or work-conditioned welfare reform in Minnesota. This is the first direct test of the guaranteed jobs component of the Carter welfare reform package, though the Supported Work results are strongly suggestive of the probable direction of effect (Rodgers et al., 1979). New Community Work Experience Program demonstrations are now being proposed by the Reagan administration to test out a decentralized local state-oriented workfare and training program for AFDC recipients.

The Employment Opportunity Pilot Project (EOPP) currently under way is also a variety of workfare. It has an even stronger test treatment of structured job search. At this time some sites are placing almost 50 percent of their eligible clients in jobs, though there appears to be wide variation in these placement rates among pilot sites (discussion with ASPER/DOL officials).

Unemployment Insurance

Historically, the analytic focus of the administrators of the Unemployment Insurance (UI) system has been on the establishment of the optimum benefit level, mainly from the standpoint of the adequacy of wage replacement. A work test, often casually or indifferently administered, is the principal technique whereby the government reflects its concern over the potential work disincentive effects of this income transfer program. In the wake of the 1975 recession, with benefit payments approaching $19 billion in fiscal year 1976, concern was expressed in some areas of the administration and in Congress over the effect on the aggregate unemployment rate of the weekly benefit level and the extension of benefits to a maximum of 65 weeks for eligible individuals. Economists in several branches of the Department of Labor funded a variety of studies to measure this impact; independent researchers conducted their own studies (Katz, 1977). While the data in these analyses were faulty and the econometric techniques used to overcome these data problems were often inadequate, the analyses did indicate that the behavior of insured workers had several effects on the measured unemployment rate. For example, the duration of unemployment among UI recipients appeared to increase as benefits and their duration increased. Hamermesh (1977) argues that the best estimate is that a 10 percent increase in weekly benefit amount will increase an individual's unemployment by about 1 week. The overall effect of the current program on the civilian unemployment rate is to increase it by about half a percentage point. Overall, however, the particular point estimate was probably not as significant in influencing policy on the UI system as was the breakthrough in this new way of looking at the UI program and the determination of the direction of effect.

Concern over the employment disincentive effects of the program, particularly problems of financing the state trust funds and determining the adequacy of UI tax rates, led to a revision of the UI legislation in the fall of 1976. However, the only efforts made to reduce disincentives to work in this legislative revision were denial of summer benefits for school employees with contracts for the forthcoming term and for school employees with a reasonable assurance of postvacation employment, and reduction of unemployment compensation benefits for retired individuals by the amount of any public or private pension based on a claimant's previous employment.

Interestingly, the current OMB recommendations, while attacking the Unemployment Insurance Extended Benefits program, do not focus on the possible disincentive effects of the program except to argue for "a more stringent work test for extended benefit claimants" (OMB, 1981). Recent announcements by the secretary of labor suggest a major refocus of UI, however (Boston Globe, 1981), and current legislative proposals for UI can be viewed as implicit recognitions of the disincentive effect.

Social Security

Evaluation research has had an interesting impact on the interpretation of the effects on labor supply of increased Social Security payments, marginal payroll tax rates, and changes in eligibility for retirement. From 1947 to 1974 the labor force participation rate of men aged 65 and over dropped from 48 percent to 22 percent. Beneficiaries within the old age and survivors' component of the Social Security Administration (SSA) rose from 15 percent to 67 percent of the total number of people aged 65 and over during the same period. Studies conducted by the SSA staff as benefits were increased or extended concluded that almost all persons retired involuntarily as a result of bad health, difficulties in finding a job, or compulsory retirement age. The basic method used in these studies was a direct questionnaire—people were asked why they retired. Since American society places considerable emphasis on the value of work as well as the social and personal obligation to work—the secularized Protestant ethic—it is not surprising that people, when asked why they retired, cited illness or business downturn (that is, socially acceptable reasons) rather than the financial and leisure opportunity associated with retirement (Munnell, 1975).

In contrast to this method of analysis, the approach of the economist is to look for evidence of revealed behavior; that is, the focus is on measurement of actual behavior and the interaction among variables affecting this behavior, rather than on direct query concerning motives and actions. Studies using economic models that include variables representing the benefit and eligibility characteristics of the SSA system find that these variables have a large economic effect on retirement decisions. Indeed, as might be expected, there is an interaction between health and financial factors (Munnell, 1975). This recognition of the voluntary nature of the retirement decision in response to increasing benefits has brought into sharper focus the financial problems of the Social Security system. The current administration is discussing changes in the retirement age and the Disability Insurance (DI) component of SSA is under OMB revision and challenge (OMB, 1981), perhaps due to OMB awareness of the above. Finally, Congress has mandated that an experiment of the Disability Insurance component be conducted to determine ways to reduce the drain on the DI funds (U.S. Code Congressional and Administrative News, 1980).

RESEARCH WITH AN IMPACT: FOLLOWING DEBATE

Training and Retraining Programs

The best example of evaluation research following the lead of policy development is in the area of training and retraining programs for both prime-age workers and youth. These programs reflect the strong belief in American society that education is the key to economic growth and the assumption, though basically unproved and unmeasured, that there are large external benefits from any type of education. Also, training programs appealed (although for different reasons) to both conservative and liberal elements in Congress and the administration. Such programs were passed with minimal political and intellectual controversy, and as a result the major evaluations of such programs came after the fact of policy development and revision. Almost every one of the evaluations of training and retraining programs have been case studies impaired by selectivity bias, lack of proper control groups, nonresponse bias, and insufficient follow-up period. Over time, however, these studies suggested that there were positive and statistically significant effects on earnings large enough, under reasonable assumptions for a social discount rate and earnings projections, to cover program costs. Nevertheless, one cannot generalize from these case studies. The inconsistency in earnings benefits across studies, linked with the growing realization that training cannot create jobs in a period of cyclical unemployment, led to a disenchantment with training as a panacea for unemployment; thus, beginning in the early 1970s, the view that retraining "did not work" became prevalent in government circles and among some academics, even though the basic evaluation results did not change (Aaron, 1978a: 65). And, indeed, it was in the mid-1970s that fairly accurate data on national samples of prime-age trainees and nontrainees were generated from SSA earnings records. Sophisticated econometric analysis of these records indicated that for males benefits averaged from $150 to $500 per year in the period immediately following retraining. The "decay rate" in those earning benefits was estimated to be about 15 percent per year. For women the benefits were between $300 and $600, with no apparent decline over the 5-year period following retraining (Ashenfelter, 1978). Given costs, the impact appeared to be marginally efficient.

However, the *presumption* that training did not work led to a major shift from a categorical program approach to the provision of a unified set of services under a decentralized program, which prime sponsors would employ in various combinations that would be more efficient and equitable. This program change was made in the absence of reliable analysis, however.

To verify that the categorical training program did not work would have required a complex set of cost-benefit analyses for different types of program treatments, as well as training courses administered to different sociodemographic target groups. Such evidence simply did not then and does not now exist. Nevertheless, the decision to decentralize the programs prevailed. The conditions whereby this decentralization would have improved the effectiveness of training were not met, however. That is, the detailed labor market information necessary to specify the appropriate training programs was no more available under CETA than it was under MDTA. Decentralization reduced federal control, a positive gain given the mood of the period. It surely did not increase program efficiency. At this time an elaborate longitudinal study of a national sample of trainees and other program participants is under way in the DOL. However, it is not designed so that one can test whether decentralization has made any difference in program effectiveness. There is only one possibility for a crude test and that is to replicate the Ashenfelter (1978) analysis with SSA earnings data for the CETA period and compare the MDTA and CETA period results.

RESEARCH WITHOUT AN IMPACT: INITIATING DEBATE

Public Service Employment

Retraining programs, job counseling, and other services for the cyclically and structurally unemployed gradually fell into relative disfavor during the early 1970s, though, as noted above, in the absence of reliable supporting evidence. The new hope for alleviating unemployment became public service employment, first authorized under the Public Employment Program of the Emergency

Employment Act of 1971 and made permanent in 1974 as the Public Sector Employment program under CETA.

Two conditions must be satisfied in order for PSE to be a socially effective method for alleviating unemployment. The more important of the two is that unemployed workers who are put to work on subsidized public sector jobs must not displace other (similar) employed workers in the public or private sector or be used to perform work that would have been performed in the absence of the PSE program. Second, the output produced by PSE workers should have some positive social value.

George Johnson, who was then director of evaluation in the office of the assistant secretary for policy, evaluation, and research, U.S. Department of Labor, pointed out that the first condition was not likely to be fulfilled. In short, displacement would not only occur, it would occur very quickly; even when state and local governments were not in fiscal straits, they had every incentive to substitute federal funds and PSE workers for their own fiscal effort. If they were in fiscal straits, their regular employees, after a period of layoffs, would be rehired as PSE workers. Such behavior was endemic in New York City, for instance. Congress was not ignorant of the fact that such displacement might occur. Indeed, "maintenance of effort" clauses are consistently written into laws such as CETA that have a revenue-sharing component. The error of Congress lay in believing that such legalisms could be enforced. To detect the extent of fiscal substitution requires a complex data set beyond the capability of local governments to provide or the federal government to finance and monitor. Both the General Accounting Office and the program auditors of the Department of Labor became cognizant of the great difficulty in measuring the degree of displacement or substitution so that maintenance of effort could be legally enforced. Ultimately, the Department of Labor auditors simply ceased to concern themselves with the problem.

Paradoxically, during the Ford administration displacement was used as an argument *against* the expansion of PSE and *for* the expansion of conventional training within CETA. The advocates at that time did not recognize or discuss the fact that under a revenue-sharing program such as CETA, displacement, or failure to maintain effort, applied to any program so funded—training as well as public service employment. And, of course, the fascinating behavior of the Reagan administration with regard to this substitution issue has been mentioned above.

With the rebirth of interest in welfare reform under Carter PSE gained a new lease on life as an integral part of a workfare program. However, the displacement issue was still a nagging concern. Widespread displacement could eliminate the effectiveness of any long-term effort to combat the structural unemployment implicit in the welfare problem. With displacement, no net reduction in overall economic dependency need occur; churning in the unskilled sector of the labor market may be the only result. This phenomenon strikes at the heart of section II-D of CETA, which is aimed at alleviating long-term structural unemployment.

RESEARCH WITHOUT AN IMPACT: FOLLOWING DEBATE

The most unfortunate recent example of social program research and data collection that has had no meaningful impact on policy debate is the analysis of the Occupational Safety and Health Act of 1970 (OSHA). At present, the Bureau of Labor Statistics expends $4.7 million annually to collect industrial accident statistics for OSHA. These data are used to help target safety inspections more efficiently. However, they are deficient in helping to evaluate the net effect of OSHA safety inspections and little of this expensive effort has helped clarify the policy cacophony that embattles this potentially useful program. Indeed, while there are a variety of data sets on industrial accidents and injuries in existence, such as state workers' compensation data, these data could not provide systematic information to guide congressional debate during the formulation of the act and such systematic information still does not exist. The proposed Schweiker amendment to OSHA (Congressional Record, 1979), for instance, referred only to aggregate time-series data on nationwide accident rates as suggestive of the "failure" of the OSHA program. With a few notable exceptions (Smith, 1979), only limited analysis of OSHA impacts exists. The Occupational Safety and Health Administration did not have a coherent research and evaluation plan between 1974 and 1977, even though this was a requirement in the annual budgeting process. During that time the OSHA administration was making no concerted effort to discover the net social impact of its policies. It was only ineffectively pressing forward selected health standards supported by ill-designed and ill-executed economic impact statements. Even so, by 1979 a total of approximately $1 billion had been spent on the administration of OSHA (Bolle, 1980). Even allowing for the extreme politicization of the agency, given the above costs plus the social costs imposed by the program on industry, it is difficult to understand that a more coherent and determined effort was not achieved to measure the effects of this program and collect more meaningful management information data.

CONCLUDING REMARKS

It is clear that social research has a considerable impact on policy formulation and execution, but not exactly in the way a fastidious scientist would prefer. It is also true that political factors define or inhibit what will be analyzed with public resources and what will be applied in any practical political context. In some cases constraints are such that it is not possible to collect appropriate descriptive data, much less to perform a critical analysis of the program in question.

Lest I overemphasize the negative side, however, let me assert that program analysis and evaluation can be an extremely valuable policy tool. In particular, I have come to believe that analysis designed to reveal the administrative and operational process of a social program can be extremely valuable. As most social scientists who become members of government discover, program processes *are not* clearly thought out or understood by the people who define and operate them. The Trade Adjustment Assistance Act, for instance, which is predicated on the reasonable assumption that those workers ought to be compensated who lose due to structural economic change, such as auto workers, has been found to be very difficult to administer since the true losers and how much they lose cannot be properly identified. Providing understanding ahead of time of how a program might work through process analysis can render an invaluable practical—as well as social—service when done correctly. A basically sound or deficient program can often be discovered by an effective process analysis. The installation of an effective work test is a prime example of where such a process analysis can be helpful, and the avoidance of the economic and political costs of TAA, discussed above, is another example.

Finally, as the level of expertise increases within the bureaucracy and Congress, more attention and resources can be paid to formulating efficient MIS systems and systematic experiments and less to shotgun approaches to program analysis as characterized by the ESEA of 1965 and the Youth Act of 1977. Gradually, experimental analysis just may gain an ascendancy which it most certainly does not now have.

REFERENCES

AARON, H. J. (1978a) Politics and the Professors. Washington, DC: Brookings Institution.
——— (1978b) On Social Welfare. Cambridge, MA: Abt Books.
——— (1975) "Cautionary notes on the experiment," in J. A. Pechman and R. M. Timpane (eds.) Work Incentives and Income Guarantees: The New Jersey Negative Income Tax Experiment. Washington, DC: Brookings Institution.
——— and J. TODD (n.d.) The Use of Income Maintenance Findings in Public Policy 1977-78. Washington, DC: Office of the Assistant Secretary for Policy and Evaluation, Department of Health, Education and Welfare.
AIGNER, D. (forthcoming) "The Residential Electricity Time-of-Use Pricing Experiments: What have we learned?" in J. Hausman and D. Wise (eds.) Social Experimentation. National Bureau of Economic Research Conference Volume.
ANDERSON, M. (1980) "Welfare reform," in P. Duignan and A. Rabuska (eds.) The United States in the 80's. Stanford, CA: Hoover Institution Press.
——— (1978) Welfare: The Political Economy of Welfare Reform in the United States. Stanford, CA: Hoover Institution Press.
ASHENFELTER, O. (1978) "Estimating the effects of training programs on earnings." Review of Economics and Statistics 60 (February).

BARTH, M. C., L. L. ORR, and J. L. PALMER (1975) "Policy implications: a positive view," in J. A. Pechman and R. M. Timpane (eds.) Work Incentives and Income Guarantees: The New Jersey Negative Income Tax Experiment. Washington, DC: Brookings Institution.

BOLLE, M. J. (1980) "Overview of S.2153 'The Safety and Health Improvements Act of 1980' (Schweiker, Williams, Church, Cranston, and Hatch) including background and pro-con analysis." Washington, DC: Congressional Research Service, Library of Congress.

BORUCH, R. F. and D. S. CORDRAY (1980) An Appraisal of Educational Program Evaluations: Federal, State, and Local Agencies. Evanston, IL: Department of Psychology, Northwestern University.

BORUS, M. E. and D. S. HAMERMESH (1978) "Estimating fiscal substitution by Public Service Employment programs." Journal of Human Resources 13 (Fall).

Boston Globe (1981) "Donovan: jobless need new careers." February 26.

CAPLAN, N. and E. BARTON (1976) Social Indicators 1973: A Study of the Relationship Between the Power of Information and Utilization by Federal Executives. Ann Arbor: Institute for Social Research, University of Michigan.

CAPLAN, N., A. MORRISON, and R. J. STAMBAUGH (1975) The Use of Social Science Knowledge in Policy Decisions at the National Level: A Report to Respondents. Ann Arbor: Center for Research on Utilization of Scientific Knowledge, Institute for Social Research, University of Michigan.

Congressional Record, Senate (1979) "Occupational Safety and Health Improvements Act of 1979." December 19.

Executive Office of the President, Office of Management and Budget [OMB] (1981) Schedule for Reagan Budget Revision. Washington, DC: Government Printing Office.

GRAMLICH, E. M. (1980) "Future research on poverty and income maintenance," in V. T. Covello (ed.) Poverty and Public Policy: An Evaluation of Social Science Research. Boston: G. K. Hall.

HALL, A. T. (1980) "The counseling and training subsidy treatments." Journal of Human Resources 15 (Fall).

HAMERMESH, D. S. (1977) Jobless Pay and the Economy. Policy Studies in Employment and Welfare 29. Baltimore: Johns Hopkins University Press.

HAVEMAN, R. H. (1977) "Introduction: poverty and social policy in the 1960s and 1970s—an overview and some speculations." in R. H. Haveman (ed.) A Decade of Federal Antipoverty Programs. New York: Academic.

JOHNSON, G. E. and J. D. TOMOLA (1977) "The fiscal substitution effects on alternative approaches to Public Service Employment policy." Journal of Human Resources 12 (Winter).

Journal of Human Resources (1980) "The Seattle and Denver Income Maintenance Experiments." Special Issue, Vol. 15 (Fall).

KATZ, A. [ed.] (1977) "The economics of Unemployment Insurance: a symposium." Industrial and Labor Relations Review 30, 4.

LEVIN, H. M. (1977) "A decade of policy developments in improving education and training for low-income populations," in R. H. Haveman (ed.) A Decade of Federal Antipoverty Programs. New York: Academic.

LEVY, F. (1978) The Harried Staffer's Guide to Current Welfare Reform Proposals. Welfare Reform Policy Analysis Series: 4. Washington, DC: Urban Institute.

LYNN, L. E., Jr. [ed.] (1978) Knowledge and Policy: The Uncertain Connection. Washington, DC: National Academy of Sciences.

——— (1977) "A decade of policy developments in the income-maintenance system," in R. H. Haveman (ed.) A Decade of Federal Antipoverty Programs. New York: Academic.

——— et al. (1979) The Carter Administration and Welfare Reform, Vols. A, B, C, D, and Sequel. Cambridge, MA: Harvard University, Kennedy School of Government.

MALLAR, C. et al. (1978) Evaluation of the Economic Impact of the Job Corps Program. First Follow-Up Report, December. Princeton, NJ: Mathematica Policy Research, Inc.

MASTERS, S. (1980) The Effect of Supported Work for the AFDC Target Group. Princeton, NJ: Mathematica Policy Research.

MUNNELL, A. H. (1975) The Future of Social Security. Washington, DC: Brookings Institution.
NATHAN, R. P. et al. (1979) Monitoring the Public Service Employment Program: The Second Round. Washington, DC: National Commission for Manpower Policy.
New York Times (1981a) "U.S. education chief disarms his critics." March 15.
——— (1981b) "Savior of the Jobs Corps was Hatch; he likes it and it's big in his state." March 13.
——— (1981c) "Support has faded for jobs programs." April 12.
——— (1981d) "'Workfare' program in California got mixed reviews." March 18.
O'NEILL, D. M. and J. A. O'NEILL (1981) "Employment, training and social services," in E. J. McAllister (ed.) Agenda for Progress: Examining Federal Spending. Washington, DC: Heritage Foundation.
RIVLIN, A. M. (1971) Systematic Thinking for Social Action. Washington, DC: Brookings Institution.
RODGERS, C. et al. (1979) Minnesota Work Equity Project: First Interim Report. Cambridge, MA: Abt Associates.
SCHILLER, B. R. (1973) "Empirical studies of welfare dependency." Journal of Human Resources 8 (Supplement).
SCHULTZE, C. L. (1968) The Politics and Economics of Public Spending. Washington, DC: Brookings Institution.
SMITH, R. S. (1980) Data Needs for Evaluating the OSHA Safety Program. Ithaca, NY: School of Industrial and Labor Relations, Cornell University. (processed)
——— (1979) "The impact of OSHA inspections on manufacturing injury rates." Journal of Human Resources 14 (Spring).
Socioeconomic Newsletter (1981) "Stockman: proposals for welfare reform." Vol. 6 (February).
SOMERS, G. and E. W. STROMSDORFER (1970) A Cost-Effectiveness Study of the In-School and Summer Neighborhood Youth Corps. Madison: University of Wisconsin, Industrial Relations Research Institute.
U.S. Code Congressional and Administrative News (1980) St. Paul, MN: West.
U.S. Congress, Congressional Budget Office [CBO] (1981) Reducing the Federal Budget: Strategies and Examples, Fiscal Years 1982-1986. Washington, DC: Government Printing Office.
——— (1977) Welfare Reform: Issues, Objectives and Approaches. Washington, DC: Government Printing Office.
——— (1976) Employment and Training Programs. Staff Working Paper. Washington, DC: Government Printing Office.
U.S. Congress, Joint Economic Committee (1979) "The effects of structural unemployment and training programs on inflation and unemployment." Hearings, 96th Congress, 1st Session. Washington, DC: Government Printing Office.
U.S. Department of Health, Education and Welfare, Office of Education (1971) Education and Training: Opportunity Through Learning. Ninth Annual Report of the Secretary of Health, Education and Welfare to the Congress on the Manpower Development and Training Act. Washington, DC: Government Printing Office.
Wall Street Journal (1981) "Reagan's plan to put welfare clients in jobs stirs much opposition." June 4.
WEISS, C. H. (1980a) "Three terms in search of reconceptualization: knowledge, utilization, and decision-making." Presented at the Conference on the Political Realization of Social Science Knowledge: Toward New Scenarios, Vienna, Austria, June 18-20.
——— (1980b) Social Science Research and Decision-Making. New York: Columbia University Press.
——— (1977) Using Social Research in Public Policy Making. Lexington, MA: D. C. Heath.

3

APPLIED SOCIAL RESEARCH?
The Use and Non-Use of Empirical Social Inquiry by British and American Governmental Commissions

*Martin Bulmer**

ABSTRACT

Governmental commissions are an established part of the British and American systems of government. To what extent are they a means by which social science can have an impact upon policy-making? To what extent do they use empirical research methods to gather evidence which influences the commissions' deliberations? What factors hinder the effective use of social science research by governmental commissions? Drawing on case studies of British Royal Commissions and Departmental Committees, and American Presidential Commissions, this article suggests that the potential effectiveness of social science is reduced by the political context in which commissions work, their preferred modes of taking evidence, the way in which commissions are staffed, and the internal dynamics of their workings.

Commissions in Britain and the United States

Independent commisions of inquiry[1] have played a significant part in the government of both Britain and the United States. Despite major differences between the political systems of the two countries, particularly in the relationship between executive and legislature, there are marked parallels between the role played by British Royal Commissions and American Presidential Commissions within each country. Governmental commissions therefore provide a valuable focus for a comparative case-study of the influence of social science upon public policy. To what extent, and in what ways, can social scientific knowledge be used by commissions to influence the course of their deliberations and help frame the conclusions which they reach? The aim of this paper is to seek answers to such questions by comparing and contrasting the influence of social science upon British and American

---

* The author is indebted to Richard A. Chapman, William Plowden, two anonymous referees and the editor for comments on an earlier version of this paper.

Reprinted from "Applied Social Research? The Use and Non-Use of Empirical Social Inquiry by British and American Governmental Commissions," 1(3) *Journal of Public Policy* 353-380 (August 1981), by Martin Bulmer, by permission of Cambridge University Press. © Cambridge University Press 1981.

commissions. The availability of case studies of particular commissions (Komarovsky, 1975; Bulmer, 1980) helps in this, but the aim is to highlight general similarities and differences.

American observers have shown a great interest in British Royal Commissions (for an excellent early survey see Gosnell, 1934), but have sometimes tended to exaggerate their differences from American Presidential Commissions. We are told, for example, that 'their symbolic, legal, constitutional, environmental, compositional and operational differences are much more important than their similarities' (Popper, 1970, 54). Another observer, Derthick, maintains that it is

misleading to liken presidential commissions in this country to British royal commissions, whose detached, impartial, apolitical character they lack. Because the President, unlike the British monarch, cannot be above politics, neither can his creatures (Derthick, 1971, 633-4).

R. K. Merton suggests, without amplification, that the two types of body 'have only a cousinly resemblance, structural and functional' (Merton, 1975). Several supposed differences are based on misunderstandings. Royal Commissions, though formally appointed by the monarch, are in fact appointed by the government of the day, and as the Webbs observed long ago, very much political creatures (Webb and Webb, 1932, 156). The degree of consensus, and success in achieving implementation of their recommendations by Royal Commissions, is not markedly greater than that of Presidential Commissions. It is not true that Royal Commissions are 'more concerned with substantive, long-range, policy' or that they can make more intensive examination of their topics because they can afford a wider perspective (Popper, 1970, 55). There are of course major differences between the political cultures of Britain and America, not least in their receptivity to social science. It may seem self-evident that if the task of commissions is to investigate a policy problem, then social science is likely to be relevant to that investigation. This depends, however, on the extent to which social science is perceived as offering a potential contribution to the policy-making process. There are very significant differences in the relative political cultures of Britain and the United States in this respect.

American society is decidedly more sympathetic and receptive to the social sciences than is British society... The epitome of the government's response to a problem in the United States is to select the professor with the highest reputation in the field, give him a generous research budget and put him on a contract. The epitome in Britain is to set up a committee of inquiry made up largely of distinguished practitioners in the chosen policy field with a token academic who may or may not be invited by his colleagues to organise research (Sharpe, 1978, 305).

The nearest analogy to a British social scientist visiting America is an English chef visiting Paris.

The differences between the two societies arise partly from the greater emphasis in American social science upon empirical research, reliable techniques and precise data, as well as the larger scale of the organisation of research, as shown for example by the presence in American campuses of survey research organisations. American politics and government is much more open to bringing in academics at a high level to advise. American politicians rely to a much greater extent than British Members of Parliament upon aides and research assistance of all kinds. Turning to academics for advice is merely an extension of this practice. The American higher civil service, moreover, is more open and less tightly-knit than the cadre of generalist administrators, most without any background in social science, who head departments and advise ministers in Britain.

Commissions have a long history on both sides of the Atlantic, going back to the origins of the Republic in America and to the early nineteenth century in Britain (Clokie and Robinson, 1937). The use of commissions to examine issues of social policy began much sooner in Britain, the most famous early example being the Poor Law Commission of 1832–4, which reorganised the historic Elizabethan system of welfare for the poor (Checkland and Checkland, 1974). This Commission made extensive use of first-hand 'empirical' inquiries by assistant commissioners around the country, but the extent of their objectivity and detachment was limited; indeed, they were grossly biased (McGregor, 1957). Nevertheless, the nineteenth-century Royal Commission was one of the mainstays of what is known as British 'blue-book sociology', the systematic collection of evidence about social conditions as part of official inquiries (Pinker, 1971, chapter 2). Karl Marx indeed praised this method of collecting objective evidence warmly in the preface to *Das Kapital* (Marx, 1959, 9).

The social facts produced by commissions were in the public domain, where they could be used to support quite different analyses of contemporary problems – in Marx's case, a critique of the capitalist system. Commissions then and now analyse social phenomena in such a way that their results can be utilised by people of sharply different philosophical and political outlook, on the commission itself or outside (cf. Skolnick, 1970, 38; Merton, 1975, 159).

The use of social science by commissions

It is, however, during the twentieth century that the part played by social science in the working of commissions has really developed. In Britain, an early landmark was Beatrice Webb's contribution to the Royal Commission on the Poor Law of 1906–9, on which she wrote a Minority Report. The Webbs were of course indefatigable social investigators and this influence was felt in the work of the commission. In the United States, commissions were first actively used as an instrument of inquiry this century by Herbert Hoover (Dean, 1969, 101–16) whose background in engineering led him to believe that scientific experts would contribute much to the workings of government. Sociologists made notable contributions to the research done for two of Hoover's inquiries, the Wickersham National Commission on Law Observance and Enforcement, 1931, and the President's Committee on Recent Social Trends, 1933. Criminologists Clifford Shaw and Henry D. McKay made a major analysis of the causes of delinquency for the former (Short, 1978, 23–49), while William F. Ogburn was Research Director and Howard Odun Assistant Director of the latter (Karl, 1959).

There are many examples of commissions in which social science has featured prominently on both sides of the Atlantic, but what conditions foster the most effective contributions of social science? It is by no means the case that commissions automatically turn to social science for evidence and insight. In Britain, those which make major use of research remain the exception rather than the rule. The mainstays are written and oral evidence, supplemented by fact-finding surveys. Yet commissions tackle public issues with a significant social science component. 'Commission reports must be judged as works of social science because commissions have been asked to do social scientist's work...they have emerged as a prominent instrument of social analysis' (Derthick, 1971, 623). A more systematic discussion of the contribution of social science will now be attempted. Its tentativeness should be emphasised, particularly the attempt to generalise about the *genus* commission on the basis of rather disparate empirical evidence. Often one seems caught between ideographic case-studies and very broad and somewhat speculative generalisations. Nevertheless the latter have some interest.

The methods of inquiry of commissions

Commissions are set up to inquire and advise. How do they set about inquiry? The answers to this question are relevant both to the types of evidence collected and to who actually does any research which the commission undertakes. As noted earlier, the main forms of evidence sought by commissions, partly explicable by their public character and dominance by lay persons, has been to invite written and oral evidence and to make visits of inspection or inquiry. The receipt of written evidence is a necessary but manageable part of their work. Visits of inspection or inquiry may or may not yield useful insights in the short time usually available for them. One British researcher has suggested that they mainly fulfil latent functions of integrating the membership and providing opportunities for relaxation in congenial surroundings (Tunstall, 1980, 137–8), though this is probably over-cynical as a generalisation. The most time-consuming activity is the receipt of oral evidence and the holding of public hearings. Here the influence of legal practice upon the work of commissions is clear. The cross-examination of witnesses is basic legal procedure, and it forms a most salient part of the work of commissions. Members of Royal Commissions are likely to be familiar with it if they have legal backgrounds, as are members and staff of Presidential Commissions. Yet it is the single activity which serves most to reduce the potential contribution of social science to commissions' work.

The inadequacy of public hearings was first pointed out fifty years ago by the Webbs:

Of all recognised sources of information, oral 'evidence'...has proved to be the least profitable. Considering the time spent in listening to it, or even in rapidly reading and analysing these interminable questions and answers – still more the money spent over them – the yield of fact is absurdly small (Webb and Webb, 1932, 142).

They argued that, unlike a court of justice, the spoken word was not superior to the written word. Commissioners in the main were not expert lawyers or skilled social investigators, skilled in taking evidence. (Though even if they were, havoc could result. Charles Booth once spent five hours of the time of the Royal Commission on the Poor Law eliciting detailed information about poor law unions in South Wales using 'the method of the interview' to the infuriation of the other members (Webb, 1948, 335–6).) Moreover, commissions lacked intelligent procedure in the selection of witnesses and in their questioning, members being more concerned to score points than to establish the truth.

These reservations about the value of oral evidence continue to be expressed. Several members of recent British Royal Commissions have considered hearings a waste of time, principally because many of those who give evidence elaborate positions they are already known to hold. An extreme instance of this is provided by the Royal Commission on the Penal System 1964–6, which was set up to make a fundamental reappraisal of national policy. One of the members, criminologist Leon Radzinowicz, was increasingly dissatisfied with the methods of working of the commission, which relied principally on written and oral evidence. 'To elicit the experience and views of the usual list of organisations and of various meritorious individuals and weigh them up in an hour or two's discussion from time to time is not enough' (quoted in Hood, 1974, 386). He favoured a much more research-based inquiry. Eventually he led the resignations of a minority of the members of the commission, leading to its disbandment. The resigning members took the view that the taking of oral evidence about penal philosophy was leading nowhere and was a waste of time.

Marvin Wolfgang and James Short argued unsuccessfully that the National Commission on the Causes and Prevention of Violence should not hold hearings, as these were likely to be unproductive and time-consuming.

They were overruled, but Short reports that 'none of the participating social scientists with whom I have talked about the matter have expressed satisfaction with the hearings' mode of inquiry' (Short, 1975, 81). The staff lawyers, on the other hand, strongly favoured the procedure. On occasion, hearings became public spectacles. The Commission on Obscenity and Pornography held few hearings, and these late in its work, but they achieved national prominence because one witness threw a cheese-cake at the unfortunate Otto Larsen, who had questioned him persistently (Larsen, 1975, 35–7), thereby supporting Skolnick's contention about the Violence Commission that:

hearings are a form of theater. Conclusions must be presented to evoke an emotional response in both the commissioners and the wider television audience. In this respect, the planners of the hearings can be likened to the author and director of a play with strategy substituting for plot (Skolnick, 1970, 36).

British practice is less flamboyant, and hearings (like Parliamentary proceedings) are not televised. In both cases, the limitations of the method detract from the potential influence of social science.

Social science input to the work of commissions

Commissions do, however, also use social science and social science research methods. How do they do so? One consideration is who they get to do the research. Is research conducted by members of the commission themselves? Or does the commission employ its own staff to carry out research? Or does it contract research to in-house government research bodies (such as the Bureau of the Census or OPCS Social Survey Division) or to research organisations outside government? Or does it employ research consultants, usually academics acting in a private capacity? All these methods have been used, often in combination. In Britain, social scientist members of commissions have played a key research role, for example, Norman Hunt on the Fulton Committee on the Civil Service (Chapman, 1973, 17–20) and Roy Parker on the Seebohm Committee on the Personal Social Services (Hall, 1980, 78–82). The appointment of a director of research on the staff is not unusual; appointment of a large research staff is. Outside bodies are frequently called upon to do factual inquiries, for example, social surveys, as for the Maud Commission on Local Government (Sharpe, 1980, 26–7) or the Younger Committee on Privacy (Rhodes, 1980, 110ff). Consultants are often used, though on a less elaborate scale than by Presidential Commissions.

Fewer members of Presidential Commissions are themselves social scientists, but commissions are much more likely to appoint social scientists to their staff. Indeed the scale on which research is organised reflects both the much greater professionalism of American social science, and the nature of the federal and continental political system within which it operates. The 'best' experts are brought in from wherever they happen to be, task-forces are established if need be on the other side of the continent, and if the co-director of research is away for a year in England, just put in a direct telephone line between his Cambridge apartment and the Commission's offices in Washington DC (Short, 1975, 67). Consultants are also used on a large scale much more widely than in Britain, reflecting the greater American faith in the social science 'expert'.

Factors favouring the use of social science research

Can one draw up a balance sheet of factors favouring, and hindering, the use of social science by commissions? Several points clearly favour the use of social science expertise. Commisions are set up to investigate a problem, and their members are keen to draw on available knowledge. In some circumstances, there may be considerable gaps in available knowledge, and also an absence of members of the public wishing to give evidence. Several commissions have therefore commissioned attitude surveys of a sample of the public, for example the Younger Committee on Privacy (Rhodes, 1980), the Redcliffe-Maud Commission on Local Government in England (Sharpe, 1980, 29) and the Kilbrandon Royal Commission on the Constitution, examining the case for regional devolution (Craven, 1978, 243ff). The more usual situation, however, is an already relatively well-researched field where the emphasis is more upon drawing together and synthesising existing knowledge for commission members.

The effectiveness of social science is clearly conditioned by the structure and methods of working of commissions. Each commission has a chairman and members, a secretariat, and possibly a staff to assist the members and to do research. Consultants may also be employed. The character and orientation of the chairman clearly plays a very important role in the extent to which social science is brought in. On the President's Commission on Obscenity and Pornography (1968–71), the chairman (a lawyer) was interested in the *empirical* conditions assumed by various types of legislation, pressed for research at the expense of other activities such as public relations, and was influenced in the conclusions he drew by the results of research. 'He read every article, research proposal, and report. He even labored on some of the questionnaires' (Larsen, 1975, 24). The Robbins Committee in Britain mounted a major research programme under the influence of its chairman, a distinguished academic economist. Such keen interest on the part of the chairman is not common, but it makes the point that he or she influences the use made of social science by the commission. The fact that so many commissions are chaired by lawyers (in Britain by judges) places the relationship between legal and social science approaches to problems at the centre of discussion, a point which recurs again and again in the following discussion.

Commissions are comprised of the chairman plus the members who are appointed for various reasons to represent various constituencies, fill different roles, and provide a mixed and wide-ranging perspective upon the problem at issue. Various typologies of commission members have been proposed, such as expert, layman, party man, official and interested party (Wheare, 1955) or expert, representative of an interest, fuse-box, advocate of a particular philosophy, consensus builder, or genial host (Donnison, 1980, 15–17). Members are not all of a kind, and only a few, if any, of them will have any detailed knowledge of social science. From that point of view they are lay people, whatever role they fill on the committee. Any social scientist on the commission, and social scientists on its staff or from outside, must therefore always be aware that they are talking to and writing for those not having background academic knowledge in their subject.

The composition of the commission is likely to influence the extent to which social science is used. Where there are one or more 'expert' members, whose views carry weight, large-scale research and investigation is made more likely. The Roskill Commission on the Third London Airport (Flowerdew, 1980), though chaired by a judge, had among its members a leading urban planner, a transport consultant, an expert in aircraft design and an academic economist. It is likely that this led to the establishment of the commission's own research team of twenty-three staff, the first commission to employ a really substantial in-house research team. Similarly, the fact that the Royal Commission on the Distribution of Income and Wealth set up an elaborate statistical and research organisation, with a staff at its peak of over thirty, was not unconnected with the fact that three out of the original nine commissioners were academic social scientists with special expertise in the study of income and wealth. The research orientation of the Presidential Commission on Obscenity and Pornography owed something to the predominance of academics or ex-academics among its membership, as well as to the interests of the chairman already mentioned.

The degree of expertise among commission members will also affect the way in which social science research findings filter through to the deliberations of the commission. In extreme cases like the Royal Commission on the Distribution of Income and Wealth, commissioners may be actively involved in advising staff on the design of research and problems of interpreting results (Bulmer, 1980a, 168). At the other extreme, if members lack expertise, research (if it is undertaken) is delegated to staff, who are then required to present the results to members in a non-technical fashion. There is evidence that academic social scientist members may play a key role on commissions in both influencing the research undertaken and more particularly in interpreting the results to their fellow commissioners. This was clearly the case on the Donovan Royal Commission on Trades Unions and Employers Associations where Hugh Clegg, an academic specialist in industrial relations, suggested that the commission undertake research, and later argued for a particular analysis of Britain's industrial relations problems using the research evidence in support. The research director, W. E. J. McCarthy, was a close associate of his from Oxford, and the industrial relations research consultants used were closely associated with their positions. 'Clegg acted as the Father, McCarthy as John the Baptist and the other researchers as their disciples' (Kilroy-Silk, 1973, 58).

Arguably this sort of influence is stronger in Britain, where the legitimacy of social science is less well-recognised. The attitude is found in official circles and among public figures that social science can contribute little of value to solving practical problems in broad areas of government policy-making. In British law, too, there is little receptivity to the introduction of social criteria in the manner of Brandeis or Frankfurter. Therefore the influence of social scientist members of commissions in persuading their lay colleagues of the value of social science may be critical. This is less likely to be the case in the United States, where the legitimacy of social science and its potential contribution to policy-making is more widely recognised. Social scientist members and staff can also play an important educative role. All commissions spend a considerable period of time getting to grips with the area they are studying. Where issues are at all technical, this is facilitated by by social scientists being part of the commission. On the Commission on Population Growth, most of the members were not experts in demography and needed to be educated in the subject (Westhoff, 1975, 49–50).

In some cases there is clear evidence that social science research directly influenced the way that commissioners reached recommendations. In the case of obscenity and pornography, the Presidential Commission took account of research findings in drawing up their policy proposals. 'On the surface, at least, effect studies by social scientists had a powerful, if not an overwhelming, impact on the Commissioners when they finally made their policy recommendations' (Larsen, 1975, 26). Opinion on the commission shifted as a result of being presented with the results of research which showed that the effects of exposure to erotic material did not lead to anti-social behaviour. The chairman, too, changed his view of the subject. As Larsen points out, social science can only be used so far. However compelling the evidence about effects and how people feel about it, the level of intervention to recommend for policy (in terms of free publication and censorship) involves considering principles and completing interests as well as simply the results of research. Even in this case with clear-cut research results, the influence of social science only extended so far.

The factors favouring the contribution of social science have to be weighed against the influences hindering its effective use. Though it is comforting to find examples of good use, the literature is full of the frustration and resignation of social scientists brought in to advise commissions whose experience has made them feel that they were less effective than they might have been. Realism is a more appropriate posture than self-congratulation, and the discussion will now examine at some length barriers to the effective use of social science by commissions.

Barriers to effective use of social science research

(*1*) **Time**

The single greatest obstacle to the use of social science is *time*, 'the discordant pacing of empirical social inquiry and of decision-making' (Merton, 1975, 163). Accounts by social science participants in the work of commissions stress this point above all others. Commissions work quickly and under pressure. If they want to draw on social science or undertake their own research, they need rapid results. The average duration of Royal Commissions since 1945 has been 2½ years (Cartwright, 1975, 190) and if research is to influence conclusions and recommendations it must be ready well before the final stage to feed into the commission's deliberations. Yet social scientists work to long time-scales, and can not necessarily adjust their schedules to fit in with short-term demands. James Short, for example, recounts how the Violence Commission set up task forces, but how slow was the process of recruiting and bringing on board senior social scientists, due to the other prior commitments. By contrast, the young lawyers who staffed the commission were there and prepared to work hard, under pressure. 'They were accustomed to the quick gathering and assimilation of concrete facts and their use in advocacy, in contrast to the social scientists' more deliberative academic style of research and preference for abstract theoretical formulations in the search for knowledge' (Short, 1975, 71). The actual experience of time constraints on commissions is variable. Sometimes major pieces of research only appear after the commission has reported. This was the case with a major survey of civil servants undertaken for the Fulton Committee on the Civil Service of 1966-8. Sometimes research is commissioned quickly and published while the commission is still deliberating, in advance of its report, as in the case of the Royal Commission on the National Health Service, 1976-9 (Farrell, 1980, 13-14).

How rapidly research can be started depends upon recruiting staff and consultants quickly at the outset. This can pose difficulties. Westhoff (1975) and Ohlin (1975) have emphasised how time of year can hinder effective recruitment. Seeking to recruit American research staff between May and October is likely to run into the problem that academics are committed for the next academic year, and cannot easily shift to a Washington post at short notice, in contrast to the much more mobile lawyers. Both the Population and Violence Commissions recruited research staff from elsewhere in government service, because they were more readily available than academics. Academic researchers were used principally to do contract research and as consultants.

(2) *Kinds of 'research'*

The timing and staff recruitment problems also affect what 'research' commissioners are able to draw on. By and large, commissions find it easier to draw on existing research than to mount new original work.

The deliberate pace of social research is incompatible with the urgency and haste under which recent commissions have operated. Under pressures of time, acceptability of findings and limitations of theory and methodology, the contributions of social scientists are reduced to...synthesising existing research and theory and preparing it for presentation (Lipsky and Olson, 1977, 197).

Donnison has emphasised how the scope for more original and fundamental inquiries on behalf of a commission is very limited, due to time constraints (Donnison, 1980, 11). Even where the commission's research draws on existing theory and fact, by exploiting existing knowledge, pressure of deadlines may prevent adequate effort being put in by consultants. On the President's Commission on Law Enforcement, many consultants

produced hasty reports that failed to identify issues clearly or failed to organise facts and theories in response to them. Almost invariably, there was a great reluctance to make policy recommendations. Most of the reports contained summaries of the literature and occasionally, ideological polemics. In other reports, analysis proceeded at too high a level of abstraction (Ohlin, 1975, 115).

Most of these failings were due to conflicts between consultants' own teaching and research work, and what they had undertaken to do for the commission in a short time-span.

Lipsky and Olson (1977, 197) argue, on the basis of their analysis of the Kerner Commission, that the conduct of original research is undertaken by commissions not because it will feed directly into the commission's work, but because it 'may contribute to public understanding through subsequent publication', after the commissioners have reached their conclusions. Thus studies produced for Kerner such as that by Fogelson and Hill refuting the riff-raff theory of riot participation made important contributions to general understanding, but were largely irrelevant to the commission's deliberations. It is recognised at the outset that such research may be 'late', but is nevertheless thought worth conducting.

(3) Funding

A further obstacle to the conduct of research may be lack of adequate resources to do so. To do 'in-house' research or engage contractors will require funding. This funding may not be readily available. Ever since the Chicago Commission on Race Relations, 1919–22, this has been a problem. Set up by the Governor of Illinois in the aftermath of the Chicago race riot of 1919, it is the classic study (1922) by a riot commission utilising social science research, and was directed by black sociologist Charles S. Johnson (Waskow, 1967; Bulmer, 1981). A good deal of the commission's time was spent trying to secure private financial support. Another example was Hoover's Committee on Recent Social Trends, 1929–33, although in that case a half-million dollar grant from the Rockefeller Foundation paid for its staff and expenses. Nevertheless, it was a committee appointed by and reporting to the President.

Another variant was for a commission to be appointed and funded by government, but for additional research for the commission to be funded privately. This was the case with the Webbs and the 1906–9 Poor Law Commission, where Beatrice initiated various empirical inquiries of her own, and firmly told the other commissioners that she intended to pursue them (Webb, 1948, 349, 371), paying for them herself or from other private sources. This practice of relying on outside resources still survives to some extent on Presidential Commissions, where in some cases commissioners who are state governors, congressmen or businessmen may rely on their own staff as well as on the staff of the commission.

The contemporary situation in Britain and America seems somewhat different. Funding is less of a problem for British Royal Commissions, where their closeness to sponsoring departments usually means that the department can either make funds available for research, or in certain cases undertake some of the research through its own internal research organisation. The Chairman or Secretary are therefore not expected to play the role of entrepreneur. In the case of Presidential Commissions, large amounts of the time of Executive and Research Directors may be spent in negotiations in Washington to secure sufficient funding for their activities (cf. Dean, 1969, 107–9). Like directors of large research institutes, much time of senior staff may have to be directed away from research management to liaison with funding agencies and efforts to keep the whole enterprise financially viable (cf. Short, 1975, 78).

(4) Predispositions of social science researchers

To what extent are commissions handicapped by having to work within a fixed time-schedule of short duration? Time of itself may in fact be less important than the underlying predispositions of academics and researchers which pressures of time bring to the surface. Several experienced commentators have pointed to the very real conflicts which may arise between social scientists and policy-makers deriving from their different outlooks. On the part of social scientists, there may be awareness of the relative indeterminacy of social science findings, a strong need to enter qualifications and reservations about any conclusions reached, awareness of values and ideological bias, and possible suspicion of the higher reaches of government (Sharpe, 1978, 76–80). On commissions, research staff 'are generally interested in particular aspects of the committee's work, in teasing out particular problems and discovering the truth about them. Often they are less concerned than the committee – sometimes scarcely concerned at all – about the final recommendations to be made. They are most unlikely to have a grasp of all features of the situation which the committee must consider before framing its recommendations' (Donnison, 1980, 11). Short states, comparing the role of lawyers and social scientists, that 'basic differences in perspective often characterised task force operation' (Short, 1975, 74). Ohlin observes that

the sociologists serving as consultants to the commission were reluctant to specify the logical implications of their analyses in the form of action recommendations for the Commission. When they did try to do this, the recommendations were often more influenced by personal ideological conviction than by appropriately organised facts and theories as arguments (Ohlin, 1975, 110).

Lord McGregor concludes an exchange with Jeremy Tunstall, a research consultant to the Royal Commission on the Press, 1974–7, which he chaired, by observing that 'his central disagreement with the Commission turns on differences of view about policy matters. Yet he seems unable to accept that the Commission, having heard what he had to say, simply disagreed with him' (McGregor, 1980, 156). Time pressures of themselves reflect more fundamental differences in outlook between academic social scientists and policy practitioners, which members of commissions inevitably become.

(5) *The staffing of commissions*

There are marked differences between Britain and the United States in the staffing of commissions and in the expertise which the staff bring to bear. Royal Commissions typically have a small secretariat of administrative personnel who are civil servants seconded to work for the commission by its sponsoring department. There will be only two or three such staff, with clerical and secretarial support, to look after the commission. Presidential commissions are usually staffed by public service lawyers, headed by an Executive Director who hires a large staff to work under him. Thus the Kerner Commission had a *senior* staff of twenty-six and a further eighty-nine support staff (Kerner, 1968, xix-xx). The National Commission on the Causes and Prevention of Violence had a *senior* staff of twenty-seven, while one task-force alone (that headed by Jerome Skolnick) had thirty-three staff, plus consultants (Violence Commission, 1970, xix, 258-9; Skolnick, 1970).

Both civil servants and public-service lawyers have distinctive characteristics which tend to hinder the use of social science by commissions, particularly in the case of Britain. The expertise of British administrative civil servants lies in running the government machine, skills which they usually apply with superb efficiency (cf. Sharpe, 1980, 27) to the workings of a commission. But they are generalists, usually with a degree in the humanities from Oxford or Cambridge, and know little or nothing either of the subject matter of the commission or of the relevance of social science to that subject. Yet the secretary and his staff may help or hinder the use of social science research crucially – for example, by preparing summaries of research findings for circulation to members. Lacking knowledge of social science and coming from universities where until recently the social sciences were taken less than seriously, yet possessing great self-confidence in their own abilities, an arrogant, blinkered and ignorant outlook on social science may in some cases characterise the senior staff of British commissions. One should not exaggerate its role as an inhibiting factor, but it is undoubtedly a feature of British government to be taken into account (Chapman and Greenaway, 1980, 158-75). Though diminishing over time, there is still an attitude found in official circles in Britain that social science can contribute little of value to solving practical problems in broad areas of general policy-making.

In the United States, the staff of commissions are dominated by public-service lawyers (Kraft, 1969). Short, for example, describes the typical process of recruitment. The lawyers

came from influential law firms throughout the country and from a variety of government agencies. Most were young, bright, confident; and they knew their way around Washington. Their recruitment was a relatively simple matter of contact by telephone between the director (or his delegate) and personal acquaintances in the firms and agencies whence they came (Short, 1975, 65).

Few, moreover, had special relevant legal experience in criminal or poverty law. They were generalists.

The explanation for the dominance of lawyers lies in their place in the American political system and in characteristics of their occupation. They are more readily available for immediate public service, and this perpetuates a tradition of public service within the guild. 'Lawyers also experience something of role-congruence between the requirements of their occupational roles and the demands of such *ad hoc* units as national commissions' (Merton, 1975, 165). The important contrasts with social scientists lie in the intellectual perspectives, styles of work and conceptions of evidence held by lawyers. Lawyers prefer sworn eye-witness testimony, sociologists favour systematic data collection, surveys and quantitative analysis of results. For the lawyer, evidence is presented and evaluated simultaneously in the hearing, whereas for the social scientist there is an elaborate system of data analysis and reporting writing, often incorporating peer review before publication, which makes the process of reaching conclusions much more long drawn-out.

It is hardly accidental that commissions' staff are so dominated by lawyers. Aside from their availability, and the fact that senior staff who are lawyers will tend to hire junior staff who are lawyers, two characteristics are of particular importance. Lawyers are generalists who work in a problem-solving context, requiring the accommodation of the interests and perspectives of clients and colleagues. These skills may be particularly advantageous at the early stages of a commission's work when issues are weakly defined and direction uncertain. Secondly, lawyers have considerable experience of working under pressure for clients regardless of personal interests. When preparing the final report, 'the most important qualities are the ability to work all day and night, to absorb endless criticism without taking personal affront and to synthesise sentiments of commissioners or anticipate and then articulate their positions on various issues' (Lipsky and Olson, 1977, 166). These qualities tend to be possessed by lawyers and are not at a premium among social scientists. The lack of effectiveness of social science may therefore arise more from the structural situation of the staff than from antipathy to social science as is more likely to be the case in Britain.

An essential distinction must be made between administrative and research staffs. Royal Commissions on occasion do have their own research staff, who are additional to the secretariat. Practice varies; sometimes there is only one research director who coordinates the work of outside consultants (cf. Kilroy-Silk, 1973, 58), sometimes he or she heads a small research team (Sharpe, 1980), more rarely a larger body of researchers is assembled (Flowerdew, 1980; Bulmer, 1980b). The secretariat itself remains small, and usually the combined staff including researchers will be less than ten. Presidential commission staff include both administrators and researchers in large numbers. Many specialist posts are established by Presidential Commissions. The Kerner Commission's staff included, for example, Directors of Investigations, Congressional Relations, Program Operations, Research Services, and Information, and a General Counsel with three assistants. Some American commissions also hire a professional writing staff. Research staff may consist of a research director and a number of supporting staff; or a research director who then draws on the services of outside academic consultants. Several US commissions have also created Task Forces, headed either by a social scientist alone or jointly with a lawyer, to investigate particular problems in depth. These task forces have also employed their own staff and consultants. Thus, on the research as well as the administrative side, Presidential Commissions, compared to Royal Commissions, are likely to have much larger staffs. This reflects both differences in the political systems of the two countries already referred to, and the more salient part played by social science in public policy in America. It does not follow, however, that Presidential Commissions are necessarily any more effective, for reasons which will be discussed shortly.

(6) Communication between staff and commissioners

The relative positions of social scientists and generalists on the staff of commissions may be explored further by examining how both relate to commission members. Both Royal and Presidential Commissions tend to have weighty legal representation as shown in the preference of judges to chair Royal Commissions or in the number of lawyers who sit on Presidential Commissions and the additional likelihood that political members will have a legal background. Thus a third of the Commission on Pornography had law degrees (Larsen, 1975, 21), while fifteen of the nineteen members of the Law Enforcement Commission were lawyers. While there is thus likely to be a predisposition in favour of legal modes of thinking among commissioners, there is much less likely to be receptivity to social science approaches. In Britain, A. R. Prest has recounted how difficult he found it to communicate fundamental principles of economics, through concepts such as 'cost' and 'externality' on a commission considering civil liability. Algebra provoked reactions of horror, and compound interest was beyond most people's comprehension. To put across social science effectively, 'what is needed is a persuasive tongue and a willingness both to repeat the same points *ad nauseam* and to rebut insubstantive objections with patience and tolerance' (Prest, 1980, 182-4).

Whereas generalist administrators or lawyers are likely to be in tune with the ways of thinking of the majority of commissioners, social scientists are not. Research workers for commissions, if of high enough calibre, have views of their own, well-established working methods and public reputations. They are not a neutral element providing technical help (Donnison, 1980, 11-12).

Similar observations are made of American Commisions.

The conceptual research and interpretive effort involved...is formidable. It takes concerted effort to convince commissioners, let alone policy-makers, that policy is not necessarily synonymous with law, or that social control can mean anything other than law enforcement (Larsen, 1975, 17).

Tradition, government sponsorship and backgrounds of commissioners make for a heavy commitment to the legal approach.

The internal politics of commissions do clearly on occasion affect the influence exercised by social science. The clearest example of this is provided by the Kerner Commission, where in the middle of its work a substantial proportion of the staff, including research workers, were dismissed at short notice. There were various factors contributing to these events, including financial difficulties, but one of the most important was disappointment among the executive staff at the quality of the research produced (Lipsky and Olson, 1977, 191). Particular controversy centred on an analytic essay by commission social scientists examining riot causation. It was a loose, imaginative document attempting to make sense of confusing events and suggest categories for future analysis. Though the executive staff had originally asked for it, it was indeed too sweeping and too far from a legal brief to be acceptable. It was too speculative and not sufficiently documented. 'To ask commissioners to put their signatures to such a document would be folly. To present the document for their consideration would seriously impair confidence in the staff' (Lipsky and Olson, 1977, 186). Instead, the executive staff's rejection of the document precipitated internal crisis, and outside criticism when dismissals were instituted.

(7) *Pressures of work*

Sweeping generalisations about the internal workings of commissions are particularly likely to be wide of the mark. Neither a picture of deep cleavages between staff and commissioners, nor that of a cosy conspiracy among all concerned to arrive at predetermined results, is near to the general state of affairs. It may be true that lawyers are more predisposed to advocacy, marshalling evidence to support a particular case, while social scientists are more likely to look at all sides of a question and to want to generate new data (Short, 1975, 74). In the actual workings of commissions, however, these differences tend to get softened in the sheer hard work involved, and the development of a common commitment to reach a final report and achieve some impact. This tendency for commissions to seek consensus was discussed earlier, but it also bears on their internal organisations.

The atmosphere of Commission activity is difficult to approximate...We worked incredibly long hours...While all of this activity seemed to occur more-or-less continuously in a frenetic melange, it was not unstructured. Staff contact with the Commissioners...was handled through the executive director ...Research directors were the chief mediators between the task forces and senior staff, though there was much direct contact among all parties...there was an active social life, among Commissioners, between Commissioners and staff, and within the staff (Short, 1975, 78-9).

A good deal of the time of the research directors, and indeed of more junior research staff, may be spent on matters not directly related to research or report preparation. For example, on Royal Commissions, the research director may be encouraged to attend hearings of witnesses, in order to be available to answer questions, though his or her time would be better spent elsewhere on research matters. These pressures bear on the chairman, too. The reminiscences of the chairman of the Royal Commission on the Poor Laws 1906-9, on which Beatrice Webb sat, record that it 'was by far the heaviest business in which I was ever engaged...The task of keeping (the members) together was very tiring and at times impossible' (Hamilton, 1922, 329). In the end, majority and minority reports were produced.

In this social process, informal groups may arise which cut across the conventional boundaries of the commission. Ohlin (1975) on the Law Enforcement Commission observed the emergence of small informal groups or cliques among members and staff, holding broadly similar but non-specific ideological positions. The existence of these groups was recognised by the chairman and executive director, and the divisions were kept firmly under control. At the same time, such differences actively performed an integrative function from the point of view of the objectives of the Commission. The chairman and executive director

maintained constant pressure to keep the recommendation closely tied to factually supported premises or to theoretical views which would be shared in common. At the same time, these informal ideological factors generated strong motivation to produce persuasive factual and theoretical support for the arguments and recommendations proposed to the full Commission (Ohlin, 1975, 111).

The formation of subcommittees or task forces may also help to achieve a similar objective. Though conflict often exists, it may be functional for the workings of the commission (cf. Coser, 1956). A full account of how commissions operate can not be confined to analysis of the different roles played by commissioners and staff, administrative or research. The dynamics of their interaction have to be considered, and the sense of purpose and group morale which an *ad hoc* commission generates appreciated.

(8) *The relevance of social science*

Although in principle social science may be relevant to the tasks facing a commission, its theory or its findings may be too arcane for members to assimilate. Indeed one may question whether commissions are suitable bodies to tackle complex theoretical issues. The extreme view is that

commissions are poor instruments for a particular purpose – explaining complicated social phenomena, which requires a high order of scientific competence. Committees are probably poor instruments for conducting scientific inquiry under any circumstances, and when the circumstances include the President's sponsorship, the close attention of the press, an atmosphere of crisis, and a subject matter inherently very difficult, they are poorer still (Derthick, 1971, 635).

An early example of such difficulties was the Wickersham Commission of 1931 in the United States. Having commissioned a number of pioneering studies of the causes of crime, including studies of juvenile delinquency causation by Shaw and McKay and a study of the ethnic origins of Chicago criminals by W. F. Ogburn, it declined to pronounce upon the scientific evidence, to favour one theory rather than another. Nearly fifty years later, the Royal Commission on the Distribution of Income and Wealth, strongly committed to research and with impressive results behind it, examined the incidence of poverty. Having received written and oral evidence on its causes, including cross examination of leading social scientists, on heredity and environmental factors in human differences, it concluded that

> questions of causation are notoriously difficult to answer in the economic and social fields... The present state of knowledge does not point with certainty to any single explanation as to why some families and individuals have lower incomes than others (Bulmer, 1980, 170).

The Chairman quite explicitly justified this position. Its task could not embrace getting involved in a vast field requiring lengthy study, which was a 'side issue' to the distribution of income and wealth. Another member of the commission drew a sharp distinction between factual and theoretic inquiry.

> The unanimity of the Commission on its presentation of its factual materials has been reached only after long discussion, and its *Reports* are the more valuable for that reason. But this experience makes me doubtful whether panels of persons of different social and political attitude and conviction can form an effective instrument of inquiry and report in questions not of fact but of social causality (Sir Henry Phelps-Brown, quoted in Bulmer, 1980a, 172).

The problems of communication and understanding of complex ideas and theoretical principles can also arise in the presentation of evidence and the explanation of methodology. One British commission, the Seebohm Committee on Personal Social Services, made little use of social research. One piece of research which they did commission, however, had little impact because not only were the results inconclusive but they were technically presented and difficult to interpret. The secretary could not summarise them and members were no more successful (Hall, 1980, 79). These difficulties of course arise more generally in making social science relevant to policy. More research does not necessarily mean clearer-cut answers to questions. It may in fact mean *less* clear-cut answers, more complex results, and a greater effort needed to interpret those results. Social science research presented to commissions is an acid test of relevance and intelligibility since staff and commission members expect material to be relevant and to be stated in such a form that the lay person can understand it.

A more general comment still on the role of social science in the work of commissions is to ask whether the most basic questions which commissions face are susceptible to answer by social science techniques. Are matters on which commissions deliberate not ultimately matters of judgement on the principles which should guide policy? The Commission on Obscenity and Pornography was criticised for relying too exclusively on social science research.

In the cases of (the commissions on) violence and obscenity, it is unlikely that social science can either show harmful effects or prove that there are no harmful effects. It is unlikely, in short, that considerations of utility or disutility can be governing. These are moral issues and ultimately all judgements about the acceptability of restrictions on various media will have to rest on political and philosophical considerations (Wilson, 1971, 61).

Westhoff considers that in the case of the Commission on Population Growth, research

probably had little effect on the philosophic spirit of the report. The same competing frames of reference would have been advanced and probably resolved in the same way because they were essentially different views of the world, largely outside the jurisdiction of scientific evaluation. Much of the rhetoric... would (also) have been the same (Westhoff, 1975, 54).

Nevertheless, research did influence some of the basic conclusions about the effects of population growth, and policy recommendations. Commissions on moral and penal questions are perhaps more likely to make recommendations resting ultimately on philosophical principles, whereas commissions on subjects like social unrest, government organisations, income and wealth, or the location of an airport may give more weight to social-science-based evidence.

(9) *Pressures to reach consensus*

What is certainly true, however, is that commissions in reaching conclusions and making recommendations take a great deal of account of the political context in which they operate.

Collectively – that is for the Commission *qua* organisation – it becomes more important to arrive at agreement than to arrive at the fullest and most accurate explanation of events; and more important to win acceptance for what is said, than to assume what is said is the closest approximation to the truth (Derthick, 1971, 629).

The emphasis upon achieving consensus among the members of the commission reflects the equation between unanimity and likely political effectiveness. A commission which produces two or more reports is less likely to be listened to carefully than one which produces a single report. The pressures to unanimity are reinforced by the socialisation and collective experience of their members, and their *esprit de corps*, but the overriding aim is based on an assessment of the political disadvantages of dissension (Wolanin, 1975, 120).

Achieving consensus without the need to present minority reports is therefore likely to be a major objective of the commission's chairman and of its secretary or executive director. Lord Rothschild, chairman of the Royal Commission on Gambling, 1975-8, observes that in order to produce a useful report, long hours of discussion led by the chairman are required. 'The ideal chairman is one who is able to blend the discordant views of his or her colleagues into a harmonious tune' (Rothschild, 1978, 11). On the American Law Enforcement Commission

the process of communication among commission and staff members was designed to forestall the development of sharply conflicting positions and to achieve a compromise position wherever possible. The chairman showed considerable ingenuity and talent in his capacity to search out and negotiate compromise positions when serious conflicts developed (Ohlin, 1975, 105).

The desire to achieve consensus may act as a constraint upon the expression of differing perspectives and their exploration through research.

A particular danger is the liability of commissions to intellectual capture, and the structuring of inquiry from the outset in particular directions. The 'capture' may be political. Derthick (1971) maintains that commissions are primarily political instruments, and that the Kerner Report, for example, became 'the orthodox Liberal textbook' for a whole range of social issues beyond race relations. Or the 'capture' may, more insidiously, be intellectual. In Britain, the Donovan Commission on Trades Unions mounted an impressive research programme, but one carried out within a specific orientation to industrial relations problems.

The authors (of the research) constituted a small inbred group sharing a similar frame of reference, what has been called the 'new Oxford group'. Most of the authors of the papers were known to be against the introduction of the law into industrial relations and most of the papers argued against it. The authors were 'fact-grubbers'. What they provided was an impressive array of facts and little in the way of attempts to link cause and effect and generalise from them. They summarised each other's work and quoted each other with approval (Kilroy-Silk, 1973, 58).

Acland (1980, 53) has suggested that despite its apparent reliance upon objective research, the influential Plowden committee used research as a device for 'stage-management', to frame and strengthen the conclusions of the liberal educationists who had most weight in the committee. It provided the setting and the scenery for an action (the commission's report) which was distinct from the research but which was framed by it.

(10) *Political acceptance or non-acceptance*

In the end, a commission's work, whatever the extent that it is social science based, will result in a report, with recommendations, which is published. Does it have any effect? Do the recommendations get implemented? Though experience is very variable, it is here perhaps that cynicism about the usefulness of commissions is most marked. As Lord Rothschild put it, 'was the sweat worth while?' Elisabeth Drew has suggested, tongue-in-cheek, five strategies for governments to deal with reports: (1) hide for as long as possible and then throw it over the White House fence; (2) postpone or play down its release; (3) dissociate or denounce the report; (4) hope the public's interest in the report has waned; or (5) ignore it. She reflects the feeling among commissioners and observers that all too often the report falls on stony ground.

A dramatic example of this was the social-science based Commission on Obscenity and Pornography, whose report was rejected by Congress as 'irresponsible' and 'degrading' and by President Nixon as 'morally bankrupt' (Larsen, 1975, 9). In both cases the word 'unacceptable' would be a more accurate description. The commission had more input than any previous one from sociologists, yet was judged almost entirely unacceptable when published. Its effect was not wholly negative (Larsen, 1975, 39–40), but it was in effect rejected out of hand by those to whom it was principally addressed. Daniel Bell (1966, 4–5) has recounted a very similar experience with the report of the Technology Commission, which the White House issued in an underhand fashion and in effect buried, because it was regarded as too controversial. Reports of British Royal Commissions can not be delayed by political interference, but their recommendations face the same hurdle as those of Presidential Commissions: political acceptance.

Conclusions

Commissions provide social scientists with an opportunity to influence the direction taken by national policy. Governments seem to set up commissions because they believe that they have public support and this support comes from the view that commissions are independent bodies, 'an instrument of truth and therefore a purveyor of justice whose siren song no government will be powerful enough to resist' (Rothschild, 1978, 9). The findings of commissions have far more impact than those of individuals. 'Facts' presenting a harshly critical appraisal of a social issue by a journalist or social scientist risk being branded as muckraking. The same facts presented in the report of a commission are likely to be seen as startling and respectable social facts. Whatever their defects, commission reports come to have a special standing within the political community (cf. Skolnick, 1970, 38). In both Britain and the United States, governmental commissions find it easier to produce bipartisan conclusions on contentious issues than do either Select Committees of the House of Commons or Congressional Committees.

Such a comparison invites the criticism that the preceding discussion neglects the differences in political structure between Britain and America, and treats governmental commissions out of context. However, the purpose of the analysis has been to identify elements in common between these bodies in the two systems, rather than to reproduce a familiar account of Anglo-American contrasts in political structure. If one considers the ten factors identified as hindering the use of social science, five of them are clearly features of the character and dynamics of commissions' working, which are similar even in different political systems, namely: time pressures; problems of communication between staff and commissioners; pressures of work; the desire to reach consensus; and the theoretical and factual complexity of social science.

Five other obstacles to the use of social science are clearly related to some extent to the nature of the political system within which the commission operates. Some of these are structural, such as problems of funding, staffing and the political acceptance of the findings of the commission. There are clear differences here between Britain and the United States. For example, commission recommendations have to commend themselves to a wider constituency in the United States and the division of powers means that the implementation is likely to be more problematical than if the government decides to act on a report in Britain.

Differences in political culture between the two societies also influence both the predispositions of commissioners, staff and social scientists toward one another, and the character of the staffs of commissions. For example, the far more extensive employment of research staff, and the scale of research carried out by American commissions undoubtedly reflects the more central position of social science in the political life of the country (Sharpe, 1978). Even so, it is not clear that the results are necessarily more influential upon the deliberations of commissions, for some of the reasons common to commissions as instruments of government. Though Royal Commissions and Presidential Commissions have a different legal and constitutional status, and operate in distinctively different political cultures, so far as their use of social science is concerned – and the obstacles to its use – the similarities are more striking than the differences.

Social scientists in both countries are concerned that their efforts in contributing to the work of commissions do not have the effects that they wish them to have. For a number of reasons, the application of social science faces many practical obstacles. Yet it may be objected that this diagnosis derives from a short-term rather than a long-term view of the influence and effectiveness of commission reports and their associated research. Just because social science does not immediately influence the views of commissioners, or because government ignores the main recommendations, does not mean that there is not longer-term influence (cf. Wolanin, 1975, 145–54).

The variable experience of the use (and non-use) of social science by commissions raises the issue of the most appropriate model for studying this policy-making process. Those who hold that social science research has a pre-eminent role to play in leading commissions toward recommendations which would be implemented quickly tend to use an 'engineering' model of the relationship between social science and social action (Janowitz, 1970, 243–59). The social scientist is seen as analogous to a doctor or engineer. A problem is presented, and the social scientist identifies the knowledge that is missing, seeks means to gather some or all of this knowledge, analyses the results, and interprets the results to make them relevant to the problem posed initially. Policy implementation follows. The foregoing discussion suggests, as others have argued (e.g. Lindblom and Cohen, 1979) that this is an oversimple view of the role of social science research, which inflates its importance and overlooks important obstacles to its influence.

An alternative approach, the 'enlightenment' model, suggests that the impact of social science upon social policy is more diffuse, and that there is a less sharp distinction between basic and applied research. The social scientist recognises that he is part of the social process and not outside of it. The advocates of the enlightenment model reject the view that social scientific knowledge produces definitive answers on which policy and professional practice can be based. Sociology is but one aspect of the social sciences, and the social sciences themselves but one type of knowledge required for policy (Janowitz, 1972, 4). An allied approach, to see social science as a means of conceptualisation (Weiss, 1977, 15–16), emphasises its importance as providing a way of looking at society, of thinking about issues, of defining and redefining 'problems', and assisting policy-makers to cope with the world.

The experience of the use (and non-use) of social science research by commissions fits much better with the 'enlightenment' than with the 'engineering' model. The influence of sociology and other social sciences lies less in being of direct utility than in providing a general perspective upon the problems and issues with which particular commissions are concerned (Bulmer, forthcoming). Moreover, theories of the policy-making process such as Lindblom's disjointed incrementalism and partisan mutual adjustment stress the interactive nature of national policy-making. The effects of many commissions, in the short run, seem to be more disjointed than incremental – i.e. they do *not* lead directly to policy change, and the members of the commission and those who observe its work become cynical and disillusioned about its effects.

This, however, is to miss a very important point. The Royal Commission on the Poor Law, 1906–9 had no immediate effect. Indeed in the short run it was largely a waste of effort, other than as a means of educating the public about the poor and giving some support to collectivist ideas which were growing in popularity at the time. Yet in the longer term the minority report, of which Beatrice Webb was the main author, anticipated many of the features of the system of welfare provision and support that became established in Britain in the middle of the twentieth century. Its effect was a long-range one, diffuse and difficult to pin down. Yet it is now recognised to have been an important landmark about social welfare in the history of British social policy. So it is with many of the subjects on which commissions report, particularly on moral issues such as censorship, obscenity, gambling, homosexuality and so on. In judging whether social science contributes effectively to the work of commissions, therefore, one also needs to take a long view.

NOTE

1 The term 'commission' is used here to refer to special *ad hoc* bodies set up to advise on specific policy problems. There are a number of bodies in both the British and American political systems with 'Commission' in their title, which are of a rather different character. They include permanent commissions such as the Canadian-American Boundary Commission, the American Battle Monuments Commission, the Royal Commission on Historical Manuscripts and the Royal Commission on Historical Monuments. There are also permanent governmental or quasi-governmental organisations such as the Federal Communication Commission, the Interstate Commerce Commission, the Civil Service Commission, the Commission for Racial Equality, the Royal Fine Arts Commission, and so on. These are not considered here. For uses of the word, see Mansfield (1968).

British Royal Commissions are bodies set up by the Queen in Council under the royal seal. There are in Britain also Departmental Committees, many of which in recent years have been as important as Royal Commissions, while some Royal Commissions have been established on trivial subjects. The term 'Royal Commission' is used to refer both to Royal Commissions proper and to important Departmental Committees, following Vernon and Mansergh (1940, 24), Rhodes (1975, chapter 2) and Cartwright (1975, chapter 2). Where the term 'Royal Commission' appears unqualified, it refers to Britain.

American Presidential Commissions are also sometimes referred to as national governmental study commissions (cf. Wolanin, 1975). They are distinguished by their importance from other bodies established by the President. Where the term 'Presidential Commission' appears unqualified in this article, it refers to the United States.

REFERENCES

Acland, H. (1980) Research as stage-management: the case of the Plowden Committee. In Bulmer (1980b, 34–57).
Bell, D. (1966) Government by Commission, *The Public Interest*, 3 (Spring), 3–9.
Bulmer, M. (1980a) The Royal Commission on the Distribution of Income & Wealth. In Bulmer (1980b, 158–79).
Bulmer, M. (ed.) (1980b) *Social Research and Royal Commissions*. London: Allen and Unwin.
Bulmer, M. (1981) Charles S. Johnson, Robert E. Park and the research methods of the

Chicago Commission on Race Relations, 1919-22, *Ethnic & Racial Studies*, 4, 289-306.
Bulmer, M. (forthcoming) *The Uses of Social Research: Social Investigation in Public Policy-making.* London: Allen and Unwin.
Cartwright, T. J. (1975) *Royal Commissions and Departmental Committees in Britain.* London: Hodder & Stoughton.
Chapman, R. A. (ed.) (1973) *The Role of Commissions in Policy-Making.* London: Allen and Unwin.
Chapman, R. A. and J. Greenaway (1980) *The Dynamics of Administrative Reform.* London: Croom Helm.
Checkland, S. and E. Checkland (1974) *The Poor Law Report of 1834.* Harmondsworth: Penguin.
Chicago Commission on Race Relations (1922) *The Negro in Chicago.* Chicago: University of Chicago Press.
Cleveland, H. (1964) Inquiry into Presidential Inquiries. In D. B. Johnson and J. L. Walker (eds.), *The Dynamics of the American Presidency.* New York: Wiley, 291-4.
Clokie, H. M. and J. W. Robinson (1937) *Royal Commissions of Inquiry.* Stanford: Stanford University Press.
Coser, L. A. (1956) *The Functions of Social Conflict.* New York: Free Press.
Craven, E. (1978) Issues on representation. In R. Davies and P. Hall (eds.), *Issues in Urban Society,* Harmondsworth: Penguin, 242-67.
Cronin, T. E. and Greenberg, S. D. (eds.) (1969) *The Presidential Advisory System.* New York: Harper.
Dean, A. L. (1969) *Ad hoc* Commissions for Policy Formulation? In Cronin and Greenberg (1969, 101-16).
Derthick, M. (1971) On Commissionship – Presidential Variety, *Public Policy*, 19, 623-38.
Dibelius, W. (1930) *England.* London: Cape.
Donnison, D. (1980) Committees and Committeemen. In Bulmer (1980b, 9-17).
Drew, E. (1968) On giving oneself a hotfoot: government by commission, *The Atlantic,* 221 (May), 45-9.
Farrell, C. (1980) The Royal Commission on the National Health Service, *Policy and Politics,* 8, 189-203.
Flowerdew, A. D. J. (1980) A Commission and a Cost-Benefit Study. In Bulmer (1980b, 85-109).
Gosnell, H. F. (1934) British Royal Commissions of Inquiry, *Political Science Quarterly,* 49, 84-118.
Hall, P. (1980) The Seebohm Committee and the under-use of research. In Bulmer (1980b, 67-84).
Hamilton, Lord George (1922) *Parliamentary Reminiscences and Reflections 1886-1906.* London: Murray.
Hanser, C. J. (1965) *Guide to Decision: the Royal Commission.* Totowa, NJ: The Bedminster Press.
Herbert, A. P. (1961) Anything but Action?: a study of the uses and abuses of committees of inquiry. In R. Harris (ed.), *Radical Reaction.* London: Hutchinson for IEA, 251-302.
Hood, R. (1974) Criminology and Penal change: a case study of the nature and impact of some recent advice to government. In R. Hood (ed.), *Crime, Criminology and Public Policy.* London: Heinemann, 375-90.
Janowitz, M. (1970) *Political Conflict.* Chicago: Quadrangle.
Janowitz, M. (1972) *Sociological Models and Social Policy.* New York: General Learning Press.
Karl, B. E. (1969) Presidential planning and social science research: Mr. Hoover's experts, *Perspectives in American History,* 3, 347-409.
Kerner Report (1968) *Report of the National Advisory Commission on Civil Disorders.* Washington DC: US Government Printing Office.
Kilroy-Silk, R. (1973) The Donovan Royal Commission on Trade Unions. In Chapman (1973, 42-80).
Komarovsky, M. (ed.) (1975) *Sociology and Public Policy: the Case of the Presidential Commissions.* New York: Elsevier.

Kraft, J. (1969) The Washington Lawyers. In Cronin and Greenberg (1969, 150–5).
Larsen, O. N. (1975) The Commission on Obscenity and Pornography: form, function and failure. In Komarovsky (1975, 9–41).
Lipsky, M. and D. J. Olson (1977) *Commission Politics: the processing of racial crisis in America*. Rutgers, NJ: Transaction.
McGregor, O. R. (1957) Social research and social policy in the nineteenth century, *British Journal of Sociology*, 8, 146–57.
McGregor, O. R. (1980) The Royal Commission on the Press, 1974–7: a note. In Bulmer (1980, 150–7).
Mansfield, H. C. (1968) Commissions, Government. In D. L. Sills (ed.), *International Encyclopaedia of the Social Sciences*, vol. III, 13–18.
Marx, K. (1959) *Capital*. Moscow: Foreign Languages Publishing House. (First published 1867.)
Merton, R. K. (1975) Social knowledge and public policy: sociological perspectives on four presidential commissions. In Komarovsky (1975, 153–77).
Ohlin, L. E. (1975) The President's Commission on Law Enforcement and the Administration of Justice. In Komarovsky (1975, 93–115).
Pinker, R. A. (1971) *Social Theory and Social Policy*. London: Heinemann.
Platt, A. (ed.) (1971) *The Politics of Riot Commissions 1917–1970*. New York: Macmillan.
Popper, F. (1970) *The President's Commissions*. New York: Twentieth Century Fund.
Prest, A. R. (1980) Royal Commission reporting. In Bulmer (1980b, 180–8).
Rhodes, G. (1975) *Committees of Inquiry*. London: Allen and Unwin.
Rhodes, G. (1980) The Younger Committee and Research. In Bulmer (1980, 110–21).
Robbins Committee (1963) *Higher Education*. London: HMSO.
Rothschild, Lord (1978) Address to the British Academy, 29 June 1978. Unpublished MS. (Briefly reported in *The Times*, 30 June 1978.)
Sharpe, L. J. (1978) The social scientist and policy-making in Britain and America: a comparison. In M. Bulmer (ed.), *Social Policy Research*. London: Macmillan, 302–12.
Sharpe, L. J. (1980) Research and the Redcliffe-Maud Commission. In Bulmer (1980b, 18–33).
Shonfield, A. (1980) In the course of investigation. In Bulmer (1980b, 58–66).
Short, J. F. Jr. (1975) The National Commission on the Causes and Prevention of Violence: the contributions of sociology and sociologists. In Komarovsky (1975, 61–91).
Short, J. F. Jr. (ed.) (1978) *Delinquency, Crime and Society*. Chicago: University of Chicago Press.
Skolnick, J. H. (1970) Violence Commission violence, *Transaction*, 7 (October), 32–8.
Sulzner, G. T. (1971) The policy process and the uses of National Governmental Study Commissions, *Western Political Quarterly*, 24, 438–48.
Thomas, H. (ed.) (1959) *The Establishment*. London: Blond.
Tunstall, J. (1980) The Royal Commission on the Press, 1974–7. In Bulmer (1980, 122–49).
Violence Commission (1970) *To Establish Justice, To Ensure Domestic Tranquility: The Final Report of the National Commission on the Causes and Prevention of Violence*. Washington DC, US Government Printing Office.
Vernon, R. V. and N. Mansergh (eds.) (1940) *Advisory Bodies*. London: Allen and Unwin.
Walker Report (1968) *Rights in Conflict: a report to the National Commission on the Causes and Prevention of Violence*. New York: Dutton.
Waskow, A. I. (1967) *From Race Riot to Sit-In: 1919 and the 1960's*. New York: Doubleday.
Webb, B. (1948) *Our Partnership*. London: Longmans.
Webb, S. and B. Webb (1932) *Methods of Social Study*. London: Longmans.
Weiss, C. H. (1977) Introduction. In C. H. Weiss (ed.), *Using Social Research in Public Policy-Making*. Farnborough: D. C. Heath, 1–22.
Westhoff, C. F. (1975) The Commission on Population Growth and the American Future: origins, operations and aftermath. In Komarovsky (1975, 43–59).
Wheare, K. C. (1955) *Government by Committee*. Oxford: Clarendon Press.

Wilson, J. Q. (1971) Violence, pornography and social science, *The Public Interest*, 22 (Winter), 45–61.

Wolanin, T. R. (1975) *Presidential Advisory Commissions: Truman to Nixon.* Madison, Wisconsin: University of Wisconsin Press.

4

POLICY ANALYSIS AND POLICY POLITICS

Robert D. Behn

The policy analyst is concerned with efficiency and outputs, and ignores sunk costs; the policy politician is concerned with distribution and inputs, and seeks to justify sunk costs. These differences, can be derived from the analyst's indifference to constituencies and the politician's devotion to them, says the author, who suggests several ways for policy analysts to increase their political influence. The complete policy analyst will not only recommend the best policy alternative but also the best political strategy for the adoption and implementation of this alternative.

In the game of public policy, to use Graham Allison's metaphor, there are two principal players: the policy analysts and the policy politicians.[1]

The policy analysts are concerned with economic efficiency, with how public policies affect society as a whole. They emphasize ex-

---

I would like to thank the National Science Foundation for their assistance in this research (Grant on the Termination of Public Policies, SOC-7719116). However, any opinions, findings, conclusions, or recommendations expressed herein are mine and do not necessarily reflect the views of the foundation. I am also grateful to Philip J. Cook, Willis D. Hawley, Giandomenico Majone, Arnold J. Meltsner, John Mendeloff, David S. Mundell, Robert H. Nelson, Allen Schick, Deborah A. Stone, and James W. Vaupel for their comments and criticisms on a working paper from which this article is excerpted. As these colleagues may note, however, their advice may have been ignored or distorted, and thus they should not be held responsible for any of my conclusions, opinions or errors. I hope to follow up on some of their suggestions in future work on this topic.

1. Graham T. Allison, *Essence of Decision* (Boston: Little, Brown, 1971), pp. 162-63. Allison suggests that policymaking be viewed as a game with each of the players playing different positions, rather than as a set-play with each actor having a different (but specified) role.

Copyright © 1981 by Robert D. Behn. Reprinted from *Policy Analysis*, Vol. 7, No. 2 (Spring 1981), pp. 199-226, by permission of the author.

plicitly defined policy objectives and conscious tradeoffs between competing objectives. They seek clear measures of outcomes—of how successfully these objectives are being realized. With a faith in their analytical techniques, the analysts draw their policy recommendations from abstract, mathematical models.[2]

In contrast, the policy politicians are concerned with distribution, with how public policies affect individuals and groups. They emphasize negotiation, bargaining and compromise, and the obscuration of competing objectives to achieve consensus. They seek the resolution of conflict between competing interests—the allocation of limited resources between such interests. With a faith in the political process, the politicians draw their policy recommendations from the intensity of their constituents' views.

This split in the world of public policy is similar to the division that C. P. Snow found in the intellectual world between the "two cultures" of the physical scientists and the literary intellectuals.[3]

2. In this article, I am distinguishing "policy analysis" from both "social science research" and "policy evaluation." Policy analysis is the examination of a particular policy problem in an effort to determine what the government should do; usually, but not always, it is prepared for a particular policymaker who wants to make, has to make, or is able to make a specific decision (or take a specific action) about the policy problem. Policy analysis addresses questions like "What should the government do about unemployment?"

Social science research and policy evaluation may also be motivated by a desire to determine what the government should do, but they approach that question only indirectly. Social science research is designed to uncover relationships—not necessarily causal—between various variables (of which none may be open to government manipulation). It addresses questions like "How is an individual's probability of being unemployed related to his or her sex, race, age, education, criminal record, previous employment record?" In contrast, policy evaluation is designed to determine the impact of existing programs. It addresses questions like "How effective is the Job Corps program in reducing unemployment?"

Social science research and policy evaluation require original research and thus are complicated by the methodological problems of research design, data collection, and data analysis. By contrast, the policy analyst, rather than initiating his own original research, often examines the results of the research of others to determine how relevant it all is to the policy problem at hand, perhaps performing some back-of-the-envelope (or on-line computer) calculations on the data or results of others to reach conclusions more directly relevant to the policy problem. Policy analysis contains an explicit, and usually detailed, recommendation for government action (or nonaction).

Much has been written about the uses of social science research. This article focuses on policy analysis.

3. C. P. Snow, *The Two Cultures and the Scientific Revolution* (Cambridge: Cambridge University Press, 1959).

Like Snow's scientist, the policy analyst is the optimist, completely convinced that the proposal that his or her analysis reveals to be the best can indeed make society better. And like the literary intellectual, the policy politician is the pessimist, as equally convinced that the analyst's newest gadget, be it benefit-cost analysis, systems analysis, PPB, MBO, or ZBB, will only make the policy process more complicated, not better, and that the sole, reasonable course is to continue to muddle through. As with Snow's two cultures, the fundamentally different values, attitudes, and emotions of the analyst and the politician cannot only inhibit communication, but also produce a caustic and pernicious antipathy between the two groups.

This dichotomy is of course an exaggeration. The analyst and the politician just described are ideal types—caricatures who define the poles of a continuous spectrum stretching from the mathematician at one end, who is fascinated with the intricacies of his models, to the self-promoting officeholder at the other end, who lavishes largess upon whatever constituency can benefit him most. But the distribution along this spectrum is curiously bimodal, with the players grouped near the two ends so that they appear almost organized into two teams (or perhaps into two leagues with the players engaged in similar games but with different rules, traditions, and scoring systems). In the following discussion, the terms *policy analyst* and *policy politician* refer strictly—it must be emphasized—to these ideal types, though the examples used to illustrate their behavior and attitudes must necessairly be drawn from the actions and words of real, more complex, policy players.

Indeed, each individual player possesses a unique combination of analytical and political skills, and for any specific policy game the players will choose up sides depending upon their talents and predilections. Thus a traditional politician may be quite analytical when considering issues that do not affect him or his constituencies; and an analyst may be quite political when viewing policies that impinge upon his interests—or upon those of the analytical community. Arnold J. Meltsner has warned of "the false division of policymaking into two incompatible camps," and the division should not be exaggerated.[4] Nevertheless, economic rationality and political rationality *are* often in conflict, and the nature of that conflict so affects the practice of policy analysis that it cannot be ignored.

4. Arnold J. Meltsner, *Policy Analysts in the Bureaucracy* (Berkeley, Calif.: University of California Press, 1976), p. 278.

THE ANALYTICAL AND POLITICAL IDEOLOGIES

Of the behavioral, attitudinal, stylistic differences listed above, a few relate most directly to the conflict between analyst and politician and to the relative influence of the two players.

Efficiency, Equity, and Distribution

The analyst's criterion for policy choice is aggregate economic efficiency.[5] The best policy is the one with the largest net benefits. Summing all the benefits and subtracting all the costs provides the analyst with a measure of the public interest.

The net social benefit criterion of course ignores questions of distribution—of who gets the benefits and who pays the costs. Even with the most efficient alternative, some individuals and groups may find that their own costs exceed their benefits. Yet, the analyst will argue, the policy alternative for which aggregate benefits most exceed aggregate costs will generate the greatest excess of benefits for compensating such losers or for achieving society's distributional objectives, whatever they may be. Using the efficiency criterion provides the best opportunity to redistribute income to whichever groups society believes to be the most worthy or most in need.

The argument that distributional objectives are best achieved by first maximizing economic efficiency can unfortunately be used to excuse a neglect of equity considerations. Under the analytical ideology, the goal of social equity is best pursued, not through the adjustment of each individual program and policy, but through an entirely separate redistributional program—preferably some form of negative income tax. That designing, enacting, and implementing such a redistributional program has proved impossible is unfortunate and troubling, but not sufficient cause to modify the efficiency

---

5. My definition of "policy analysis"—as it is practiced rather than as it should be practiced—emphasizes the discipline of economics rather than statistics, operations research, urban planning, or even "policy analysis" as it is now being taught at the newly created schools of public policy. That is because (1) economics provides the criterion by which most policy analysts make their judgments, and (2) most of today's analysts either came to their work with a significant background in economics, or quickly obtained one. Note, for example, that President Carter's original cabinet of twelve department heads contained five economists (or analysts: Blumenthal, Brown, Kreps, Marshall, and Schlesinger), five lawyers (or politicians: Adams, Bell, Califano, Harris, and Vance) and two "others" (who, as proof that you can make it in Washington without a college degree, also fit in the politician category: Andrus and Bergland).

criterion when analyzing questions of pollution control, mass transit, health manpower, water resource management, or defense procurement. Identifying those who will lose from a new policy, and the size of their loss, and designing a practical mechanism for compensating them may be quite difficult, but the theoretical possibility of doing so is sufficient for adoption of the efficiency criterion. The analyst is deeply concerned about social equity; this is one of the reasons the analyst argues so vigorously for the most efficient alternative: to provide the most excess benefits for redistribution. But having professed concern, the analyst leaves the problem of equity for another day.[6]

That efficiency dominates equity as an analytical value is quite explicable. For efficiency, there exists a single, simple measure: net social benefits. In contrast, equity can only be described, and then merely obliquely, in terms of Lorenz curves and Gini coefficients. There exists no simple, single measure for determining whether any distribution of income or assets is more equitable than another. Further, regardless of how difficult it is to determine total costs and total benefits, it will always be harder to identify their distribution.[7] Many benefits may be quite focused and direct, but most of the costs

6. Henry Rosen writes: "Should equity issues be dealt with in each policy decision, or should they be dealt with through a separate income distribution policy? (The usual procedure in cost-benefit analyses, of course, is to neglect distributional consequences and limit the analysis to a measure of aggregate efficiency—one reason that policy makers show little enthusiasm for such analyses.) . . . In specific cases there usually is no way to identify all of the gainers and losers, and the information costs of attempting such identification are often high. Moreover, the mechanisms for compensating losers are weak or nonexistent. . . . An analysis which omits distributional effects and discusses only aggregate efficiency deals with a part of the decision maker's problem, and perhaps only a small part" ("The Role of Cost-Benefit Analysis in Policy Making," in *Cost Benefit Analysis and Water Pollution Policy*, ed. Henry M. Peskin and Eugene P. Seskin [Washington, D.C.: Urban Institute, 1975]), pp. 367–68.

7. Robert H. Haveman and Julius Margolis cite this as one of the arguments against a formal weighting of benefits and costs to reflect who benefits and who pays: "Obtaining accurate data on the distributional impact of public expenditures is often difficult. Not only must the distribution of the benefits be ascertained, but also the distribution of costs to taxpayers and true resource suppliers. Because of the difficulty of accurately estimating these patterns with existing knowledge, it is not yet appropriate to incorporate equity weights into formal benefit and cost estimates" ("Public Expenditure and Policy Analysis: An Overview," in *Public Expenditure and Policy Analysis*, 2d ed., ed. Haveman and Margolis [Chicago: Rand McNally, 1977]), p. 19).

(to the taxpayer and to the consumer, through an increase in the national debt and the resulting inflation) will inevitably be dispersed and indirect. Because efficiency is a simple, single, specific, measurable criterion, it is more adaptable than equity to analytical work.

In contrast to the analyst, the politician is most interested in distribution. Political influence is exercised not by individual citizens but through the intermediation of organized constituencies, and as an elected official or the political appointee of one, the policy politician is responsive to constituencies—not to the analyst's abstract notion of aggregate public welfare. The politician is deeply concerned about how much his constituents will benefit and how much they will pay.[8] Writes Robert H. Haveman,

> While policy analysis focuses on the costs and benefits of policy measures to society as a whole, few individual policymakers find the social benefit criterion relevant to their more limited objectives. If the legislator takes the costs of a decision and spreads them widely over citizens or in some other way camouflages them, while he concentrates the benefits on a vested group whose support he seeks, the fact that aggregate costs are greatly in excess of benefits is of little interest to him. In effect, policy analysis answers questions that few legislative policymakers are interested in either asking or having asked.[9]

And the politicians, not the analysts, make most of the important policy decisions.

This difference in perspectives is illustrated by the recent controversies over water resource policy and the construction of dams, irrigation systems, and flood control projects. Using the standard techniques of benefit-cost analysis, the analyst concludes that many water projects are inefficient—that their total costs are greater than their total benefits—and thus should not be built.[10] The benefits of

8. That is why Harold D. Lasswell entitled his book that examines politics from the "standpoint" of "the working attitudes of practicing politicians" *Politics: Who Gets What, When, How* (New York: McGraw-Hill, 1936).
9. Robert H. Haveman, "Policy Analysis and the Congress: An Economist's View," *Policy Analysis* 2 (Spring 1976): 247.
10. See the White House press release of 18 April 1977, "Statement on Water Projects," for the benefit-cost ratios of the thirty-two water resource projects on President Carter's various "hit lists." For seventeen of these projects, the ratio of remaining benefits to remaining costs was less than 1.0. For a critical view of the benefit-cost analysis of one project, see Steve H.

such projects are, however, quite concentrated (and obvious), while the costs are widely distributed (and unperceived), thus providing some groups with significantly positive net benefits despite the aggregate inefficiency of the projects. Responding then to the views of his most vocal constituents, the politician concludes that the projects are most valuable for them—which indeed they are—and therefore ought to be built. There is no constituency to complain about so dispersed a cost, and that the benefits are obvious while the costs are unperceived further weighs against the analytical perspective. The view of the politician triumphs.

One economist writes: "Many public programs are administered with little attention to their distributional impact. It should not surprise us then when these programs exhibit perverse distributional consequences."[11] Certainly we should not be surprised, but for different reasons. It is arrogant to believe that the analyst's neglect of distributional issues is emulated by the other players in the policy game. Indeed, the reasons that the distributional consequences are so perverse is precisely because someone—the politician—pays the utmost attention to distributional impact. Policies with perverse distributional consequences are enacted not out of ignorance, but out of a combination of knowledge and apathy: knowledge by the few who benefit substantially from the perverse distribution, and thus push hard for "their" program, and apathy by the many who pay for it, but for whom the cost is, individually, so small that major efforts to resist are not worthwhile. Indeed, the losers may actually support the program in exchange for the winners' backing for another program (with a different set of perverse distributional consequences) that benefits the first program's losers.

The policy politician's attention to distributional impact clearly does not reflect a concern for equity. Precisely the opposite. The politician's distributional interest is strictly parochial, while the analyst's is merely theoretical. The politician's interest is, however, a response to the realties of the policy game—to the conflicts between

---

Hanke and Richard A. Walker, "Benefit-Cost Analysis Reconsidered: An Evaluation of the Mid-State Project," *Water Resources Research*, 10, no. 5 (1974): 898–908.

11. James T. Bonnen, "The Absence of Knowledge of Distributional Impacts: An Obstacle to Effective Policy Analysis and Decisions," in Robert H. Haveman and Julius Margolis, *Public Expenditure and Policy Analysis*, 1st ed., ed. Haveman and Margolis (Chicago: Rand McNally, 1970), p. 246.

groups and the competition for government largess. Little wonder that the politician's interests dominate the process, or that the distributional consequences are so perverse.

Inputs, Outputs, and Benefits

A basic tenet of policy analysis is that the outputs of a public policy provide the proper basis for evaluating its accomplishments. The apprentice analyst is constantly cautioned against mistakenly using inputs as a measure of program benefits. Benefits can be correctly assessed only from how much you get out of a program, not by how much you put in. To evaluate, for example, the programs of the U.S. Navy, an analyst does not count (or weigh) the number of sailors, ships, planes, and missiles, but assesses the navy's ability to carry out various missions—sea life support, amphibious assault, air strikes, anti-submarine search and destroy—in a variety of theaters.

In contrast, the policy politician often finds that, for his purposes, inputs provide the appropriate measure of program benefits. To the analyst, for example, the benefits of military programs are the outputs (national security) and the policy question is how much defense is obtained from the different kinds and levels of military expenditures. To the politician, however, the benefits of military programs are the inputs (dollars and jobs) and the policy question is how much profit and employment is obtained (by his constituents—don't forget the distribution) for various kinds and levels of military expenditures. The politician may feel compelled to argue for his favorite weapons system in terms of national defense (output), but his evaluation is often based on dollars and jobs (inputs).

This difference in perspective helps explain the policy politician's resistance to program budgeting. To the analyst, a program budget is most helpful for making public expenditure decisions because it explicitly relates expenditures to program outputs. For analogous reasons, the politician likes the line-item budget, for it is organized in terms of inputs. The politician and the analyst each prefers the budgetary format that displays what he perceives as program benefits.

Unfortunately, conceptual, methodological, and practical complications often make it difficult to define, measure, and predict the important outputs of any policy. It is usually easier to identify the inputs than the outputs. Evaluating a weapons system in terms of the profits and jobs produced is much less demanding than evaluating it in terms of its (marginal) contribution to national security. Thus the analyst needs to be always alert for the very human proclivity to think that inputs are an adequate expression of benefits.

James R. Schlesinger, in his now classic article on "Systems Analysis and the Political Process," states that one of "the guiding principles of systems analysis" is the orientation of analysis and allocation decisions toward output rather than input categories," and cautions that "in the real world of political decision it is immensely difficult to concentrate on outputs rather than inputs.[12] Yet, less than a decade after writing that, Schlesinger himself was unable to avoid the trap. In an effort to document "the tipping of military balance" from the United States to the Soviet Union, Schlesinger cited a number of "comparative statistics" nearly all of which were input measures:

> Since fiscal year 1968, U.S. military manpower has declined by 1.5 million men. It is now approximately 600,000 men below the pre-Vietnam level. Indeed, it is almost 500,000 men lower than during the Eisenhower years. . . . In fiscal year 1968 the Navy had 976 ships. This fiscal year [1976] it will be down to 483 ships. . . . Since 1960, Soviet military manpower has grown from approximately three million men to 4.4 million—more than twice the size of the U.S. military establishment. The Soviets devote at least 15 percent of the national effort to defense activities. . . . In fighter aircraft, [Soviet] production rates exceed those for the U.S. Air Force by a factor of four. . . . According to intelligence estimates, the Soviets now outspend the United States in virtually all major categories. In the aggregate, the CIA estimates, the Soviets outspend the United States in dollar equivalents by about 45 percent.[13]

Incredibly, Schlesinger, the advocate of analysis, makes no effort to compare the capabilities—the outputs—of the American and Soviet military forces.

Policy decisions can clearly depend upon whether one uses the analyst's or the politician's definition of program benefits. Consider

12. James R. Schlesinger, "System Analysis and the Political Process," *Journal of Law and Economics* 11 (October 1968): 285–86.
13. James R. Schlesinger, "A Testing Time for America," *Fortune*, (February 1976), pp. 147–49.

the hypothetical rodent control problem designed by Edith Stokey and Richard Zeckhauser to illustrate cost-effectiveness analysis. A city has 500 rat-infested apartments, a $10,000 financial constraint, and two possible rodent control programs; Method A costs $100 per apartment and is 90 percent effective; Method B costs only $40 per apartment, but is only 50 percent effective. Simple arithmetic reveals that with Method A the city can treat 100 apartments and expect to eliminate the rats from 90 of the 500 infested units. Using Method B, 250 apartments will be treated with the expected result that the rates are eliminated from 125 of the 500 units. Using the output of the program, the number of apartment from which the rats are eliminated, as the measure of the program's benefit, the policy analyst clearly prefers Method B.[14]

Now introduce another hypothetical program: Method P costs only $20 per unit, but then it is only 10 percent effective. Since Method P would be expected to eliminate the rats from only 50 units, the policy analyst would clearly rank it below either A or B.

The policy politician, however, looks at the problem differently. Using the input of the program, the number of apartments treated, as the measure of program benefits, the politician determines that Method A "benefits" only 100 apartments and Method B "benefits" 250 apartments, while Method P "benefits" all 500 units. Given the inputs as the measure of benefits—and a concern for distribution— the politician prefers Method P.

The analyst, of course, scoffs at the politician's reasoning: "Method P offers only good intentions—not results." But there is a certain political, if not analytical, logic to the politician's preference for P, particularly given his professional incentives. For one, the outputs may be difficult to predict. It may be possible only to estimate how effective each program will be. And, for any given set of effectiveness estimates, there is some uncertainty about the exact output of all three programs (though, given a binomial probability model, not very much.[15] It is possible to argue about the extent of the output-

14. Edith Stokey and Richard Zeckhauser, *A Primer for Policy Analysis* (New York: W. W. Norton, 1978), pp. 154–55.

15. For example, there is less than a 7 percent chance that Method P will eliminate the rats from 60 or more housing units and less than a 0.2 percent chance that it will eliminate rats from 70 or more units. Similarly, there is less than a 3 percent chance that Method B will eliminate the rats from less than 110 units, and less than a 0.1 percent chance that it will eliminate them from less than 100 units.

benefits for any of the three programs. In contrast, the input-benefits can be predicted precisely.

Moreover, outputs may be more difficult to perceive and measure. People may not know from how many apartments on their block the rats have been eliminated; they will have a much better sense of how many have been treated. Citywide, the rat control agency will know exactly how many apartments it has treated, though six months later it may be unable to report to the city council exactly how many apartments have been freed of rats as a direct result of the program.

Finally, there are questions of distribution and equity. Methods A and B are quite equitable on an a priori basis: before a lottery is drawn to determine who will get the treatment, every household has a 50 percent chance of getting the treatment and a 25 percent chance of having its rats eliminated. But once the apartments to receive Method B have been selected, half of the households have a 50 percent chance of having the rodents eliminated and the other half have no chance. With Method P, however, every household has a 100 percent chance of getting the treatment and thus always the exact same chance—even if it is only 10 percent—of having its rats eliminated. (Though there was never any accusation that the draft lottery was rigged, it was nevertheless widely perceived as unfair.) The politician will have less trouble explaining support for a program with only a 10 percent chance of eliminating the rats, than explaining support for a program that treated only half the apartments. Even though the policy politician's preferred program is the least efficient, it is supported by political logic that can easily overwhelm analytical arguments.

Although this example is hypothetical, the contrasting values and behavior that it illustrates are quite real. In the U.S. Department of Agriculture, reports Charles L. Schultze, there is "a program subcategory called 'agricultural production capacity,' which covers those programs aimed at increasing farm efficiency and productivity. Some of the activities in this subcategory are research efforts, such as control of crop-destroying pests and research into better seed strains."[16] To the analyst, the benefit of this program is measured by how much it increases the productive capacity of American agriculture. Schultze notes, however, that the appropriations committees

---

16. Charles L. Schulze, *The Politics and Economics of Public Spending* (Washington, D.C.: Brookings Institution, 1968), p. 28.

of Congress dispense the operating funds for this program "to hundreds of small agricultural research stations judiciously scattered throughout the country—stations which are often too small to be efficient."[17]

With efficiency as the decision criterion and output as the measure of benefit, the policy analyst often concludes that it is best to concentrate resources. Total output-benefits are maximized by focusing inputs where the marginal returns will be the greatest.

In contrast, with a concern for distribution and with input as the measure of benefits, the policy politician prefers to disperse resources widely. The distribution of input-benefits can be maximized by dispensing them where there are none. This leads to what Schultze calls "functional logrolling,":

> It is difficult to enact programs, particularly those of a public investment character, that are targeted to a specific geographically limited problem. Federal investment programs, designed to meet specific problems of the inner city, are broadened by congressional amendments to include rural areas. Conversely, programs tested to specific rural needs are often broadened to include metropolitan areas. . . . The present legislative process, and the packaging of administration proposals, encourages logrolling of projects strictly within functional lines.[18]

The Model Cities program, conceived as an experiment to learn about the impact of concentrating resources in small neighborhoods of a few cities, was broadened to cover all major cities.[19] Northeastern governors, jealous of the funds devoted to irrigating the arid West and converting inland southern cities into seaports, demand not an end to such boondoggles but a further dispersion of water resource monies to rebuild their own neglected and ailing municipal water systems. "We've got to get some of the pork-barrel back East," said one gubernatorial aide.[20]

17. Ibid., p. 29.
18. Ibid., p. 134.
19. Edward C. Banfield, "Making a New Federal Program: Model Cities, 1964–68," in *Policy and Politics in America: Six Case Studies*, ed. Allan P. Sindler (Boston: Little, Brown, 1973), pp. 124–58.
20. Margot Hornblower, "East's Rumblings Alter Politics of Water," *Washington Post*, 11 April 1978.

In the policy game, the politician's interest in distribution and inputs usually wins over the analyst's concern for efficiency and outputs.

Sunk Costs

To the policy analyst, sunk costs don't count. Liabilities incurred, whether they be payments already made or irrevocable commitments to make future payments, cannot be recovered, regardless of the alternatives chosen. Thus, to the analyst, the only costs of a project that count are the opportunity cost, as measured by the value of whatever future opportunities must be forgone to complete the project. Sunk costs represent opportunities that have already been forgone, and, although the decision to commit those costs (and thus to give-up the now lost opportunities) may with hindsight appear regrettable, it is too late to do anything about it.

The policy politician has a different attitude, however. The analyst seeks to justify them. Argued U.S. Congressman Melvin Price, over the question of terminating the nuclear plane, "It is hard to see why the Defense Department won't move ahead and get a flying aircraft after making such a substantial investment."[21] Similarly, Congressman Nick Galifianakis complained about the failure of the National Park Service to continue its erosion control program at Cape Hatteras, "It seems to me that we are diluting the investment that we already have there."[22]

Work on the National Visitor Center at Union Station in Washington, D.C., has continued because of the politician's desire to justify sunk costs. One member of Congress considers it "a blight on the community . . . practically useless." Another confesses it is "a mess . . . an eyesore." Yet both support completion. Why? Because $45 million has already been spent. "The problem is, it's there," explained Congressman Elliott H. Levitas, chairman of the House Subcommittee on Public Buildings and Grounds, which is re-

21. Price is quoted by W. Henry Lambright, *Shooting Down the Nuclear Plane* (Indianapolis and New York: Inter-University Case Program and Bobbs-Merrill, 1967), p. 18.
22. U.S., Congress, House *Second Supplemental Appropriations Bill, 1971*, Hearings before Subcommittees of the Committee on Appropriations, 92d Cong., 1st sess. (Washington, D.C.: Government Printing Office, 1971), p. 260.

sponsible for the visitor center. "We must either finish it or leave it as a monument to how bad government can be." So in May 1979 the committee voted to authorize another $39 million.[23]

Not that sunk costs do not provide the analyst with useful information. If large sunk costs are to be subtracted from a *fixed* total expenditure, then the larger the sunk costs the less resources required to complete the project and the more sense it will make to do so. If, however, large sunk costs imply a *growing* total expenditure, significantly above the cost estimates originally made, then large sunk costs are significant not only because of what they tell about prior expenditures invested in the project, but for what they imply about future expenditures necessary to complete it.

Thus, when evaluating a project, the analyst compares *remaining* costs to *remaining* benefits. Before anything is done, all benefits and costs are remaining. But, since most of the benefits will not be realized until the project is completed, while most of the costs will be committed before then, the ratio of remaining benefits to remaining costs will go up as work progresses. Consequently, because of sunk costs, it often makes sense to complete half-finished projects even if, using hindsight, it is obvious that the project did not make sense at the beginning.

Yet, even if the analysis of a half-completed project reveals that remaining costs exceed remaining benefits, the policy politician may well favor completing the project. In 1977, for example, the Carter Administration undertook to reevaluate thirty-two water resource projects. After completing this analysis, it recommended the continuation of nine projects "without modification," even though it had calculated the ratio of remaining benefits to remaining costs to be less than 1.0 for eight of these nine projects. One continued project (Lyman in Wyoming) was two-thirds complete, but still had a ratio of remaining benefits to remaining costs of only 0.5. Among the "factors of decision" for Lyman, the Carter Administration listed "the percentage completion of the project (the sunk costs of the project) and the fact that irrigation repayment depends on completion."[24] One official in the U.S. Department of the Interior, when asked why the eight projects with ratios of remaining benefits to re-

23. Donald P. Baker, "Criticized Visitor Center Still Voted $39 Million," *Washington Post* 10 May 1979.
24. White House "Statement on Water Projects," p. 34.

maining costs of less than 1.0 were not terminated, kept insisting that they were "just too far along."[25] Explained one White House aide, "It's a matter of expectation. . . . People have a right to expect the federal government to finish what it starts."[26]

The Tennessee Valley Authority's Tellico Dam provides a final example. The infamous snail darter aside, it did not make sense—from the analyst's perspective—to finish the project. Why? Because the benefits to be gained were exceeded by the costs, which included both $35.2 million in out-of-pocket capital costs *and* $40 million in opportunity costs for the very valuable farm land that would be flooded if the dam was finished. The Endangered Species Act of 1973 had been amended in 1978 to establish the Endangered Species Committee to consider exemptions if (among other things) the benefits of a project are clearly greater than those for alternatives that would permit a species to be saved. Since the net benefits of Tellico were negative, they clearly were not greater than those for the do-nothing alternative, and the Endangered Species Committee decided not to grant an exemption.[27] Yet with $103 million already sunk into the project, politicians pressed for completion. Argued Senator Howard Baker of Tennessee, "I simply cannot stand idly by and see a stultification of common sense, to see this act stop a dam that was finished, virtually, before the [Endangered Species] Act was passed and before the fish was discovered."[28]

In addition to the emphasis on outputs rather than inputs, another of James Schlesinger's "guiding principles of systems analysis" is "the avoidance of foot-in-the-door techniques leading to an unintended commitment to large expenditures."[29] Yet, why should the foot-in-the-door technique be so effective? Because of the desire to

25. Personal interview, 26 January 1978.
26. Personal interview, 20 June 1978.
27. For an analysis of the costs and benefits of completing the Tellico Dam see U.S., Department of the Interior, Office of Policy Analysis, "Tellico Dam and Reservoir, Staff Report to the Endangered Species Committee," mimeographed (Washington, D.C., 1979), esp. pp. 2.14–2.15. Incredibly, the TVA argues that since the farm land behind the dam has already been purchased, the value of this land should be considered a sunk cost, even though the land has yet to be flooded and could be resold as farm land if the project was not completed.
28. Baker is quoted in "Snail Darter Wins Another Victory on Senate Floor Vote," *Congressional Quarterly* 24 (16 June 1979): 1143.
29. Schlesinger, "Systems Analysis and the Political Process," p. 285.

justify sunk costs. The reasoning may seem circular, but the full circle is rarely in view. With a concern for distribution, the politician seeks to provide as many constituents as possible with benefits. And although it is difficult to provide everyone with immediate output benefits (because of the need to concentrate resources to obtain such outputs), inputs can be distributed quickly and widely. Even with limited resources, everyone can be provided with some, small but real, input benefits. And of course the output benefits inevitably follow—the foot-in-the-door technique works—because otherwise those initial (sunk) inputs would be wasted.

To the analyst, sunk cost is an economic variable. But sunk cost is also a political variable; it indicates how much of the prestige of the government and its senior officials is invested in the project. And sunk cost provides a measure of the power and expectations of the constituency that will benefit from the completion of the enterprise. Writes Allen Schick, "What economics writes off as sunk costs, politics rewards as a vested interest."[30] If the sunk costs are large enough—in either absolute or percentage terms—the policy politician will favor completion of the project.[31]

The Imperative of Constituency

These differences between the analyst and the politician can be derived from the analyst's indifference to organized constituencies and the politician's devotion to them. The politician seeks to satisfy people's explicitly expressed "wants"; the analyst is concerned about what people "need."[32] The analyst believes that it should not be necessary for individuals to organize themselves to prove that a policy is desirable; the politician believes that it is sufficient. Stokey and Zeckhauser summarize well the Weltanschauung of the analyst:

30. Allen Schick, "Systems Politics and Systems Budgeting," *Public Administration Review* 29, 2 (March/April 1969): 148.
31. Individuals of course do not always ignore sunk costs either. Richard Thaler argues that when consumers make a decision they weigh the pleasure to be gained against the pain of knowing that a sunk cost was wasted ("Toward a Positive Theory of Consumer Choice," *Journal of Economic Behavior and Organizations*, forthcoming). Consequently, individual citizens may not be too sympathetic with the analyst's dictum to ignore sunk costs; indeed, politicians seek to justify sunk costs precisely because they know they will be ridiculed by the citizenry if they appear to have been wasteful by ignoring them.
32. I am indebted to Willis D. Hawley for this observation.

One of the great virtues of the benefit-cost approach, as informed by willingness-to-pay calculations, is that the interests of individuals who are poorly organized or less closely involved are counted. (This contrasts with most political decision making procedures. Even when pushed by powerful interest groups, projects whose benefits do not outweigh their costs will be shown to be undesirable. The benefits and costs accruing to all—to the highway builders, the environmentalists, the 'little people,' the users and the providers of services, the taxpaying public—will be counted on a dollar-for-dollar basis. Benefit-cost analysis is a methodology with which we pursue efficiency and which has the effect of limiting the vagaries of the political process.[33]

The virtue of analysis is that it ignores the distorting influence of organized constituencies. Yet this is also a liability. The analyst's indifference to constituencies means that there may be no organized interest capable of advocating the conclusions of the analysis and mobilizing support in the political arena where the policy decisions are finally made. With disturbing regularity, one reads in the policy analysis literature sentences like "Political resistance to the proposal was, unfortunately, underestimated."[34] The analyst's indifference to constituencies—and the existing policy arrangements that created and sustain them—helps explain why analysts are often blind to the opposition that will, quite predictably, challenge any effort to change these arrangements and why they are often oblivious to what must be done to overcome or placate these opponents.

POLITICS, ANALYSIS, AND INFLUENCE

Analysts, even if they do not like it or accept it, are political players in the policy game. Their analysis will be used by politicians to support or oppose policy proposals. Indeed, if the politicians do not somehow use their analyses—either to make or to justify decisions—the labors of the analysts will be irrelevant.

Actually, politicians have a number of incentives to become familiar with policy analysis. They may wish to use analysis to im-

---

33. Stokey and Zeckhauser, *Primer*, p. 151.
34. For example, "although the opposition of most job agents to the incentive plan had been known, the political power they could wield was not fully evident until after the system had been formulated" (David Greenberg, Al Lipson, and Bernard Rostker, "Technical Success, Political Failure: The Incentive Pay Plan for California Job Agents," *Policy Analysis* 2 [Fall 1976]: p. 568).

prove public policy decisions, or they may fear being at the mercy of some analysis they cannot comprehend, or they may hope to employ analysis to support their own preconceived views. Thus politicians will hire analytical staff and seek the advice of outside analysts. And some will attempt to use analysis to legitimize their favorite programs by subtly manipulating the methods of analysis (such as dictating an absurdly low discount rate) to bias the analytical conclusions.

Similarly, analysts need to become more familiar with the work of politicians. As one congressional aide comments, "They [the analysts] don't really know what pressures we [the politicians] are under. And they don't care."[35] Writes Lawrence E. Lynn, Jr., "systems analysis often does not matter in decision making because system analysts do not know what matters to decision makers. The usefulness of analysis will increase to the extent that analysts develop better understanding of decision-making contexts and conduct their work in the light of that understanding."[36] Unless policy analysts are willing to be the mercenaries of political patrons—the expert witnesses testifying on behalf of whomever's policy their current analysis supports—and to have their analytical principles shamelessly manipulated, they will need a better understanding of politics. The motive may be defensive or offensive—to prevent the abuse of their analysis, or to make their analytical voices more influential—but analysts still need to increase their political sophistication.

NO LOBBY FOR EFFICIENCY?

As economists who venture into the political world so often lament, there is no lobby for efficiency.[37] The purpose of any interest group is to secure large and direct benefits for its members. And the benefits of efficiency, though large in the aggregate, are perceived (if at all) by the members of society to be small and indirect. That no organization exists to lobby in Washington, the state capitols, and the city halls for the benefits of general economic efficiency is there-

35. Interview, 6 November 1978.
36. Laurence E. Lynn, Jr., "Systems Analysis: Pitfalls from the User's Perspective," in *Handbook of Applied Systems Analysis*, ed. E. S. Quade (Laxenburg, Austria: Institute for Applied Systems Analysis, forthcoming).
37. For example, Haveman writes, "except for a few recent efforts, there exists no effective group to lobby for economic efficiency" ("Policy Analysis and the Congress," p. 247).

fore not surprising. Only the most naive analyst will expect that the alternative he has demonstrated to be most efficient will be automatically and effectively championed in the political arena.

Still, there is hope. Although it will be impossible to build a permanent organization *to support general economic efficiency*, it may be possible to mobilize a temporary coalition *to oppose a specific inefficiency*. For any inefficient program, some group must be obtaining benefits that exceed its own costs (otherwise there would be no political support for the inefficiency), and, as a result, the net excess costs for the rest of society must be even greater than those calculated for the program as a whole. Some (indeed most) people are paying the bills and receiving few (or no) benefits. The political task is to identify those paying net costs, arouse their displeasure, motivate them to action, and to provide them with a vehicle for opposition.

The difficulty is, as Mancur Olson has observed, that for any individual or group the costs of opposing the inefficiency may exceed the costs imposed on them by the inefficient program.[38] Weighing such costs, and the uncertainty of winning any political struggle, may convince people that the inefficiency simply does not warrant a battle. But political action can be motivated by passion as well as by rational calculation—particularly when the numbers necessary to make the calculation are obscure—and stimulating emotional opposition may not be difficult. Still, it is best to identify an aggrieved affinity group, a natural coalition for which net costs are obvious (even if not necessarily large) and which has a history of political action or a potential for it.

Such a group will not be motivated by an altruistic concern for economic efficiency, but by a personal concern for its own costs. Yet the appeal should be patriotic, not parochial. We all want to believe that we are working for society's benefit, not just our own. (Even those who seek personal gain by imposing an inefficient program on society will emphasize societal benefits.) The trick is to identify the proper group, one that once it begins to think about the inefficiency of the policy will realize that it is getting gypped. The task is not so much to explain to the group how much it is losing as to get it thinking about a policy in which it has not previously perceived any stake.

The Carter Administration's effort in 1977 to terminate various

38. Mancur Olson, Jr., *The Logic of Collective Action* (Cambridge: Harvard University Press, 1965).

water resource projects provided an excellent opportunity for using this approach. Many of the environmentally destructive projects marked for termination were quite inefficient—though each one did provide net benefits to some region in either the South or the West. Thus, in a speech to the Detroit Economic Club, President Carter could have undertaken to explain the inefficiencies of a few, specific projects. (He need never have mentioned that the Northeast and Midwest were paying costs that substantially exceeded their benefits.) Such a deliberate and public attack on the economic inefficiency of the projects (with their adverse environmental impacts completely ignored) could well have generated opposition from corporate executives—Can you think of a group more receptive to a presidential attack on economic inefficiency?—throughout the Northeast and Midwest. Certainly it would have had more impact than merely listing the benefit-cost ratios in the back of a press release.

If policy analysts are, as Charles Schultze conceived them, "partisan efficiency advocates," they need to advocate their cause to the most receptive audience.[39] Recognizing that economic efficiency itself has no constituency, and that in each situation it will be necessary to identify those individuals and groups who have a self-interest in supporting the most efficient policy alternative, is the analyst's first step towards increased political influence.

Making Analysis Persuasive

Creating coalitions to support efficient policies requires a communication of the analyst's reasoning. The need, however, is not merely for a translation from analytical to political language, though that certainly can help. (After all, although the analyst's jargon may mesmerize, it will rarely convince.) Nor is the task one of educating political players in the ethos and techniques of analysis.

What is required is a complete transformation of the analyst's reasoning from the coordinates of an analytical mind into the reference system in which the audience thinks. Anyone who customarily conceives of physical space in linear, cartesian coordinates (x, y, z) and finds it difficult to locate a point expressed in polar coordinates (r, Θ, Φ), except by transforming the polar coordinates back to linear

39. Schultze, *Public Spending*, p. 96.

ones, should recognize the importance of transforming analytical reasoning into the audience's own frame of reference rather than attempting to teach them to think in the analyst's coordinate system. Writing about the problem of communicating analysis, Arnold Meltsner emphasizes the need for the analyst to "increase the degree of similarity between himself and his audience." Experienced analysts, he writes, "try skillfully to couch their arguments in terms that increase the appearance of shared values."[40]

Although the analyst may believe that his own principles of reasoning, the analytical paradigm, is the only rational approach to public policy making, he needs to recognize that this view is not universal. Indeed, some fundamental analytical concepts such as using opportunity costs rather than out-of-pocket costs, are alien to most people; they simply do not think in terms of opportunities forgone.[41] Consequently, any analytical argument that depends upon simplified illustrations of the opportunity-cost principle to establish the validity of a more complicated policy proposal will be very unpersuasive.

Take the task of explaining to the Detroit Economic Club why a particular water resource project is economically inefficient. The temptation is to begin with a simple, superficial explanation of benefit-cost analysis. After all, these are corporate executives—people who deal every day with analysis of costs and profits and who understand (at least implicitly) that if they invest their firms' resources in one project they will have to forgo other investment opportunities. But no matter how intelligent these executives and no matter how clever your explanation of benefit-cost analysis (and do not forget it must be delivered by the president or a cabinet officer), the final recitation of the benefit-cost ratios for various projects will have absolutely no meaning. This audience thinks in the reference system of business, not in the one of policy analysis. Thus the inefficiencies of the projects need to be explained in business, not analytical, terms.

Fortunately, in this case at least, this is quite possible—for many water resource projects provide mostly private, not public, goods.

40. Arnold J. Meltsner, "Don't Slight Communications: Some Problems of Analytical Practice," *Policy Analysis* 5 (Summer 1979): 379.
41. See Thaler, "Toward a Positive Theory."

Benefit-cost analysis is necessary to ensure that all the benefits of public goods (valued in terms of each individual's willingness to pay) are included when evaluating a public investment project. For many reclamation projects, however, most of the goods are private; the individuals and firms who benefit can be easily identified and charged, so that the evaluation of these benefits can be based not on some mysterious estimate of willingness to pay, but on actual payments.

Thus the government could contract-out the construction of a dam and the aqueducts to connect the reservoir with the cities, farms, and industries that will buy the water. A construction firm, such as Brown and Root, could calculate how much of an annual fee it would pay the government for the right to build the dam, collect a specified amount of water, and sell it in a specified region. Or, if the firm concludes that it could not pay the government and still make a reasonable return on its investment, it could submit a negative bid: the subsidy it would require to cover nonvendable benefits, such as recreation and flood control.

In principle, such a corporate analysis is equivalent to a public investment (benefit-cost) analysis, though the mental framework is quite different. Using the corporate investment approach, however, the president could explain to the Detroit Economic Club exactly how economically inefficient a water project is. For example, if a private firm were to build the Central Arizona Project and receive an annual, federal subsidy of $30.7 million (to cover flood control, recreational, fish and wildlife, and other public benefits) it would have to charge $106 per acre-foot of water to earn a 6.375 percent return on its investment amortized over 100 years. What corporation would be willing to invest $2 billion to make only a 6.375 percent return—and then only over a 100-year period? None. Anyway, no one could actually do that, since water is currently selling in central Arizona at from $10 to $50 per acre-foot. To a corporate executive this kind of explanation better dramatizes the inefficiency of the project than does saying that the benefit-cost ratio is only 0.58.[42]

Emphasizing the importance of analysis that persuades, Giandomenico Majone asserts that "policy makers need retrospective (postdecision) analysis at least as much as they need prospective

42. U.S., Department of the Interior, "Water Projects Review: Central Arizona Project," mimeographed (Washington, D.C., 1977), pp. 6–9.

(or predecision) analysis, and probably more."[43] Frequently, of course, analysts are called upon to undertake such retrospective analyses, though they usually find it a dishonorable chore (particularly when they disagree with the decision). The role of policy analysis, however, is not only to help determine the best alternative but also to ensure that this alternative is adopted and implemented by the government. Once a political decision maker has accepted the analyst's recommendation (if, perhaps, for some slightly different reasons) the analyst has an obligation to ensure that the wisdom of his advice is recognized by those with the power to push it.

For the policy analyst to have influence, he must be more than just technically correct; he must be convincing—not only to his fellow analysts, but also to an influential constituency.

The Need for Political Strategy

Too narrow a definition of the analyst's responsibility and field of competence can isolate him from political reality and inhibit his policy influence. If an analyst is known for the excellence of his economic logic and the reliability of his statistical inferences, but also for the vacuity of his (implicit) political assumptions, his work will be dismissed as irrelevant by the responsible policymakers. Yet, once he has developed a policy proposal that can generate significant benefits, the analyst should not be disinterested in having those benefits realized. Indeed, if honest, neutral analysis reveals that one or several alternatives are preferable (or that one or several alternatives are highly undesirable), the policy analyst has a clear obligation to maximize the chances for their adoption. How then should the policy analyst fulfill his political responsibility?

The analyst can begin by assessing the political feasibility of each alternative. Yet an alternative's political feasibility is not some in-

---

43. Giandomenico Majone, "The Uses of Policy Analysis," in *The Future and the Past: Essays on Programs and the Annual Report 1976–1977* (New York: Russell Sage Foundation, 1978), p. 207. Majone sees a major role for the analyst as "a producer of policy arguments . . . more similar to a lawyer . . . than to a problem solver" (p. 213). To convert the policy analyst into the policy lawyer would threaten both the credibility of analysis and the analyst, however, just as the use of benefit-cost analysis not as a prospective tool to help make better water resource decisions but strictly as a retrospective tool to justify them has not only made the shameless manipulation of such analysis inevitable, but has also created wide-spread distrust of the value of any such analysis and of the morals of the analyst.

herent, fixed characteristic, like one of a policy's many genes that is merely waiting to be located, deciphered, and reported. The political feasibility of an alternative is clearly dependent upon the ingenuity of the political strategy designed to obtain its adoption and upon the dedication and skill of those who would implement the strategy. Consequently, *the analyst's responsibility extends beyond the mere passive determination of political feasibility to the active creation of a political strategy. The complete policy analyst will not only recommend the best policy alternative but also the best political strategy with which the client can win the adoption and implementation of this alternative.* After all, how can a policy alternative be the "best" unless it is actually adopted and implemented?

By itself, analysis is politically impotent. It becomes an effective political instrument only when it is incorporated into a political strategy that is designed to achieve adoption of its recommendations. And developing such a strategy is, indeed, part of the analyst's responsibility.

A traditional analyst might demur, claiming that such overt political thinking is beyond his competence. That may be true—but it should not be. The analyst who has thoroughly studied a policy problem should be as familiar with its political complications as its economic ones; the two issues are not independent. An analyst who has paid attention to the distributional questions should be well aware of both the obvious antagonists and the potential allies. Consequently, it would be disingenuous—indeed, unethical—for the analyst to present his client with a policy recommendation that will generate much opposition and little support without also offering a political recommendation as to how the client could (1) avoid a damaging, futile battle, and (2) achieve the policy goal. Can the analyst really send his client into the political arena without explaining what perils are likely to appear and what weapons the client will find most effective?

Iterating between Analysis and Politics

Political infeasibility is all too easy to recognize—indeed, to overrate. A passive and uncritical examination of a proposal's chances for acceptance and adoption will typically reveal that all is hopeless. The proposal is not really a new idea; it has been offered before, but made little progress against the opposition of influential and powerful interests.

Yet, too often, it is the mythology of power that confers upon a policy proposal that status of "political infeasibility." Previous attempts to have the proposal adopted may have been imaginary, casual, or incompetent. The influence, prestige, and authority of interest groups is often sustained through an unwillingness to challenge a reputation rather than by a frequent and serious testing.

For example, every president since Franklin D. Roosevelt openly opposed the 200-year-old policy of free use of the inland waterways. Yet nothing happened. Thus the "political infeasibility" of charging for commercial use of the canals, locks, and dredged rivers that the U.S. Army Corps of Engineers builds and maintains became a legend in Washington, D.C. And the barge operator acquired the mythical powers of some motorized Neptune who could swiftly banish with a jab of his omnipotent trident anyone who suggested imposing a fee, tax, or toll.

Then, amazingly, in 1978 Congress passed a tax, albeit a modest one. What happened? Did a new president struggle to change the policy? Did congressional leaders courageously decide it was time for a change? Did the public demand action? Did the barge operators withdraw from political combat? No. Congress acted primarily as a result of the efforts of a single, junior senator from the minority party, Pete V. Domenici of New Mexico.

What was Domenici's secret? He actually tried. He made an intelligent and dedicated effort to get his proposal adopted. Mentioning a policy proposal in a budget submission or in a congressional message or even in a television address does not imply a major presidential endeavor. Every president since FDR may well have opposed free use of the inland waterways, but none of them made a truly serious attempt to change the policy. That, of course, is because everyone knew that getting the change adopted was "politically infeasible"—everyone, that is, but Domenici. He and his staff undertook not a passive examination of feasibility but an active search for strategy. And they persevered. Thus (with some inconstant White House support, excellent rapport with his fellow legislators, and some luck) Domenici was able to scuttle the barge operators.[44]

If the best policy politicians can be caught in the "infeasibility trap," the analyst must certainly be careful. For, paradoxically, the

---

44. For a summary of this legislation see "Waterway Use Tax Cleared in Final Days," *Congressional Quarterly Almanac* 24 (1978): 513–15.

analyst's ability to influence policy may be limited by his being too political—or at least prematurely so. The anxious analyst, apprehensive lest his recommendations be rejected by his client as infeasible, may prematurely preclude from consideration those alternatives for which he anticipates the largest and most obvious opposition.

Yet, as has already been emphasized, political feasibility is not some intrinsic, binary variable; it is not a quality that a policy alternative somehow either does or does not possess. Like any other characteristic of a policy proposal, it can be affected by modifying the proposal itself or by influencing other, outside but related variables. The analyst needs to identify the constraints to adoption, and to determine the costs of eliminating them: both the economic opportunity costs of other policy goals that must be foregone to obtain the economic resources required to modify the proposal to make it politically acceptable, and the political opportunity costs of other policy goals that must be sacrificed in exchange for the necessary political backing for this initiative.

Deciding how the political constraints to adoption of a policy proposal can be most cheaply removed—and whether that price is worth paying—is both an analytical and a political responsibility. The policy game is not a relay with the analyst running the first (analytical) leg and then turning the baton over to the politician to run the last (political) lap while the analyst watches passively (if painfully) from the sidelines. If the analyst drops out after the first lap, he will discover that his recommendations are gradually modified, compromised, and discarded so that the final, adopted policy hardly resembles his proposal.

This is what happened with President Carter's 1977 review of the water resource projects. A water projects review office was established, and analysts were assigned to teams to review different projects. When these analyses were complete, they were turned over to the politicians, who decided which projects to continue, which to modify, and which to recommend for deletion from the budget. At this decisionmaking stage, the analysts—having done their "job" of preparing the background papers—were ignored and the decisions were based solely on political considerations. Whether a project had benefits greater or less than costs was irrelevant. Even when an analysis provided a particularly illuminating and dramatic description of a project's economic inefficiency—such as the above explanation for the Central Arizona Project—the information was neither used to make the decision in private nor to defend it in public.

In this case, it was not that the analysts refused to participate in the political decisionmaking, but that the politicians simply ignored them. At the same time, the politicians undoubtedly ignored them because previous experience with (other) analysts had convinced them that the analysts had little to contribute to political decisionmaking.

To overcome their profession's reputation for political naivete, policy analysts will need to devote more attention to the role of constituencies—to identify the constituencies that stand to lose (either substantively or symbolically) from each alternative, to determine the intensity of their interest, and to evaluate their strengths (both actual and mythological). At the same time, analysts need to identify constituencies, including latent ones, that can benefit from each proposal. Constituencies are not permanent features of the political landscape carved in stone aeons ago by some mysterious force that political archeology has yet to identify. Constituencies must be created, organized, motivated, and mobilized. They can also be disarranged, confused, demoralized, and thwarted.

Constituency building, the traditional analyst might argue, is the responsibility of the policy politicians. It is. But the policy analyst has a responsibility to assess how it can best be done. After all, getting a policy adopted by the authoritative executive and legislative policy makers involves not only generating political support for the analytically superior alternative and defeating or neutralizing opponents; it also involves modifying alternatives to attract supporters and placate opponents. If this is done solely by the politician, the substantive policy sacrifices will be dictated solely by politics—not by trade-offs between substantive and political considerations.

John Mendeloff has written that the insights of policy analysis "can be generated by bounding back and forth among the [economic and political] perspectives, which requires either a multidisciplinary team or a multidisciplinary head."[45] I believe that the complete policy analyst needs a multidisciplinary *head*. Selecting public policies, and getting them adopted and implemented, requires re-

45. John Mendeloff, *Regulating Safety* (Cambridge: MIT press, 1979), p. x.

peated iterations between the analytical and the political. Unless analysts are willing to watch as essential components of carefully crafted policy alternatives are discarded to placate various constituencies, they must improve their understanding of the political part of the game. Only the complete policy analyst, who knows what compromises to make to build support or neutralize opposition and what sacrifices to resist because of insufficient political gains, will win the confidence of the key political players and become a full member of the policy-making team.

5

SOCIAL SCIENCE AND
THE REAGAN ADMINISTRATION

Irving Louis Horowitz

Never has a presidential candidate, much less a president, made more use of social scientific personnel than has Ronald Reagan. With equal certainty, not in recent times has any president cut so deeply into the budgetary bases of "soft money" funding and support for this sector of the intellectual elite. Therein lies a paradox.

After the defeat of the Republican party by a slim vote in 1976, the Reagan campaign made extensive use of social scientists to develop policy operations that would broaden its base. The Center for Strategic and International Studies, the American Enterprise Association, and the Institute for Contemporary Studies have drawn on an impressive roster of social scientists for ideas on health and welfare, minority employment, and school busing.

The same emphasis appears in the pattern of appointments in the present administration. Political scientists are, if anything, better represented than in the past: Jeane J. Kirkpatrick at the cabinet rank post of United States Representative to the United Nations, Ernest W. Lefever as the proposed Assistant Secretary of State for Human Rights, and Fred C. Ikle as Under Secretary of Defense for Policy, indicate an ongoing social science presence in the new administration.

Why then were the cuts so deep in the National Science Foundation budget for social science? A large part of the reason is the absence of a policy thrust in most of the theoretical work done with the Foundation's support. The Reagan administration has taken the position that policy-oriented social science deserves more consideration than theoretical work; and further that such policy-oriented efforts should be supported within the framework of mainline federal agencies.

The budget cuts suggested for fiscal years 1981–1982 with respect to the National Science Foundation are a good indicator of this situation. The overall federal budgetary cuts are roughly 3.5 percent; the cuts to the physical sciences may average between 5 and 10 percent; the cuts to the National Endowment for the Humanities work out to roughly 50 percent; in contrast, the cuts to the social sciences, specifically sociology and economics, are in the area of 65 to 75 percent. One can surmise that such budgetary cutbacks are not intended to limit social scientific activities *per se*, but reflect a movement sharply away from theoretical issues and toward practical, policy concerns.

The crisis in social science funding derives not only from the actual amounts cut, but also from how these decisions were made.

From Irving Louis Horowitz, "Social Science and the Reagan Administration," 1(1) *Journal of Policy Analysis and Management* 125–129 (1981). Copyright © 1981 by the Association for Public Policy Analysis and Management. Reprinted by permission of John Wiley & Sons, Inc.

New levels of funding support for the social sciences were not resolved through the interaction of agencies in consultation with the scientific community, but by a virtual mandate establishing new guidelines and priorities. The new OMB pattern represents a decisive shift from the government's traditional willingness to allow the scientific community to determine the direction of its government-supported research. The consequences of this new style of government policymaking for the sciences could well be greater than the actual fiscal decisions rendered.

Budgetary cutbacks in the area of social science research presumably will be compensated for, at least in part by an increase in funding support by the private sector. It is anticipated that conservative agencies, which achieved a high level of prominence in the Reagan victory—such as the Heritage Foundation, the American Enterprise Association, and the Olin Foundation—will make up the deficit of their older liberal counterparts: Ford, Rockefeller, and Carnegie.

Relying on a shift from governmental to private financing represents a gamble consistent in spirit with the general approach of supply-side economics; in principle, activities that enlarge private sector participation will be viewed with greater favor than those that do not. The presumption is that resulting private sector activity itself will make legitimate the character of social science research. Of course, the success of the gamble depends on whether the private sector will view spending on social science research as beneficial. It has been so long since anyone has raised the question of what the private sector wants in the way of social research that there is a reasonable question whether that sector itself even knows. It is one thing to hope that the private sector will fill a void in, say, computer technology applications; it is quite another to count on its filling a void in poverty research, especially in a period when philanthropic giving will be in short supply.

Along with a decrease in the federal budget is a rerouting of funds to state and city governments, in accord with the Republican party platform of 1980. Through state and city governments, the funds that formerly went to the study of energy, environment, and education—the three Es of policy research—may well continue to be expanded. Centers of social and policy research unquestionably will have to work harder for funds and more directly under parochial supervision than in the past. The allocation of funds will be different: state and local rather than federal and international. Also, the amount of money allocated per contract will probably be less. As a result, more immediately affected segments of the social science community may well be such think tanks as Mershon, Bendix, Rand, Abt, and Mathematica—organizations with anywhere from $15,000,000 to $35,000,000 annual budgets largely dependent on federal support—rather than specialized agencies like the Social Science Research Council and Russell Sage, capable of operating with fewer dollars and smaller-scale projects.

At some level, budgetary issues are ideological in character although they are fought out at organizational levels. The cutbacks at the National Science Foundation and the National Endowment for the Humanities are no exception. Disciplines such as sociology, anthropology, psychology, and, to a lesser extent, economics and political science, from the New Deal to the Great Society, have been concerned with stating the case for a large, amorphous, but quite real underclass: retirees and people living on fixed incomes, historically exploited racial and ethnic minorities, very young children subject to physical abuse, and so on. In this regard, whatever their political proclivities, social scientists have tended to support constituencies of the Democratic party. The social science community too is subject to the iron law of politics: To the victor belong the spoils, to the vanquished belong the ashes.

In other ways, too, the behavior of the social science community has been a factor contributing to the shift in federal research priorities. A curious schizophrenia is evident among social researchers. On one side are strong impulses toward self-deprecation in the guise of modesty or self-criticism, while on the other side are demands for increased funding to overcome such inherited weaknesses. Social science began to expect rewards for failure rather than success, to acknowledge almost eagerly how little a research undertaking had actually discovered or resolved—but to insist nonetheless that past failures were a ground for expecting yet more government support. Their physical science counterparts, on the other hand, held to a model of reward based on success.

The present structure of the social science community perhaps can be described best as one of balkanization, a fragmentation of immense proportions. Any primary journal within the major social sciences exhibits a range of articles of such diversity and such different levels of methodological sophistication that it would tax a schizophrenic to read such a publication from start to finish. This is not intended to argue that we should determine *a priori* who is right or who is wrong, or which theoretical framework is inferior or superior; it is only to assert that the social sciences are being assaulted, not only from the edges inward, but from the innermost core outward. The capacity of social scientists themselves to resist cutbacks has become measurably weakened by such internal conflict; hence the present administration's reductions of social science funding have met with relatively little pressure group response.

Without question, the most important consequence of the present budgetary situation is the pending reorganization of social science itself. Such a reconstruction, long overdue, is not a function of self-criticism or self-reflection, but as in all basic choices a response to real world issues: the limitations of resources on the one hand, and questions raised about the utility of social science on the other. The social sciences must confront the fact that every major problem which they address has become interdisciplinary. Whether the subject is crime, health, or foreign policy, the character of research and the definition of expertise have gone far beyond older disciplinary boundaries. Budgetary patterns, on the other hand, have been locked into older patterns of disciplinary boundaries that no longer are relevant or justifiable.

What we can expect in the near future is a large-scale reorganization of social science with increased focus on specialized agencies and programs and decreased commitment to social science research for its own sake. Social science was nurtured in a period of relative splendid isolation in the nearly semifeudal atmosphere of the university in which the cares of the world were only partially heard. Increasingly, the market will determine the utility of social science projects. If support for the social sciences is to be maintained even at reduced levels, such aid will involve making policy itself a central end, not an accoutrement to the research design. Increasingly, the thread that may hold us together is the policy implications of the work being done.

The actual impact of federal cutbacks to the social sciences could well be muted by a variety of factors: reorganization of programs, increased foundation support, and new programs in expanding divisions. However, the research that survives will be the research that bears most directly on policy and program.

A policy agenda for the social sciences is clearly a top priority for those who, in halcyon years gone by, were used to determining policy priorities for others. My agenda would include the following points:

Local, community, city, and state constituencies must be addressed and cultivated. Linkages to subfederal levels no longer must be viewed as parochial or insignificant in character. If decentralization is to retain its democratic properties, then social research must contribute to that effort at its fundamental root sources.

Social research must reflect the ongoing demographic and employment shift; the need to contribute to problems of new environments and new careers should be considered equal in value to the solution of old problems in older centers of population and power.

Social scientists must begin to develop more subtle relationships with the political process, not just as policy advisors playing positivistic mandarin roles, but as party operatives in all major (or if ideology so dictates, minor) parties. It is time for a declaration of independence from one party, and an equally firm pledge to participate actively in the political process as a whole.

Social scientists must begin to view employment opportunities outside the academy as equal in status and worth to those inside the university department. Increasingly, employment and career opportunities in every walk of life—from hospital administration to scholarly publishing—are becoming accessible to the sorts of special talents exhibited by social scientists.

These suggestions for a social scientific revitalization are neither exclusive nor exhaustive. They do indicate, however, both the possibility as well as the need to move beyond the present movement of widespread discontent and demoralization to a higher ground of integration.

The author would like to express his appreciation to Kenneth Prewitt, Jiri Nehnevajsa, Otto N. Larsen, and Ruth S. Hanft for their suggestions on how to improve this statement. Needless to say, they are in no way responsible for the positions the author takes or the narrative itself.

IRVING LOUIS HOROWITZ is Distinguished Professor of Sociology and Political Science at Rutgers University, Hannah Arendt Chair, and Director of Studies in Comparative International Development.

PART II

POLICY ISSUES AND POLICY STUDIES

Income Support Policy

Much discussion during the Reagan administration has centered on a "safety net" for those most vulnerable to poverty, loss of income, and lack of access to the essentials. While the merits of the various proposals of the administration in this area are vigorously contested, it is interesting from a policy perspective that, regardless of the rhetoric, there are but two fundamental aspects to a government-sponsored safety net: an income support policy and a social services policy. Further, what becomes apparent in comparing the proposals of recent administrations is that each has focused on some change in the mix or relative emphasis of these two approaches. Since Roosevelt and the New Deal, successive administrations have seen these two policy areas as interrelated and complementary, not mutually exclusive. This section addresses income support, while another section will address social service policy.

As the name implies, income support focuses on the monetary aspect of a person's or family's well-being. Income support can be of several types: direct cash transfers, as in certain welfare and retirement programs; indirect transfers, which allow persons to retain income that otherwise would be collected in taxes; or through a guaranteed income floor to eligible persons, with government subsidies to those whose incomes fall below that designated level. Considerable attention has been paid of late to this policy area. The costs of income support programs designated as "entitlements" (as in social security) and that have remained discretionary (as in Aid to Families with Dependent Children) have grown considerably. The issue now is either to contain these costs or find new ways to finance the programs.

The articles in this section explore a number of the aspects of income support policy, both in the United States and in Britain. Danziger, Haveman, and Plotnick challenge the assumption that the income support policy in the United States has been so successful in drastically reducing poverty and other aspects of economic vulnerability that any further expansion will do nothing but reduce the incentive to work, save, and contribute to the economic growth of the society. This assumption, widely shared by key policymakers in the Reagan administration, is thought by the authors to be overstated. They argue not for a retrenchment in income support, but rather for a reorientation to link such policy more closely to employment policy. In this manner, the concern over disincentives in the system could be addressed while not allowing persons currently covered to fall back into poverty.

Burkhauser and Smeeding examine the U.S. policy of a universal income floor for the low-income elderly through the Supplemental Security Income (SSI) and social security (OASI). Because these two programs are linked through a regressive taxation process—SSI taxes income from OASI at virtually 100 percent—the overall safety net under the elderly low-income worker is considerably more fragile and frayed than may first be apparent. The authors focus on the negative interaction between these two support policies and the consequences for the equity and efficiency of the current OASI-SSI system.

Butler provides a comparative analysis of the British experience with price and income policies and the implications for comparable efforts in the United States. British efforts to control wage and price escalations with both voluntary and mandatory policies are carefully assessed as to their impact and level of success. With voluntary controls a proven failure and full-scale controls politically unacceptable, the need is to devise a strategy somewhere between the two extremes. The findings from the British effort in this regard are particularly instructive for the United States.

Johnson and Pencavel present a model that enables policymakers to forecast the changes in net earnings or hours worked that would accrue from the introduction of a negative income tax (NIT) program. Drawing on data from the Seattle-Denver Income Maintenance Experiments, the authors conclude that one of the reservations expressed by some regarding the NIT—that such a program would reduce the incentive to work—has some support, but not as much as perhaps anticipated. The key finding from their study was that the wage rate of an individual covered by an NIT program affected not the hours worked by that individual, but the number of hours worked by the individual's spouse.

6

RETRENCHMENT OR REORIENTATION
Options for Income Support Policy

*Sheldon Danziger, Robert Haveman, and Robert Plotnick**

Income support and other social welfare programs have grown rapidly since 1965. Their growth has had important beneficial impacts—protection against income losses, guaranteeing access to essentials, and the reduction of poverty. This growth has also been accompanied by some reduction in work effort and perhaps savings. Because of these side effects, some have argued that the programs be curtailed. The evidence presented in this paper suggests a reorientation of policy rather than a simple retrenchment. First, the income support system is described and its growth documented. Then, the role of the system is appraised. This review of the evidence culminates in a summary scorecard which includes the impact of the postwar growth of the income support system on poverty, work, savings, and economic growth. The scorecard also describes how additional growth in the system would affect these same variables. The conclusions of this analysis provide the basis for a reorientation strategy that emphasizes programs to enhance earnings and employment in the private sector as a complement to income support. In such a reorientation, earnings would be substituted for cash support, and the inefficiencies created by minimum wage laws, work disincentives, and other labor market, constraints would be offset.

The past three decades, and particularly the last fifteen years, have

*The research reported here was supported by funds granted to the Institute for Research on Poverty at the University of Wisconsin-Madison by the Department of Health, Education and Welfare pursuant to the provisions of the Economic Opportunity Act of 1964. The authors wish to thank Irwin Garfinkel, George Jakibson, Robert Lampman, and Eugene Smolensky for challenging comments on a previous draft. The conclusions expressed herein are those of the authors.

From Sheldon Danziger et al., "Retrenchment or Reorientation: Options for Income Support Policy," 28(4) *Public Policy* 473-490 (1980). Copyright © 1980 by the President and Fellows of Harvard College. Reprinted by permission of John Wiley & Sons, Inc.

witnessed explosive growth in income support and other social welfare programs. These programs accomplish important objectives: They prevent large losses in economic well being because of uncontrollable events that destroy earnings capacity or disrupt earnings. They guarantee access to indispensable goods and services. They reduce poverty, thereby narrowing the income gap between rich and poor.

The gains achieved in all of these areas are substantial, yet some feel that the income transfer system has grown too large. Income poverty is now all but erased, they claim, and the undesirable side effects are enormous. Work incentives have been eroded—for both the poor and the rich. The incentive to save has been weakened, and as a result, economic growth is impeded and productivity retarded. Some of those taking this position argue that the growth of these programs should be curtailed; others want the programs themselves to be scaled back or eliminated.

In this paper, we offer a quite different evaluation of the income support system. In our view, the evidence does not sustain the claim that retrenchment is in order, even though all is not as it should be. Critics have overstated the gains against poverty and the costs of work and savings disincentives. Although the War on Poverty has not been won, progress has been made. And while the policies have increased disincentives to work and save, the magnitude of these effects poses no serious threat to the efficiency of the economy. From our reading of the evidence, reorientation rather than retrenchment is the appropriate policy response. Retrenchment could no doubt promote efficiency, but it will also increase poverty. What is required is to integrate the income support system into the labor market. Such a reorientation would both promote efficiency and reduce poverty.

We begin by describing the income support system and documenting its growth. Then we describe the role of the system in reducing poverty, and appraise its effects on work and savings. This review of the evidence culminates in a summary scorecard. In it, we present our evaluation of how the postwar growth of the income support system has affected poverty, work, savings, and economic growth, and how additional growth in the system would affect these same variables. The conclusions of this scorecard provide the basis for a reorientation strategy that emphasizes programs to enhance earnings and employment in the private sector as a complement to income support. Only through such a reorientation can earnings be substituted for cash support, and the inefficiencies created by minimum wage laws, work disincentives, and other labor market constraints be offset.

Income Support Programs and Their Growth

Public expenditures for income support totalled $200 billion in 1978—10 percent of GNP. These programs, listed in Table 1, are divided into two groups: social insurance and income assistance. Eligibility for the social insurance programs depends on past contributions and some identifiable problem, such as disability, un-

Table 1. MAJOR INCOME SUPPORT PROGRAMS, 1978

	Expenditures (in $ billion)
Social Insurance Programs	$152.1
Old Age and Survivors Insurance ⎫	81.2
Disability Insurance ⎬ OASDHI	12.7
Medicare ⎭	25.2
Unemployment Insurance	11.8
Workers Compensation	10.0
Veterans Disability Compensation	6.2
Railroad Retirement	4.0
Black Lung	1.0
Income Assistance Programs (Welfare)	$ 51.9
Medicaid	18.9
Aid to Families with Dependent Children (AFDC)	11.9
Supplemental Security Income (SSI)	7.4
Food Stamps	5.5
Veterans Pensions	3.3
General Assistance	1.2
Housing Assistance	3.7
Total	$204.0

Source: *The Budget of the United States Government, Fiscal Year, 1980,* Appendix.

employment, or old age. In contrast, the income assistance programs do not require past contributions. Their benefits are income-tested, in that they are available only to those whose incomes from private sources and social insurance are very low. The income assistance programs, taken together, form the "welfare system." Programs of each type provide cash (e.g., Social Security and AFDC) and in-kind support (e.g., Medicare and Food Stamps). Some are federal programs, others are joint federal-state ventures or state-local programs.

Income support programs provide aid to households on a scale far larger than is usually perceived. Presently, about half of the nation's households (indeed, 80 percent of all poor ones) receive cash or in-kind income from one or more programs; the mean cash benefit for households receiving benefits exceeds $3400. About 35 percent of households receive social insurance income; 12 to 15 percent participate in one or more welfare programs.[1]

Several characteristics of the income support system should be emphasized. First, it is a categorical system, in that it deals differentially with people having the same needs but different characteristics. For example, there are separate programs for single-parent families, veterans, the aged, blind, and disabled, the unemployed, and the working poor. Most, though not all, of this categorization is a response to the issue of work incentives. Those who are expected to work are treated differently from those who are not. Food Stamps is the only program that assists all persons with low income. Second, expenditures for social insurance are substantially larger than for welfare; they account for nearly three-quarters of the expenditures. Consequently, social insurance lifts more people out of poverty than does welfare, even though a larger proportion of welfare benefits go to the poor. Third, although many consider AFDC to be synonymous with "welfare," AFDC accounts for only a fifth of all expenditures on income assistance. Medicaid is by far the largest welfare program.

In 1950, public spending for income support equalled 2 percent of GNP, 4 percent of personal income, and 14 percent of govern-

---

[1] See S. Danziger, R. Haveman, and R. Plotnick, "Income Transfer Programs in the United States: An Analysis of Their Structure and Impacts," in U.S. Congress, Joint Economic Committee, *Special Studies of Economic Change*, 1980.

ment spending. After 25 years of rapid growth, these shares had increased to 10, 13, and 32 percent, respectively. This growth had several causes. First, the increased affluence of the post-World War II period led citizens to revise upward their notions of what constitutes a minimally decent standard of living. As a result, more families were judged to require assistance, and this aid was directed toward those with the lowest incomes. Second, programs automatically grew as they matured. For example, Social Security expenditures were low for many years because few qualified for retirement benefits. As a larger fraction of retirees became eligible, outlays increased. Finally, several programs were initiated or expanded after 1965, particularly Medicare, Medicaid, and Food Stamps. Social Security payments for both retirement and disability grew rapidly as, in a series of measures between 1967 and 1974, Congress increased benefits by 90 percent. By way of comparison, average personal income grew by only 43 percent over this period.[2]

The Antipoverty Impacts of Income Transfers

Rapid growth in coverage and benefit levels of income support programs has significantly reduced the incidence of poverty. Table 2, column 1, presents the changes in income poverty from 1965 to 1976 if all cash receipts, including cash income support payments, are taken into account. These data, the official Census poverty statistics, show that poverty fell by 25 percent between 1965 and 1972, but that there has been no real progress since. The second column adjusts Census data for underreporting of incomes, payment of federal income and payroll taxes, and the receipt of in-kind transfers, and shows that poverty when income is so defined declined by almost 50 percent. The adjusted poverty data suggest a less-serious problem in each year, but also show no real progress since 1972. Nonetheless, an incidence of 6.5 percent means that 14 million persons remain poor, and among some groups, even adjusted poverty levels remain shockingly high. About one-third of black female households, one-fifth of white female households, and one-tenth of black male households remain poor.

[2] See R. Plotnick, "Social Welfare Expenditures: How Much Help for the Poor?" *Policy Analysis*, 5 (Summer 1979): 271-289.

Table 2. TREND IN THE INCIDENCE OF POVERTY AMONG PERSONS, 1965-1976

	% of Population below Poverty Line	
Year	Census Income	Adjusted Income
1965	15.6	12.1
1968	12.8	10.1
1970	12.6	9.4
1972	11.9	6.2
1974	11.6	7.8
1976	11.8	6.5
% change, 1965-1976	-24.4	-46.2

Source: Robert Plotnick and Timothy Smeeding, "Poverty and Income Transfers: Past Trends and Future Prospects," *Public Policy*, 27 (Summer 1979): 259.

Poverty declined, but not because the programs of the War on Poverty successfully provided a "hand up" to enable the poor to earn their way out of poverty. If only income from private sources is counted, the percentage of the population below the poverty line—the "pretransfer poor"—has remained almost constant at about 20 percent since 1965. Cash and in-kind benefits, not increased earnings, account for all the progress.

While absolute poverty has declined, overall income inequality has remained remarkably stable. If support payments had not increased, the distribution of income would actually have become more unequal during the past twenty-five years.[3]

Clearly, income support payments vastly improve the living standards of our poorest citizens. For those who want to and are able to work, however, the increased support payments do not provide economic independence. One consequence of the growth in income support is increased dependence on government programs for an increasing percentage of the population.

[3] Several papers have demonstrated this conclusion. See especially S. Danziger and R. Plotnick, "Demographic Change, Government Transfers, and the Distribution of Income," *Monthly Labor Review*, 100 (April 1977): 7-11. See also A. Blinder, "The Level and Distribution of Economic Well-being," to appear in M. Feldstein, editor, *Postwar Changes in the American Economy*, (National Bureau of Economic Research, Cambridge, Mass., 1981); T. Smeeding, "On the Distribution of Net Income: Comment," *Southern Economic Journal*, 45 (January 1979): 932-934; M. Reynolds and E. Smolensky, *Public Expenditures, Taxes, and The Distribution of Income* (Academy Press, New York, 1977).

To some extent the growth of income support payments has contributed to pretransfer poverty. Without improved benefits, some recipients would have worked more, and, as a result, pretransfer poverty would have been lower.[4] Similarly, if benefits had not grown, some persons with relatively low market incomes (e.g., single mothers or the elderly) might not have established independent households that are counted among the pretransfer poor.[5] Still, our research suggests that these effects, while present, are not sufficiently large to challenge our main conclusion: if income support payments had not increased, poverty would not have declined.

Effects of Income Transfers on Work and Saving

In addition to enhancing security and reducing poverty, income support programs create incentives that adversely affect economic behavior. These incentives have received substantial attention in recent years. Whether referred to as supply-side effects or Laffer-curve impacts, or whether discussed in the scholarly journals or in the press, the critical issue concerns the impact on economic growth. At its core, this case against existing income support policy can be paraphrased as follows[6]:

> Because of the incentives in income support programs, and the taxes required to finance them, work effort is discouraged and savings and investments are reduced. Thus, the growth in the income support system has played a significant role in the sluggish performance of the economy. Further expansion would have increasingly negative effects.

A large number of recent studies has sought to quantify the

---

[4] See R. Plotnick, "Income Support Programs, Income Redistribution, and Labor Supply: A Simulation Analysis," mimeo, 1979.

[5] See S. Danziger, G. Jakubson, S. Schwartz, and E. Smolensky, "Work and Welfare as Determinants of Female Household Headship," Institute for Research on Poverty Discussion Paper, mimeo, 1980.

[6] For examples of such arguments, see A. Laffer and J. Seymour, *The Economics of the Tax Revolt: A Reader* (Harcourt Brace, New York, 1979); see also the section on "Domestic Issues" in *The United States in the 1980s* P. Duignan and A. Rabushka, Eds. (Hoover Institution, Stanford, 1980).

magnitude of the negative work and savings incentives. This literature provides the basis for judging the extent of the behavioral responses generated by income support policy.

Consider first work effort. While almost any aspect of an income support program might cause beneficiaries to alter their work effort, two key financial characteristics—the guarantee and the benefit-reduction rate—are most important. The guarantee, which often varies with family size, is the maximum payment that a person or family could receive. For example, a family of four with no other income might be guaranteed a cash grant of $4000. The benefit-reduction rate is the percentage by which this payment is reduced as earnings increase. For example, if benefit payments are reduced by 60 cents for each dollar of earnings, the benefit-reduction rate is 60 percent. In most income support programs—for example, Aid to Families with Dependent Children, Supplemental Security Income, Unemployment Insurance, and Old Age Insurance (OAI) for those younger than age 72—these benefit-reduction rates are positive and rather high. In several programs, however, benefits do not depend on earnings; neither OAI benefits for those over 72 nor veterans' disability payments are reduced as earnings rise.

Economic theory predicts that both the guarantee and the benefit-reduction rate will reduce work effort. The guarantee, by providing an income cushion, enables beneficiaries who value activities other than work to substitute these for work. The benefit-reduction rate also reduces work effort—in this case by effectively cutting the wage rate by which the worker is rewarded. While this effect may be somewhat offset because the benefit-reduction rate also limits the total income available, it is clear that an increase in both the guarantee and the benefit-reduction rate would reduce work effort. And, in recent years, both guarantees and benefit-reduction rates have been rising.

Numerous studies—both social experiments and more conventional analyses of data—have confirmed the existence of these guarantee and benefit-reduction rate effects.[7] From these studies,

---

[7] The most prominent of these studies are: G. Cain and H. Watts, *Income Maintenance and Labor Supply* (Markham, Chicago, 1973); S. Masters and I. Garfinkel, *Estimating the Labor Supply Effects of Income Maintenance Alternatives* (Academic Press, New York, 1978); M. Keeley et al., "The Estimation of Labor Supply Models Using Experimental

it is possible to estimate—in a rough fashion—the total impact of the income support system on work effort. This estimate must be rough, however, because the studies tend to focus on individual programs and not on the entire income support system. When an entire system of many programs is put into place, some fundamental behavioral changes may occur. People's evaluation of the benefits and costs of working (or working hard), the benefits and costs of entering the labor force early when young (or leaving later when old), the benefits and costs of avoiding layoffs or terminations, the benefits and costs of hurrying back to work when laid off, and the benefits and costs of seeking advancement and promotions may all be altered. All of these changes must be considered in evaluating the total effect on work of the support system.

Robert Lampman's "guesstimate" of the effect of the expansion of all social welfare expenditures on total work effort concluded that the system's expansion from 1950 to 1976—from 9 to 21 percent of GNP—caused hours worked to decline by 7 percent from what they would have been if the system had not expanded.[8] This rather high number resulted because the effects of some programs (e.g., public education) not in the income support system (Table 1) were included in the study. Moreover, the effect on work of the taxes required to finance the expansion was also included.

Our approach is somewhat different. Statistical estimates of the work responses of various groups to guarantees and benefit-reduction rates are now available. These responses, when applied to programs serving specific groups, yield estimates of the work reduction attributable to each program. By reviewing the effect on work of each of the programs in Table 1, an aggregate effect can be obtained. Our procedure suggests a total work reduction of about 3 percent. This result is consistent with the 7 percent figure

---

Data," *American Economic Review*, 68 (December 1978): 873-887; M. Keeley et al., "The Labor Supply Effects and Costs of Alternative Negative Income Tax Programs," *Journal of Human Resources*, 13 (Winter 1978): 3-36; J. Heckman, M. Killingsworth, and T. MaCurdy, "Recent Theoretical and Empirical Studies of Labor Supply," prepared for a conference at Magdalen College, September, 1979, mimeo; and D. Hamermesh, *Jobless Pay and the Economy* (Johns Hopkins, Baltimore, 1977).

[8] R. Lampman, "Labor Supply and Social Welfare Benefits in the United States," Institute for Research on Poverty Special Report 22, 1978. It should be noted that Lampman's estimate is of the labor supply effect of all social welfare benefits (including housing, manpower training, and education programs), rather than just income transfers.

obtained by Lampman, because the programs in Table 1 exclude some major components of total social welfare expenditures. Moreover, we did not include the disincentive effect of the increased taxes required to finance the outlays.[9]

Neither of these estimates supports the view that increased income support or social welfare spending has seriously disrupted the functioning of the labor market. The percentage reduction in total economic activity caused by these disincentives will be less than either the 7 percent or 3 percent reduction in time worked because the earnings of most recipients are well below the average of U.S. workers.

The effect of the income support system on thrift and savings has also been studied. The expansion of benefits has been found to decrease total savings. This occurs because income is transferred to lower-income people, who have higher propensities to consume, and away from higher-income people, who tend to save more. In an economy with slack resources, this expansion in consumption would result in greater output and employment. These increases at least partially offset losses in production due to work disincentives and may induce greater investment. In a fully employed economy, however, the increased consumption could come only at the expense of investment, and would result in some slackening of production and growth.

This possibility has been widely discussed, especially with respect to the impact of Social Security on savings. Three possible mechanisms by which Social Security benefits interact with the savings rate have been identified. First, the expectation of Social Security benefits may lead citizens to save less for their retirement. Because the system operates on a pay-as-you-go basis, public saving does not occur to offset the reduced private saving. As a result, total saving in the economy is likely to fall. The second effect may partially offset this. Because of Social Security, some people may retire earlier and hence require more retirement income than otherwise. This may cause them to save more in their preretirement years, thus increasing total saving in the economy. Finally, again because the Social Security system is on a pay-as-you-go

---

[9] The estimates on which we relied in arriving at this conclusion are described in S. Danziger, R. Haveman, and R. Plotnick, op. cit.

basis, income is being transferred from young people to older people. If parents wish to leave a bequest to children, they may increase its amount to offset the increased tax burden on children caused by the Social Security System. The result may be an increase in saving, thus reinforcing the second effect.

In recent years a larger number of researchers have addressed the Social Security-savings nexus.[10] An impressive array of variables and empirical equations have been mustered in the "regression wars" among these contenders. The general result—and perhaps the current consensus among economists—is that Social Security has depressed private savings by a small amount, but that this amount has not yet been measured precisely.

These studies, it should be noted, focus on Social Security alone, not on the effect of the entire income support system, and they do so in the context of a fully employed economy. As noted above, for a slack economy the case is quite different. Given the failure of the American economy to achieve full employment over most of the postwar period, we conclude that the overall effect of the income support system on the level of savings—and hence on the growth rate of GNP—may well have been slightly positive and no worse than neutral.

The Effects of Income Support Programs—A Summary

The entries in Table 3 reflect our reading of the empirical studies and summarize our judgments on the effects of the income support system. The first column is backward-looking—it appraises the effects of the actual expansion of the system from its size and composition in 1950. The first entry, for example, indicates that income poverty today is 50 to 60 percent smaller than it would have been if the 1950 income support system had been maintained.

---

[10] See M. Feldstein, "Social Security, Induced Retirement, and Aggregate Capital Accumulation," *Journal of Political Economy*, 82 (October 1974): 905-926; R. Barro, "Are Government Bonds Net Wealth?" *Journal of Political Economy*, 82 (November/December 1974): 1095-1117; R. Barro, *The Impact of Social Security on Private Saving: Evidence from the U.S. Time Series* (American Enterprise Institute, Washington, D.C., 1978); A. Munnell, "The Impact of Social Security on Personal Saving," *National Tax Journal*, 27 (December 1974): 553-567. A useful review of the time-series studies is Louis Esposito, "Effect of Social Security on Saving: Review of Studies Using U.S. Time Series Data," *Social Security Bulletin*, 41 (May 1978): 9-17.

Table 3. EFFECTS OF INCOME SUPPORT PROGRAMS.

	Effect of Support Programs, Relative to 1950 System	Effect of Marginal Expansion, Relative to Current System
Income Poverty	Reduction by 50 to 60 percent	Not large, as most easy gains have been made
Work Effort	Reduction by 3 to 7 percent	Negative
Savings	Modest reduction, assuming full employment; otherwise a small increase	Neutral or slightly negative; slight expansion if less than full employment
GNP Growth	Modest reduction, assuming full employment; otherwise a small increase	Slightly negative; neutral if less than full employment

The second column is prospective. It reflects our judgment regarding the effects of a modest proportional expansion of the system from its current state. For example, such an expansion is not likely to produce a noticeable reduction in the number of poor people. Most of the additional support payments would go to recipients who already are above the poverty line. Our estimates indicate that a proportional expansion in benefits would reduce the gap between the incomes of the poor and the poverty line by merely 5 cents for every dollar spent. The easy gains have already been made, and the groups remaining poor today will not be substantially helped by a proportional expansion of existing programs.

Past growth of the system has significantly reduced poverty while only modestly reducing work effort, savings, and GNP growth. Continued growth, however, means a less-favorable trade-off. Proportional expansion of existing programs will secure few redistributive gains and cause further erosion of work effort and savings.

Our conclusion differs substantially from an alternative view, that holds (1) the War on Poverty has been won, in large part, because of the rapid growth in income support payments, and (2) the disincentive effects of the current system are so large that the answer to "How much more equality can we afford?" is "Not any more."[11] This view overstates both the positive antipoverty and negative work and savings effects of the current system. Though poverty has declined substantially, a significant problem remains; while the system does create some disincentives to work and save, their modest size currently poses no serious threat to the growth of the economy.

New Directions for Income Support Policy

What then is called for? Some observers argue that we have moved too far along the "Laffer curve," that economic growth is needed, even at the cost of increased inequalities, and that a retrenchment is required. The elimination of Food Stamps and an end to the automatic inflation adjustments of benefit levels in Social Security and other programs have been suggested. The evidence does not justify these conclusions. Reductions in income support would lose much and gain little. However, changes in the current system designed to emphasize work opportunities could simultaneously improve incentives, enhance economic growth, and improve the position of those with poor education and few skills, whether they are poor or near poor.

This reorientation of the system would not involve cutbacks in income support to those who are not expected to work—the aged, disabled, or those with substantial child care responsibilities. It would emphasize policies—of which employment subsidies are a primary example—designed to enhance earnings and employment opportunities in the labor market for low-skill workers. Through such a strategy, the structural unemployment caused by minimum wages (and other gaps between worker productivity and the wage costs borne by employers) would be reduced. Those expected to work—that 30 percent of all income-poor household heads—would experience improved labor market options. These improved market conditions would also benefit those who are not expected to work—many of whom wish to, and indeed do, work.

[11] M. Anderson, *Welfare*, (Hoover Institution, Stanford, 1977); M. Paglin, "How Effective is Our Multiple Benefit Anti-Poverty Program?" paper presented at Middlebury College Conference on Welfare Reform, April 1980; E. Browning, "How Much More Equality Can We Afford?" *Public Interest*, No. 43 (Spring 1976): 90-110.

Our reorientation does not represent a comprehensive reform of the entire income support system.[12] We do not, for example, address Social Security reform, reforms in health insurance or unemployment compensation, or reforms for those not expected to work, to name a few. Nonetheless, policies to enhance earnings and employment warrant attention for two major reasons. First, reductions in work induced by the current system are its most significant negative effect. These reductions entail real economic losses and generate vociferous public dissatisfaction. Second, the major lesson that we draw from the policy debates of the past decade is that a welfare reform of the negative income tax variety that does not promote independence from support payments cannot solve the "welfare mess." To do so requires that we reduce poverty not by providing more income support payments, but by providing more job opportunities and higher earnings.

Several recent policy initiatives suggest that such an employment-based reorientation is already under way. A major thrust of President Carter's welfare reform plans (the unsuccessful 1977 Program for Better Jobs and Income, and the postponed 1979 reforms) was to reduce welfare's work disincentives.[13] The reforms would have reduced the benefit-reduction rate for recipients who worked and provided public employment to stimulate the *demand* for recipients who could not find private jobs.

Although welfare was not reformed, Congress did legislate programs to increase both the work effort of recipients and the demand for their labor. In 1977 and 1978, public employment was rapidly expanded under the Comprehensive Employment and Training Act (CETA). Many of these jobs were filled by low-skilled and disadvantaged workers. The Tax Reform Act of 1978 further encouraged increased work by expanding the Earned Income Tax Credit. It now provides a subsidy that increases with earnings up to a maximum of $500 for a family head with low earnings, and

---

[12] Additional discussion of the nature of this reorientation and of some other aspects of reform are presented in S. Danziger, I. Garfinkel, and R. Haveman, "Poverty, Welfare, and Earnings: A New Approach," *Challenge*, 22 (Sept.-Oct. 1979): 28-34; and R. Haveman, "Direct Job Creation: Potentials and Realities," in *Employing the Unemployed: Assessment of Federal Programs*, E. Ginsberg, ed., (Basic Books, New York, 1980).

[13] See S. Danziger, R. Haveman, and E. Smolensky, "The Program for Better Jobs and Income—A Guide and Critique," U.S. Congress, Joint Economic Committee, February 1978.

reduces taxes for all families with children and with incomes below $11,000. Because the credit is based on earned income, it makes work, relative to benefit recipiency, more attractive than before, and thus reduces the adverse impact of support programs on work effort.

Two other recent developments focus on earned income and the labor market determinants of pretransfer poverty. In 1976, Congress adopted the New Jobs Tax Credit, which subsidized employment over and above 102 percent of the previous year's employment level. Because this credit only subsidized 50 percent of the first $6000 of earnings, employers were given a substantial incentive to hire low-skill (relative to high-skill) workers and to substitute labor for capital. Evaluations have suggested a major job creation impact from this program. In the construction and retailing industries, for example, 20 percent of the 1977-78 employment increase has been attributed to the New Jobs Tax Credit, and many of the added employees were low-skill, low-wage workers.[14] Second, Congress passed the Targeted Jobs Tax Credit in late 1978. This credit subsidizes 50 percent of the first $6000 of wages of certain target groups of workers, including disabled workers, youths from disadvantaged families, disadvantaged Vietnam-era veterans, ex-offenders, and recipients of SSI and General Assistance.

These developments recognize the connections among poverty, income support programs, and the labor market. All but the Earned Income Tax Credit aim at directly altering the demand for labor by reducing the cost of hiring additional workers. These subsidies can offset existing biases against employment—such as the investment tax credit, minimum wages, and employment costs of pensions, unemployment insurance, and mandated health and safety regulations. If successful, the subsidies will cause employers to substitute workers in the target group for both capital and nontargeted workers. Such altered incentives help to counteract the work disincentives of support programs and form the core of a fundamental reorientation of the income support system.

These programs have other effects that are likely to make them

---

[14] See J. Bishop and R. Haveman, "Employment Subsidies: Can Okun's Law be Repealed?" *American Economic Review*, 69 (May 1979): 124-130, and J. Perloff and M. Wachter, "The New Jobs Tax Credit: An Evaluation of the 1977-78 Wage Subsidy Program," *American Economic Review*, 69 (May, 1979): 173-179.

more popular than increased income support. If job creation efforts are targeted on groups with high unemployment or low labor-force participation, output and employment will increase without creating inflationary pressure. This effect has been called "cheating the Phillips curve." Moreover, taxpayers will benefit from the increased taxes paid by the newly hired workers as well as from the reduced support payments. Both poverty and dependency will be reduced, and the self-respect of the newly employed should increase. Targeted job creation will also shift the composition of employment toward low-skill, low-wage workers. If smaller disparities in unemployment rates and market incomes are desired, this is a major benefit.

While such a reorientation of income support policy has a strong rationale, the effective design and implementation of programs to stimulate the demand for low productivity workers are not straightforward. "Displacement effects"—the reduction of employment somewhere else that offsets the jobs created directly by the program—are a major problem. If there is displacement, the *net* job creation impact will be smaller than the *gross* number of workers hired or subsidized. Another problem involves the high resource and budget costs of the net jobs created by this approach. A recent estimate (based on an assumed displacement rate of 20 percent in public and 80 percent in private job creation programs) suggests a cost per job of about $6500 for private sector programs and over $9000 for public sector programs. These estimates suggest that the taxpayer cost per job created is close to if not in excess of the net earnings of the new employees. A third problem concerns whether the value of the output produced exceeds the real costs of creating the jobs. These real costs include both the value of the equipment and materials used and the value of what the worker would have been doing if the program had not existed (e.g., child care, other market work, or leisure activities).

Job creation programs in the public sector (e.g., CETA) are likely to differ from those in the private sector (e.g., the New Jobs Tax Credit). Economic theory suggests that the private sector will be more efficient. Private employers already have established production processes and marketing channels for their products, whereas public employment programs are often undertaken with no clear definition of expected output and no easy measure of productivity. Partially off-setting this is the fact that, through competition, privately marketed outputs are more likely to displace other production than public outputs designed to fill an unoccupied economic niche. Moreover, if private employers use the subsidy to retain workers whom they otherwise would have laid off, the opportunity cost of the workers retained will be low. Although private sector efforts targeted on low-skill workers are likely to be more efficient, all attempts to create jobs may encounter some of these difficulties.[15]

As we enter the 1980s, the reorientation of income support policy toward increasing the demand for low productivity workers would appear to have both political appeal and an economic rationale. Major domestic problems of the 1980s are likely to include continued inflation; structural unemployment of women, minorities, and the low-skilled; and economic dislocation due to higher energy prices and changing retirement patterns. Policies to enhance employment and earnings, in particular employment subsidies, have an important role to play in such an environment. The Full Employment and Balanced Growth Act of 1978 already provides a legislative mandate to directly use such federal policies to meet these problems.

While this employment generation approach is basic to a more effective income support system, it in no way constitutes a complete reform. With it, the work disincentives in the existing system could be reduced. Serious problems of program integration and administration, horizontal inequities among families of different types and in different locations, and incentives for migration and family break-up would still characterize the existing system. Making employment the core of the system, however, would influence the direction of future, more general reforms.

Clearly, such a reorientation requires a great deal more knowledge about the benefits, costs, and administrative design of specific initiatives. Additional research on these issues should be high on the policy agenda for the early 1980s. The results from these studies could serve as the basis for an efficient expansion of employment subsidies and, perhaps, public employment programs.

[15] For a full discussion of the potentials and problems of public employment and wage subsidy policies, see *Creating Jobs: Public Employment and Wage Subsidies*, J. Palmer, ed. (The Brookings Institution, Washington, 1978).

A reorientation of the support system that emphasizes earnings and employment can induce the low-skilled to increase their work effort and employers to increase their demands for such workers. It offers the potential for reducing poverty and dependence on government payments and increasing work, savings, and economic growth. The sacrifice of this potential in the interest of retrenchment would miss an opportunity for meaningful reform.

7

THE NET IMPACT OF THE SOCIAL SECURITY SYSTEM ON THE POOR

Richard V. Burkhauser and Timothy M. Smeeding

Since 1974, Supplemental Security Income (SSI) has provided a universal income floor for the low-income aged. A major feature of this "social welfare" program, however, is that it taxes income from social security (OASI) at virtually 100%. In this article we show that the current structure of SSI has altered significantly the "social insurance-social welfare" nature of OASI for many low-income workers. Using data from the 1973 Social Security Exact Match File we find that lifetime contributions paid into OASI by low earners make them only slightly better off than would be the case had they relied solely on SSI. Moreover, we show that while a reduction in the net tax (benefit reduction) rate on OASI in SSI would increase SSI expenditure, it would also result in removing a large number of low-income elderly people from the poverty rolls. The consequences of this negative interaction of SSI on OASI lead to serious questions about the equity and efficiency of the current OASI-SSI system and about the likelihood of continuing political support for it.

This research was begun while both authors were at the Institute for Research on Poverty, University of Wisconsin-Madison, and was supported by funds granted to the Institute by the Department of Health, Education and Welfare pursuant to the Provisions of the Economic Opportunity Act of 1964. The authors wish to thank Jennifer Warlick, John Bishop, and other members of the Institute workshop for helpful comments on previous drafts of this article. A preliminary version of this article was presented to the American Economic Association on December 28, 1979.

From Richard V. Burkhauser and Timothy M. Smeeding, "The Net Impact of the Social Security System on the Poor," 29(2) *Public Policy* 159-178 (Spring 1981). Copyright © 1981 by the President and Fellows of Harvard College. Reprinted by permission of John Wiley & Sons, Inc.

> If this low-income worker is going to be a welfare person to begin with, when he winds up with social security benefits he is getting the minimum. . .[If] you then proceed to give him the welfare payment to bring that up to what you think his income ought to be when he retires, the result is that he really does not get anything from social security because he would have gotten that much from welfare.
>
> U.S. Senator Russell Long (La.)
> Hearing Before Senate Finance Committee
> July 29, 1971 (Storey, 1975)

I. Introduction

In 1974, when the Supplemental Security Income program for the aged, blind, and disabled replaced Federal grants to States for old-age assistance, aid to the blind, and aid to the permanently and totally disabled, it was believed that this federally funded plan would strengthen the third leg of the traditional Federal "three-legged stool" approach toward the income support of the aged.[1] As this policy is usually presented, the first leg consists of Federal encouragement (through deferred taxes, etc.) of private saving and retirement plans that allow individuals to provide for their own retirement. The second leg consists of social security benefits (OASI) that provide "social insurance" to workers based on taxes they pay into the system over their lifetime. The third leg consists of "social welfare," that provides income transfers to the poor aged regardless of past tax payments.[2] SSI is now the principal Federal support program in this area of public policy toward the aged. Together, these programs attempt to guarantee adequate (nonpoverty) income levels for all aged persons. But the metaphor of the three-legged stool has a major shortcoming. So, indeed, does the public policy approach it represents. Neither adequately takes into account the fact that programs developed in each of these

---

[1] In this article we concentrate exclusively on federal income policy toward the aged. Our arguments are equally relevant, however, for the interaction between SSI-disability and OASI-disability insurance.

[2] For an example that applies the metaphor of the three-legged stool to income support, see Schulz (1977).

three neatly compartmentalized areas interact with each other. Recent criticism of this interaction in the economics literature has concentrated on the negative impact of OASI on private saving and pension plans.[3]

In this article we look at an interaction that is less understood—that between OASI and the newly created SSI program. In the remainder of this section we discuss our approach to judging the impact of SSI on the equity, economic efficiency, and political backing of current Federal income support policy. Section II describes the interaction between OASI and SSI, our data base, and the model that we use to analyze these issues. Section III presents the results of our analyses, while Sec. IV presents one alternative to the current OASI-SSI interaction and its impact on the elderly poor.

In understanding the interaction of SSI with OASI it is important to recognize that although OASI is not a "pure social insurance" program, it does contain a life cycle relationship between taxes paid into the system at younger ages and benefits received at older ages. In establishing this relationship, OASI delicately balances social insurance goals with income distribution goals. As social insurance, OASI relates future benefits to previous contributions in an intertemporal sense. But unlike "pure social insurance," expected benefits do not exactly match contributions. Traditionally this has been the case for two reasons. First, within any given age cohort, features of the OASI program—for instance, a progressive benefit formula, a minimum benefit, a uniform dependent's benefit, and a work test—attempt to redistribute income from high earners to low earners. Second, from almost the beginning, the pay-as-you-go nature of the system permitted the payment of benefits to virtually everyone in excess of their contributions, resulting in large across-generation transfers to both high- and low-wage earners. Burkhauser and Warlick (in press) show that up to 1972 (the last year of their data) this across-generation distribution dominated within-generation distribution. Thus, the expected present value of benefits has exceeded that of a fair return on individual lifetime contributions for all income cohorts who were eligible for OASI benefits in 1972.

[3] See especially Feldstein (1974) and Munnell (1977).

Since SSI guarantees a minimum annual income to all persons aged 65 and over, regardless of past tax payments or OASI eligibility status, it is a "pure social welfare" program with no direct intertemporal relationship. But it will become apparent that SSI, through its impact on OASI, plays a potentially significant role in work and saving behavior over life. At first glance, guaranteeing low-income people a minimum income level regardless of their OASI status seems a wholly positive achievement.[4] A more careful consideration of the interaction of this social welfare program with the social insurance component of OASI suggests, however, that it has been accomplished only at a significant cost: it has altered the value of OASI for low-wage earners.

As SSI is presently structured, it replaces OASI benefits to the low-income elderly dollar for dollar, save for a small disregard of $20 per month. In other words, for those aged 65 and over, with current incomes low enough to qualify for SSI, OASI benefits are taxed at 100%. The consequence, we shall argue, is to reduce significantly the marginal value of the OASI system to workers with a history of low wages.

In fact, low earners who make OASI contributions during their working years will receive little more in benefits at older ages than would be the case had they relied on SSI alone. Thus the coverage that they obtain with their OASI social insurance contributions is redundant, to the extent that SSI already provides this coverage. From an equity standpoint, the introduction of SSI has tilted the redistributive aspect of OASI away from low earners. The impact of such a change on economic efficiency is also clear. For low earners who make contributions for redundant OASI coverage, such contributions are truly "taxes." Over the life cycle we predict such a tax will yield at least three types of behavioral responses by long-term low earners:

(1) an incentive to reduce work effort when younger[5] ;
(2) an incentive to retire and claim OASI benefits at age 62, in

---

[4] The earlier old-age assistance program that SSI both upgraded and superseded provided something of an income floor for the elderly, although on an uneven and haphazard basis, state by state. SSI, in contrast, represents the first explicit recognition of a nationwide, federally guaranteed, minimum income for all elderly, regardless of the state in which they live.

[5] For an empirical estimate of the effect of OASI on distribution of work effort over the life cycle, see Burkhauser and Turner (1978).

order to recoup previous payroll tax contributions otherwise lost at age 65 due to the redundancy caused by SSI[6];

(3) an incentive to "hide" earnings in illegal activities and/or casual (non-IRS-reported) jobs, in order to avoid the OASI payroll tax.

In addition, the SSI liquid asset test discourages saving on the part of those who would otherwise qualify for SSI because of their low current income. Measuring the magnitude of these behavioral responses is beyond the scope of this article; nevertheless, they do indeed exist, and may be quite important for some earners.

The political importance of this interaction is clear. As potential low-income retirees and political leaders sympathetic to their economic situation come to realize, first, that the OASI taxes of low earners yield them little marginal return and second, that these taxes indirectly benefit retired high-wage earners, as we will show, an erosion of their political support for OASI must follow.[7]

II. The Interaction of SSI with OASI

A. SUPPLEMENTAL SECURITY INCOME

SSI provides benefits to those aged 65 and over on the basis of the characteristics of the filing unit (marital status and housing) and of sources and size of other current income. In general, couples with both spouses eligible (i.e., both 65 or older) are entitled to 1.5 times the benefit for a single individual.[8] Benefits are reduced by one-third if a filing unit lives in the home of another (e.g., that of a son or daughter). The actual Federal guarantees in 1974 for the six types of SSI filing units considered here are shown in Table 1,

---

[6] This point is made by Tolley and Burkhauser (1977), who argue that the 100% tax on OASI benefits by SSI effectively removes the actuarial penalty for early OASI acceptance. Hence those eligible for SSI are induced to accept OASI at ages 62-64.

[7] The current "earned income tax credit" uses general revenues from the income tax to refund, in effect, some portion of OASI taxes to low-income families with dependent children. This provision can be interpreted as evidence that lawmakers are already sensitive to this issue.

[8] No benefit is paid for a spouse under age 65 who is not blind or disabled, or for dependent children of the beneficiary, unless that dependent is necessary for the care and well-being of the beneficiary, i.e., is an "essential person," in SSI terminology. In that case, the dependent is treated as an eligible spouse.

Table 1. SSI BENEFITS FEDERAL GUARANTEE LEVELS FOR DIFFERENT TYPES OF FILING UNITS

Type of Filing Unit	Federal Guarantee Per Year	
	1974	1972[a]
Single person living in own home	$1716	$1456
Couple, both eligible, living in own home	2574	2184
Single person living in the home of others	1144	970
Couple, both eligible, living in the home of others	1716	1456
Couple, spouse ineligible, living in own home	1716	1456
Couple, spouse ineligible, living in the home of others	1144	970

[a]Value of 1974 guarantee in 1972 dollars.
Source: U.S. Congress, Joint Economic Committee, 1974.

together with these guarantee values in 1972 dollars. The vast majority of beneficiaries (70%) are in the first two groups, while the number of recipients who are couples (with or without an eligible spouse) living in the homes of others is virtually zero.

In 1974, 30 states supplemented the Federal minimum SSI benefit for at least one of the six categories of recipients. These supplements ranged from a few dollars in some states to supplemental benefits that equaled, and in the case of California exceeded, the Federal guarantee. Thus in some high-supplement states, the Federal minimums of Table 1 were doubled.

The current interaction of SSI with OASI arises from the differential treatment of income in the SSI means test. Wage earnings have a $65 per month disregard; for every dollar of additional earnings, SSI benefits are reduced by 50 cents. Virtually all non-wage earnings, including OASI, reduce SSI benefits dollar for dollar after a $20 per month disregard.[9]

B. SOCIAL SECURITY (OASI)

OASI bases benefits on past contributions, but the relationship is not exact. Like SSI, OASI has, in effect, a "means test." The disregard for wage earnings in 1972 was $175 per month—nearly three times the SSI disregard. As is the case with SSI, every dollar

---

[9] The only exception is a veteran's pension. This is discussed in Sec. IV.

of earnings above the disregard reduces OASI benefits by 50 cents. Unlike SSI, OASI does not test nonwage income. As we shall see, the lack of a means test on nonwage earnings has effectively prevented the type of interaction between OASI and private pension plans that we describe here between SSI and OASI.

C. DATA BASE

We use the 1973 Social Security Exact Match Data File, which merges individual records from the 1973 Current Population Survey (CPS) with OASI earnings and benefit records. With these data, the pattern of actual OASI benefits, as well as lifetime contributions into the system by all individuals, can be found. Such a data base permits us to separate the social welfare and social insurance aspects of OASI for individual filing units. Further, because it includes CPS demographic, locational, and other income data, we can simulate SSI benefit levels across the entire SSI eligible population and thus measure the impact of SSI on OASI.

D. SIMULATIONS

Two sets of SSI benefits were simulated for the six types of SSI filing units shown in Table 1. Since SSI did not begin until 1974, our simulations (which assume that SSI began in 1972) use real benefit levels equivalent to those that were in effect on July 1, 1974. Official federal income disregards, exclusions, and earnings tests were applied to the potentially eligible population (i.e., filing units with at least one member 65 or older) in order to determine SSI eligibility and federal benefit levels. On this basis, 4.915 million elderly (30% of the elderly population) would have been eligible for $3.33 billion in SSI benefits in 1972, had the program then been in effect.[10]

---

[10] We assume that participation in SSI is 100% by all eligibles, despite the fact that actual SSI participation is much lower. In fact, only 50-60% of those eligible participated in 1974, the first year of the program (Warlick, 1978). The SSI participation rate should increase as the program becomes better known and publicized. If participation rates are low because of lack of information on the SSI program (or about applying for benefits), the value of SSI to an eligible person would be, dollar for dollar, equal to OASI benefits. If, however, those who do not participate in SSI are responding to the "welfare" stigma associated with the program, we may overestimate the value that they place on SSI; for them, it is an irrelevant alternative. Operationally, this means that we value SSI benefits at 100% for those currently eligible for such benefits. In addition, it

A second set of simulations took state supplementation into account. The basic 1972 Federal guarantees were increased for beneficiaries according to the type of filing units and the state of residence, according to the ratio of the total state guarantee (including supplements and Federal minimum) to the Federal minimum on July 1, 1974.[11] Using the new guarantees we then recomputed eligibility and benefit amounts. As a result, 6.9% more aged persons—6.042 million in all—became eligible for $4.96 billion in SSI benefits in 1972.

In measuring the life cycle effect of SSI on the OASI system, we split actual OASI benefits into two components: (1) an annuity or social insurance component and (2) a social welfare or intergenerational transfer component. The annuity is equal to the amount that beneficiaries would have received upon retirement, in annual yearly payments until death, had they placed their OASI contributions in an investment portfolio that produced income equal to the average yield on stocks (dividends plus capital gains) over the period during which they were contributing to OASI. Hence this aspect of the calculation converts OASI contributions into an actuarily fair pension. The difference between actual benefits received and actuarily fair benefits is then defined as the social welfare component of OASI.[12]

III. Simulation Results

Table 2 presents the result of our calculations. Column 0 shows SSI benefits in the absence of OASI income for the mean filing unit characteristics as described in Sec. II. In column 1, we record

---

should be noted that we value SSI benefits at zero for those not currently eligible for them. Clearly, in a behavioral sense, this overestimates potential SSI benefits to those actually getting them and underestimates SSI benefits to those not currently getting them.

[11] Because the Social Security Exact Match File includes only noninstitutionalized persons, the 4.1% of aged SSI recipients in nursing homes (Sherman, 1979) were not counted in our simulations.

[12] The reader interested in a more explicit explanation of these calculations should consult Burkhauser and Warlick (in press). It should be noted, however, that the value of a fair annuity is markedly affected by the interest rate chosen to discount future benefits. By assuming that the interest rate is constant across income groups, we may overstate the value of such an annuity for low earners with potentially higher rates of discount.

Table 2. THE DISTRIBUTION OF OASI AND FEDERAL SSI: MEAN BENEFITS BY INCOME CLASS, 1972

Income[a] Class	Mean Benefits[b]			Net OASI (1)+(2) −(0) = (3)	Annuity Value (4)	Life Cycle Transfer (3)−(4) = (5)	Population	
	SSI without OASI (0)	OASI (1)	SSI with OASI (2)				Percentage Aged in Class (6)	Percentage in Class Eligible for SSI (7)
$0	$1288	$0	$1288	$0	$0	$0	2.0	100.0
1–500	1328	47	1314	33	4	29	1.0	100.0
501–1000	1237	619	794	176	36	140	6.5	100.0
1001–1500	1181	943	540	302	109	193	10.7	87.7
1501–2000	686	1344	216	874	252	622	12.3	47.6
2001–2500	482	1548	170	1236	351	885	11.0	30.6
2501–3000	257	1766	90	1599	426	1173	7.6	12.3
3001–3500	117	2031	40	1954	518	1436	6.0	8.3
3501–4000	42	2190	17	2165	673	1492	5.1	3.1
4001–4500	16	2288	8	2280	708	1572	4.8	1.5
4501–5000	26	2326	6	2306	758	1548	4.2	1.6
5001–7500	2	2320	1	2319	792	1527	12.7	0.2
7501–10,000	2	1990	1	1989	731	1258	6.5	0.2
10,001 or more	0	1800	0	1800	602	1198	9.7	0.0
Total[c]		$27.1	$3.3	$23.7	$7.4	$16.12	100.0	30.0

[a]Census money income, net of Old Age Assistance (OAA) benefits; 1972 cash values.
[b]These are explained in Sec. III of the text.
[c]Total amounts in billions of dollars.

the mean of OASI benefits actually received by income class.[13] They include retired worker benefits, spouse benefits, or widow benefits as appropriate.[14] Benefits in column 2 are the SSI benefits that the mean filing unit in each income class would receive, given the mean OASI benefits.[15] Benefits in column 3 are the sum of columns 1 and 2 minus SSI benefits in the absence of OASI. For instance, the mean filing unit of income class $1501–$2000 receives $1344 in OASI benefits (column 1). Given these benefits and all other income and mean class characteristics the filing unit is eligible for $216 in SSI benefits (column 2). But if that filing unit received no OASI benefits it would be eligible for $686 in Federal SSI benefits, as shown in column 0. Thus net OASI benefits equal $874 (1344 + 216 - 686).[16] Column 4 is the value of a fair annuity based on lifetime contributions by both employee and employer into OASI. Column 5 is the net life cycle

---

[13] There is some question about the "correct" income perspective from which to approach this problem: should we use current or permanent income? SSI eligibility and benefits are based on current, not permanent, income. It would seem, however, that the earnings-based behavioral response to the SSI–OASI interaction is particularly important for long-term low earners. Two observations may effectively mute this controversy. First, those eligible for SSI on the basis of current low income, who also receive OASI and other pensions, have most likely been low earners over their working lives. If their incomes had been higher for a long time, private pensions, interest income, savings, etc., would tend to make them ineligible. Hence, among the elderly, current and permanent low income should be highly correlated. Second, while we chose to use the current income rankings in this article, we are not constrained to rank by current income. Our data base provides us with at least ten years of earnings history for most elderly. Using this information it was possible to construct a rough measure of permanent income, and on that basis we found that the probability of becoming eligible for SSI exceeds 50% for those who have up to $2000 of permanent wage earnings. Although the probability of low earnings at older ages is nonzero for those with high permanent incomes, it is relatively low.

[14] Those currently eligible but not receiving benefits and those still working and subject to the earnings test receive less than they otherwise could in 1972. In that year the social security earnings test taxed benefits at 50% for those aged 62–71 who were earning above $2100.

[15] Algebraically: SSI = G – ADED and ADED = (OASI + NWINC –240) + 0.5(EARN –780); where the annual SSI benefit equals the federal guarantee (G), or federal guarantee plus state supplementation in Tables 3 and 4, minus allowable annual deductions (ADED). ADED equals OASI benefits (from column 1) plus other nonwage income (interest, rent, dividends, and other pensions) net of the $240 nonwage income disregard, plus one-half of earnings (EARN) net of a $780 disregard. If earnings are less than $780 no earnings are deducted.

[16] Algebraically: NET OASI = OASI + SSI –SSIN, and SSIN = G –DED, where DED = (NWINC –240) + 0.5 (EARN –780). Thus NET OASI benefits equal current income (OASI in column 1 plus SSI in column 2) minus SSIN, or SSI benefits if OASI were zero (column 0). SSIN is calculated exactly as is SSI in column 2 (see fn 15) except that OASI is ignored in determining the SSI benefit.

transfer component of OASI. It is the difference between the amount that the mean filing unit in each income class would have received in a pure social insurance system and what it actually receives, net of SSI. This is the social welfare component of OASI.

The values in Table 2 are calculated for all elderly filing units, based only on the Federal SSI guarantee. Comparing columns 1 and 3, we see that the effect of SSI is to reduce total OASI benefits below what the individual would otherwise have received, given his or her other income. Clearly the major impact of SSI is on low-income classes, especially those below the $2500 range. It is the long-term low-wage earners in these income classes who have contributed to OASI throughout their working lives who are most seriously affected, for the net life cycle transfer that they receive is reduced (column 5). Thus the net redistributive effect of SSI is to make net life cycle transfers in the OASI system significantly smaller for low-income households. While it is still true that mean OASI benefits continue to exceed the return for a fair annuity, the "social welfare" benefit for high-income elderly is substantially higher than it is for low-income elderly—a fact that is more than slightly ironic. The negative effect of SSI on OASI is greatest for those in the $501-$2500 brackets which contain over 40% of all elderly people, the large majority of whom are poor.[17] On the average, the greatest reduction is $641 ($943 - $302) or 68% of gross OASI benefits for the 10.7% of the elderly in the $1001-1500 income bracket. All told, 30% of the elderly are eligible for SSI. Looking only at the Federal portion of SSI, Table 2 shows its impact on OASI is both widespread and substantial. The aggregate total reduction in OASI benefits due to Federal SSI is $3.439 billion (column 1 minus column 3).

Table 3, following the same format as Table 2, shows the simulated impact when both Federal and state portions of SSI are included. The most striking result is that state supplements increase the interaction impact of SSI on OASI. Mean and total SSI benefits are now larger in column 2, and a greater proportion of the elderly are adversely affected (37% as against 30% earlier).

---

[17] The official government poverty lines for the elderly in 1972 were $1994 for a single individual and $2505 for a couple (U.S. Bureau of the Census, 1973:143).

Table 3. THE DISTRIBUTION OF OASI AND FEDERAL-STATE SSI: MEAN BENEFITS (INCLUDING STATE SSI SUPPLEMENTS) BY INCOME CLASS, 1972

Income[a] Class	Mean Benefits[b]			Net OASI (1) + (2) −(0) = (3)	Annuity Value (4)	Life Cycle Transfer (3)−(4) = (5)	Population	
	SSI without OASI (0)	OASI (1)	SSI with OASI (2)				Percentage Aged in Class (6)	Percentage in Class Eligible for SSI (7)
$0	$1439	$0	$1439	$0	$0	$0	2.0	100.0
1−500	1476	47	1462	33	4	29	1.0	100.0
501−1000	1379	619	936	176	36	140	6.5	100.0
1001−1500	1340	943	698	301	109	192	10.7	87.8
1501−2000	1185	1344	447	606	252	354	12.3	66.2
2001−2500	884	1548	325	989	351	638	11.0	45.0
2501−3000	695	1766	225	1296	425	871	7.6	33.1
3001−3500	454	2031	139	1716	518	1198	6.0	19.3
3501−4000	322	2190	89	1957	673	1284	5.1	11.9
4001−4500	164	2288	43	2167	708	1459	4.8	6.1
4501−5000	126	2326	42	2242	758	1484	4.2	4.6
5001−7500	30	2320	7	2297	792	1505	12.7	1.4
7501−10,000	10	1990	4	1984	731	1253	6.5	1.2
10,001 or more	0	1800	0	1800	602	1198	9.7	0.0
Total[c]	$27.1		$5.0	$21.7	$7.4	$14.2	100.0	36.9

[a] Census money income, net of Old Age Assistance (OAA) benefits; 1972 cash values.
[b] These are explained in Sec. III of the text.
[c] Total amounts in billions of dollars.

148

Note that column 3 is exactly the same at income levels below $1501. This comes about because in Table 2 SSI had already replaced 100% of OASI benefits for these people, so that the higher SSI benefits simulated in Table 3 cannot replace any greater amount of OASI. Above the $1500 income level, however, the interaction effect increases as more aged become eligible for SSI. For instance, the maximum impact is now $738 ($1344 - $606), or 55% between $1501 and $2000, compared with only $470 ($1344 - $874), or 35% of OASI benefits, in Table 2. Ironically, then, while state supplementation increases the guarantee level for SSI recipients, it also increases the size of the SSI-OASI interaction. The aggregate total OASI reduction is now $5.4 billion ($27.1 - $21.7 billion). Once again all the values in column 5 are positive, so that even with the SSI interaction, a positive social welfare component of OASI continues for all income classes (partly because of the $360 per year disregard). But for an even larger portion of low earners, SSI reduces net OASI benefits.

In a state such as California where supplements are very high, the marginal benefits to low earners are most profoundly reduced. Our simulations for 1972 do not find negative transfers (i.e., less than actuarily fair OASI returns) for mean income groups, but some negative returns for individual low earners were found. In addition, the across-generation portion of OASI benefits is falling over time as people contribute into OASI over their entire lifetimes.[18] Those just reaching age 65 in 1981 may well have contributed into the system for over 40 years. Thus it is likely that in many high-supplement states the net return to such low-income aged is already negative.

IV. Policy Alternatives

The creation of SSI has guaranteed households a minimum income in old age, but not without raising serious equity questions by significantly altering the social insurance-social welfare character of OASI. As we have just demonstrated, one of the implications of

---

[18] In cross tabulations that are not shown, the annuity portion of OASI increases from an average of 10% for those filing units with a head aged 80 and over to 50% for those with a head aged 66-68 in 1972.

our current SSI program is its erosion of the marginal benefit from OASI contributions made by low-income workers. In response to a similar equity problem that might arise from the interaction of OASI and private pension, OASI *does not* reduce its benefit payments to those receiving private pension income, even though OASI has a significant social welfare component.

Currently, both OASI and SSI respond to wage earnings by taxing benefits (above the disregard) at 50%. Limiting the tax rate to 50% shows a real concern for efficiency, for such taxes potentially distort labor supply adversely. In this article we have posited that the 100% tax on OASI benefits by SSI also has potentially adverse effects on labor supply across the entire life cycle.[19] Therefore, it can be argued that on grounds of both efficiency and equity, a reduction in this 100% rate should be considered. Even within SSI this would not be precedent setting since veterans' benefits are currently taxes at 60%; clearly Congress has been willing to give certain nonwage income preferential treatment.

In Table 4, we simulate the effects of a proposal to reduce the SSI tax rate on OASI to 50%.[20] The major result of this change is, not unexpectedly, to increase the net return on OASI for lower-income SSI recipients. Looking at column 2 we see that reducing the tax on OASI benefits significantly increases the size of the SSI program. The largest portion of these funds, however, goes to workers with low OASI earning histories; for the most part, they are in lower-income classes. Furthermore, as column 5 shows, the social insurance—social welfare aspect now changes. The transfer share of OASI increases for those in the $501-$2500 income classes— those considered at or below the poverty level in 1972, but reducing the tax on OASI benefits makes more filing units in the $2501-and-over income classes eligible for SSI, thus reducing the OASI transfer portion for these higher-income classes.

[19] We have emphasized throughout the negative substitution effect of this tax on work. It should be recognized that its removal or reduction would also have an income effect that would offset to some degree any increased work incentives. This is especially the case for the current cohort of older workers who would experience a significant and unexpected increase in lifetime wealth. But this unexpected increase would be less important for the future aged since it would be spread over a longer period and would allow for greater adjustment in their work behavior.

[20] In addition to reducing the marginal tax to 50% we also eliminate the $240 disregard. These proposed changes are among those suggested by Munnell (1977).

Table 4. THE DISTRIBUTION OF OASI AND FEDERAL-STATE SSI WITH A 50% TAX RATE FOR OASI MEAN BENEFITS BY INCOME CLASS, 1979

Income[a] Class	Mean Benefits[b]						Population	
	SSI without OASI[d] (0)	OASI (1)	SSI with OASI (2)	Net OASI (1)+(2)−(0) = (3)	Annuity Value (4)	Life Cycle Transfer (3)−(4) = (5)	Percentage Aged in Class (6)	Percentage in Class Eligible for SSI (7)
$0	$1439	$0	$1439	$0	$0	$0	2.0	100.0
1–500	1476	47	1462	33	4	29	1.0	100.0
501–1000	1379	619	1244	484	36	448	6.5	100.0
1001–1500	1454	943	1154	643	109	534	10.7	99.4
1501–2000	1519	1344	1011	836	252	584	12.3	96.5
2001–2500	1429	1548	833	952	351	601	11.0	88.4
2501–3000	1324	1766	713	1155	425	730	7.6	74.2
3001–3500	1166	2031	576	1441	518	923	6.0	59.1
3501–4000	1134	2190	473	1529	673	856	5.1	56.9
4001–4500	738	2288	266	1816	708	1108	4.8	38.1
4501–5000	617	2326	220	1929	758	1171	4.2	13.2
5001–7500	144	2320	49	2225	792	1433	12.7	8.2
7501–10,000	34	1990	12	1968	731	1237	6.5	1.8
10,001 or more	0	1800	0	1800	602	1198	9.7	0.0
Total[c]		$27.1	$9.9	$21.4	$7.4	$14.0	100.0	58.3

[a] Census money income, net of Old Age Assistance (OAA) benefits; 1972 cash values.
[b] These are explained in Sec. III of the text.
[c] Total amounts in billions of dollars.
[d] Mean SSI benefit levels without OASI are higher in Table 4 than in Table 3 because a greater share of the population of each income class above $1500 is eligible for SSI benefits. See fn 10.

Another major result of this change would be its impact on the ability of the social security system as a whole to provide protection from poverty for the aged population. Because OASI is based on a social insurance concept, some people, especially those who were low-wage earners over their entire lifetime, may not receive benefits sufficient to raise them above a poverty level in old age. This was the original justification for a separate SSI program. Since the 1960s a major benchmark for measuring the effectiveness of public policy has been the degree to which social programs have removed people from poverty. The poverty line is defined as the minimum level of income necessary to provide an adequate living for a family of some given size.[21] It has been argued that the social security system at a minimum should provide sufficient income support to guarantee that no worker should fall into poverty in old age. Table 5 shows that OASI benefits alone were not sufficient to keep 6.3 million or 28% of the aged above the poverty line in 1972. One method of reducing poverty in this age group would be to increase OASI benefits. SSI is an alternative method of providing transfers to the poor, and Table 5 shows that if it had been instituted in 1972 and all the eligible poor had accepted benefits, those in poverty would have fallen to 3.9 million or 17% of the aged population. This is a drop in the poverty population of 2.5 million or 39%.

A major ongoing debate concerns the best method of decreasing the aged poverty population. Clearly OASI has a major redistributive component and any increase in OASI benefits would aid all aged recipients including the poor.[22] Increases in SSI would more closely target money to the low-income aged.[23] Table 4 shows

---

[21] The measures of poverty used in this simulation are the official government poverty lines as indicated in fn 17. A less than 100% participation rate in SSI would certainly lower its antipoverty impact. Warlick (1978) has shown, however, that SSI participation is positively related to the net income gain. Thus, whatever the SSI participation rate under the current program, the large SSI benefits produced by a lower OASI tax rate would probably increase participation in the SSI program. If this is the case, adjusting for participation in the SSI program would widen the differential antipoverty impact of SSI with a 50% OASI tax rate as compared to SSI with a 100% tax rate.

[22] Those who advocate increasing the redistributive aspects of OASI argue that it provides the most politically palatable method of channeling funds to the low-income aged. One method of increasing redistribution within OASI would be through a "double-decker" plan that provides a fixed demogrant to every aged person, with additional benefits based on contributions added on top. See Garfinkle, Warlick, and Berry (in press) for a discussion of this plan.

[23] It is argued that OASI's method of redistributing income is neither equitable nor efficient and that it should return to its social insurance principles. Those who argue for

Table 5.   IMPACT OF THE SOCIAL SECURITY SYSTEM ON POVERTY AMONG THE ELDERLY, 1972

			Marginal Impact of SSI Program	
Income Definitions	Number of Elderly Poor (millions)	Poverty Rate	Reduction in Poor (millions)	Percentage Reduction in Poverty Rate
OASI[a]	6.3	28		
SSI program[b] under current rules	3.9	17	−2.4	39
Proposed SSI program[c]	1.6	7	−4.7	75
Total aged population[d]	22.5			

[a] Actual OASI benefits plus all other sources of money income exclusive of SSI or other welfare programs. In-kind income is not counted.

[b] Same as definition a but including potential 1972 SSI benefits (both federal and state) and assuming 100% participation. This is equivalent to definition used in Table 3.

[c] Same as definition a but including potential SSI benefit when the tax on OASI benefits is 50%. This is equivalent to definition used in Table 4.

[d] Potential SSI population in 1972. It includes single people aged 65 and over and married couples in which at least one member is aged 65. It excludes those residing in institutions.

that reducing the current 100% tax rate on OASI benefits of SSI recipients to 50% would have increased program costs by nearly $5 billion. Table 5 shows the impact of this adjustment in OASI-SSI interaction on the poverty population. The number of elderly poor falls to 1.6 million or 7% of the aged population. An SSI program that allowed the working poor this increased return on their lifetime contribution to OASI would have resulted in a 75% drop in the poverty population rather than the 39% decline due to the current SSI system.[24] In a period of increased pressure to hold the line on OASI payroll taxes such an alternative method of income distribution has significant appeal.

Here, we do not advocate this or any other particular policy change, but simply illustrate the tradeoffs inherent in the treat-

---

a "two-tier" system would like to see SSI take over the redistributive aspects of OASI. See Munnell and Stiglin (in press) for a discussion of this plan.

[24] These are only first approximations of the potential effect of such a change on both program costs and the poverty population since no behavioral responses to this change in SSI were considered. They do provide, however, a rough measure of the tradeoff between reduction in the poverty population and program costs.

ment of OASI income. The major point is that the interaction between OASI and SSI that now exists most severely affects low-wage earners. Small changes in the structure of SSI can change this interaction significantly while also changing the antipoverty impact of the social security system as a whole. Clearly, a more thoughtful consideration of such interactions is necessary for evaluating policy proposals for the aged.

V. Conclusions

Current Federal income support policy attempts to ensure economic security for the aged population. It does so through encouragement of private saving and pension programs and through social insurance and social welfare programs. The effects of this policy cannot be found simply by looking at each program in isolation. Rather, we have shown here that particular program features affect the goals of the program and elicit behavioral responses far beyond their particular spheres of reference. SSI, which attempts to provide an income floor for the aged poor, has an effect not only on the poor in a given period but also on the social insurance–social welfare nature of OASI and, through OASI, potentially on labor supply and savings decisions across the life cycle. Moreover, changes in the SSI-OASI interaction (such as decreasing the SSI tax rate on OASI to 50%) offer a viable alternative to increases in overall OASI benefits as a method of insuring systemwide protection against falling below the poverty lines. Ultimately, such interactions may be translated into changes in public support for OASI itself. Unless this is recognized and its impact included in studies of the equity, efficiency, and "popularity" of individual programs, such studies will miss these important effects on both behavior and distribution.

BIBLIOGRAPHY

Burkhauser, R., and Turner, J. A. (1978): "A time series analysis on Social Security and its effect on the market work of men at younger ages," *Journal of Political Economy,* 85(701): 715.

Burkhauser, R., and Warlick, J. (in press): "Disentangling the annuity from the redistribution aspects of Social Security," *Journal of Income and Wealth.*

Feldstein, M. (1974): "Social Security Induced Retirement and Aggregate Capital Accumulation," *Journal of Political Economy,* 82: 5(September/October).

Garfinkel, I., Warlick, J., and Berry, D. (in press): "The Distributional Effects of the Double-Decker Alternative for Eliminating Dependency in Social Security." In *A Challenge to Social Security – The Changing Rules of Women and Men in American Society,* R. V. Burkhauser and K. Holden (Eds.). New York: Academic.

Munnell, A. (1977): *The Future of Social Security.* Washington, D.C.: The Brookings Institution.

Munnell, A., and Stiglin, Laura (in press): "Women and a Two-Tier Social Security System." In *A Challenge to Social Security – The Changing Roles of Women and Men in American Society,* R. V. Burkhauser and K. Holden (Eds.). New York: Academic.

Schulz, J. (1977): "Public Policy and the Future Roles of Public and Private Pensions." In *Income Support Policies for the Aged,* G. S. Tolley and R. Burkhauser (Eds.). Cambridge, MA: Ballinger, pp. 11-36.

Sherman, S. (1979): "Comparison of Aged OASI and SSI Recipients, 1974," *Social Security Bulletin,* January: 39-44.

Storey, J. (1975): "The New Supplemental Security Income— Implication for Other Benefit Programs," *Policy Sciences,* 6: 359-374.

Tolley, G. S., and Burkhauser, R. V. (1977): "Integrating Social Security into an income policy." In *Income Support Policies for the Aged,* G. S. Tolley and R. V. Burkhauser (Eds.). Cambridge, MA: Ballinger.

U.S. Congress, Joint Economic Committee (December 1974): *Handbook of Public Income Transfer Programs,* Studies in Public Welfare, Paper No. 20. Washington, D.C.: U.S. GPO.

U.S. Department of Commerce, Bureau of the Census (December 1973): *Characteristics of the Low Income Population 1972.* Current Population Reports, Series P-60, No. 91. Washington, D.C.: U.S. GPO.

U.S. Department of Commerce, Bureau of the Census (July 1973a): *Household Money Income in 1972.* Current Population Reports, Series P-60, No. 89. Washington, D.C.: U.S. GPO.

U.S. Department of Health, Education and Welfare (February 1979): *Social Security and the Changing Roles of Men and Women.* Washington, D.C.: DHEW.

Warlick, J. (November 1978): "An Empirical Analysis of Participation in the Supplemental Security Income Program Among Eligible Aged Persons." Prepared for the Annual Meetings of the Gerontological Society.

8

PRICES AND INCOMES POLICY OPTIONS
Problems Arising from the British Experience

Eamonn Butler

Throughout history, attempts have been made by governments to control inflation or at least to modify its impact, by the imposition of wage and price controls. As recently as October 1978, President Carter announced a policy which he hoped would limit the rise in the Consumer Price Index to 5.75 percent in the succeeding year. The U.S. Administration's guidelines were complex, but set absolute maxima of 7 percent on wage increases and 9.5 percent on prices. Yet there was immediate protest from many sides, such as the labor unions,(1) and it was plainly becoming more and more difficult to adhere to the policy as time went on. Economists who had established their positions for (2) or against controls (3) now took their debate to the mass communications media. (4) Underlying the debate was the widespread feeling that voluntary controls were insufficient to stem increases in wages and prices. The questions now raised are whether statutory controls are more efficient, and whether they would be politically feasible anyway. In this environment, it is not surprising that the U.S. Administration might look towards non-statutory methods of control with more bite than a straightforward voluntary agreement.

A voluntary set of guidelines backed up by non-statutory guidelines is, however, nothing new. In Britain, such a system operated until abolished by the Conservative government which came to power in May 1979. Clearly it is worth an examination of this control system, to see whether it suggests any policy options — or warnings — in respect of the American economy.

Britain's Experience of Controls

It is unwise to generalise too enthusiastically from one country to another before establishing that they are truly analogous. A survey of the wage and price policies in Britain should suffice to show that the experience of controls is, in fact, remarkably similar and has been so for two decades.

From Eamonn Butler, "Prices and Incomes Policy Options: Problems Arising from the British Experience," 5(3) *Journal of Social and Political Studies* 179-197 (1980). Copyright 1980 by the Council for Social and Economic Studies. Reprinted by permission.

Wage controls

In mid-1961, the British government countered a large increase in wages around the country by the announcement of a 'pay pause' on increases in wages, salaries and even dividends. In February 1962, a White Paper (government policy document) was published, (5) which was intended to convert the pay pause into a lasting form of incomes policy. A 'guiding light' of 2-2½ percent average increase in wage and salary increases, based on a trend analysis of past productivity figures, was set. To this extent the policy was remarkably similar to the wage-price guideposts introduced in the United States a year earlier. But in Britain, circumstances conspired to obscure a 'guiding light' based on past trends. The National Economic Development Council reported that a future rate of increase in productivity of 3¼ percent could be attained. If this were so, it was felt that 3-3½ percent would be more appropriate a target figure than 2-2½ percent, and the National Incomes Commission, a pay-claim review agency, confirmed this view officially.

The election of a Labour Party government brought a new approach to incomes policy in April 1965. (6) Using once again *projections* for future productivity, a norm of 3-3½ percent was set. Increases over the norm would have to be balanced by increases below the norm to maintain the overall trend in line with the productivity estimates. Three of the conditions under which a higher than average settlement could be permitted were essentially similar to the 1962 criteria for movement above the norm; these related to increased output per worker in an enterprise, manpower shortages, and differences in payment for comparable work. To these, the Labour government added an exception providing for larger increases to lower paid workers. Another innovation was to tie wage controls much more closely to prices policy, which will be outlined below.

On the incomes front, however, the experience of the United Kingdom had been very close to that in the United States. David Smith commented:

"Both the criteria for wages and salaries, as they were announced in 1962 and modified in 1965, and the criteria for prices bore a striking resemblance to the wage-price guideposts announced in the United States in 1962. In both countries the appropriate movement of average earnings was linked to a trend in national productivity; in the United Kingdom the trend was based on a projection, and in the United States on an average of past changes in productivity. Exceptions to these norms were to be justified by productivity, labor shortage, or low wage considerations. The British criteria added another exception for cases in which it was generally recognized to be in the national interest for the pay of a group of workers to be in line with remuneration for similar work. Also, in both countries, increases and decreases in individual prices were to depend on changes in output per employee in relation to the national average, on changes in nonlabor costs, and on the ability to attract capital."(7)

From April 1965 until June 1966, these guidelines operated on a voluntary basis, although agreement did not come easily. The 1966 sterling crisis, however, brought forth a statutory policy, with a six-month freeze on wages and strict controls on prices, followed by a further six months of 'severe restraint.' During this latter period, the criteria adopted in 1965 were brought back into play, but were interpreted much more closely than before. The serious economic situation was cited as a reason for setting no pay increase norms, although its demise was something of a relief to the government, since the norm had by then come to be taken as a minimum and not an average, since most groups at the bargaining table thought their own claims to be more legitimate than the average. (8) Other elements of the policy were intended to help the slow-down; new negotiations over pay and hours were to take place at a minimum period of a year since the last round; justified increases were to be awarded in stages; there was to be no compensation for income lost during the six month freeze. Restraints were also put upon price increases.

In March 1968 came a new statutory initiative with the passing of the Price and Incomes Act, which followed another sterling crisis and devaluation in November 1977. While setting new controls on prices, the government affirmed its faith in a ceiling of 3½ percent on incomes. Yet the powerful unions had already wrought substantial legal privileges from the Labour government in exchange for their adherence to voluntary policies over the previous few years, and found themselves in a position to circumvent this new attempt at control. (9) By the end of 1969, the government had approved several pay settlements above the norm in the public sector, and in the words of the Confederation of British Industry, "appeared to have abandoned its policies." (10) New policies were being shaped when the government was defeated in the general election of 1970.

The Conservative Party, under Edward Heath, came to office committed to oppose wage and price controls and to abolish the National Board for Prices and Incomes which had institutionalized the policies of the late sixties. Within a year, however, the government found that prices were rising at a disturbingly high rate (which is now accepted as being the consequence of too rapid a stimulation of the economy and a substantial increase in monetary aggregates). Employers were calling for a new agreement with the unions. Unions were complaining about prices. Eventually in 1972, the Conservative government felt compelled to introduce legislation on incomes and prices policy.

Once again, there was a remarkable closeness between these controls and the Nixon Administration's policy following 1971. Nixon's 'Phases' became Britain's 'Stages', which were longer and supplemented by an extra one, but the general policy of a Stage 1 freeze for six months, followed by gradual relaxation, was similar. The statutory policy continued until the defeat of the Conservatives in 1974. The freeze was followed by Stage 2 pay limits of £1 per week plus 4 percent (to favour the lower paid), and after November 1973, this was eased to 7 percent or £2.25 per week, whichever was greater. This policy inspired little confidence, however, because prices and wage demands continued to rise at record levels, and the policy was brought to a swift end when the government were defeated in a confrontation with the powerful miners' union in February 1974. From then, the controls became voluntary. The Labour government entered into a 'solemn and binding' but unwritten agreement with the Trades Union Congress to cooperate in voluntary wage restraint. This 'Social Contract' itself came under strain very quickly; the unions wanted to make up for their losses under the previous government, and earnings rose by 21 percent in 1974, and 30 percent in 1975, compared with 13 percent under the last year of statutory controls.

Gradually, inflation subsided from its peak of over 28 percent, but this was probably due more to the government's adherence to strict fiscal and monetary guidelines than to the

Social Contract. Yet the rate of increase of prices was still high; and in mid-1977, a new, rigid policy was adopted with an across-the-board limit on pay awards, backed up by the threat of government economic sanctions against companies which conceded to higher claims. This was a new and innovative development in pay policy, and is perhaps instructive for the current American situation. Previously in Britain, governments had tried a rigid freeze, followed by gradual relaxation. The Labour government of 1974-9 was the only one which began with voluntary controls and then discovered that it had to toughen its policy. The similarity with the Carter Administration is plain, and accordingly the British experience with these economic sanctions will be examined in greater detail below.

Prices policy

Much of this continuing attempt to reduce the pressure of wage demands has been pegged to prices policy, since it is the level of prices, and not of wages, which was the real object of the policy instruments. The 1962 policy contained little emphasis on prices, but the new Labour government, in its incomes policy of 1965, placed much more emphasis on the role of price increases in prompting further wage demands. Accordingly, in the policy of 1966, prices were to be held constant for the most part, and control was based on the voluntary cooperation of businesses and unions in prenotifying increases in prices to the government. The policy, which was first spelt out in the White Paper of April 1965, specified a number of criteria upon which individual price rises were acceptable. These were situations in which the enterprise was faced with unavoidable costs in wages, materials or capital which could not be offset by increased productivity or by the company's own efforts; or, if having made such efforts, the company was still unable to attract sufficient capital to meet home and overseas demand.(11)

Although a voluntary policy, it was given official status by the creation of the National Board for Prices and Incomes, to which the government could refer price increase proposals at its discretion. This agency went through several metamorphoses. Until the sterling crisis of 1966, the NBPI carried no legal force; then came the freeze and period of 'severe restraint' on wages and prices. From July 1967 to March 1968, a 'period of moderation' as it was called by the government returned prices and incomes policy once again to the voluntary side, although it should be noted that any prenotified price increase could be delayed for over six months while investigations by government and the NBPI were undertaken, and if the NBPI recommended a restraint upon the individual price. The 1968 Prices and Incomes Act gave the government increased powers to stall prenotified price increases, and even to *reduce* prices upon recommendation by the NBPI. Like its equivalent on pay, this policy proved remarkably difficult to enforce.

The Heath government took its lesson from the United States when it established a single agency to which policing and control of prices were entrusted, called the Price Commission. This was a little different from the American Price Commission and the Cost of Living Council, since the latter were subordinate law-making bodies with the power to make regulations having the force of law. The British system required Parliament to agree to any proposed changes in the Price Code, making the system much more cumbersome.

The Price Code was detailed and rigid. In its final 1976 form, it contained some 150 clauses and a further 130 pages of explanation. It worked in two ways. Firstly, the Code limited the net profit margin of all enterprises to its historic level made in the twelve months before April 1973. If the net margin exceeded this level, then price reductions were ordered or proposed price increases prenotified to the Commission were held up. Initially, prenotification was required from only the largest companies, but by November 1973, medium-sized companies were also required to prenotify. Secondly, an overall gross margin limit was imposed on distributors, and prices from manufacturing or service companies were to be allowed only to the extent that they could be justified by certain specified 'allowable' cost increases which could not be absorbed by the enterprise. Needless to say, these controls were very unpopular with business and with investors, since any net increase in productivity made by a firm as a result of capital investment or reorganization would have to be met by a *reduction* in prices to redress the profit margin to its historic level. This would mean a lower absolute level of profits in many cases, and this was hardly a spur to new investment, and had a depressive effect on the normal expansion of profit margins during the rise of the business cycle, reducing the expansionary effect of the government's other stimulative policies. Other 'allowable cost' rules seemed somewhat arbitrary. In 1973, for instance, only one-half of any increase in wages could be passed on to consumers as an allowable cost, although this was increased to 80 percent in 1974 and finally abolished in July of 1976.

It is certainly true that Britain's unfortunate experience with these controls set British politicians, economists and electors more firmly against them than their American counterparts, although some of those who were trying to maintain wage and price controls in the United States did experience a similar disappointment in their efforts. (12) In Britain, however, the controls had an obvious effect on profitability — the Price Commission estimated that the allowable cost rules had depressed profits by between £3,500 million and £8,000 million (13) — and little effect on prices. Even the Chairman of the Commission until 1977, Sir Arthur (now Lord) Cockfield, concluded that the record of the Commission in controlling prices was "a bitter disappointment." (14) The Commission frankly admitted that "the best estimate we can make is that, at the peak, price control reduced prices by 3 or 4 percent . . ." (15) even though retail prices rose by more than 100 percent over the duration of the Pay Code. In fact, because of the distortions in investment and other economic activity which were unforeseen consequences of the Code, (16) there was a decline in competition and an upward pressure on prices at the same time that the Commission was attempting to keep prices down.

With the failure of this system came the most recent phase in Britain's attempts at price control. The Price Commission Act of 1977 retained the Commission without the rigidity of a Price Code, so that a discretionary, rather than a general pricing policy, came into effect. This 'investigatory system' allowed the Commission to engage in two kinds of enquiry. Investigations could be made into prenotified price increases in the case of the larger companies, or into actual price increases by others, or into the margins of distribution companies. Alternatively, at the request of the government, the Commission could make a 'sector' inquiry into the pricing policies of a large section of industry or particular trade. Any prenotified price increase was frozen for up to four months pending the Commission's report, unless the Commission specifically exempted it, and at the end

INDUSTRIAL AND COMMERCIAL COMPANIES REAL PRE-RATE OF RETURN (SEASONALLY ADJUSTED)

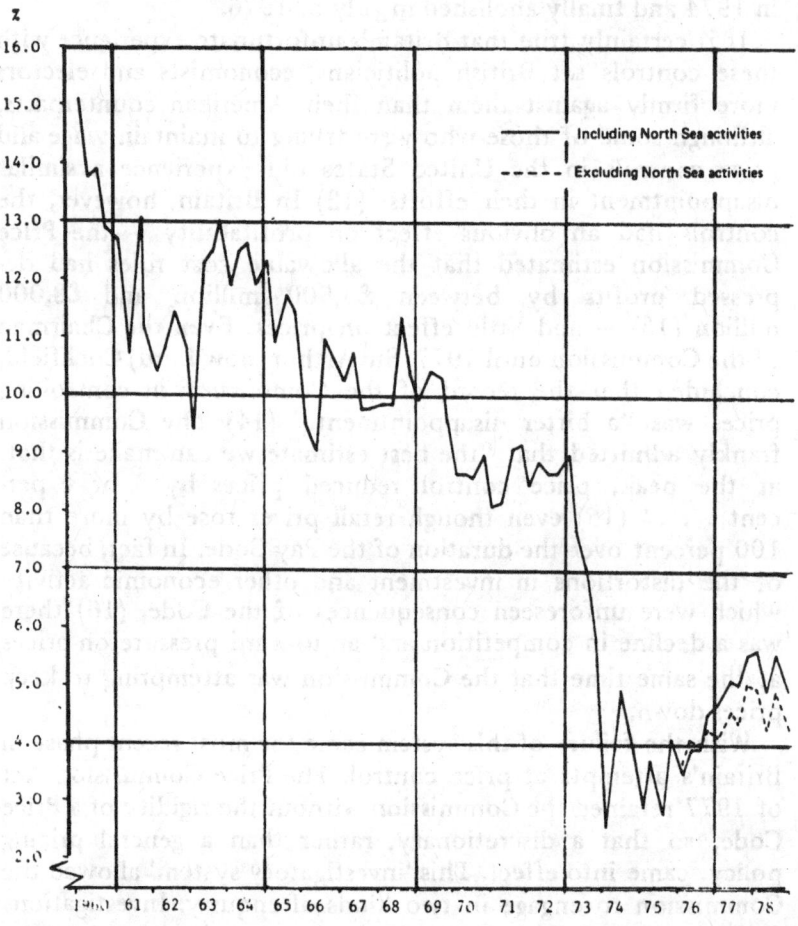

Source: Derived from National Income and Expenditure 'Blue Books' and CSO statistics.

Notes: Gross trading profits plus rent less stock appreciation less capital consumption at current replacement cost as a percentage of net fixed capital stock at current replacement cost plus book value of stocks.

of that period, the Commission could recommend the government to freeze the price increase for a further nine months. After conducting a sector enquiry, the Commission had the power to recommend a reduction in prices for a period of up to one year, and parliamentary approval could be sought to extend the freeze or reduction for a longer period. Eventually, the incoming Conservative government of 1979 announced the abolition of the Commission within a few days of taking office.

The implementation of the policies

From this survey it can be seen that Britain has not found it possible to adhere to any fixed set of wage or price limits or of criteria to justify increases in wages or prices. Given that Britain has been coping with higher rates of inflation, her people have been able to draw much less confidence about the effect of controls, but the problem of maintaining limits has hit successive administrations in the United States almost as much.

Like the United States, Britain has been best able to maintain controls at a time of crisis, when the need for 'pulling together' was widely perceived; but it has been difficult in both countries to maintain the policy in a coherent form much past a six-month freeze or a twelve-month period of restraint. The 1962 criteria in Britain had been circumvented by negotiations to shorten hours and to increase paid holidays, and by more frequent negotiations about pay. The norm was quickly perceived as an average, and pressure mounted for earnings increases to be related to the cost of living. After the freeze of 1966, unions attempted to make up what they perceived as earnings increases lost through the statutory controls, and the 'period of severe restraint' was moderated to a 'period of moderation.' Strike threats by major public sector unions caused the emphasis to be shifted from wages to prices, with the rest of the policy being gradually eased into cold storage.

While the success of controls in the 1940's and 1950's are often seen as a source of success by economists including Phillips and Lipsey, (17) tests show that there has been less cause of congratulation in the last two decades. Work by Brechling, using quarterly equations for the rate of increase of wage rates, found evidence that controls may have reduced wage increases by up to 2 percent in 1964-5, although equations for the rates of increase of wholesale prices and the GNP implicit price deflator reveal no significant impact of incomes policies up to 1965.(18) Yet it must be remembered that Britain in the sixties experienced considerable wage drift, so it is possible that earnings were not depressed as far as the wage rate data would suggest.

It is difficult to apply the same sort of analysis to the data from the 1973 series of controls, since the background rate of inflation was so large. Statutory and voluntary controls existed together with the greatest rate of increase in the retail price index that Britain had ever known.

TABLE 1

Inflation in Britain, 1970-78

Year	% increase in the RPI in June over previous year
1970	5.9
1971	10.3
1972	6.1
1973	9.3
1974	16.5
1976	26.1
1977	17.7
1978	7.4

Source: *Winning the battle against inflation*: Supplement to the Economic Progress Report, August, 1978, H. M. Treasury

Businesses during this period evolved their own methods for circumventing price controls. Thus old products were made 'new' products by subtle changes in packaging, weight, or style, so that prices could be raised without attracting the notice of the Commission. Another ingenious development was that of the 'list price', which with the subsidence of the inflation has now almost entirely disappeared. Businesses would set 'list prices,' the prices which appeared on their published catalogues (although the usual practice was to publish prices separately to avoid frequent catalogue reprinting) at an artificially high level. This price was the one which would be subject to control. Then, the firm would offer a 'discount' to consumers. The actual price charged thus bore no relation to the — controlled — 'list price.' This was but one of the mechanisms devised to beat the controls. On the wage side, there were regular innovations, many coming to the relief of government, for avoiding the set limits.

We have already noted the effect of those controls on profitability and the pattern of investment. The real pre-rate of return for industrial and commercial companies, seasonally adjusted, plummeted from around 9 percent in 1972 to under 3 percent in 1973, levelling off to about 4 percent in the following years. (19) No other economic factor can explain such a substantial fall. Further observations on this point will be made when we come to consider the policy options open to the U.S. Administration, below.

From this review of the British experience, it is clear that there are many guidelines to American policy. The history of the two countries has been similar in terms of the application of controls, although not of course in terms of demand management, monetary and fiscal policies. This is perhaps a reason why controls have come to be regarded in Britain as much more of a failure than they have in the United States. Yet the inflationary situation in Britain has led to the persistence of some form of controls, voluntary or otherwise, until 1979. Furthermore, Britain has experimented much more with non-statutory forms of control, ranging from simple voluntary measures to more sophisticated non-statutory sanctions, as yet untried in the United States. This recent history, and in particular the operation of sanctions and the working of the Price Commission, is worth particular attention when we come to consider the Administration's options.

Policy Options in the United States: The British Experience

In deciding its next step in counter-inflation policy, the Administration may consider the following proposals.

The continuation of voluntary policies

The British experience with voluntary prices and incomes policy is that it is eroded comparatively quickly, particularly on the incomes side. The guidelines established in 1962 were quickly adjusted under pressure, and the 'Social Contract' which was supposed to be binding but which lasted only a short time after 1974 was soon pronounced dead by the General Secretary of the Trades Union Congress, despite political circumstances which were threatening an electoral defeat to his colleagues in Parliament.

This rapid erosion of the Contract was not just the result of the increasing power of the unions in a critical economic situation. Rather, it was the belief among unions that the government was not living up to its promises to limit prices effectively. This concession was an inevitable one if the voluntary policy was to continue: after an initial period of restraint, wage earners demanded that their earnings should at least keep pace with the rise in prices. After all, real output and productivity were increasing, and it was believed that there was no reason why anyone should take a cut in real income in such circumstances. So great was this pressure that even the Heath government felt compelled to build special cost-of-living bonuses into its own State 2 formulation, although that government had always argued for a tougher line on wages than had Labour administrations.

Should a United States Administration decide to enforce a voluntary system of controls, it could well find itself forced to accept this kind of cost-of-living agreement in order for the policy to be approached by earners. Yet this is difficult to justify on the logic of controls themselves; for wage and price policies assume a cost-push theory of inflation whereby rising wages force higher prices and higher prices prompt greater wage demands. The impasse is ended only if one concedes that other factors, such as monetary variables and the management of demand, are powerful agents in the determination of prices; but under this view, controls are something of an irrelevance anyway. In Britain, the curbing of corporate profits has to some extent engineered a situation to the liking of the unions, where earnings were indeed outstripping prices, but it is doubtful whether American unions have the power to exert such a pressure. While in Britain, then, the cost-of-living-agreement impasse could be explained away under the need for more efficiency and lower rates of profit, it is doubtful whether this explanation would survive long in the United States.

It seems, then, that if voluntary controls are to be a feature of U.S. policy for some time, that pressure will be mounted to insert some kind of cost-of-living arrangement or productivity deal. But such an arrangement will be ridiculed as quite circular, making some tougher, perhaps statutory controls relatively more attractive. The attractiveness of a tough policy will be further increased by the phenomenon well known in Britain and alluded to above, namely that all norms tend to be seen as minima.

Non-statutory sanctions

To avoid the unpopularity of full-fledged statutory controls, a form of non-statutory sanctions might seem attractive. Good behaviour can be rewarded with tax concessions or with government aid and contracts, while behaviour which is contrary to the government's guidelines can be punished by the withdrawal of aid or contracts. This system has been used often before in the United States to consolidate all kinds of Administration policy.

In Britain in 1977, the government was facing the apparent failure of its Social Contract to keep down prices, and a series of criticisms, chiefly from union leaders, and in other ways was in a situation much like that facing the current Administration. It shifted the responsibility for keeping wage increases down to private business. It set across-the-board guidelines (which were gradually but unwillingly raised from eight per cent through nine and then ten percent) and announced that any company awarding larger increases would face economic sanctions in the form of withdrawal of aid or of government contracts.

In order for this to be perceived as a non-statutory attempt at prices and incomes policy, however, there could be no formal system. New government contracts contained clauses requiring the contractor to adhere to the guidelines, but no statutory mechanism of control could be devised — the working of the system relied on the discretion of the government. As a result, the government had complete discretion to interpret the guidelines and to decide who had broken them and whether sanctions should be taken; and further, there was no appeal against a government decision. While many people thought it perfectly reasonable that the government should refuse to help firms who were breaking its pay guidelines, the informality of the system led to an increasingly arbitrary and concealed use of sanctions against companies. Threats delivered verbally replaced clear, written guidelines. The 'blacklist' of companies which were denied contracts was kept, but its existence strenuously denied by the Prime Minister, (20) and even Members of Parliament were denied access to it. (21) Some companies did not know they had been sanctioned, or why, and since the list was informal, even those companies mistakenly included were unable to obtain any legal compensation.

A few examples will illustrate the dubious nature of this informal, non-statutory system. MacKie and Company, a shipbuilding firm in competition with the government-controlled Harland and Wolff, was denied export credit guarantees because its wage increases exceeded the government guidelines, despite the fact that it was more efficient than Harland and Wolff, and had been losing labour to them as a result of massive public subsidies to the latter. The economic dislocation caused by such cases is clear. Again, in pay discussions with the public sector miners, who had brought down the Conservative government and who were a powerful component in the Labour Party, the guidelines were put aside in favour of 'productivity deals' which allowed the net earnings per worker to rise by a total of 24 percent over the year 1977-78. (22) Lastly, the Ford Motor Company, which was the most successful automobile manufacturer in Britain, was willing to pay its workers an increase substantially above the guidelines. Concerned that intervention would lose the support of the Transport Union which represented the workforce at Fords and which was one of the most powerful supporters of the government, the Chancellor of the Exchequer backed down and allowed a 12 percent settlement to pass without discretionary action. One year later, however, Ford decided to stick to the guidelines in its next pay round, since it was clear that the government could not sustain another assault on its policies. The workers reacted with a nine-week stoppage of work, and eventually a 17 percent settlement was offered by the company, whereupon the government imposed the sanction of a total boycott of Ford products. At this point, however, the union-sponsored Labour Members of Parliament, together with the Opposition, brought a defeat to the whole sanction policy in Parliament in December 1978.

It seems likely that a similar charge of arbitrariness in government would face any attempt by any United States President to introduce a non-statutory sanctions policy, and the nature of American politics is such that this would be more difficult for an Administration to resist than in Britain. In addition, more militant unionism could be encouraged by the controls, as it was in Britain, where the unions saw the guidelines as something of a challenge to be tackled and a minimum basis for a settlement if the more militant unions were not to lose face. Complaints can also be expected from businesses, who will, as in Britain, find it difficult to attract labour if they are not allowed to pay sufficiently without incurring sanctions, and who will not relish their position as policing agents for the Administration, nor being made the scapegoats for any failure in the controls.

The system of sanctions could, then, be seriously considered as a solution to the gradual erosion of a voluntary control system by businesses and wage earners who perceive that restraint is to their economic detriment. The experience from Britain would seem to be unequivocal, however, that such a system is surrounded in pitfalls and is difficult or impossible to prosecute fairly.

Weak statutory controls

The next option would be a system of weak statutory controls, far from the unpopular Nixon-style controls, but having the force of law. The nearest equivalent in Britain would be the investigatory system operated by the Price Commission after 1977. It is frequently suggested that if the market behaviour of the largest firms can be controlled, then the behaviour of the other firms in the market will follow, and hence that a statutory framework of controls can be attempted without a great administrative mechanism. (23) This argument makes statutory controls attractive, but the experience from Britain would seem to be that control of the largest firms is not sufficient to alter the behaviour of others. As noted already, prenotification controls on large companies in 1973 were quickly extended to medium-sized companies, and the requirement was made for all these companies to keep careful records which could be inspected by the Price Commission. Even with this measure of control, market behaviour was difficult for the Commission to change effectively.

Profit margin controls are one example of a form of control which could be operated by an institution such as the Price Commission. The Commission's effect on profitability in Britain is, however, a cause for much concern. Price controls in Britain seem to have a small effect on total prices, but a serious effect on profitability, which is a small percentage of the totality of an individual price and which have been the main elements in price restraint. In the United Kingdom, a ten percent reduction in the profits of commercial and industrial enterprises would account for 0.8 percent reduction in consumer prices, which suggests a lack of wisdom in attempting to trim prices by trimming profits. Yet the policy in Britain reduced margins in several ways. During an investigation, prices were restrained; restrictions could be imposed after an investigation; oligopolistic behaviour by firms, each anxious to avoid investigations by keeping price rises down, has also trimmed profits across markets; the bureaucratic costs to companies having to deal with Commission investigations has lowered profits; and in other ways, the net effect has been depressive. The chart shows the full extent of this decline in profitability during the years of controls.

The selective, discretionary system of price controls through Price Commission activity might also have tended to depress, rather than augment, industrial efficiency in Britain. This is certainly a factor in investment, since lower prices and reduced profit margins caused many firms to reappraise their investment schedules, and the existence of the Price Commission, with its discretionary powers was a source of uncertainty which firms had to plan for instead of being able to devote all their energies to industrial performance freely. There is also a problem that an agency with powers to enforce price reductions or restrictions on one hand is faced with an uneasy partner when it attempts to suggest, on the other, improvements in efficiency to businesses. In Britain, the business view was that even where the Commission detected what it took to be serious inefficiencies, its remarks were usually inaccurate and oversimplified, and that such intervention and the squeeze on profits was not the best way to increase efficiency. (24)

Britain found other objections from business in the way that price investigations were conducted. In the first place, to establish the justifiability of a prenotified price increase, the Commission would have to have access to confidential company data, as would any consultants they chose to employ on the case, and this caused grave concern to business. In the published reports, information was made available to competitors about company operation and marketing strategy. Undoubtedly in any similar system proposed in the United States there will be a similar need for the government to explain its decisions, and similar protest from industry that competitors, particularly foreign competitors, are being helped. Lastly, the press coverage given to the Commission's criticisms gave a feeling of widespread incompetence in business and a lack of confidence in the market system, although this was exaggerated by the headlines. This again made it difficult for business to expand with confidence, but seems to be an inevitable feature of this form of control.

Conclusions

These, then, are the main policy instruments which the Carter Administration might consider as the next stage in its counter-inflation policy, apart from fully-fledged 1971-type controls, with which most American economists will be familiar. The British experience is that there are severe problems with all of them, and it remains open to question in political circles whether the problems are outweighed by the economic advantages.

Voluntary controls have failed to work effectively in Britain, despite a feeling of national crisis, a highly centralised pay bargaining system, and a Labour government with strong union support. Inevitably exceptions and 'special cases' have arisen — often, as in the case of nurses in Britain, with strong national support — to erode the policy, and militant unions have regarded it as something of a challenge. Non-statutory controls in the form of sanctions have had a similar demise, and have led to accusations of arbitrariness in their enforcement in addition to their being gradually eroded by special cases. Weak statutory controls of a discretionary nature have increased business uncertainty while reducing the funds available for new investment, research and development.

It will be instructive to see whether the Thatcher government will be able to live without some form of price or wage controls as its predecessor under Edward Heath promised to do in 1970 and abandoned just over a year later. The signs are that the government has the resolve to resist the use of controls, but some kind of productivity deal for public sector workers is probably too attractive to resist.

As far as the United States is concerned, there is probably more faith in statutory controls of some kind than in Britain. Nevertheless, the similarity between the two countries in their experience with controls up to about 1976 should suggest that the recent history of controls in Britain deserves close scrutiny by American policy makers.

FOOTNOTES

(1) See, for example, the letter by George Meany to the *Washington Post*, November 3, 1978.

(2) For an extensive bibliography on this subject, see Feliz Chin and Edward Knight, *Government Policy Relating to Wages and Prices, 1974: A Selected Bibliography*. Washington, D.C.: Library of Congress Congressional Research Service, 1976.

(3) For bibliography of this kind see the Fraser Institute's *The Illusion of Wage and Price Control*. Vancouver: The Fraser Institute, 1976. See also Samuel Brittan and Peter Lilley, *The Delusion of Income Policy*, London: Maurice Temple Smith, 1976. Another useful bibliography appears in Schuettinger, Robert, and Eamonn Butler, *Forty Centuries of Wage and Price Controls*, Washington, DC: Heritage Foundation, 1979.

(4) See for example, Robert Lekachman, 'The Case for Controls' *The New Republic*, October 14th, 1978, and Lekachman and Lyle Gramley, "Mandatory Wage-Price Controls?" *U.S. News & World Report*, June 18th, 1979.

(5) H. M. Treasury, *Incomes Policy: The Next Step*, London: Her Majesty's Stationery Office, Cmnd. 1626, 1962.

(6) Department of Economic Affairs, *Prices and Incomes Policy*, London: HMSO, Cmnd. 2639, 1965.

(7) David Smith, 'Incomes Policy' in Richard Caves, *Britain's Economic Prospects*, London: George Allen & Unwin, for the Brookings Institution, 1968, pp 123-4.

(8) For official evidence on this see Department of Economic Affairs, *Prices and Incomes Policy After 30th June, 1967*, London: HMSO, Cmnd 3235, 1967.

(9) For a review of the gradual increase in power of the union movement during the period of these controls, see John Burton, *The Trojan Horse: Union Power in British Politics*, London: Adam Smith Institute, 1979.

(10) Confederation of British Industry, *Price Controls and the Price Commission: The Business View*, London: CBI, 1979.

(11) Department of Economic Affairs, *Prices and Incomes Policy*, London: HMSO Cmnd. 2639, 1965, p. 7.

(12) See for example, C. Jackson Grayson, *Confessions of a Price Controller*, New York: Dow-Jones, Irwin, 1974. And by the same author, 'Controls are not the Answer', *Challenge*, vol. 17, November-December 1974, pp 9-12, and his 'The US Economic Stabilisation Program 1971-74' in the Fraser Institute's *The Illusion of Wage and Price Control*, op. cit.

(13) The lower estimate is based by the Commission on the assumption that its recommendations delayed scheduled price increases for one year, while the upper figure assumes that the loss to the company was permanent. Unfortunately the Commission did not have records sufficient to check where in the range is the most likely actual figure.

(14) Sir Arthur Cockfield, 'The Price Commission and the Price Control. *Three Banks Review*, March 1978, p. 17.

(15) *Ibid.*

(16) For examples of such economic distortions, see D.R. Glynn, in the *CBI Review*, London: Confederation of British Industry, April 1976.

(17) A. W. Phillips, "The Relation between Unemployment and the Rate of Change of Money Wage Rates in the United Kingdom, 1861-57", *Economica*, vol. 25, November 1958, pp 283-99. See also Richard G. Lipsey, "The Relation between Unemployment and the Rate of Change of Money wage Rates in the United Kingdom, 1861-1957: A Further Analysis," *Economica*, vol. 27, February 1960, pp. 1-31.

(18) Frank Brechling, "Some Empirical Evidence on the Effectiveness of Prices and Incomes Policies" quoted in David C. Smith, *op cit*.

(19) These figures according to National Income and Expenditure Blue Books, various years.

(20) *Hansard* (Parliamentary record), vol. 960, column 747, January 1978.

(21) Michael Latham, M.P., reported in *The Daily Telegraph*, 9th January, 1978.

(22) *Hansard*, vol. 960, column 781.

(23) A similar situation to that predicted by George L. Perry, 'Wages and the Guideposts,' *American Economic Review*, vol. 57, September 1967, pp. 897-904.

(24) *Price Controls and the Price Commission: The Business View*, Confederation of British Industry, *op cit*.

9

FORECASTING THE EFFECTS OF A NEGATIVE INCOME TAX PROGRAM

Terry R. Johnson and John H. Pencavel*

This paper outlines a scheme that forecasts the change in net earnings or in hours worked that results from the introduction of a negative income tax (NIT) program. The authors illustrate this scheme by estimating labor supply functions for married men, married women, and single women who participated in the Seattle-Denver Income Maintenance Experiments. These functions are then used to simulate the effects of several NIT programs. The findings suggest that changes in the wage rate of an individual covered by an NIT program result in important changes in the hours of work of the individual's spouse.

THE purpose of this paper is to present an analysis of the labor supply responses of husband-and-wife families and of single females to the Seattle-Denver Income Maintenance Experiments (SIME/DIME).[1] Our analysis of the effects of the experiment combines two distinct features. One involves exploiting the experimental nature of the data by relating the change in hours worked over some period to the change in the family's budget constraint induced by the negative income tax (NIT), as calculated on the basis of preexperimental observations. As a short-hand expression, we dub this the "impact approach." This scheme was proposed by Ashenfelter and Heckman and is somewhat analogous to the methods used in laboratory sciences in that a treatment is applied at one moment and a reaction is measured over a subsequent period of time.[2] Thus, in the NIT experiment, the treatment is measured at preexperimental values of the relevant variables and the response is measured one or two years later. This approach is especially valuable in that it provides a scheme for forecasting the effect of any given NIT program.

---

*Terry R. Johnson is a senior economist and manager of the Employment and Training Research Program at SRI International and John H. Pencavel is a professor of economics at Stanford University and is affiliated with the National Bureau of Economic Research. The resourceful and unstinting research assistance of Susan McNicoll and the comments of Richard West on a preliminary draft of this paper are gratefully acknowledged. The research reported in this paper was performed under contracts with the states of Washington and Colorado, prime contractors for the Department of Health, Education, and Welfare.

[1] A brief description of SIME/DIME may be found in Michael C. Keeley et al., "The Estimation of Labor Supply Models Using Experimental Data," *American Economic Review*, Vol. 68, No. 5 (December 1978), pp. 873–87.

[2] Orley Ashenfelter and James J. Heckman, "Estimating Labor Supply Functions," in Glen G. Cain and Harold W. Watts, eds., *Income Maintenance and Labor Supply* (Chicago: Rand McNally, 1973), pp. 265–78.

Reprinted with permission from the *Industrial and Labor Relations Review*, Vol. 35, No. 2 (January 1982). Copyright 1982 by Cornell University. All rights reserved.

In previous applications of this approach, the conventional model of labor supply has been drawn upon only to distinguish the effects on hours of work of changes in after-tax wage rates from the effects of changes in nonwage income.[3] Yet, of course, this theory generates a number of restrictions on behavior. For instance, the utility-constant effect on the husband's hours of work of a small increase in the wife's wage rate should equal the utility-constant effect on the wife's hours of work of a small increase in the husband's wage rate (the symmetry condition) or the effect of an equiproportionate change in commodity prices, wage rates, and nonwage income should leave each individual's hours of work unchanged (the homogeneity condition). It therefore seems natural to inquire whether more powerful inferences concerning the effects of the NIT experiment can be gleaned from more careful attention to the empirical implications of the conventional model. Operationally this means specifying a particular form for the direct or indirect utility function of the representative household and then estimating the labor supply functions implied by the preference structure. Therefore, the second feature of our study is that it adopts an explicit expression for the utility function of the representative household.

The advantage of specifying an explicit utility function is that with the information it provides of a family's preferences for work and for consumption, we do not require separate (and perhaps mutually inconsistent) studies into the effects of an NIT on the decision to work, the decision of how many hours to work, and the decision to participate in the scheme by being below the breakeven level of income. Instead, all these aspects of the effects of an NIT program can be resolved once the family's utility function is known. Although the specification of a particular representation of preferences may appear at first sight to be a somewhat demanding procedure, in fact some such assumption is inevitable even though it may not be made explicit. When certain integrability conditions are satisfied, any fitted labor supply equation may be interpreted as implying a particular form for or approximation of family preferences. In view of this, for those who intend to take the conventional theory of labor supply seriously, the relevant issue is not one of whether a functional form for preferences should or should not be made, but rather which forms of labor supply functions or preference functions are most useful for the purposes at hand.

In this paper, therefore, the impact approach to measuring the labor supply effects of the NIT experiment is imbedded in an explicit utility function framework. As we shall show, this framework allows each family to be different in having its own additive "fixed effect" (or permanent component), but otherwise families share the same parameters of a particular utility function. Operationally, we relate the *change* in net earnings to the various NIT program parameters. In essence, the procedure involves comparing the behavior of families during the experiment with their preexperimental behavior and investigating whether any differences in their behavior may be associated with their experimental treatment.

The Model

A forecasting scheme. In this section we outline the features of an impact analysis of SIME/DIME that is designed primarily as a device for forecasting the effects of any given NIT program. To understand our use of the term impact analysis, consider a rep-

---

[3] We are aware of two major research efforts that use this approach: Orley Ashenfelter, "The Labor Supply Response of Wage Earners," in John L. Palmer and Joseph A. Peckman, eds., *Welfare in Rural Areas: The North Carolina-Iowa Income Maintenance Experiment* (Washington, D.C.: The Brookings Institution, 1978), pp. 109–38; and Keeley et al., "The Estimation of Labor Supply Models Using Experimental Data" (and several other papers by Keeley et al.). The Ashenfelter study used data from the rural income maintenance experiment and Keeley et al. examined SIME/DIME data. Ashenfelter's work yielded the counterintuitive result that non-market time is an inferior good, but his parameters were not estimated precisely. Keeley et al. produced interesting results, and although they couch their argument in terms of *changes* of hours, in fact they fit an equation in which the dependent variable is the level of hours of work. Their procedures and results are discussed further below.

resentative two-worker family in which the subscript 1 indicates the husband's characteristics and subscript 2, the wife's. In the pre-NIT situation (indicated by the subscript 0), their gross wage rates are w_{10} and w_{20}, their gross nonwage income is y_0, their tax rate is t_0, and their hours of work are h_{10} and h_{20}. Suppose an NIT program is now introduced which leaves gross wage rates unchanged, but which changes the tax rate to t_e and replaces net nonwage income of $(1-t_0)y_0$ with $S + (1-t_e)y_0$ where S is the NIT support level.[4] The NIT-induced change in net wage rates is thus $(t_0-t_e)w_{10}$ and $(t_0-t_e)w_{20}$ and the change in net nonwage income is $S - (t_e-t_0)y_0$. This change in their opportunities is likely to induce these individuals to alter their work patterns. After a passage of time to allow individuals to make the required adjustments, each individual's hours of work, h_{1e} and h_{2e}, are recorded as are his or her net earnings which, if gross wage rates are unchanged, are given by $(1-t_e)w_{10}h_{1e}$ and $(1-t_e)w_{20}h_{2e}$. It is appropriate to concentrate on net earnings since the NIT-induced change in earnings is proportional to the excess transfer cost of the program over the cost calculated on the basis of pre-experimental incomes alone.[5]

A scheme that would be of value in forecasting the change in net earnings as a consequence of the NIT program would be one that makes use of information known prior to the implementation of the NIT and information on the characteristics of the particular NIT program to be introduced. That is, a scheme for forecasting the difference between the net earnings of, say, the husband in the presence of an NIT—namely, $(1-t_e)w_{10}h_{1e}$—and current net earnings $(1-t_0)w_{10}h_{10}$ may be characterized as

(1) $\Delta E_1 = f[(t_0-t_e)w_{10}, (t_0-t_e)w_{20}, S - (t_e-t_0)y_0, X_{10}, X_{20}]$

where

$\Delta E_1 = (1-t_e)w_{10}h_{1e} - (1-t_0)w_{10}h_{10}$,

and where X_{10} and X_{20} stand for other attributes of the husband and wife, respectively, in the pre-NIT situation that may be relevant for forecasting purposes. If the f function and program participation were known, then Equation 1 could be used to predict the change in net earnings accompanying any NIT program characterized by a tax rate t_e and a support level S.

The Stone-Geary utility function. In choosing among different possible representations of the f function, we required that it should be simple and tractable and that it should be consistent with the economist's conventional notions of purposive behavior. A natural choice satisfying these two conditions is the linear expenditure system in which the variables appear in f in a straightforward linear form and which is consistent with the following representation of a family's preferences for commodity consumption (x) and work:

(2) $U(x, h_1, h_2) = (1-B_1-B_2)\ln(x-\gamma_0) + \sum_{i=1}^{2} B_i \ln(\gamma_i - h_i)$,

where

$x > \gamma_0$ and $\gamma_i > h_i$.

(For single females, B_2 is set equal to zero.) This Stone-Geary function can claim an excellent pedigree in empirical work on the analysis of consumer behavior, and it is being applied increasingly to labor supply behavior.[6] Its tractability, however, comes

---

[4] In fact, in the design of the experiment, the tax rate applied to nonwage income is not independent of the source of that income. We have ignored this wrinkle in the exposition here although it is taken into account in the construction of the variables and in the empirical work.

[5] This is straightforward to demonstrate. See, for instance, Ashenfelter, "The Labor Supply Response of Wage Earners," p. 133.

[6] For instance, on consumer demand, see the studies cited in A. Brown and A. Deaton, "Models of Consumer Behaviour: A Survey," *Economic Journal*, Vol. 82, No. 328 (December 1972), pp. 1145–1236; or the more recent monograph by Angus Deaton, *Models and Projections of Demand in Post-War Britain* (London: Cambridge Studies in Applied Econometrics, 1975). On labor supply applications of the Stone-Geary, see Michael Abbott and Orley Ashenfelter, "Labour Supply, Commodity Demand, and the Allocation of Time," *Review of Economic Studies*, Vol. 42, No. 3 (October 1976), pp. 389–411; or Louis Phlips, "The Demand for Leisure and Money," *Econometrica*, Vol. 46, No. 5 (September 1978), pp. 1125–44.

at a price: its additive form implies that a utility-constant increase in one adult's wage rate must reduce the other adult's working hours, and the own-wage elasticity of each hours-of-work function is approximately proportional to its nonwage income elasticity.[7] Whether hours-of-work functions actually warrant these restrictions is an issue that, to the best of our knowledge, has yet to be examined.

Suppose the family may be characterized as choosing its consumption of commodities and its working behavior to maximize Equation 2, subject to its budget constraint $x = (1-t)(\Sigma w_i h_i + y)$ where the price of commodities has been normalized to unity. Under these circumstances, the net earnings of each individual will satisfy the following expression:

(3) $\quad (1-t)w_i h_i = \gamma_i (1-t)w_i$
$\quad - B_i [(1-t)(y + \Sigma_i w_i \gamma_i)$
$\quad - \gamma_0] \quad i = 1, 2.$

The expression on the right-hand side in square brackets represents the excess of "maximum net family income" over "minimum consumption expenditure" and may be called the "discretionary full income." Simple differentiation of Equation 3 with respect to $(1-t)y$ reveals B_i to be the fraction of any small increase in exogenous net income that is "spent" by individual i working less and earning less labor income (or individual i's marginal propensity to consume "leisure").

An equivalent expression for, say, the husband's net earnings is as follows:

(4) $\quad (1-t)w_1 h_1 = (1-B_1) \gamma_1 (1-t)w_1$
$\quad - B_1 \gamma_2 (1-t)w_2 + B_1 \gamma_0 - B_1 (1-t)y,$

which makes clear the *linear* dependence of the husband's net earnings on his own net wage rate, on his wife's net wage rate, and on net nonwage income. Writing Equation 4 for the pre-NIT situation (subscripted by o) and for the NIT situation (subscripted by e)

[7]See Angus Deaton, "A Reconsideration of the Empirical Implications of Additive Preferences," *Economic Journal*, Vol. 84, No. 334 (June 1974), pp. 338–48.

and forming the forecasting equation described by Equation 1, we derive the following expression for the effect of an NIT on the husband's net earnings evaluated at pre-NIT gross income:

(5) $\quad \Delta E_1 = (1-B_1) \gamma_1 (t_0 - t_e)w_{10}$
$\quad - B_1 \gamma_2 (t_0 - t_e)w_{20} - B_1 [S - (t_e - t_0)y_0],$

where, as before,

$\Delta E_1 = (1-t_e)w_{10}h_{1e} - (1-t_0)w_{10}h_{10}.$

Alternatively, for those eligible for NIT payments, the payment associated with a particular NIT program is $P = S - (t_e - t_0) (\Sigma w_{i0} h_{i0} + y_0)$ when evaluated at pre-NIT gross income. Hence, the previous expression may be rewritten as

(6) $\quad \Delta E_1 = (1-B_1) \gamma_1 (t_0 - t_e)w_{10}$
$\quad - B_1 \gamma_2 (t_0 - t_e)w_{20}$
$\quad - B_1 [P + (t_e - t_0) \Sigma_i w_{i0} h_{i0}].$

In arriving at this expression, a linear budget constraint was assumed whereas in both the pre-NIT and the NIT situations some nonlinear budget constraints obtain. Our response to this problem is the familiar one of replacing the nonlinear budget constraint with that linear constraint which is tangent to the nonlinear constraint at the observed pre-NIT hours of work. The experimental tax rate, t_e, and the NIT payments, P, are imputed on the basis of each family's preexperimental income. Measurement errors in this imputation are discussed in the next section. Our procedures with respect to the budget constraint variables are evident from the Figure.

NIT program participation. Equation 6 is a forecasting device for the NIT-induced change in net earnings where all right-hand side variables are measured at their observed, pre-NIT, values. As it stands, the device presumes that individuals actually participate in the NIT program and receive payments. It is natural for forecasting purposes to set the probability of NIT program participation equal to one for those individuals whose pre-NIT income is below the tax breakeven since these individuals can increase both commodity consumption and leisure by participating in the program.

Figure
NIT and Pre-NIT Budget Constraints

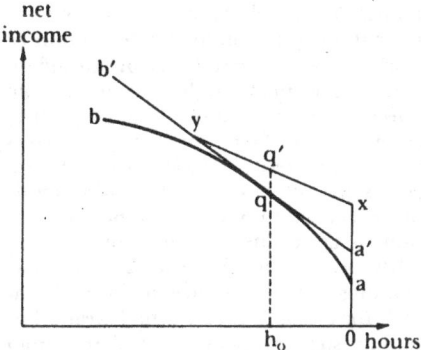

The pre-NIT budget constraint for this individual is given by the (concave from below) line Oab. This assumes a tax rate that increases throughout with income. The corresponding linearized budget constraint at the point q (which corresponds to observed pre-NIT hours of work h_o) is Oa'b'. The superimposed NIT budget constraint (assuming a fixed tax rate NIT program) is Oxyb'. The difference between the slopes of xy and a'y represents $(t_o - t_e) w_o$, while the vertical distance qq' is the level of NIT payments evaluated at pre-NIT hours of work (called P in the text).

But for individuals above the tax breakeven on the basis of pre-NIT income, the probability of NIT program participation lies between zero and one. For these individuals Equation 6 is an inadequate description of behavior since such individuals' predicted NIT payments (P) are zero and their imputed change in tax rates is zero ($t_e = t_o$). They can become eligible for NIT payments, however, by reducing their consumption of commodities sufficiently and by increasing their leisure time. To accommodate such behavior on the part of those individuals who are above the tax breakeven level on the basis of their pre-NIT income, Equation 6 was augmented with variables related to the probability of NIT program participation.[8] The modified equation is as follows:

$$(7) \quad \Delta E_1 = (1 - B_1) \gamma_1 (t_o - t_e) w_{1o}$$
$$- B_1 \gamma_2 (t_o - t_e) w_{2o}$$
$$- B_1 [P + (t_e - t_o) \sum_i w_{io} h_{io}] + b_1 A$$
$$+ b_2 (T_e \cdot A) + b_3 (R \cdot A) + b_4 (S \cdot A),$$

where A takes the value of unity for those experimental families whose pre-NIT income is above the tax breakeven level and zero otherwise. T_e is the initial tax rate of the NIT program to which the experimental family is assigned.[9] R is a dichotomous variable taking the value of unity for individuals assigned to the nonconstant tax rate programs and zero otherwise, and S is the family-size-adjusted support level of the NIT program to which the experimental family is assigned. Interacting A with the experimental tax program parameters, T_e, R, and S, the specification in Equation 7 relates the probability of NIT participation for a family initially above the breakeven level of income to the financial incentives for consuming leisure. Estimates of the coefficients b_1 to b_4 provide an estimate of the effect of different NIT programs on the net earnings of those whose pre-NIT incomes were above the tax breakeven level. For such families, these coefficients combine the effects of the program parameters on the probability of NIT participation and on the change in net earnings conditional upon NIT participation.

Estimation Issues

The development of the model in the previous section was entirely in a deterministic setting. Now we will consider issues concerning the stochastic structure.

---

[8] Of course, the utility-based approach may also be used to determine the functional form for the program-participation probability. In the case of the Stone-Geary, however, the expression is not particularly tractable; so the simple procedure employed in Equation 7 should be understood to be an approximation to this more convoluted expression.

[9] By "initial" tax rate, we mean the tax rate corresponding to zero taxable income. For the fixed tax rate programs, $T_e = t_e$. For the nonconstant tax rate programs, the individual's actual NIT tax rate will normally differ from the initial tax rate.

The most convenient procedure is to suppose in Equation 3 that the consumption parameter, γ_0, is not the same for all families, but instead for each family consists of three components: one, Ψ_i, is fixed and unique to each family; a second is fixed and common to all families, $\overline{\gamma}_0$; and a third is a random component, u_{it}, that varies by family and over time. Upon differencing the net earnings equation, the fixed components Ψ_i and $\overline{\gamma}_0$ drop out of the equation and the error term is $v_i = B_1(u_{ie} - u_{i0})$. There are two reasons for believing that the error term, v_i, is not distributed independently of the regressors in Equation 7.

First, whenever the budget constraint is nonlinear, net wage rates are jointly determined with hours of work. The procedure of linearizing the budget constraint around preexperimental hours of work implies that the variables describing the preexperimental budget constraint are endogenous with respect to preexperimental hours of work. The experimental budget constraint is also nonlinear for all experimental families because of the kink at the tax breakeven level and, in particular, for families below the breakeven on the nonconstant tax rate program. Moreover, imputing the experimental tax rate and the level of NIT payments on the basis of preexperimental hours of work will result in measuring the experimental budget constraint with error. Also note that because we estimate net earnings equations, any errors in measuring net wage rates will appear both in the left-hand and right-hand side variables. For all these reasons, it seems inappropriate to treat the error term in the earnings change equations as distributed independently of the variables $(t_0 - t_e)w_{10}$, $(t_0 - t_e)w_{20}$, and $P + (t_e - t_0) \sum_i w_{i0} h_{i0}$. A natural limited information method for responding to this problem is to replace these variables with their corresponding predicted values from prior regressions on a set of exogenous variables. The scheme retains its use as a forecasting device, provided the instruments use information from the preexperimental year only.

A second class of problems concerns the fact that Equation 7 (the forecasting equation) is derived from Equation 3 (a net earnings equation), describing the decisions of individuals working a positive number of hours. As is well known, restricting the estimation of Equation 7 to the sample of workers normally results in a biased and inconsistent estimator unless the nonrandom selection of the sample is appropriately accounted for. Our procedure here makes use of a proposal of Heckman's.[10] This involves first estimating over the entire sample of workers and nonworkers a probit equation to determine the conditional probability of both the husband and the wife working in both the preexperimental year and the second experimental year. The second step involves constructing from this probit equation the reciprocal of the Mills ratio, λ_i (the ratio of the ordinate of the estimated standard normal to the estimated tail area of the distribution) and entering λ_i into Equation 7 fitted over the sample of individuals working in both years.[11] This procedure avoids confusing the parameters of the function determining the decision to work with the parameters of the hours-of-work function for workers only.[12] The least-squares estimator of Equation 7 containing λ_i is consistent, but not fully efficient.[13]

[10]James J. Heckman, "The Common Structure of Statistical Models of Truncation, Sample Selection, and Limited Dependent Variables and a Simple Estimator for Such Models," *Annals of Economic and Social Measurement*, Vol. 5, No. 4 (Fall 1976), pp. 475–92.

[11]Thus, if $\hat{I}_i$ is the predicted value of the index from a fitted probit on the determinants of the husband and wife working preexperimentally and in the second experimental year and if F is the standard cumulative normal distribution function, then $\lambda_i = f(\hat{I}_i)/F(\hat{I}_i)$. Since we condition on both the husband and wife working, what is required here is not a univariate but a bivariate probit. In fact, since virtually all of the husbands work, the potential selection biases with respect to husbands are unimportant.

[12]The two functions would differ, for instance, in the presence of fixed costs of working. See John F. Cogan, "Labor Supply with Time and Money Costs of Participation," Rand Report R-2044-HEW (Los Angeles: The Rand Corporation: October 1977); or Giora Hanoch, "Hours and Weeks in the Theory of Labor Supply," Rand Report R-1787-HEW, August 1976.

[13]More precisely, the variance of the disturbances of Equation 7 supplemented with λ_i is heteroskedastic unless the disturbances in the probit equation are independent of the error term in Equation 7.

Finally, we take note of the fact that the experimental treatment was not applied in a purely random manner (so that inferences from unadjusted experimental-control comparisons may be quite misleading). Instead, husband-wife families and single females were each stratified by "normal income" level,[14] by race (black, white, Chicano), and by site (Denver, Seattle). Moreover, the families were assigned to the eleven different NIT plans as well as to the control status randomly *within* each of these categories. To account for any effect of this assignment design on changes in net earnings, dummy variables for site, race, and "normal income" categories were included as regressors in the estimated equation.[15] Hence the final form of the estimating equation may be written for husbands as follows:

$$(8) \quad \Delta E_1 = (1 - B_1) \gamma_1 [(t_0 - t_e)w_{10}]$$
$$- B_1 \gamma_2 [(t_0 - t_e)w_{20}]$$
$$- B_1 [P + (t_e - t_0)\sum_i w_{i0} h_{i0}]$$
$$+ b_1 A + b_2(T_e \cdot A) + b_3(R \cdot A) + b_4(S \cdot A)$$
$$+ c_1 Z + c_2 \lambda + v,$$

where Z represents the vector of assignment dummy variables,[16] λ is the inverse of Mills' ratio, and v is a stochastic disturbance term.

The Results

The earnings change equations described above are estimated using data on husband-wife households and on single females that satisfied the following criteria: each household completed the interviews necessary for constructing three years of information (one year of preexperimental data and the first two years of the experiment); each household experienced no marital change during the three-year period; and none of the household's adults was self-employed or in the military during this period. The first condition combines the effect of attrition with missing interviews; the second condition was imposed to avoid problems caused by changing households; and the third condition was applied to avoid using unreliable wage-rate and hours-worked data. The analysis sample consists of 1,678 husband-wife households and 1,339 single females.

Annual measures of the hourly wage rate and working hours are constructed from quarterly values. To form annual hours worked we sum the number of hours worked during each quarter. The gross wage rate in the preexperimental year is calculated as the weighted average of the individual's quarterly gross wage rate on the main job where the weights used are the hours worked on the main job in the particular quarter. The annual marginal tax rate in the preexperimental year is a weighted average of the quarterly values where the weights used are the relevant quarterly values of the family's gross reported earnings. The quarterly marginal tax rates take into account federal and state income taxes, Social Security taxes, and any welfare programs (AFDC or Food Stamps) that families chose to participate in preexperimentally as well as the interaction among these programs.

The husband's and the wife's equations are estimated jointly by a nonlinear least squares procedure that takes account of the cross-equation restrictions; the single females' earnings change equation involves estimating an exactly identified equation.[17] The first step is to construct the λ for the husbands' and wives' equations and the λ for the single females' equation. The fitted

---

[14]Each family's "normal income" was determined from data collected prior to enrollment into the experiment.

[15]The conditions under which this will appropriately account for nonrandom assignment are spelled out in Michael C. Keeley and Philip K. Robins, "The Design of Social Experiments: A Critique of the Conlisk-Watts Assignment Model," in Ronald G. Ehrenberg, ed., *Research in Labor Economics* (Greenwich, Conn.: JAI Press, 1981).

[16]Three dummy variables for the three manpower programs that accompanied the NIT experiment are also included in Z.

[17]No account is taken of the heteroskedasticity of the error term introduced by the presence of the λ terms, a fact that suggests caution in drawing statistical inferences from the estimates. The numerical maximization procedure is the Davidon-Fletcher-Powell method. A description of this method can be found in any standard text on numerical optimization procedures; for example, see G. S. G. Beveridge and R. S. Schechter, *Optimization: Theory and Practice* (New York: McGraw-Hill, 1970).

Table 1. Parameter Estimates of the Net Earnings Change Equation 8.

Coefficients		Husband	Wife	Single Females
Estimated coefficients:	B_1	.288* (.136)		.129 (.118)
	B_2		.088 (.173)	
	γ_1	2222* (471)		1711* (314)
	γ_2		1403* (484)	
Coefficients on variables:	A	316 (1617)	2997 (2075)	1488 (898)
	$T_e \cdot A$	522 (2398)	−2358 (3078)	−2146 (1327)
	$R \cdot A$	−70 (573)	296 (735)	526 (279)
	$S \cdot A$	−.248 (.204)	−.383 (.262)	−.085 (.128)
	λ	266.1 (252.1)	−934.3* (323.6)	77.5 (164.1)
−2 log. of likelihood		3713.3		2494.3

Note: Estimated asymptotic standard errors are in parentheses beneath the coefficients. For ease of reading, an asterisk has been placed next to coefficients more than 1.96 times their estimated standard errors.

probit equations from which each λ is constructed are presented in the Appendix. There are 498 husbands and wives both of whom work in the preexperimental and the second experimental years and there are 706 single females who work in both years. These are the samples over which the earnings equations are fitted. Each individual enters once in the sample. The estimates of the parameters of Equation 8 for husbands, for wives, and for single females are presented in Table 1. It should be remembered that each estimated equation includes twelve more variables than are listed in Table 1: these are the assignment variables (Z). Thus, there are twenty explanatory variables in all. Since $(t_o - t_e)w_{1o}$ and $(t_o - t_e)w_{2o}$ are necessarily highly correlated and since variables such as the imputed level of payments and the imputed change in wage rates are by construction correlated with S, T_e and R (as well as with the assignment variables since assignment to treatment was not random),[18] collinearity among the right-hand side variables is clearly affecting our ability to draw confident inferences from these estimates.

Before turning to the utility function parameters, consider the implications for

[18] Recall that the experimental impact variables $(t_o - t_e)w_{1o}$, $(t_o - t_e)w_{2o}$, and $P + (t_e - t_o) \Sigma_i w_{io} h_{io}$ are all predicted from prior ordinary least-squares regressions. The exogenous variables in these prior equations are as follows: dummy variables for each of the eleven different NIT plans; a dummy variable for those experimental families on the three-year program; two dummy variables for race (black and Chicano) and one for site (Denver); years of schooling, age, age squared, and a permanently disabled dummy for the husband and for the wife; a dummy variable for the presence of any preschool-aged children; and, finally, all the other right-hand side variables in Equation 7. The equivalent equations for single females are the same except for the absence of the characteristics of the spouse. Incidentally, observe that Equation 8 is estimated without an intercept. The addition of a constant term, in fact, leaves the estimates in Table 1 practically unaltered.

the change in net earnings of the estimated coefficients on the program participation variables (that is, on those variables involving A). Inserting the mean values of T_e, R, and S for these workers over experimentals predicted to be above the breakeven on the basis of their preexperimental income,[19] the mean change in annual net earnings for this group is forecasted to be $-\$425$ for husbands, $-\$167$ for wives, and $-\$135$ for single females. These decreases in net earnings combine the effects of these program variables (T_e, R, and S) on the probability of being below the breakeven and the reduction in work effort conditional upon being below the breakeven. Expressed as a fraction of mean preexperimental net earnings for these workers, these represent decreases of 8.9 percent for husbands, 7.3 percent for wives, and 5.8 percent for single females.

The estimates of the utility function parameters (B_1, B_2, γ_1, and γ_2) are perhaps best understood with reference to their implications for the slopes of the hours-of-work functions. These are given in the upper half of Table 2 for husbands and wives and in the first line of Table 3 for single females. The uncompensated hours-of-work function for the husband is negatively sloped with respect to his own net wage rate and, at the point at which these slopes are evaluated,[20] this implies an own-wage elasticity of $-.159$. This estimate sits comfortably within the range of estimates of this elasticity from nonexperimental data. A one thousand dollar increase in family nonwage income reduces his annual hours of work by 126 hours. Alternatively, $-w_1(\partial h_1 / \partial y) = B_1 = .288$, which implies that the husband allocates .29 of each additional dollar of exogenous income to the purchase of nonmarket time. This is again fully in line with estimates from nonexperimental data.[21]

By contrast, the wife's uncompensated hours-of-work function is positively sloped with respect to changes in her own wage rate with an implied own-wage elasticity of .062. The wife "spends" $.088$ $(B_2 = -w_2 \cdot \partial h_2 / \partial y)$ of each additional dollar of nonwage income on consuming nonmarket time. The husband's and wife's results indicate relatively small compensated cross-effects of changes in one spouse's wage rate on the hours worked by the other spouse. The uncompensated cross-wage effects are much larger and, as we shall see, of some consequence for the operation of an NIT.

The slopes of the hours-of-work functions for single females as given in Table 3

---

[19] For these working husband-wife families, the means are as follows: $T_e = .669$, $S = 4328$, and $R = .242$. For single females the means are as follows: $T_e = .678$, $S = 4085$, and $R = .341$. In performing this simple simulation exercise, none of the other right-hand side variables in Equation 8 is being "turned on." Consequently, the predicted change in net earnings describes white workers in Seattle not on any manpower program and whose "normal income" is either not determined or in the E7 category (that is, $11,000 – $13,000).

[20] The values of hours of work and of wage rates at which these slopes are calculated are given beneath Tables 2 and 3. These values represent the mean values of these variables for experimental workers predicted to be below the breakeven in Keeley and Robins, "The Design of Social Experiments." By evaluating the functions at the same point, differences between the results of this study and that of Keeley and Robins are attributable solely to the estimates and not to the evaluation points. If the parameter estimates in Table 1 were evaluated at our sample means, the slopes of the labor supply functions would be similar to those in Tables 2 and 3. The Keeley and Robins study represents the application of the estimation strategy outlined in Keeley et al., "The Estimation of Labor Supply Models Using Experimental Data." We compare our results with the Keeley and Robins study because the sample used there includes Chicanos as does ours, whereas the Keeley et al. paper works with a sample that excludes Chicanos.

[21] For instance, Ashenfelter and Heckman, "Estimating Labor Supply Functions," use the 1967 Survey of Economic Opportunity for 3,203 male workers and obtain an estimate of .27 in this context; David H. Greenberg and Marvin Kosters, "Income Guarantees and the Working Poor: The Effect of Income Maintenance Programs on the Hours of Work of Male Family Heads," in Glen G. Cain and Harold W. Watts, eds., *Income Maintenance and Labor Supply* (Chicago: Rand McNally, 1973), pp. 14–101, obtain an estimate of .29. Also, George J. Borjas and James J. Heckman, "Labor Supply Estimates for Public Policy Evaluation," Industrial Relations Research Association, *Proceedings of the Thirty-first Annual Meeting, August 29–31, 1978*, (Madison, Wis.: IRRA, 1979), pp. 320–31, review male labor supply functions estimated with nonexperimental data and suggest a range of uncompensated own-wage elasticities from $-.19$ to $-.07$. Our own estimate of $-.159$ sits comfortably within this range.

Table 2. Estimated Wage and Income Effects on Hours of Work: Husbands and Wives.

Researcher	Husband's Wage		Wife's Wage		Nonlabor Income
	Uncompensated	Compensated	Uncompensated	Compensated	
Johnson and Pencavel					
Hours of work of husband	−130.5	106.1	−176.4	−19.7	−125.8
Hours of work of wife	−128.6	−19.7	49.2	118.9	−57.9
Keeley and Robins					
Hours of work of husband	−73.5	41.1	−73.4	0*	−60.9
Hours of work of wife	−208.4	0*	−1.5	132.0	−110.8

Notes: The asterisk indicates that these coefficients were constrained to zero, which implies that the cross-wage effects ($\partial h_i / \partial w_j$) in Keeley and Robins, "The Design of Social Experiments: A Critique of the Conlisk-Watts Assignment Model," in Ronald G. Ehrenberg, ed., Research in Labor Economics (Greenwich, Conn.: JAI Press, 1981), are given by h_j ($\partial h_i / \partial y$). The wage effects are measured in terms of annual hours per dollar increase in the wage rate and the income effects in terms of annual hours per thousand dollar increase in nonlabor income. To facilitate comparison between the two studies, all effects are measured at the same values: h_1=1880.97; h_2=1204.69; net wage of husband=2.293; and net wage of wife=1.521. These represent the sample means in the preexperimental period of workers only in the Keeley and Robins study for experimentals predicted to be below the tax breakeven.

Table 3. Estimated Wage and Income Effects on Hours of Work: Single Females.

Researcher	Uncompensated Wage Effect	Compensated Wage Effect	Income Effect
Johnson and Pencavel:	−58.7	78.8	−87.2
Keeley and Robins:	−81.0	75.9	−99.5

Notes: These estimates are evaluated at the following values for female heads of families: hours of work = 1577.24 and net wage rate = $1.48. Again, these are the preexperimental means for workers in the Keeley and Robins study who are experimentals predicted to be below the tax breakeven. See Table 2 for citation.

suggest an own-wage elasticity of −.056 with a marginal propensity to consume nonmarket time of .129. In fact, these estimates for single females lie between those for husbands and those for wives and it is as if, as far as hours-of-work functions are concerned, single females possess the characteristics of the averaged married husbands and wives!

For husbands and wives these responses are broadly consistent with the stylized facts on labor supply from the nonexperimental literature, although exact comparisons with previous work are difficult to make in view of the differences in research methods, definitions of variables, and data sets. In the case of single females, little seems to be known from nonexperimental data. Perhaps the closest and most natural comparison would be one with other hours-of-work functions fitted to these SIME/DIME families and here the studies of Keeley et al.[22] and Keeley and Robins merit discussion.[23] Although their estimation strategy (like ours) involves measuring right-hand side variables at their preexperimental values, unlike our treatment, errors in measuring these variables in this way are ignored. That is, they treat the equations' stochastic terms as distributed independently of their regressors. They assume that fixed costs of work-

[22] Keeley et al., "The Estimation of Labor Supply Models Using Experimental Data."
[23] Keeley and Robins, "The Design of Social Experiments."

ing are zero so that individuals at a corner solution (nonworkers) and those at an interior solution (workers) are pooled together and conventional Tobit procedures are applied to a much larger sample than that to which our Equation 8 was fitted. As is well known, this Tobit scheme may be characterized as a special case of our λ procedure.[24] Finally, their functional form neglects substitution effects of changes in one spouse's wage rate on the other spouse's work decisions.[25]

The lower part of Table 2 and the second line of Table 3 present the slopes of the hours-of-work functions as estimated in the Keeley and Robins study. For single females, the two sets of estimates in Table 3 are very close and they are mapping out the same basic relationship. The correspondence between the estimates reported in this paper and those of Keeley and Robins is less apparent for husbands and wives. Their hours-of-work function for husbands is less negatively sloped (or "backward sloping") than ours while they report, surprisingly, an inelastic hours-of-work function for wives. Clearly, more work is called for to account for the discrepancies for husbands and wives between our estimates and theirs.[26]

As a rough indication of the sort of implications for a negative income tax program suggested by our parameter estimates, consider working adults with values of the relevant variables given by the means in the preexperimental year for experimental families predicted to be below the breakeven level of income. The predicted change in net earnings for these individuals is given by Equation 5 with the values of the utility function parameters given in Table 1 used to simulate different NIT programs.[27] Table 4 presents the implied proportionate changes in net earnings for each adult as a consequence of applying different NIT plans. Of course, these reductions in net earnings combine the effects of applying a higher tax rate to a given level of before-tax earnings with the behavioral (hours-of-work) response to these changes in tax rates. To provide some idea of the magnitude of the automatic reductions in net earnings, we have calculated in the last line of Table 4, la-

---

[24]See Heckman, "The Common Structure of Statistical Models of Truncation."

[25]In addition to these differences between our work and the Keeley and Robins paper, which may generate diverse estimates of income and substitution effects, there are some differences in variable definitions as well. We are aware of at least three differences within the category of variable definitions. First, our definition of the change in disposable income variable (evaluated at preexperimental hours of work) does not allow the value of the variable to be negative. For instance, if a person who is on AFDC has a value of preexperimental disposable income that is greater than what he or she would receive from SIME/DIME, we define the value of the change in disposable income variable as equal to the minimum SIME/DIME payment, whereas Keeley and Robins subtract from the payment the amount of AFDC income received, a procedure that would result in a negative value for this variable. Second, we predict whether a person is above or below the breakeven on a quarterly basis and turn on the *FABOVE* dummy variable only if the household is predicted to be above the breakeven in all four quarters; Keeley and Robins define this variable on the basis of an annual computation. Finally, our definitions of annual marginal tax rates differ for two reasons.

First, they use an arithmetic average of the quarterly marginal tax rates, whereas we use an earnings-weighted average. Second, Keeley and Robins add the full AFDC marginal tax rate for AFDC recipients to the average annual federal and state marginal tax rate even if the individual participated in AFDC for only one quarter; our procedure is to determine AFDC participation within the quarter and modify the quarterly marginal tax rate only for those quarters in which the individuals participate.

[26]If there are important husband-wife interactions, an alternative interpretation of the Keeley et al. model may be offered to the one they propose. According to this alternative interpretation, if $w_{20} = kw_{10}$ is a good approximation of the data, then the coefficient on $(t_0 - t_e)w_{10}$ in the husband's equation measures a weighted sum (involving k) of the husband's own-substitution and the husband-wife's cross-substitution effects. Correspondingly, the coefficient on $(t_0 - t_e)w_{20}$ in the wife's equation measures a weighted sum of the wife's own-substitution and the husband-wife's cross-substitution effects. Even on this line of reasoning, however, their estimates and our estimates are no closer. In fact, this alternative interpretation seems rather strained in view of the weak association between w_{10} and w_{20} for these 498 husbands and wives: the simple correlation between w_{10} and w_{20} is .104.

[27]To be explicit, for husbands and wives in the following simulations, $t_0 = .256$, $y_0 = \$1,301$, $w_{10} = \$3.226$, and $w_{20} = \$2.170$. For single females, $t_0 = .324$, $y_0 = \$1,856$, and $w_0 = \$2.362$. The mean of net earnings in the preexperimental year for these husbands is \$4,848, for wives it is \$1,994, and for single females it is \$2,776.

Table 4. Simulated Proportionate Change in Net Earnings Corresponding to Different NIT Programs.

Support Level	Husband		Wife		Single Female	
	$t_e=.5$	$t_e=.7$	$t_e=.5$	$t_e=.7$	$t_e=.5$	$t_e=.7$
S = $3800	−.420	−.579	−.416	−.620	−.385	−.621
S = $4800	−.479	−.638	−.460	−.664	−.431	−.667
S = $5600	−.527	−.685	−.496	−.699	−.468	−.704
Fixed hours	−.305	−.555	−.320	−.582	−.236	−.505

Notes: These proportionate changes in net earnings are derived by inserting the parameter estimates given in Table 1 and the values of exogenous variables given in Footnote 27 into Equation 5 and expressing the result as a fraction of preexperimental net earnings.

belled "fixed hours," the reduction in net earnings resulting from a higher tax rate with hours of work unchanged.[28] Thus, for the "typical" husband examined in this table, the nonbehavioral reduction in net earnings attributable to raising the tax rate on his income to .5 is 30.5 percent of preexperimental net earnings. Augmenting this automatic reduction with the behavioral response that results from allowing his hours of work to adjust to his new budget constraint results in a total reduction in net earnings of 42.0 percent of preexperimental net earnings (when the annual support level is $3,800 in 1971 dollars).

The changes in net earnings in Table 4 are very similar for the three types of adults, although women are slightly more sensitive to differences in tax rates than are husbands. It should be emphasized that, although the differences between some of the entries in the "fixed hours" row and the entries in other rows appear small for the husband and the wife, this does not mean that their behavioral responses are negligible. On the contrary, the important husband-wife cross-wage effects we have estimated imply that the higher NIT tax rates applied to each individual's wage rate induce each spouse to work more hours, not fewer, and this behavioral response attenuates the reduction in hours worked by each individual as a consequence of the decline in his or her own net wage rate and as a consequence of an increase in nonwage income.

To be specific, for the "typical" husband subject to an NIT tax rate of .7 and with a support level of $3,800, the total reduction in his net earnings is 57.9 percent of his preexperimental net earnings while the automatic reduction in his net earnings is 55.5 percent (as given in the "fixed hours" line in Table 4). In this instance, if the cross-wage effect on the husband's hours of the reduction in his wife's net wage were set to zero, the reduction in the husband's net earnings would be 65.9 percent.[29] The cross-wage effects that we have estimated, therefore, appear to have practical importance and are not a trifling theoretical nicety. Of course, the numbers in Table 4 depend very much upon the particular values of the exogenous variables chosen for this illustration. A more complete simulation exercise would involve applying Equation 5 to all individuals in the relevant population.

Conclusions

This paper has implemented a scheme that has potential value for policy purposes

---

[28] That is, for each individual we calculated $(t_0 - t_e) w_0 h_0$ and then expressed this as a ratio of preexperimental net earnings, the values for which are given in the previous footnote. The values for h_0 used in these calculations are those given in the notes to Tables 2 and 3.

[29] To provide other examples, if cross-wage effects between husbands and wives were set to zero, then for a tax rate of .5 and a support level of $3,800, the proportionate reductions in the net earnings of the husband would be .464 and of the wife .506; or for $t_e=.7$ and S=$3,800, the corresponding figures would be .659 for the husband and .760 for the wife.

in forecasting the change in net earnings for each individual that would result from the implementation of an NIT program. In developing this scheme, we have tried to remain faithful to the economist's notion of purposive behavior by specifying a functional form for this forecasting device that can be derived from an explicit representation of a household's preferences for work and nonmarket time. The estimates of these preferences using data from the Seattle-Denver Income Maintenance Experiments are consistent with the stylized facts on the nature of labor supply functions as estimated from nonexperimental data. That is, at the average values of the relevant variables, for husbands we derive hours-of-work functions that are negatively sloped with respect to their own wage rates while for wives we derive hours-of-work functions that are positively sloped with respect to their own wage rates.

However, this correspondence between our results and those from nonexperimental data could be satisfied with a wide variety of estimates and it hardly provides a rigorous yardstick with which to evaluate these results. Moreover, the impetus for undertaking these experiments was the dissatisfaction with the estimates from the nonexperimental literature; so it seems somewhat inappropriate subsequently to judge the soundness of the results from the experimental data in terms of their correspondence with the estimates from the nonexperimental data.

By another yardstick, namely, that provided by the results from the Keeley and Robins analysis of SIME/DIME, our point estimates correspond closely in the case of single females but diverge for husbands and wives. One reason for this divergence may be that our procedure explicitly allows for one individual's wage rate to affect his or her spouse's hours of work. Moreover, our simulation exercises indicated that these cross-wage effects were nontrivial in measuring the impact of an NIT on an individual's net earnings. The degree to which these cross-wage effects are robust with respect to alternative specifications of a household's preferences (and, in particular, with respect to specifications that do not restrict the husband's and the wife's nonmarket time to be net substitutes as does our specification) would appear to be an important and well-defined item on the agenda for future research.[30]

Finally, it is evident from the standard errors accompanying our parameter estimates that a wide range of income and substitution effects are compatible with the data. This is unfortunate, since an assessment of the consequences of alternative NIT schemes requires knowledge of the income and substitution effects separately. In these circumstances, considerably more analysis of the experimental data using different procedures and assumptions is required before estimates from these experiments can be applied confidently to simulate the effects of different NIT programs.

[30] For a recent survey of the joint labor supply of husbands and of wives that emphasizes how little we know concerning the sign and sizes of the cross-wage effects, see Marjorie B. McElroy, "Empirical Results from Estimates of Joint Labor Supply Functions of Husbands and Wives," in Ronald G. Ehrenberg, ed., *Research in Labor Economics*, Vol. 4 (Greenwich, Conn.: JAI Press, 1981).

Appendix

Table. Estimates of the Probit Parameters Determining the Probability of Working in Both the Preexperimental Year and the Second Experimental Year.

Variable			Both Husband and Wife Working	Single Female Working
Constant			.320	−2.063***
NIT financial program:	F1		−.370*	−.272*
	F2		−.008	−.039
	F3		−.148	−.277
	F4		−.050	−.003
	F5		−.262	−.265
	F6		−.203	−.384**
	F7		−.083	−.560***
	F8		−.263	−.148
	F9		−.085	.056
	F10		−.317	−.471**
	F11		.118	−.394*
Black x Denver dummy			.582***	.709***
Black x Seattle dummy			.442***	.237*
White x Denver dummy			.165	.564***
Chicano dummy			.211*	.451***
Homeownership dummy			−.088	.365***
3-year financial dummy			.013	.152
Husband:	permanently disabled		−.705**	
	age		−.111***	
	age squared		.0013**	
	years of schooling		.019	
Wife:	permanently disabled		−1.198***	−1.212***
	age		.070	.049
	age squared		−.0011*	−.0005
	years of schooling		.078***	.074***
Preschool age child dummy			−.606***	−.444***
Any children dummy			.073**	.004
Manpower program:	M1		−.147	.156
	M2		−.240***	−.027
	M3		.007	−.166
"Normal" income:	E1	($1,000)	−1.369***	−.942***
	E2	($1-3,000)	−1.512***	−.158
	E3	($3-5,000)	−1.160***	.453**
	E4	($5-7,000)	−.869***	.797***
	E5	($7-9,000)	−.767***	1.132***
	E6	($9-11,000)	−.193	2.957*
−2 log. of likelihood			336.54	555.52

Notes: There are 1,678 observations for the husband and wife sample and 1,339 observations of single females. All variables are defined as of the preexperimental year. The NIT financial program variables are all dichotomous and they correspond to the programs listed in Table 1 of Keeley et al. Similarly, the manpower program variables and the "normal" income variables are also dichotomous. M1 takes the value of unity for individuals eligible to receive manpower counseling. M2 is unity for individuals eligible for counseling and a 50% education and training subsidy. M3 is unity for individuals eligible for counseling and a 100% education and training subsidy.

*Significant at the .10 level, two-tailed test.
**Significant at the .05 level, two-tailed test.
***Significant at the .01 level, two-tailed test.

The Block Grant Mechanism

A fundamental purpose of the federal government is to collect revenues and taxes and distribute these monies to other levels of government (state and local), individual recipients, and the private sector for activities, agencies, and programs meriting governmental support. The mechanisms for transferring these funds have varied widely. The fact that there has been such variation in the distributive mechanisms indicates an unresolved tension in the federal system as to how these fiscal transfers ought to occur. The tension, succinctly stated, is between accountability and autonomy.

The tension is evident in programs funded either through categorical grants or through general revenue sharing. Categorical grants carry clear stipulations and requirements as to who is eligible to receive the funds and for what purposes the funds are to be spent. General revenue-sharing funds are disbursed with few requirements, and local government may make decisions appropriate to local conditions.

What has emerged in recent years is an accommodation of these two approaches through what is known as the block grant. Here, funds from various categorical programs in a broad area—such as health, education, criminal justice, and social welfare—are combined into large "block" grants and then distributed to state and local governments for redistribution. The goal in this process is to achieve broad national policy objectives, but with state and local governments allocating the resources and making program implementation decisions. The rationale for the block grant funding mechanism has three components: to decentralize the decision-making process and thus enhance flexibility and program responsiveness; to increase citizen participation in decisions regarding distribution of governmental resources; and to lessen administrative costs and burdens. While there is little evaluative evidence to support (or refute) these assumptions about citizen participation and program processes, the strategy continues to gain in popularity, particularly with the Reagan administration. The policy implications of this funding mechanism are explored in the chapters in this section.

The section opens with recent congressional testimony of the Advisory Commission on Intergovernmental Relations (ACIR). The commission argues that there is a place for the block grant mechanism in the federal system, and that it should be utilized when funding demands and constraints make it the most viable of the three general options available. The paper charts the three funding strategies and compares them according to several key variables, thereby more crisply defining the options for policymakers—and this is no small contribution. The chapter by Nathan provides additional information and analysis on the varying funding mechanisms available to the government. The clear message in Nathan's piece is that no single (or simple) solution exists as to which allocation process should be used to respond to the multiple demands on government. Block grants are not the final word on fiscal transfer policy; they are but one technique in a needed repertoire of techniques.

Two articles in this section take up the application of block grants to individual content areas. Greenberg addresses the Partnership for Health Act that created a block grant in

1966 in three states—Michigan, Pennsylvania, and Alabama. Fifteen years of experience with this block grant are examined. The central conclusion is that limitations of the block grant mechanism ought to be considered fully before this strategy is employed. Chernick suggests in his analysis that using the block grant mechanism, in contrast to a categorical grant, which requires matching funds from state or local government, means that available resources will most likely decline. The AFDC program serves as an example of the trade-off between increased state discretion and lessened requirements for state matching funds, and indicates that the level of benefits for participants will decrease as the state contribution declines.

Finally, the chapter by Chelimsky posits eighteen procedures that could be implemented by the Congress to ensure that the national policy objectives inherent in the block grants are being met. Acknowledging the tension between accountability and autonomy, the chapter nonetheless suggests that the presence of such tension does not exclude or neutralize consideration of accountability. The chapter carefully distinguishes among the several accountability questions that can be posed, specifically, "accountability to whom," "accountability by whom," and "accountability for what." Establishing accountability procedures is not a cost-free effort. Demands of time, staff, resources, and trustworthy data must be considered; and with each block grant, stated objectives and accountability requirements must be reconciled carefully.

10

THE CONCEPT OF BLOCK GRANTS

The Advisory Commission on Intergovernmental Relations

The term "block grants" has suddenly become almost a household term this year. After years of developing this concept and advocating the benefits of block grants, ACIR is gratified to see this rising popularity. Unfortunately, a great deal of confusion surrounds this popularization of the block grant concept.

I am happy, therefore, to have this opportunity to help clarify what our Commission means by block grants, and how these grants compare with other forms of intergovernmental fiscal transfers, such as categorical grants and revenue sharing. ACIR believes that there is a place in our federal system for all three types of grants, and that conscious choices should be made about which type should be used in each situation. The choice should be based upon the national purposes involved and the locus of political accountability desired. The fiscal, policy, and administrative features of the grant program, then, should serve these basic national purpose and accountability objectives. Varying political judgments and shifting budget circumstances also substantially affect the choice of grant mechanisms.

My purpose in this presentation is not to analyze, in detail, the numerous specific proposals for block grants now pending before Congress. Clearly, a number of these will be enacted, given the positive action on several in both the Senate and House reconciliation bills. But how many will be enacted ultimately, and what their essential design features will be, are questions that cannot be answered now. My purpose then, is to suggest the major factors which should be considered by the Congress in making its political judgments about the type of grant mechanisms most appropriate for achieving varying program, fiscal, and administrative objectives.

A comparison of block features in relation to those of categorical grants and revenue sharing will be presented first. Then, some of the common variations on the block grant concept which tend to confuse it with the other two basic types of grants will be probed. And finally, two primary intergovernmental issues arising out of the use of block grants—state channeling and budget consequences—will be examined briefly.

BLOCK GRANTS COMPARED TO OTHER TYPES OF GRANTS

In the spectrum of the types of grants available for use by the federal government, block grants are near the center of the continuum. Categorical grants, with

---

Presented by David B. Walker, Assistant Director of the Advisory Commission on Intergovernmental Relations, before the Joint Economic Committee of the Congress of the United States, Washington, D.C., July 15, 1981.

their high specific national program purposes and rigid compliance requirements, are at one end. General revenue sharing, with its total lack of program purposes and minimal policy and administrative requirements, is at the other. Since they fall midway between these two extremes, block grants reflect important national purposes of a general nature and require compliance with a variety of national policy requirements. But they also allow recipient governments to make most of the decisions about project priorities and the best means of complying with national policies while still meeting state and local objectives most effectively and efficiently and in a manner most acceptable to their own constituencies.

These, of course, are the ideal goals of these programs. Actual block grants tend to mix the features of these three basic types. And that is where most of the confusion about block grants arises. Yet, a focusing on these normative traits can help to clarify the key intergovernmental issues involved in choosing the appropriate type of grant mechanism.

Fundamental Factors of Choice

Choosing the appropriate grant mechanisms should begin with an explicit consideration of the national purposes involved. Revenue-sharing programs, for example, are designed to deliver money, not programs. In theory, their objective is to help match the fiscal capacity of the aided governments to their fiscal needs. No program purposes are stated.

At the opposite extreme, categorical grants seek to achieve very specific program results from the subnational levels of government or other providers. The federal government, itself, specifies very specific program objectives and even the means of achieving them in many cases. While formula categorical grants may be used to support state or local programs, project grants are used in a more experimental fashion to demonstrate the feasibility of certain results in many fewer places. Thus the national purposes reflected in categoricals may range from supporting research and the development of new capacities to govern at the subnational levels to supporting ongoing but narrowly defined program activities. Quite often, categorical grants have been used as incentives for state and local governments to pursue activities which they otherwise would be unlikely to pursue on their own. Moreover, the continuing tendency to have basically national programs administered by the subnational governments has been another major goal of a number of big categorical grant programs.

Much more general national purposes usually underpin block grants. The enactment of such a grant generally reflects a willingness on the part of the federal government to share in the financing of a broad functional program. Sometimes these are programs of nationwide scope in which the federal government has an interest in supporting at least minimal levels of service throughout all the states. It might be the national purpose, for example, to support the development of more integrated criminal justice systems, rather than specific judicial, corrections, and police systems, as was the case with the Safe Streets Act. Another example might be to specify the national purpose that the needy shall be provided with adequate social services, according to their individual needs, rather than that there be a series of individual types of social services which must be sought out separately (as the Title XX program in part seeks to do). Under such block grants, recipient governments would detail the particular types of criminal justice or social services needed in any particular locale in order to satisfy the generally stated national purpose. Block grants work best, so the theory goes, when they encompass most, if not all, of the federal aid in the particular functional area. This gives maximum latitude for the state and local governments to meet the needs as they actually occur, without artificially determined program rigidities imposed from Washington.

The political ideas on which these diverse formulations of national purpose are based range widely. The philosophy of revenue sharing, at one end of the spectrum, is that the federal, state, and local governments are separate levels of government, entitled to act largely independent of one another in the programmatic sense, and capable of doing so. In short, it reflects a devolutionary philosophy.

On the other hand, the categorical grant philosophy is that the federal government needs to dominate program policy and specify the means of accomplishment, in order to ensure the achievement of national objectives. This is a philosophy of federal superiority and supremacy.

The block grant philosophy is more like one of shared objectives and responsibilities, equal partnership, and mutual trust among the levels of government. In short, it represents a more nearly cooperative concept of federalism. It recognizes the interdependencies among the levels of government, and it works best when each of the levels of government is capable and committed to similar goals in the functional program area addressed by the block grant.

These differences in national purposes and philosophies call for corresponding distinctions among grant recipients. The tendency of categorical programs to specify exactly what is to be done and how, and to promote the creation of specific organizational structures for narrow program purposes, is associated with the practice of providing these grants to specialized units within states or local government or to specialized nongovernmental service providers. The narrow purpose of the program is served directly by this choice of recipients. Political accountability for program results runs directly from the grant recipient to the federal government. While certain nods may be made in the direction of citizen participation and the involvement of elected officials, these "outside parties" frequently are involved in a largely pro forma way.

The much greater reliance on the decision-making process of the governments receiving block grants and revenue sharing leads to the conclusion that in most cases these types of grants should be made to general purpose governments—the governor and legislature at the state level, and the chief executive and governing bodies of county and municipal governments at the local level. The major exception would be block grants to independent school districts (which normally are established apart from city and county governments throughout most of the nation).

Under block grants, the recipient is accountable more or less equally to its own political process and to the federal government. Under revenue sharing, accountability is almost exclusively to the recipient government's own political processes. It is important, therefore, in these two grant mechanisms, that the recipient should have broad decision-making power and direct accountability to the people through the election of its own decision makers.

These issues, concerning national purpose and the locus of accountability, clearly are the fundamental considerations in choosing among the three basic types of grant mechanisms. Revenue sharing should be used when the federal government is seeking only to share its superior financial base with needy subnational governments in accordance with their fiscal needs, and when the federal government is satisfied that most of the state and local governments receiving these funds will know best what program results to pursue and how to pursue them. Block grants should be used (1) when the federal government's own program priorities are such that it desires to supplement the service levels in certain broad program areas traditionally provided under state and local jurisdiction, (2) when it seeks to establish nationwide minimum levels of service in these areas, (3) when broad national objectives are consistent with diverse state and local program objectives, and/or (4) when the federal government is satisfied that state and local governments know best how to set subordinate priorities and administer the program. Finally, categorical grants should be used when the federal government has very specific national objectives in mind which call for innovative or politically controversial programs at the state and/or local levels which are not likely to be undertaken without highly conditioned federal incentives.

Other Major Features of Grant Programs

Once the basic decision has been made about which type of grant to use—based upon national purpose and accountability considerations—other features of the grant program should be enacted with that basic choice in mind. This helps to ensure that the basic philosophy of the program will be carried out as intended.

With respect to its financial provisions, revenue sharing should be allocated exclusively on the basis of formulas related to measures of fiscal need. Block grant funds should be allocated by formulas designed to emphasize program needs—with the exception that certain discretionary or related categorical grant funds might be set aside to meet research, recipient training, technical assistance, or unusually acute program needs. Categorical grant funds may be allocated among recipients either by formulas, preferably related to some measure of program need, or on the basis of project application competitions. Even when the funds are allocated by formula, such funds are released only upon approval of specific plans for directly eligible project activities.

Matching funds, contributed by recipient governments in proportion to federal grant amounts, are not required for revenue-sharing programs. Tax cuts by recipients and overall reductions in governmental spending are acceptable results in revenue-sharing programs, if that determination is made by recipient governments in response to their own political processes.

Matching funds, on the other hand, may be required at modest levels in block grant programs. Alternatively, it is quite common to require in block grants that the past level of spending in the aided program area not be reduced because of the federal supplementation (the so-called maintenance of effort requirement).

Matching requirements frequently are a major feature of categorical grant programs. This is a natural outcome of the national purpose in these grants for stimulating new subnational governmental activities. Matching ratios may run anywhere from one dollar of the recipient's funds for each nine dollars of federal money, to two dollars of the recipient's funds for every one dollar of federal financing—depending upon the degree of stimulation desired by Congress and the president.

Application and planning requirements also vary greatly for these three types of grant mechanisms. There are no application or planning requirements for revenue sharing, since eligibility is determined by federal law and there are no program requirements to which recipients must adhere. Organizational and administrative requirements are also minimal in revenue sharing. Any state and almost any county or municipality with even minimal public servicing, reporting, and budgeting processes would qualify. Also, very few general policy requirements apply to revenue sharing—the principal one being civil rights protections. The idea here is to minimize the federal administration effort involved in distributing funds, while at the same time minimizing red tape for the recipient governments.

Categorical grants, again, are at the other extreme. Application, planning, organizational, and administrative requirements are so detailed and specific that the documents submitted by recipients prior to the authorization of federal funds frequently run into the hundreds of pages. The recipient's eligibility and organizational structure must be specifically documented and usually justified each year for each project. The project must be shown to be in accordance with specified types of plans and planning processes, and numerous requirements for reporting, auditing, and other types of administrative activities must be met. In addition, most categorical grants are subject to a broad array of general policy requirements relating to nondiscrimination, protection of the environment, equitable treatment of persons and businesses displaced by grant activities, merit principles for employment on the project, citizen participation, and the use of prevailing wages for construction workers under contract in the project. Categorical grant applications must show, in detail, how each of these requirements will be met. All of the application information must be reviewed and approved by the grant-making agency before federal funds can flow. Frequently, this is a long and arduous process.

Block grants have simplified application and administrative requirements. Greater reliance is placed upon the recipient governments' own organizational structure and planning processes. Most of the same general policy requirements which apply to categorical grants also apply to block grants, but recipients frequently may certify and show evidence, only once, that their own political and administrative processes meet these requirements, rather than demonstrating how each requirement is met specifically in each project. Emphasis is placed upon planning documents submitted with the application to show that federal funds will be used in a manner consistent with national program objectives and in a reasonable relationship to demonstrated state and/or local needs, desires, and priorities. Postaudits of program results and finances are used to ensure compliance with federal conditions. Overall, though, administrative burdens are much less for block grants than for categoricals and recipients have much more flexibility in meeting their own needs with federal funds.

The major purposes and features of revenue sharing, block grants, and categorical grants—as described above—are briefly summarized in the following table. Although somewhat oversimplified, this table is designed to provide a quick and easy checklist for decision makers who must choose appropriate grant mechanisms to match their purposes.

TYPES OF PROGRAMS OFTEN CONFUSED WITH BLOCK GRANTS

Block grants which have been enacted or proposed frequently do not follow rigorously the design described above. Some variations are only slight, but others diverge widely. For example, some consolidations of categorical programs result only in a somewhat more broadly defined categorical program, such as the Education Amendments of 1974 and the Comprehensive Older Americans Act Amendments of 1978. Even those block grant programs originally enacted with rather broad discretion for recipient decision making frequently are recategorized by legislative amendments which focus them more narrowly or earmark funds within the block for specific purposes. For example, over the years, the community development block grant was more narrowly targeted to distressed neighborhoods; law enforcement assistance acquired special funding set-asides for juvenile justice; and public service jobs were set up as a separate category within the comprehensive employment and training program, with eligibility requirements which became increasingly restrictive.

Another divergence is that many functionally related categorical programs frequently have remained outside the block grant programs. For example, youth employment has remained outside of CETA; special services for the aging have remained outside the social services block grant; many community development programs have remained outside the block grant in that area; and the Partnership for Health block grant has encompassed only a small part of the aid in that field.

Major Features, Three Basic Types of Federal Grant Programs

Features	Revenue Sharing	Types of Programs	
		Block Grants	Categorical Grants
Purpose	delivering money, not programs	generalized program objectives in a broad functional area; systematic financial support of all appropriate jurisdictions; most of the relevant federal aid encompassed in the block	very specific program objectives and requirements; developing capabilities and activities lacking or deficient among recipients; demonstrating program innovations
Political philosophy	separate levels of government, largely independent in the programmatic sense DEVOLUTION	shared objectives; equal partnership; mutual trust among levels of government SHARED RESPONSIBILITY	federal government dominates program policy and specifies means of accomplishment; often tends toward FEDERAL SUPERIORITY
Recipient	general purpose state and local governments	usually general purpose state and local governments, or school districts	general purpose units or specialized agencies of state or local government, plus nongovernmental service providers
Recipient accountability	to own political process	equally to own political process and to the federal government	to the federal government, first and foremost
Allocation of funds	formula based on recipient fiscal capacity and tax effort	formula based on program needs	formula based on program needs, or project competition (grantsmanship)
Matching funds	none required (tax cuts allowed)	none, or few, required; maintenance of effort often required (supplementation of activity)	usually required (stimulation of activity)
Application and planning requirements	none	moderate; emphasis upon recipient's own planning process	extensive and detailed; little flexibility available to recipients

(continued)

Major Features, Three Basic Types of Federal Grant Programs (continued)

Types of Programs

Features	Revenue Sharing	Block Grants	Categorical Grants
Organizational and administrative requirements	minimal	moderate (as compared with categorical grants)	extensive and detailed
General policy conditions (beyond program policies)	minimal; postaudit	substantial; process certification	substantial; detailed preapproval
When to use	when fiscal concerns are virtually the only ones under consideration	when supporting traditional or well-established programs which exist nationwide and engender little or no political disagreement among governmental levels about the need for such programs	when supporting innovative and/or politically controversial programs not likely to be undertaken by recipients without federal incentives; often target to specific population groups
Principal advantage to recipient government	extra funds with which to govern own affairs	substantial flexibility to meet own as well as national objectives	freedom to undertake costly and controversial programs, with the federal government taking most of the financial or political risks

Nevertheless, the five existing block grants—social services, community development, employment and training, law enforcement, and Partnership for Health—share some of the typical block grant features. Save for the Partnership for Health program, all require federal approval of grantee plans and maintenance of grantee fiscal effort. All five require compliance with a wide range of generally applicable national policy requirements—including civil rights, uniform relocation, environmental impact, merit personnel, and prevailing wages for construction workers.

In contrast, a number of major program consolidations proposed by President Nixon in the early 1970s would have omitted these types of conditions. They would have folded 129 categorical programs into 6 broad programs referred to as special revenue sharing—because of their general lack of federally imposed conditions. The 6 would have been for education, transportation, urban community development, rural community development, manpower training, and law enforcement. Only the urban community development and manpower proposals passed, but both were transformed by Congress into conditional block grants more like the block grant model described above rather than the revenue-sharing model.

This record of past enactments and proposals illustrates the tensions which exist among the three ideal types of grant programs. As a result, a single program often exhibits features most appropriate to more than one of these mechanisms. Congress then should be clear and consistent in designing grant programs so that they can be administered faithfully in accordance with legislative intent.

STATE CHANNELING OF BLOCK GRANTS

Another lesson learned from the experience with existing block grants is that when they are given first to the states, for eventual use by local recipients, the tendency is for them to lose their block grant features before they reach the local level. For example, a large share of the funds passed through to local governments under the law enforcement assistance program were awarded in the form of specific project grants accompanied by additional matching and administrative requirements in the best traditions of the categorical grant mechanism. If Congress, then, desires the ultimate recipients to receive funds under the block grant format, it probably should consider specifying this intent in the law. Otherwise, red tape taken away by the federal program may be added back by the states and program flexibility afforded by the federal program may not affect the localities.

ACIR has recommended, recently, that the federal government consider taking on full financial responsibility for a number of grant programs now providing direct benefits to needy individuals. In return, the federal government would terminate a large number of grant programs designed to assist state and local governments in programs where these subnational units already provide the bulk of public sending and decision making. This would be a fiscally neutral way of reducing the number of grant programs and making the federal grant system more manageable. The political implications of full federal financial responsibility for income maintenance programs would be akin to those for many categorical grants. Specific national purposes would be at stake, and the congruence of interest among the Congress, the bureaucracies, and the program interests would be felt. Political support at the federal level, very likely, would be strong.

As budget situations tighten and loosen from time to time, Congress should consider these budget consequences as it restructures the grant system. Support for these programs usually is high because of the congruence of concerns among the Congress, the bureaucracy, and the program interest groups and beneficiaries.

Block grants would be expected to lead to somewhat less expansion of public spending, since their role is to encourage minimum standards and supplement well-established functions of government, rather than to aggressively stimulate new activities.

Revenue sharing would be expected to have little overall effect on recipient government spending, or perhaps even a dampening effect. This arises from the lack of requirements for either program innovations or matching funds, combined with the acceptability of tax reductions by receiving governments.

Experience with existing block grants and the general revenue-sharing program indicates that the federal government is less likely to fund these two types of programs as generously as it does the categorical programs. The national purposes simply are not as direct and compelling in the more generalized programs. Hence, their political support is not as strong.

State administration of broad block grants also raises the significant question of who will gain and who will lose benefits under the new program. Unless the beneficiary pattern is clearly specified in the block grant legislation—often not a desirable practice—potential winners and losers will fight it out at the state level to determine how funds will be distributed below the state level. This can be a time-consuming and politically difficult process, but it is inherent in the flexibility normally accorded through the block grant mechanism. Some general federal guidelines may be stated in the block grant legislation, and perhaps even a few earmarks for critical eligibility categories may be established, as was the case with LEAA. Yet, too much of this will have the affect of recategorizing the block grant. Congress should carefully consider and clearly state its intent in this regard.

BUDGET CONSEQUENCES OF GRANT TYPES

Categorical grants have tended to support relatively high and increasing levels of public funding for the programs involved. Their very purpose is to stimulate new activity and to require added expenditures by recipient governments (matching funds).

CONCLUSION

The administration's current proposals for restructuring the grant system, although mostly described under the heading of "block grants," really fit the revenue-sharing model much more closely than ACIR's model of block grants. Most rely upon public information reports about planned and actual use of funds, biennial audits by the states, no matching or maintenance of effort requirements, and certifications by grant recipients that discrimination will be prohibited in the disbursement of aid funds. These provisions are very similar to those in the existing general revenue-sharing program.

The design features of those "block grants" included in the Senate and House omnibus reconciliation bills reflect everything from the "special revenue sharing" approach to the enlarged categorical grant device. Clarity and consistency are not among the hallmarks of these bills, and questions legitimately may be raised regarding the national purposes and pattern of accountability reflected in them. Hopefully, the approaching final phase of the reconciliation process will clarify these crucial questions.

11

BLOCK GRANTS AND STATE DISCRETION
A Study of the Implementation of the Partnership for Health Act in Three States

George D. Greenberg*

ABSTRACT

This article examines the use of federal funds provided to state health departments under a grant consolidation of eight previously categorical health programs in Michigan, Pennsylvania, and Alabama in a comparative context. The primary question addressed is why the three states chose to describe their allocations of funds within the total health department budget differently, and what political, administrative, and bureaucratic factors explained the differences. Although certain factors were found to be at work in all states (e.g. each had an incentive to concentrate the reported use of federal funds to simplify federal audits) these factors combined with circumstances unique to each state to produce different expenditure patterns. After examining the experience of three states, general hypotheses are developed. For example, it is hypothesized that more volatile changes in allocations will result from grant consolidations in policy areas which do not address basic service needs. Finally the decision-making process with respect to block grant funds is characterized as one in which a small group of professionals determined allocations autonomously with relatively little input from interest groups or other actors within state government; nevertheless, the external political and administrative environment severely limited the possibilities of realistic choice in each of the three states studied.

---

* I wish to thank the National Center for Health Services Research which supported this study under grant HS 01495. I am indebted to the state health department officials in Alabama, Michigan, and Pennsylvania who made this research possible. I would also like to thank Leonard Robins, Janet Shikles, William Schmalzreid, Bruce Vladeck, John Kingdon and Robert Baitty for comments on an earlier draft. Of course the views expressed are my own and in no way reflect the positions of the Department of Health and Human Services.

From George D. Greenberg, "Block Grants and State Discretion: A Study of the Implementation of the Partnership for Health Act in Three States," 13(2) *Policy Sciences* 153-181 (1981). Copyright 1981 by Elsevier Scientific Publishing Company. Reprinted by permission.

Introduction

This study addresses the question of why state allocations of federal dollars differ. In the American system states are not merely administrative units of the federal government; they reflect independent constellations of political and economic forces. If states (and localities) are delegated resources by the federal government to perform tasks, they will attempt to use those resources and perform the tasks in ways which ease their own political, administrative, and economic problems. The actions they ultimately take may or may not coincide with the original federal goals and intentions. Thus new federal dollars and new federal programs enter a unique policy environment in each state. The purpose of this research is to describe that environment in three states and to understand the manner in which it affected state decisions on the use of health block grant funds.

The Partnership for Health Act

The block grant created by The Partnership for Health Act [Section 314(d) of the Public Health Service Act] was chosen for study because of the wide budgetary discretion it allows states. The Partnership for Health Block Grant was created in 1966 as part of the strategy known as 'Creative Federalism'. Congress combined the formula grant which supported general health department activities with eight other state formula grants to form a block grant for community health services. [1]. The general goal of the 314(d) block grant was to encourage program innovation and shifts by states away from previous funding patterns established under the earlier system of categorical grants.

The block grant gave considerable flexibility to states in the allocation of Public Health Service Act 314(d) funds. Compared with the previous system of nine categorical grants, funds could be shifted freely from one use to another without violating federal requirements that a minimum had to be spent in each area. The likelihood of funds lapsing because a state could not spend them appropriately in a given area diminished. Nevertheless, the 314(d) block grant was not entirely free of federal controls despite the added flexibility given states. Regulations prohibited the use of block grant funds for air pollution, inpatient hospital care, research or capital expenditures. Fifteen percent of the total was earmarked for mental health. In 1967 a requirement was added that 70% of all 314(d) expenditures support direct delivery of services (hereinafter called the 70% requirement). However, direct delivery of services was interpreted to mean state health department activities which supported delivery of services such as analyzing pap smears in the state laboratory. Therefore a pass through of 70% of the funds to local health departments was avoided. At the same time, state reporting requirements were reduced. Instead of submitting annual reports, states simply had to assure that records would be available for audit if necessary.

At the same time that the Partnership for Health created the section 314(d) block grant, state comprehensive planning agencies [314(a) agencies], sub-state regional planning bodies [314(b) agencies], consolidated project grant authorities [314(e) funding], authority to train health planners, and authority to exchange Public Health Service personnel with state health department personnel were established. The different provisions of the act were designed to work in tandem to reorient the Public Health Service and states away from narrow disease categories and towards comprehensive and integrated community services. The funding flexibility provided by the block grant was to help implement the plans of the state planning [314(a)] agencies. Federal funding of innovative 314(e) projects was to be approved by the 314(a) agency, and state experimentation would be encouraged as the innovative 314(e) projects would be spun off to the states who were expected to continue to fund them under an expanding 314(d) block grant.

Unhappily this ambitious agenda for reorienting the health care delivery system soon fell apart. Political support for categorical health programs where beneficiaries can be specifically identified is much greater than the support for less visible general health services which benefit the entire population. As a result 314(d) funding did not expand as envisioned. New categorical programs for rat control, migrant health, drug addiction, etc. were passed by the Congress instead of expanding the 314(d) block grant. Funding for the 314(e) project grants did expand somewhat, but federal officials paid little attention to state 314(a) agencies when deciding what projects within a state to accept. The state health departments which usually controlled the 314(d) funds also paid little attention to the 314(a) agency plans even when the 314(a) agency was itself within the health department. The fact that the entire 314(d) block grant typically constituted less than 10% of a health department's budget, meant that there was little incentive for a state to attempt to plan comprehensively across the bulk of the remaining federal categorical grants.

The Partnership for Health collapsed in part because of some inherent tensions in its basic design. The Partnership rested on an assumption that states would act as instruments of the federal government in achieving national goals. Thus it was assumed that state administrative flexibility in the use of funds would serve federal goals of innovation, experimentation, and attempts to reform the health care delivery system. But states are separate political entities with their own goals and are not simply administrative arms of the federal government. When goals diverged federal officials used the project grant authorities they controlled to fund their own priorities, and the states used the administrative flexibility under the block grant to further their own internal needs and not necessarily the experimentation, innovation, and rationalization of health services the federal government desired. What was left of the original concept from the state point of view was the increased administrative flexibility afforded them by the consolidation of the former categorical grants.

Recent legislative changes have not affected this basic flexibility; however, over time, federal officials became less supportive of 314(d) expenditures as it was perceived to serve state goals and not their own agendas. The Nixon administration tried to eliminate 314(d) funding and the Carter administration has also recommended its elimination in order to help balance the FY 81 budget [2].

Selection of States

The states chosen for study were Michigan, Pennsylvania, and Alabama. Michigan was chosen because the original research site was Ann Arbor. Pennsylvania and Alabama were chosen to afford meaningful comparisons with Michigan. Selection of Alabama allowed variation among sampled states in the formal control over health department decisions given to the state medical society. In Alabama, by state cnstitution, the state medical society selects 12 of 15 members of the State Committee on Public Health which directly oversees the health department. In Pennsylvania there is an advisory health board of 12 members appointed by the governor, five of whom must be physicians. In Michigan there is an eight-member Public Health Advisory Council appointed by the governor, with no required physician representation. Selection of Pennsylvania allowed variation among sampled states in the extent to which the county health department formed the basic unit of delivering public health services within the state. In Pennsylvania only seven of 67 counties have their own health departments. District and regional offices of the state health department provide for the public health needs of the other 60. By contrast, in both Michigan and Alabama, the county health department is the basic unit of service delivery. Although the plan of analysis called for the political and administrative factors which influenced the allocation of 314(d) funds to emerge inductively from the research, the composition of the state medical society and the structure of local health services delivery were a priori felt to be important factors.

Several other factors entered into the final selection of states. A southern state was chosen because the need for public health services is greater in the South where there are fewer private physicians. For example, in 1971, 22% of pregnant women in Alabama received their pre-natal care from the county health department [3]. States were also selected on the basis of an analysis of per capita health and hospital expenditures regressed against per capita income in order that a high health spending, an average health spending, and a low health spending state could be selected after having controlled for state wealth. Alabama was high, Michigan average, and Pennsylvania low. The purpose of the regression was to assure that states which had made conscious decisions to emphasize or de-emphasize public health were chosen, and that variations in state performance did not simply reflect such mundane factors as relative state wealth. States were not chosen on the basis of their performance in allocating funds under 314(d). Nevertheless, each states allocation of 314(d) funds turned out to be unique.

Plan of Analysis

The effect of allocating 314(d) funds to one function in the state health department budget is to free state funds for use in other areas. Given their "fungibility" in state health department budgets, it is difficult to trace the "true impact" of federal funds [4]. In effect, the Partnership for Health constituted a general revenue source supporting health department budgets and not a program. Thus it can most accurately be said that if 314(d) funds constituted 10% of the total health department budget, it constituted 10% of the support for every health department program within the budget, no matter where the health department reported 314(d) expenditures to the federal government. As Leonard Robbins has argued, it is impossible to tell from examing state budget data alone whether changes in where 314(d) funds were reported had any real relationship with observed changes in overall health department budgets [5].

Nevertheless, interesting questions remain and important analysis can be done. A few states budget 314(d) funds separately [6]. Moreover, other states do report that 314(d) funds support certain activities and not others. It is important to ask why states chose to claim that 314(d) supported certain activities especially when these reports differ from state to state. Thus the question the allocation of 314(d) raises is why states have chosen to label certain expenditures as supported by 314(d) when their true fiscal effect is general support of the entire state health department budget. A second question is whether the creation of a block grant led to greater change in the overall state health department budget and greater innovation that might have occurred in the absence of the block grant.

In this report, the extent to which states show 314(d) funds in high priority areas of the state health department budget is analyzed by comparing the rate of budget growth of programs in the state's 314(d) plan with overall health department budget growth. Moreover, inferences can be made as to whether changes in 314(d) funding for a program are related to the budget priorities of the health department by comparing changes in the overall growth of a program with changes in the amount of 314(d) funds reported in that program. For example, if 314(d) funding in an area was increasing at the same time that the overall budget for that area was declining, an inference might be drawn that 314(d) funds were reported by the state in support of a low priority budget item. Such analysis was conducted for each state studied to the extent that the availability of state expenditure reports and budget documents allowed.

Based on the experience of three states, hypotheses will be developed about the implementation of The Partnership for Health Act in all 50 states and more generally about the process of implementation in an intergovernmental system characterized by state political autonomy and administrative discretion.

Michigan

Overview

The 314(d) funding pattern in Michigan is a series of relatively small and complex shifts over time within a funding pattern which is relatively stable. The shifts occur because of the need to meet federal audit requirements and the need to maximize the budget given the relatively detailed appropriations made by the state legislature. Program innovation has occurred in a few areas. The needs of state health officials in dealing with the legislature, administrative convenience in meeting federal requirements, and the generation of federal matching funds appear to be more important in the aggregate in determining 314(d) allocations than budget priorities placed on individual programs. The dominant effect of the block grant appears to have been to give state health department officials the administrative flexibility to accommodate these pressures.

Michigan's 314(d) funding process

314(d) dollars are not kept budgetarily separate within the state and individual expenditures cannot be traced to the 314(d) dollar. As 314(d) funds enter Michigan they are commingled with other state and federal funds which support state health department activities in the state treasury. Nevertheless, the annual appropriation's bill for the state health department shows 314(d) funds in support of broad program areas (e.g. maternal and child health), and reports filed with the federal government are even more specific.

The state legislature sets a total expenditure level for each specific program and within programs for objects of expenditure (e.g. salaries) in the health department's budget. Although specific sources of federal funds such as 314(d) are shown in the annual appropriation's bills in support of specific programs, the health department can decide at the end of the fiscal year to shift programs from state funds to federal funds and vice versa as long as the total dollar amount budgeted for each program is not exceeded. Since other federal funds are restricted to categorical uses, only 314(d) funds and state funds can be shifted around from program to program at the time of an audit so that federal matching and other requirements can be more easily met. For example, if a federal auditor questioned whether a 314(d) expenditure for an environmental health program met the 70% requirement, the health department could list the 314(d) funds as supporting a different program which clearly met the requirement and then show state funds from that program in support of the environmental program.

Since 314(d) funds constituted only 3.4% of Michigan's health department budget in FY 1975, it is relatively easy to shift funds around in this manner to meet audit requirements. According to one Michigan health department official, "You can label something a 'd' expenditure depending upon what the 'feds' wanted to see. As long as 314(d) is only 3% of the budget we're home free. We could even show the 314(d) dollar supporting some programs to the 'feds' and other programs to the state (legislature) with no problems given the system" [7]. Thus the allocation process in Michigan is essentially a labeling process in which certain programs are given a 314(d) label because that helps the state pass an expenditure audit.

Michigan's 314(d) allocations — Interview and Documentary Evidence

Although 314(d) funds have not shifted dramatically from their previous uses under the preceding categorical programs, the added flexibility has led to some changes in the use of funds.

According to a 1970 state report on 314(d) expenditures, "Since past categorical funds were directed at priority targets, it is not reasonable to expect that there would be significant redirection of funds and with only a marginal (dollar) increase, substantial new programming cannot be supported." [8]. Close examination of apparent shifts in the budget often reveal that the activities supported remain the same [9].

Nevertheless, several instances of the use of 314(d) flexibility can be found in Michigan to fund innovative new programs or to institute new procedures which would have been difficult under the old categorical funding system. In FY 1968-1969 314(d) money was redirected to purchase rubella vaccine to begin a vaccination program which was subsequently continued with state funds. In FY 1970-1971 Michigan began funding "regional teams". Rural health departments had trouble attracting full-time health officers and personnel, thus the state began hiring personnel and assigning them to these counties. Since the health officials hired might be engaged in the entire range of health department activity, the old categorical funds could not have been used for this purpose. Michigan also combined 314(d) funds with maternal and child health funds into a new formula distribution within the state to support county health department services. Under the older system of categorical grants, there were a series of small project grants to local health departments for various categorical purposes. These project funds were replaced by a single distribution of funds to all county health departments on a per capita basis. The accounting requirements for each of the former categorical programs would have made this impossible.

Despite the examples of the flexible use of 314(d) funds just cited, the Deputy Director of Michigan's Health Department warns against attempting to infer the priorities in Michigan's health department budget by observing which items received increases in 314(d) funding. According to him (1) federal administrative requirements, (2) the need to free state dollars to match in other federal programs, (3) the relative glamour of programs, and (4) the need to support certain basic research and development efforts play at least as important a part in determining which programs receive increases in 314(d) funding as health department budget priorities.

(1) *Federal administrative requirements.* The 70% requirement had to be satisfied. At

one point Michigan considered putting all its 314(d) money into the laboratories to ease reporting burden. According to the Deputy Director, "the auditors would come in and ask where is your 314(d)? And we could say it's all in the laboratory. That is a direct service to people and here is the output, here's the performance measure and its all locked up. There is the package. Now go on home" [10]. Although this option was rejected, the state laboratory does receive a large percentage of Michigan's 314(d) allocation.

The 70% requirement also causes shifts in what are labeled 314(d) expenditures at the end of the year in the process described above. According to the Deputy Director, "Now kidney disease has been a kind of back-up in this, if you will, because it's about a $500,000 program, it's a state program, but it is sometimes included in the program mix that is called the "d" part of the plan. So you have $500,000 in direct services which if an auditor comes through and contests anything else you can say the contested program was not supported in part by 314(d) and you can say the kidney program was. If they say regulation of local water supplies is not a direct service to people, OK, then we'll move the 314(d) out of that and place it under the kidney program. So you just can't draw heavy programmatic conclusions out of this. It's dangerous" [11].

(2) *The need to free state dollars to match in other federal programs.* The need to show greater amounts of state dollars in certain programs to match federal categorical grants affects health department budgeting. In FY 1972-1973 approximately $ 400 000 of 314(d) funds were rebudgeted from the Detroit Maternity and Infant Care (DMIC) Project to the state laboratory because it was learned that additional state funds in the DMIC budget could generate federal matching funds under Title IVA of the Social Security Act. The money was re-allocated to the laboratory for the reasons just explained.

(3) *The relative glamour of programs.* It is sometimes desired to show certain state expenditures as supported by "d" funds because of federal officials' interest in them. According to one official, "We supported the Community Health and Social Services Project in Detroit on 314(d). That was shortly after the big burning (the Detroit riots) and talk about that sort of thing was good. In addition, I think some areas such as migrant health have a particular amount of visibility and pizzazz at the national level" [12].

The relative glamour of programs also affects budgetary politics with the state legislature. One strategy is to budget relatively high glamour programs on 314(d). Once a budget level has been established the 314(d) money might be switched elsewhere and the state legislature might continue to support the program on state dollars if it is relatively glamourous. The opposite ploy is to gain state legislature support for an unpopular program by saying it will primarily be supported on the federal 314(d) dollar. The legislature is not taken in by this claim since it appropriates both state and federal money to all programs simultaneously, establishing a total expenditure level for each. However, it may make it politically palatable to show a less popular program supported by federal dollars. According to a health department official. "Well we show them the 'd' is there and we put those federal dollars there to cough up more general funds. We're honest about it but it makes it easier for the policy makers if they're uncertain and say, well, if you can put this on federal, OK. But if we've got to go scratch then we're going to look at it more closely" [13].

(4) *The need to support basic research and development.* Basic R and D efforts for which it is otherwise difficult to obtain political support are sometimes supported on 314(d). An ongoing survey project designed to better identify local health department needs, called ECHO, was supported on 314(d) in Michigan.

Although examples were cited of the use of 314(d) funds to support high priority and innovative projects in Michigan, the flexibility provided under the block grant appears to be primarily used to solve the particular political and administrative problems health department officials face when accounting for expenditures to federal auditors or when drawing up their budget presentation for the state legislature.

Michigan's 314(d) funding allocations — budget data analysis

Table 1 lists the distribution of Michigan's 314(d) funds across budget areas for FYs 1967-1973 and 1975. It reveals a large degree of stability over time. In FY 1969, the five budget areas of statistics and vital records, local health, salaries to support state staff in disease control, general environmental health, and the state laboratories received 45% of all 314(d) funds. In FY 1973 these same areas received 57%, although there were shifts among them. Despite these shifts and some additional shifting into and out of the area of maternal and child health, "d" funds apparently remained in the programs in which they began.

There were 11 program areas in the Michigan budget which received 314(d) funds in FY 1967-1968 and 13 in FY 1972-1973 listed in Table 2. One area funded in FY 1967-1968 was not funded in FY 1972-1973 and there were three new areas the latter year. Of 14 areas of expenditure with "d" funding in either FY 1968 or FY 1973, eight experienced total budget growth greater than the average growth of the state health department (see Table 2). 314(d) funds were more likely to be spent on high priority budget areas than on low priority budget areas, but the margin of difference is hardly better than chance.

Large shifts in 314(d) dollars do not necessarily reflect what is happening to the total budget of a program receiving 314(d) funds. For example, consider the Detroit Maternity and Infant Care Project discussed earlier. The total budget for DMIC remained at about $ 2 million despite the removal of $400,000 in 314(d) funds in FY 1973. The "d" funds were replaced by state funds in order to match federal funds available under Title IVA of the Social Security Act. In the same year, the "d" funds were rebudgeted to the state laboratories. However, the total budget for the laboratories increased only approximately $ 100 000 as state money was removed to provide state matching dollars to DMIC.

Pennsylvania

Overview

The tale of 314(d) funding is easiest to tell for Pennsylvania because change has been minimal and one criterion of allocation, administrative convenience, dominates. The 314(d) dollar continued to support direct delivery of services at a time when the stated priority of the director of the health department was to reduce Pennsylvania's involvement in the direct delivery of services. The flexibility gained under the block grant appears not to have been very much used in Pennsylvania.

Pennsylvania's 314(d) funding process

314(d) expenditures are not separately identifiable in Pennsylvania's fiscal management system. 314(d) funds are commingled with other state and federal funds in the state's general fund. The legislature then budgets to the health department in broad categories. The FY 1974-1975 appropriations to the health department were made in 16 appropriations, and one of these, for general government operations, in the amount of $ 25 175 000 accounted for 45% of total health department allotments. A second appropriation for school health examinations accounted for an additional 25%.

There is no specific legislative allocation of 314(d) funds to health department programs although 314(d) funds are calculated into the total amount of incoming revenues available for health department activities. 314(d) allocations are determined in a post hoc fashion by health department personnel for purposes of accounting to the federal government. Certain state programs are labeled as receiving 314(d) support. Programs identified in previous years as supported by 314(d) are usually chosen again.

The accounting system of the health department is weak. Expenditures are calculated across programs, after the fact, by means of a time sample of regional and central health department personnel. Once the total amount spent on a program is calculated by means of the time sample, the percentage of a specific program supported by 314(d) can also be determined. 314(d) expenditures represented 4.3% of Pennsylvania's total health department budget in FY 1975.

Pennsylvania's 314(d) allocations—Interviews and Documentary Evidence

There has been minimal change in Pennsylvania's allocation of 314(d) funds recently. The state maintains a system of district health department offices organized into a regional system to provide basic health services to 60 of Pennsylvania's 67 counties. The allocation of the bulk of Pennsylvania's funds both in FY 1967 (the last year of the old categorical system) and in FY 1975 supported this system of direct services in the regions. The local services supported by 314(d) were in adult programs (primarily alcoholism, venereal disease, tuberculosis, heart disease, and cancer).

TABLE 1

Michigan's Distribution of 314(d) Funding Across Programs
[Selected Fiscal Years (in thousands)]*

Budget Category	1966	1967	1968	1969	1970	1971	1972	1973	1974	1975
Admin. Services	190.7	264.7	305.6	326.0	352.7	531.0	566.2		588.7	
Executive	5.0	16.2	22.5							
Management services	70.0	44.0	48.0	72.6	58.6	63.7	63.7			
Statistics and vital records	64.3	92.4	88.0	101.9	127.8	291.7	323.0			
Information and education	50.0	112.0	147.0	151.5	166.4	175.6	179.3			
Medical Care Admin.	14.0									
Community Health	1211.8	1093.4	1311.6	1659.5	1353.0	1161.1	1175.0		1177.6	
Admin. and consultant services	764.2	481.9	528.9	769.3	748.9	657.6	577.9		708.3	
Salaries	(372.3)	(143.0)	(188.0)	(200.0)	(138.0)	(146.3)	(66.0)		(708.3)	
Local health	(308.9)	(338.9)	(338.9)	(476.0)	(476.0)	(461.3)	(461.3)			
Special projects				(93.3)	(133.0)	(50.0)	(50.0)			
Training	(83.0)									
Disease control	437.0	611.6	782.7	890.2	333.9	287.8	287.8		287.8	
Salaries	(437.0)	(281.0)	(265.0)	(340.0)	(134.0)	(86.0)	(87.8)			
Chronic disease project		(330.5)	(426.7)							

Measles				(90.0)				
TB					(371.0)			
Renal					(167.1)			
Direct federal projects						(200.0)	(200.0)	
Ghetto health						100.0	14.8	100.0
Regional teams						170.0	200.9	209.3	181.5
Maternal and Child Health				297.0	400.0	400.0		
Environmental Health	101.2	101.2	178.0	320.1	428.1	476.8	497.0	435.1
General environmental health		4.2	38.1	148.8	150.1	170.9	178.5	115.7
Salaries	15.5			(61.8)	(63.1)	(67.2)	(70.4)	(7.6)
Migrant health				(87.0)	(87.0)	(103.7)	(108.1)	(108.1)
Water supply			32.2		21.0	22.0	22.4	143.9
Wastewater			102.8	34.7	98.5	115.9	121.0	
Radiological health	63.5	97.0		136.6	158.5	168.8	175.5	175.5
Technical and support services			5.0					
Laboratories	124.8	130.5	138.2	167.8	197.7	208.6	508.5	508.5
Total	1642.5	1584.0	1934.0	2770.0	2731.0	2278.0	2747.0	2710.0

* Missing information sometimes results in the sub-breaks not adding to the totals.

Sources: Account Structure by Sources of Funds, Michigan Department of Public Health, for FYs 1967 1968 to 1972 1973; FY 1975 data taken from Health Program Reporting System. Inventory of Programs and Expenditures Publication No 36. Association of State and Territorial Health Officers. Nov. 1976. p. 27.

TABLE 2

Michigan Budget growth FY 1967 1968 to 1972 1973

Total. Health Department Budget 314(d) FY 1967 1968 = $49 680 000   % Growth = 43%
1972 1973 = $71 153 000

Budget Category	1	2	3(%)	4(%)	5	6(%)	7	8(%)	9(%)	10(%)	11(%)
Administrative Services											
Executive	166.8	16.2	10	1	131.1	21	0	100	0	10	0
Management services	366.2	44.0	12	2.8	711.0	94	63.7	44	9	3	2.3
Statistics and vital records	593.4	92.4	16	6	1321.5	123	323.0	249	24	8	12
Information and education	333.8	112.0	34	7	420.4	26	179.3	60	43	9	7
Community Health											
Administrative and consultative services	2786.5	481.9	17	30	7910.0	184	887.2	84	11	6	32
(Salaries)	(368.4)	(143.0)	39	9	(458.7)	25	(66.6)	53	15	24	(2)
(Local health)	(2331.0)	(338.9)	15	21	(2828.2)	30	(461.3)	36	16	1	(17)
(Other)	(86.3)	(0)	0	0	(4623.1)	NA	(359.3)	NA	8	8	(13)
Disease control	8283.8	611.5	7	39	7665.8	7	287.8	53	4	3	10
(Salaries)	(1022.4)	(281.0)	27	18	(1026.3)	0	(87.8)	69	8	19	(3)
(Other)	(7261.4)	(330.5)	5	20	(6659.5)	1	(200.0)	39	3	2	(7)

216

	1	2	3	4	5	6	7	8	9	10	11
Environmental Health											
General environmental health	483.7	4.2	1	0.2	1405.7	191	178.5	4350	13	12	6
Water supply	189.9	0	0	0	404.5	113	22.4	NA	6	6	1
Wastewater	123.1	0	0	0	460.4	274	121.0	NA	26	26	4
Radiological health	405.6	97.0	24	6	991.8	144	175.5	81	18	-6	6
Laboratories											
Laboratories	1184.3	130.5	11	8	2083.5	76	508.5	290	24	13	19

1 = Total FY 1968 budget for this category.
2 = 314(d) allocation to this category in FY 1968.
3 = The percentage of the category supported by 314(d) in FY 1968 = 2/1.
4 = The percentage of the FY 1968 314(d) grant allocated to this category = 2/total 68 d.
5 = Total FY 1973 budget for this category.
6 = Percentage growth in this category = (5 − 1)/1.
7 = 314(d) allocation to this category in FY 1973.
8 = The percentage growth in 314(d) funds allocated to this category = (7 − 2)/2.
9 = The percentage of the category supported by 314(d) in FY 1973 = 7/5.
10 = The change in the percentage of the category supported by 314(d) funds = 9 − 3.
11 = The percentage of the FY 1973 314(d) grant allocated to this category = 7/total 73 d.

Sources: Account Structure by Sources of Funds, Michigan Department of Public Health, FYs 1967 1968 and 1972 1973.

Since there has been practically no change in the justification of 314(d) funding, the primary question is why? The answer essentially is administrative convenience. Past justifications of 314(d) have passed federal audit and any changes might bring a challenge. According to an earlier account, "The reason for this (lack of change) was that there was no additional state money available to replace the federal funding for the former categorical grants, and second, that it would be an accounting nightmare to report 314(d) expenditures if they were spread across many programs. The state had purposefully, therefore, restricted the identification of 314(d) support to a set number of programs to reduce problems which could be encountered in reporting or a potential audit" [14].

Given Pennsylvania's lack of strong health department accounting system, we can understand why labeling a large number of programs as receiving "d" support would produce an accounting "nightmare" for the state. The weak accounting systems explain why 314(d) funds are allocated to only a few "safe" program areas.

For example, maternal and child health activities supported with federal Title V funds do not also receive 314(d) support in Pennsylvania. Pennsylvania officials argue that Congress did not "intend" 314(d) money to be used for maternal and child health activities since they had already established a separate categorical program in that area. Equally to the point, however, is the fact that Pennsylvania runs its entire maternal and child health effort on federal dollars. The state matching money is comprised of two separate state programs. Title V Crippled Children's funds are matched by $ 4 million in expenditures at the state home for crippled children in Elizabethtown. Title V Maternal and Child health funds are matched by the approximately $ 15 million the state spends on its school health program. In order to show 314(d) expenditures on maternal and child health activities, an accounting system would have to be developed to determine which school health activities and which activities at the state home were matching the federal Title V dollar and which were matching 314(d) since a single state expenditure cannot be used to match in two different federal programs. Since such a system does not exist and would be expensive to develop, it is easier for the state to allocate 314(d) funds to programs which do not receive other federal funds.

A similar problem occurs in programs which generate federal re-imbursements or user fees. For example, 314(d) funds are not used to support the state's vital statistics effort because over 50% of the expenditures for that program are generated by fees. Although the remaining 50% could be shown as state match for 314(d), it would have to be shown that federal 314(d) dollars and the user fees were not supporting the same activities.

Other characteristics of Pennsylvania's health department further restricted the allocation of 314(d) funds. In 1971 a separate Environmental Protection Agency was established in Pennsylvania and all environmental programs were transferred from the health department. In 1967 three environmental programs were included in Pennsylvania's 314(d) plan. The loss of environmental programs meant there were

TABLE 3

Pennsylvania's Distribution of 314(d) Funding Across Programs
[Selected Fiscal Years (in thousands)]

Budget Category	1966 1967	1971 1972	1972 1973	1973 1974	1974 1975
Administration	288.4	205.0	118.0	115.0	115.0
Bureau management	118.4	61.0			
Procurement			100.0		
Central services and stores				100.0	100.0
Planning, evaluation, research	25.0				
State Civil service	6.4				
Educational activities	131.9	86.0			
Sponsored professional training	6.7	18.0	18.0	15.0	15.0
Administration of the regional system		40.0			
Adult Chronic Diseases	434.1	245.0	245.0	295.0	275.0
Administration	28.8				
Heart disease	79.0	30.0	30.0	(?)	(?)
Cancer	156.0	105.0	105.0	(?)	(?)
Chronic illness and arthritis	170.3	110.0	110.0	(?)	(?)
Adult Chronic Respiratory Disease	169.8	927.9	978.0	1068.0	1053.0
General		84.0	84.0	(?)	(?)
TB control	169.8	223.9	249.0	(?)	(?)
TB-allegheny		225.0	225.0	(?)	(?)
TB-phila.		395.0	420.0	(?)	(?)
Laboratories	76.8	64.0			
Local Health	957.3	2105.0	2198.8	2017.6	2073.5
Environmental	141.1				
Radiological health	111.9				
Sanitation	14.2				
Environmental safety	14.0				
Maternal and Child Health	114.7				
Dental	40.9				
Children's cardiac program	73.8				
Other	148.0			30.0	
Licensing				30.0	
Public health nursing	10.6				
Home health services	87.4				
Communicable disease	40.0				
Drug control	10.0				
Total	2330.32	3546.9	3539.8	3528.1	3516.5

Sources: Budget tables provided by the Budget Section of the Division of Business Management, Pennsylvania Department of Health for FY 1971-1972 to 1974-1975. Data for FY 1966-1967 obtained from Report of Expenditures for Health Services, Budget Bureau Form No. 68-R408, submitted by Pennsylvania to the Public Health Service 15 Aug. 1967.

fewer programs supported on state dollars with which to demonstrate the 314(d) dollar had been matched and earned.

A large part of Pennsylvania's tuberculosis program consists of the provision of inpatient hospital care, but 314(d) regulations prohibit expenditures in this area. 314(d) regulations required that expenditures could only be made in jurisdictions or programs where minimum merit system standards had been met. Parts of the Office of the Director of the Health Department were under patronage in Pennsylvania.

According to the business manager of the health department, there are only two considerations in preparing the 314(d) budget, "Can we meet the 70% requirement, and can we provide a state dollar to mach every federal dollar. Other than that we don't really concern ourselves" [15]. The Director of the Bureau of Administrative Services states the health department was trying to reduce the number of areas in which 314(d) funds were justified in order to simplify requirements and because it was "administratively inconvenient" to put 314(d) money in "all those places" [16].

Because of the desire to minimize the auditing and administrative burdens on the state, 314(d) expenditures have been justified year after year in the same programs with little change. The bulk of the old categorical dollar was spent on direct services by state health department and regional office staff in adult disease programs. The elimination of environmental programs from the department in 1971 increased the concentration of 314(d) dollars in these programs and inflationary pressures pushed further towards consolidation. (Given inflation, fewer programs and activities can be supported for the same amount of money.) When 314(e) tuberculosis money was folded into the block grant, Pennsylvania continued to channel the same amount of money to the tuberculosis projects in Philadelphia and Pittsburgh which were formerly supported by the "e" money. The tuberculosis projects have become a permanent part of the chronic respiratory disease portion of the 314(d) state plan. The result has been described as the "recategorization" of the (d) block grant funds in Pennsylvania. According to Janet Shikles, "In the case of Pennsylvania where the (d) funds have been associated or reported as supporting specific programs for such a long time, administrative flexibility - one of the supposedly key features of the block grant - may have been lost" [17].

Pennsylvania's 314(d) allocations – budget data analysis

Table 3 lists the distribution of 314(d) funds across program areas for FY 1966-1967 and FYs 1971-1972 to 1974-1975. Table 3 shows a more stable funding pattern than Table 1 showed for Michigan. The vast majority of 314(d) funds can be found in four program areas: the system of district and regional services of the health department (local health), state level support for adult chronic disease programs, state level support for adult chronic respiratory disease programs, and state administration. These four items comprised 77% of the 314(d) total in 1967, 98% in FY 1971-1972, and 100% in FY 1974-1975. In 1967 there were a total of 21 budget areas receiving "d"

TABLE 4

Pennsylvania Budget Growth FY 1971-1972 to 1974-1975
(in thousands)

Total Health Department Budget FY 1971-1972 = $57 593 000   % Growth = 39%
1974-1975 = $80 057 000

314(d) FY 1971-1972 = $3 546 900
FY 1974-1975 = $3 516 500

Budget Category	1	2	3	4	5	6	7	8	9	10	11
Bureau management	481.6	61.0	13%	2%	406.0	16%	0	100%	0%	-13%	0%
Public health education	342.6	86.0	25%	2%	465.0	35%	0	100%	0%	-25%	0%
Training	18.0	18.0	100%	0.5%	15.0	17%	15.0	17%	100%	0%	0.5%
Central services and stores	708.7	0	0%	0%	915.0	29%	100.0	NA	11%	11%	3%
Adult chronic diseases	513.4	245.0	48%	7%	383.0	-25%	275.0	12%	72%	24%	8%
Adult chronic respiratory diseases	1777.2	927.9	52%	26%	2875.0	62%	1053.0	13%	37%	-15%	30%
Administration of the regional system	213.3	40.0	19%	1%	337.0	58%	0	100%	0%	-19%	0%
Laboratories	1225.1	64.0	5%	2%	2161.9	72%	0	-100%	0%	-5%	0%
Local health	8080.8	2105.1	26%	59%	11817.5	48%	2073.5	1%	18%	-8%	59%

1 = Total FY 1972 budget for this category.
2 = 314(d) allocation to this category in FY 1972.
3 = The percentage of the category supported by 314(d) in FY 1972 = 2/1.
4 = The percentage of the FY 1972 314(d) grant allocated to this category = 2/total 72 d.
5 = Total FY 1975 budget for this category.
6 = Percentage growth in this category = (5 - 1)/1.
7 = 314(d) allocation to this category in FY 1975.
8 = The percentage growth in 314(d) funds allocated to this category = (7 - 2)/2.
9 = The percentage of the category supported by 314(d) in FY 1975 = 7/5.
10 = The change in the percentage of the category supported by 314(d) funds = 9 - 3.
11 = The percentage of the FY 1975 314(d) grant allocated to this category = 7/total 75 d.

Sources: General Fund Budget Statement for the State of Pennsylvania FYs 1971 and 1975. Budget tables provided by the Budget Section of the Division of Management, Pennsylvania Department of Health.

support, in FY 1971-72 there were thirteen, and in FY 1974-1975 there were only five [18].

Of nine areas supported with "d" funds either in FY 1971-1972 or FY 1974-1975, only four were growing as rapidly as the average growth of the total state health department budget. Of these four, only one showed absolute growth in 314(d) funding and this growth was only 13% (see Table 4). Two of the four "growth" areas did not receive any "d" funding in FY 1974-1975. 314(d) funds appear to be flowing out of high priority areas into relatively low priority areas in Pennsylvania.

Alabama

Overview

Over a 10-year period Alabama's reported use of 314(d) funds has changed dramatically. From an even distribution of funds across 15 program areas, Alabama now concentrates 67% of its funds in one program and only funds four. The new 314(d) funding allocations are primarily determined by political criteria although the desire to reduce accounting and auditing requirements also helps explain some of the consolidation.

Alabama's 314(d) funding process

Unlike Michigan or Pennsylvania, Alabama's 314(d) funds are kept within a separate account within the health department's financial management system. Individual expenditures are charged to this account which shows a beginning and ending balance for each fiscal year. The decisions on which expenditures to charge to this account are made by state health department officials, and state legislative involvement in 314(d) funding and budgeting is minor. Nevertheless, as in Michigan and Pennsylvania, the way the legislature budgets for the health department affects health department officials' calculations of how to show and account for 314(d) expenditures.

The Alabama legislature budgets all federal funds by a single general authorization to spend federal funds each fiscal year. A separate limit on the expenditure of federal Medicaid funds is usually passed. By contrast appropriations of state funds are quite detailed. There are usually over 30 separate appropriations of state funds to the health department. Legislative failure to consider or appropriate federal funds in any detail gives state health department officials flexibility in deciding which programs and activities will receive federal support. However, the other side of the coin is that there is no state commitment to continue expenditures if federal funds are withdrawn. 314(d) funds represented 4.8% of Alabama's total health department budget in FY 1975.

Alabama's 314(d) allocations – Interview and Documentary Evidence

Over 67% of Alabama's 314(d) dollar in FY 1975 went to support the system of eight branch laboratories attached to the central state laboratory. Another 25% supports the formula distribution to county health departments to support basic local health services. Nevertheless, the total amount of "d" funds going to the counties has declined in recent years as all available funds have been shifted into the branch laboratories.

There are several reasons which operate in conjunction to determine this allocation of funds. As in Michigan and Pennsylvania, the 70% requirement and the need to account for federal funds are important considerations and both the branch laboratories and the formula distribution meet audit requirements. According to the Director of the Health Department, "We try to keep the 314(d) funds 'clean' since we have to account for them. If an expenditure is vague such as administrative overhead, we try to keep that on state money" [19]. As in Michigan and Pennsylvania, inflation has also meant that fewer activities can be supported on a 314(d) grant of constant size. However, funds have primarily been concentrated in the branch laboratories in order to (1) make sure there is minimal disruption to high priority state and local health department activities if federal funding for 314(d) ends, and (2) place in jeopardy a program state health department officials have been politically unable to cut back. In order to understand these reasons, the character of state health department-local health department relationships and the impact of the 314(d) block grant upon those relationships must first be described.

Alabama supports a relatively large percentage of county health department budgets by means of its formula distribution to county health departments. In FY 1974-1975, federal and state funds accounted for 25% of total funds (excluding fees and reimbursements) received by county health units in Alabama compared with approximately 12% in Pennsylvania and 6.5% in Michigan [20]. Jefferson County (Birmingham) received only 8% of its budget from non-county funds in FY 1971, but a small rural county (Lowndes) received approximately 60%. 314(d) funds constituted approximately 10% of the formula distribution to county health departments in FY 1975. Thus, in a rural Alabama county, a significant percentage of the total budget consists of 314(d) funds.

The total county health department budget for a rural Alabama county might only be $ 25 000. This might allow for one nurse and one sanitarian. At the county level, all available funds are commingled to support two or three positions. If only $ 2000 in federal funds were lost to such a county, the remaining dollars would not be enough to continue to support the full-time nurse and sanitarian. The county might be threatened with the loss of even basic health services. If the remaining funds were rebudgeted to another use, the nurse or sanitarian could not be rehired if federal funds again became available.

Since the state legislature budgets only state funds, loss of federal funds could only be restored if the legislature passed a supplemental appropriation for that purpose. In recent years the legislature has said they would not do this although their resolve has not been tested since Congress restored proposed cuts of 314(d) in Nixon administration budgets. Nevertheless, the uncertainty of continued federal 314(d) funding combined with the posture of the legislature has created a dilemma for Alabama state health officials.

As federal funds became more uncertain, the state health department began to seek out program activities in which to concentrate 314(d) dollars where the impact would not be too damaging if 314(d) funds were lost since it was not clear the state legislature would replace them. On the other hand, 314(d) funding could not be withdrawn too abrubtly from the formula distribution without severely disrupting the program of basic services given the relative dependence of rural Alabama health departments on state and federal funds. The result has been a moderate decline of the flow of 314(d) dollars into the formula distribution in the last few years as increases in state and local support for county health departments took up some of the slack. 314(d) funds were channeled out of other areas and into the state health department system of eight branch laboratories. For many years the state health department had been urging consolidation of branch laboratory services into the central laboratory, but had been blocked by local political pressures. By funding a low priority program on 314(d), a cutback in federal funds would help solve the health department's political problems in trying to close the branch laboratories. Moreover, the branch laboratories possessed a local constituency that would create pressure on Alabama's congressional delegation to restore 314(d) funds. Concentrating the funds in the branch laboratories had the additional advantage of simplifying audit requirements. According to an Alabama health department official, "Since the branch laboratories met the 70% local requirement, we decided this would be the best place to allocate 314(d) funds. If the "feds" cut the money out, it would be the place where the most squawking would be. It was the place we'd have a power base to make an appeal to the Congress. On the other hand, you can't put the money in areas where you would really have a disastrous effect on public health in the state if the funds were eliminated, but you have to put it in areas of high visibility. It's hard tightrope to walk . . . By putting the funds in the branch laboratories, a cutback would solve our political problems, but at the same time we're nervous because if the 314(d) were to go we'd also have to cut back major services instantly" [21].

As a result Alabama's health department officials feel they have lost flexibility under 314(d) [22]. The exigencies of dealing with the legislature, the counties, state fiscal arrangements, and past political agendas create so many constraints that officials feel the branch laboratories are the only place they can safely allocate 314(d) funds. Thus they feel "locked in". These perceptions are ironic since it is the very flexibility created by the removal of the old categories that allowed concentration of block grant funds in the branch laboratories to begin with.

TABLE 5

Alabama's Distribution of 314(d) Funding Across Programs
[Selected Fiscal Years (in thousands)]

Budget Category	66 67	67 68	68 69	69 70	70 71	74 75
County Health Departments	468.0	424.4	535.7	481.4	481.4	327.0
Formula	(235.0)	(?)	(531.4)	(466.0)	(466.0)	(327.0)
Direct assistance	(233.0)	(?)	(4.3)	(15.4)	(15.4)	(0)
Laboratories	48.4	101.5	399.3	485.6	602.6	876.2
Central Lab.	(?)	(?)	(?)	(32.8)	(94.1)	(?)
Branch Labs.	(?)	(?)	(?)	(452.8)	(508.5)	(?)
Administration	12.7	52.5	45.6	10.0	20.0	88.4
Fringe Benefits	25.5	37.0	44.9	53.7	57.3	
Tuberculosis	52.9	57.3		439.9	221.2	
Casefinding	(?)	(?)		(?)	(191.2)	
Drugs	(?)	(?)		(?)	(30.0)	
Drugs	50.4	62.3	119.8	66.2	58.2	25.6
Heart	(27.8)	(42.3)	(40.0)	(26.0)	(29.2)	(25.6)
Other	(22.6)	(20.0)	(79.8)	(40.2)	(29.0)	(0)
Environmental				18.4	18.4	
Construction	11.5					
Nursing	21.5					
Cancer	59.3	40.0				
Dental	9.5	18.1				
Chronic	65.4	128.8				
Licensure	4.9					
Radiological Health	39.8	36.2				
Inspection		106.1				
Total	869.8	1064.2	1145.3	1555.2	1459.1	1317.2

Source: Data for FY 1966 1967 obtained from Report of Expenditures for Health Services, Budget Bureau Form No. 68-R408, submitted by Alabama to the Public Health Service; data for FY 1967 1968 to FY 1970-1971 obtained from copies of federal reports on file in the finance division of the Alabama Health Department; FY 1974 1975 data taken from Inventory of Programs and Expenditures, Publication #36, Health Program Reporting System, Association of State and Territorial Health Officers, Nov. 1976, p. 6.

Alabama's 314(d) Allocations — Budget data Analysis

Table 5 lists the distribution of Alabama's 314(d) funds across progam areas for FYs 1967 - 1971 and FY 1975. Table 5 shows an increasing concentration of 314(d) funds over time. In 1967 the laboratory system received only 5% of total categorical expenditures. In FY 1975 the laboratories received 67%. The state formula distribution to county health departments still continues to receive 314(d) funds; however, after an initial increase that share has declined from a high of 54% of all 314(d) funds in 1967 to 24% in 1975. The number of budget areas receiving 314(d) support declined from 15 in 1967 to four in 1975. Funds were evenly distributed across the 15 areas in 1967; but by 1975 funds were highly concentrated, with the branch laboratories and

TABLE 6

Alabama Budget Growth FY 1969 1970 to 1974 1975
(in thousands)

Total Health Department Budget FY 1969 1970 = $22 919 850   % Growth = 42
                                 1974 1975 = $32 536 211

314(d) FY 1971 1972 = $1 555 300
       FY 1974 1975 = $1 317 178

Budget Category	1	2	3	4	5	6	7	8	9	10	11
Administration	872.6	10.0	1%	.5%	1048.2	20%	88.4	784%	8%	7%	7%
Central and branch labs.	1297.4	485.6	37%	31%	2472.1	90%	876.2	80%	35%	2%	67%
Drugs (heart, diabetes, VD)	267.1	66.3	25%	4%	?	?	25.7	156%	?	?	2%
Heart	(?)	(26.0)	(?)	2%	(25.7)	?	(25.7)	0%	100%	?	(2%)
Fringe benefits	322.7	53.7	17%	3%	?	?	0	100%	0%	17%	0%
Country health departments	1896.4	481.4	25%	31%	3557.8	88%	326.9	32%	9%	16%	25%
Environmental health	951.6	18.4	2%	1%	3312.5	250%	0	100%	0%	2%	0%
Tuberculosis	585.2	439.9	75%	28%	1487.2	154%	0	100%	0%	75%	0%

1 = Total FY 1970 budget for this category.
2 = 314(d) allocation to this category in FY 1970.
3 = The percentage of the category supported in 314(d) grant allocated to this category = 2   1.
4 = The percentage of the FY 1970 314(d) grant allocated to this category = 2 total 70 d.
5 = Total FY 1975 budget for this category.
6 = Percentage growth in this category = (5   1) 1.
7 = 314(d) allocation to this category in FY 1975.
8 = The percentage growth in 314(d) funds allocated to this category = (7   2) 2.
9 = The percentage of the category supported by 314(d) in FY 1975 = 7 5.
10 = The change in the percentage of the category supported by 314(d) funds = 9   3.
11 = The percentage of the FY 1975 314(d) grant allocated to this category = 7; total 75 d.
? = Reporting category dropped

Sources: FY 1974 1975 data taken from Inventory of Programs and Expenditures, Publication No. 36, Health Program Reporting System, Association of State and Territorial Health Officers, Nov. 1976, p. 6; FY 1969 1970 data obtained from copies of federal reports on file in the financed division of the Health Department and the annual expenditures report of the health department for FY 1969 1970.

the formula distribution to county health departments accounting for 92% of the funds.

There are eight areas of expenditure that received 314(d) funding in either FY 1970 or FY 1975 (see Table 6). Of these, budget growth can be calculated for five from state financial reports. Of these, four experienced budget growth greater than the state health department average. However, only one, the state laboratories, showed an absolute growth in "d" funding. Two of these areas did not receive any 314(d) funds in 1975. 314(d) funds appear to be flowing out of higher priority areas in Alabama into the system of branch laboratories. Although the laboratory system as a whole grew more rapidly than the state health department average, we know from interviews that "d" funds supported the low priority branch laboratories and not the high priority central laboratory.

Comparative Analysis of State Experience Under 314(d)

In both Pennsylvania and Alabama, the number of programs receiving 314(d) support declined over time; in Michigan the number increased slightly. In Pennsylvania and Alabama funds were flowing from high priority to low priority areas but in Michigan they were flowing to high priority areas. In Michigan, there was evidence that administrative flexibility was used to fund new priorities and respond flexibly to problems; there was no such evidence from Pennsylvania and Alabama. Both Michigan and Pennsylvania exhibited continuity over time in the programs supported on 314(d) although there was a slight dispersion in Michigan and a marked concentration in Pennsylvania. By contrast, in Alabama, a program receiving 5% of the total in 1967 received 67% in 1975.

Certain factors appeared to be at work in all three states; however, combination with unique factors at work in each state produced different results. The desire to reduce exposure of state expenditures to federal audit produced a tendency to concentrate 314(d) funds in all three states. However, this tendency was overridden in Michigan by equally powerful incentives resulting from the character of the state budget process. The effects of inflation on a constant 314(d) dollar also produced tendencies towards concentration in all three states. The tendencies were overridden in Michigan. The impact of the old categories was also strong in all three states. Only Alabama drastically changed prior funding patterns.

Differences in state budget processes help to account for these differences. Michigan's legislature set the state health department budget in a relatively detailed manner establishing an overall spending ceiling for each program regardless of whether funding was from state or federal funds. Pennsylvania's legislature also set total program levels but appropriated in a few broad accounts. Alabama's legislature presented a mixture, appropriating state funds in a relatively detailed manner like Michigan and appropriating federal funds all at once in a single amount. Michigan health department officials had an incentive to use proposed 314(d) allocations to assure that both state and federal funds were budgeted in the proper places to both maximize federal matching funds and to obtain future legislative support for health department priorities. These incentives did not exist in Pennsylvania and Alabama because of the differences in legislative treatment of the health department budget. Tendencies towards the concentration of 314(d) funds were therefore partially countered in Michigan. On the other hand, legislative failure to rebudget federal funds and create a total expenditure ceiling for each health department program meant that there was no legislative commitment to a total program level if federal funds were withdrawn in Alabama. The uncertainty led state health department officials to concentrate 314(d) funds into areas where a cutoff would cause minimal damage to the state's overall program.

Variation in state accounting and financial patterns also helps to account for differences. In Michigan, 314(d) dollars were transferred out of the Detroit Maternity and Infant Care Project in order to generate increased federal match by replacing federal dollars with state dollars. There would have been no comparable opportunity in Pennsylvania since the state's maternal and child health program is run entirely on federal dollars while state matching dollars are kept separately in two distinct programs. Moreover, Pennsylvania's accounting system could not distinguish which of these program activities might be used to match federal maternal and child health dollars and which used to match elsewhere even if this were not the case. Thus 314(d) funds in Pennsylvania were allocated to program areas where there were no other sources of federal funds.

Variation in state health department relationships with county health departments also accounts for differences. In Alabama, historic funding patterns meant that health departments in poor, rural counties were heavily dependent on state and federal aid to support basic services. As a result, uncertainty of federal funding which affected all states, had unique impacts in Alabama.

Finally there were unique factors in each state which helped to determine outcomes. Pennsylvania had undergone a reorganization in 1971 which stripped the health department of all environmental programs. This generated further impetus to consolidation in Pennsylvania, as many of the programs formerly supported on 314(d) were removed [23]. In addition, there were fewer opportunities compared with Michigan to switch 314(d) funds across programs, since there were fewer programs.

Each of the factors identified at work in all three states combines with factors unique to each state to produce a pattern of reported 314(d) expenditures which is also unique. Without prior knowledge of the variables, their strength, and the unique ways they combine within a state to produce an environment of choice for health department decision-makers, it would have been impossible to predict the impact of the creation of the 314(d) block grant in any state.

Hypotheses

Although it is impossible to generalize on the basis of three cases, the following hypotheses concerning the allocation of discretionary block grant funds can be derived from the experience of Michigan, Pennsylvania, and Alabama. These hypotheses may be tested against the experience of other grant consolidations or in other states for 314(d).

(1) The flexibility created by the formation of a block grant will not produce a large shift of funds to high priority areas or to new innovative programs.

(2) The flexibility created by the formation of a block grant will produce funding shifts to accommodate the political and administrative needs of state agency officials which will take priority over the desire to encourage new innovations or to meet new programmatic needs.

(3) The smaller the size of the block grant in relationship to total agency funding, the more likely block grant funds will be used to satisfy political and administrative constraints and the less likelihood they will be allocated to high priority areas.

(4) The creation of a block grant will lead to the concentration of funds into fewer and fewer program areas as long as some federal restrictions on their use remain requiring audits.

(5) If the funding level of a block grant remains constant, inflation will produce tendencies to concentrate funds.

(6) Allocations under a block grant change slowly because the need for basic services does not go away. Therefore, patterns of funding will be more volatile in program areas which do not address basic service needs.

(7) Uncertainty of continued block grant funding will reduce allocations of block grant funds to high priority areas within the budget.

(8) The allocative flexibility obtained from the creation of block grants is gained at the cost of uncertainty of future funding resulting from the loss of political support for undifferentiated and unidentified expenditures. Uncertainty of funding creates administrative problems as severe as the problems solved by the ending of categorization.

Conclusion

The primary effect of the Partnership for Health Act was to give states greater administrative flexibility in the use of funds, but greater administrative flexibility did not necessarily result in program innovation or the rebudgeting of funds to high priority areas as needs arose [24]. Nevertheless, a survey of 50 state health departments indicated that health officers ranked the flexibility of the block grant in meeting new priorities or needs as they arose as the most valued component of the block grant and administrative convenience a distant second [25]. Although states may value their hypothetical ability to re-order budget priorities, they do not appear to be doing so in fact, at least in three states.

314(d) funds were more often shifted for reasons of administrative convenience or political advantage than for reasons of program priority. If 314(d) funds could be legally applied to almost the entire range of health department activities (except for the relatively few restrictions mentioned above), they were functionally equivalent to state dollars. If state and federal dollars were virtually interchangeable, an increase in 314(d) funding for a program did not necessarily indicate a state priority, unless total funding for the program was increasing more rapidly than in other health department programs. When this test was applied, it appeared that only in Michigan were 314(d) funds flowing towards higher priority programs and, even in Michigan, political and administrative factors appeared to outweigh budget priorities in determining allocations.

Several explanatory factors were found to work in conjunction to explain the pattern of reported uses of 314(d) funds in three states. These included (1) state budgeting and funding processes, (2) funding patterns between state health departments and county health departments, (3) uncertainty of future federal support, (4) the desire to simplify administrative and accounting arrangements, (5) remaining federal restrictions, and (6) historic patterns of the use of funds within the state health department.

A relatively small group of state health department decision-makers in each state controlled and understood the reported and actual uses of 314(d) money. This group included the director of the health department and his or her deputy, the financial officer, and one or two other members of the management staff. Specific involvement by the governor's office or the legislature was minimal although the degree of detail in which the legislature considered the overall health department budget affected the decisions of this relatively small group of people [26].

Although a small group of decision-makers was relatively autonomous in the allocations of block grant funds they chose to make, their decisions were heavily influenced by constraints established by the external environment on their choices. Thus the dependence of rural county health departments in Alabama on outside aid, the lack of state legislature commitment to continue federal funds, and the threatened cutbacks in federal 314(d) support in Presidential budgets combined to create a context of decision-making which was very different from the environment of choice in Michigan or Pennsylvania. Similarly the loss of environmental programs in a prior reorganization coupled with weak state accounting procedures and the manner in which other programs such as maternal and child health were financed combined to create a unique context of choice in Pennsylvania. In Michigan, legislative involvement in setting a total spending ceiling for a large number of detailed programs gave health department officials incentives to use 314(d) allocations to influence the manner in which these ceilings were set. These patterns dictated by the external environments differ from state to state, hence the different patterns in the reported uses of 314(d). This remains true even though there were factors such as the uncertainty of federal funds which operated in all 50 states.

Decision-makers in any organization are faced with problems which they need to solve. If an outside observer wishes to understand the uses to which such decision-makers put discretionary funds or resources, the first step is to understand the problems they face in conducting their daily business. These problems are set by the necessity to deal with external actors who control the resources needed to accomplish agency missions. Available discretionary resources are used to help ease these relations. Thus the first step in understanding the allocation of discretionary funds and the implementation of federal programs in autonomous state environments is to learn the particular problems faced by the decision-makers who control these choices in each.

Notes

1. The eight other categorical programs were for cancer, chronic illness and the aged, dental health, heart disease, home health services, mental health, radiological health, and tuberculosis.
2. P.L. 94 63 passed 29 July 1975 and P.L. 95 626 passed 10 November 1978 amended section 314(d). The principal changes of the former were to drop state matching and maintenance of effort requirements and to bring 314(d) planning provisions into conformity with the state health planning structure established under P.L. 93 641. The principal changes of the latter were to develop an allocation formula within states in lieu of the 70% requirement and to shift to a uniform national reporting system. This study covers the period FY 1968 1975 and therefore is not affected by these changes.
3. Maternal and Child Health Services of State and Local Health Departments, FY 1972, DHEW Publication No. (HSA) 74 5801, MCHS Statistical series No. 7, Table 5.
4. Fungibility refers to the ease in which funds can be transferred among and within state and local budgetary accounts. For a discussion of how fungibility makes difficult the tracing of the fiscal effects of federal aid, see R. Nathan, A. Manvel and S. Calkins (1975). *Monitoring Revenue Sharing*, Washington, D.C.: Brookings, pp. 7 9 and 181 192.
5. Leonard Robins (1974). "The Conversion of Categorical Into Block Grants: A Case Study of the 314(d) Block Grant in the Partnership for Health Act," Ph.D. dissertation, Department of Political Science, The University of Minnesota, pp. 107 109.
6. *The Partnership for Health Act: Lessons from a Pioneering Block Grant*, Advisory Commission on Intergovernmental Relations Report No A-56, January 1977, pp. 44 45. Two states claimed that federal and state matching funds were administered as a discrete program on a 50 state questionnaire.
7. Personal interview, 17 February 1977.
8. "Progress Report on the Use of PHS 314(d) Grant Funds for Health Services in Michigan 1969 1970," Michigan Department of Public Health, p. 1.
9. According to the Review of Michigan Plan for Health Services, 27 June, 1969, ". . . the major shift in funding involves moving some funds from special projects in the Bureau of Community Health to the General Environmental Health Program in the Bureau of Environmental Health. In the current fiscal year these funds are being used largely for local environmental health special projects; in the forthcoming year, these funds will be used for established environmental health programs which are local in focus. While the funds have shifted in the budget, neither the plan nor the character of the expenditure have been altered". (see p. 2).
10. Personal interview, 3 June, 1975.
11. Personal interview, 3 June, 1975.
12. Personal interview, 3 June, 1975.
13. Personal interview, 3 June, 1975.
14. Janet Shikles, "Examination of the Use of section 314(d) funds by State and Local Agencies," Report issued by the Office of Planning, Evaluation and Legislation, Health Services Administration under Contract No. SA-5994 75, Department of Health, Education and Welfare, July 1975, pp. 38 39.

15 Personal interview, 20 June, 1975
16 Personal interview, 23 June, 1975.
17 See Note 14, p. 44.
18 Adult chronic diseases and adult chronic respiratory diseases are each counted as one program in each year (see Table 3).
19 Personal interview, 23 July, 1975.
20 Pennsylvania has only seven county health departments in 67 counties. State aid represents 12% of their budgets.
21 Personal interview, summer, 1975
22 Alabama is only one of two states which stated that relationships with local health departments had deteriorated and one of only three states which reported less discretion than under the previous system of categorical grants on the Advisory Commission of Intergovernmental Relations' survey of 50 states. Both answers capture the frustration of state health officials with the instability of 314(d) as a funding source for local health services.
23 Michigan also established a separate environmental agency in 1974 but only air pollution and wastewater programs were transferred to it. Water supply, restaurant inspection, sanitation, occupational safety and health and other programs were left with the health department. Thus the environmental area could remain a high priority area within the budget of the Michigan state health department.
24 In a previous study Leonard Robins classified funding changes that states attributed to the flexibility afforded under 314(d) and found only 14 to be substantial. Further analysis revealed that there was little relationship between states which had reordered priorities and states which reported the old categorical system of grants had created a great deal of hindrance to them. See Note 5, p. 178.
25 ACIR, *The Partnership for Health Act*, pp. 80 83.
26 Ten states reported that the governor played a major role in the allocation of 314(d) funds and 14 states reported that their appropriations committees played a major role. (See the ACIR study, pp. 52 53). Michigan reported that both the governor as well as the appropriation's committees played major roles; Pennsylvania and Alabama did not. However, in Michigan, the interview evidence indicates that the influence of the governor and the legislature results from overall determination of program by program expenditure limits. Neither actor appears to specifically allocate 314(d) funds.

12

"REFORMING" THE FEDERAL GRANT-IN-AID SYSTEM FOR STATES AND LOCALITIES

Richard P. Nathan

THE title asigned for this paper is "Reforming the Federal Grant-in-Aid System for States and Localities." The first word of the title, "reform," is an uplifting word which means to shape anew. It is typically used to describe proposals, or a program of proposals, predicated on the assumption that whatever is being reformed is fundamentally flawed, in need of basic change.

I would not have picked this title for myself. I do not believe the federal aid system is fundamentally flawed, despite the din of organizations and experts who obviously do not agree.

A Dynamic System

The U.S. federal aid system is constantly changing; the whole history of federal fiscal flows and for that matter of American federalism is one of fluidity and change. Some observers consider this to be one of the problems. Indeed, few experts on the current system of federal grants-in-aid to state and local governments have a good word to say about the frequent changes in the amount and character of federal grant programs. It is therefore important to state clearly at the outset that I believe the dynamism of the federal aid system is one of its strengths. This dynamic quality has significance not just for intergovernmental fiscal relationships, but for the American governmental system as a whole.

The current period provides a good illustration. The American public is undergoing an historic shift in its attitude toward government, demonstrating a strongly felt desire to reduce both its size and its influence. In my reading, the turning point for federal aid was not the 1980 election as much as the eastward movement of the sentiment expressed by California voters in June 1978 to reduce local property taxes.

This is by no means the only time that fundamental change has taken place in the American federal aid system. The Great Society programs of the mid-sixties provide another example. The changes made under President Nixon's New Federalism program, largely as a reaction to perceived weakness of the Great Society programs, also involved a substantial change in diretion of domestic policy.

The Values of Federalism

There is an intellectual dilemma here. The adaptability of the American intergovernment aid system embodies the Madisonian belief in the desirability of the active involvement of many factions (Federalist 10). Probably the most enduring characteristic of the American political system is its openness and competitiveness. Anybody can play government and almost everybody does at one time or another. The number of players and their intensity of feeling produces, said Tocqueville, "a picture of power, somewhat wild perhaps, but robust, and a life liable to mishaps but full of striving and animation."[1]

Yet this competitiveness of the U.S. political system, reflected in the constant pulling and hauling that results in policy change, is not compatible with two important political values that underlie the programs of many of those who would "reform" the federal aid system. The first is *rationality*, as reflected in proposals for allocating functional responsibilities on a basis that reflects a coherent theory as to the most logical or efficient arrangement for governmental institutions and operations. The second value is *stability*, as reflected in demands for less frequent shifts in policies relating to the ways in which domestic government is organized and operates. The essential problem is that the pluralism sought by Madison and responsiveness to change praised by Tocqueville are not necessarily consistent with these

---

From Richard P. Nathan, "'Reforming' the Federal Grant-in-Aid System for States and Localities," 34(3) *National Tax Journal* 321-326 (September 1981). Copyright 1981 by the National Tax Association-Tax Institute of America. Reprinted by permission.

two values of many reformers.

Another political value needs to be added to this picture—the Jeffersonian concept of *localism*. The planners' desire for rationality and stability at the center of the political system are not easily squared with diversity and opportunities for political self expression at the periphery. All of these political ideas—pluralism, flexibility, rationality, stability, and localism—can conflict with one another. Domestic policy making is a constant process of balancing these ideas, as well as others.

Many advocates of reform of the federal aid system call for a "sorting out" of governmental responsibilities, overlooking the fact that we are constantly sorting out governmental responsibilities. There is no single sorting-out process for all times.

This is the perspective I want to highlight in this paper. Perhaps we should pass a law requiring a label on proposals for reforming the federal aid system like that on cigarette packs, to the effect that such proposals can be dangerous to the health of our political system.

Status of Federal Grants

President Carter's budget for fiscal year 1982 proposed $99.8 billion in federal grants to states and localities. Before the Stockman deluge, the reasonable expectation was that federal grants would go over the symbolic $100 billion mark in the coming year. The Reagan plan now envisions a reduction in federal grants to $86.4 billion.

This is $8.2 billion less in grant spending than is budgeted for fiscal 1981. If the administration's optimistic estimate of the inflation rate is used to adjust these figures, this reduction translates into a decline between 1981 and 1982 of over 17 percent in real spending for federal grants-in-aid to states and localities. The Reagan administration proposes even more sharply to reduce grants to states and localities for their own programs and services (that is, for other than welfare or entitlement programs); these would drop by about one-quarter in real terms from 1981 to 1982. The biggest cuts come in grants to states and localities for social programs. Grants for education, training and employment programs, and social services are projected to drop by 40 percent in real terms.

The Reagan program is indeed a radical shift for domestic policy. It also involves changes in the form of federal grants.

The Form of Grants

Reformers often state as a first premise that the federal aid system is unmanageable, and that aid programs have, in the word that is almost always used in this context, "proliferated." Again, some perspective is needed. I recently presented a paper that listed seven myths of the federal aid system.[2] One of the myths was that federal aid has been growing wildly. In fact, since 1978, when Proposition 13 was adopted, there has been a falling off in federal grants, as shown in table 1. The idea of cutting federal grants was not patented by the Reagan administration.

Another myth is that federal grants-in-aid have "proliferated" (that word again) like rabbits. The proliferation school of federal aid tends to count watermelons and peanuts in the same way: A huge program like Medicaid is considered equal to a small grant for summer camp safety or rat control.

True, the Carter administration introduced some new categorical programs,

TABLE 1
PERCENT CHANGE IN REAL FEDERAL AID TO STATE AND LOCAL GOVERNMENTS, 1960-1982

Five-Year Period Annual Average	Percent Change
1960–1965	7.1
1965–1970	12.3
1970–1975	8.6
Annual	
1975–1976	11.1
1976–1977	8.6
1977–1978	5.9
1978–1979	-1.6
1979–1980	1.3
1980–1981	-5.0 (est.)
1981–1982	-17.1 (est.)

Source: U.S. Office of Management and Budget

particularly in the youth employment field. Despite these developments, the fact of the matter is that more than one-third of all nonwelfare grant funds to states and localities currently is in the form of what the U.S. Office of Management and Budget classifies as "general-purpose" and "broad-based" grants. If one adds to that federal aid for public service employment administered through the CETA block grant system, general and broad-based grants acounted for over half of all nonwelfare grants in 1978. Nixon's brand of New Federalism is very much with us. The domestic program of the Nixon years was one of expenditure growth and quite fundamental changes in policy to achieve decentralization through the adoption of broader and less conditional grants. These changes have made their mark on our political and governmental system.

Another myth is that federal grants-in-aid, particularly "categorical" grants, are intrusive and tightly controlled by "pointy-headed bureaucrats." This is one of my favorites. I suggest that the best therapy for persons afflicted with this myth is to try to get information about what is happening under any one of your favorite federal grant-in-aid programs. The feds in many cases simply do not know. Not only do they lack sophisticated control mechanisms with which to implement grandiose plans, they simply do not know what is being done. Even if they have information about the allocations to major functional areas by recipient jurisdictions under a particular grant program, they are likely to have relatively little information about the specific programmatic uses of these funds and even less information about the effects and effectiveness of the dollars spent.

I do not mean to disparage either federal bureaucrats or state and local officials. I do not believe that federal bureaucrats can, or necessarily should, know how every federal grant dollar is spent. Under many programs the cost of finding out would be four or five times the amount spent on the progam. Again, this lack of central control reflects the essential character of our federalism. It is a highly pluralistic, open, and competitive system. Personally, I like it that way. I have only sympathy for federal officials called on the carpet by a congressional committee because they have limited knowledge of what happens under a particular federal grant program.

Four Approaches to "Reform"

Four approaches have been advocated for "reforming" the federal aid system. They are:
(1) The "Henny Penny School of federalism" which holds that the sky is falling, thus we urgently need to adopt basic institutional and programmatic reforms.
(2) The block grant approach, which began under Nixon and is now proposed to be extended into new—and I will argue, in some cases, inappropriate—functional areas.
(3) The turn-back school of federal aid reform, which is almost as old as money and equally hard to deflate.
(4) The idea that budget reduction is reform, which may indeed be the real Ronald Reagan position on the federal aid system.

(1) The Henny Penny School of Federalism

The first approach, the Henny Penny School of federal aid reform, is often reflected in reports written by Washington experts associated with organizations like the U.S. Advisory Commission on Intergovernmental Relations, in speeches by national political figures (most frequently Republican) and by planners at every level.[3] Such statements feature horror stories and favored inefficiencies; they call for basic changes, some of which may be good.

Many who share this perspective, for example, propose that we assign all welfare programs (that is, entitlement or income-transfer programs) to the national government. The word "assign" in this context is usually interpreted broadly. Conceptually, one can identify three dimensions of domestic programs—policy making, financing, and execution. Many reformers of the "Henny Penny" school propose giving the federal government responsibility for all three tasks.

In exchange for taking on responsibility for welfare, the national government would gracefully withdraw from other fields, which should, so the theory goes, be fully the responsibility of state and local governments. These include education, public safety, highways and mass transit, and public health. The arguments sound good and sometimes are made effectively. But we have to remember what Morton Grodzins taught us over twenty-five years ago. The federal system has always been a system of *shared* responsibilities. Daniel Elazar traced this thesis all the way back to the Articles of Confederation. The idea of some tidy rearrangement where some functions belong to the central government, some to the states, and some to local governments is attractive, but the world of government, not to mention the rest of the world, is more complicated than that.

I have been (justifiably) accused of overusing an idea attributed to H. L. Mencken; "For every human problem, there is a solution which is simple, neat, and wrong." Without going into more detail, I would just say that the "Henny Penny" school tends to reach for simplistic and holistic reforms of the governmental system that do not fit the values underlying this system. Madison lives: The idea of checks and balances and of achieving political equilibrium through extensive interaction (call it citizen participation) should not be jettisoned on the grounds that the modern world doesn't permit the luxury of sometimes slow and often untidy decision-making.

Take as an example the operation of local public transit systems. We are told that this is a local function if ever there was one. The Reagan budget revisions propose a five-year phase-out of federal aid for this purpose, which amounted to $1 billion in 1978. Yet operating grants from the federal government for public mass transit systems are one of the most important sources of external support to the nation's older urban centers, precisely those places that have the most serious fiscal, economic, and social problems.

So here is another value conflict—*equity* (often called "targeting" in the federal aid context) versus *rationality*. A strong concern for the former is the reason why big-city mayors, Ed Koch is particular, are upset about the proposed phase-out of transit operating subsidies. Intellectual tidiness and the planners' view of rationality are nowhere near as important to them a money—in this case money that is concentrated on the most distressed cities.

(2) Grant Blocking

Some reformers propose to cut the red tape connected with federal grants and reduce their proliferation by creating block grants. The first point that has to be made about grant blocking, alluded to earlier, is that we have already done a lot of it. That means there are not as many opportunities to do more. Grant blocking is seen by its proponents as a way of providing more scope for discretion to state and local governments. Our research and that of others has demonstrated that the community development block grant, for example, has achieved this decentralization purpose.[4]

The Reagan administration proposes to create additional block grants for social services (including health services) and education. The former, social services, involves a functional area in which we already have something that many people consider a block grant, namely the Title XX program. Moreover, the idea of a block grant for education is one that both the Nixon and Ford administrations tried to achieve, but came up short because of strong interest groups with deep feelings to the contrary.

The Reagan administration is also reported to be planning additional block grants for functions that I believe are inappropriate for grant blocking—welfare and possibly also medicaid and housing. The case against block grants in these areas is based on the premise that the federal government should have the predominant responsibility for setting policy for income-transfer or entitlement programs, though not necessarily for administering such programs. Central policy making is needed to achieve equity from state to state, although perhaps with different payment levels to reflect regional differences in costs of living and wages.

A brief discussion of the aid to families with dependent children (AFDC) program in this context helps to fill in the argument. A potential and very serious adverse effect of blocking the AFDC program would be to create competition among the states to reduce benefits for the most controversial group among the poor—working-age people with children. This might be a way to achieve the purpose of the McGill Commission report (the President's Commission for a National Agenda for the Eighties), which urged the adoption of policies that provide incentives to people to move from depressed to better-off communities, but the hardship to individuals that such a competition would cause suggests that this is probably not what the McGill what the McGill Commission had in mind.

In fact, such a policy would work in just the opposite way of what the McGill Commission envisioned. It would be likely to increase the incentives for people to locate or remain in the most distressed states and urban communities because these places tend to provide the relatively highest benefits.

The irony of the Reagan proposals for block grants in social services and education is that this technique is currently seen as a method for budget cutting. Eight years ago when the last big push for block grants was underway, it was assumed that the only way new block grants could pass was if extra funds were added as a "sweetener." *What was once an instrument (intended or not) of budget expansion is now regarded as a way to achieve budget reductions!*

(3) The Turn-back Approach

The turn-back approach has deep roots but absolutely no record of success. The idea here is that the federal government would relinquish specific tax resources, and in exchange state and local governments would pick up certain functions now funded in full or in part by federal grants. President Eisenhower, who was attracted by this idea, set up an "action committee" to study this subject; it came up with proposals that never got anywhere.

The turn-back approach to federal aid reform is a tricky one because the places that now pay the largest shares of the taxes that would be reduced or eliminated are not always the same places that have the greatest needs for the services that would no longer be federally aided. The net result is that this approach is pretty much a dry hole. Few people are talking about it seriously at this time, which is a good thing.

(4) The Budget Cutting Approach

A final way to change the federal grant system is simply to cut federal grants. This is what is happening now. However, the rationale given by budget cutters applied primarily to the condition of the federal budget. Demographic pressures on the social security system, the desire to increase real levels of defense spending, and high interest rates on the federal debt are seen as leaving no other options except to cut fiscal subventions to state and local governments, if federal spending it to be significantly reduced.

Studies conducted at the Brookings Institution and Princeton University on the effects of federal grants (both of individual programs and case studies) suggest that the most fiscally distressed jurisdictions will be hardest hit by these federal aid reductions. These studies show that the most important variable for predicting the effect of federal aid on local finances is the fiscal condition of the recipient jurisdiction.[5] Fiscally hard-pressed jurisdictions tend to be much more dependent on federal aid than other governmments because they are more likely to use these funds for basic or primary services. Better jurisdictions, for various reasons, tend to use most of their federal aid for purposes that are clearly identified as federally supported. That way, local officials can escape with less politial responsibility should changes in federal grant levels or policies force them to eliminate or reduce the aided services.

It is ironic that although this type of change in the federal grant system is the one that is most likely to occur, it is the only one of the four options reviewed here that is not put forward as an instrument for correcting flaws in American federalism. Yet grant reduction is the subject of the hour. If it succeeds, it will have profound effects on American federalism and intergovernmental relations.

* * *

The lesson I draw from all of this is: Beware of simple solutions. Be careful in tampering with political institutions. Recognize the tradeoffs between democratic political values and rational or planners' values. Do not overlook the strength and resiliency of the political system of which federal grants-in-aid are now so intrinsically a part.

This is not to say that changes should be avoided. But, because of the way the political system works, in order to achieve change, one is often tempted to dramatize the problems that are felt to require it. The natural tendency is to overdramatize. For some liberals interested in federal aid reform, this temptation has become a trap. They have been blind-sided by the administration's domestic budget cuts, which skillfully, but only partially, have been justified as encompassing ideas that can help to relieve the widely advertised (I would say overadvertised) flaws and problems of the American federal aid system.

FOOTNOTES

[1] As quoted by Martin Diamond in "The Ends of Federalism," *Publius*, Fall 1973, vol. 3, no. 2, Center for the Study of Federalism, Temple University. I am especially indebted to Diamond for his excellent interpretive writing on American federalism.

[2] "Federal Grants-in-aid: How are they Working?" in *Cities Under Stress: The Fiscal Crises of Urban America*, Robert W. Burchess and David Listokin, eds., The Center for Urban Policy Research, Rutgers University, 1981.

[3] The mention here of the ACIR in reference to the "Henny Penny" school of federalism obliges the author to offer some documentation. Several examples are given in this footnote.

The quarterly periodical, *Intergovernmental Perspective*, published by the ACIR, featured articles in the Winter 1980 issue on the subject, "A System Overloaded." The cover graphic was a Rube Goldberg-type cartoon depicting an apparatus combining the Capitol dome and a human heart with tubes and paraphernalia attached suggesting great complexity and confusion. The lead article stated that the tax expenditure movement "reveals much about the breakdown of the processes of representative government." The final paragraph of the article, referring to the new decade of the 1980s, stated that "the most disturbing trend involves the future direction of representative government." The article concluded: "considering the dramatic changes that have occurred over the past 20 years, and the current domestic and international challenges confronting the nation, the restoration of trust in representative goverment is crucial to the course of federalism in the years ahead."

Writing in the same journal in the Fall 1979 issue, other ACIR staff members referred to the federal government as "Leviathan run amuck." One article asserted, "Evidence of systematic overload is everywhere in Washington (and across the land)."

Similar hyperbole is reflected in an ACIR statement presented at the Council of State Government Annual Meeting in Las Vegas in 1980. The statement referred to "the current network of intergovernmental relations [as] dangerously overloaded, to the point that American federalism's most trumpeted strengths—flexibility and workability—are criticallly endangered."

ACIR reports abound in lists of problems with concluding statements, such as "These, then, are some of the major trends that have emerged during the past decade, and they combine to support the summary generalization that never has the maze of fiscal, functional, regulatory and administrative links between and among the federal government, the states, and all substate units been more complex, costly, and convoluted than it is now." *Summary and Concluding Observations, The Intergovernmental Grant System: An Assessment and Proposed Policies*, Washington, June 1978, A-62, pp. 67–68.

Writing about the literature on intergovernmental relations, political scientist Thomas J. Anton has identified what he calls the "new professionals of despair," for whom, "the leading issue is no longer 'how intergovernmental relations work' but 'why intergovernmental relations fail.'" Anton associates a number of ACIR publications with this point of view. He maintains that "few of the writers who express global judgements of despair pay much attention to the large number of detailed, empirical investigations of governmental interactions." Thomas J. Anton, "Intergovernmental Change in the United States: Myth and Reality," (January 1980, processed), pp. 4–5.

[4] See, for example: Richard P. Nathan and others, *Block Grants for Community Development*, 1977, and Paul R. Dommel and others, *Decentralizing Community Development*, June 1978. (Both reports are listed in the appendix to this paper.)

[5] See the list of publications on these studies contained in the appendix to this paper.

13

BLOCK GRANTS FOR THE NEEDY
The Case of AFDC

Howard Chernick

Abstract

Changes in the federal program of Aid to Families with Dependent Children have been considered which would alter the program from one in which federal dollars match state and local contributions, to a program in which the federal contributions are fixed in the form of a block grant. A review of econometric evidence suggests that under a block grant scheme, the federal contribution must be substantially greater than under a matching grant if the program's beneficiaries are to receive the same level of benefits. If the federal government seeks to maintain benefits unchanged in real terms, the states' share of total welfare expenditures will decline.

Since the launching of the great society program in the 1960s, the federal government has generated hundreds of programs that have been targeted for the support of some narrowly defined category of recipients or activity, from grants for the construction of sewerage systems in rural areas to aid for the education of handicapped children. As of 1975, the Advisory Commission on Intergovernmental Relations counted a total of 442 such grants to state and local governments.[1]

The proliferation of categorical grant programs has generated widespread complaints of administrative complexity, program duplication, and unwarranted distortion of local priorities. In response to this dissatisfaction with categorical grants, considerable momentum has developed in support of a restructuring of the grant system, with increased emphasis on the use of block grants. Block grants occupy an intermediate position in the grant-in-aid system. They provide greater local discretion and certainty of funding than categorical grants, but unlike general revenue sharing they are still tied to some identified national problem, such as community development or social services for welfare recipients.

The growth of block grants in recent years has been significant. Between 1972 and 1978 federal grants-in-aid that were sufficiently

---

From Howard Chernick, "Block Grants for the Needy: The Case of AFDC," 1(2) *Journal of Policy Analysis and Management* 209-222 (1982). Copyright © 1982 by the Association for Public Policy Analysis and Management. Reprinted by permission of John Wiley & Sons, Inc.

broad to be classified as block grants increased by $8.5 billion, going from 8.4 to 14.7 percent of all federal grants.[2] One major program which has been considered for block grant funding is the Aid to Families with Dependent Children program (AFDC), and measures to that end have had considerable support in both houses of Congress. As I shall demonstrate, the block grant approach promises to generate a new set of issues and questions, which should be considered carefully in future AFDC proposals.

ADVANTAGES AND DISADVANTAGES OF BLOCK GRANTS Most block grants have the following basic design elements: Aid is authorized for a wide range of activities within a single functional area; the state or local governments that receive the grant identify problems and design programs according to their individual needs; there is a minimum of federal regulations and reporting requirements. Moreover, federal aid is distributed by statutory formula rather than on a project-by-project basis, with the maximum amount of aid to any eligible government strictly defined and the total federal outlay carefully limited. With few exceptions, recipients of block grants are not required to match federal aid with additional contributions of their own, or even to maintain their prior levels of expenditures on the aided activity. Finally, the grants are steered away from specialized agencies of state or local government toward units that serve general purposes, hence away from specialists toward elected officials and administrative generalists.[3]

Categorical grants, by contrast, usually target funds to a single activity such as the control of rodents or the training of librarians. Federal administrators exercise a much closer control over the design of the program and its execution. Most categorical grants are distributed on a project-by-project basis to eligible recipients, which often include agencies specialized in the specific activities and nonprofit organizations. However, aid under the largest categorical programs is allocated via statutory formulas. Though most categorical grants are strictly limited in total amount, two of the most important, AFDC and Medicaid, contain no such limits. Categorical programs are much more likely to require local matching or maintenance of local effort as a condition of grant receipt than the broader block grants.

The arguments for block grants are based on their decentralizing effect and their administrative simplicity. By reducing grant administration and compliance costs and by consolidating fragmented and frequently overlapping programs, block grants can increase the cost effectiveness of government expenditures. In addition, the greater funding certainty of the block grant promotes more rational planning. The increase in freedom of choice, and the shift in power toward elected officials can also alter spending decisions.* The result, it is contended, is to make programs more

---

*In the first two years of the Department of Housing and Urban Development's Community Development Block Grant, for example, less than 30 percent of the funds were used to finance activities previously supported by the categorical system.[4]

responsive to the needs and preferences of all the citizens of the locality, and to reduce the power of special interest groups.

In retaining some accountability for the use of funds, block grants still promote national objectives by providing for areas of general concern. Thus, according to the argument, they provide a useful complement to general revenue sharing, under which the government makes wholly unrestricted grants to lower levels of government. Moreover, block grants may be distributed by special allocation formulas that allow more precise targeting of grant funds to reflect special needs, for example in old industrial areas. Such differences in need cannot be captured adequately by a single formula, which must, of political necessity, be based on broad factors such as population and per capita income.

The weakness of the block grant approach is the weakness that always attaches to unguided local spending. Some of the benefits of local spending spill over into other spending jurisdictions. An obvious example would be public health programs to combat communicable diseases. Because the local government does not place sufficient value on the risks that such diseases would generate for nonresidents, too little will be spent on the programs. To correct for this underspending, according to the usual theory, a subsidy from a higher level of government is called for, at a rate determined by the importance of the spillover to other localities. By lowering the cost of the specific good or service, the grant provides a direct incentive for the local government to increase the provision of the good or service.

Where block grants are used, they may increase the resources available to the recipient government, but they do not provide any special incentive to increase spending on the good or service that generates the spillover; accordingly the block grant can simply be used to displace local spending. To be sure, the grant may be made subject to provisions that the local government must maintain its prior rate of expenditure. However, the effectiveness of such requirements diminishes sharply over time. The greater possibilities for displacement mean that the block grant is more likely to be used to increase programs other than the one generating the spillover, or even to support local tax relief. Viewed in this way, the block grant is inefficient. It may stimulate too little spending on the good generating the spillover, at too great a cost to the federal government. Problems such as these have contributed to the political instability of block grants. Programs which began on a block grant basis, as for example the Law Enforcement Assistance Program, have been encumbered over time with a series of restrictions and with the reimposition of categories within the block.

Another problem with the block grant is that the distribution of aid by broad formulas may not succeed in targeting resources to jurisdictions with the greatest needs. If need is defined in terms of very specific problems, such as the lack of sanitary sewerage systems, then the distribution criteria for the categorical program can be specified so as to insure that localities with the most severe deprivation will receive the largest share of the funds. Block grant formulas have tended more toward equal per capita distributions of assistance. Though block grant formulas may permit slightly better targeting than a single revenue-sharing program, they may still be inferior to categorical aids in their distributional effects.

BLOCK GRANTS FOR AFDC The arguments for and against block grants can be illuminated by applying them to a specific program—AFDC.

AFDC provides grants to states to subsidize their cash payments to eligible categories of recipients. These grants provide that the federal government will match any level of payments made by the various states at rates that, for most states, lie between 50 and 78 percent. The financial structure of AFDC grants is open-ended, in that the state's choice of benefit levels and asset eligibility determines total payments, and so determines the federal contribution. There is no legal maximum on the federal grant to any state. The various block grant proposals typically provide a fixed amount to each state which would grow with inflation and population increases. Matching requirements would be eliminated along with federal program rules. As a result, the federal government would no longer concern itself with rules regarding income eligibility, provisions concerning the effect of earnings in the calculation of recipient's benefits, and provisions regarding work requirement for beneficiaries.

Backers of the block grant proposal stress the advantages that accrue to the federal government from the change in the financial structure of the grant, and the benefits that the states would derive from the relaxation in federal rules. For the federal government, the block grant would place a cap on outlays in support of AFDC. For the states, it is argued, the block grant will allow the development of innovative program models, such as experiments with various types of work requirements. The result will be to reduce the number of able-bodied workers on the rolls. By allowing states to keep all of the savings, the block grants will increase the state's incentive to reduce payment errors and to remove ineligibles from the rolls. It is also contended that the block grant will simplify administrative procedures and allow greater state discretion over programs, in part by insulating governments from the power of the national welfare lobby.

One argument against the block grant is couched primarily in terms of the effect on recipients. The block grant discourages states from raising benefit levels, because the states must bear the full cost of any increase in the number of eligible recipients. Moreover, the block grant encourages underspending because of the spillover problem discussed earlier. Even if the majority of citizens in the nation want to provide certain minimum support levels to the poor, each state is inhibited from responding because of the threat that businesses and higher-income residents might flee the state in order to avoid the fiscal burden. Proponents' response to this concern is that inadequacy of benefits is really a problem in only a few states. To deal with these states, the formula for the distribution of federal aid through block grants can be adjusted to provide additional funds, subject to the condition that such states raise their benefit levels.

A second argument against block grants goes to the issue of state cost and financial exposure. States argue that in the absence of federal cost sharing, any unanticipated increase in case loads will hit the states much harder. The result is to increase the fiscal vulnerability of the state to fluctuations in its economy. Two lines of solution have been proposed from various quarters: to fix the block grants at a level that somewhat exceeds the matching grants they displace, thereby providing fiscal relief to hard-hit states; and to tie changes in individual state allocations to various proxies for need, such as population growth and unemployment rates.

THE EVIDENCE In the end, the choice between block grants and matching grants must be made on the basis of many factors, including not only the fiscal implications of the choice, but also questions of administrative efficiency and policy flexibility. The evaluation that follows is limited to the fiscal implications. In terms of those implications alone, what the evidence suggests in brief is that the block grant proposals present policymakers with a difficult problem of choosing between two outcomes: sustaining reduced benefits to the recipients on the one hand or sustaining increased costs to the federal government on the other.

From a fiscal point of view, grants from the federal government may have various effects on the budgetary behavior of state and local governments. They may be stimulative by leading the states to increase their own expenditures on the aided program over and above the federal funds; they may be additive by supplementing an unchanged level of contributions from the state; or they may be fully or partially substitutive by being accompanied by a reduction or cancellation of the state contribution.

To see how states might respond to a switch from matching grants to unmatched block grants, it helps to lay out the possibilities in graphic terms. Conceptually such a switch represents an increase in the unrestricted resources available through grants to the recipient government; at the same time, it represents an increase in the cost to the state of raising benefits. In Figure 1, the horizontal axis represents total outlays on AFDC, while the vertical axis represents the state's outlays on all other government goods and services.

$A'A$ is the state's budget constraint in the absence of any grants, portraying expenditure based on its own fiscal resources. $A'G$ defines the state's possibilities under an open-ended matching grant for welfare. $A'B'B$ portrays those possibilities if the matching grant were replaced with a block grant equal to the state's current matching grant and if that grant carried the sole condition that it must be spent on welfare. CD represents the funds received from the federal government, whether as a matching grant or as an equivalent block grant. Finally, Figure 1 also portrays the pos-

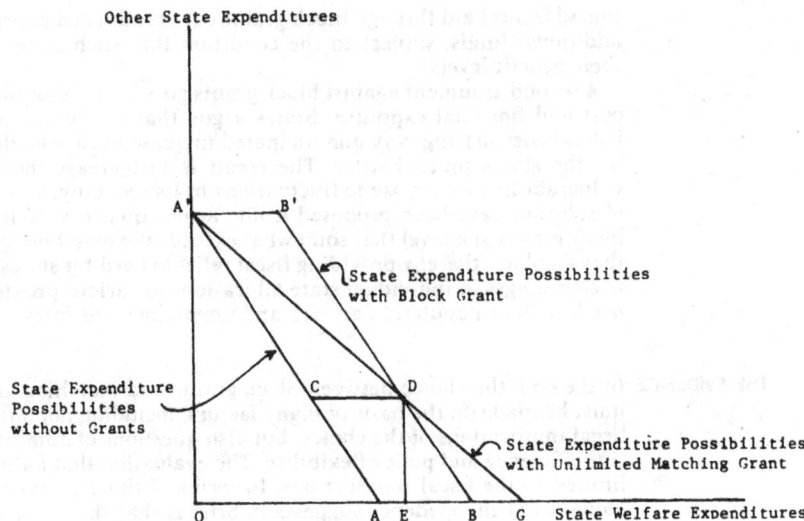

Figure 1. State expenditure possibilities associated with different types of federal welfare grants.

sibilities if states were required to maintain the current level of benefits, shown in Figure 1 as *OE*; if such a condition were imposed and if there were no change in the number of families served, then the possible expenditure patterns would be *A'CDB*.

How would the states actually respond to a shift in terms of the AFDC grant from a matching basis to a block, unmatched basis? To answer this question it would be helpful to evaluate past experience with similar types of changes in federal grant structures. Unfortunately, there has been relatively little experience with this kind of change. However, there have been a number of studies of changes in state spending behavior associated with the introduction of the AFDC matching grant. The best of these studies is that of Larry Orr[5] on AFDC benefit level determination. Orr finds that the AFDC matching grant has been partially substitutive, with about one-third of the grant used to increase benefit levels, and the rest released for other budgetary purposes and for tax relief.* However, the entire effect of the grant on the level of benefits is found to stem from the effect of matching state expenditures at the margin. If the matching requirement were eliminated, and if fixed dollar grants

---

*The Orr result is based on a careful statistical specification of the way in which AFDC matching rates affect the cost to the state's taxpayers of assuring given levels of income support for the poor. Though other studies of the effect of welfare grants have produced matching rate estimates ranging all the way from zero to greater than one, all except the Orr study are beset with statistical problems which make their estimates unreliable.

were made instead, his model predicts that over several years average real benefit levels would decline by about 16 percent.

The implication of the Orr analysis is that a greater dollar amount of block grant aid would probably be required to maintain real benefits at their current level than under the matching grant scheme. How much more would depend on the type of requirement imposed on the state for maintenance of levels of expenditure, on the case load effects of block grants, and on each state's marginal propensity to spend for welfare from unrestricted grant resources.

Figure 2 illustrates the relative expenditure effects of block and matching grants. Suppose that in the absence of the matching grant, with initial expenditure possibilities AA', the state would have spent OD on welfare. The matching grant changes the possibilities to $A'G$, and increases welfare spending by an amount DE, to a total level of OE. The Orr study suggests that for the AFDC program the increase in benefit levels per dollar of matching grant, or DE/FE, is about one-third. Thus, the matching grant has displaced an amount FD of local spending, leaving OF as the level of state outlays on welfare.

Suppose that the current matching structure were replaced by a block grant of equal dollar magnitude. What maintenance-of-effort requirement would be necessary to prevent a decline in benefit levels? If there were no change in case loads, then it is clear the state must continue to spend OF of its own resources. Thus, a requirement that the state maintain its own expenditures at their current level would be needed.

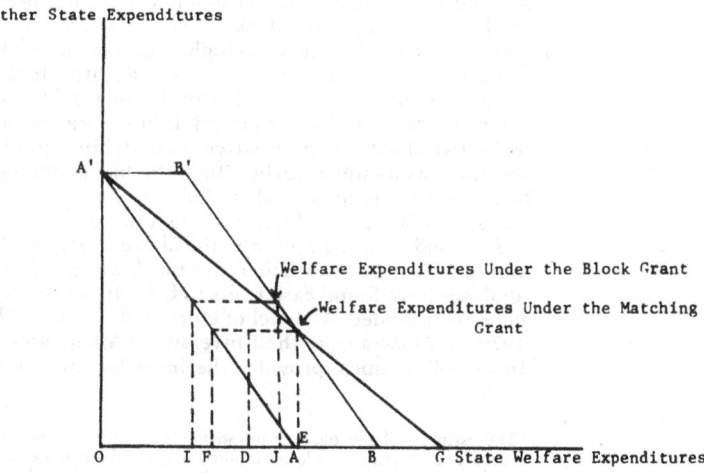

Figure 2. State expenditures under block grants and matching grants compared.

How effective would a maintenance-of-effort requirement be over time in maintaining benefit levels at the matching grant level? To answer this question, it is necessary to know what would have been the level of benefits if the matching grant structure had not been disturbed. In the past, nominal benefit levels have increased steadily; if that trend could have been expected to continue, then the maintenance-of-effort requirement would not have been constraining on aggregate expenditures. Therefore, the Orr model predicts that over time a fixed dollar grant would lead to a level of benefits lower than the level that would exist with matching grants. This long-run displacement is illustrated in Figure 2 by a reduction in welfare expenditures from OE to OJ, and an increase in displacement from FD to ID.

By how much would a block grant have to exceed a matching grant in order to prevent any decline in benefit levels? The answer depends on various factors: on the relative stimulus to benefit levels provided by the two different types of grant; on the predicted rate of increase of benefit levels under the matching program; and on the number of years that have elapsed since the introduction of the block grant.

Make several assumptions: that a dollar of AFDC matching aid is three times as stimulative as a dollar of AFDC block grant aid*; that nominal AFDC benefits would continue to increase at the 1974–1980 rate of 5 percent per year; and that case loads would be unchanged under the block grant. On those assumptions, we estimate that in order to maintain benefit levels, the average block grant would have to be about 9 percent higher than the matching grant after the first year, and about 43 percent higher after five years. (The formula for making these computations is given in the Appendix.) As the maintenance-of-effort requirement becomes less binding over time, the block grant would have to increase to an equilibrium level three times higher than the matching grant level.

These estimates are obviously quite sensitive to the assumptions made as to the relative fiscal stimulus of a dollar of matching aid versus a dollar of block grant aid. If block grants for AFDC proved to be two-thirds as stimulative as matching grants, rather than one-third as assumed earlier, then the block amounts would have to be only 11 percent higher than the matching grant after five years, and 50 percent higher in the long run.

A second key assumption in the above analysis is that case loads would be unchanged under the block grant. However, previous analyses have found case loads to be quite sensitive to the level of benefits provided. A model of entry and exit into AFDC, using the 1970–1971 data from the University of Michigan's Panel Study of Income Dynamics, provides the basis for an estimate. From the

---

*The estimate of the block grant spending response is derived from published estimates of the state and local response to general aid, under the assumption that the labeling of a block grant as a welfare grant would induce a slightly higher welfare spending response by the state than would a completely untied grant to the state.

model, it appears that among families headed by a single female parent, a 10-percent increase in maximum benefits leads to a 17-percent increase in the proportion that participated in AFDC during a given year. If the same relationship applies when maximum benefits fall, then such a fall would produce a substantial decline in the number of families on the AFDC rolls. To be sure, this case load decline might in turn reduce the amount by which benefit levels would be lowered, by decreasing the total budgetary outlay required to maintain a given level. But the new equilibrium under the block grant would still generate lower benefit levels.

So far, we have explored the effects of maintenance-of-effort requirements as if those requirements were couched in terms of maintaining nominal dollar expenditures or benefit levels. Suppose, however, that the maintenance-of-effort requirement were made more stringent by requiring that the real—that is, the inflation-adjusted—value of benefits be maintained under the block grant. Would a block grant equal in dollar amount to the matching grant then be sufficient to protect benefit levels? Not surprisingly, the answer again depends on the pattern of growth in the level of benefits that would have occurred under the matching grant. Suppose that benefits were expected to rise in real terms, as they did in the 1960s. In this case, even a maintenance requirement in real terms would not be sufficient to prevent a long-run reduction in benefit levels. If, however, real benefits were falling, as they did in the 1970s, then the situation could be reversed; in that situation, a block grant that was equal to the matching grant and that was coupled with the more stringent maintenance requirement might conceivably be superior to the current matching structure in protecting clients from further erosion of benefit levels. As discussed in the next section, the political difficulties in constraining state expenditure choices in this way have so far prevented this stringent maintenance requirement from being incorporated in any of the recent block grant proposals.

To summarize, the available evidence suggests that maintaining the long-run pattern of growth in the real level of benefits implies a considerable increase in the block grant. To be sure, the matching grant has not been particularly stimulative of AFDC expenditures and nominal benefit levels have increased quite slowly over the past five years. Nevertheless, in the long run the block grant might still have to be as much as 1.5 to 3 times higher than the total amount of matching aid in order to maintain benefits at the level that would be achieved by the matching grant.

Another aspect of the switch from matching grants to block grants is the differential effect of such a change on the various states. Any such switch would have a substantially different impact from one state to the next. The greatest relative decline is likely to occur in those states that already have the lowest benefit levels. This expectation stems from the fact that the current matching formula provides for higher matching rates in states with low levels of per capital income, and these are the states which tend to have the lowest benefit levels. Accordingly, these states would suffer the greatest relative increase in the marginal cost of welfare. For example, Mississippi, whose AFDC benefit levels are among the lowest in the country, would go from a marginal cost of 22¢ per dollar of AFDC spending to a full dollar, while California would face only 50¢ increase. If the block grant to each state were equal to its prior matching grant, the Orr model predicts that the relative decline in benefit levels in Mississippi would be much greater than in California. Not only is this widening undesirable on equity grounds; it would also increase the incentive for AFDC recipients to migrate to high-benefit states. To prevent this widening, the block grant formula would have to provide proportionally more aid to the poorest states.

The problems generated by a widening of differentials between states illustrate the nature of the tradeoff between benefit adequacy and federal cost that must be faced in establishing a distribution formula for block grants. Under the open-ended matching grant, heretofore used in AFDC, the amount of aid going to each state depends on two factors: the state's own expenditure decisions and the rate at which expenditures are matched by the federal government. Under any formula that would provide block grants at the level formerly provided by matching grants, those states with the lowest benefit levels would receive smaller grants, thereby increasing the fiscal pressure to cut benefit levels. On the other hand, if the block grant formula provided relatively more funds to low-benefit states, high-benefit states in effect would be penalized for the generosity of their payments. As I show below, different legislative proposals resolve this tradeoff in quite different ways.

RECENT BLOCK GRANT PROPOSALS

The current effort to fund AFDC with block grants began in 1978 when Senators Moynihan, Cranston, and Long introduced S.3470 as a modest alternative to President Carter's "Better Jobs and Income" plan. Their plan was quickly adopted as the conservative alternative to the President's proposal, and developed into a comprehensive welfare reform package. The block grant concept has had growing support in both houses of Congress, as well as the express support of the incumbent head of the Department of Health and Human Services.

Most recent proposals would implement the block grant by providing each state with an amount equal to its current matching grant although at least one proposal would begin to reduce grants by 2 percent per year after five years. It is typically provided that the basic grant would grow at the rate of inflation, and would change proportionately with the state's population. Moreover, some of the proposals would add a supplement for states with high unemployment. In addition, the proposals typically include added amounts intended for the fiscal relief of all the states, as well as sums intended as an incentive for low-benefit states to raise their benefit levels. The funds for fiscal relief are proposed for distribution on the basis of the state's current share of AFDC and revenue-sharing funds in some cases, or on the basis of state population in others. The criterion of AFDC share is of course more favorable to the states with high welfare expenditures, such as New York and California. These two states received almost 30 percent of federal AFDC funds in 1979, as compared with a population share of only 18 percent. Incentive payments are tied to an increase in benefit levels in some proposals or proposed without any such requirement in others.

In order to analyze the implications of these proposals for the size and allocation of future AFDC block grants, the actual pattern of the grants made from 1975 to 1979 under the existing matching formulas was compared to the growth that would have occurred had a block grant been implemented in 1975. Each state's initial block grant was set at a level equal to its 1975 matching grant amount, plus its 1979 fiscal relief allotment, deflated to 1975 dollars. The grant was assumed to grow at a rate equal to the growth in the Consumer Price Index, plus the growth rate in the state's population. The results of this exercise show that by 1979 the total federal outlay would have been 42 percent higher under the block grant than the amount actually recorded under the matching grants.

These results stem from the fact that in this statistical exercise the block grant is indexed to the rate of inflation plus population growth. In actual fact, during the recent era of matching grants, benefit levels have grown more slowly than the rate of inflation, and the number of recipients has been almost stable. Projecting future costs under the assumption that current rates of inflation and benefit level growth persist over the next six years, the total AFDC block grant would range from $2.3 to $4.5 billion higher than the actual matching grant, depending on the amount of fiscal relief included in the block grant. Thus, the fact that federal outlays in any one year are capped under the block grant is overshadowed by the significantly higher growth rate under full indexing.

What are the implications of the block grant formula for the sharing of welfare expenditures between the federal government and the states? In part, this depends on the requirements relating to the maintenance of state expenditures. All of the proposals require states to use federal funds for "payments of AFDC and other social welfare purposes." However, requirements for the maintenance of benefits are quite varied. Some proposals have no requirements at all; others call for passing through to recipients the increase in the federal block grant which is due to inflation; still others require that state expenditures be maintained at existing levels. None of the existing proposals would require maintenance of benefits in real terms. It therefore follows from the argument in the preceding section that the block grant is likely to lead to the displacement of some portion of the increase in state welfare expenditures that otherwise would have occurred.

The result of introducing the block grant concept, therefore, should be a substantial increase in the federal share of total AFDC expenditures, and a decline in the states' share. If existing proposals are adopted as proposed, the growth in block grants over the years would probably be sufficient to prevent the decline in benefit levels. If the block grants do not grow after all, however, benefits will decline.

Meanwhile, attempts to protect individual states from the effects of changes in the size of their case loads, which are incorporated in all block grant proposals, seem unlikely to produce the desired results. Formulas for the allocation of block grants among the states include a factor to reflect population growth and another to reflect periods of high unemployment. But the data show that during the period from 1975 to 1979 population growth was negatively correlated with case load growth, while insured unemployment showed a positive but weak correlation with growth in case loads. Other alternatives, such as the change in the number of poor families or poor children, would almost certainly be superior to population change or unemployment rates as proxies for state need. However, at present the lack of reliable annual data on a state-by-state basis precludes the use of these variables. If block grants for AFDC are introduced, therefore, there may be considerable payoff from collecting more reliable data on the extent of poverty by states.*

One way to reduce the high federal cost of the AFDC block grant is to limit its growth to some fraction of the inflation rate, and make the fiscal relief a one-time-only supplement. For example, for the 1975–1979 period, a federal block grant scheme would have produced funds equal to the matching grants of that period if the block grant had been adjusted automatically by the sum of two factors: population growth plus 44 percent of the inflation rate. On the other hand, large differences would have occurred in the distribution of the funds by states; block grants would have been 24 percent less than matching funds in Florida and Mississippi, for example, and 69 percent greater in Texas and Arizona. In general a partially indexed block grant typically produces lower figures than the actual matching grants in those states whose benefit levels increased at above-average rates relative to their population growth.

Wide variations from state to state in the growth of benefit levels, in AFDC case loads, and in population, when coupled with the fact that there is not much correlation between these various factors, mean that no single region would be a clearcut gainer or loser under the block grant distribution as compared with matching grant allocations. To illustrate, the rapid population growth in many southern states tends to increase their share under a block grant. However, in states such as Mississippi, the population

---

*A precedent for this type of data collection exists. In 1975, Congress charged the Survey of Income and Education, a large census-like survey, with the goal of providing reliable estimates of the number of poor children in each state. This information was to be used for the distribution of compensatory education funds under Title I of the Elementary and Secondary Education Act.

growth factor has been offset by substantial benefit level increases, which has tended to increase matching grant allocations. Other states, such as Georgia, combined an above-average level increase in benefit levels over the 1975–1979 period with an above-average decline in case loads. The net result was a relatively slow growth in the matching grant amount, a result that contrasts with a 44-percent increase in federal funding that would have been generated by a block grant program of the same total size for the nation as a whole. As noted earlier, fiscal flows under the block grant do not consistently favor the states with low benefits; accordingly, the block grant formula is likely to result in a widening of interstate benefit differentials. That result can be avoided only if a strong incentive for raising low benefit levels were incorporated in the block grant allocation formula.

CONCLUSION A review of the econometric evidence suggests that over time states are likely to respond to the change in fiscal incentives under the block grant by reducing benefit levels in AFDC programs. Federally imposed requirements for the maintenance of state effort can only slow the rate of decline; they cannot prevent the decline from occurring. To compensate for the decline in state expenditures, the level of block grant funding would have to be substantially higher than the amount required under matching grants. The net result would be a shift in the composition of welfare spending, with an increase in the federal share and a decline in that of the states.

An analysis of recent block grant proposals for AFDC reveals that just such a pattern is likely. Had the block grant been implemented in 1975 along lines now being proposed, the provisions for offsetting inflation in these proposals would have increased federal outlays considerably above their matching grant level, and led to an increase in the federal share of AFDC costs. If the inflation adjustment is reduced so that the growth rate of block grants no longer exceeds the growth rate for matching grants, the distribution of grants among the states would be changed greatly from existing patterns. These disparities point to the difficulty of finding a block grant formula that can duplicate the fiscal flows resulting from case load changes and payment decisions of the individual states. The consequence is painful adjustments for some states and a probable widening in the benefit level disparities among the states.

The decisions of the Congress in choosing between block grants and matching grants will entail other factors as well, including questions of administrative efficiency and policy flexibility, subjects that this article does not address. The critical point to be recognized here is that without a large reduction in the number of participants in a transfer program such as AFDC, it is not possible for a block grant simultaneously to lower federal cost, lower state cost, and protect benefit levels for participating families. Since a block grant scheme for AFDC almost certainly implies a different combination of outcomes than a program based on matching grants, it is important for policymakers to consider these tradeoffs in weighing the consequences of the shift.

The author would like to acknowledge the substantial contribution to this article made by David Carroll of the Office of Income Security Policy, Department of Health and Human Services, who performed much of the research on recent block grant proposals, and made helpful suggestions throughout the analysis. He would also like to thank Richard Kasten, Daniel Weinberg, and Martin Holmer, all of the Office of Income Security Policy, and Barbara Boyle Torrey for many helpful suggestions. The views expressed in the article are those of the author. They in no way reflect the official position of the Department of Health and Human Services.

APPENDIX
The Ratio of Block Grant Dollars to Matching Grant Dollars

To determine the ratio of block grant dollars to matching dollars which would be required to maintain benefit levels over time, I divide welfare expenditures into two parts, the original portion mandated by the maintenance-of-effort requirement, and the increase that must be coaxed out of block grant dollars rather than matching dollars. Define terms as follows: G_B and G_m are the block grant and matching grant amounts, b_B and b_m are the spending response coefficients per dollar of block and matching aid, r is the expected growth rate of AFDC benefits under the matching scheme, and t is the number of years since the introduction of the block grant. Then the expression for the ratio of block grant to matching grant dollars is

$$\frac{G_B}{G_m} = \frac{1 + (b_m/b_B)[(1 + r)^t - 1]}{(1 + r)^t}$$

HOWARD CHERNICK, who holds a Ph.D. from the University of Pennsylvania, is an economist with the U.S. Department of Health and Human Services.

NOTES
1. Advisory Commission on Intergovernmental Relations, *The Intergovernmental Grant System: An Assessment and Proposed Policies; Summary and Concluding Observations* (Washington, DC: U.S. GPO, June 1978), p. 4.
2. Break, George F., *Financing Government in a Federal System* (Washington, DC: The Brookings Institution, 1980), p. 124.
3. Advisory Commission on Intergovernmental Relations, *Block Grants: A Comparative Analysis* (Washington, DC: U.S. GPO, 1977), p. 6.
4. Nathan, Richard P., Dommel, Paul R., Leibschutz, Sarah F., Mossir, Milton D., "Monitoring the block grant program for community development," *Political Science Quarterly*, 92(2) (Summer 1977): 226.
5. Orr, Larry, "Income transfers as a public good: An application to AFDC," *American Economic Review* (June 1976): 359–371.
6. Hutchens, Robert, "Entry and exit transitions in a government transfer program: The case of Aid to Families with Dependent Children," *Journal of Human Resources*, 16(2) (Spring 1981): 217–237.

14

MAKING BLOCK GRANTS ACCOUNTABLE

Eleanor Chelimsky

The proposal by President Reagan to consolidate 84 categorical grant programs, transform them into six block grants in the areas of health, education, social services, and emergency energy aid, and simultaneously cut the overall funding for those grants in differing amounts, arises from a groundswell of public criticism of federal spending. This criticism, which had developed over a number of years, contained strong ideological and federalist components among the diversity of complaints articulated, and focused heavily on the categorical grants which have formed the backbone of federal expenditure for social programs over the years. The criticism peaked sharply in California with the Proposition 13 referendum of June 1978, and again nationally in November 1980 with the conservative success in the general elections.

The question of which sectors of the budget would be cut was never open to much doubt, given the campaign concentration on "wasteful social programs" and "inflexible categorical grants," and given also the conservative character of the new administration. Conservatives have long argued for minimum involvement of the government in the lives of citizens except in support of the social order[1] (that is, to maintain the rule of law, established institutions, a strong military defense, and the right to acquire, retain, and inherit property); and for minimum taxation to assure only those public functions which cannot be handled by the private sector. "Big" government,

AUTHOR'S NOTE: The views and opinions expressed by the author of this chapter are her own and should not be construed to be the policy or position of the General Accounting Office.

From Eleanor Chelimsky, "Making Block Grants Accountable," in Lois-ellin Datta (ed.) *Evaluation in Change: Meeting New Government Needs.* Copyright 1981 by Sage Publications, Inc.

heavy taxes, and the resource redistribution favored by liberals have been seen by conservatives as harmful to the economy, destructive of the "work ethic," and generally damaging to social institutions.

Given these views, it was perfectly predictable that the budget cuts proposed by a conservative administration should have heavily affected social programs which seek to equalize or redistribute income or other resources, rather than, say, defense programs. In addition, it was also natural that budget constraints should focus on categorical grant programs, given that these are of such relatively recent vintage, had grown so rapidly during the 1970s, and had received so much criticism from federalist, as well as conservative, perspectives.

Specific federalist criticism of categorical grant programs has been, first, that too much power is vested in the national government at the expense of states and localities; and second, that this overweening power (expressed, they feel, in red tape, overlapping jurisdictions, and uncoordinated requirements at the national level) has made it impossible for states and localities to carry out the programs effectively.

In sum, categorical grants have received criticism emanating from both ideological and federalist perspectives; however, the boundaries of the current critique of these grants extends far beyond those perspectives.

THE CURRENT CRITIQUE OF CATEGORICAL GRANT PROGRAMS

One place where both federalist and ideological criticisms have converged is in the area of categorical program goals, many of which are likely to be unacceptable, a priori, to conservatives and to certain (states' rights) federalists. Six different kinds of goals can be distinguished:

(1) Case transfers or transfers-in-kind of collective goods (such as social or mental health services) to low income or other target population groups;
(2) The diffusion of innovations in the delivery of public services (to increase productivity via the introduction of modern information processing equipment, for example);
(3) The development of needed skills and capabilities at state and local levels, and within the labor force generally (often also called "capacity-building" or "-sharing");
(4) The dissemination of information and the attempt to influence local consumer preferences in accordance with national policy (vaccination, speed-limit, anti-alcohol or anti-smoking campaigns, for example);
(5) The improvement of the bargaining power of the poor, of minorities, and of the disadvantaged at the local level (via employment training or unemployment compensation, for example); and

(6) The removal of obstacles (usually through grants for multijurisdictional planning, or through 100 percent funding, where required) raised by jurisdictional boundaries [adapted from Schultze, 1974: 183-185].

All of these goals, however whether or not they are acceptable to everyone derive either from traditional kinds of collaboration which have always existed within the federal system (Elazar, 1962), or from more recent income redistribution policies begun in 1913 (made possible, in fact, by the income tax, which was a straightforwardly redistributive measure). Service programs such as Medicare and Medicaid, or Aid to Families with Dependent Children (AFDC), clearly embody and crystallize one or more of these objectives.

Despite its somewhat hallowed traditions, however, the categorical grant program as a policy mechanism is now the subject of criticism coming not only from conservatives and states' rights federalists but from every ideological direction and every level of the federal system. This was *not* the case for service programs developed under the liberal New Deal. Contemporary criticism of those programs (such as accusations of socialism, interventionism, academism, red tape, confusion and waste, on the one hand, or of irrelevance and irrationality resulting from an unwillingness to attack "the root causes" of social problems, on the other hand) had typically come either from conservatives who were politically weakened by the Great Depression, or from ephemeral, "share-the-wealth" Populists (under Huey Long) and from a small, splintered radical movement. President Roosevelt's overwhelmingly dominant liberal reform movement could thus fend off most of these accusations, although it did make some efforts to placate the Populists during their period of political ascension. Again, in the 1960s, the Kennedy/Johnson "massive innovative wave" (Sundquist with Davis, 1969: 261) would give short shrift to the complaints of conservative doubters generally, and at state and local levels in particular (Martin, 1965: 77), but did lend an ear to (domestic) radical movements which appeared to be gathering political momentum on its left.

What is different today, then, is that much of the current criticism of categorical grant programs derives from liberals who were the architects and supporters of the very programs under attack. This criticism has, of course, occurred on the basis of performance, not of ideology. But these liberals thus join the ranks of conservatives, who would normally be expected to oppose the programs on ideological grounds (although many have also voiced criticisms of program performance), and of those intergovernmental system practitioners, administrators, and legislators who have come to see in service programs a glaring exposition of the flaws in the current ability of the intergovernmental network to act effectively in response to public problems.

One of the inferences which may be drawn from the above discussion is that a problem with liberal thinking in the past may have been a failure to recognize the importance and power of the federal system framework in the implementation of categorical programs. This failure, however, appears to have been both integral to certain liberal beliefs and goals, and a predictable result of them. The liberal faith in centralization, given the conservative stance taken by many states and local governments with regard to social reform (a stance which may have closed liberal ears to any validity in their criticisms), the inability of reform governments to maintain the integrity of needed program planning, and the liberal preoccupation with national objectives which was so intense and exclusive as to divert talented liberal attention from focusing also on the means for achieving them, are all factors which impeded awareness of growing state and local criticism.

This is not, of course, to assert that failures of implementation are restricted to liberal social programs, categorical or otherwise. The mindset attending the Three Mile Island nuclear plant system design, with its inattention to the most ordinary needs of operational procedures, and the implementation-monitoring difficulties prevalent in service program activities championed by conservatives (crime control or court-delay reduction efforts, for example) illustrate adequately that implementation failures are neither a social nor a liberal nor a governmental monopoly. They are, however, of particular concern to liberals insofar as liberals have identified themselves with social reform and are hence responsible for the federal initiatives especially categorical grant programs—implemented in pursuit of that reform.

The implementation deficits which have occurred in many programs are now well recognized by the least some liberals. In the words of Senator Levin (1979):

> My fear is that the programs I so strongly support are going to be doomed not by a flaw in intent but by a flaw in implementation.

It is not clear, however, that the failure of the categorical grant concept to integrate the federalist administrative and practitioner network—which is a major component of the "flaw in implementation"—is as well recognized or understood. Nonetheless, this failure figures prominently among performance criticisms currently leveled at categorical programs.

In addition to failures of planning, of implementation, of networking, and of evaluation, however, categorical grant programs have helped to produce an unanticipated side effect: the creation and multiplication of interest groups. This development has become the source of an important (and newer) criticism leveled at categorical grant programs: to wit, that service providers and service beneficiaries have evolved into stakeholders, that new organizational structures have been built and new political alignments or coalitions have developed because of them, and that the public, in general, is no longer well served in these circumstances. The War on Poverty, for example, supplied

Mayor John Lindsay of New York with a surrogate for the party support he lacked. (As Lindsay remarked, "The community corporations cracked up traditional systems ... the traditional Democrats were more fearful than my crowd. I supported the Poverty Program, the black community knew I would support it ... now I don't have to call them for payoffs. They'll support me in the fall" [Tolchin and Tolchin, 1972: 77-80].) Other city officials have used categorical programs to prevent the organizations which elected them from dissolving (as an example, Mayor Ivan Allen of Atlanta, who was elected by "an unstable coalition of blacks and businessmen," cemented that coalition "primarily through his ability to get and give federal patronage in the form of grants for the benefit of both groups" [Tolchin and Tolchin, 1972: 67].)

Not only have categorical programs influenced the development and viability of interest groups, however; interest groups have also influenced the development and viability of categorical programs. Intervention by stakeholder groups at the program planning stage may mean that legislation is postponed or never enacted, as was the case with President Kennedy's "bold new approach" to mental health centers in 1963, according to Lucy Ozarin:

> The hearings went forth, both in the Senate and in the House. The original proposal was for legislation that would provide money to build mental health centers and also staff them. Now, at that time, the American Medical Association was very much against what they called socialized medicine, and they saw the staffing provision - money to hire staff as smacking of socialized medicine. Building was all right, however; there'd been the Hill-Burton program for years to build hospitals and health facilities. The AMA was able once again to swing enough weight, to object strongly enough, so that the final legislation which emerged in 1963 was a construction program. For two years, that's what we had [Chelimsky, 1979: 810].

Interventions by stakeholder groups at the program implementation stage have been equally powerful. If programs to increase productivity in a city agency, in the classroom, or in a police district, for example, are opposed by municipal, teacher, or police unions which can paralyze city operations with strikes, or control state legislatures with campaign funds, these programs are not likely to be either well implemented or institutionalized.

These circular interactions between categorical programs and interest groups mean that: (1) these programs (and other federal policy mechanisms) have enormous obstacles to overcome in areas where stakeholders are both opposed to the program and entrenched; (2) where programs address goals desired by powerful stakeholder groups, federal efforts will be facilitated in the Congress (and also at state and local levels, insofar as stakeholder influence is reflected in individual state and local power structures); (3)

federal agencies are stimulated to work very closely with stakeholder groups and the relevant congressional committees, thereby forming (and contributing to the multiplication of) "iron triangles";[2] and finally, (4) units of general state and local government—at least partly in reaction to these developments and relationships—now find themselves taking on (willingly or defensively) some of the characteristics of stakeholder groups. This last point is of importance because the federalist perspective of state and local units which are *also* stakeholders is likely to be different from the perspective of those which are not.

The increasing dependence of state and local governments on federal aid, along with the increase in number, strength, and scope of stakeholder groups, has now blurred earlier distinctions between governmental and lobby groups. States, cities, counties, regional councils of government, all have built staffs in Washington to try to shape the federal grant formulas to their benefit and to achieve a more dominant voice in federal policy. Almost half the states now maintain grantspersons in Washington, "to look for more federal money" for their own state (Herbers, 1978). But the dependence which such a relationship has generated was recently made clear when the states were warned by U.S. Senator Muskie about their efforts to develop a budget-balancing amendment:

> It's not a threat, but a matter of arithmetic. We could save $31 billion . . . merely by killing revenue sharing, education grants, sewerage construction and block grants [Pine, 1979].

All of these factors—the growth in numbers and influence of stakeholder groups (whether hostile or supportive); the fact that the responsibility for this growth is at least partly attributable to categorical grant programs; and the transformations which that growth appears to have engendered in the nature of governmental relationships and in the character of the programs themselves—have notably added to current criticisms of categorical programs.

In summary, ideological and federalist criticism of categorical grant programs has been joined more recently by a public critique of the stakeholder or interest group phenomenon. Beyond the predictable focus of conservative criticism on program goals, there has also been a strong conservative critique of program *performance*, involving the effects of programs and program regulations on market operations, on the economy, on personal or corporate freedom, and on the social order (impacts of public assistance on the "work ethic," for example). The criticism of interest group influence has tended to reinforce the conservative critique by bringing evidence to bear that the liberal goal of achieving social reform through innovative programs may have been transformed, at least for some programs, into the less avowable goal of achieving affluence and influence for some stakeholder groups. On the other hand, some liberal and federal system critics while rejecting the view that program goals were wrong, illusory, or inappropriate have now come to view many categorical programs as inadequately realized, based on the experience of program performance over the past 15 years, and have become concerned as well about the increasing development of interest groups.

The following 14 criticisms present some of the major complaints about categorical grant performance which have been most frequently heard over the last few years. Categorical grants are accused of being:

(1) *Ineffective in achieving their goals* (examples typically given here are the AFDC, job training, environment-saving or federal crime control programs which are alleged neither to have reduced dependence on public assistance, nor moved well-trained people into private sector jobs, nor reduced air, water, and noise pollution, nor made the streets safe, as they had promised, or had been expected, to do);

(2) *Inefficient in their operations*, involving both poor management and waste by agency administrators, and also abuse both by service providers and beneficiaries (examples given are the Medicaid program, where fraud is reported as considerable on the part of health care providers and where services are said to be of unacceptably quality; or the Comprehensive Employment and Training Administration program, where local control and accountability have been considered inadequate; or the AFDC program, where recipient abuse is thought to be unacceptably high);

(3) *Excessively centralized and controlled at the national level*, thereby decreasing proper and constitutional state and local political independence and decreasing as well both the likelihood of program and service appropriateness, and the quality of implementation at the local level;

(4) *Distortive of state and local priorities* in the pursuit of national priorities: that is, the criticism is that categorical grants force state and local governments to find matching money they would not otherwise have been spent without the existence of the federal funding; that they create dependence upon the national government (states and localities are often called "federal junkies" in this regard); and that their planning requirements use up many man-hours of local government time and scarce expertise;

(5) *Substantively fragmented and uncontrolled across topical areas at the national level* (both *among* and *within* agencies) due to the proliferation of similar or overlapping programs, thereby causing major problems of administration at local, state, and national levels (fragmentation, or lack of coordination *among* agencies has meant that the federal agency manager of each program may pose different and complex requirements, despite simultaneous or concurrent juris-

diction with other agencies which operate independently; a recent example involves the town of Junior, West Virginia, which has spent seven years trying to conciliate the conflicting demands of six federal agencies involved in its effort to build a sewage treatment plant [Herbers, 1979a]; fragmentation *within* federal agencies has meant that the responsible management of public programs can become extremely difficult, if not impossible, to accomplish);

(6) *Underfunded,* such that success, in terms of stated objectives, is not a realistic possibility (a basic failure of public housing, for example, is that demand vastly exceeds supply; the same is true for day care and public service jobs);

(7) *Inequitable,* when the supposed beneficiaries benefit little, if at all, versus other populations (public housing, urban renewal, and manpower or employment training programs are most often cited as examples: it is claimed that "urban-renewal programs have destroyed twice as many dwellings as they have built" [Wilcox, 1969: 282]; that they benefit developers and the affluent who move into "luxury hotels and apartments" created with money from HUD rather than the needy; that public housing serves the "nonthreatening" elderly of the 3.2 million people now living in 1.2 million public housing units, 48 percent are elderly rather than low-income, and especially minority, families; and that public employment and training programs have typically benefited populations other than the poor, as, for example, in the CETA program, where federal funds have been used [or misused] to rehire teachers, police officers, and firefighters whom municipalities could no longer afford to pay, or in earlier programs where "less than half the participants in public service jobs were economically disadvantaged" [Mayor Ernest N. Morial of New Orleans in Joint Economic Committee, 1978]); in particular, and very significantly, it is claimed that categorical grant programs have often done more to stimulate the growth of state and local bureaucracies than they have to affect substantively the social problem addressed;

(8) *Generative of decreased* (or decreasingly rising) *national economic productivity,* as a result of the induced expansion of the public sector whose contribution to economic productivity, although difficult to quantify, is typically calculated as low relative to the private sector;

(9) Productive of *overgreat expectations:* that is, the promise of equality implied by federal service programs is in fact a disservice to those they purport to serve, in that they raise hopes which cannot be fulfilled (as, for example in the effort to reduce current rates of unemployment among inner-city minority youths which far exceed those of the Great Depression; the point here is that while job skills can be taught and learned, if the real problem for these youths in getting and holding jobs in the private sector is that the economy

"doesn't really need these kids" [Sar Levitan in The Economist, 1978: 52], then the teaching and learning of these skills are futile exercises);

(10) *Value-eroding* (that is, service programs are not only productive of disappointment because of underfunding, inequitability, and illusory expectations of utopian equality, but they also tend to demean the idea of merit and of reward for merit; the pursuit of equality, in this sense, is said to have reversed the old humanist idea that justly earned rewards should not be *denied* because of race, creed, sex, or age, and converted it to one in which those rewards are claimed *because* of race, creed, sex, or age, as opposed to merit [Daniel Bell in Greider and Kotz, 1973]);

(11) *Bureaucratizing:* that is, tending to substitute compliance with bureaucratic rules and regulations for the achievement of substantive and formally targeted program outcomes;

(12) *Nonterminable and noncontrollable,* because of the enduring power of their constituencies, and productive of additional interest groups, either developed at state and local levels because of categorical grant funding, or constituted nationally as the result of new programs (programs for the elderly and the handicapped, for example);

(13) *Wasteful,* in terms of increasing the use of public monies for salaries and administrative expenses; and, finally,

(14) *Self-interested:* that is, categorical grants are said to enhance a tendency on the part of agencies and service-providers, themselves stakeholders, to be inward-looking, and to put their own interests ahead of those of program beneficiaries.

This synthesis of the defects ascribed to categorical grant programs, most of which have been frequently repeated in the literature of the past few years,[3] gives rise inevitably to the question: If these programs are so bad, why have they been in vogue for so long? In effect, in weighing the shift to block grants, it is also important to ask what qualities and advantages categorical grants may possess that explain their survival to date despite such a chorus of disapproval.

First, there is unquestionably the matter of *national objective,* of legislative intent. The characteristics of the current categorical grant system reflect decisions made by the Congress to serve national goals as defined by the Congress. When these grants are administered and controlled at the national level, it is possible to target very specifically the kinds of problems (such as poverty, sickness, inner-city housing deterioration) which the administration and the Congress feel must be addressed nationwide as matters of national policy and priority, as well as the kinds of populations (such as children, elderly, the mentally ill, crime victims) who have the greatest need of help, even using conservative criteria for government activity (see note 1).

Second, there is the matter of direct *accountability for federal funds*. Since categorical grants have typically been quite clear about what the national objective is, this allows various functions to occur which bring knowledge of whether the implemented program at state and local levels is faithful to the national purpose; whether the program is well implemented and well managed, according to that purpose; and whether the program made any difference. Since the basic concept is that of a contract, there is an obligation and a quid pro quo on each side. As one federal administrator has expressed it:

> A large proportion of categorical grants provide a specific sum of money, with a very high federal matching ratio (80, 90, or 100 percent) for a very particular purpose, and specify the delivery of very particular forms of collective goods.... [M]any of these grants are a means by which the federal government uses state and local governments (or in some cases local non-profit organizations) as agents or subcontractors to produce centrally determined amounts and kinds of collective goods, since, for a number of reasons, principally historical and political, the federal government itself virtually never delivers collective goods or services at the local level [Schultze, 1974: 182-183].

With categorical grants, therefore, there is, at least theoretically, a kind of bargain-exchange situation which specifies both expectations and willingness to perform on the part of the contracting parties. This builds in understandings of anticipated performance, measurement of that performance, and remedies for lack of performance if the need should arise. In short, categorical grants try to assure that the public gets value for its money; yet it is this very effort which has been responsible for many of the complaints leveled at categorical grants: red tape, data collection, performance forms and questionnaires to fill out, applications to file, plans to rationalize, and so on.

Third, there is the matter of *national capability and expertise*. Although there is, of course, variability in different substantive areas, the national government, its civil servants, and its research arms have a long record of capability and demonstrated technical skills in administering complex programs. Categorical grant programs have especially benefited from this institutional expertise, and, above all, from the continuity of that expertise, at the national level. Although some states and localities may have equal expertise, this is not true of all states and localities. In particular, it is difficult to compare state and local programs with national programs because most of the former are never evaluated.

Fourth, there is the matter of program *information at important decision points*. The presence of evaluation staff and evaluation mandates in national-level agencies has permitted the preparation and planned coordination of nationwide program reports for the use of executive branch and legislative branch decision makers. In this way, information about program status is generally available, and both sets of users are assured that the data developed at state and local levels can be planned for and designed in terms of their relevance to user information needs and decision-points; and that the reliability and validity of evaluative information developed at state and local levels can be checked.

Fifth, there is the matter of *program integrity*. Categorical grant managers, who are responsible at the national level to the President and the Congress, are required to monitor programs carefully to ensure ongoing knowledge of management problems. Audit staff at the national level can be held responsible under categorical grants for reporting on the maintenance of adequate accounting and inventory systems at state and local levels. This signifies a national check on whether state and local agency accounting, inventory, and unallowable expenditure problems are being identified and corrected, and on whether financial status reports, for example, are accurate.

Sixth, there is the matter of national *program standards*. The categorical grant system features a reasonable level of similarity among state or local programs. This diminishes the incentive for program clients to cross state lines to obtain better (or different) benefits, and it ensures some equality among states with regard to federal programs.

Seventh, there is the matter of *interstate control*. Categorical grant programs can assure coordination across states in topical areas such as disease or pollution, which do not respect state boundaries. Interstate tracking of "neighborhood or external effects" such as public health risks has always been a national-level responsibility, even under the most conservative criteria (see note 1).

Finally, there is the matter of topical areas involving *shared responsibility*, such as the health care or criminal justice "systems." The categorical grant system can ensure that federal monies are targeted according to need and so as to promote coordination and interdependence (when the national policy so dictates) by settling the issue of "Who gets how much" outside the framework of historical organization and power at the state level.

In summary, although categorical grants have been heavily criticized for defects of implementation, they also present major qualities which may be important to try to retain. As the shift to block grants is contemplated and debated, it is therefore useful not only to examine which of the 14 problems outlined above are likely to be improved or solved, but also, which of the 8 advantages may be degraded or lost. Some categorical programs, after all, have achieved major successes in meeting their objectives. The Food Stamp program, Head Start, Education for the Handicapped, all have done a lot of what they set out to do. The point here, however, is that the reason why their success has in fact been demonstrated through audit and evaluation is that audits and evaluations were among the conditions that recipients had to accept in order to receive their categorical grants. Eliminating these conditions, then, carries the major risk that the performance of federally funded programs will remain essentially unknown.

BLOCK GRANT PROGRAMS AS A REMEDY TO THE CRITIQUE OF CATEGORICAL GRANT PROGRAMS

In analyzing prospectively what block grants are likely to mean vis-à-vis the problems and advantages of categorical grants discussed above, it is first necessary to pinpoint what a block grant is. To say that it occupies the midpoint between the "no-strings-attached" approach of revenue sharing and the "tight national control" of categorical grants does not characterize the mechanism with much precision. Furthermore, it is not even clear that a block grant does occupy such a midpoint, given that there are so many different forms of block grants, some closer to revenue sharing, some closer to categorical grants. The focus of that "midpoint" is even harder to situate over time if the experience of the past is any guide: in effect, as problems of accountability of one sort or another have arisen in the block grants of the 1970s, a phenomenon known as "creeping categorization" has ensued as the Congress has struggled to exercise some control over the federal funds. Thus, a block grant which starts out in life as a transfer mechanism whose purpose is to increase recipient discretion over spending decisions may not, over time, end up doing so. In general, block grants can be more accurately described as occupying "a span of policy space within which shifts may occur reflecting a balance between national (state) and local program preferences and power" (Dommel, 1981:1).

The Advisory Commission on Intergovernmental Relations (ACIR) has identified five design characteristics which help to distinguish block grants from other types of federal transfer (1977: 6; emphasis added):

(1) Federal aid is authorized for a wide range of activities *within a broadly defined functional area.*
(2) Recipients have substantial discretion in identifying problems, designing programs, and allocating resources to deal with them.
(3) Administrative, fiscal reporting, planning, and other federally imposed requirements are kept to *the minimum amount necessary to ensure that national goals are being accomplished.*
(4) Federal aid is distributed on the basis of a statutory formula which results in narrowing federal administrators' discretion and providing a sense of *fiscal certainty* to recipients.

(5) Eligibility provisions are statutorily specified and favor general-purpose governmental units as recipients, and elected officials and administrative generalists as decisionmakers.

Thus, a block grant may be defined as "a program by which funds are provided to general-purpose governmental units in accordance with a statutory formula for use in a broad functional area largely at the recipient's discretion." However, it is important to note that block grants neither fail to express the national objective sought in funding a program (Reagan, 1972: 63), nor do they eliminate (a) state and local accountability for the funds received, or (b) national responsibility for the appropriate use of national revenues (Dommel, 1981: 1).

If evaluations are done so that a record of ongoing experience with block grants is developed, it should be possible to say whether the worst fears or most optimistic expectations have been realized. While it is hard to imagine that the block grants will eliminate all 14 of the problems cited in categorical funding, it is equally hard to imagine that a number of successes will not occur. However, the absence of retrospective information does not preclude prospective examination of the likely ability of block grants to cope with the problems experienced by categorical grants. To begin with, it would appear that there are three problems which the block grant can be expected to affect favorably:

(1) *Excessive centralization and control at the national level* should certainly be reduced by block grants; that is one of their major purposes. But while block grants are almost certain to address this criticism, it remains to be seen whether more local discretion will lead to better local implementation and management (see Netzer, 1974). Further, it is not clear that "excessive centralization and control" at the state level will not be substituted for that of the national level. As the U.S. General Accounting Office (GAO) has pointed out (1979: 23), "Federal formula block grants to states often are transformed into discretionary categorical grants to local governments from the state."

(2) *Fragmentation and loss of control across topical areas* are likely to be improved by the use of block grants, *but only if there is proper, continuous, and careful oversight at the national level* (see Herbers, 1979a).

(3) With regard to *overgreat expectations*, it seems that the move to block grants, especially accompanied by large budget cuts, should reduce, not raise expectations. While it is true that the reduction of social expectations may not be cost-free, it is nonetheless clear that block grants accompanied by major budget cuts are certainly a step toward such a reduction.

On the other hand, it would appear likely that some problems may get worse. In particular, both logic and experience point to two problems which have not benefited from decentralization in the past:

(4) *Inefficiency in operations* ("inefficiency" involves poor management, waste, fraud, and abuse; see item 2 in the list of categorical grant complaints) is likely to be aggravated by moving to block grants. It is true that state and local programs are sometimes well managed, sometimes not, as is the case for federal programs. Again, corruption among officials is a problem on which no level of government has a monopoly. However, the experience of both the LEAA and CETA block grant programs has been that waste, fraud, and abuse of federal dollars became so widespread, flagrant, and uncontrollable without built-in elements of accountability, that the Congress eventually voted to increase the national control over recipient discretion. It is also important to recognize that initial cost savings (such as those potentially achievable through "cutting out layers of bureaucracy") are not the only factors in efficient management. The assurance of such management (one which can control costs and allocate resources effectively over the long term) requires, among other things, good record systems, performance standards, and the ability to compare management results with those of other managements. Unfortunately, under block grants, decentralization or local autonomy has often meant notably different record systems and performance standards, with the consequent inability to know what is happening in a given management system, and to compare across managements. An illustration of the multiplicity and dissimilarity of local systems is given by the property tax which is "the only tax for which there exists more than 70,000 different legal tax rates, hundreds of thousands of distinctive effective rates because of assessment nonuniformity and probably, when all the overlaying local taxing units are added up, several *million* distinctive effective tax rate combinations" (Netzer, 1974: 231). In sum, the experience of the past, along with the problems of local differentiation and uncertain instruments of accountability, all suggest that block grants are more likely to exacerbate than improve inefficiency.

(5) *Inequitability* might have been expected to improve under block grants, because it seems reasonable that decentralization should help to target monies better on needy local populations; unfortunately, experience once again has shown that needy populations may not have the organization and power to wrest those monies from state and local governments where they have little or no representation, if accountability mechanisms are not present. Under revenue sharing, for example, which represents the "no-strings" extreme, civil rights violation complaints have been numerous (770 were declared as

"pending" in 1979), yet the Treasury Department, which administers revenue sharing, does not have the necessary personnel to evaluate these complaints nor to "sort out all the inequities" of which Department officials are aware. (Herbers, 1979b). Since block grants must serve whatever target populations are indicated in the law, it seems at first glance that they would have lesser problems with equity than would revenue sharing similar problems, in fact, to those existing with categorical grants. There are, however, the additional difficulties that given "minimal," or lessened, accountability (1) the target populations intended and specified by the law may not actually be the ones served, and (2) without evaluation mechanisms, it may be nearly impossible to find this out. Block grants are thus likely to be more, not less, inequitable than categorical grants because of the ability of state and local bureaucracies to support their requests for funds effectively, and because of the "minimal" national accountability which has often accompanied block grants.

On four problems, uncertainty exists. Although the block grant may have some potential for impact in these areas, there are strong arguments for both positive and negative effects:

(6) The *decreased productivity* claimed for categorical grants could theoretically improve under block grants if the latter were to cause a reduction in public sector employment. However, it is not clear that this will occur for several reasons: (a) Some of the programs that are targeted for block grants have never been administered by the states and will therefore require "wholly new state bureaucracies" (Stanfield, 1981: 828). (b) The trend in federal programs has been toward increased (not decreased) bureaucracies as program control increases. Finally, (c) even "minimal" requirements for accountability at state levels will mean increased work as states take over the federal responsibilities for such things as processing local applications, grant decision-making, the checking of local financial and performance reports, or the conduct of audits and evaluations, for example.

(7) *Wastefulness* may be no better under block grants. At this time, it is not clear whether administrative expenses will in fact be lessened or not, and, as discussed above, it is certainly not likely that inefficiency, fraud and abuse will decrease under block grants.

(8) *Distortion of state and local priorities* may occur just as well under block grants as under categorical grants if national funds continue to be sought whose purposes are not state or local purposes. Certainly, the *national* objectives may be less well served if the activities chosen by states and localities for implementation under the grant are peripheral or noninstrumental to those objectives. While it is true

this would imply at least some reduction of state and local priority distortion, it would certainly increase national priority distortion in comparison with categorical grants. Whatever the outcome, it seems likely that any immediate improvement gained through block grants in adhering to state and local priorities might be bought at the risk of more fundamental long-term distortion because of "fiscal certainty," a design characteristic presented by block grants. Such fiscal certainty provided to recipients is likely to increase, rather than decrease, their dependence upon the national government and distort their priorities on a long-term basis. Block grants do not seem able, in and of themselves, to help with this problem, and they could increase it.

(9) *Noncontrollability and nonterminability of grants*, a problem due to *current* constituent power, may not continue to be the case under block grants. First, the national lobbies may not be represented in the same proportions or with the same power in the different states. Second, the block grant concept could force constituencies such as the disadvantaged and handicapped to compete with each other for federal funds. However, *other constituencies* the traditionally strong ones in individual states could quickly develop the same stranglehold on federal funds in block form as the national lobbies exercise on federal funds in categorical form. Also, at a higher level, if one perceives state and local governments themselves as stakeholders or constituencies, and grants are given with "fiscal certainty," then there is not likely to be much improvement in either the controllability or terminability of federal programs under the block grant mechanism.

Finally, for five of the categorical grant problems cited, the problem does not appear susceptible to being addressed via a change in the grant mechanism:

(10) The *self-interest* of agencies is a property of units at all levels of government. It would be surprising if block grants could help.

(11) *Underfunding* is a criticism which seems entirely unrelated to funding mechanisms. Block grants can neither help nor hurt.

(12) *Ineffectiveness in achieving program goals* is related to so many profound difficulties other than the intergovernmental transfer mechanism (such as the intractability of the problem addressed, the lack of understanding of the problem, the failure to pilot-test proposed program-solutions, and so on) that it would be hard to see why or how changing the mechanism could help. Block grants would seem to be neutral for this problem.

(13) *Value-erosion* is not likely to change under block grants since the same purposes or national objectives would continue to be served; only the transfer mechanism would differ.

(14) *Bureaucratization* is no better or worse in state or local agencies than at the national level. Rules, regulations, and rituals are normal aspects of agency activity. Block grants are not likely to change that.

The analysis of problems encountered in implementing a system cannot, of course, be the only focus of prospective comparison between categorical and block grants. In the previous section, eight advantages were ascribed to the categorical grant system and it is also useful to question the ability of block grants to encompass these assets while concurrently bringing a new set of strengths. The argument can be set forth as follows:

First, with regard to the *national objective*, this would still be spelled out under block grants. It might be more broadly defined, and it is certain that much more discretion would be allowed to state and local officials with regard to the choice of activities, but the fact that the national objective is explicitly specified means that national revenues *should* continue to go to national priorities, *given the presence of adequate accountability measures*. However, efforts to reverse prior "distortion of state and local priorities" may lead to some distortion of the national objective (see item 8 in the list above) and further, the fungibility resulting from the greater discretion accorded would also be expected to cause at least some leakage from the grant purpose. The difficulty involved in tracking any such leakage again points to the need for accountability in this area.

Second, the *accountability for federal funds* still exists under block grants, not only at state and local but also at national levels. However, the effort to achieve "minimal" reporting requirements may make it difficult or impossible to find out (1) whether activities are implemented which are directly relevant to achieving the national objective, and (2) whether the results of those activities reveal that they are effective and useful.

Third, the loss of *national capabilities and expertise* are likely to be sorely missed. There is much debate about the capacity of *all* states and localities to take on the new responsibilities implied in the block grant proposal. The general view, however, is unfavorable, given the concurrent budget reductions, the existing skills and expertise in some states, and the timing of the shift which is planned to occur with great rapidity. Asking for the "maximum lead time possible" in testimony before the Senate Labor and Human Resources Committee in April, North Carolina's Governor Hunt (Chairman of the National Governors' Association's Human Resources Committee) said the proposed cuts in expenditure, given the speed with which the administration wants to implement them, leaves "little doubt that the block grants proposed will result in a reduction of services" (Stanfield, 1981: 829). If this occurs, however, it will be very difficult to say which part of the reduction in services is attributable to budget cuts, and which to the state and local capacity to operate and account for complex programs.

Fourth, *decision-point information* may not be available at all under block grants. The potential loss of all information about program effectiveness appears to involve so much more important risks in terms of congressional oversight and accountability responsibilities that it appears likely the "minimal" requirements will need to focus on those, to the detriment of ordinary, generalized program status information. However, the Congress can in fact ensure that such information is both collected and made available, even under block grants.

Fifth, given past experience, it seems likely that *program integrity* would suffer under block grants unless a major effort at coordination were made by the national agency responsible (see the discussion under "inefficiency" above).

Sixth, national *program standards* or guidelines for performance would now be missing, and it is predictable that there would be considerable variability in state and local programs implemented with block grant funds, setting up incentives for "program-hopping" among some beneficiaries and reinforcing the likelihood of increased fraud and abuse.

Seventh, unless the national agency responsible in the topical program area were given the authority, it is not clear how *interstate problems* could be handled.

Finally, with regard to program areas requiring *shared responsibility*, it seems that little progress is likely to be made. The data available from the LEAA block grant program, for example, make clear that the lack of strong authority at the national level precluded any real development of integrated relationships among the police, prosecutorial, judicial, and correctional functions. In ACIR's words, (1977: 91), on reviewing the LEAA block grant experience over 8 years:

> Despite growing recognition that crime needs to be dealt with by a functionally and jurisdictionally integrated criminal justice system, the Safe Streets program has been unable to develop strong ties among its component parts.

In summary, in addressing the 14 performance problems identified here for which categorical grants are most often criticized, one may reasonably speculate that block grants are likely to be: *useful* in trying to improve three problems (those of "excessive centralization and control at the national level," "fragmentation and lack of control across topical areas," and "overgreat expectations"); *neutral* in the case of five problems (those of "ineffectiveness of achieving program goals," "underfunding," "value-erosion," "bureaucratization," and "agency self-interest"); *hurtful* with respect to two problems (those of "operational inefficiency" and "inequitability"); and *uncertain* with regard to four problems (those of "decreased productivity," "wastefulness," "distortion of state and local priorities," and "constituency uncontrollability").

Turning to the categorical grant advantages enumerated above, it appears that the only one likely to survive more or less intact is the specification of national objectives. It is uncertain what the state and local capacity will be for handling block grant responsibilities, or how and if interstate problems will be dealt with under block grants. Finally, it seems probable that program standards, decision-related information, shared responsibilities, and program integrity will all suffer notable erosion or will fail to be maintained without special action by the Congress under block grants.

Thus, in moving to block grants, only 3 of the 14 major problems found with categorical grant programs seem likely to improve. Past experience predicts that problems of inefficiency including problems of integrity such as fraud and abuse and problems of inequitability are likely to worsen notably due to the weakening of the accountability mechanisms present in categorical grant programs. It is therefore especially important to examine what can be done to improve accountability in block grant programs, without restricting unduly the increased recipient discretion, flexibility, and control they promise, as compared with categorical grant programs.

MAKING BLOCK GRANTS ACCOUNTABLE

The preceding effort to compare categorical grants and block grants in a general way suggests that there are some important problems encountered by categorical grants which either do not appear to be addressable by block grants or may well be worsened by the adoption of this mechanism. At the same time, the President and the Congress are likely to lose at least some of their ability to judge what is happening in these programs because many of the advantages of categorical grants chief among which, surely, is the assurance of recipient and national-level accountability for federal funds will have been lost.

If the Congress should decide to adopt the President's proposal for budget cuts coupled with the consolidation of categorical grants and their transformation into block grants, and if the rapid implementation schedule for that effort is not modified, it will probably be important to look very carefully at the accountability measures provided in the proposal and to decide whether or not they are adequate for national policy-making purposes.

Before beginning an examination of those measures, and of the various existing alternative measures which could potentially bolster their effectiveness, it may be useful to discuss the concept of accountability very briefly here, so as to be a little bit more precise about what it signifies. Accountability is, of course, defined by the dictionary as "the condition of being answerable, responsible, obliged to account for one's acts," presumably, to *someone else*. But if there *is* someone else, the accountability implies a relationship: one person is accountable to another (or to many others) with regard to something entrusted to that person's care; the "something" is, of course, taxpayers' money, the accountability is for public funds.

The accountability relationship, then, is a little like a contract, which is "a bargain or agreement voluntarily made upon good consideration between two or more persons capable of contracting to do, or forbear to do, some lawful act" (Justice v. Lang, 42 N.Y. 493, 1 Am. R. 576). Such a contractual agreement creates rights and duties on both sides (as in the accountability relationship where the person receiving funds from the public purse is answerable for those funds to the appropriating entity and through that entity to the public). Further, these rights and duties are legally binding; that is, they are recognized and enforced by the courts.

Accountability on the part of one party thus implies at least some measure of control on the part of the other, since the duties of one are the rights of the other. In this way, because accountability signifies accounting to someone for something, the proper receiver of that accounting must be in a position to control or ensure both its delivery and quality. Mosher (1979: 234) points out that three requirements need to be met for the accountability relationship to exist effectively. There must be:

(1) *Information* about the actions and decisions of the individuals and organizations who are held accountable (transmitted) to those who are holding them to account.... The nature and usefulness of the information provided—its honesty and accuracy, completeness, specificity, relevance, adequacy, and timeliness—have always been critical attributes of accountability.
(2) *Receivers of the information*, who are able and willing to examine it, investigate it if necessary, digest it, and report it or initiate appropriate action based on it.
(3) *Recourse* on the basis of such information, to correct deficiencies and improve performance and/or to reward honorable and effective performance or penalize dishonesty, concealment, fraud, inefficiency, or ineffectiveness.

Accountability without adequate information from the accounting party, or without adequate oversight on the part of the receiver, or without at least potential recourse to sanctions in case of problems, is merely symbolic accountability, a kind of gesture in the right direction without real significance. As Etzioni (1975: 279) phrases it:

> The hallmark of "accountability as gesture" is that that it is pure norm with little or no instrumentality attached. That is, the speaker or writer advocating accountability fails to follow up the use of the term by outlining specific arrangements.

Fortunately, the block grant mechanism (unlike revenue sharing, as discussed above) provides for real accountability, and the administration has recognized this. While the block grant programs proposed vary somewhat in their provisions, they do presently contain elements of accountability. Most frequently, these include clauses requiring reports on intended and actual use of funds and periodic financial audits, as well as prohibitions against using those funds for buying land or constructing buildings, for satisfying matching requirements of other federal programs, or in a way which discriminates on the basis of race, sex, age, or physical handicaps. Some also include "maintenance-of-effort" provisions of various sorts.

Generally, however, these elements of accountability relate almost exclusively to financial responsibility and to equitable treatment issues; they do not provide an adequate basis for judging: (a) the match of the actual programmatic focus with the legislative intent regarding the program, (b) the quality of management and implementation in the program, (c) the delivery of services in the program, or (d) the outcomes or effectiveness of the program.

It is true that the Reagan proposal represents one way of addressing some of the complaints raised against the categorical grant system; however, simplification and consolidation do not require that the issues of the fidelity of program focus or program effectiveness be disregarded. In fact, in times when budgetary constraints require the elimination or drastic reduction of numerous existing programs, means for determining the relatively less effective programs become extremely important. Further, it is clear from the "creeping categorization" experience of many block grant programs of the past not only that such accountability is possible without diminishing the special advantages of the block grant mechanism, but also that if accountability is not provided for from the beginning of the block grant legislation, then the Congress will need to move toward this effort later on, with the greater cost and loss of information that this entails.

This section therefore begins what probably should be an ongoing effort to list the various elements and tools of accountability which currently exist, with the idea that such a typology would be helpful for examining the current block grant proposal. Such elements or tools must obviously address the requirements for accountability given above:

- instruments for obtaining *information* of the relevant kind and quality;
- instruments by which *receivers* can investigate and control the information collected and/or delivered; and
- instruments for *recourse* in the event of failures of accountability.

Many questions need to be confronted in beginning to structure such a typology for use with block grants, not least of which are: Accountability to whom? Accountability by whom? Accountability for what? How much accountability?

The first question, "Accountability to whom?" is a somewhat more difficult one for block grants than for categorical grants. With the latter, it is assumed that all accountability to the public will be through the Congress. With block grants, accountability to the public takes two forms: through the Congress, with regard to the national objective, through the state legislature and/or judiciary with regard to state and local objectives.

The second question, "Accountability by whom?" is a fairly straightforward one to answer since the people who are accountable under block grants are the same ones who are accountable under categorical programs. In the words of one analyst:

> Block grants eliminate neither state and local (or recipient) accountability for the money nor federal responsibility for assuring proper use of federally collected revenues [Dommel, 1981: 1].

The third question, however, "Accountability for what?" is a vastly more complex matter which the foregoing examination was intended to address. To recapitulate the findings of the prospective analysis which has been performed here, it seems likely, under block grants, that—given the larger discretion available at state and local levels—there is some danger of *inequitability* with regard to national target populations, and some danger of *irrelevance to the national program purpose* with regard to the selected activities. It seems likely, further, that—depending on how the Congress construes "minimal" accountability—there is some danger of *lack of information* at the national level with regard to *program performance* and with regard to *program costs*. It seems likely, finally, that, given state and local government variability, given lack of uniform standards or definitions, given the difficulty of assuring formal reporting across states, and given the painful historical experience, there is danger of *increased inefficiency, waste, fraud, and abuse* in block grant programs.

Block grant programs, then, need to gear their accountability instruments to the areas where they are most likely to be vulnerable and, if this analysis is correct, "accountability for what?" should thus focus on three issues:

(1) Accountability for achieving the *national objective* in funding the program; this issue focuses on (a) whether the program has followed the legislative intent (with regard to activities and target populations, if specified, for example) and (b) whether it has proven effective in meeting the broad national objective;

(2) Accountability for achieving *state and local objectives;* given that recognition of such objectives is a major reason for adopting the block grant mechanism, this issue focuses on whether specific state and local activities are effective in meeting *their* objectives (this, of course, is a responsibility for the recipient to decide, but it is important to envisage the possibility so as not to frustrate or preclude this accountability in the federal design of the block grant); and

(3) Accountability for *program integrity and efficiency;* this issue focuses on whether sound program management is ensuring that objectives are pursued in the least costly way and with the internal controls over eligibility and expenditure needed to prevent waste, fraud, and abuse.

With regard to the fourth question, "How much accountability?" it is clear that the Congress will want to vary accountability measures and especially degrees of accountability within those measures based upon its own priorities for a particular program, upon acceptability to the administration and to state and local governments, and upon the objectives, structure, functions, and a host of other factors in the block grant. This question, then, is one which the Congress must decide and which will need to be addressed on a case-by-case basis.

While it is thus impossible to be specific here with regard to the degrees of accountability which may need to be incorporated in particular block grant programs, and while other work currently in progress will help to characterize the needed accountability framework, it is probably not premature to sketch out some of the elements or tools of accountability which could be embodied in block grant programs, and which should respond both to accountability *requirements* (that is, information, receiver control, and recourse instruments) and accountability *issues* (national program intent and effectiveness; state and local objectives and effectiveness; program management efficiency and integrity).

There are many elements of accountability and degrees of accountability within those elements which the Congress can possibly consider in addressing the three accountability requirements and the three "accountability for what?" issues, depending on: the substance and type of the program, the particular program history (that is, the problems and successes it has already encountered), and the congressional sense of special priorities and accountability requirements within the program.

Clearly, the Congress will feel differently about different block grants. For some, experience will have shown that the national intent and/or target population are less likely to be well served at state and local levels than for others. Certain block grants will have demonstrated a high susceptibility to fraud and abuse; others will not. Thus, elements of accountability (and degrees of accountability within those elements) need to be targeted to block grants in terms of (a) the Congress' expectations and priorities for a particular program, and (b) the ability of the elements to measure and report this information.

All elements of accountability have special characteristics and applicability. Some may have seemed ineffective in some programs but might be useful in others. Eighteen of them are presented here in the effort to begin a typology of elements which can lead to improved flexibility while maintaining needed controls in block grants.

(1) *Specification by the Congress of the National Objective Sought in Funding the Program.*

This first element is the foundation for accountability at the national level. Without specification of the national objective (and, as discussed earlier, block grants can accommodate various shades of specificity moving from extremely broad definition to relatively detailed precisions about eligible activities and populations, for example), no accountability is possible on whether implementation moves in the desired national direction (since that direction is not clearly given), or on whether the program is effective (since effectiveness is only meaningful with regard to an objective). This element addresses the first accountability issue and is a prerequisite both for the generation of information and for receiver control.

(2) *Requirement by the Congress that Decisions on the Use of Block Grant Funds be Made Through Whatever Budget Process the State or Locality Uses for Its Own Funds.*

This element, if selected, would address the second and third accountability issues and ensure that block grant funds will produce at least the same budgetary and accounting information as other state and local funds. This is a minimal level of accountability at state/local levels.

(3) *Provision by the Congress that Block Grant Funds be Disbursed Through an Auditable Accounting System.*

This element would address the second and third accountability issues and ensure the production of good expenditure information. If the system were also made subject to periodic independent audit, then that would help to fulfill the second accountability requirement, that of receiver control. Degrees of accountability can vary with the frequency and type of the audit.

(4) *Requirement by the Congress for the Submission of State Plans to the Relevant Federal Agency Detailing the State's Intended Strategies and Activities in Implementing the National Objective.*

This element seeks to address the first accountability issue and might be selected as a fairly stringent means of ensuring the survival of the national objective in the 50 state programs by obtaining state attention to that objective in the development of the plan. It produces both information and receiver control. Various degrees of accountability can be ensured here by using other accountability elements jointly with the plan (through the means of guidelines by the federal agency on project eligibility or expenditure controls, for example, or through plan review and/or approval at the federal level, or through citizen participation in the development of the plan). This element also develops information on state activities which is important for the later performance of evaluation at either recipient or national levels. However, state plans are costly to prepare, have generated major problems (in the LEAA block grant program, for example) and may not be as useful for evaluation as are individual project applications featuring an evaluation component, for example.

(5) *Requirement by the Congress for a Formal Application Process by Which Potential Recipients Explain What They Will Do With Funds Received Under the Program and Why.*

This element if chosen, would represent a fairly stringent effort to ensure (a) the understanding and acceptance of the national objective at the recipient level; (b) the development of state and federal-level information about how the national objective is being implemented and what funding decisions are being made; and (c) the state or federal ability to sanction recipient misuse of funds with regard to the recipient's own assertions of intent. Degrees of stringency in this accountabiity element can be determined through differing review and approval processes.

(6) *Provision for Citizen Participation in State and/or Local Level Planning and/or Program Review.*

This element represents one possible way of addressing the problem of inequitability in the case of a specified target population, that is, the first accountability issue. It could be chosen in an attempt to ensure that the largest number of state and local voices will be heard, and that the programs implemented at state and local levels will in fact reflect state and local priorities within the broad national objective. Degrees of accountability within this element concern the types of citizen participation employed (public hearings, advisory planning, councils, citizen review boards), and the uses to which that participation is put within the program (input to state plans, voluntary assistance in service delivery, opinion surveys). This element, however, which has been a feature of both revenue sharing and block grants, tends to generate new constituencies and special interest groups; accordingly, there have been problems at state and local agency and provider levels in dealing effectively with citizen participation as a tool for accountability.

(7) *Requirement for a Recipient Report (to the State Agency or the State Legislature or the Congress or the Federal Agency) on the Use of Funds.*
This element, which calls only for performance data and does not require assessment, can be selected for two reasons. It provides retrospective information on how the block grant funds have been expended and it addresses the first two accountability issues.

(8) *Requirement by the Congress for Monitoring of Recipient Implementation by State and/or Federal Agencies.*
This element provides for receiver control of recipient-generated information. It can be chosen to address at least partially all three accountability issues (national and recipient objectives as well as management), if that were desired. Monitoring is also useful as a prerequisite for more sophisticated information, since evaluation depends on implementation monitoring to report on effectiveness. This then is an extremely important element of accountability, because the lack of provision for any implementation monitoring would signify first, that little reliable status information on program progress could be available in a timely manner either to state agencies, executive branch agencies, state legislatures, or the Congress; and second, that each audit or evaluation performed will be more expensive in that it must first proceed to the development of information on the status of implementation. Degrees of accountability can be specified in the comprehensiveness of the monitoring information sought, in the frequency of its performance, and in the procedures for assessing the reliability of the information produced (analysis, control, on-site visits, and so forth).

(9) *Requirement by the Congress for a Recipient Performance Report on Effectiveness Based on Independent Audit and/or Evaluation.*
This element can be used to address the three accountability issues. It provides both information and receiver control to those to whom the recipient is accountable. The usefulness of the information and the degree of confidence which the receiver may place in it are both dependent, however, on the quality of that information.

(10) *Provision for Technical Assistance in Accounting and Evaluation to Recipients by Federal and/or State Agencies.*
This element can be included so that less technically advanced localities/recipients may provide higher quality information to re-

ceivers. It thus can address both the problem of inequitability (by ensuring that eligible receipients are not denied help because of inadequate "grantsmanship"), and the first and third accountability issues. Further, if evaluation and audit (which report on program quality and integrity) are to be performed, they will both need good planning, data collection, and accounting systems in place if they are to address accountability objectives. Depending on the amount of audit and evaluation information deemed necessary by the Congress in a particular program, various degrees of accountability can be developed through the use of technical assistance.

(11) *Requirement by the Congress for the Audit of Recipient or Federal Agency Program Management.*

This element can be chosen so as to address all three accountability issues. Its use would have two purposes: first, the knowledge that there is provision for audit in a program tends to deter unsound management practices; second, the audit itself provides both information and receiver control to decision makers on program costs, implementation, management, and performance. Degrees of accountability are provided via the frequency, comprehensiveness, and program level of the audit.

(12) *Requirement by the Congress for Federal Agency Performance of Program Evaluation at Recipient or National Levels on the Effectiveness of Recipient Activities.*

This element, like audit, could be selected to address all three accountability issues but is especially useful in (a) the provision of empirical evidence of program effectiveness in terms of the national objective sought; (b) the pilot testing of new programs, management systems, or technology; and (c) the synthesis of retrospective information for policy use. Again, the prospect of evaluation constitutes the program equivalent of Mencken's "still, small voice that tells us someone is watching." Thus, the knowledge of a mandate for evaluation tends to deter deviations from expected courses of action. Degrees of accountability are afforded by the frequency, scope, duration, and level of the evaluation.

(13) *Requirement for Project Reports by Local Agencies to the State.*

This element could address, on a case basis, all three accountability issues and provide detailed information from the site level on a particular project useful for both state and federal receiver control. Degrees of accountability in this element concern the subject matter of the report, its frequency, and the methods of checking on its validity.

(14) *Provision for the Issuance of Program Standards or Guidelines by Federal or State Agencies.*

This element might be used to ensure that there will be some uniformity either across state programs or across level program within a state with regard to program substance, internal controls and sanctions to deter fraud and abuse, and program reporting. Such uniformity assists all three accountability issues by building the national and/or recipient objectives into the standards or guidelines; by helping to ensure the development of cross-site information on program substance and quality; and by reducing the likelihood of unsound management. Varying degrees of stringency can occur here based on the type and specificity of the guidelines and standards; the number, frequency, and detail of program reporting requested; and the monitoring, audit, and evaluation functions called for to check on individual program status and uniformity across sites and programs.

(15) *Requirement by the Congress for an Annual Performance Report by the State to the Executive Branch Agency.*

This element can be used to provide information on program progress for an entire state to the federal agency, thus fulfilling two accountability requirements and addressing two issues. Degrees of accountability in this element relate essentially to the subject matter of the report (this can cover a range of materials moving from a recapitulation of state plans, a description of what was implemented, an explanation of how complete the various projects were in achieving coverage of the objective, through a summary of state and local evaluation, audit, and monitoring findings, to a set of state conclusions and recommendations based on the results of funded activities and the problems encountered), and to the methods adopted by the federal agency (or the Congress) for checking or analyzing its validity.

(16) *Requirement by the Congress for an Annual Performance Report by the Executive Branch Agency to the Congress.*

This element can be selected to hold the executive branch agency accountable to the Congress in the oversight process. The performance report may involve degrees of accountability ranging from the inclusion of simple status report information for each state (establishing the degree to which the block grant activities are faithful to the national program objective) through the provision of national monitoring, auditing, and evaluation reports generating information on program effectiveness, costs, and management integrity, to the recommendation of proposed changes in substance, procedures, and funding. Stringency in this element may be increased by congressional mandates for independent audit or evaluation of the federal agency program. This element can thus fulfill two (or even three) accountability requirements, depending on whatever independent reviews are accomplished, and can address all the accountability issues.

(17) *Requirement by the Congress for a Performance Report from an Independent Agency (for example, GAO) on Recipient Activities, Covering Integrity, Efficiency, and Effectiveness.*
This element can be used to ensure a high level of accountability with regard to the first and third accountability issues, and to provide both information and receiver control.

(18) *Specification of Sanctions for Failures of Accountability at Any Level and of Rewards for Effective Performance.*
This element can be selected to deter malfeasance and to provide incentives for sound performance; it serves the recourse requirement presented earlier. As Mosher (1979: 235) states:

> Among the cruder tools for enforcing accountability (historically)... have been death, replacement, removal, demotion, elimination or reduction of authorities or resources, and legal action, either civil or criminal or both, to redress grievances. Less extreme but still significant instruments to penalize failures in performance include reprimands, loss of repute among superiors, peers, and subordinates, social penalties on self and family, and countless others. Instrumental to all these, and increasingly potent unto itself, is simply disclosure and publication. The key to accountability is thus, quite simply, information the openness with which an individual or agency operates and the access to information by persons outside who are in a position to do something about it, if necessary, and the ways in which relevant information is selected, processed and utilized.

To recapitulate briefly, this section has developed 18 accountability elements which range from minimal to stringent and which can be selected to assure accountability in block grants based on the degree of specificity of the national objective; and the importance attached by the Congress and the administration to the determination of whether or not it is being accomplished. As specificity and importance increase, it seems natural to move up the ladder in *stringency*, going from a self-reporting system (providing information without receiver control), through a national agency reporting system (providing two levels of information and one level of receiver control) to an independent national-level reporting system (providing two levels of information and two levels of receiver control). In the same way, within a single type of reporting system, the elements move up the ladder in *rigor*, going from monitoring through audit to evaluation at either recipient or national levels.

SUMMARY

In conclusion, then, this chapter has sought to make five points:

(1) that the criticisms leveled at categorical grants may not all be addressed by turning the programs into block grants;
(2) that some aspects of current programs notably their equitability, efficiency, and integrity may be worsened by the block grant mechanism's loss of uniformity, definition, reporting and coordination across state programs at the national level;
(3) that measures are needed to ensure appropriate accountability by federal, state, and local personnel for the use of federal funds based on accountability requirements for:

- relevant information,
- an entity to receive and control the information, and
- recourse in case of failure;

and based on the accountability issues of:

- the achievement of the national objective;
- the achievement of the recipient objective; and
- program integrity and efficiency.

(4) the accountability measures are consistent both with the basic concept of the block grant and with the duty of policymakers to assure the proper use of federal funds; and finally,
(5) that at least 18 elements of accountability exist which can be considered by the Congress in varying degrees of stringency, depending upon the particular program involved, the specificity of the national objective, and the congressional view of the importance of knowing whether or not that objective is being accomplished.

Accountability, of course, is not cost-free. Some constraints and restrictions on program administration are unavoidable in any effort to monitor and assess program performance. Without "strings" of some sort, there will be no valid and reliable data by which to follow program activity, and no established criteria by which to judge program results. On the other hand, there is no reason to assume that the kinds of structure and demands imposed by the present largely categorical system are the only (or best) means to assure accountability. The costs which that system imposes in administrative inflexibility and fragmentation are real. The question that needs to be posed is what sort of requirements of national, state, and local governments will provide the information and criteria necessary for accountability in a particular program with a minimum of administrative overload to state and local program administrators.

NOTES

1. Milton Friedman (1962: 22-36), for example, has distinguished four reasons for governmental action in a free society: to make rules and to serve as umpire; to prevent or counter monopoly; to overcome "neighborhood" or external effects; and to protect those who cannot protect themselves, such as the insane or children.

2. The operation of an "iron triangle" usually involves a smooth and solid relationship among an administrative federal agency, the relevant legislative committees and subcommittees, and an intercessor client group or lobby.

3. In particular, the synthesis was developed using materials from Chelimsky (1979), the proceedings of a symposium which was jointly funded by the National Institute of Education, the National Institute of Justice, and the MITRE Corporation. This symposium brought together national, state, and local government program managers with evaluators and auditors in an effort to examine federal program problems and discuss ways of addressing them.

REFERENCES

Advisory Commission on Intergovernmental Relations (1977) "Safe Streets reconsidered: the block grant experience, 1968-1975." (unpublished)
    (1977b) "Block grants: a comparative analysis." (unpublished)
CHELIMSKY, E. (1979) Proceedings of a Symposium on the Institutionalization of Federal Programs at the Local Level. Washington, DC: MITRE Corporation.
DOMMEL, P. R. (1981) "Statement prepared for the Senate Committee on Labor and Human Resources." Washington, DC: The Brookings Institution.
The Economist (1978) "Does CETA work?" April 29: 52.
ELAZAR, D. J. (1962) The American Partnership. Chicago: University of Chicago Press.
ETZIONI, A. (1975) "Alternative conceptions of accountability: the example of health administration." Public Administration Review (May/June): 279.
FRIEDMAN, M. (1962) Capitalism and Freedom. Chicago: University of Chicago Press.
GREIDER, W. and N. KOTZ (1973) "False hopes and faulty panaceas." Washington Post, April 8.
HERBERS, J. (1979a) "Washington, an insider's game." New York Times Magazine, April 22.
    (1979b) "End to federal revenue-sharing expected in forthcoming budget." New York Times, July 9.
    (1978) "Deep government disunity alarms many U.S. leaders." New York Times, November 12.
Joint Economic Committee (1978) "Hearing on Structural Unemployment and Public Policy." Washington, DC: Government Printing Office.
LEVIN, C. (1979) "Keepers of the dream." Washington Post, August 2.
MARTIN, R. C. (1965) The Cities and the Federal System. New York: Atherton Press.
MOSHER, F. C. (1979) The GAO: The Quest for Accountability in the American Government. Boulder, CO: Westview Press.

NETZER, R. (1974) "Discussion of 'The Property Tax: Progressive or Regressive.'" American Economic Review (May): 231.

PINE, A. (1979) "Senator Muskie criticizes states on budget-balancing moves." Washington Post, February 14.

REAGAN, M. D. (1972) The New Federalism. New York: Oxford University Press.

SCHULTZE, C. L. (1974) "The Great Society versus the New Federalism: sorting out the social grant programs." American Economic Review (May): 183-185.

STANFIELD, R. L. (1981) "Block grants look fine to states; it's the money that's the problem." National Journal, May 9.

SUNDQUIST, J. L. with D. W. DAVIS (1969) Making Federalism Work. Washington, DC: The Brookings Institute.

TOLCHIN, M. and S. TOLCHIN (1972) To The Victor. New York: Vintage.

U.S. General Accounting Office (1979) Perspective on Intergovernmental Policy and Fiscal Relations. (GGD-79-62). Washington, DC: Government Printing Office.

WILCOX, C. (1969) Toward Social Welfare. Homewood, IL: Irwin.

Targeting Federal Funds

As noted in the previous introductory section on the block grant mechanism, tensions persist in the federal government in the area of what form intergovernmental fiscal aid should take. The trend toward block grants has become evident in recent years but is by no means predominant or pervasive. Indeed, all three strategies of intergovernmental fiscal aid (categorical grants, block grants, and general revenue sharing) are alive and well, though one could argue that general revenue sharing is showing signs of becoming anemic. The presence of this continuing ambivalence clearly affects governmental policy: Programs find themselves being shifted from one fiscal strategy to another and often back again. Forward planning, program continuity, and administrative functioning in such a context is difficult at best.

The degree to which federal funds should be targeted to specific geographic locations, organizations, or groups of citizens is, in the final analysis, a political question. Targeting for any particular funding strategy is among the most sensitive of the policy decisions legislatures have to make. On the basis of such decisions, large groups of individuals, portions of the country, and types of organizations will find themselves included or excluded from the opportunity to draw on the fiscal resources.

An additional concern in this area must not be overlooked: the concern of diluting versus concentrating program resources as they influence program outcomes. Stated succinctly, the tighter the targeting requirements, the more narrowly defined the eligible recipients, and the more likely the ability to demonstrate some impact as a result of more concentrated use of funding. Keeping the parameters of the program tight through clear and precise targeting requirements is one means to increase the likelihood that the available funds will be used for the intended group. However, the trade-offs between tighter versus more open eligibility requirements are never resolved once and for all. (One might suggest, somewhat cynically, that the persistent pressure at the federal level to accommodate conflicting claims has taken its toll. The federal government is now willing to pass along these problems to state and local governments through the creation of the block grant mechanism. The federal government states the national objective, but leaves it to the state and local governments to find the means of implementation.) The more precise the targeting, the more likely that those currently excluded will press to expand the eligibility requirements, while those favored by the requirements will resist any relaxation.

The manner in which various agencies of the federal government have responded to the targeting issue is the focus of the three articles in this section. Farnham focuses on the transformation of a number of categorical grant-in-aid programs in the Department of Housing and Urban Development (HUD) into the Community Development Block Grant (CDBG) program. Having traced out the rationale for this shift, the findings are provocative: It is not evident that a key justification for targeting—local discrimination—was occurring or that those for whom the categorical grants were intended were, in fact, the actual recipients.

The analysis of the Urban Development Action Grant (UDAG) program by Webman is informative, for it illuminates one targeting strategy that has been used to assist distressed urban areas: specifically, liberally defining eligible urban areas but establishing tough criteria for actual program participation. Because public and private sectors are required to agree beforehand on what economic development will occur and what the explicit contributions of both partners will be, potential participants have incentives and also constraints. The targeting in this instance is self-selective among those urban areas that have previously worked to develop collaborative relations between the public and private sectors.

Finally, the article by Hargrove and Dean suggests that the block grant mechanism is a means to put issues of targeting square in the lap of local officials. What the CETA system sought to institutionalize was a decentralized and flexible response to local labor market requirements. This flexibility meant variations in targeting, in objectives for local programs, and in decision-making procedures. Yet the ambivalence of federal CETA officials to those variations often resulted in calling into question the decisions made at the local level. In the current period of counterreform, the demand on scarce resources will grow. Thus the targeting question comes to the center of the policy process. To ask, "Who shall be served?" is to pose a question with no final answer.

15

THE TARGETING OF FEDERAL AID
Continued Ambivalence

Paul G. Farnham

The issue of the targeting of federal intergovernmental aid on certain groups in the population has been widely discussed over the past two decades. Although there has been a trend toward the lessening of federal control over grant-in-aid programs, all affected groups have exhibited ambivalent attitudes on this question. This paper illustrates the reasons for this ambivalence by examining both the process by which U.S. Department of Housing and Urban Development categorical grants for urban and community development were transformed into the community development block grant program and the debate that has occurred over the implementation and renewal of this legislation.

How much control should Congress and the administration exert over federal intergovernmental grants? That question has been widely debated in both academic and governmental circles for the past twenty years. The tendency over this period has been toward decentralization and the lessening of federal control over grant-in-aid programs, as reflected in the shift from the Great Society philosophy of the Johnson administration to the New Federalism of the Nixon and Ford administrations and the efficiency-in-government emphasis of the Carter Administration. Congress, administration officials, and other affected parties continue, however, to exhibit ambivalent attitudes on this question. To illustrate the reasons for this ambivalence, this paper examines both the process by which U.S. Department of Housing and Urban Devel-

I would like to thank Arthur Schreiber and George Cluff for comments on an earlier draft of this paper. Research on the paper was partially supported by the Research Program Committee of the College of Business Administration, Georgia State University.

opment (HUD) categorical grants for urban and community development were transformed into the community development block grant program and the resulting debate over program implementation and renewal. The analysis will indicate the areas where either increased knowledge of program effects or a greater consensus on policy goals is needed to minimize future policy shifts.

The Need for Targeting

Categorical grants have traditionally been the form of aid used by the federal government to stimulate expenditure by lower levels of government on certain functions or toward specific groups of people such as minority or low-income groups. These grants usually require a matching contribution by the local government or demonstration of some minimum level of spending in a designated area. Local governments are required to submit applications, which are often long and detailed, in order to obtain the categorical funds.

The *Housing and Community Development Act of 1974* folded seven HUD categorical grants into the community development block grant program: urban renewal; open-space land grants; public facility loans; water and sewer facilities grants; neighborhood facilities grants; the Model Cities program; and neighborhood development grants. A total of $16.5 million had been spent under these programs in the period 1949 to 1973. The programs ranged in size from $9.5 million for urban renewal to $0.2 million for neighborhood facilities grants.[1]

Urban renewal, the oldest program, had been under attack almost since its inception in 1949. Major criticisms focused on its physical-development orientation which resulted in slum clearance and the destruction of much of the housing stock for minority and low-income groups in many cities. Critics also emphasized the lack of coordination between urban renewal and other local activities and the lack of involvement of community residents in designing urban renewal projects. The physical development approach, how-

[1] Richard P. Nathan et al., *Block Grants for Community Development* (U.S. Department of Housing and Urban Development, Washington, January 1977), p. 22.

ever, was appealing to local politicians who were concerned about the aesthetic qualities of their cities and the preservation of local tax bases. This approach was supplemented by the other categorical grant programs instituted in the early 1960s: open-space grants; public facility loans; and water and sewer facility grants.

The Model Cities program of 1966 was designed to confront many of the problems in the existing community development programs. The primary goal of Model Cities was to show that significant improvement could be achieved in dealing with both physical and social urban problems by the concentration of federal funds on deteriorated areas in selected demonstration cities. A second goal was to increase the involvement of residents of these target areas in the decision-making process. During this period increased emphasis on minority and low-income areas was also being stressed in the other HUD categorical programs such as the open-space grants. Priority selection systems that gave greater weight to projects in low-income areas were instituted. Regulations called for the coordination of projects under these other grants with the development of programs in the Model Cities neighborhoods. Thus program coordination and targeting were becoming key issues in community development in the late 1960s.

These issues were one part of the ongoing general debate at all levels of government over the effectiveness and usefulness of the categorical grant approach to stimulate the provision of local government services that had either not been provided at all or that allegedly had not been provided to minority and low-income groups. The matching requirements of these grants did appear to have created excessive amounts of red tape and bureaucratic delay as well as incentives for falsifying or stretching the interpretation of the requirements in various ways. The tremendous increase in the number of grants throughout the 1960s created a chaotic situation for many local governments since numerous city departments might be involved in applying for and administering the grants. There was often little coordination among the departments in these efforts. In many cases no single official or agency knew what types of grants the local government was receiving or how much money was involved. For example, in 1972 Mayor Norman Mineta of San Jose, California, hired an assistant who spent a year and a $200,000 federal grant assembling a book that specified the sources and amounts of federal grants to the various city agencies.[2] A federal interagency task force attempted to undertake the same project for Oakland, California. However, in its publication, *Federal Decision Making and Impact in Urban Areas: A Study of Oakland*, the task force spent most of its time discussing the reasons why such a project could not be completed. These reasons included factors such as differences in geographical data bases and reporting periods among the federal agencies and broad variations in the methods of reporting and recording program funding information.[3] Other examples abound throughout both academic literature and records of government hearings.

These problems, combined with the traditional Republican party distrust of federal government interference in local affairs, led to the development of the New Federalism philosophy of the Nixon administration. Proponents of this philosophy argued that locally elected government officials have a greater knowledge of local problems than do federal officials in Washington and that they should be given the freedom to allocate grant funds according to their own priorities. In 1971 this philosophy culminated in the Nixon administration's proposal for special revenue sharing in which categorical grants in specific areas such as community development, education, and manpower training would be consolidated. Funds for each of these broad areas would be allocated to communities by statutory formula. Local governments would then be free to make their own decisions about expenditures on projects within these broad program areas. There would be no matching requirements under special revenue sharing.

These special revenue sharing proposals encountered great opposition from Congress which was not as willing to relinquish control over the grant funds as was the Administration. Critics argued that local governments traditionally undersupplied the public services consumed principally by low-income residents. If categorical grants were combined into special revenue sharing legislation, these governments would have the opportunity to revert back to their traditional spending patterns. The argument

---

[2] Timothy B. Clark, John K. Igelhart, William Lilley, "The New Federalism: Theory, Practice, Problems—A Special Report," *National Journal* (March 1973), p. 39.
[3] Oakland Task Force, San Francisco Executive Board, *Federal Decision Making and Impact in Urban Areas: A Study of Oakland* (Praeger, New York, 1970), pp. 53-56.

made by Richard LeGates and Mary C. Morgan was typical: "The broad range of discretion left to local officials [under special revenue sharing] and the absence of federal priorities virtually ensures that less and less money will go toward meeting the problems of urban decay. . . . There are many indications that the Better Communities Act [special revenue sharing] will eliminate the current role—as limited as it is—of poverty neighborhoods in the planning and execution of redevelopment programs. Control of revenue sharing funds will pass to local government officials traditionally unresponsive or hostile to the needs of the urban poor."[4]

Congressional debate over the decentralization issue and the targeting question was one of the major reasons why passage of the community development special revenue sharing legislation was delayed from 1971 until 1974. When this legislation was finally included in the *Housing and Community Development Act of 1974*, the name of the program had been changed to community development block grants and the legislation contained more restrictions on the use of the funds than the administration had proposed. The legislation did consolidate the seven categorical programs with no local matching of funds required. In addition, the bill contained a series of national objectives for the block grant program. These included (1) elimination of slums and blight and the prevention of the deterioration of property and community facilities, especially those for low- and moderate-income persons; (2) the elimination of conditions detrimental to health, safety, and public welfare through code enforcement, demolition, etc.; (3) the conservation and expansion of the nation's housing stock to provide a decent home for all persons, but principally those of low and moderate income; (4) the expansion and improvement of the quality and quantity of community services, principally for persons of low and moderate income, that are essential for sound community development and for the development of viable urban communities. Local governments would submit a single, broad application that included a three-year community development

---

[4] Richard T. LeGates and Mary C. Morgan, "The Perils of Special Revenue Sharing for Community Development," *Journal of the American Institute of Planners*, 39 (July 1973): 260.

plan summary, a one-year action program, a housing assistance plan, and a budget. They would have to assure the Department of Housing and Urban Development that they had given "maximum feasible priority" to activities that would benefit low- and moderate-income families or aid in the prevention of slums or blight and that they had provided for "adequate" citizen participation and had complied with the nondiscrimination provisions of the act.[5]

The inclusion of these restrictions in the block grant program shows that distributional and targeting considerations were of utmost importance in the minds of the legislators. Their arguments against the administration's special revenue sharing proposals appear to have been based on two assumptions: (1) Local governments had been insensitive to the needs of minority and low-income groups. In particular, they had biased the distribution of municipal public services in favor of middle- and upper-income classes in response to the voting and political power of these groups. This practice should be ended both to correct past inequities and to prevent racial disturbances in the future.[6] (2) The restrictions on the categorical grants were assumed to be effective in aiding the targeted populations. Neither of these points, however, has been conclusively demonstrated.

Missing the Target?

The theoretical and empirical literature on intergovernmental grants is vast.[7] Most of these studies are concerned with the impact on local expenditures and taxes of various types of grants and matching ratios. The outcomes, even in the theoretical analyses, depend upon the underlying income and price elasticities

[5] Nathan et al., ftn. 1, pp. 53-54.
[6] Reports by the Kerner Commission and the National Commission on Urban Problems had cited the lack of adequate municipal services in minority and low-income neighborhoods as one of the causes of the racial disturbances in the late 1960s.
[7] The following studies are representative examples of this literature: James A. Wilde, "Grants-in-Aid: The Analytics of Design and Response," *National Tax Journal*, 24 (June 1974): 143-155; Wallace Oates, *Fiscal Federalism* (Harcourt Brace Jovanovich, New York, 1972), pp. 65-118; Edward M. Gramlich and Harvey Galper, "State and Local Fiscal Behavior and Federal Grant Policy," *Brookings Papers on Economic Activity*, 1 (1973): 15-58.

of the communities for the subsidized goods and upon whether grants are open-ended or closed. The assumption is also made that communities are maximizing some concept of social welfare. Recent studies have become more sophisticated in their development of models of local government behavior and in their treatment of the variety of ways by which grants can affect local expenditures. For example, McGuire uses an indirect statistical method to analyze the shape of a local government's post-subsidy budget constraint because, he argues, the true effect of a subsidy on the recipient's resource constraint cannot be determined from the nominal administrative requirements of the grant program.[8]

The empirical work in the grant studies has usually been carried out on an aggregate level with samples such as the forty-eight states, metropolitan areas, etc. Grant displacement of local funds has been identified at this level. Little work has been done, however, on measuring the distributional effect of the grants within a locality or city. One of the most respected students of intergovernmental grants, Edward Gramlich, has argued on several occasions that grants research must go beyond the question of measuring the overall impact of the funds to the more difficult issue of whether the desired type of spending for the programs' specified clientele is actually achieved.[9] It is often the case that most of the expenditure that is targeted on low-income neighborhoods is used to hire persons who live elsewhere to provide services to target-area residents. How much the target-area residents benefit from this spending is a question for detailed, disaggregated analysis of the transformation of federal dollar inputs into local public service outputs. The utility maximization models used in most of the traditional grants studies are inappropriate for an analysis of the monetary and nonmonetary factors that influence the allocation of public expenditure among neighborhoods within a city and for an evaluation of program impact.

Although many evaluations of the Great Society categorical

---

[8] Martin McGuire, "A Method for Estimating the Effect of a Subsidy on the Receiver's Resource Constraint: With an Application to U.S. Local Governments 1964-1971," *Journal of Public Economics,* 10 (August 1978): 25-44.

[9] Edward M. Gramlich, "Intergovernmental Grants: A Review of the Empirical Literature," *The Political Economy of Fiscal Federalism,* edited by Wallace Oates (Lexington Books, Lexington, MA, 1977), pp. 234-235.

grant programs were undertaken, they tended to focus more on the process of funding than on the impact of the grants. In the community development area there are no systematic evaluations of the impact of even large programs such as Model Cities. The reasons for the lack of evaluation in the Model Cities program are discussed extensively by Bernard J. Frieden and Marshall Kaplan in *The Politics of Neglect: Urban Aid From Model Cities to Revenue Sharing*. One of the major factors that prevented the undertaking of systematic evaluations was the political need for immediate measures of program impact. Frieden and Kaplan write that "while long-term critical analyses that would generate an understanding of impact and institutional behavior patterns were accepted as important, [Assistant Secretary for Community Development] Hyde could not wait for the conclusion of lengthy studies. He also did not care much whether evaluative techniques were 'pure,' 'academically' acceptable, or complete. Analyses, to be useful to him, needed to be converted, almost while in process, into amended strategies."[10]

The question of bias in the intracity distribution of local public services remains controversial largely because it has not been well researched. Many charges of discrimination were raised in the 1960s before organizations such as the Kerner Commission and the National Commission on Urban Problems. In a recent paper, Frieden and Kaplan argue that the poor lacked the political clout to benefit from municipal public works programs in the 1930s. During the sixties, when federal requirements worked in their favor, the emphasis changed from hardware to software and innovative social programs. Now, under the community development block grant program, hardware is again fashionable, but the authors argue that low-income groups continue to lose out when dealing with city hall since they still lack political power and there are no strict targeting requirements in the legislation.[11] A similar view was expressed by the authors in *The Politics of Neglect*. In

[10] Bernard J. Frieden and Marshall Kaplan, *The Politics of Neglect: Urban Aid From Model Cities to Revenue Sharing* (M.I.T. Press, Cambridge, MA, 1975), p. 180.

[11] Bernard J. Frieden and Marshall Kaplan, "Community Development and the Model Cities Legacy," Working Paper No. 42, November 1976, cited in U.S. Congress, House Subcommittee on Housing and Community Development of the Committee on Banking, Finance, and Urban Affairs, *Hearings, Housing and Community Development Act of 1977*, 95th Congress, 1st Session, 1977, pp. 650–654.

a review of that book, however, Christopher DeMuth argues that Frieden and Kaplan "do not attempt to compare with Model Cities the *total* effect of general and special revenue sharing on the level of public expenditures benefiting model neighborhoods nor do they explain how citizen participation has changed (or may be expected to change) from what it was under Model Cities." DeMuth also argues that he knows of nothing "that suggests that Model Cities actually brought either a measurable concentration of public funds into model neighborhoods or the kind of mobilization of local initiative envisioned by the program's framers. . . ."[12] Similar controversy over discrimination in municipal service provision has been raised by the National Revenue Sharing Monitoring Project in Washington, D.C., in connection with spending under the general revenue sharing program.[13] In all of these cases the issues revolve around the question of local behavior regarding the provision of public services in the absence of federal restrictions and targeting requirements.

Legal cases involving charges of discrimination in the provision of public services have not lived up to what was expected to be a precedent-setting case: *Hawkins vs. Town of Shaw* (1971). In that case the Fifth Circuit Court of Appeals found the town of Shaw, Mississippi, guilty of racial discrimination in the provision of a number of services and ordered town officials to provide black residents with services equal to those already provided to whites. This case has had only limited applicability elsewhere, however, because it was litigated on the basis of a near absolute deprivation. There were large differences between the services provided to blacks and to whites. Furthermore, documentation in the case was relatively easy given that there was rigid residential segregation in the town and that the small size of the community (population 2,500) permitted an exhaustive inventory of the public services.[14]

The literature on the intracity distribution of local public services has developed only in recent years and is still quite small.

---

[12] Christopher DeMuth, "Deregulating the Cities," *The Public Interest*, 44 (Summer 1976): 123-124.

[13] National Revenue Sharing Monitoring Project, *General Revenue Sharing: The Case for Reform* (Center for National Policy Review, Washington, 1976), p. 8.

[14] Astrid E. Merget, "Equalizing Municipal Services: Issues for Policy Analysis," *Policy Studies Journal*, 4 (Spring 1976): 300.

Carl Shoup provided the basic framework for this type of research in 1964 by illustrating the equity-efficiency conflict that can result in allocating police protection services within a city.[15] In 1970, Werner Hirsch noted that relatively little is known about the actual distribution of state and local public services by such categories as location, income, and race because records are not kept in those terms and because officials do not want discriminatory practices known to the public if they exist.[16] Other researchers have argued that local government records do contain the basic public service data which must then be combined with census and socioeconomic data for this type of research.

Some empirical work measuring the distribution of various local public services has been undertaken. This research, which usually consists of case studies of particular services in selected cities, has shown the complexities involved in defining and measuring the distribution of local public services. The results, especially those regarding the question of services in minority and low-income areas, are mixed. Frank Levy and his associates found an allocation of resources that favored both high- and low-income groups over the middle class in the Oakland school district for the year 1969-70. This reflected, at least in part, the influence of the federal compensatory programs begun in the 1960s.[17] In the education studies summarized by Hirsch, some measures favored the "privileged" districts while others favored the "underprivileged" districts.[18] Donald Fisk and Cynthia Lancer were unable to find *prima facie* evidence of discrimination against a low-income neighborhood in the provision of recreation services in Washington, D.C., in 1972.[19] Steven Gold concluded in a 1968 study that service levels in areas designated by the Detroit Department of Parks and Recreation as "most in need" were not consistently

---

[15] Carl S. Shoup, "Standards for Distributing a Free Governmental Service: Crime Prevention," *Public Finance*, 19 (1964): 383-392.

[16] Werner Z. Hirsch, *The Economics of State and Local Government* (McGraw-Hill, New York, 1970), p. 195.

[17] Frank Levy, Arnold Meltsner, and Aaron Wildavsky, *Urban Outcomes: Schools, Streets, and Libraries* (University of California Press, Berkeley, 1974), pp. 67-78.

[18] Hirsch, ftn. 16, pp. 195-197.

[19] D. M. Fisk and C. A. Lancer, *Equality of Distribution of Recreation Services: A Case Study of Washington, D.C.* (The Urban Institute, Washington, 1974).

lower than elsewhere in the city.[20] Robert Lineberry found that residents in high density, heavily ethnic census tracts with low socioeconomic status had the greatest proximity to libraries and fire stations in San Antonio in 1970.[21]

These studies are cited not to show that no bias or discrimination in the provision of public services exists, but rather that it cannot automatically be assumed to be present. In his summary of the literature covering large cities such as New York, Chicago, Washington, Oakland, and Houston, Lineberry argues that "distribution studies are more likely than not to find either roughly equal or even compensatory patterns than to find discriminatory patterns. . . .*Pockets* of discrimination can be found, but probably not *patterns* of discrimination. There are no doubt dozens of ways municipal governments discriminate against the urban underclass, including zoning decisions, the *treatment* of citizens by bureaucracies, and educational disadvantages. But the weight of evidence compels the conclusion that overt, measurable discrimination in the distribution in conventional city services has been overstated by anecdotal commentary and conventional wisdom."[22]

It must be remembered that all of these studies are limited by the availability of adequate data. This limitation is the most serious with regard to the measurement of differential quality of public services among neighborhoods. Furthermore, the impact of any public service distribution can change substantially over time since significant population shifts are occurring in most of the country's major cities. The existence of this literature, however, does raise questions regarding the benefits of federal targeting requirements to equalize public service distribution and the way these benefits compare with the increased costs of decision making that the requirements entail. Differing perceptions of these benefits and costs on the part of the Nixon administration and Congress were central to the original debate over the community development block grant program. These differences have con-

---

[20] Steven D. Gold, "The Distribution of Urban Government Services in Theory and Practice: The Case of Recreation in Detroit," *Public Finance Quarterly*, 2 (January 1974): 123.

[21] Robert L. Lineberry, *Equality and Urban Policy. The Distribution of Municipal Public Services* (Sage Publications, Beverly Hills, 1977), pp. 117-125.

[22] Lineberry, ftn. 21, p. 186.

tinued to play a role in the implementation and renewal of the program.

Target Setting

In 1974 Congress appropriated funding for the community development block grant program for only three years. Although much of the discussion in the Congressional hearings on the renewal of the program in 1977 focused on the overall allocation formula, significant concern was once again expressed about the targeting issue. Several studies of the community development block grant program had been undertaken almost as soon as the program began operation. These studies, which were cited in the Congressional hearings, differed in their conclusions about the impact of the block grant program on low-income and minority groups. A Brookings Institution study directed by Richard Nathan found that a majority of the fund allocations in the 62 sample jurisdictions in the first year of the program provided direct benefits to low- and moderate-income persons. One-quarter of the funds were assigned for community-wide purposes.[23] The National Association of Housing and Redevelopment Officials (NAHRO) studied 149 communities and concluded that the proportion of block grant funds targeted to low- and moderate-income census tracts in the communities was 51 percent in the first year and 44 percent in the second year.[24] The Southern Regional Council, on the other hand, concluded from its on-the-spot investigations in 26 communities in the first year of the program and an additional 20 cities in the second year that very few cities spend the bulk of their community development allocations on projects that were of greatest benefit to low- and moderate-income citizens. The Council, an activist civil rights group, charged that Congress and HUD had allowed an interpretation of the national objectives in the block grant program that permitted "the construction of tennis courts,

[23] Richard P. Nathan, Paul R. Dommel, Sarah F. Liebschutz, and Milton D. Morris, "Monitoring the Block Grant Program for Community Development," *Political Science Quarterly*, 92 (Summer 1977): 226-227.

[24] "Administration Targets Aid to Aging Cities," *Congressional Quarterly Weekly Reports*, 35 (March 5, 1977): 419.

swimming pools, baseball parks and other frivolous activities as 'urgent needs,' while other, more pressing priorities such as code enforcement and housing rehabilitation have not been encouraged."[25]

These varying conclusions result from differences in methodologies and definitions of benefits and from the different samples employed in the impact studies. The Brookings researchers acknowledge that the on-the-scene benefit assessments made by their research associates were only measures of direct, near-term benefits and that there may also be long-term and more indirect benefits to low-income persons from the program. Both the Brookings study and the NAHRO study reached conclusions by analyzing data on the block grant applications. Experience with other types of grants has shown that there can be major discrepancies between the projects listed on grant applications and those that are actually undertaken and completed.

In its own monitoring of the block grant program, HUD has utilized three methods for estimating program benefits in low-income neighborhoods. The city-attested method uses the benefit levels reported by cities in their applications. Under this approach cities can allocate all of the funds budgeted for a given activity, regardless of the area where it is located, to the low- and moderate-income priority category as long as at least 51 percent of the funds for the activity are planned to benefit low- and moderate-income persons. The SMSA median income method totals up all program dollars planned for census tracts with median incomes that are 80 percent or less of the SMSA median income. This method excludes both funding not specifically directed to low- and moderate-income neighborhoods and non-area-specific activities that could benefit low- and moderate-income persons. The adjusted SMSA median income method is similar to the previous method except that adjustments are made for non-area-specific activities.[26] Under

---

[25] Prepared statement of Wayne A. Clark, Southern Regional Council, Atlanta, Georgia, cited in U.S. Congress, House Subcommittee on Housing and Community Development of the Committee on Banking, Finance, and Urban Affairs, *Hearings, Housing and Community Development Act of 1977*, 95th Congress, 1st Session, 1977, p. 768.

[26] U.S. Department of Housing and Urban Development, Office of Community Planning and Development, *Fifth Annual Community Development Block Grant Report* (U.S. Government Printing Office, Washington, D.C., 1980), p. III-3.

the second and third methods, HUD estimates that approximately 64 percent of all block grant funds from 1975 to 1979 have benefited low- and moderate-income persons. For 1979 (the only year for which data are available), the city-attested method allocates 94 percent of the funds to low- and moderate-income groups.[27] The arbitrariness of all these methods shows why conclusions regarding the recipients of program benefits can vary widely. The methods illustrate the problems involved in determining whether any types of targeting requirements have an effect on local government behavior.

The arguments over the targeting issue in the block grant renewal hearings were very similar to those that had occurred from 1971 to 1974 in the hearings on the original act. They also demonstrated the same ambivalence over the issue of the benefits versus the costs of targeting. Critics of the block grant program, such as the Southern Regional Council, argued that they were not advocating a return to the complex application procedures of the categorical grants but that local officials should be held more accountable through additional performance standards. Frieden and Kaplan favored the approach of establishing in the law a specific minimum percentage of funds to be used for low- and moderate-income persons and the tightening of standards for resident involvement in community development programs. An 80 percent rule had been included in the original act by the Senate but it was deleted by the conference committee. A similar situation occurred during the passage of the 1977 renewal legislation. Senator William Proxmire included several proposals to restrict funds to low- and moderate-income groups but they were not approved by Congress.

The focus of this debate switched to the executive branch two weeks after the *Housing and Community Development Act of 1977* was signed in October 1977. HUD Secretary Patricia Harris proposed a set of regulations to implement the act that included a rule that 75 percent of each recipient's grant should be spent on low- and moderate-income persons. This rule immediately brought charges that HUD was attempting to change the block grant program by administrative fiat. Much concern was expressed over maintaining local flexibility under the program. The attitudes expressed in a December 1977 position paper by the National League of Cities were typical of those of many interest groups. The League argued that the block grant program had fostered a more workable relationship between the federal and local levels of government in the achievement of national housing and community development objectives and had provided greater flexibility to communities in establishing local priorities. However, the "concept of a block grant program may be destroyed if restrictive regulations continue to be developed and applied nationwide without regard to diverse local and regional considerations."[28] According to the League, HUD should restrict itself to the administration of the law and not add complications and red tape by voluminous interpretations. The League argued for more program monitoring to determine whether communities were complying with the provisions of the act.

This argument that the 75 percent rule would be unnecessarily restrictive and costly prevailed with the passage of the *Housing and Community Development Amendments of 1978*.[29] That legislation prohibits the Secretary of HUD from disapproving a community development application on the basis that it addresses any one of the block grant program's primary purposes—that assisted activities principally benefit persons of low and moderate income or aid in the prevention or elimination of slums or blight or meet other community development needs having a particular urgency—to a greater or lesser degree than any other. An application can be disapproved if the Secretary determines that the extent to which a primary purpose is addressed is "plainly inappropriate to meeting the needs and objectives which are consistent with the community's efforts to achieve the block grant program's primary objective—the development of viable urban communities by providing decent housing and a suitable living environment and expanding economic

---

[28] National League of Cities, "Community Development Policy," December 7, 1977, cited in U.S. Congress, House Subcommittee on Housing and Community Development of the Committee on Banking, Finance, and Urban Affairs, *Hearings, Housing and Community Development Amendments of 1978*, 95th Congress, 2nd Session, 1978, p. 299.

[29] For a detailed discussion of the events leading to the passage of these amendments, see Paul R. Dommel, Victor E. Bach, Sarah J. Liebschutz, Leonard S. Rubinowitz, and Associates, *Targeting Community Development* (U.S. Government Printing Office, Washington, D.C., 1980), pp. 14-21.

opportunities, principally for persons of low or moderate income.[30] Thus the Secretary's responsibility has been statutorily defined by Congress. According to the joint explanatory statement of the conference committee, "the amendment is designed to make clear that a determination to disapprove cannot be made simply because an application gives greater or lesser weight to one spending priority in relation to the others, and that any percentage limitation on the level of funds to be allocated shall be strictly avoided, except for review purposes, in order to take account of unique community needs."[31] Therefore, even though Congress was never willing to accept the original "no strings attached" special revenue sharing concept, it has also been unwilling to set a precise targeting formula or to permit an executive agency to do so.

Benefits and Costs of Targeting

It is questionable whether increased targeting of federal funds can be achieved without a return to sets of procedures and a level of federal involvement at the local level similar to that under the categorical grant programs. If federal intergovernmental legislation is going to include national objectives that differ substantially from local objectives, the legislation must include targeting requirements and monitoring processes that are strong enough to change local behavior. There has been substantial testimony by local officials that federal requirements help absorb some of the political heat generated in the attempt to implement national objectives at the local level. Achieving these goals, however, will entail substantial administrative and compliance costs at all levels of government and a loss of flexibility at the local level. The issue then becomes a question of whether the benefits from additional regulation are greater or less than the costs involved in enforcing compliance.

[30] U.S. Congress, House Subcommittee on Housing and Community Development of the Committee on Banking, Finance, and Urban Affairs, *Compilation of the Housing and Community Development Amendments of 1978*, 95th Congress, 2nd Session, 1978, p. 53.
[31] U.S. Congress, House Subcommittee on Housing and Community Development, *Compilation of the Housing and Community Development Amendments of 1978*, p. 90.

It has been shown that Congressional legislators have been most reluctant to release control over federal intergovernmental grants. It may also be the case that even if restrictions are loosened by legislation, they tend to gradually reappear in various forms in the implementation process. Evidence on this conclusion was derived by Richard Nathan and his associates at the Brookings Institution from the second year findings of their monitoring study of the block grant program. Of the 61 jurisdictions included in the Brookings study, 32 reported either a substantially greater or a somewhat greater role by HUD at the local level when comparing the second year of the program with the first year of operation. Furthermore, when officials in the 44 jurisdictions with prior HUD categorical grant experience were asked to compare the amount of red tape under the block grant program with their previous experience, only half of those responding (21 out of 43) reported a decrease in red tape.[32]

Nathan and his associates argued that the increased HUD involvement in the second year of the program may have resulted from the fact that program implementation was rushed in the first year and that performance monitoring reviews and program evaluations were not conducted until the second year. It has already been shown, however, that HUD attempted on its own to institute stronger targeting requirements than Congress mandated and that many interest groups have called for more effective program monitoring. Further evidence on the increasing role of HUD is provided in the Brookings research on the third and fourth years of the block grant program. The Brookings field associates reported that "HUD's role expanded in almost half of the [monitored] jurisdictions in the third year and in half the fourth year. This increase occurred in all types of jurisdictions, with a somewhat greater expansion of HUD's role in suburban jurisdictions in the third year. The associates' comments indicate that the expansion of HUD's role in the suburbs was often related to the issue of program benefits to low- and moderate-income groups."[33]

Although the Brookings researchers are skeptical that "recategorization" of the block grants is occurring, much of the evidence

---

[32] Richard P. Nathan and Paul R. Dommel, "Federal-Local Relations Under Block Grants," *Political Science Quarterly*, 93 (Fall 1978): 426-429.

[33] Dommel et al., ftn. 29, p. 37.

they present supports the conclusion that there are significant steps in that direction. The shift in policy instituted by Secretary Harris is described as follows: "Before the shift, decisions about CDBG spending were made in two stages: Local governments formulated their plans, and HUD reviewed those plans on technical and legal criteria. After the shift, decisions were made in three stages: First HUD defines program objectives; then local decisionmakers establish priorities and formulate programs within the HUD guidelines; and finally HUD reviews the local application to see if it appropriately interprets the national program goals."[34] Although the Brookings researchers argue that this policy is based on administrative choice and is therefore subject to change, they also point out that, according to their measures, the policy appears to have been successful in increasing benefits to low- and moderate-income neighborhoods.[35] Since this is one of the goals in the program legislation, it is very plausible to argue that the federal role, accompanied by larger decision-making costs, will continue to increase.

With regard to the benefits of stronger targeting requirements, evidence has been presented that one of the justifications for federal targeting, the problem of discrimination in the provision of local public services, does not appear to be as great a problem as it was thought or assumed to be. Moreover, the evidence on who actually benefits when federal funds are spent on targeted neighborhoods is contradictory and inconclusive. This is not to deny that the other problems dealt with in the community development block grant program, such as poor quality housing and the lack of economic opportunity for low- and moderate-income citizens, do exist. These problems, however, may be handled more efficiently by programs designed to directly affect the distribution of income among individuals as opposed to programs attempting to target expenditure on areas or neighborhoods.

What can be concluded from this analysis is that policy instruments must be appropriate for the intended goals and that any federal response to local problems must be considered from the viewpoint of its expected benefits and costs. Unfortunately, in many cases our knowledge of these factors is quite rudimentary.

[34] *Ibid.*, p. 36.
[35] *Ibid.*, p. 167

16

UDAG
Targeting Urban Economic Development

Jerry A. Webman

The Urban Development Action Grant (UDAG) program, the principal urban policy innovation of the Carter administration, was intended to stimulate economic recovery in America's most distressed urban areas. Enacted in October 1977 as section 119 of the Housing and Community Development Act of 1977, it provided $400 million in each of its first two years of operation, fiscal 1978 and 1979. Congress increased funding to $675 million for fiscal 1980. Popular among the nation's mayors, UDAG survived the Reagan fiscal 1982 budget cuts despite initial inclusion among doomed programs.

In authorizing the program, Congress provided specific instructions concerning who was to receive action grants, but said little about what recipients could do with the money. The law states that UDAG funds should go "to severely distressed cities and urban counties to help alleviate physical and economic deterioration through reclamation of neighborhoods having excessive housing abandonment or deterioration, and through community revitalization in areas with population outmigration or a stagnating or declining tax base."[1] Relative levels of "severe distress" and "excessive" deterioration were to be measured by "factors such as age and condition of housing stock, including residential abandonment; average income; population outmigration; and a stagnating or declining tax base."[2] Congress clearly intended that eligibility be narrowly restricted and that eligibility criteria emphasize physical aspects of urban deterioration.

---

[1] Housing and Community Development Act of 1977, sec. 119 (a), 91 Stat. 1125 (1977).
[2] Ibid., sec. 119 (b).

JERRY A. WEBMAN is assistant professor of politics and public affairs at Princeton University and director of the cross-national research project on the politics and implementation of urban economic development policy. He is the author of a forthcoming book on urban redevelopment in two Western European cities.

Reprinted with permission from the *Political Science Quarterly* 96 (Summer 1981): 189-207.

By contrast, the law is remarkably vague and permissive in describing how action grants are to help alleviate distress. Applications are to "describe a concentrated urban development action program setting forth a comprehensive action plan and strategy to alleviate physical and economic distress through systematic change." In its strongest hint about what such programs should include, Congress required that they "be developed as to take advantage of unique opportunities to attract private investment, stimulate investment in restoration of deteriorated or abandoned housing stock, or solve critical problems resulting from population outmigration or a stagnating or declining tax base."[3] Congress intended, in short, that UDAG be a highly targeted program. But it did not specify that the program should focus primarily on private investments as its way of stimulating economic development.

This focus is nonetheless the distinctive feature of the UDAG program. This approach flows not from the authorizing legislation but from Department of Housing and Urban Development (HUD) rules and regulations. Using the law's "unique opportunity" provision, HUD officials wrote regulations stating that "no project will be funded . . . unless there is a firm commitment of private resources to the proposed project."[4] With this provision, HUD shaped the action grant program as an instrument for achieving public goals by securing the cooperation and active participation of private business. HUD's first annual report on UDAG explains the strategy behind the requirement for private commitments.

> This is a fundamental principle distinguishing the Action Grant program from previous urban revitalization efforts. This requirement is based on the recognition that public funds, alone, are not sufficient to revitalize distressed cities. The private sector is essential, working in partnership with local government, to carry out economic development and neighborhood revitalization projects.[5]

These regulations mean that action grants cannot fund just any activity that would "help alleviate deterioration," but can only support projects that stimulate new private economic activity in distressed urban areas. Applications must contain legally binding commitments for private investment: no UDAG money can be spent until private funds begin to flow.

In sum, the law specifies who can receive UDAG grants; the regulations specify what can be done with them. Together, these legislative and administrative requirements define the two principle goals of the UDAG program: to stimulate private economic activity, and to do so in the nation's most distressed urban areas. This article assesses how well the program met these goals in the first two years of its operation. It uses two sources of information: data provided by HUD on the 520 grants that were awarded between April 1978 and January

---

[3] Ibid., sec. 119 (c) (2).
[4] *Federal Register*, vol. 43, no. 6 (19 January 1977), p. 1608.
[5] U.S. Department of Housing and Urban Development, Office of Evaluation, *Urban Development Action Grant Program: First Annual Report* (Washington, D.C.: Government Printing Office, 1979), p. 4.

1980; and case studies of eight UDAG projects in five New Jersey cities—four projects in Newark and one each in Paterson, Morristown, New Brunswick, and Salem.

The Mechanics of Action Grants

To obtain an Urban Development Action Grant, an eligible city or urban county must put together a financial package. This package is the central component of a UDAG application, and understanding the process of putting together the package is the key to understanding how the UDAG program works.

In brief, an application must show first that government officials and prospective private investors have worked out a project that would be viable if a specific problem were solved, and second that an action grant to the municipality can reasonably be expected to solve that problem. The application must also estimate how many jobs the project will create, predict how the project will affect the municipality's fiscal position, show how much experience the local government has had with similar undertakings, and provide information on how distressed the municipality is. In choosing which projects to fund from among those submitted in each calendar quarter, HUD looks at all the supporting information. But first HUD officials review the plans for the specific project and the information provided on a specific problem to be solved by an action grant.

Action grants can be used to solve a wide range of problems connected with new private investment projects. Like traditional public works and community development grant programs, action grants can be used to provide infrastructure, access, or public facilities for a proposed project. Like urban renewal, funds from UDAG may be used to assemble and discount developable tracts of land. Other uses for action grants have more in common with Economic Development Administration and Small Business Administration programs. In these cases, a grant can enable a municipality to extend direct financial assistance to a potential investor.

This last form of assistance requires some elaboration. In a pattern HUD has encouraged, cities have lent or occasionally given UDAG funds directly to project developers.[6] Often private investors have found land and adequate public facilities in declining cities, but have claimed that they could not raise adequate capital cheaply enough to make the project feasible and attractive. In such cases, cities, often acting through quasi-independent development corporations, can provide UDAG money in the form of loans to private developers. Such loans usually take the form of a subordinated second mortgage on land and buildings. The most common form of subsidization is to charge interest below the market rate. Such "soft" loans, as illustrated by the New Jersey case studies, can amount to a substantial subsidy.

[6] David Cordish, "Overview of UDAG," in *The Urban Development Action Grant Program: Papers and Proceedings on Its First Two Years of Operation*, eds. Richard P. Nathan and Jerry A. Webman (Princeton, N.J.: Princeton Urban Regional Research Center, 1981), p. 16.

The variability in uses for UDAG money is an important attribute of the program. Cities, their development corporations and consultants, and potential investors have considerable flexibility in developing financial packages for proposed projects.

The advantages of this flexibility for an economic development program can be seen by contrasts with the urban renewal program, a predecessor of UDAG.[7] Urban renewal also attempted to help revitalize declining cities by subsidizing private investment in blighted areas. Before it ended in 1974, the urban renewal program had attracted $9.15 billion in private investment in various renewal projects; federal grants and public investment in the same areas amounted to $9.03 billion.[8] Despite this accomplishment, the program was a rather blunt instrument for economic development. The urban renewal program could provide money to local redevelopment authorities that allowed them to buy land and sell it at greatly reduced prices to developers. It could also provide some indirect aid for infrastructure and public facilities. But it could not give direct aid to a business in return for an investment in a renewal area. One of the strengths of the UDAG program is the ability to adapt to a specific firm's investment needs.

This flexibility is particularly significant when considered together with another major way in which UDAG differs from previous urban development programs, namely the HUD requirement that UDAG projects be "wired"—that is, that both the local government and the private investor be committed in advance—before grants are approved. Under the urban renewal program, local renewal authorities were required to dispose of redevelopment land through competitive bidding. Projects could not be tailored to fit a specific developer's needs. The urban renewal program had a mixed record in attracting developers. Some redevelopment agencies offered land that was so attractive that developers did compete for its use; in other cases the agency had to quietly make arrangements with a developer before the project proceeded. In many cities, however, redevelopment agencies assembled and cleared land but could find no private developer to buy and use it. Some of these sites were eventually used for public facilities, but many sat empty.[9]

In fact, many of the UDAG projects that were funded in the first two years of the program were built on land that had been acquired under the urban renewal program but had been vacant for several years. As the UDAG program con-

---

[7] For comparisons see, M. Carter McFarland, *Federal Government and Urban Problems: HUD: Success, Failures, and the Fate of Our Cities* (Boulder, Colo.: Westview Press, 1978), p. 94.

[8] U.S., Congress, Senate, Committee on Banking, Housing and Urban Affairs, Subcommittee on Housing and Urban Affairs, *The Central City Problem and Urban Renewal Policy*, Committee Print, 93rd Cong., 1st sess., 1973, p. 65.

[9] A legion of urban renewal case studies could be cited. Those dealing in particular with implementation problems include Roger Montgomery, "Improving the Design Process in Urban Renewal," in *Urban Renewal: The Record and the Controversy*, ed. James Q. Wilson (Cambridge, Mass.: MIT Press, 1966), pp. 454–87; Harold Kaplan, *Urban Renewal Politics: Slum Clearance in Newark* (New York: Columbia University Press, 1963); and Jean L. Stinchcombe, *Reform and Reaction: City Politics in Toledo* (Belmont, Calif.: Wadsworth Publishing Co., 1968).

tinues, some municipalities may eventually run out of such publicly owned land. If this happens, local governments may find in some cases that to make a deal with a private business they must offer the business a tract of land, and that before they can make such an offer they must acquire the land. As the urban renewal program showed, land acquisition can take years and create tremendous controversy. In this way, the UDAG program's requirement that packages be agreed upon in advance may in some places slow the program's implementation; analysts cannot know whether this problem will actually arise, however, until more UDAG projects are built.

HUD's requirement of an advance commitment has had another effect that is already clear. This effect is related to the process of developing projects. By requiring that deals be "wired," the UDAG program brings private investors directly and publicly into the political process. Business people willing to invest in eligible cities thus become major participants in the design of development projects. The result is a development package that brings together the local government's concern for economic development and a private developer's evaluation of the potentials and requirements for a specific investment at a specific location.

The local government and the developer are not the only participants in the UDAG development process. The UDAG office in HUD's Washington headquarters reviews each proposal for an action grant, evaluating what is being proposed and how the proposed project will be carried out. HUD thus has extensive influence over the details of a project. This approach is the opposite of the funding method used in other recent urban aid programs, such as the Community Development Block Grant (CDBG) program and activities funded under the Comprehensive Employment and Training Act (CETA). Those programs leave local governments more flexibility in deciding what projects to fund with federal money.

Approved UDAG projects, in sum, reflect an amalgam of the requirements and interests of local government, HUD officials, and private investors. Thus, the balancing and negotiation needed to prepare a successful package must affect the content of approved projects.

Does UDAG Attract New Private Investment in Declining Urban Areas?

As noted earlier, one of the UDAG program's two principal goals is to stimulate new economic activity. HUD's regulations state that a grant should be made only where it will pin down an investment that otherwise would not have been undertaken in that particular jurisdiction. Some critics of the UDAG approach have argued that a significant portion of the private investments that applicants claim were stimulated by action grants would actually have been made without a grant to sweeten the deal.[10] In response, HUD officials have required local govern-

---

[10] U.S. General Accounting Office, *Improvements Needed in Selecting and Processing Urban Development Action Grants* (Washington, D.C.: General Accounting Office, 1979).

ment officials and developers to sign in their applications what amounts to an oath that the proposed project would not go forward "but for" the UDAG grant. As a result, the issue is often referred to as the "but-for" issue.[11]

In most previous discussions, the "but-for" question has been considered in terms of particular grants for particular projects at particular sites. It is also necessary to discuss the more general issue: Do action grants support a pattern of investment that is different from current trends? Is UDAG altering, however marginally, the locational patterns that have led to urban economic decline?

In discussing these questions, we are stepping back from the "but-for" question. Unfortunately, there are not yet enough reliable data to allow a comprehensive assessment of the record of UDAG in affecting investors' decisions on whether to locate a business in one place or another. This article suggests an approach that could eventually be used in making such assessments. For now, it is instructive to review information on the kinds of places that businesses have been favoring in recent years and to determine whether private investments tied to UDAG projects are going to the same or different kinds of places.

Action Grants and General Investment Trends

Trends in the location of private investment can be briefly summarized: Older central cities are losing economic activity; less built-up areas—suburbs, rural areas, growing cities—are gaining such activity. The process is not simply the movement of existing enterprises; it also involves a bias in the choice of location of new activities. Various explanations for this shift have been offered; the economic factors are most important for assessing the UDAG program.

In brief, the transportation, infrastructure, density, and other advantages of the older cities no longer outweigh the advantages of other more dispersed places—the suburbs, rural areas, and newer cities in the South and West. No longer do manufacturers need to be near the railroads and waterways that brought them their raw materials and carried their goods to customers. No longer do most manufacturing firms find it economical to use multistory factories to save on land costs. Now these firms bring in their raw materials and send out their finished products by truck or air, using factories built on one level on open, cheaper land, in keeping with the most modern production techniques.

This dispersion of business began with manufacturing firms but has extended to business services and retail and personal services as well. As manufacturing has declined, many older large cities have lost population, jobs, and large parts of their tax base. Because the law authorizing UDAG uses several of these factors in measuring distress, many of the cities eligible for UDAG aid are those that have experienced this pattern of decline.

Yet other locational forces are at work as well. The same large cities that have lost manufacturing still offer advantages to other types of businesses. Many service activities still require center-city locations that facilitate "face-to-face" con-

---

[11] Cordish, "Overview of UDAG," p. 10.

TABLE 1

Average Percentage Change in Value Added, Sales and Receipts, 53 U.S. Cities, 1967-1977

Activity	Percentage Change, 1967-1977
Value added by manufacturing	+80.8
Wholesale sales	+98.0
Retail sales	+93.3
Selected Service receipts	+190.0

Source: James W. Fossett and Richard P. Nathan, "The Prospects for Urban Renewal," in *Urban Government Finance in the 1980s*, ed. Roy Bahl (Beverly Hills, Calif.: Sage Publications, 1981), p. 77.

tacts. These activities include finance, advertising, publishing, information services, law, specialized medicine, and government.[12] Several older cities have experienced growth in their central business areas, even though other areas have declined—a pattern of "islands of prosperity" surrounded by decline.[13]

The same locational forces have affected smaller cities of the Northeast and Midwest, some of which had prospered in the past because they were close to raw materials or power sources. These cities have declined as old industries have either moved away or grown smaller; but some have other advantages, such as good transportation and skilled workers, that could attract new industries.

Impressions of these trends are more readily available than are hard measures of their magnitude.[14] Table 1, which shows data for fifty-three of the fifty-seven largest U.S. cities, provides evidence of a shift in all central cities from manufacturing to service activity. Similarly, Varaiya and Wiseman conclude from a study of thirty metropolitan areas that "in old and intermediate aged cities such [high-wage] services constitute the only source of significant employment growth other than local government. For cities in all classes, the share of employment in this category has doubled between 1958 and 1972."[15] In central

---

[12] This process has been well documented and discussed at length. For a recent example see James W. Fossett and Richard P. Nathan, "The Prospects for Urban Renewal," in *Urban Government Finance in the 1980s*, ed. Roy Bahl (Beverly Hills, Calif.: Sage Publications, 1981). For a classic overview, see Raymond Vernon, *The Myth and Reality of Our Urban Problems* (Cambridge: Harvard University Press, 1966), esp. pp. 20-22 and 46-51. Others would add an explicitly political explanation for these patterns. For example, see David Gordon, "Capitalist Development and the History of American Cities," in *Marxism and the Metropolis: New Perspectives in Urban Political Economy*, eds. William K. Tabb and Larry Sawers (New York: Oxford University Press, 1978), pp. 25-63.

[13] Anthony Downs, "Urban Policy," in *Setting National Priorities: The 1979 Budget*, ed. Joseph A. Pechman (Washington, D.C.: Brookings Institution, 1978), p. 168.

[14] For example see John Herbers, "Urban Center's Population Drift Creating a Countryside Harvest," *New York Times*, 23 March 1980, and idem, "Commuter Travel Stretches with Metropolitan Areas' Spread to Countryside," *New York Times*, 24 March 1980.

[15] Pravin Varaiya and Michael Wiseman, "The Age of Cities, the Employment Effects of Business Cycles, and Public Service Employment," in *Studies in Public Service Employment: Project Report*, ed. Michael Wiseman (Berkeley: Institute of Industrial Relations, University of California, 1978), p. 36.

TABLE 2
Change in Manufacturing Employment by Area, 1967-1973

Area	Number of Manufacturing Jobs (thousands)		Change, 1967-1973 (thousands)	
	1967	1973	Number	Percentage
United States	18,569.3	18,710.0	+145.7	+0.8
Metropolitan	13,482.0	13,054.5	−427.5	−3.2
Nonmetropolitan	5,082.0	5,655.0	+573.0	+11.3

Source: M. F. Petrulis, "Regional Manufacturing Growth Patterns," U.S. Department of Agriculture, Rural Development Research Reports, no. 13 (June 1979).

cities, rich and poor, service activities and service employment constitute the major point of growth.

Manufacturing activity, in contrast, has become more dispersed. Furthermore, between 1967 and 1973 manufacturing employment increased very little in the United States as a whole (see Table 2). What increases did occur were concentrated *outside* metropolitan areas. During this period central cities and suburbs alike were largely unable to attract enough new manufacturing activity to offset the loss of jobs caused by disinvestment and more capital-intensive production techniques. Although comparable employment data are not yet available for subsequent years, nonmetropolitan areas have continued to outstrip cities and suburbs in population growth (see Table 3). Because population and jobs have generally shifted from metropolitan to nonmetropolitan areas at similar rates, it can be assumed that the population figures mean that jobs are still shifting.

Does UDAG support investments that counteract these trends? Figures 1 and 2 indicate that it does not. These charts use figures for the program's first two years and compare two things: the proportions of *all* grants and *all* private investments that went to central cities, suburbs, and nonmetropolitan areas; and

TABLE 3
Changes in Population of Standard Metropolitan Statistical Areas (SMSA) and Nonmetropolitan Counties, 1970-1977

Type of Area*	Population (thousands)		Population Change, 1970-1977 (thousands)	
	1970	1977	Number	Percentage
Metropolitan	137,058	143,107	6,049	4.4
Nonmetropolitan	62,761	69,459	6,698	10.7

* Data use the Census Bureau's definitions of SMSAs as of 1970.

Source: U.S. Department of Commerce, Bureau of the Census, "Social and Economic Characteristics of Metropolitan and Non-Metropolitan Population: 1977 and 1970," Current Population Reports, Special Studies P-23, No. 75 (November 1978).

FIGURE 1
Proportions of All UDAG Funds, 1978-1979

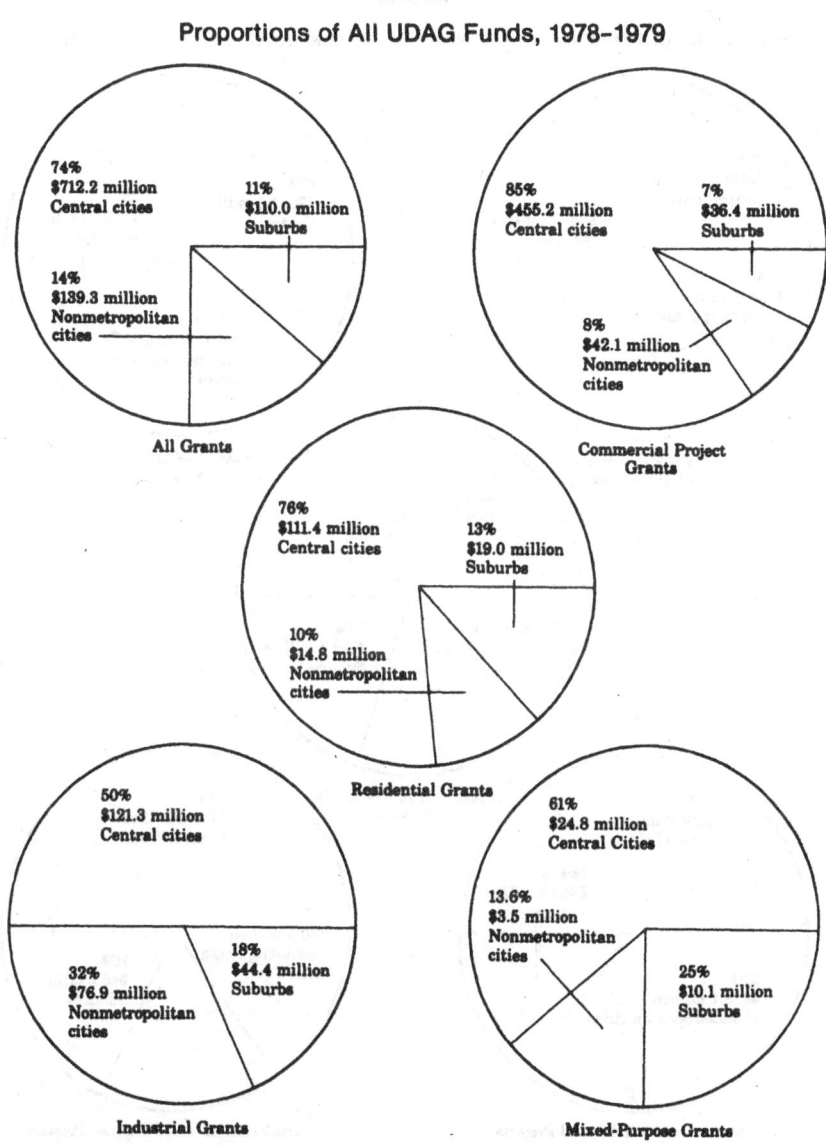

Source: U.S. Department of Housing and Urban Development, Office of Evaluation, *Urban Development Action Grant Program: First Annual Report* (Washington, D.C.: Government Printing Office, 1979); HUD news releases; and HUD Action Grant Information Service.

the proportions of each of four different *types* of UDAG grants and private investments that went to each of the three types of jurisdictions. The four investment types are commercial, industrial, residential, and mixed use. In effect, the figures compare the whole with its parts—that is, the locational pattern for all

FIGURE 2

Proportions of All Private Investment Committed to UDAG Projects, 1978-1979

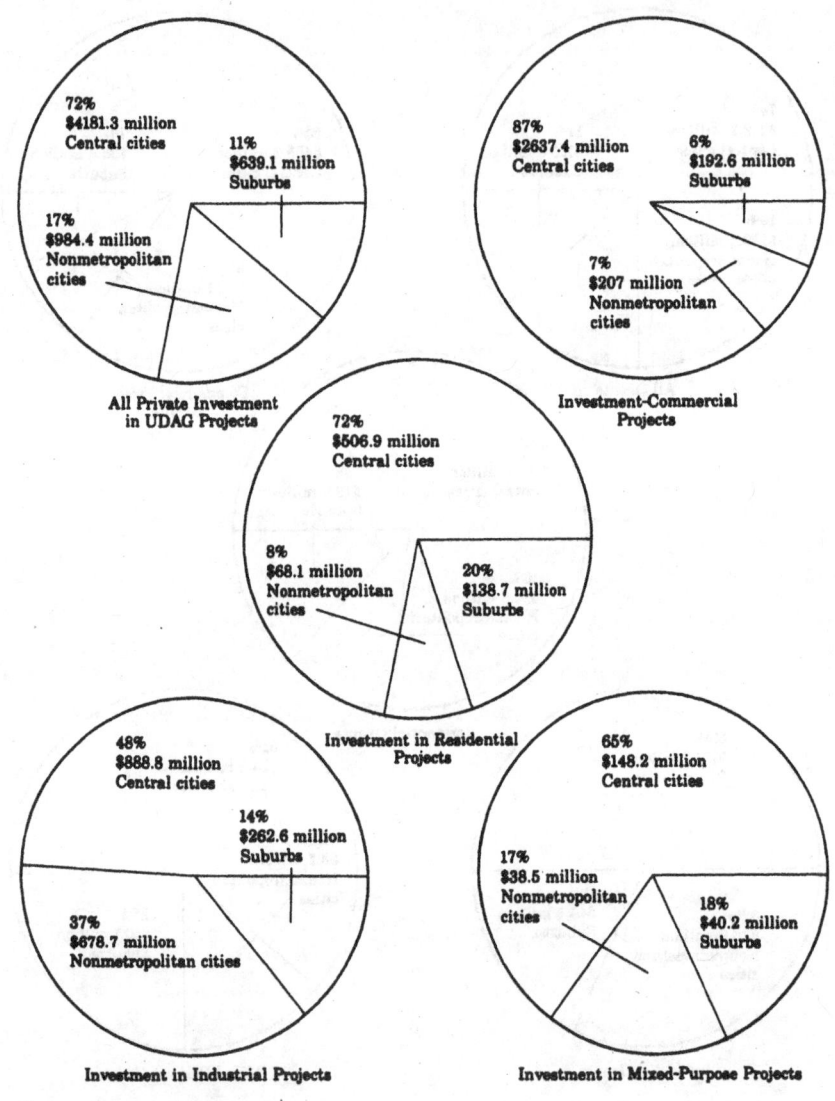

Source: Same as Figure 1.

UDAG grants and all private investments is compared with the pattern for each separate type of grant and investment.

By concentrating on the two categories most directly related to economic development, it can be seen from the charts that, compared with their share of overall grants (74 percent) and investments (72 percent), central cities attracted a disproportionately large amount of commercial activity (85 percent of grants,

87 percent of investments) and a disproportionately small amount of industrial activity (50 percent of grants, 48 percent of investments). Commercial activity includes offices, hotels, and retail stores. For the same types of projects, nonmetropolitan cities reversed the pattern: Relative to these cities' overall shares of grants (14 percent) and investments (17 percent), industrial projects proved disproportionately important (32 percent of grants and 37 percent of investments) and commercial projects disproportionately unimportant (8 percent of grants, 7 percent of investments). Distressed suburban cities showed a slightly greater tendency to attract industrial grants (18 percent) and residential investments (20 percent) than overall patterns would predict, but otherwise remained close to their overall share for each type of project (11 percent).

These findings suggest that action grants support the general *kinds* of locational choices investors have been making in the program's absence. UDAG tends to follow rather than to counter current urbanization patterns. Thus, one should not dismiss UDAG's impact on distressed cities, but rather stress that its impact does not constitute a reversal of the current and dominant patterns in American urbanization. The location of the projects that action grants support reflects the existing locational advantages of the distressed cities—a point that can be illustrated with examples from the New Jersey case studies, which demonstrate the advantages of central business districts for commercial development and the attraction of peripheral areas for expanded industry.[16]

Newark is New Jersey's business, legal, and financial center, although that city's dominance in these activities has certainly diminished in the past fifteen years. The city's Washington Park UDAG project provides a $10 million second mortgage to help finance a $35 million office building in Newark's central business district. This will be only the second speculative office building constructed in Newark in more than a decade. The completed project is to provide retail space, parking, and facilities for a corporate headquarters and for legal and financial offices—that is, the sort of activities that are still drawn to the downtowns of central cities, but that increasingly find suburban and nonmetropolitan "campus" sites a suitable alternative. Modern downtown office space can help maintain the relative attractiveness of central-city locations.

Twenty miles west of Newark, Morristown is using a $5 million action grant to build a foundation and provide subsidized parking for a $60 million office, retail, and hotel project. Because it is on the edge of the northern New Jersey metropolitan area, Morristown and its environs have been attractive locations for "exurban" corporate headquarters and business services—some of which were previously situated in Newark. The problem that the UDAG project deals with is the growing attractiveness of the environs at the expense of the aging center of Morristown itself. By subsidizing construction costs, the action grant allows the project's developers to benefit from Morristown's existing commer-

---

[16] These eight case studies were conducted between June and November 1979. For details of history, financial package, and implementation prospects, see Jerry A. Webman, "UDAG Case Studies," in *The Urban Development Action Grant Program*, Nathan and Webman, pp. 25-39.

cial and business locational advantages and still charge rents competitive with outlying sites.

New Brunswick varies the theme slightly. The action grant will help finance a hotel-conference center project, which abuts the new Johnson and Johnson Corporation headquarters, Rutgers University, the county offices, and a medical center. This combination of research, business, government, and medical services is not typical of the traditional downtown area. It is an example of the kind of central-city concentration that is becoming more common. UDAG helps provide an additional facility appropriate to the kind of urban development New Brunswick is experiencing, but once again the project builds on inherent strengths rather than attempting to reorient the city's economy.

These three cases illustrate growth in nonmanufacturing activity in cities. There is, however, one case under study that is out of keeping with prevailing trends: a $5.8 million project to restore a traditional, central-city, multistory industrial building. The restoration will accommodate a number of small manufacturers and distributors in the buildings of a bankrupt brewery in Newark. Manufacturing may indeed be "no longer an urban-seeking sector of our economy,"[17] but the demand for inner-city industrial space has not entirely disappeared—as some 15 percent of UDAG investment indicates.

Still, the most attractive sites for industrial expansion remain those with open land and easy access to transportation, especially by road. Accordingly, other industrial UDAG projects in Newark and in Paterson use sites that are more characteristic of suburbs and nonmetropolitan areas than of central cities. In both instances, developers will locate industry on undeveloped or underdeveloped sites on the edge of the cities near major interstate highways. Sites like these are hard to find in central cities, but they do show the kind of locational advantages industry will likely seek.

This point is made more clearly by a $730,000 industrial project in Salem, a city of 7,000 in the southern part of New Jersey, outside the state's metropolitan areas. Located near tomato fields, factories in Salem once made both catsup and the bottles to put it in. As New Jersey agriculture declined, Salem's factories closed and the city's unemployment rate rose to 18 percent. The UDAG project helped finance the rehabilitation of an abandoned linoleum factory near a state highway on the edge of town. The new owner is using it to make military electronics components. With an experienced labor force and good road transportation in Salem, this factory can take advantage of the availability of land and the ease of access found in an essentially rural location. Available studies reveal less about development patterns in nonmetropolitan areas. It is known, however, that well over one-third of investment in industrial UDAG projects has been directed to such locations.

---

[17]Academy for Contemporary Problems, *Revitalizing the Northeastern Economy: A Survey for Action: General Summary and Recommendations* (Columbus, Ohio: The Academy for Contemporary Problems, 1977), p. 43.

Action Grants and Particular Investment Decisions

To summarize, the kinds of places where commercial and industrial UDAG projects are locating are very similar to the kinds of places where commercial and industrial firms are making unsubsidized investments. But this does not mean that businesses benefiting from UDAG aid are getting windfalls for doing what they would have done anyway: Action grants may *influence* the location of investments, but only within the bounds of dominant nationwide patterns of economic development.

These general patterns help to clarify what effect UDAG has on particular investors' decisions to locate particular facilities in particular places. From the viewpoint of local governments—and of public-policy analysts—this is an important issue. The owner of a small electronics manufacturing firm may look at several sites and find that two or three of them are equally attractive, but it makes a big difference whether the firm moves to an economically distressed town like Salem or to a nearby "green field" site or a less distressed city. Similarly, a developer interested in putting up a speculative office project may find that a traditional urban center like Newark or Morristown offers the advantage of easy face-to-face contacts while a campus-like site near an expressway has the advantages of easier access and more space. For both the electronics firm and the office developer, a subsidy package made possible by UDAG can tip the scales in favor of the fiscally distressed city.

Whether or not an investor locates in a distressed city is important to that city for two reasons. First, the investment can bring jobs closer to relatively immobile disadvantaged people. Of course, a firm that locates in a jurisdiction with large numbers of disadvantaged people may or may not actually hire those people. But if the firm were to locate in a more prosperous location, the exclusionary residential policies in force in many such communities may well assure that disadvantaged people from other jurisdictions would *not* benefit.[18] Second, new economic activity may have a positive effect on municipal finance, although local tax abatements may limit the impact. An improved tax base provides municipal government with some relief from the widespread problems of fiscal stress.

These benefits can be attributed to UDAG only if the enterprise in question, or another one with similar fiscal and employment characteristics, would not have selected the given location without an action grant. It is difficult to determine that nothing as good or better would have occurred without the UDAG grant. The aggregate data on general patterns of investment do not help here; the case studies of individual projects enable analysts to make preliminary judgments about those projects, but these judgments cannot be generalized to other projects.

In short, one cannot now assess whether, in specific cases, the UDAG pro-

---

[18] Michael N. Danielson, *The Politics of Exclusion* (New York: Columbia University Press, 1976)

gram makes a difference in investors' decisions about where to locate new or expanded enterprises. But this is an important issue in evaluating UDAG. What is needed is a more continuous and larger research effort than has so far occurred. Such a project would consider the history, financial package, and local economic environment of a representative sample of UDAG projects and would gather information over a period of several years. This information would then provide the basis for uniformly structured and well-informed judgments about the stimulative effects of the action grants. If such studies were carried out in enough cases for a long enough time, according to sufficiently uniform research and analysis procedures, then conclusions could be drawn about the locational impact of the program.

ARE ACTION GRANTS AWARDED TO THE MOST DISTRESSED CITIES?

The basic purpose of the UDAG program implies that grants should be targeted to the most distressed urban areas. The law setting up the program mandates that UDAG money is to be "targeted"—that is, directed toward the most distressed cities—in two ways. First, eligibility standards allow only the most distressed urban areas to compete for action grants. Under HUD regulations, 2,067 towns and cities are eligible to apply.[19] Second, in choosing among applications HUD is supposed to give preference to the most distressed eligible cities that apply. The law states that the selection criteria must include "as the primary criterion, the comparative degree of physical and economic distress among applicants as measured (in the case of a metropolitan city or urban county) by the differences in the extent of growth lag, the extent of poverty, and the adjusted age of housing in the metropolitan city or urban county."[20] In principle, UDAG is a "worst first" program.

How has HUD put this principle into practice? To help choose among eligible metropolitan cities, HUD has devised an "impaction index." This approach takes into account the percentage of housing built before 1940 (weighted 0.5), the percentage of the local population with incomes below the poverty line (weighted 0.3), and the percentage rate of population growth (or decline) between 1960 and 1975 (weighted 0.2). Using this index, HUD has ranked eligible metropolitan cities from 1 (most distressed) through 322 (least distressed).[21]

Do heavily distressed eligible cities benefit more from UDAG than relatively better-off cities? The answer is yes with a qualification, considering the relative amounts of private investment. Table 4 indicates that the most distressed cities did receive a disproportionate share of grants. The most distressed quartile, in fact, received nearly four times as many grants as the least distressed quartile.

[19] As data extend through the last round of UDAG awards made before the 1980 revision of the program, this discussion of targeting ignores the "pockets of poverty" provision added to the program in 1980.

[20] Housing and Community Development Act of 1977, sec. 119 (e).

[21] HUD has excluded from this ranking cities eligible for the small cities (less than 50,000 population) set-aside.

TABLE 4

Distribution of Approved UDAG Projects by Impaction Ranking of Cities

Impaction Ranking of Cities	Number of Approved Projects	Percentage of Total Projects
Most distressed quartile (n = 80)	122	44.8
Next most distressed quartile (n = 80)	84	30.9
Next most distressed quartile (n = 80)	32	11.8
Least distressed quartile (n = 78)	34	12.5
Total projects	272	100.0

Source: HUD eligibility rankings; U.S. Department of Housing and Urban Development, Office of Evaluation, *Urban Development Action Grant Program: First Annual Report* (Washington, D.C.: Government Printing Office, 1979); and HUD news releases.

These findings, however, do not take into account the likely effects of a city's size on success in winning action grants. Larger cities are likely to have more economic activity, a larger administrative staff, and more experience with federal grant programs than smaller cities and thus win more action grants whatever their levels of distress may be. A multivariable analysis allows analysts not only to hold population constant but also to estimate the effects for particular cities of relative levels of distress.

Equation I in Table 5 displays the results of such an analysis for the number of grants cities received. Clearly, population is an important determinant of how many grants a city received. But even with population held constant, the impaction index is still strongly related to this measure of program benefits. (Recall that the impaction index runs from the most distressed to the least distressed city, so that a negative regression coefficient indicates that HUD favors more distressed cities.) Thus with population held constant, a city with the median score on the impaction index received an additional .8 of a grant and the most distressed city an additional 1.6 grants over the least distressed city.

The results suggest that more distressed cities did measurably better in the UDAG contest than did their relatively less distressed competitors. But how much was this success worth? HUD administrators may have some measure of control over who gets an award ahead of whom; they may have less control over how much each award is worth.

Because action grants are tied closely to the amount of private investment they supposedly leverage, the size of grants will vary to some extent with the amount of money private investors are willing to risk in a city.[22] The most distressed cities are in difficulty in part because they are not desirable places in which to invest. As a result, the most distressed cities might end up applying for and receiving more but smaller action grants. Thus, better-off cities might

---

[22] Levels of private investment are based on applicants' estimates and are probably somewhat inflated for purposes of strengthening applications. In the remainder of this analysis, I have assumed that this bias is constant across all cities. Less distressed cities are as optimistic as more distressed ones.

TABLE 5

Regression Equations: Effects of Population and Impaction Ranking of UDAG Recipients on Number of Grants Recipient Received, Total UDAG Funds Recipient Received, and Private Investment Received, 1978-1979, Metropolitan Cities (in dollars)

Equation		Regression Coefficient	Standard Error	Significance
I. Number of grants city received, 1978-1979 =				
1. City's population plus (thousands)	×	.0017	.00015	.00001
2. City's ranking on impaction index plus	×	−0.005	.00123	.00001
3. Intercept		2.01		
$R^2 = .50$				
N = 149				
II. Total UDAG funds city was awarded, 1978-1979 =				
1. City's population plus	×	$4.144	0.5702	.00001
2. City's ranking on impaction index plus	×	$−9,111.00	4,713.5	.05
3. Intercept		$5,202,302		
$R^2 = .28$				
N = 149				
III. Total private investment committed to city's UDAG projects, 1978-1979 =				
1. City's population plus	×	$5.87	3.0	.01
2. City's ranking on impaction index plus	×	$61,973.29	21,171.20	.005
3. City's total of awarded UDAG funds plus	×	$6.33	0.37	.00001
4. Intercept		$−13,022,760		
$R^2 = .76$				
N = .49				

Source: HUD UDAG eligibility rankings; HUD, *UDAG: First Annual Report*; HUD news releases.

receive more in total dollars from the program even though more distressed cities might receive more grants.

The findings reported in equation II of Table 5 indicate that this problem is less severe than might be expected. Total UDAG funds are strongly related to the impaction index when population is held constant. According to these estimates for a "typical" city of 500,000, the difference between being the most and the least distressed eligible city amounted to about $2.9 million over the course of two program years.

Clearly UDAG grants are awarded in a way that provides disproportionate benefits to heavily distressed cities. But what about the private investments that these grants "leverage"? The evidence in equation III suggests that the pattern is reversed for private grants: with both population and action grant money held constant, less distressed cities attracted more private investment than more distressed cities. For a city of 500,000 with the predicted relative success rate for winning UDAG funds, being the *least* distressed rather than the most distressed was worth an additional $1.4 million over two years in private investment within UDAG projects.

Equation III also indicates that although grant money is targeted to more distressed cities, private investment in UDAG projects is less targeted. This equation uses data from HUD, which are based on cities' own estimates of how much private money will be invested in a project. Although these estimates are likely to be inflated, there is no reason to believe that estimates from cities at one end of the impaction ranking will be any more or less inflated than estimates from cities at the other end of the ranking. As a result, the figures are probably reliable for making comparisons. Thus, despite relative success rates in winning UDAG funds, better-off cities will still attract more private investment than worse-off cities. The program, as noted earlier, may counter but will not alone reverse prevailing urban development trends.

One caution implicit in this discussion of targeting is that these estimates of the effect of relative distress on UDAG funding assume that all factors besides population and distress ranking are equal among recipient cities. Obviously they are not. Calculated percentages of variance explained in numbers of grants and funding levels (the R^2 statistics) indicate that the other factors are important determinants of relative levels of UDAG funding. Among these factors are likely to be relative political influence, differences in experience with federal grant programs, and HUD administrative procedures. These and similar explanations may be important and are candidates for further research. Even so, the importance of other factors, whether proven or assumed, does not diminish the impact of distress as it has been estimated here. That impact is considerable.

Conclusion

During its first two years, was the UDAG program implemented in a way that was consistent with the targeting and economic development goals set by Congress and HUD? With some caution, one can conclude from available evidence that it was. Action grants did subsidize private investment in America's most distressed urban places. They subsidized this investment more heavily where distress was more severe, although not heavily enough to compensate for greater private investment in better-off cities.

The question, however, does imply that this private investment was somehow "new"—that is, different from what would otherwise have occurred. Here the evidence is much weaker. General trends suggest that UDAG projects build on existing locational advantages rather than attempt to create new ones.

Still, these advantages may have gone unexploited in the absence of the grant. A grant, for example, probably was required before Paterson's well-located but underutilized industrial space would attract new investment. Land assembly and capital costs might have remained too high for the small firms involved. In contrast, Morristown's city-center tract would probably have been developed without UDAG. The alternative may have been smaller and thus less competitive with suburban facilities, but some development would probably have occurred. Judgments of this sort will have to be made more systematically for a larger number of cases over several years before the program's overall effectiveness can be assessed. Nevertheless, UDAG does offer an innovative approach to urban policy and has important political and economic implications.

UDAG introduces two major innovations to federal urban policy. First, the program takes an explicitly economic approach to issues of urban decline. HUD has limited action grants to projects that seem likely to create or maintain economic activity in cities whose economic base has been eroded. The second innovation follows from the first. The program's economic objectives are to be realized not solely through governmental action, but through a public-private partnership. A city government agrees to apply for grants (and probably to provide other services and facilities) and the federal government agrees to award a grant because a private business commits itself to invest in industry, commerce, or housing in that city. This partnership for economic development in distressed urban areas defines both the potentials and the limitations of the UDAG program.

UDAG's potential may lie less in its influence on the location of specific investments than in the incentives it provides for cities and private firms to work together. A financial package to which HUD, a municipal government, and a private developer will all agree must provide a balance among public—that is, local and federal—and private interests. Negotiating this financial package can bring the city's economic development problems squarely before policymakers. These findings on the program's first two years suggest that UDAG will especially encourage this process in the most distressed cities.

Furthermore, UDAG will be most effective where existing conditions and other subsidies attract the private investor. As shown earlier, the general locational pattern of UDAG investments matches the locational pattern of unsubsidized growth. The UDAG program will not restore large numbers of manufacturing jobs to most declining metropolitan areas. Only in rare instances can action grants be expected to provide investors with a locational incentive big enough to overcome the forces that have led to shifts in economic activity from the North and Midwest to the West and South, and from large central cities to suburban areas.[23]

[23] For a summary of these trends, see George Sternlieb and James W. Hughes, "New

UDAG must be considered as one of a number of available types of aid to distressed cities and to the people who live in them. By encouraging shifts in investment among areas, UDAG can speed the transition of distressed areas to new—if reduced—economic functions. If UDAG indeed shifts investment to distressed areas where it would not otherwise occur, and if UDAG continues its "worst first" strategy in awarding grants, then the program can play an important role in this adjustment process.

Further assessment of the UDAG program as an element in federal urban policy must take account of three aspects of the program: UDAG as *subsidy*, as *symbol*, and as *process*.

This article has concentrated on UDAG as a subsidy and has raised several public-policy questions about the way funds are dispersed. We could ask other questions. For example, what exactly is the federal government buying with action grants: economic transformation, support of lame-duck industries, or help for low-income households? Answers to these questions must await a longer record of implemented projects. Once again a longitudinal study of a large sample of action grant projects would be needed to provide data for analysis of these issues.

UDAG and the action grant office in HUD symbolize the federal commitment to distressed urban areas. The extent, durability, and appropriateness of that commitment may be questioned. The program, nevertheless, does help to maintain the visibility of this commitment.

The UDAG program must also be appraised for its effect on the process of urban policymaking. The program not only subsidizes private firms, but also brings them into a bargaining process with public officials. The bargains that are struck in this process are the basis for the program. Further study of the UDAG program must consider the political results of the program and the effects of these public-private partnerships in the realization of public objectives for distressed cities.*

Metropolitan and Regional Realities in America," *Journal of the American Institute of Planners* 43 (July 1977): 227–41.

* This article is based on a research project conducted by the Princeton Urban and Regional Research Center and partially supported by the Department of Housing and Urban Development. Special thanks for comments and assistance are due to David L. Aiken, Professor R. Douglas Arnold, William Natbony, and Professor Richard P. Nathan. Mr. Natbony, Uday Mehta, Michael Multari, and Michael Spies assisted in preparing the New Jersey case studies.

17

FEDERAL AUTHORITY AND GRASS-ROOTS ACCOUNTABILITY
The Case of CETA

Erwin C. Hargrove and Gillian Dean

The Comprehensive Employment and Training Act of 1973 assumed that prime sponsors would join local political accountability and planning for local labor market needs. The new federal role was to be technical assistance in this task. Similar assumptions guided other block grant programs. A comparison of these programs concludes that the bureaucratic political incentives of implementors were initially ignored, but that program failings can be improved by appealing to such incentives.

The designers of the Comprehensive Employment and Training Act (CETA) of 1973 assumed that the new law would bring about certain institutional changes at all levels of government. Most of these expectations have not been confirmed by the actual delivery of services under CETA. Were the initial expectations unrealistic, or are other explanations more appropriate?

Insight about how the structure of block grant programs may affect the behavior of governments can be gained by comparing CETA to two other similarly structured programs. The CETA legislation, passed in December 1973, was a successful compromise between a Republican administration, which sought special revenue sharing, and a Democratically controlled Congress, which sought to retain federal authority while increasing the capability of local gov-

This paper was originally prepared at the request of the National Commission for Manpower Policy.

ernments to plan service programs. The Title XX amendments to the Social Security Act and the Better Communities Act were both passed in 1974 under similar compromises.

An analysis and comparison of how these three programs have actually worked may permit us to assess the validity of the assumptions on which they were based. This is a good point of departure for asking how the programs might be improved or revised.

CETA EXPECTATIONS AND CETA REALITY

CETA restructured the nation's job training delivery system to transfer training and employment responsibilities to the local level. Under Title I of the act, approximately 550 governmental units could qualify as prime sponsors and receive federal funds to plan and operate employment and training programs matched to local labor market needs. Prime sponsors would have to meet certain broad, federal guidelines and be subject to federal criticism if their plans were inadequate. They would also be the potential recipients of technical assistance from federal officials.

Funds were to be allocated to areas by a formula based on unemployment, a poverty index, and previous aid levels. Prime sponsors might be cities or counties of more than 100,000 population or consortia that were combinations of governmental units in which one member had a population of at least 10,000. States could be prime sponsors for areas not covered by local governments.

Title I did not create new training services, but consolidated more than seventeen existing categorical programs. Prime sponsors could continue to operate programs that had been federally established, but CETA also provided flexibility for prime sponsors to establish services that would best fit local preferences. National offices of the U.S. Department of Labor (DOL) would no longer make contacts directly with local community colleges, Urban League units and other service providers, nor would they operate local employment and training programs themselves. Prime sponsors, rather than federal officials, would decide what services should be offered, who should provide them, and how well they were being delivered.

CETA contains a number of categorical titles, the most important being those for public employment and youth. We assess the influence of those titles upon the implementation of the program, but our primary focus is upon the decategorized Title I for training the work force.[1]

The aims of CETA were based on preferences about the way employment and training services should be delivered and on expectations about what would actually happen when national programs were administratively decentralized and substantively decategorized. Our analysis examines four key expectations.[2]

- Policy goals, plans, and programs would be formulated and administered at the local level.
- The elimination of categorical training programs would permit local plans and programs to be designed according to local employment needs through a comprehensive plan.
- Prime sponsors would be responsive to local demands for employment and job training programs through advisory councils representing consumers, providers, and publics.
- The federal role would be substantially altered, the aim of decentralization being to reduce federal involvement in local employment and training policy while at the same time retaining sufficient authority for oversight and technical assistance to support local efforts.[3]

One can find a model of rational economic planning implicit in the CETA legislation and program organization, which assumed that prime sponsors would plan services and evaluate them in a systematic fashion according to the employment needs of local labor

---

1. Several new programs have been added to the original CETA legislation. In 1974 provisions for more public service jobs were added; 1977 saw several amendments aimed at unemployed youth (such as the Young Adult Conservation Corps), and during the 1978 CETA reauthorization Congress added a program to promote cooperation with private sector employers. The numbering of CETA titles has continually been rearranged; now Title I training program provisions are incorporated into Title II.

2. See U.S., *Manpower Report of the President* (Washington, D.C.: Government Printing Office, 1974), pp. 37–44; and U.S., National Commission for Manpower Policy, *CETA: An Analysis of the Issues*, NMCP 1–8–78 (Washington, D.C.: National Commission for Manpower Policy, 1978), chs. 1 and 2.

3. See Robert Guttman, "Intergovernmental Relations under the New Manpower Act," *Monthly Labor Review* 97 (June 1974): 12; and Carl E. Van Horn, "Implementing CETA: The Federal Role," *Policy Analysis* (Spring 1978): 159–84.

market areas; that planning and grass roots politics would be congruent, so that planners would be held accountable by local citizens for their efforts; and that the federal government's role would shift from a predominantly checking and supervising role to one of technical assistance, in which the development of planning and evaluation capabilities in prime sponsors was the main objective. This rational planning model was articulated in the desire to get beyond the incoherence and fragmentation of the previous categorical program structure. It thus served specific rhetorical purposes and was never presented in a systematic fashion as a model of future authority relationships. The assumptions are fairly clear, however. The early CETA experience has both confirmed and denied these original expectations.[4]

- *Programs are planned and operated locally but planning is weak.* One of the clearest results of CETA has been that decision making has shifted to the prime sponsors. Prime sponsors have developed their own employment and training goals and plans and have determined, contracted for, and operated their own sets of programs. These plans are often little more than ritual appendages to funding, however; they are neither comprehensive nor specifically aimed at meeting local labor market needs.[5]

- *Categorical ties have not been quickly abandoned.* Legal decategorization aims were realized rapidly. Prime sponsors are no longer required to operate programs of the era of the Manpower Development and Training Act (1962) and the Equal Opportunity Act (1964). In practice this new flexibility had limited initial im-

---

4. Two caveats concerning efforts to assess CETA are in order. Only early implementation assessments are available for this relatively new program, and these cannot distinguish with certainty start-up problems and continuing constraints. A second factor that clouds generalizations about CETA is the extreme diversity of experience among prime sponsors. Diversity, in fact, is one of the striking findings of the early CETA assessments. See, for example, Irwin L. Hernstadt, Morris A. Horowitz, and Marlene B. Seltzer, *The Implementation of CETA in Boston—1974–1977*, (Washington, D.C.: U.S. Department of Labor, Employment and Training Administration, 1977); and Randall B. Ripley, *The Implementation of CETA in Ohio* (Washington, D.C.: U.S. Government Printing Office, 1977).

5. See a report by the Committee on Evaluation of Employment and Training Programs of the National Research Council's Assembly of Behavioral and Social Sciences: William Mirengoff and Lester Rindler, *CETA: Manpower Programs Under Local Control* (Washington, D.C.: National Academy of Sciences, 1978), ch. 2, p. 42.

pact, however. At the local level, prime sponsors have often stayed with the old categorical training programs rather than adopt new ones. At the federal level, CETA has remained categorical in broad outline. Massive infusions of funds into public service employment in response to unemployment and recession have riveted local CETA attention in that direction, and Title III created new categorical programs for various minority groups and for young people.[6]

- *Plans are responsive to a limited set of local demands.* CETA's expectation that local elected officials would be responsive to a broad popular constituency has not been met. Local participation in decision making has increased over pre-CETA days, but local officials appear to distribute Title I funds in accordance with their own political incentives and in response to the urgings of local community-based service providers.

- *A new federal role has been only partially achieved.* National and regional office involvement in local manpower program planning and operations have diminished appreciably, although there is wide variation in the intrusiveness of federal officials. It appears that, across the board, federal staffs do not provide much broad substantive advice to prime sponsors but do maintain a strong interest in procedural accountability.

These descriptions of what has happened do not tell us whether the initial assumptions about institutional development incorporated into the CETA legislation were mistaken or whether more time is needed to realize the original goals. For example, is prime sponsor planning weak for intrinsic reasons or simply because it takes time to learn how to plan?

CETA AND THE SEARCH FOR NEW PATTERNS OF GOVERNMENT

The success of any change in the structure of program delivery hinges on the new patterns of government that emerge. The block grant strategy of CETA relies strongly on accountability at the state and local levels. Federal authority and dollars are used to equalize resources among governments, but program effectiveness depends on accompanying changes in governmental institutions at these levels—changes in what they do, how they do it, and for whom.

The ability of prime sponsors to tailor manpower services to locally defined needs is dependent on the ability, authority, and po-

6. Mirengoff and Rindler, *CETA,* pp. 26–28.

litical will of the sponsors. Therefore an understanding of the implementation of CETA should build on three key concerns: the institutional capabilities of prime sponsors for planning; the patterns of accountability that emerge as a consequence of the devolution of authority from the federal level to the local level; the nature of intergovernmental authority relationships.

Planning

Many prime sponsors have not had staffs previously experienced with employment and training programs, and thus have lacked the expertise needed for comprehensive and effective policy development. During the early CETA years, policy goals set at the local level were for the most part vague and general. Plans seldom offered rational or substantive criteria for ascertaining whether one program was more effective than another. In the first year of CETA, plans often called for sets of services not very different from previous years. Since then, plans have departed somewhat from the inherited program mix. Inexperienced planning continues to be compounded, however, by tight federal deadlines, lack of timely technical assistance, and continuing changes in requirements stemming from congressional appropriation adjustments and new legislation. More recently, planners have given increased attention to the actual performance of program operators, but there continues to be little analysis that combines long-term goals and current training efforts.[7]

Administrative weakness at the local level has also tended to undermine CETA decategorization aims. Few prime sponsors responded to the new latitude by planning new mixes of services or developing innovative programs that meshed well with existing programs and needs. Most prime sponsors implemented preexisting programs, often making contracts with the providers for those programs. Prime sponsors were not prepared to monitor the work of providers closely, evaluate the effectiveness of individual programs, or tie future funding decisions to assessment results. As an example, the Cleveland area prime sponsor funded service deliverers in 1975

7. These issues are discussed by William Mirengoff and Lester Rindler, *The Comprehensive Employment and Training Act: Impact on People, Places, Programs: An Interim Report*, staff paper prepared for the Committee of Employment and Training Programs, Assembly of Behavioral and Social Sciences, National Research Council (Washington, D.C.: National Academy of Sciences, 1976), ch. 1; and by Mirengoff and Rindler, *CETA*, chs. 2 and 5.

and 1976 without evaluating their efficiency or placement success. When prodded by DOL to select program operators competitively, Cleveland terminated two previously funded programs. Although located on the spot, prime sponsors have often known little about local needs or effective service strategies. High rates of staff turnover, exacerbated by inadequate management information systems, have impeded administrative improvement.[8]

The fact that CETA sponsors operate completely within a local political setting has influenced the shape of the institutional capacities of prime sponsors. Public service employment (PSE) titles of CETA receive greater funding than training programs, and local political leaders have given less attention to training than to PSE, particularly in areas of high unemployment. In some areas, the rapid growth of PSE funding has led to administrative separation of training and employment efforts, often with little coordination between the two.[9] The political need to respond to economic downturns has meant that the priorities of sponsors give primary attention to enrolling large numbers of CETA participants and only secondary attention to the task of building administrative capabilities for long-term job training policies.

Increasingly, prime sponsors are starting to operate programs directly; more than one-third of the existing CETA programs are run by sponsors.[10] Regulations that allow prime sponsors to operate programs themselves also allow fledgling local agencies to respond to organizational incentives for growth. The difficulties of negotiating with private providers of training also stimulate local prime sponsors to take on more and more training operations themselves. There is also evidence that, over time, Title I funds are being used somewhat less for classroom and on-the-job training; instead there has been a shift toward more politically visible work experience and other subsidized employment programs.[11]

Regional offices have put virtually no emphasis on assisting spon-

8. For discussion of Cleveland's use of providers and problems with staff turnover, see "Status of Improving Cleveland's Management of Its Employment and Training Programs: Letter Report to Representative Mary Rose Oakar," HRD-78-126 (Washington, D.C.: U.S. General Accounting Office, 7 June 1978), pp. 5–6 and ch. 4. See also Mirengoff and Rindler, *CETA*, ch. 4.
9. Mirengoff and Rindler, *CETA*, ch. 4, p. 57.
10. Mirengoff and Rindler, *Comprehensive Employment and Training Act*, p. 117.
11. Mirengoff and Rindler, *CETA*, ch. 5, pp. 27–28.

sors to develop their institutional capacities. The strong legacy of the Manpower Development and Training Act of 1962 has left regional offices with only limited concern for local program effectiveness. The lack of historical experience with this program structure leaves DOL staffs poorly versed in strategies for developing local staffs and for making optimal use of local planning councils.[12] In sum, a lack of institutional strength at the state and local level has often meant that decentralization is not accompanied by high-quality planning and programs.

Accountability

Proponents of CETA anticipated that devolution of authority to the local level through block grants would lead to stronger and closer grass-roots accountability for service delivery. The general public would have an increased say in what programs were established and a better opportunity to lodge complaints if funds were being spent ineffectively.

Provisions concerning citizen participation require sponsors to establish manpower planning councils (MPCs). These councils were to include interested citizens who would see to it that community interests, such as those of poor and ethnic groups, were represented. In practice, however, prime sponsors have exercised wide discretion in determining who serves on the MPCs and have often been quite relaxed about following MPC suggestions. These efforts to mandate change in accountability have not succeeded in involving the general public in planning employment and training programs. Persons and groups not already closely involved in such programs are rarely appointed to MPCs or included in decision making. MPCs are more likely to be dominated by provider groups that represent their clients only quite indirectly. Providers have a stronger interest in pressing their own organizational needs than in presenting the preferences of the groups to whom they deliver services.

The CETA experience shows that although planning councils are becoming more active, members are still essentially volunteers who have limited time to give to council matters. Councils are heavily influenced by fulltime CETA staffs and have only modest independent substantive influence, although provider influence can also work through less formal channels in the fluid local political set-

12. Mirengoff and Rindler, *CETA*, ch. 5.

ting.[13] The influence of politically savvy program operators can be seen in prime sponsors' continuation of courses that have had low placement rates and that labor market surveys forecast as low-demand areas.[14]

The providers by whom prime sponsors are strongly influenced are likely to be those who are politically articulate and experienced in delivering employment and training services and in presenting the case that their services are needed. The early experience of CETA showed that community-based organizations have fared well as program operators; prime sponsors have tended to keep programs run by local churches, colleges, and employment/training centers.[15] Prime sponsors are less apt to make contracts with public employment service units than was the case in pre-CETA days, despite the efforts of regional officials to encourage contracts with these units. By contrast, local vocational education agencies are continuing to train workers, although prime sponsors are increasingly using CETA funds to purchase training slots in schools rather than funding whole projects to be operated by schools.[16]

The emphasis of the New Federalism on diffuse, popular participation in program decision making at the local level was based on inaccurate assumptions about the nature of citizen interest and action. The hope that local elected officials could and would be held accountable for employment and training programs via the ballot box assumed incorrectly that voters in general are interested in issues related to training the work force. In fact, the emphasis on ballot box accountability has allowed CETA training efforts to be virtually swamped by public service employment. When CETA first started, training programs were the focus of funding ($1.5 billion for CETA Title I in 1974 and $400 million for Title II public service employment). As the economy turned downward in the mid-1970s, however, funding priorities changed, and by 1977 training

13. See Bonnie B. Snedeker and David M. Snedeker, *CETA: Decentralization on Trial* (Salt Lake City: Olympus Publishing Company, 1978), pp. 76–77.

14. General Accounting Office, "Status," p. 15.

15. For an opposing view, see "Community Based Organizations in Manpower Programs and Policies," National Commission for Manpower Policies, Special Report no. 16 (Washington, D.C.: U.S. Government Printing Office, 1977).

16. Mirengoff and Rindler, *Comprehensive Employment and Training Act*, ch. 5; Mirengoff and Rindler, *CETA*, ch. 10.

funds had increased only marginally and PSE money was at $7.5 billion. When there is a great deal of money available for PSE, local officials devote more time and attention to PSE because it is politically more beneficial and publicly more salient. Assessment of CETA operations during the second year shows that Title VI public service employment funds awakened considerable interest among elected officials. Local CETA administrators, attuned to the preferences of these officials, wielded their considerable influence in CETA operations to put emphasis on PSE planning and administration.[17]

Efforts to build ballot box accountability into CETA by lodging program responsibility in the hands of elected officials have also contributed to a broadening of the clientele of CETA training programs. This change is also influenced by the wider distribution of CETA funds to suburban areas and by changes in client eligibility provisions from the MDTA era. Services are now distributed more widely and are less closely targeted to the disadvantaged.[18] CETA sponsors can set their own eligibility standards, and under new broader standards program operators are likely to select for training those applicants who are most likely to succeed. This "creaming" is not constrained by prime sponsors and is not monitored or controlled by federal oversight.

Changing Authority Relationships

The legal aspects of intergovernmental relationships have been changed easily. Now prime sponsors formulate their own Title I plans; these are almost never disapproved or questioned by federal officers of the DOL's Employment and Training Administration (ETA). National and regional offices do not write Title I contracts; program operators deal directly with prime sponsors.[19]

The extent to which CETA achieves effective decentralization is dependent on actual, as opposed to legal, changes in relations between federal officers and local prime sponsors. Early assessments of CETA suggest that national involvement has been reduced, but

17. Mirengoff and Rindler, *CETA*, pp. 75–79.
18. Donald C. Baumer, Carl E. Van Horn, and Mary Marvel, "Examining Benefit Distribution in CETA Programs," *Journal of Human Resources: Education, Manpower and Welfare Policies* 14 (Spring 1979): 171–96.
19. Mirengoff and Rindler, *Comprehensive Employment and Training Act*, pp. 71–72.

that a new strategy for technical assistance to prime sponsors has not been readily adopted.[20] The managerial style of federal officials and their interpretation of how to carry out altered federal responsibilities has varied widely across regions. Federal influence ranges from domination to a hands-off approach. Prime sponsor reactions to regional offices also vary: there are complaints about unwillingness to offer help, frustration over excessive regulations, and appreciation for assistance.

Overall, the new federal role appears to be not so new. Regional offices stress the monitoring of procedures over technical assistance.[21] Staffs have not readily abandoned pre-CETA authoritative roles in allocating funds and determining program tactics; they also have not developed capacities for providing technical assistance and guidance. The mix of questions to which they address their attention has remained about the same because local sponsors have not adopted a new and more demanding stance. The federal role has been reduced, but not strongly reoriented.

Limited change in federal-local relations tends to undercut decategorization under Title I. Regional staffs, familiar with pre-CETA programs, often encourage prime sponsors to keep traditional services and operators. This has in effect served to reinforce local allegiance to categorical-era training programs.[22] Continued categorization at the national level has also had its effects. The growth of public service employment has curtailed potential federal help in monitoring and evaluating local training programs. The content of training has not caused national political controversies, but the PSE aspect of CETA has tempted some local governments to use federal funds as fiscal transfers by hiring ineligible workers

20. Van Horn, "Implementing CETA"; Ripley, *CETA in Ohio*; Mirengoff and Rindler, *Comprehensive Employment and Training Act*; Mirengoff and Rindler, *CETA*.

21. See U.S., Advisory Commission on Intergovernmental Relations, *The Comprehensive Employment and Training Act: Early Readings from a Hybrid Block Grant* (Washington, D.C.: Government Printing Office, 1977); idem, *In Brief: The Intergovernmental Grant System, an Assessment and Proposed Policies* (Washington, D.C.: Government Printing Office, 1978); Harry Katz and Michael Wiseman, "An Essay on Subsidized Employment in the Public Sector," in *Job Creation Through Public Service Employment, An Interim Report to the Congress of the National Commission for Manpower Policy* 3 (March 1979): 204–206; and Mirengoff and Rindler, *CETA*, ch. 4. p. 59.

22. Van Horn, "Implementing CETA," p. 167.

to do jobs that would have been done anyway.[23] This has caused a national controversy and has obscured the question of whether national and local program goals coincide in Title I.

OTHER BLOCK GRANT PROGRAMS

During the years when CETA was developing, block grant strategies emerged in two other policy areas—social services and urban development. Both block grants were established by merging previously separate categorical programs, and both shared the four basic premises of CETA: recipients would have wide planning and program operation authority that had formerly been in federal hands; this new authority would include flexibility to design services to fit local needs; elected officials responsible for programs would be responsive to citizen demands; and limitations of federal administrative discretion would reduce federal intrusiveness.

Title XX

Federal financial support for social services has been provided by the Social Security Act. The Title XX amendments created block grants to the states for social services such as day care, foster care of children, drug counseling, and so forth.

Planning—The federal government has been strongly influenced by the tradition of localism in the delivery of public welfare income and services and does not require states to provide specific services at specified levels of adequacy. States are required, however, to submit for federal approval a comprehensive annual services program (CASP) plan stating what services will be provided, to whom, and where, as well as whether services will be provided by the agency or whether they will be purchased from another public or private agency. The CASP plan must be published for public review and comment and modified on the basis of these comments.

For the most part, the states have lacked strong administrative resources for planning social service delivery. State officials were happy about their opportunity to put together approved plans, but interviews with state officials have revealed a catalog of negative features of the planning process.[24] In almost half the states, for ex-

---

23. Katz and Wiseman, "An Essay," p. 207.
24. Jerry Turem et al., *The Implementation of Title XX: The First Year's Experience* (Washington, D.C.: Urban Institute, 1976), p. 33.

ample, observers noted a serious lack of prerequisites for proper planning, including needs assessments, management information systems and planning staff competence. In effect, Title XX called for a new set of staff abilities and competencies that did not exist in most state agencies.

Accountability—Efforts to build local accountability into Title XX programs have foundered on the nature of group politics. Locally powerful private service providers do not put a very high priority on careful planning, and they have exerted substantial pressure on state agencies to retain categorical-era loyalties rather than develop policy flexibility.

Title XX is essentially a state program, in that the legislation places responsibility for planning and program operation in the hands of state government, as opposed to local units; but the legislation explicitly "opens" the planning process to persons outside the state social services department. These new participants can include local governments, local departments, and local units of state administered social service programs. Preliminary evidence indicated that local influence over state social service planning did increase, but that much of this increase occurred, not in local general-purpose governments, but in regional, district, or area offices of the state agencies. Social service professionals remain strong.

Title XX also attempts to mandate service accountability to the general public. The effects have been that a large number of provider groups are active in exercising influence over these decisions. There is little meaningful participation by low-income consumers of social services.[25]

Authority—Title XX specified a new role for regional offices. Planning decisions were to be made exclusively at the state level; there was to be no second-guessing by regional and national officials. Early experiences showed national officials to be less intrusive; they offered somewhat more technical assistance, and made efforts to help state agencies take on new planning and evaluation tasks.[26] There was wide variation across regions, however, in state-level response to the mandated shift in authority patterns. Some state officials felt that planning quality was impeded by the lack of definitive

25. Turem et al., *Title XX*, p. 103; Robert B. Hudson, "A Political Perspective on Title XX," mimeographed (Waltham, Mass.: Brandeis University. Heller School, 1977).
26. Turem et al., *Title XX*, p. 145.

and stable guidelines, while others complained about excessive intervention by federal staffs. The short start-up time for Title XX provided both state and regional offices little time to rethink their roles. There were no major changes in personnel, and state and federal civil servants tended to interact as they had previously.[27] Federal officials were eager to interpret any ambiguities in the legislative definition of their role as calls for a stance that did not appreciably lessen their bureaucratic terrain or disturb their established patterns of interaction.

Better Communities Act

The Better Communities Act (BCA), passed in August 1974, authorized $8.3 billion over three years to be distributed by the U.S. Department of Housing and Urban Development (HUD) in the form of broad, flexible payments made to qualifying local governments. The local units were to be general-purpose governments rather than autonomous or semiautonomous agencies (such as redevelopment agencies, housing authorities and Model Cities' community development agencies) that had been receiving urban program funds in the past. The community development block grant took seven previously established federal assistance programs and folded them into a single new grant package. The "folded-in" grants were urban renewal, model cities, water and sewer facilities, open spaces, neighborhood facilities, rehabilitation loans, and public facility loans.

Planning—Legislative compromises surrounding BCA established both substantive and procedural requirements. Each participating city and urban county were required to submit for approval an application containing a three-year community development plan, an annual development plan, and a housing assistance plan. Recipients were also required to provide information to citizens and to encourage citizen participation. The act outlined broad national goals and permissible uses for the funds; high priority was to go to projects that would benefit low- or moderate-income families.

An implementation monitoring study by The Brookings Institution found that BCA has prompted administrative reorganization that has, in a number of cases, increased local capacities for planning and policy development. In the first years of the block grant this potential was not fully realized; programs closely followed the

---

27. Turem et al., *Title XX*, p. 12.

patterns set in previous years. As a result BCA operations were largely channeled through existing local departments or special agencies. The ability of local governments to devise new administrative strategies was not taxed.[28]

BCA provided more money, with fewer strings, than had previous urban development programs. Local generalist officials began to take a more lively interest in questions that had previously been assigned to specialists. Chief executives quickly became involved in BCA application work. Legislative bodies, which were authorized to approve applications, started in some cases to take a more active role. This was especially true in large urban areas where prior experience with community development allowed legislatures to take action even in the face of short and rigid deadlines.[29]

Accountability—Citizen participation requirements under BCA are not specific and they do not focus particularly on low- or moderate-income groups. The act mandates that local governments give people the opportunity to be heard, but stops short of requiring officials to take account of the views of citizens. General citizen participation has been neither extensive nor meaningful; nor have the disadvantaged fared well in representation.[30] The major effect of mandating participation on a community-wide basis has been that urban development planning has become politically more open and competitive among organized groups. Neighborhood organizations have been particularly vocal and active. In some cities, a consensus has emerged in favor of concentrated efforts at development in limited geographic areas. More generally, however, the participation of organized groups appears to have reinforced a tendency to spread funds across a large number of areas and over many types of activities in order to satisfy the newly enlarged set of demands; the Brookings study of BCA's first year suggests that extensive group participation may work at cross purposes with the objective of comprehensive planning for community development.[31] This conflict between politics and planning is particularly prevalent in communities where local officials view citizen participation as an important part of the BCA strategy.

28. Richard P. Nathan et al., *Block Grants for Community Development* (Washington, D.C.: Brookings Institution, 1976), p. 407, ch. 7.
29. Nathan et al., *Block Grants*, pp. 373–84.
30. Tom Gale, *The New Housing Program—Who Benefits?* (New York: National Urban League, 1977).
31. Nathan et al., *Block Grants*, p. 486–87.

Authority—BCA legislation was obscure about the nature of the federal role, especially about HUD's role. At the outset, HUD adopted a minimal-involvement strategy. Reviews of local decisions were to be "Spartan."[32] At one point the external hands-off stance of federal officials allowed several cities to ignore broadly established federal guidelines. Locally formulated housing assistance plans were required to include an explicit commitment to low- and moderate-income housing. Local elected officials, however, mindful of their constituencies, were often reluctant to acquiesce to these nationally established goals. When federal officials gave BCA funds to cities that did not agree to having low- and moderate-income housing, representatives of the poor and minority groups pressed for more vigorous federal controls. But this pressure was applied through alternative channels—courts and the national HUD offices —because local elected officials and Congress were often not responsive to the needs of low- and moderate-income families.

A COMPARISON OF THE THREE BLOCK GRANT PROGRAMS

The workings of these three block grant programs are very similar. The structural changes in legal authority and program design occasioned by CETA, Title XX, and BCA stimulated many of the same general political and bureaucratic patterns: (1) It has proved difficult to create, as intended, institutional arrangements at the grass-roots level that allow programs to be planned in a comprehensive way. (2) The search for accountability to local publics has resulted primarily in responsiveness to organized groups— whether service providers, specific clientele, or other government bureaucracies. (3) Federal officials have had difficulty transferring their procedural authority to local governments, but at the same time have been slow to develop new substantive roles as advisers to local governments in methods of service delivery. The result is that the development of local institutional capabilities has lagged. This is less the case with BCA than with the other two programs, because BCA is more of a program to allocate monies than to deliver services.

These conclusions are no great surprise to a political scientist. Programs are not decentralized into a vacuum but into live, ongoing, local political processes. Economic planning in terms of labor mar-

32. Nathan et al., *Block Grants*, p. 68.

ket needs must give way to politics as the basis for resource allocation.[33]

Americans are organized much more as producers than as consumers in interest group representations to government. Citizens at large are not inclined to organize to seek a diffuse public good.[34] When groups of citizens do organize as consumers of policy, some are usually better organized than others and possess disproportionate political resources.

The goals of these block grant programs have been selected to meet the political incentives of elected officials. This is different from responding to the claims of provider groups. A common theme seen in all these cases is the effort to increase the range of constituencies served, often to the detriment of disadvantaged people. Thus the pattern of representation is necessarily partial.[35]

One must not immediately blame politics, however. It is not clear that planners would know what to do even if political pressures were totally absent. For example, one can imagine more than one reasonable and comprehensive CETA plan for a given labor market area. Planning is a function of values and knowledge. It is difficult to engage in comprehensive planning because of planners' disagreement about goals. This is complicated by deficiencies in knowledge. Therefore what appears to be planning is more often an incremental process of goal setting through bargaining and of goal revision through the continual infusion of new, but always incomplete, information. Statutory language does not provide criteria for the resolution of value conflicts inherent in the several purposes of a complex program. The knowledge of the relative effectiveness of different service deliverers and programmatic strategies is also quite deficient in each of these areas.[36] Given these constraints on planning, it is in fact very "rational" for local governments to respond to the existing demand structure in their communities as they develop programs.

33. See Robert A. Dahl, *A Preface to Democratic Theory* (Chicago: University of Chicago Press, 1956), ch. 5.
34. See Mancur Olson, Jr., *The Logic of Collective Action: Public Goods and the Theory of Groups,* rev. ed. (New York: Schocken Books, 1971).
35. See Anthony Downs, *An Economic Theory of Democracy* (New York: Harper and Row, 1957), ch. 4.
36. See David Braybrooke and Charles E. Lindblom, *A Strategy of Decision: Policy Evaluation as a Social Process* (New York: The Free Press, 1963), chs. 1–6.

One might argue that the slowness of changes in the federal role in all three cases discussed here is due to the tension between nationally and locally determined goals. Federal concerns about compliance with the law dictate a strong supervisory posture. This has been true in regard to the public employment provisions of CETA and the blatant neglect of projects for disadvantaged populations in the BCA. But the objectives of CETA, Title XX, and BCA are cast so broadly in the statutes that there is only a limited place for an authoritative federal role in pursuit of substantive goals. This suggests that the chief impediment to the shift from a supervisory federal role to one of technical assistance is to be found in the difficulties of changing the skills and orientations of federal program managers.

It might have been possible to develop an implementation estimate in 1973 from social science research about how CETA could have been expected to work in practice. For example, the literature on citizen participation in social programs could have been cited, probably in a disillusioning way. Again, the likely effect of the political incentives of local officials on the clients selected could have been predicted.[37] And the capacity of prime sponsors for developing good planning and evaluation could have been measured against the prior knowledge of the limitations of these functions in all human organizations.[38]

One cannot now answer the question of whether such "implementation estimates" would or should have brought about a differently structured program at the outset. A more interesting question is whether the programs, as they stand today, reflect flawed assumptions about how institutions can be expected to work.

We do not conclude that this is the case. The model of "rational

37. See George E. Hale, "The Political Implications of National Manpower Policy," *American Behavioral Scientist* 4 (March/April 1974): 555–71; Judith May, *Citizen Participation: A Review of the Literature* (Davis, California: Institute for Government Affairs, 1971); Edie Goldenberg, "Citizen Participation in General Revenue Sharing," in *The Economic and Political Impact of General Revenue Sharing*, ed. F. Thomas Juster (Washington, D.C.: Government Printing Office, 1976): 165–82; and Hudson, "A Political Perspective."

38. Robert A. Dahl and Charles E. Lindblom, *Politics, Economics and Welfare* (New York: Harper, 1953); and Robert A. Levine, *Public Planning: Failure and Redirection* (New York: Basic Books, 1972).

planning" implicit in all three programs is not rigid and can be adapted to the limitations of planning and the realities of politics. If it is thought that the manifest goals of programs, which were to be achieved through planning, are being diverted by politics, then one antidote is to find a way to structure the bureaucratic and political incentives of the implementors in a way that is congruent with program goals. We now turn to that task in regard to CETA.

CETA'S FUTURE: PREDICTIONS AND PRESCRIPTIONS

The following predictions about CETA are likely to be valid if the federal government continues current policies and administration without significant changes.

Prime sponsors will determine which clients to serve according to the political incentives of local elected officials, as these officials perceive them.

What appear to be contradictory behaviors by prime sponsors may result. On the one hand, the majority of prime sponsors may resist federal efforts to direct, by rule, that the disadvantaged be the primary recipients of training services. Such a goal would conflict with a wider distribution of services that better serves the desire for reelection of local elected officials. On the other hand, local officials are likely to press the federal government to maintain and extend the national categorical program of public employment that also serves the political incentives of local officials. This is not really a contradiction, because local officials have sought maximum latitude in the disposition of funds for public employment and have resisted federal efforts to have the program serve primarily the disadvantaged. Local officials are opposed not so much to categorical programs as to any federal targets that limit their own political purposes.

Ambiguity and tension between the federal government and prime sponsors will continue in regard to whether the program should serve national or local objectives.

We can expect prime sponsors to act on the Congress through elected officials of state and local governments to assert their increasing independence from federal authority. This is part of an expanding pattern of representation through the federal system in which state and local governments have become primary actors in representation to Congress. It was perhaps the political strength of these actors that made the passage of CETA possible.[39] But we can also expect that well-organized interest groups that speak for the disadvantaged will seek the increase of federal authority on their behalf if they lose out at the grass roots. This tension and ambiguity about the proper locus of authority are really questions about the goals of the program, and there is not likely to be agreement about that.

Many prime sponsors will try to improve their planning and evaluation capabilities in order to strengthen themselves against the pressures of provider groups and to increase their own control over local plans.

This trend is not uniformly strong, and there may be a number of prime sponsors that cannot improve their institutional capabilities without federal assistance. This development would be strengthened if the federal role were to be predominantly one of technical assistance to prime sponsors. As we have seen, such a reorientation has not been achieved.

In the light of our findings and predictions, what prescriptions might be advanced for shaping the future development of CETA? The suggestions below accept the purposes and general framework of CETA as good, and prescribe improvements.

Increasing the Institutional Capabilities of Prime Sponsors

The Employment and Training Administration should take the steps necessary to incorporate the use of knowledge derived from research about service delivery into the work of ETA professionals. This can be done by extensive training of professional staffs, but such training must be put into practice in the field. Thus it is crucial for the regional offices to be so staffed that they are regarded as a valuable resource by prime sponsors.

It might be argued that ETA personnel who are not involved in day-to-day service delivery are never likely to have credibility for those who are. Therefore they would do better to concentrate on the administrative problems of prime sponsors, which could include the tasks of planning and evaluation. We think that nothing would be lost and much might be gained, however, if ETA program offi-

---

39. See Samuel H. Beer, "Federalism, Nationalism, and Democracy in America," *The American Political Science Review* 72 (March 1978): 9–21.

cials were moved toward a concern with service delivery questions. Assistance to prime sponsors in planning and evaluation would be strengthened by such an effort. Prime sponsors are anxious to develop their own planning and evaluation capacities so that they can exert more control over competing program operators. Prime sponsors are also increasingly interested in building a larger set of sponsor-operated programs and will seek federal technical assistance on this front if it is offered with a clear disclaimer of federal control.[40]

Accountability

The federal government should take steps to widen the scope of representation at the local level. This will not be accomplished with ease, but a useful beginning step would be keeping providers off the councils and adding representatives of client groups.

General citizen interest in CETA training programs is low and most likely cannot be increased. Therefore the best route to widening participation in planning and operation lies in increasing the access of groups who receive employment and training services. The political system assures provider groups a strong voice. Institutional modifications are now needed to improve accountability to recipients. In addition, local planning councils, now largely dominated by CETA administrators and only moderately influential in substantive decision making, might be strengthened by providing them with independent, competent staff assistance. Such wider representation might of course be congruent with the political incentives of local officials to distribute services widely. The disadvantaged might suffer. But if the disadvantaged were more fully represented in a formal way in the planning of employment and training programs, they would be in a better position to help themselves. It should also be pointed out that this ambiguity about who CETA should serve is a part of the statute itself rather than a result of administrative discretion.

Prime sponsors should be encouraged to strengthen efforts to place their trainee graduates in nonsubsidized jobs. Despite the

---

40. See National Academy of Sciences, *Knowledge and Policy in Manpower: A Study of the Manpower Research and Development Program in the Department of Labor* (Washington, D.C.: 1975), ch. 9; and Charles L. Schultze, *The Public Use of Private Interest* (Washington, D.C.: The Brookings Institution, 1977), pp. 45–46, 62.

trend toward increased use of Title I funds for work experience and public service employment, there is little evidence that the reason for these changes has been that prime sponsors believe such training improves individual employability. In fact, these shifts have not been accompanied by significant efforts to move trainees into nonsubsidized employment.[41] The placing of trainee graduates would strengthen accountability in three ways: the efficacy of training would be tested in a market; a visible good that follows from training would be apparent to potential recipients of services and the base of applicants might thereby be broadened; other institutions in the labor market, particularly employers, would become consumers of CETA activities, which might enable prime sponsors to plan more effectively for labor market needs.

The negative aspect of this prescription is that the incentives of prime sponsors to select the most promising trainees might be increased. Those with severe problems would be ignored. All human services organizations face this problem, and the remedy, if there is one, could be applied to CETA in ways we cannot anticipate. Prime sponsors need not compete with the U.S. Employment Service in placement activities; but such competition might increase the credibility of the Employment Service if it were to compete effectively. We endorse the model of competition in bureaucracy in the absence of a market test of the value of services.

Reconciling National and Local Authority

The authority relationship between the federal government and the prime sponsors is best left ambiguous. The ETA should maintain and exercise selectively its authority to approve local plans and to monitor local fulfillment of approved plans. This selectivity should be guided by the extent to which locally determined programs tend to deviate from national goals, by the extent to which alternative programs are available and known to meet national objectives, and by the extent to which the national office can feasibly influence prime sponsor behavior. A positive example is the ETA effort to get sponsors to cooperate more effectively with local Employment Service offices. ETA's decentralized program structure should not be obliterated by an overbearing federal presence. CETA

41. Mirengoff and Rindler, *CETA*, ch. 5, pp. 27–28.

can remain strongly decentralized, however, if federal control efforts are well focused on a limited set of specific goals.

CONCLUSIONS

Capable institutions develop slowly and are subtly molded by political and organizational contexts. We see the nurturing of such institutions as the primary federal task. Yet it is difficult to create effective planning and service delivery capacities at the local level. The specification of legal requirements and procedures is not sufficient, since expectations embedded in the legislated structure of a program often are not borne out in reality. Unless such assumptions are evaluated and compared to performance it is impossible to administer a program well or improve its design.

Health Care Policy

The health care area does not suffer from a lack of policy research and analysis. Indeed, studies on the many aspects of this issue proliferate. The vast majority of these studies can be categorized into three areas: cost containment, regulation, and access. The articles in this section fall into these three general areas.

Containing the cost of health care in the United States has become a policy matter of paramount importance. Constantly escalating resources are being devoted to hospital care, physical fees, and ancillary services. However, the multiple efforts to put a cap on these costs have been marginally successful at best. Both Brown and Mechanic explore several of the attempts at cost containment and assess the reasons for the lack of persistent or widespread success. Two explanations are particularly persuasive: Costs cannot be contained because of competing and conflicting interests among the key actors in the medical area, and because the policy analysis that has been conducted has been both overabundant and often lacking in clarity.

It is in this politically sensitive atmosphere that budget cuts are being made in existing programs, on the assumption that cost cutting in and of itself will resolve the basic tensions and paradoxes. The article by Estes and Lee demonstrates that this approach has important consequences for groups in our society who rely on government support to obtain health care. According to their analysis of policy shifts, the contributions from various levels of government will shrink over time, and the level of care available to the elderly will thus decline.

What is apparent in considering these three key policy areas—cost containment, regulation, and access—is that they are intricately linked and interdependent. Cost containment is of highest priority; deregulations and access are frequently seen to be the areas in which costs can best be controlled. The complex web of linkages among various actors and components in the system make any change extremely difficult. Because these linkages are not complementary, they create the dilemmas and cross-pressures documented in a number of these articles. McMenamin, for example, analyzes the second most costly aspect of health care—physician fees. Increasing fees affect who is to be served, how well they are served, and where the fundings for such services are to be found. The policy tradeoffs in this area are multiple and not easily attained.

Finally, the article by Reinhardt on the health care system in the Federal Republic of Germany is informative as a case study. West Germany has developed a health care system more generous and comprehensive than that found in the United States, but with no greater proportion of the gross national product (GNP) devoted to health care costs. This alternative way to organize the delivery, cost, and access of health care merits the careful attention of those who have come to believe that the U.S. system is out of control and deficient in the service it renders to its citizens. The West German case makes it clear that the problems plaguing the American system are not the result of too many or too few resources (funds, personnel, or facilities), but rather the result of the decisions and policies made regarding allocation of these resources.

18

COMPETITION AND HEALTH COST CONTAINMENT
Cautions and Conjectures

Lawrence D. Brown

Competition makes for better health care. It's just that simple.
—DONALD S. MACNAUGHTON, Chairman of the Board, Health Corporation of America, advertisement in *The Wall Street Journal*, January 23, 1981

We have no valid basis from which to project the effect of competition on the traditional system.
—DEPARTMENT OF HEALTH, EDUCATION, AND WELFARE (in U.S. House of Representatives, Interstate and Foreign Commerce Committee, 1972)

Any economist's assessment of the workability of competition is likely to have a highly provisional and even personal character and is likely to rest heavily on the ad hoc assessment of obvious alternatives in given situations.
—JOE BAIN, 1950 (quoted in Katzman, 1980)

LIKE OTHER WESTERN NATIONS WITH UNIVERSAL OR near-universal health insurance coverage, the United States has debated at length about public policies to contain health care costs. Unlike other western nations, however, the United States has shown intense interest in "market approaches" based on "incen-

---

From Lawrence D. Brown, "Competition and Health Cost Containment: Cautions and Conjectures," 59(2) *Milbank Memorial Fund Quarterly/Health and Society* 145-189 (1981). Copyright 1981 by The Brookings Institution. Reprinted by permission.

tives" and "competition." Two market approaches have received close attention. One would manipulate consumer cost-sharing, especially deductibles and copayments, in order to bring a larger share of the cost of health services to bear on consumers and thereby encourage them to shop around carefully for "efficient" providers when they seek care. The second approach would design incentives for consumers to join efficient, organized health care systems, usually health maintenance organizations (HMO) or some other variant of prepaid group practice (PGP).

Consumer cost-sharing is a familiar feature of United States health insurance—consumers pay directly about 32 percent of health care costs. Specifically, in 1979 consumers paid directly for 8 percent of hospital, 37 percent of physician, 73 percent of dental, and 84 percent of drug expenditures (Gibson, 1980:1, 8). Apart from various federal financing programs, however, cost-sharing in insurance has not been incorporated in public policy, much less made the foundation of a market approach to cost containment. Development of HMOs, on the other hand, has been the aim of various federal policy efforts since 1970, and the search for policies to enlarge the number of HMOs and HMO-like entities goes on earnestly.

These market approaches appear to share three basic assumptions: first, that more efficient health plans (whether innovations along traditional indemnity lines or organized systems like HMOs) would be developed on a large scale if consumer demand for them were stronger; second, that the presence of these efficient plans would introduce vigorous price competition into health care markets, and therewith cost containment without extensive public regulation; and third, that the major obstacles in the way of these desirable developments are public policies reflecting the failure of consumer-voters to recognize their true collective interest in less expensive health care arrangements.

Although the reasoning behind market approaches is largely theoretical and deductive—which is to say, conjectural—it has been advanced and elaborated in some quarters with evangelical zeal. This paper attempts neither to refute these propositions nor to argue against market approaches. Its purpose is rather to offer some cautions and counterconjectures, calling attention to political, institutional, and organizational considerations largely ignored or assigned to the sidelines in the individualistic images of the market advocates. This essay will argue that the translation of reformed incentives and demand patterns into efficient health care organizations is by no means a simple or straightforward process, that there is now little basis for estimating the cost containment potential of competition among health care plans, and that the consumer's interest in efficiency—and therefore in new organizational forms and in competition—is very poorly understood. In sum, the appeals of the market approaches are not "just that simple."

It may be objected that yet another explication of the complexity of it all is neither an original nor a useful contribution to policy analysis. It is impossible not to admire the parsimony of incentives disembodied from their organizational, institutional, and political contexts and spun out in an elegant causal web weaving together consumer calculations, organizational formation, interorganizational behavior, and a more efficient health care system. Yet, not all analytical simplifications useful for generating policy *ideas* are also useful for generating policy *strategies*. Especially in today's high tide of political enthusiasm for market approaches to cost containment, there may be some point in recalling the obvious: that some simplifications are simplistic and therefore possibly misleading to policy makers.

This paper will draw upon certain aspects of public policy experience with HMOs to raise its cautions and conjectures. HMOs are a useful focus for three reasons. First, most practical experience with market approaches derives from HMO development efforts. Second, some proposed market approaches depend heavily on HMO-like entities to embody the right incentives and to trigger the competition which revitalized markets are thought to demand. Third, some market advocates believe that HMOs are the best means of overcoming the many well-known deviations of health care markets from perfect or normal market behavior. For example, it does not matter that physician suppliers tend to define the degree and type of consumer demand or that consumers lack the information and interest to shop around for efficient suppliers of care if physicians, by going to work for an HMO, and consumers, by subscribing to one, can be led to "precommit" (Fuchs, 1979:170) themselves to efficiency.

The origins of the federal HMO development strategy need no more than a brief review here. Faced with the need to do something about rising health care costs, but unwilling to adopt extensive regulation, consumer cost-sharing, or national health insurance, the Nixon administration was persuaded in 1970 that an attempt to build health maintenance organizations, entities which took the "skeleton" of famous prepaid group practices such as the Kaiser-Permanente Plans and implanted it in highly diverse and flexible organizational forms was an attractive market approach. In 1970 the administration asked Congress to create a new HMO option for Medicare recipients. In 1971 it began using discretionary funds to plan the development of about 100 HMOs around the country. In the same year it proposed that Congress create a special HMO development program. If this were done, the Department of Health, Education, and Welfare (HEW) argued, there might be 1700 HMOs within a few years with perhaps 40 million people enrolled (U.S. Department of Health, Education and Welfare, 1971:37). After long debate Congress passed an HMO development program in 1973; the program, amended in 1976 and 1978, remains in existence today. Results, however, have been relatively unimpressive: today there are about 230 HMOs, enrolling about 4 percent of the population (about 9 million people). Some believe that the federal government itself is largely to blame for these modest accomplishments: the 1973 law, it is said, was unworkable, and administration of the program was poor. Not until the amendments of 1976 and an administrative reorganization in 1977 did the program get a fair chance. This essay cannot evaluate this view in detail. An alternative explanation is worth considering however: that the policy analysis behind the HMO development effort was flawed in important ways, that a rapid growth in HMO numbers and enrollment was simply not an outcome the federal government was equipped to bring about.

Incentives and Institutions

Throughout the 1970s, federal policy makers dealing with HMOs cheerfully relied on two code words reiterated by policy analysts—incentives and competition—tied together conceptually by a third code term, market approach. To professional economists who use these terms regularly, they denote—at least sometimes—processes with rigorous definitions and concomitants. To many of the policy analysts and policy makers engaged in HMO-building, these terms had a host of vague and imprecise, but nevertheless ambitious and seductive, connotations. HMOs promised such all-American ends as pluralism, choice, efficiency, and reorganization achieved by such all-American means as markets, incentives, and competition. The correct manipulation of conceptual elements produced a strategy that would yield both cost containment, attractive to all but especially to conservatives, and a challenge to fee-for-service (FFS) medicine, attractive to the innovation- and reform-minded. Equally important, it appeared to ensure that rarity—a solution that would satisfy both ideological camps. According to HMO proponents, the organizations would contain costs, improve access, and enhance quality of care, without trade-offs among these goals and at little cost to the federal government. Policy makers seldom encounter so compact and glowing a package of policy assets, and it is no wonder that they rushed to embrace it.

HMO advocates extrapolated basic assumptions and relationships of economic theory to the health field and to HMOs in particular, promising that the combination of new incentives and reinvigorated competition would produce market conditions that would lead in turn to a better and more efficient health care system. This economic reasoning gained force from its close coincidence with the two major reformist strains of that school of thought within the health community that has long argued for a reorganization or restructuring of the health care system not by means of government rules but rather by means of changes in financial incentives.

The first school of reformers calls for "industrialization" of the health care system. In this view it is socially and economically absurd that a highly specialized, high-technology field like medicine should continue to be organized in small "cottage industry" units of solo practitioners integrated ad hoc with hospitals, payment mechanisms, medical centers, and other institutional fragments in need of coordination on behalf of care of the whole person. The reformers view a rearrangement and coordination of the fragments in larger-unit organizations, which would make the scale of production conform to the technology of the industry, as the logical solution. The HMO, an organization that combines in one setting doctors, clinics, hospitals, administrators, and consumers (or at any rate brings them together in one plan) and, under a central financial administration, assumes full responsibility for the comprehensive health care needs of members struck some as the ideal embodiment of this reorganization (Ellwood et al., 1971).

The second reformist strain calls for the replacement of FFS payment modes with thoroughgoing prepayment. The critique is straightforward: FFS reimbursement gives physicians an incentive to supply excessive care to the consumer. Requiring doctors to provide care on a fixed budget set in advance and to share in the risk of exceeding that budget, as in an HMO, reverses the illogical incentive system of FFS. At the same time, the organizations' need to compete for customers assures not only that doctors will avoid giving too little care for economic reasons but that on the contrary they will treat patients early, indeed keep them well, in order to hold down costs.

The synthesis in one organization of comprehensive delivery and prepaid financing yielded a rational, self-regulating entity which, when set down in the larger system, would by the competitive pressures of its efficiency, force that system to change its ways: the result would be improved health care through the self-regulation of the market. This image, a fusion of reformist thinking popular among many progressive health professionals since the reports of the Committee on the Costs of Medical Care in the 1930s and of arguments widespread among health economists, generated the reasoning that the HMO proponents advanced and the politicians accepted.

To these analysts, to high-level Health, Education, and Welfare (HEW) officials in the Nixon administration, and to many legislators, the logic of the HMO initiatives seemed to be almost intuitively obvious. Clearly the incentives of the FFS, third-party system were illogical, the reverse of what they ought to be. Doctors were getting paid to treat the sick; and the more they treated them, the richer the providers grew. Obviously the federal government should attempt to "leverage" change to unite prepaid financing and group practice in responsible organizations that would reward doctors financially for keeping patients well and thereby embody correct and logical incentives. Once put in place, economic laws governing the HMO's internal incentive system would lead to competition in the larger system and, thereby, would produce high-quality, accessible care, efficiently delivered, in the system as a whole. Small federal sums to cover the start-up costs of HMOs might therefore go a long way.

The proponents were too ready to accept the assurances of the literal model of HMOs that economic processes would reconcile quality, access, and cost in the highly desirable ways predicted. But, even if one granted the proponents their predictions, the difficulty remained that they took for granted the most problematic element of the exercise, the organization-building process, those coordinated contributions needed to put an HMO together in the first place. In George

Homans' words, economic theory may have considerable success at explaining "behavior once the institutions are given," but "it is much more difficult to explain the institutional conditions themselves." Although economic theory may be, as Homans put it, "lucky in being able to take institutions pretty much for granted" (Homans, 1967), those who resort to economic theory for policy analyses may enjoy no such luck. The HMO episode demonstrates a central irony and limitation of economics-based policy analysis in the health care field, namely, that an orientation that takes so little direct account of the institution-building process generates so often and so enthusiastically recommendations that presuppose heroic institution-building efforts.

Under the spell of the model, policy makers failed carefully to consider the HMO as an organization, as a system of contributions. Instead they tended to view it as some unitary entity the existence of which was contingent mainly on the right amounts and composition of federal aid. In the eyes of the administration many HMOs—indeed 1700—could be launched with small federal sums because, so long as requirements were kept few and flexible, private sponsors would rush in with private capital. To Senator Edward M. Kennedy (D-Mass.) and other liberals, an indefinitely large number of HMOs could be started if only the federal government put up enough billions of dollars. Debate then turned to the problem of finding middle ground between these unacceptable extremes. What should be the relative importance of grants versus loans? What, if any, role should subsidies play in the program? What type of plan should be eligible for what type of aid, and so forth? Between the abstractions of the policy analysts and the details of the lawmakers, basic "middle-range" questions were largely overlooked—assuming the presence of federal funds, large or small, who would want to claim them? What would they do with them? What results could be expected?

Unfortunately, the plausibility of the HMO concept as a policy strategy depended heavily on answers to precisely such questions as these. Why would sponsors launch HMOs? Why would physicians go to work for them? Why would consumers subscribe to them? Why would hospitals cooperate with them? Even if one granted that the incentives of the ideal-typical HMO would work as intended *if* these contributors contributed, what incentives did the proposal offer them *to* contribute and to keep contributing in harmonious interaction over time?

This simple question had an equally simple answer: few. But except for some program specialists in the Social Security Administration and the Health Services and Mental Health Administration, whose advice on the HMO proposal was sought as a matter of politeness and then ignored, no one appears fully to have recognized the importance of these questions. The questions did not fit the analysts' model, which addressed the behavior, not the creation, of institutions; nor did they enter the early deliberations of politicians more accustomed to thinking expansively about the formidable leverage of federal grants than about their limits. As events soon showed, however, neglect of these questions proved to be a severe deficiency in the HMO strategy.

A little familiarity with the evolution of the United States health care system, or for that matter a little rumination, detached from the ideology of markets, incentives, and competition, might have shown not only that it was unlikely that key contributors would find themselves strongly induced to form and support HMOs but also that they faced strong disincentives to do so. Basic, bedrock trends in the health care system—not by-products of faulty incentives, but deeply-rooted elements of consumer psychology, professional culture, and organizational character—worked against the growth and development of HMOs. First, the tendency in the United States (and indeed in most of Europe) to entrust the financing and delivery of care to separate hands made it unlikely that *sponsors* (some of which, such as hospitals, dealt only with one of these functions, and others of which, such as industrial firms, dealt directly with neither) would attempt to integrate both functions in an HMO under their own auspices. Second, the growth of FFS group practices allows *physicians* to enjoy most of the advantages of prepaid group practices while accepting few of their constraints. Third, steady expansion of third-party payment health insurance plans, encompassing an ever-larger share of medical bills (including outpatient bills) and reducing the consumer's direct share of costs, undercuts the HMO's appeals to potential *subscribers*. Fourth, the tendency to perform more medical functions of an increasingly complex and costly technological character in *hospitals* sets hospitals that have based their organizational arrangements and budgetary expectations on this trend at odds with the decreases in inpatient use (and therefore in revenues) that an HMO's accustomed mode of operation entails. For these and other reasons, these contributors have strong interests in keeping separated processes the HMO internalizes. In theory, industrialization—pulling together into one organization processes previously performed by interaction among several—is a highly rational and responsible approach to reforming the system. In practice, incorporating matters handled by interorganizational relations within an intraorganizational framework may raise levels of interdependence, problems of coordination and control, and therefore conflict to levels that potential participants find unacceptable and therefore face a strong incentive to avoid.

American policy makers might have made more realistic judgments about the prospects of the HMO strategy if they had considered European experience. In Europe, PGP arrangements were once widespread. Health care was provided under the auspices of unions, churches, fraternal groups, and other voluntary associations that contracted with doctors for fixed prepaid sums on behalf of their members (Glaser, 1970). But these arrangements rarely survived the introduction of national health insurance, with basic benefit entitlements and free choice of physician for most of the population.

One lesson of this experience is that, although much of the population will accept, indeed welcome, care provided by PGP-like arrangements in the absence of universal coverage, broad entitlements lead to a demand for freedom of choice of provider. Another is that the principle of free choice of providers—the precept that any qualified physician can treat any entitled beneficiary—is also very important to doctors. In Germany, "from 1892 on, these issues, the physicians' access to sickness fund practice and the patients' freedom-of-choice, dominated discussion between sickness funds and the medical profession" (Blanpain et al., 1978); and "freedom" steadily gained ground, as it has also in other European nations.

To be sure, the United States differs from Europe in an important way: the privatism and diversity of American health insurance policies permit extensive competition among insurers. By offering more value for the subscriber's dollar, it has been argued, HMOs might attract a sizable market share. Even so, comparative analysis suggests that it is unlikely that the United States population, increasingly well covered by third-party plans allowing freedom of choice of provider and financed in ever-larger degree by employer contributions, will foresake their freedom for closed panel plans. Comparison also shows the implausibility of the view that doctors, many of them resistant to group practice of any sort, will move in large numbers to *prepaid* group practices, or that many of them will voluntarily foresake FFS reimbursement for salaries or capitation.

The moral—simple, unsubtle, but pertinent—is that incentive-based syllogisms that derive conclusions from a chain of highly problematic institution-building processes should not be taken for finished and plausible pieces of policy analysis. The fundamental weakness of the HMO proposal was that it rested on an uncritical application of the concept of incentives. This concept is, of course, one of the most useful and widely used in the social sciences and perhaps the most widely used in policy analysis, but it is not the all-purpose tool it is sometimes taken to be. That policy should "change the incentives" to bring behavior into line with what government seeks has the ring of unassailable insight, eternal truth, elegant simplicity. Not surprisingly, some policy analysts have apparently persuaded themselves that the merest flick of an incentive system can, like Sumner's mores, make anything right. The right incentives, one is assured, will lead businesses back into central cities (the "urbank" and "urban enterprise zone" proposals); make companies produce and consumers buy much less gasoline (decontrol of gas prices); lead polluting firms to pollute "optimally" (pollution taxes, fees, and "rights"); make lower-class persons behave like solid, hard-working middle-class citizens (improved "objective opportunities"); and lead doctors who, poor benighted souls, would otherwise treat patients only when they have become ill, to suddenly start keeping them well (HMOs). Very likely, incentives are capable of doing some of these things to some degree and others very little or not at all; however, the fact is that remarkably little is now known about what policy problems successfully lend themselves to what types of incentive-based solutions.

An incentive is simply a reward or penalty. It is, of course, an elementary and powerful psychosocial truth that people tend to respond to rewards and penalties. This truth, however, cannot be applied wholesale and unrefined to policy analysis and translated directly into useful practical advice. Individuals face incentives; systems have properties. Although system properties are not wholly distinct from individual incentives, they are not wholly reducible to them either. Incentives are embodied in sociopolitical and psychocultural contexts, embedded in institutions, in a word. In some cases, this fact may be disregarded without harm; in others, reliance on disembodied incentives may render policy advice useless or worse. It is therefore highly apposite to seek principles that distinguish between these situations.

Of any proposal to manipulate incentives as a policy device, three questions should be asked at the outset. First, who must be made subject to the incentives if the desired outcome is to occur? Second, how do these individuals define rewards and penalties; that is, how do their values bear on the incentives under discussion? Third, how large must the inducement be to bring about the desired outcome? The first question is institutional: that is, it requires a canvass of the major participants in the delivery systems (or whatever) to be changed. The latter two are psychological and cultural: they require an analysis of values and norms. Unless the answers to these questions are relatively straightforward and favorable, the postulated play of incentives is likely to be hindered, and the incentive approach may not work.

In cases where it is reasonable at least for analytic purposes to picture the policy problem as one of bringing about the proper relationship between government and individual, the three questions may have direct and actionable answers. For instance James Q. Wilson has shown that in thinking about crime it can be useful to disengage from deep causal issues, look at the problem as one of the available measures government may take vis-à-vis criminals, and then ask what incentives (in this case, deterrents) government possesses. The "who" is the criminal, the "what" is the loss of freedom, and the "how great" involves deprivations of liberty of greater or lesser periods (Wilson, 1977).

Most relationships government attempts to influence by means of policy are more complex. Education, for example, is a policy area in which research has pointed out the presence and importance of previously unrecognized patterns of influence. This discovery led in turn to newly-perceived perplexities in policy-making. The findings of James Coleman and his associates (1966) on the correlates of educational achievement among elementary and secondary school students introduced into what had generally been regarded as a relationship among government, school, and student a fourth powerful variable—family background. Coleman (1972) threw new light on the relationship between government policy and educational achievement precisely because he refused to eschew causal analysis in favor of policy analysis, insisting instead on searching for the influence of hidden forces behind accepted images. The be sure, the Coleman findings made the policy question appear far less actionable than it had seemed before. Had the researchers limited themselves to policy analysis in the narrow sense, however—to discussion of readily available "policy tools" for the "manipulation of objective conditions" (Wilson, 1977:159, 161)—they would have missed what may be the heart of the matter.

Failure to appreciate the nature and complexity of health care institutions and their implications for the HMO-building effort is the most important explanation for the disappointments of the HMO strategy. Eyes fixed on the theoretical virtues of the HMO as an institution, the analysts gave too little thought to the complexities of bringing these institutions into being. It was apparently thought sufficient that government dangle seed money (an incentive) before the eyes of entrepreneurs. But the organization-building process was far more complex than this: government must attract sponsors who must recruit and socialize providers (physicians and hospitals) and then attract and place under the (properly functioning) providers' care a sizable number of consumers. In a fair assessment of the plausibility of this strategy, the trio of questions mentioned above—who, what, and how large—was crucial but almost entirely neglected by the analysts' model. The dependence of the comprehensive, responsible HMO on four sets of actors—sponsors, doctors, subscribers, and hospitals; the complex interplay of economic, political, cultural, psychological, and organizational variables in forming the tastes of each group for what an HMO offered them; and the strong forces working against building and joining HMOs were central to assessing the proposal's promise.

HMOs, in short, should be viewed as complex organizational coalitions. Their formation and stability require not only that consumers demand them (whatever this means in practice) but also that this demand be felt strongly by sponsors, physicians, and hospitals, which may have strong preferences against building or participating in HMOs. Then consumers who demand HMOs in general must accept and select them in concrete choice situations—quite another matter. Had these factors been taken into account, the exercise would have disrupted the advocates' agenda. The contingent and high-risk nature of the strategy would have been exposed; goals and expectations would have been scaled down; a system-wide reorganization would have been neither promised nor predicted; the "numbers game" would have appeared foolish; and politicians might have lost interest.

Competition and Complexity

Even if health maintenance organizations could be built effortlessly and in large numbers, it is unclear what policy impact they would have. HMO proponents generally took for granted that the competitive presence of HMOs in the larger system would create incentives that would actualize the theoretical virtues claimed on behalf of competition. Unfortunately, the outcome the analysts confidently predicted lies mainly in the realm of the deductive.

Although the analysts' theories relied on a bilateral image to deduce the benefits that the presence of cost conscious HMOs would bring about—the HMO versus its FFS competition—the process is in reality multiordered, highly complex, and only partially responsive to economic and competitive forces. To accomplish their postulated effects, HMOs must make their presence felt on each of five variables, each subject to a complicated mix of competitive and noncompetitive, monetary and nonmonetary forces of varying strengths. These variables are consumers, technology, physicians, hospitals, and third-party payers. In the health field, there is no single, personalized object—the benefit-cost-balancing criminal to be deterred, for example—at whom the government may beam its incentives. There are instead five loosely-linked elements each of which is driven by forces significantly distinct from those driving others and each of which is therefore differently susceptible to diverse types and strengths of governmental incentives. To understand the impact of an HMO or of other types of competition, one must explore the values each of these five variables assumes in the presence of the new competitor. Only in this way can one predict whether an input injected at the beginning of the complex chain of cause and effect may be expected to generate the predicted and desired output, or indeed any recognizable output at all. All five variables should be kept simultaneously in view. Insofar as they fail to set HMOs in their full institutional setting and thereby fail to keep interdependence and interaction constantly in view, analysts will fail to get an accurate reading of the efficacy of an HMO's competitive incentives. Unfortunately, however, not enough is known about the values of these five variables to support confident policy analysis, much less the bold promises of the HMO advocates.

Put simply, health care expenditures reflect five forces: (1) the nature and extent of consumer expectations; (2) the nature and extent of medical technologies; (3) the number and behavior of physicians; (4) the number and organizational character of hospitals; and (5) the structure and scope of third-party payment mechanisms. These variables interact with one another in local delivery systems and therefore must be taken into account in formulating policies at the federal level designed to change these systems. Over time, all five variables have assumed values that call for more and better medical care. Larger numbers of consumers (some of whom find care newly accessible as a result of federal programs) bring ever-higher expectations to the system. The growth of medical knowledge and the diffusion of medical technologies generate an ever-larger number of more costly procedures which become part of popular and professional definitions of good care. A growing number of doctors, facing these expanding consumer expectations and technological opportunities, have a strong professional and economic interest in giving each patient the most and the best. Hospitals in search of organizational prestige and high-caliber medical staffs have expanded their beds, facilities, equipment, and services—and therewith their costs. The growth of third-party payment plans, in which insurers tend to reimburse providers with less than a sharply critical eye, has added fuel to all these expansive, expensive developments.

The number of variables and the complexity of their interactions place great obstacles in the way of policy analysis, that is, recommendations for governmental action based on some combination of theory and research. Sound analyses should neglect none of the five variables, but the variables embody processes very different from one another and therefore disrupt lines of disciplinary specialization. Physician behavior should be viewed not only from the standpoint of economics but also from those of the sociology of professions and even anthropology. Consumer expectations and behavior require the insights of psychology, sociology, and economics. Understanding medical technology demands these disciplines and an admixture of natural science. Hospital and insurance firm behavior is probably best illuminated by organizational analysis. Taking variables out of context and examining them in the light of one discipline alone (say economics) guarantees distortion. But examining the full range of variables in the light of several pertinent disciplines mainly exposes the complexity of it all, induces humility and restraint in the student, and leads to cautious and circumscribed policy analyses or to none at all. Those who understand the system most fully tend therefore to be least entrepreneurial in their recommendations and tend least to seize or attract the ear of policy makers. Conversely, policy advocacy in the health field presupposes a capacity for gross simplifications.

Unfortunately, the simplifications of the policy analysts may lead to misunderstandings; for, if complexity may be willed away in the analytic world, it keeps breaking into the real world. A policy analytic input in the health field must make its way through five "black boxes"—consumers, technology, physicians, hospitals, and insurers—each with different institutional properties that skew and distort the input as surely as a prism skews and distorts a ray of light beamed through it.

The HMO strategy works insofar as it injects competitive pressures that break into and restructure the interinstitutional processes that uncritically favor more and "better"—and more costly—medical care. The problems, then, are to specify how and how far these processes are subject to competitive pressures and how and how likely HMOs are to exert such pressures. The question, in sum, is how might HMOs affect the market characteristics of the United States health care system?

Judging by the confidence with which HMO proponents and other advocates of competitive solutions to medical care inflation advance their various proposals, one might conclude that the market behavior of the medical care system is well understood. This is not the case. Indeed, in the cases of consumer and physician behavior, there does not exist even a well-developed vocabulary with which to name and describe processes, let alone a model that links processes to one another in patterns useful to policy makers. As a policy tool, however, competition presupposes consistent behavior and an ability to make refined predictions about it, and it works if, and only if, it affects the major variables in anticipated and desired directions. The literal theory of HMOs promises precisely this: HMOs, offering broader benefits at substantial savings over FFS competitors, will pressure third-party payers, physicians, and hospitals into curbing their own costs and thereby altering both their uncritical uses of technology and the efficiency of the care they offer consumers. But it is doubtful that any of the five variables is highly susceptible to competition in the sense in which the term has traditionally been used in economics and in which the literal HMO theory used it.

For one thing, the proposal presupposes that HMO efficiencies can be brought to bear directly on the financial calculations of the consumer and that the consumer will respond primarily to these financial considerations. But as conventional third-party plans financed increasingly by employer contributions to employee health premiums have spread, the individual's share of the cost of his health coverage has declined, thereby reducing his incentive to choose the efficient plan. In 1977, employers contributed 100 percent of employee health insurance premiums in 57 percent of cases (Phelps, 1980:62). Second, although the HMO may be the efficient plan, it is in many places also the more expensive plan, often demanding a payroll deduction larger than that required to join the competition. Although the HMO may offer more coverage for each dollar, consumers may not value the additional coverage enough to be willing to incur the deduction. Third, consumers do not choose health insurance on financial grounds alone. Matters of style and taste—for one's present physician, against "clinic medicine," for freedom of choice in general, or against the HMO's hospital in particular, for example—also affect the decision. Little is known about these elements of consumer choice. It is therefore little more than guesswork to try to predict how a change in a financial incentive aimed at the consumer's pocketbook—in this case, introduction of an HMO—will affect his health care coverage decisions.

Nor is it clear that competition among plans will alter medical norms so as to make the technological imperative less powerful. In the quest for a competitive edge, HMOs may substitute less for more technically intensive care, but here too noneconomic variables intervene. Unless the plan offers the most and the best and gives physicians a reasonably free hand to practice good medicine as defined by their professional training and outlook, it will have difficulty attracting and retaining good physicians. Also pertinent are the consumer's expectations that membership in an HMO will not oblige him to forgo the advances of modern medicine, and physicians' risk of malpractice suits if they fail to do "all they could."

Moreover, unless the HMO owns or controls its own hospitals, it will share in the costs of the acquisition and use of technology along with the hospital's other clients. In the quest for organizational prominence hospitals will, unless constrained by public regulation, seek to be the first in town with the latest medical gadget. If they acquire it, they will try to use it; and, to the degree that they succeed, HMOs relying on that hospital will partake of the costs. Perhaps sustained HMO competition could have some impact on the diffusion and use of technology by doctors, hospitals, and insurers in the larger system. How such competition works, and how large its effects might be under different circumstances are unclear, however.

If competition is to be felt and acted on, these feelings and responses must come from providers of medical care and coverage; namely, doctors, hospitals, and insurers. These providers display odd blends of competitive and noncompetitive processes, however, about which much remains to be learned. In most places, health insurance is a competitive business: the competition takes place mainly between nonprofit Blue Cross and Blue Shield plans and profit-making commercial plans seeking the business of large purchasers (notably employers and unions); and it is carried on in the economic media of premiums, costs, and benefits offered. Hospital costs, on the other hand, are usually driven by competition of a very different type—among predominantly nonprofit institutions that advance their organizational interests by competition not in the currency of price but of quality, or at any rate the technological and professional trappings of quality. The production functions of the quality- or image-competitive hospitals and the costs that ensue naturally complicate the economic logic of predicting the behavior of the price-competitive insurers called upon to pay hospital bills.

Physician behavior responds to still other forces; the degree to which the term competition accurately captures these forces has been little studied and is little understood. Physicians are often said to monopolize the provision of medical care services, and from this it is often thought to follow that new competition would be a good and efficient thing. This assessment of the problem, however, rests on an uncritical use of language. Throughout the United States economy, Lester Thurow (1980) writes, "it is becoming . . . less and less clear what a monopoly means." In the health care sector, "which in the main consists of a multitude of relatively small private service units" (Mott, 1977:238), the meaning of the term has never been clear.

The basic problem is not that physicians monopolize services in the traditional economic sense (indeed those who charge monopoly often acknowledge in the next breath that medicine in the United States is a cottage industry) but rather that physicians claim expertise over the proper application of medical care in general and over the amounts and types of care that particular consumers ought to demand and that physicians ought to supply. The problem, in Freidson's (1970) words, is "professional dominance" not "monopoly." Using the latter term enthrones lack of competition as the central cost problem by semantic fiat. If monopoly is the problem, then breaking the monopoly must be the corrective. Viewing the problem as one of the demand-defining capacities of professional suppliers places the question in a very different conceptual and practical light.

Physician behavior is a complex tapestry of professional (including personal, cognitive, peer-related, and ethical) and financial considerations about which abstract economic reasoning conceals at least as much as it clarifies. This complexity presumably explains the remarkable disagreement among policy-oriented economists on the effects of increasing the supply of physicians. Some argue that such a step would be a disastrous invitation to enormous increases in treatments and costs as physicians used their demand-defining powers to maintain "target incomes," that is, those incomes they believe they have a right to achieve as a consequence of years spent in acquiring expertise. Others contend that the competition engendered by an increased supply of physicians would drive charges down and thereby strike a blow for cost containment. The disagreement cannot be resolved because the nature and consequences of competition in physicians' behavior have not been well explored.

Despite the predominance of economists in the health policy literature, surprisingly little careful empirical attention has been given to exploring what such terms as "markets," "competition," and "well-functioning market competition" mean or might mean in health care services and what their actual or possible meanings mean in turn for public policy. Those accustomed to envying economists for analytical and empirical rigor can only marvel at their widespread disagreement over seemingly elementary descriptive matters in the health field.

One analyst will cite the private character of the United States health care system, apparently taking it for granted that nonpublic and market-based are synonymous. A second will compile long lists of the ways in which health care services deviate from the assumptions that support classical market theory and take an agnostic or highly cautious position on policy solutions. A third analyst, looking at the very same list of deviations, will offer heated assurances that policy makers can solve their problems only by strengthening or introducing competition, market forces, cost consciousness, and the like. A fourth will declare firmly that markets and market forces do not and cannot work in a field with the peculiar properties of health care, while a fifth bitterly deplores the American tendency to treat health care as a commodity to be bought and sold.

It is far from clear what should be expected from increased competition in the health care field. Empirically, only two competitive effects stand forth clearly: first, in the largely nonprice-competitive hospital sector, organizational competition has fueled an "arm's race" for newer and better technology without much regard for costs; and second, in the reasonably price-competitive insurance sector, competition has made it difficult for poor risks, those with unfortunate actuarial attributes or an unfortunate health history, to get coverage—in short, it has promoted skimming and creaming. Competition with experience-rated commercial insurance plans forced Blue Cross to abandon most of its community rating long ago, thereby creating problems that made the case for government intervention by way of Medicare and Medicaid. Neither competitive effect is socially desirable, yet no others may be clearly attributed to competition in the health care field.

Given this institutional context, one should be skeptical of theoretical assertions that the introduction of an HMO into the larger system will produce all manner of reforms and improvements. A realistic assessment of the prospects requires answers to two questions. First, to what extent and how do HMOs compete? Second, to what extent and how do conventional plans respond to this competition? Answers come less easily than one might think.

The same factors that make HMOs difficult to build by blueprint also make it difficult to explain in general terms what makes them competitive. Competitiveness turns on highly particular and local aspects of a plan's setting: location, the attitudes of employers and employees, the generosity of employers' contributions to the health coverage of their workers, and others. It also turns on highly particular strategic choices of management: staffing decisions, the appearance and design of facilities, utilization controls, marketing assessments and efforts, and others. The "correct" interaction and balance among these many variables define a plan that is *able* to compete. But the list of variables yields no general formula for competitiveness that applies equally to all plans. Some will be more competitive than others for reasons of time, place, and circumstance.

Obviously HMOs must in some sense compete; this truism means nothing more than that HMOs cannot be indifferent to how the price and contents of their product compare with those of other products. Fewer conclusions follow logically from this fact than is sometimes supposed, however. It takes at least two parties to create a competitive setting; and, if one or both of the potential competitors is substantially insulated from the ordeals of competition, competitive discipline relaxes for the other too. Ability, will, and need to compete are different matters. None follows directly from the others.

Competition may be expected to have its intended effects only if, first, both competitors must absorb their own true costs over time and, second, both can control their costs. Medical care markets frequently violate both assumptions, at least in the case of the HMO's major competitor which is usually, though not always, a Blue Cross plan and which will be designated here by the shorthand term "Blue Cross." Blue Cross plans convert increased costs into higher premiums passed mainly along to employers and then to workers in the form of smaller wage increases and to the public at large in the consumer price index. Not all—indeed sometimes not any—of the increases are borne directly by the individuals whose coverage the premium purchases. Nor are these plans well suited to control costs. Although they may monitor and investigate claims for payment submitted by enrollees and providers, too much fastidiousness and too many disallowances generate conflict and may be worse for business than premium increases. These important areas of competitive insulation in Blue Cross operations define in turn the competitive challenge faced by HMOs.

If the HMO's competitors are themselves inflationary and lax, the HMO can loosen up too and still remain competitive. So long as the HMO offers broader benefits for not a great deal more money, it will be, everything else being equal, competitive even if it does not maximize its savings, indeed even if it is almost as inefficient as the competition.

The literal theory of HMO competition assumes that HMOs will attempt to maximize savings—that is, exploit to the hilt the various efficiencies inherent in the HMO structure; but plans may often prefer, in Herbert Simon's term, to "satisfice." If a plan is attempting to reach the break-even enrollment point or to grow very rapidly, it does indeed face incentives to maximize, that is, to offer the broadest possible benefits for the smallest possible price. There are high organizational costs as a result of maximizing, however; and a plan that is running in the black and growing as fast as its facilities and preferences dictate will weigh these costs carefully. Two costs of maximizing are of special importance: first, the strict utilization controls required to ensure that care is allocated tightly and in accord with least-costs principles may alienate doctors and set them in conflict with the administration; second, strict economies and efficiencies might give members the impression that HMO care is a bargain basement brand with distinctively different norms from those prevailing in the mainstream. Plans with very well socialized physicians and members may be able to maximize savings without incurring these costs, but no economic laws ensure that these human elements will behave as they should. Moreover, even plans in urgent need of building enrollment in order to break even need not force costs and premiums to their lowest feasible levels in order to do so. Instead, they may mount an aggressive marketing campaign by expanding contacts with unions and employers or step up their advertising. These qualifications to the maximizing model—that stable plans need not maximize, that to maximize carries high organizational costs, and that alternatives to it exist—should be considered in estimates of the strength and nature of competitive pressures exerted by HMOs. The notion that HMOs may be satisficers has received little analytical attention. To the degree that they do satisfice, however, injecting HMOs into the larger system is unlikely to have the direct, sizable results foreseen by adherents of the maximizing model.

A reasonable assessment of the competitive impact of HMOs should, in short, take close account of the market positions and organizational characters of both HMOs and their competition. A priori, one might expect competition to be most vigorous between young HMOs in search of a break-even enrollment and well-disciplined, comparatively efficient Blue Cross operations, that is, those with the least slack. Conversely, one would expect competition to be least vigorous between stable HMOs content with their market shares and growth rates and poorly disciplined, comparatively lax Blue Cross plans. Even as hypotheses, however, these generalizations are suggestive at best; organizational idiosyncracies and management philosophies in both HMOs and Blue Cross plans are of major, perhaps central, importance; and these factors lie outside the scope of economic laws. One assumes, for example, that the Kaiser plans are tough competitors not mainly because they fear going under if they run a somewhat less tight ship but primarily because of their long standing, deeply ingrained allegiance to practices of sound management.

It may be expected that the vigor of competition will depend too on the market share of the HMOs. It would be strange indeed if the Blue Cross plans of California did not feel strong competitive pressure from the two Kaiser plans in that state, both of which have been in business for more than thirty years and each of which has a membership of more than one million. It would be even stranger, however, if these strong competitive pressures automatically accompanied HMOs of whatever age and size around the country.

Although a recent study of the competitive effects of HMOs by the Federal Trade Commission (FTC) (1977) found evidence of competition between HMOs and Blue Cross in the western states, where Kaiser and some other plans are strong and long established, little evidence could be found of competition in other areas of the country. Some of the areas studied are the sites of old and comparatively large HMOs: Washington, D.C., for example, houses the Group Health Association (GHA), a forty-year-old plan of roughly 110,000 members; and New York City is the home of the Health Insurance Plan of Greater New York (HIP), a thirty-year-old plan with about 770,000 members. The FTC study shows that the usual maximizing assumption that any HMO able to survive over time must compete is simplistic. Plans like GHA and HIP survive but apparently do not compete, at least not aggressively, indeed, judging by the FTC findings, not even noticeably. On satisficing assumptions, this is perfectly natural behavior for settled plans which for reasons of facility size, managerial philosophy, or some other reason either are not eager to expand or conclude that the likelihood of significant expansion is too small to justify the organizational costs required to make savings as great, premiums as low, or benefits as broad as possible.

These considerations have led some HMO proponents to argue that the benefits of competition will be best and perhaps only realized in areas where HMOs compete vigorously with each other. When this happens, it is argued, an HMO cannot use Blue Cross inefficiency as an excuse for laxity of its own; instead, efficiency will breed further pressure for efficiency. Recent experience in Minneapolis, where seven HMOs compete with one another, has received a wide press (Christianson and McClure, 1979); but the results of this competition are unclear. Harold Luft (1980) observed that, despite a doubling of HMO enrollment in Minneapolis-St. Paul between 1975 and 1977 and HMO hospital use averaging 42 percent below the Blue Cross group average, overall hospital use in the area "stayed constant or increased slightly"; whereas the HMO reductions should have produced an areawide decrease of 15 days per 1000, even *apart* from a competitive effect. The result, Luft remarks, might be explained in many ways but is "consistent with both the notions of no major competitive response and the selective enrollment of low utilizers in the HMOs."

Competition among HMOs may be expected to have its intended effects only if several conditions are met. First, the entrepreneurs and managers of HMOs must be willing to compete with each other. Unfortunately, there is no good reason why they would be. Most HMO executives want to succeed, not test academic notions about competition. They succeed by building strong, stable organizations, not by subjecting themselves to the risk of failing a fair market test. HMO administrators, like most other executives, tend to be highly averse to risks to their organization's stability and therewith to their own reputations and careers. Competition is a very salient risk.

For this reason, HMO founders and executives tend to analyze markets carefully before they plunge in and tend to be wary of fragmenting HMO markets of uncertain strength. If they do enter a market already populated by HMOs, they will often try to differentiate their product. One approach is to specialize by location. In Massachusetts, for example, the state insurance commissioner licensed the state's first open panel HMO only after requiring that its application be rewritten to insure that it and other HMOs would not "be like the Mafia, dividing the state into families." (Boston Evening Globe, 1978). Another strategy is to specialize by "taste," challenging an HMO not with another similarly structured HMO but with an IPA, for instance. In short, HMOs may deliberately choose not to challenge each other's markets. This possibility poses obvious problems for the theory of competition. According to Walter McClure (1980), "the worst realistic scenario occurs if the first few health care plans in an area become content with their market share after they have acquired 20–30,000 enrollees or so to assure stability. Then, relatively few consumers, unions, and employers understand or demand fair market choice." This worst realistic scenario is also the most realistic scenario. As one HMO administrator put it in an interview, "many HMOs would be happy to get 25,000 and just leave it right there. It's easier to manage."

Second, if HMOs are to compete with one another, employers must be willing to offer more than one HMO and perhaps also to promote them to their employees. To the degree that HMOs specialize by area, this may be difficult. Employers are reluctant to bear the administrative costs of offering plans remote from work or convenient to the homes of only a few of their workers. Even if the plans are well located, employers may be diffident. Some resist the costs and inconvenience of reprogramming health offerings in any way. Others will do so to meet the legal requirement that they offer a federally qualified HMO if and when one exists in their area but will not offer another HMO before or afterward. Even employers willing to offer multiple HMOs may decline to promote them; many consider it prudent not to meddle in employees' health care decisions. In all these respects, Minneapolis appears to be quite distinctive if not unique: there several major employers have taken a lead not only in offering but also in promoting several HMOs (Iglehart, 1978).

Third, competitive HMOs presuppose that unions bargaining collectively on behalf of employees will welcome multiple HMOs and will leave the choice of particular plans to their individual members. Unions sometimes welcome an HMO option as a bargaining chip with conventional plans (the threat of taking their business elsewhere may thus become credible). Occasionally unions welcome a new HMO as a club to hold over an established HMO in which membership is heavily enrolled and dissatisfied. Usually, however, they prefer to commit their membership to and consolidate their influence with one plan, not fragment both among several.

Fourth, to be a durable policy solution competition among HMOs must in some sense be self-stabilizing. One requirement of a sound competitive system is that strong competitors be induced to compete by the prospect of enjoying the fruits of superior performance, including the development of a commanding market share by beating the competition. Another requirement is that competitors be prevented from achieving monopoly power. Balancing these requirements is no simple matter, as FTC and other antitrust experience shows. If aggressively competitive HMOs rout their competition, will the weak HMOs be allowed to fail? Or will they be bailed out, sacrificing efficiency for a competition justified in the name of efficiency?

The analytical point of these reflections is that competition in health care should be treated not simply as an economic process, but also as a product (or casualty) of the interests of actors in formal organizations, especially HMO sponsors and managers, employers, unions, and those government agencies that oversee and regulate competition. The practical point is that the conditions required to support vigorous competition among HMOs are unlikely to be met for extended periods in many places.

Even if HMOs (one or several) came out seeking a knockout, so to speak, one should consider the separate questions of the ability, need, and will of Blue Cross to respond. If competition is an infallible road to lower costs, it may be asked, why has the persistent price-based competition between Blue Cross and commercial insurers not led to lower costs over time? Apparently competition per se is not enough. The usual answer to this puzzle is that third-party payers are irresponsible, that is, they lack control over and responsibility for the behavior of the doctors whose treatment decisions they largely ratify. Because third-party payers tolerate inefficient treatments, pay the bills, raise their premiums, and then market mainly to employers who pay much or most or all of these higher premiums and pass the costs along to the public and because both Blue Cross and its commercial competition are on an equal footing in this respect, neither has an incentive for efficiency. An HMO, by contrast, can control its providers and must absorb its own costs in responsible fashion and therefore does face incentives for efficiency. The presence of an HMO, therefore, will have effects on a third-party payer different from those of another third-party competitor.

This reasoning makes questionable assumptions about both the HMO's demand for competition and the ability of Blue Cross to supply it. As noted above, it may be argued that the same lack of internal discipline that HMO competition is expected to combat may establish a ceiling or norm of maximum acceptable inflation which the HMO may find it more comfortable to hover around or just below than drastically to undercut. On the supply side, it is surely not evident—and to an organization theorist not even plausible—that the presence of an HMO with, say, 20,000 members will make a Blue Cross plan long accustomed to, and content with, permissiveness suddenly begin fighting with doctors, hospitals, and enrollees over appropriate treatment and unwarranted claims. It is quite likely that the fundamental dynamic here too is organizational, not merely financial; it is a question of the strength of leadership and the nature of management philosophy in the highly varied Blue Cross plans. Even if an HMO is highly efficient (that is, able to offer a wider set of benefits at a cost well below that of the competition), Blue Cross officials may find it less costly on the whole to lose some members (it would be remarkable if an HMO's penetration rate in many areas exceeded 20 percent, after all, and extraordinary indeed if it grew large enough to threaten a Blue Cross plan's survival) than to battle doctors, hospitals, and enrollees in an effort to drive costs and premiums sharply downward. Nothing follows automatically from the injection of competition, at least not from competition of the type and on the scale that HMOs now generally offer. If HMOs were set down amidst all 69 Blue Cross plans, the result would probably be 69 different competitive responses ranging from none at all to vigorous, with most falling somewhere in between but closer to none.

The argument offered here is not that Blue Cross plans will not respond competitively to the presence of an HMO, but rather that they need not and may not do so. The hypothesis that responses are a function not of economic laws but rather of organizational politics and managerial policies specific to each plan suggests the corollary that the most efficient Blue Cross plans may offer the most competitive responses. That is, one might expect the tough competitors, those Blue Cross plans well run by executives who pride themselves on achieving and maintaining a high penetration rate and on offering an attractive product, who "hate to lose one member" (in the words of an HMO official describing the attitudes of the tough Blue Cross competition he faced) and who are determined to run a tight ship, to be most willing to take on doctors and other claimants in the interests of sound management and HMOs in the interests of organizational maintenance.

If these hypotheses are sound, analysts should guard against spuriously attributing to competition behavior that derives mainly from managerial philosophy and organizational politics. In the United States health care system, plans everywhere compete to some degree. This competition takes no single form and has no determinate result, however, but rather many forms and results. Competitors may take one another carefully into account, as apparently happens in California where the two Kaiser plans are very large and achieve high penetration rates in the San Francisco and Los Angeles metropolitan areas; or they may largely ignore one another, as apparently happens in Washington, D.C., and in New York City. Some plans facing sharp competition appear to be efficient; others less so. Correlation should not be mistaken for causation: one should no more automatically attribute to the presence of an HMO the efficiencies of competitors than one should conclude that continued inefficiencies in conventional plans faced with HMO competition are caused by the presence of an HMO.

If competition is contingent on organizational politics, Blue Cross plans with similar market shares might react quite differently to the entry of an HMO into their service areas. This does seem to be the case. In example, the Blue Cross plans serving Rochester, New York; Providence, Rhode Island; and Cleveland, Ohio, all command a strong share of the local health insurance market. Yet, whereas Blue Cross of northwestern New York helped to establish HMOs in Rochester, Rhode Island's Blue Cross plan has been mildly supportive but not greatly enthusiastic about plans in Providence; and the Blue Cross plan serving Cleveland was described by one former HMO executive as uncooperative and hostile to HMOs. In short, Blue Cross responses vary with the managerial outlooks of their executives; to these executives, as to everyone else, HMOs are Rorschach tests into which one reads what one will. Some executives have resisted them strongly; some have welcomed them in hopes that they would fail and vindicate the *status quo;* some have become involved in them as means of cornering a share of the potential HMO market for themselves; some have participated in HMO development in the interests of product diversification; some have entered the field to demonstrate to the government and to the public the flexibility and open-mindedness of the insurance industry; and others have become involved, or have declined to get involved, for still other reasons. No abstract model describing the ideal-typical HMO locked in competition with the ideal-typical Blue Cross firm to the greater efficiency of both begins to fit the facts. Useful models wait not upon the elaboration and refinement of economic laws of competition but rather upon careful qualitative research into organizational behavior in health insurance plans.

But, even if HMOs could be made to compete aggressively and Blue Cross plans could be made to respond with fear and trembling and efficiency, the effects of such competition would not be clear, and some of them might not be desirable. For one thing, competition can lead to underservice and abuse. This happened in California where the Reagan administration unleashed very vigorous competition among prepaid health plans (PHP) and between PHPs and FFS physicians for Medicaid recipients in the same area. Reagan "relied on the market place to develop competition, believing the good would drive the bad out. It just didn't work that way," Elizabeth Owen, director of a prepaid health project in the California Health Department, recently observed (Group Health News, 1980:3). Although the California PHP experience had several unusual properties, the facts remain that one major means of competing is to hold premiums down, that one major way to do this is to realize internal economies, that some ways to do this are to underserve and to ration or restrict access to care, and that these possibilities will never be entirely absent from the minds of physicians and executives whose main attachment to prepaid plans is money. Exclusively money-minded executives and the abuses they practice may be few. Even solid and decent plans may give rise to questions about the source and consequences of internal economies, however. For example, Harold Luft's (1978) finding that HMOs achieve savings by reducing hospital admissions for nondiscretionary as well as for discretionary procedures by no means convicts HMOs of underservice, but it does raise questions worthy of further research.

One should also consider what may be termed the "adaptive" costs of competition. HMO competition may, for example, lead Blue Cross to broaden its own benefits, thereby encouraging utilization. California may offer an instructive example. The FTC study (1977:77, n. 3) notes that Blue Cross of Northern California claims to have "the broadest outpatient benefits package of any Blue Cross plan," a development that the authors view as a "competitive step" to meet the appeal of the huge Northern California Kaiser plan. Luft (1980:304) points out that, although California ranks forty-sixth among states in the share of its expenditures for hospital care, it nonetheless stood third in per capita health spending in 1969, the last year for which such data were available. The explanation, he writes, is that "perhaps as a result of the improved ambulatory care coverage by conventional insurers, California ranked second in the share of per capita expenditures for physicians' services." He concludes that "by some standards the mix of medical services bought by Californians may be more efficient, but there is no evidence that even massive HMO enrollment has resulted in overall cost containment."

Another possible cost of adaptation to competition is that hospitals "may raise rates to compensate for reduced utilization" brought on by the presence of an HMO (FTC, 1977:117, n. 1). Consider, for example, the case of Washington, D.C., a city with three HMOs in 1978, a forty-year-old giant of over 100,000 members, a rapidly growing plan of about 43,000 members, and a smaller HMO of about 15,000. In 1978 the *Washington Post* reported that the average cost of a day of care in Washington hospitals was rising 50 percent faster than the national average of 18.5 percent. (In Maryland, which has a strong rate-setting commission, the article noted, the increase had been held to 8.2 percent.) The reason appeared to be low occupancy and resulting "high unit costs, since many expenses remain the same even when some beds or wards are not being used."

It is doubtful that the presence of the HMOs affected this situation much one way or another. Yet, the workings of vigorous competition might be expected to reduce occupancy further. The interesting policy question is: What happens then? Will hospitals voluntarily redefine their services and facilities by means of cutbacks, mergers, and closures? Will they cling to their underused facilities and continue to cover rising unit costs in their per diem charges? Will competition by itself brake this tendency and induce a more efficient hospital sector? Or will the assistance of public regulation—rate-setting, decertification, and the like—be required, and perhaps more urgently and on a larger scale? The fact is that no one knows what effect HMO competition will have on costs, or even if it will be downward or upward. Likewise no one knows whether competition will prove to be an alternative to regulation or an invitation to further and more stringent regulation.

Insurance and Efficiency

In the 1970s the federal government launched in earnest the search for acceptable health care cost controls, beginning with decentralized approaches, both incentive-based and regulatory. In the 1980s there will be debate over more centralized measures toward which the efforts of the 1970s may prove to be transitional.

The debate over centralization grew intense in 1977 when the Carter administration proposed that Congress enact a health care cost containment plan that would impose federal revenue and capital caps on hospitals. Congress rejected the plan decisively in 1979. Meanwhile, pricked by the threat of this escalation of regulatory power, opponents of regulation have scrambled with new urgency to devise or revise incentive-based alternatives.

It is not surprising that these efforts have repeatedly returned to HMOs. As the 1970s closed, however, incentive theorists increasingly recognized the limits of a decentralized organization-building strategy. An effective HMO strategy would at the very least require changes in financial incentives initiated by the central government; these changes might reinforce, but would remain essentially independent of, the HMO strategy. This reconceptualization of the requisites of an effective incentive-based strategy is one of the more important products of the HMO experience of the 1970s. In the 1970s, policy logic took the form: "*If* HMOs are launched (with modest federal start-up aid), *then* consequences X, Y, and Z will follow." Increasingly today policy logic takes the form: "*If* the federal government makes changes A, B, and C in programs and laws D, E, and F, *then* HMOs may catch on in greater numbers, and *then* consequences X, Y, and Z, including the elimination of many of the obstacles to market competition, will follow." This belated acknowledgement that the HMO strategy is not free-standing and independent of painful change is an important step toward realism. What is realistic is not necessarily feasible or desirable, however.

The proposals to use federal law to encourage market approaches to cost containment are complex, diverse, and difficult to summarize. (In part this results from the tendency of the authors of these measures to rush to the hopper with their solutions, reflect afterward on the full complexity of what they have proposed, and then modify their proposals substantially.) Most, though not all, of these proposals build on three basic elements. First, they would require that all employers who offer health benefits to a workforce above a certain size offer multiple choices, usually meaning two or three distinct plans. Second, so that employees have not only a choice but also an incentive to choose the inexpensive option, they would require that employers make equal contributions to the various offerings. Employees choosing more expensive options would pay for the extras out-of-pocket. Third, in order to sharpen the incentive to choose the inexpensive plan, the proposals would depart from present practice and treat employer contributions to employee health insurance premiums above a certain dollar limit as taxable income to the employee. Some versions would give a tax rebate to employees choosing cheaper plans. These measures, it is argued, will guarantee that consumers have both a choice among plans and an incentive to choose the more efficient plans. The result would be price competition among plans. (See U.S. Senate Finance Committee, 1980; Enthoven, 1980; but also Seidman, 1980, for a different approach.)

It will be very difficult to translate these principles into legislation for four major reasons. First, the approach is not likely to be highly popular with the electorate. One may assume that most people view their insurance purchases as acts of prudence, not extravagance; that they regard their present direct share of health expenses as an adequate or perhaps even excessive check on frivolous use; and that they will not be pleased to see the tax code manipulated to manipulate their coverage decisions while other tax cuts are promised. Moreover, these proposals would greatly disrupt established collective bargaining prerogatives and are strongly opposed by organized labor.

Second, the proposals raise many seemingly small questions that assume great significance when viewed through the eyes of major organizations affected by them. For example, what will be the minimum number of employees in firms before they become subject to the multiple choice requirement? How does the choice of one or another number affect administrative costs to employers and carriers, ability to experience rate, bargaining leverage, and other factors? What is to constitute a distinct offering? Can one carrier—for instance, Blue Cross—offer separate plans or must the plans be offered by separate carriers? Must one or more of the offerings be an HMO? Must one or all HMO offerings be federally qualified? Or state qualified? How is the precise dollar cap on employer contributions excluded from federal tax to be derived? Can a national cap work, or must regional caps be installed to compensate for variations in costs?

Third, using the tax code for purposes of health cost containment may prove to be highly frustrating to government and citizen alike. In Herbert Kaufman's words (1977:84–85): "It does not take a vivid imagination to visualize the consequences of using taxation for purposes besides raising revenue. The multiplication of categories would itself necessitate a flood of instructions, which would be followed by more instructions as unanticipated ambiguities presented new problems." There would follow "requests for advisory opinions," "complaints about the length of time needed to get answers," appeals and court battles, and "a larger body of enforcement agents." Kaufman also notes that "taxation has already become one of the major sources of what people think of as red tape. The more purposes it is made to serve, the worse it is likely to get."

Finally, even assuming that agreement could be reached on all these details, there is a fourth element contained in some market approach proposals, notably, Alain Enthoven's consumer choice plan, but absent from others, that elicits strong controversy. This is the requirement that all of the multiple plans offered market a minimum, federally defined, benefit package and observe other federally imposed constraints on rate-setting and recruitment. This provision would protect HMOs and other comprehensive plans from the adverse selection likely to occur in a purely competitive setting. Under the market approach, offerings may be expected to run from very inexpensive indemnity-type plans with high deductibles and copayments and many exclusions and limitations to HMOs offering wide benefits with few deductibles, copayments, exclusions, or limitations, but charging a higher premium. Given a choice and financial incentives (a tax rebate and a loss of tax exclusion) tied to premium levels, healthier people with good health histories and little expected need for care may be expected to choose the cheap indemnity plans while sicker people expecting to use much care may opt for the HMO. Over time, indemnity costs will fall while HMO costs rise, eventually driving HMOs from the market. The only way to avoid this outcome is to define a minimum benefit package and require that all eligible plans offer it (Enthoven, 1980:78–82).

This proposal has created great dissension within the ranks of those who support market approaches and consumer choice in general. Proponents of cost-sharing argue in essence that, although HMOs have their uses and merits, there is no good reason to circumscribe the limits of free competition so sharply simply to protect them. The point of a market approach should be, in the words of Alfred Kahn, "to see the market free to offer consumers the widest range of choices they are willing to select" (U.S. Senate Finance Committee, 1980:192).

The prospect that cost-sharing will be the main outcome of free markets and wide choices has in turn evoked a long list of familiar objections. Cost-sharing, opponents contend, deters relatively inexpensive preventive and outpatient care and may actually raise costs over time by increasing the need for hospitalization, indiscriminately deters beneficial medical procedures along with ones of little expected benefit, inequitably imposes higher costs on those with the greatest needs, asks people to make complex benefit-cost calculations in moments of anxiety and stress, and invites privately purchased supplementary insurance plans to fill gaps in the primary policies. However, the Enthoven approach—multiple offerings, equal contributions, and a tax cap combined with minimum benefit packages and other regulatory measures designed to make the world safe for HMOs and other comprehensive, organized systems—seems to some market builders to put unacceptable limits on the free play of market competition.

Even if these various difficulties could be overcome, no one knows what effect a market approach would have if it were adopted. As Karen Davis explained, "there is little evidence to indicate that these efforts can provide substantial immediate relief from health care inflation or that competitive approaches can effect more than marginal changes in the health care system," for "we have little practical experience which shows how the majority of consumers would actually behave in such circumstances" (U.S. Senate Finance Committee, 1980:37).

Evidence from the Federal Employees Health Benefits Plan (FEHBP), sometimes cited as a rough prototype of a consumer choice plan, suggests that responses may be small. The federal plan offers workers a choice among Blue Cross, commercial plans, and HMOs (where available); requires that the plans meet certain minimum requirements; and pays 60 percent of the average of premiums of a sample of major plans but no more than 75 percent of the premium of any plan selected. HMOs have been offered since the program began in 1960, and the number of HMOs offered jumped from 21 in 1960 to 64 in 1978. Yet, the number of program beneficiaries enrolled in HMOs has grown only slightly over time, from 5.8 percent in 1960 to 8.4 percent in 1978. Moreover, the Kaiser Plans have all along accounted for about half of this enrollment. There is no reason to assume that the general population will prove more Pavlovian in responding to FEHBP-like financial incentives than has the federal work force.

None of these incentive approaches is the answer their proponents sometimes take them to be. Indeed, no one has the slightest idea how any of them would work if put into practice. Their principal contribution is that when scrutinized closely they dispel the illusion that simple, painless, inoffensive federal strategies can be devised to improve the efficiency of the health care system by means of HMOs or otherwise. Modest sums of seed money and manipulation of financial incentives at the margin will not do. If the incentives are just incentives—that is, one more benefit or cost added at the margin of freely taken decisions—they may well turn out to be too small to accomplish their purpose. To meet its objectives, the federal government must be prepared to manipulate the particulars of the tax code and of financing programs strongly and unequivocally toward HMOs or toward other exemplars of efficiency. That is, it must award windfalls or impose burdens large enough reliably to constrain decisions on a large scale. But then it will no longer be benignly manipulating incentives; it will instead be authoritatively withdrawing familiar benefits such as tax exclusions or first dollar coverage and thereby imposing costs and disincentives to continue accustomed and widely accepted behavior. To some, this approach to efficiency is preferable to regulation. Be this as it may, calling it an incentive approach strains language severely. To put the point in the plain Benthamite language it deserves, both regulatory and market approaches work by means of governmental imposition of various types and degrees of pain. The policy choice lies, therefore, not between a libertarian, freespirited, incentive approach honoring consumer choice and an oppressive, coercive, regulatory approach forcing narrow options down the throats of a resistant populace, but rather between types and degrees of publicly imposed pain. Efforts to achieve efficiency and cost control by means of incentives, markets, and competition would not be, if taken seriously, an inconspicuous exercise in constructing new consumer choices. They would instead demand extensive social engineering that would impose large changes on the structure of the American health care system. To work, these efforts must penalize significantly the vast majority of the population, which has given no indication whatever that it wishes to be forced to be free to choose between extensive cost-sharing that renders meaningless its accompanying freedom of choice of providers and comprehensive coverage in closed panel HMOs.

The current habit of describing the incentive approaches discussed above with the hallowed term markets confers an undeserved respectability on approaches that share little in common with markets as traditionally understood and obscures the enormous differences between new markets and old. Traditionally, a market approach has denoted social arrangements that facilitate the aggregation and channel the expression of decentralized, "atomized," individually taken preferences within broad and general public rules of conduct (contracts shall be upheld, fraud and violence are prohibited, and so forth). The so-called market approaches recommended to policy makers today as a means of employing private interests in the service of public ends have a very different character. These approaches invite the central government to design with care and specificity a set of top-down rewards and penalties which, when applied to the system from above, may be depended on to change millions of individual choices significantly in directions that government prefers and that the individuals affected hitherto rejected. The object of the old markets was to express preferences; that of the new markets is to shape them. Old markets facilitated expression of a range of choice limited mainly by individuals' willingness and ability to pay, with institutions held constant, so to speak. New markets construct a range of choices and then stack the deck, by manipulating incentives toward what government defines as the right choice, with the explicit intention of producing institutional change. If the new approach were described accurately—as, for example, "centrally planned social engineering by the federal government involving the manipulation of material rewards and penalties to trigger major behavioral changes"—instead of in code words with ancient and honored libertarian connotations, the nature of the enterprise and of the policy options would be much clearer.

It is logically possible that some market approach to cost containment that does not suffer from the drawbacks discussed here could be devised. This logical possibility is unlikely to come to pass in practice, however, because at bottom these approaches, however ingenious or theoretically elegant, rest on questionable assumptions about the nature of the demand for health insurance. The usual image portrays consumers whose principal concern is the dollar cost to them of health insurance and whose overriding interest lies in achieving as much of a free ride as possible, that is, in acquiring for themselves as much coverage with as few limitations as possible at the lowest possible out-of-pocket costs, thereby removing financial deterrents to their consumption, and waste, of care. This problem, wherein consumers lose interest in restricting the amount of care they receive because third parties pay most of the bill, is called "moral hazard."

This image of the demand for health insurance and of the effects of moral hazard on the consumption of health care is open to question. For example, although the cost the consumer bears is certainly one relevant aspect of his choice among health insurance plans, it is not the only aspect. Matters of taste and style of care also enter in, especially when, as in the case of the choice between an HMO and a conventional competitor, choosing the health coverage offered by the HMO entails choosing its delivery system also. This has always been a major obstacle to HMO growth despite the tendency of HMOs to offer broad benefits and to impose lower out-of-pocket costs on consumers. For this reason, the propensity to join HMOs cannot be predicted or manipulated by financial incentives alone.

Nor are present health insurance patterns adequately pictured as a product of thoroughgoing moral hazard, of free riders run riot. One might begin by distinguishing between two types of free rider problems. The first describes a situation in which some ride free at the expense of others because the former class has somehow exempted or insulated itself from the costs of goods or services generally (collectively) enjoyed. Group A enjoys a benefit but pays little or nothing, allowing group B to bear all the costs of providing the benefit. In this situation there are two groups, one which rides free and one which is taken for a ride. The problem is that the nature of the collective good itself prevents group A from being excluded from its provision even though the group declines to contribute to the costs of its production.

Although the problems arising from widespread third-party payment of health care costs are sometimes described in similar terms, the description is misleading. The two classes that constitute the classic collective-good free-rider problem do not exist in the case of health care services and costs. For no one is health care a "free collective good"; everyone pays for health care—in higher insurance premiums, higher taxes, higher out-of-pocket costs, higher prices, foregone wage increases, or in all of these and in other ways—and everyone knows it. And in one respect the problem is the reverse of the classic free rider problem: whereas the classic problem is that nonpayers cannot be excluded from collective benefits, in the health insurance case it sometimes happens that certain payers are excluded from the collective good—some unemployed or self-employed persons, for example, who bear health related increases in taxes, prices, and other ways but who have declined to purchase or have been denied health insurance.

Most analysts of moral hazard, however, have in mind a second, different version of the free rider problem. This problem is not that there exist two classes, one of exploiters and one of the exploited, but rather that under third-party payment each member of the single-payer-consumer class lacks a personal financial incentive to restrain the amount of care he consumes, if and when he consumes care, because abstinence on his part would not be emulated by others and would therefore make a merely imperceptible dent in the total social cost of medical care. In this sense, it is said, each rides free at the expense of all. The rational solution, it is argued, is to devise arrangements forcing more of the true costs of care directly onto consumers so as to require them to weigh possible costs of care against the likely benefit or value of care as measured by their own willingness to pay for it.

As critics of this economic reasoning have often pointed out, the analysis overlooks important elements in the interplay between individual decision-making and the peculiar properties of medical care. Concrete evaluations of the benefits and costs of particular services carrying particular costs "at the point of service delivery" are largely beside the point when the point is to achieve *insurance* against *risk*. Health care is not merely another valued product or consumer good. As Bruce Vladeck argues,

> the theoretical proposition that free goods tend to be overconsumed and that eliminating "moral hazard" will reduce consumption has considerable intuitive appeal, especially to those naturally sympathetic to economic models of human behavior. As applied to medical care, however, it is an insidious principle, imposing hardship on

the healthy and sick alike, violating the very purposes of medical assistance programs, and perpetuating the linkage between access to care and ability to pay. If, as a society, we choose to treat health care as a merit good, then it is absurd to assume that its demand function resembles that for ice cream. (Vladeck, 1976:497–498)

One insures against risk precisely because one does not want to be confronted with such willingness-to-pay questions in the unhappy event of illness. People buy health insurance, first, because one never knows what objective conditions (illnesses) may strike; second, because one never knows exactly how one will feel about the value of alternative treatments for various objective conditions of various degrees of severity; and, third, because one does not feel capable of deciding and does not want to be forced to compute benefit-cost ratios attaching to various treatment-illness combinations when an illness poses these questions. Anxiety levels are apt to be too high and the professional expertise of the patient too low to permit rational decision-making at such a time.

The result is that all (or most) purchase generous insurance benefits so that all (or most) may ride free *if* something unfortunate happens. The favored political status of health spending lies here. In William Glaser's words (1982), "most other spending programs are transfers to other persons, but health spending is viewed as a potential benefit to one's self when it is urgently needed." To some critics this social behavior is the irrational, irresponsible log-rolling that defines moral hazard. From another point of view, however, it is a highly rational, or at any rate entirely understandable, form of collective risk spreading and sharing. To be sure, consumers ride free when they partake of the most and best care available because they do not bear a burdensome share of the costs. On the other hand, consumers buy the right to enjoy such care with awareness of the aggregate costs of their (collective) decisions—everyone knows that health care is expensive and that it is wrong to waste it—and in the expectation and hope that they will never be forced to exercise their right. Although there are no doubt some Scrooges fully convinced that third-party payment of health services leads consumers to seek care recklessly and for the sheer perverse fun of it, in this respect, too, medical insurance departs from the usual free rider problem, wherein the consumers' incentive to consume varies positively and directly with the scope of third-party coverage. Thus, in its second sense too the free rider diagnosis misses the mark. Analyses of health insurance that see in it only or mainly the perversities of heedlessness and waste-shifting set policy discussion off in misleading directions.

The usual analyses of health insurance today offer neither useful policy advice nor convincing explanations of prevailing patterns. These analyses either over- or underexplain present arrangements. If moral hazard is indeed the central dynamic and the universe of consumers is peopled with crafty, wasteful free riders, it is difficult to explain why this universe, acting in the political marketplace, did not bring about in its self-interest some cradle-to-grave program of national health insurance (NHI) some time ago. This would be the logical outcome of the moral hazard, free rider diagnosis; but it is one the United States has resisted. Instead the United States relies on a mix of public and private arrangements that generally offer less than comprehensive benefits and less than first-dollar coverage for care and that generally incorporate some cost-sharing features, of which the market theorists would like to see more.

There is no obvious explanation for this electoral self-restraint, but a reasonable hypothesis is that the electorate fears that the enactment of comprehensive NHI might lead most or many citizens to start acting as economic theory says they now act and that it fears the collective costs of this. But if consumer-voters show this much cost consciousness and self-restraint, why do they not show more? That is, why does the same willingness to avoid the temptations of NHI not generate a cost-containing, efficiency-favoring set of arrangements, including truly deterrent cost-sharing provisions, such as many economists recommend? Reasonable hypotheses are that, although the electorate wants something less than comprehensive services at very high costs, it wants very full coverage for the most intensive and costly services, notably inpatient and surgical services, and that, although it does not demand full first-dollar coverage (at least not by way of public financing), it wants enough coverage to insure that out-of-pocket costs do not become truly burdensome. The result of these preferences would be a middle ground between the two logical extremes to which the theoretical assumptions of the moral hazard theorists lead. And it is this illogical middle ground that United States coverage patterns occupy.

Several derivative hypotheses follow. First, consumers may make a distinction between consumer-initiated and physician-initiated treatments; and whereas they tend to be willing to bear a sizable share of the cost of the former (as a check on extravagance), they wish to bear few of the costs of the latter (as a check on anxiety and inexpertise). Second, this distinction will correspond very roughly to that between outpatient care (consumer-initiated) and inpatient care (physician-initiated). Consumers may prefer to see the two treated differently in insurance arrangements. Although they may be willing to continue to bear some share of the cost of the former, they may strongly resist schemes that impose large costs of the latter on them. If so, schemes that merge the two modes and entitle the consumer to government aid after he has incurred from his own pocket costs (for whichever purpose) established by a sliding income-related scale may prove to be highly unpopular.

As for HMOs, consumers may in general prefer good coverage for inpatient procedures combined with some risk of incurring out-of-pocket costs for outpatient procedures to the comprehensive bargain offered by an HMO, especially when HMO care restricts the consumer to the staff and facilities of the plan itself. Finally, consumers are likely to resist strongly any scheme that obliges them to incur large out-of-pocket costs for either outpatient or inpatient care.

It is a mistake to assume that the patterns described here can only be explained by the absence of consumer choice, meaning the consumer's ability to choose coverage from sources more efficient than FFS, third-party-payment-based plans like Blue Cross. In the United States consumers exercise choice in many ways—notably, through their choice of health plans in the workplace or in the market, through collective bargaining, and through the political process. An efficient system of cost-sharing provisions or incentives encouraging HMOs could be widely in place within a few months—if consumer-voters wanted it and were willing so to instruct insurance agents, employers, union representatives, and politicians. The same may be said of comprehensive NHI. The problem is not that consumers cannot choose among alternative modes of care but that they have chosen, for good and sufficient if little understood reasons of their own, alternatives of which some analysts disapprove and that they have exercised those choices by means of nonmarket decision mechanisms which these analysts distrust.

It should be emphasized that the arguments advanced here are crude hypotheses and that, unfortunately, very little is known about consumer attitudes and preferences on any of these matters. Policy analysts have become so entangled in the counterfactual logic of trying to devise ways in which consumers would convey what they might be willing to pay for health care services, if battered, creaky health care markets could be made to resemble the handsome creature in the texts, that they have devoted almost no attention to studying—by means of interviews, surveys, and other empirical research techniques—what people do in fact want from a health insurance system and how they prefer to pay for it.

Conclusion

Much of the policy analysis behind market approaches to health cost containment has suffered from confusion over the differences among fact, hypothesis, and evidence. This confusion has (to recall Bain's words) made the analysts' assessments of the workability of competition in the health field even more provisional and personal than they must unavoidably be.

When Paul Ellwood devised and top HEW officials decided to promote an HMO strategy, they knew of the experiences of a few PGPs, notably the Kaiser plans. They knew, in short, a few facts. That the essence of the Kaiser accomplishment lay in the union of prepaid financing and group practice and that these accomplishments could be duplicated wherever prepayment and group practice were conjoined were hypotheses. Hypotheses of at least equal plausibility were that various idiosyncracies in the history, location, staffing, structure, and other circumstances of these plans were important to their success and that these peculiarities could not easily be duplicated on a large scale elsewhere. Instead of attempting patiently to develop evidence that might help one choose among these competing hypotheses, the policy advocates moved adroitly into the realm of metaphor by speaking confidently of the "skeleton" of PGP and of "prototypes." The central question remained, however: is it true that any combination of prepayment and group practice, from the largely self-contained Kaiser system to the jerrybuilt IPA, could replicate the

Kaiser achievements? After a decade of federal encouragement to HMOs, the answer is still unclear. Everyone knows what everyone knew before the HMO strategy was launched: HMOs have impressively low rates of hospital use. But the extent of savings by IPAs is disputed, the degree to which HMO inpatient economies are explained by self-selection or offset by other costs is debated, and little is known about the quality of care in these younger plans.

Nevertheless, HMOs are now trotted out as a "prototype" of the possibilities of comprehensive and organized health care systems in a greatly rearranged, competitive health insurance system. Consumers who resist such rearrangements because they believe that good care is expensive are said to be mistaken: organized systems such as Kaiser show that it is possible to cut cost without cutting the quality of care (Enthoven, 1980:xix). However, the *fact* that good care can be inexpensive implies neither that good care is always or usually inexpensive nor that inexpensive care is always or usually good. That care is good and inexpensive at Kaiser does not even mean that it is good and inexpensive also at the 230-odd other HMOs and IPAs; these organizations, after all, are very different from Kaiser. In Rashi Fein's words (1980:362), "We lack accepted norms of what is and what is not appropriate." Despite the extreme recklessness with which the term efficiency is tossed about in such discussions, the fact is that the correlates of physician (or other provider) effiency are not well understood. In short, a judgment on whether or not the relationship between quality and cost in the Kaiser Plans is an interesting datum or a prototype ripe for generalization depends on amassing and analyzing much more evidence.

Competitive proposals exhibit the same conceptual problems. That competition appears to work in Minneapolis-St. Paul, Hawaii, and Clackamas County, Oregon (Enthoven, in Senate Finance Committee, 1980:59) is an interesting fact. That these situations contain basic principles that may be generalized nationwide is a hypothesis. A hypothesis of at least equal plausibility is that these situations are idiosyncratic, highly dependent on local community, medical, and organizational leadership and coalitions and on other supportive social structures to be found in few other places. At this stage in the development of market approaches in the health field, policy *advocacy* should take a distant back seat to policy *analysis;* that is, to the patient and dispassionate search for empirical evidence that bears clearly on hypotheses founded on a mere handful of interesting facts.

References

Bain, J. 1950. Workable Competition in Oligopoly: Theoretical Considerations and Some Empirical Evidence. *American Economic Review* 40:37; quoted in Katzman, 1980:47.

Blanpain, J. et al. 1978. *National Health Insurance and Health Resources: The European Experience.* Cambridge, Mass.: Harvard University Press.

Boston Evening Globe. 1978. Doctors' Medical Program Wins Approval from Stone. September 19.

Christianson, J.B., and McClure, W. 1979. Competition in the Delivery of Medical Care. *New England Journal of Medicine* 301:812–818.

Coleman, J.S., et al. 1966. *Equality of Educational Opportunity.* Office of Education, U.S. Department of Health, Education, and Welfare. Washington, D.C.: U.S. Government Printing Office.

———. 1972. The Evaluation of *Equality of Educational Opportunity.* In *On Equality of Educational Opportunity,* edited by F. Mosteller and D.P. Moynihan. New York: Vintage Books.

Ellwood, P.M., et al. 1971. Health Maintenance Strategy. *Medical Care* 9 (May/June).

Enthoven, A.C. 1980. *Health Plan: The Only Practical Solution to the Soaring Cost of Medical Care.* Reading, Mass.: Addison-Wesley.

Federal Trade Commission. 1977. *Staff Report on the Health Maintenance Organization and Its Effects on Competition,* by L.G. Goldberg and W. Greenberg.

Fein, R. 1980. Social and Economic Attitudes Shaping American Health Policy. *Milbank Memorial Fund Quarterly/Health and Society* 58:349–385.

Freidson, E. 1970. *Professional Dominance: The Social Structure of Medical Care.* New York: Atherton Press.

Fuchs, V.R. 1979. Economics, Health and Post-Industrial Society. *Milbank Memorial Fund Quarterly/Health and Society* 57:153–182.

Gibson, R. 1980. National Health Expenditures, 1979. *Health Care Financing Review* 2 (Summer):1 and 8.

Glaser, W.A. 1970. *Paying the Doctor.* Baltimore: The Johns Hopkins Press.

———. 1982. Health Politics—Lessons from Abroad. In *Health Politics, Policy and the Public Interest*, edited by T.J. Litman and L.S. Robings. New York: John Wiley and Sons. In press.

Group Health News. 1980. December; p. 3.

Homans, G. 1967. *The Nature of Social Science*. New York: Harbinger.

Iglehart, J.K. 1978. HMOs Are Alive and Well in the Twin Cities Region. *National Journal* (July 22):1160–1165.

Katzman, R.A. 1980. *Regulatory Bureaucracy*. Cambridge, Mass.: The MIT Press.

Kaufman, H. 1977. *Red Tape*. Washington, D.C.: The Brookings Institution.

Luft, H.S. 1980. Health Maintenance Organizations, Competition, Cost Containment, and National Health Insurance. In *National Health Insurance: What Now, What Later, What Never?*, edited by M.V. Pauly. Washington, D.C.: American Enterprise Institute for Public Policy Research.

McClure, W. 1980. *Comprehensive and Regulatory Strategies for Medical Care*. Excelsior, Minn.: InterStudy.

Mott, B.J.F. 1977. The New Health Planning System. In *Health Services: The Local Perspective*, edited by A. Levin. Proceedings of the Academy of Political Science 32, New York.

Phelps, C.E. 1980. National Health Insurance by Regulation: Mandated Employee Benefits. In *National Health Insurance: What Now, What Later, What Never?*, edited by M.V. Pauly. Washington, D.C.: American Enterprise Institute for Public Policy Research.

Seidman, L.S. Income-Related Consumer Cost Sharing: A Strategy for the Health Sector. In *National Health Insurance: What Now, What Later, What Never?*, edited by M.V. Pauly. Washington, D.C.: American Enterprise Institute for Public Policy Research.

Thurow, L.C. 1980. Let's Abolish the Antitrust Laws. *New York Times* (October 19).

U.S. Department of Health, Education, and Welfare. 1971. *Towards a Comprehensive Health Policy for the 1970's: A White Paper*. Washington, D.C.

———. 1972. U.S., Congress, Senate. Subcommittee on Public Health and Environment of the Committee on Interstate and Foreign Commerce. *Hearings on Health Maintenance Organizations*. 92nd Cong., 2d sess., pt. 1, p. 93.

U.S. Congress, Senate. 1980. Committee on Health, Subcommittee on Finance. *Hearings on Proposals to Stimulate Health Care Competition*. 96th Cong., 2d sess.

Vladeck, B.C. 1976. On Cutting the Cost of Medical Assistance. *Policy Analysis* 2 (Summer):497–498.

Washington Post. 1978. December 30.
Wilson, J.Q. 1977. *Thinking about Crime*. New York: Vintage Books.

Address correspondence to: Lawrence D. Brown, Research Associate, Governmental Studies Program, The Brookings Institution, 1775 Massachusetts Avenue, N.W., Washington, D.C. 20036.

19

SOME DILEMMAS IN HEALTH CARE POLICY

David Mechanic

Health care policy in the United States does not suffer from inattention. The volume of analyses, research studies, proposals, option papers, and interpretations of the latest crises is staggering. The amount of information produced, however, contributes little toward resolution of policy questions because the policy problem is not insufficient information or analyses but rather an inability to resolve the conflicting and competing interests among powerful actors (Alford, 1975) who dig in for the battle more deeply as the economic constraints on continuing expansion become more clear.

In the discussion that follows, I examine the increased complexity of the health care system in relation to competing interest groups and changing economic circumstances. With an emphasis on cost containment, it is difficult to promote the interests of some groups without taking resources or other advantages from those who already have them, and this establishes considerable tension in the policy-making arena. Many of the dilemmas faced arise from the unwillingness to directly confront the core issues and tensions, and the arrangements we develop to work around them. The result is that we do not resolve central problems, and our ineffectual interventions create further problems.

Although there are many data on various aspects of performance

---

From David Mechanic, "Some Dilemmas in Health Care Policy," 59(1) *Milbank Memorial Fund Quarterly/Health and Society* 1-15 (1981). Copyright 1981 by David Mechanic. Reprinted by permission.

of alternative forms of medical organization and delivery systems, as well as excellent information on the clinical advantages and costs of alternative therapeutic regimens, the intangibility of the medical effort and the lack of agreement as to what constitutes quality of care allow the debate to persist quite independently of the massive evidence that exists. The clinical mentality, with its commitment to the value of the individual experience and the personal judgment of the medical professional (Freidson, 1970), reinforces a great deal of anti-intellectualism, denial of aggregate experience, and self-serving rhetoric. Although the facts may show little benefit from surgical interventions, technological innovations, or expensive new approaches, the self-interested retort of the professional who insists that the procedure saves lives usually carries the day. Thus, for example, replicated controlled clinical trials and other studies call into serious doubt the value of enormous expenditures to develop coronary intensive care units (Waitzkin, 1979), but the personal beliefs of the hospital administrators who organize such units and the clinicians who run them are given greater credence. Whether their firm convictions reflect their self-interest or their unique perspective and view of patient care need not concern us here. The irony is that the reasoned decision not to use such services as coronary intensive care, given the public perception of such technologies, makes physicians who choose such a course vulnerable to allegations of incompetence and malpractice.

The debate on health policy proceeds alongside a growing appreciation that the value of increased medical efforts and improved technology is probably less than the public believes (Powles, 1974). Despite the enormous expenditures made for medical care, and their acceleration in the past two decades, the public continues to support increased expenditures and the further development of medical technology (Mechanic, 1979a). The public gives higher priority to the growth of medical investment than to expenditures for education, transportation, or urban problems. However jaundiced the medical care experts have become about the excesses, inefficiencies, ineffectiveness, and irrelevance of much of medical care, the fact is that the public does not share this perspective. Increased investment in medical care continues to be highly valued by the public.

If there is any point of agreement among politicians, health service researchers, the public, and medical practitioners, it is that medical care costs a great deal. Politicians and government officials face the greatest pressures of cost because, with the government responsible for two-fifths of medical care expenditures, the tax burden is large, and the trade-offs among competing demands are difficult. Thus there is alarm about the tap on the public purse, and strong incentives exist to introduce cost containment. These incentives are buttressed by a skepticism that further investments in medical care will provide returns justifying the cost. Although most Americans don't really feel the direct pressures of cost because third-party insurance or public programs pay most of the bills, even that small proportion of the total that is out-of-pocket is disturbing. Consumers, responding in terms of where costs hurt them, naturally want more front-end coverage—more comprehensive insurance. Given the way medical payment is structured in our society, the solution to the individual consumer's perceived cost problem is to shift the basis of payment to tax-supported governmental methods.

The psychology of illness, and the importance that consumers give to their own medical care, make policy formulation particularly difficult. Reasonable consumers can see the logic of more efficient distribution and organization of services, more parsimonious use of laboratories and technologies, and allocating resources in some relation to expected benefits, but when sick they want the best that medical science makes possible, and these wants are reinforced under a third-party payment system. While most people agree, in principle, that excess hospital beds should be converted or eliminated, in practice they want the principle to apply only to other people's hospitals. There is agreement that frivolous utilization and expenditures should be discouraged, but few patients ever think their own problems frivolous or unworthy of the best care available.

Population surveys suggest that most patients see physicians as responsible for rising costs and feel that they make little effort to curb high expenditures (Mechanic, 1979a). These perceptions probably arise from the public's disapproval of the high fees physicians charge, which most people become aware of only through required out-of-pocket expenditures for that portion not covered by third parties. There seems to be little awareness of, or concern for, high fees that have been paid by an insurance plan. The very high and increasing incomes of physicians, which are well advertised, also probably contribute to a sense that doctors are not sufficiently concerned. But most people tend to distinguish doctors in general from their own, and have more charitable views toward physicians with whom they have a personal relationship. Feeling highly dependent on such relationships, the typical patient has a strong need to see the doctor as an ally. It is such needs and feelings that reinforce the strong political influence of physicians.

From an economic perspective, consumer concerns about physicians' fees are poorly focused because such fees constitute little more than a fifth of total expenditures. Although they may be excessive, not much saving can be achieved in this sphere. More central to the problem of increasing costs are costs resulting from physician decisions, for example, the accumulation of laboratory and ancillary services, unnecessary admissions to hospitals, and excessive lengths of stay. Government policy shows recognition of this fact, as reflected in efforts toward hospital cost containment, the promotion of health maintenance organizations, and the encouragement of family practice, but such policies, with the exception of the last, have received little of the kind of public support translatable into political capital. Where public support has been intense, as in the encouragement of family practice residency programs, there has been a dramatic growth of such residencies and budgetary support for them.

Surveys of physicians, in contrast, while they reflect realization of the increasing costs of medical care, give little evidence that physicians see their responsibility clearly, and there is a disconcerting tendency for physicians to attribute mounting medical care expenditures to the poor health behavior of consumers or their tendency to misuse medical services. There is little evidence that physicians who practice under fee-for-service reimbursement are taking positive steps to limit the use of procedures of marginal value, nor is there strong indication that professional standards review organizations (PSROs) are contributing in any substantial way to cost control, despite their focus on utilization review (Congressional Budget Office, 1979). In short, neither patients nor physicians are doing a great deal about growing costs, improving the rationality of medical services, or asking hard questions about the value of existing patterns. They have little incentive to do so, and when they do it is with a clear awareness of their own economic interests.

The hospital, of course, is the focal point of most attention, but it is besieged by a growing number of conflicting pressures. With an excess of hospital beds and increased demands to reduce hospital utilization, hospital administrators are more than ever sensitive to maintaining bed occupancy rates. This fact alone makes them responsive to demands and expectations of those physicians who can keep the beds filled. Hospitals are no more immune than other organizations to rising prices (and particularly to increased energy costs), and their administrators must struggle to gain control over decision processes that have not traditionally been theirs. The disappointing experience of incentive reimbursement experiments in hospitals is probably attributable to the faulty assumption that administrators could control the decisions of their institutions—a tenuous assumption, given the powers and prerogatives of the medical staff. To add to the troubles of hospitals is the growing unionization and militancy of many workers, including house staff. Collective bargaining agreements, and the need to conform with a wide variety of guidelines and regulations, have shifted some important economic decisions from administrative control to other parties, making the management of hospitals and priority-setting more complicated. Hospitals have been pushed into a defensive posture from which they struggle to escape. External pressures demanding accountability and more efficient operation result in a growth of the administrative component and increased centralization of decision-making. Although the intent of regulators is often to increase the range and quality of service, as well as reduce costs, under pressure administrators tend to seek risk reduction and are hesitant to innovate. The result is a reluctant accommodation to the varying pressures rather than a careful assessment and establishment of needs and priorities. Much effort goes into maintaining the illusion of compliance with demands for accountability without a fundamental change in how the hospital deals with daily demands. As pressures heighten, hospitals, like bank robbers, go where the money is, and that isn't where the most needy reside.

The Response of Government

Although much lip service is given to issues such as quality and access, when budgets get tight, cost replaces competing concerns. The name of the government game in medical care is "cost control," and when cuts have to be made they inevitably occur at the points of least resistance. In simpler terms, this means that the poor, the old, and the chronically ill suffer. It is these groups that are funded by budgets more vulnerable to attack, and these groups have poor political organization and limited power. The low public esteem for welfare ensures that the Medicaid program and other public programs for the poor will be scrutinized first, and the evidence is already clear that eligibility is being tightened as states and localities struggle with the need to contain cost. While the gray lobby is more effective than the representatives of the poor and minorities, Medicare is also in danger of increased co-insurance and deductibles and other limitations. When the affluent are not gaining, there is little charity. Discussions of national health insurance at such a time have risks because if it does succeed the outcome is likely to be a limited plan responsive to the vast middle class and not to the disenfranchised. If we were to bet on the likelihood of competing proposals, the odds would be in favor of catastrophic insurance, which would provide many of the wrong incentives for doctors, hospitals, and purveyors of technology (Fuchs, 1974). It is worthwhile for a society to consider and plan for the impact of catastrophic illness, but it is not wise to do so outside a broader framework of care that sees catastrophe in its proper place. But the odds are against this.

Beyond the strategy of cutting vulnerable budgets, the approach to cost has largely been at the regulatory level: utilization review, certificate of need, modification of bases for reimbursement, review of eligibility criteria, and the like. The data are not yet in, but the net savings from such efforts, if any, are probably marginal. Tightening up on the number of hospital beds leads hospitals to invest in other areas such as technology (Salkever and Bice, 1976); making it difficult for hospitals to purchase new equipment encourages physicians to organize to do so in their private offices. The medical system is a leaky vessel and plugging a hole or two displaces the pressures elsewhere.

The displacement game is played in government as well as in the private sector. Each responsible unit is concerned about its own costs and not about aggregate expenditures. Cutbacks in Medicaid eligibility may force more old people into hospitals to get their care, but someone else is paying. Dumping mental patients in the community transfers mental health costs to the social services sector, but on the health ledger it appears to be a savings. Cutbacks in support for residency training in fields such as psychiatry require new sources of funding, and departments adjust by turning away from community programs and toward more lucrative hospital care to generate such funds internally. Physicians and medical institutions are remarkably adaptable, and they have the funds, the expertise, and the security of considerable public support to play the game well. It is primarily the marginal institutions and practitioners serving the poor that falter.

The Dilemmas of Regulation

Medicine in the United States is highly regulated and is increasingly bureaucratized, with a significant growth in its administrative infrastructure. This trend affects not only all institutional providers and units of government but also smaller medical care practices, including the individual office-based physician. Although there is a strong ideology concerning the autonomy and freedom of the physician, in fact American doctors are more highly monitored and regulated than doctors in many other countries. Such regulation comes from all units of government, reimbursement programs, and private professional groups. Comparison with the English National Health Service, a system of care believed to be highly regulated in a manner interfering with professional freedom, would indicate that American doctors are significantly more burdened with detailed rules and guidelines relating to their modes of practice and clinical work than are their English counterparts. While the English administratively establish general constraints on the economics of care, they intervene less at the level of patient care than we do. In fact, physician regulation in the United States is very extensive and applied in a way that is costly and burdensome. The need to maintain the mirage of a private sector of medical care in the United States, I believe, results in consequences opposite to those desired—a rather heavy hand of government on the process of medical care. Government must set constraints, but it need not intrude into the details of patient care.

The growth of medical bureaucracy in the United States arises from two sources. First is the need to reimburse on an individual fee-for-service, or on a cost-reimbursement basis, large numbers of professionals and organizational providers. The billing process itself, and the paperwork necessary to monitor numerous and complex third-party insurance contracts—with varying co-insurance, deductibles, and maximum benefit schedules and with widely varying coverage and criteria for major medical payments—boggle the mind and would have been impossible without the development of sophisticated computer systems. Although this complexity may serve insurance companies in preventing consumer comparisons, it assuredly confuses both patients and their doctors. It would be interesting to know how many covered benefits are never paid, simply because consumers are baffled or have too much inertia to contest disputed claims. In the case of professionals and institutions, the cash flow of third-party reimbursement is often a significant problem, and there are often major failures to collect available reimbursement in public institutions.

More complex than billing are the efforts of government to correct for obvious failures of the existing structure of services to deal with problems of access, cost, and quality. Since government intervention takes place within the context of vigorous interest-group politics and within a value system critical of such government intrusions, governmental inputs tend to occur at the margins rather than at the core of problems, and government activity is characterized by attempts to achieve change primarily through economic incentives. Since government pays two-fifths of the total bill, and even a larger proportion of hospital costs, the medical sector is dependent on government for its survival.

Government involvement comes, however, not through a few broad strokes but rather through hundreds of programs and thousands of guidelines and special criteria. Each program developed to attack some special categorical or administrative concern has its own specifications, conditions for eligibility, and administrative guidelines. Garnering these funds, therefore, not only takes enormous effort in information monitoring, planning, and application preparation but also requires sophistication that varies widely among localities and institutions. Even when programs are organized to assist the most needy, it is the needy with the most sophistication and organizational capacity who are best able to capture available resources.

In each instance the specific criteria and guidelines promulgated can be justified, but in the aggregate they often work at cross-purposes, and the cost involved in monitoring and compliance can be staggering. The prevalent perspective is that rules are salutory, and little consideration is given to matching up the benefits with the costs of new regulatory activity. Rules proliferate at a rapid rate, are frequently unenforceable, and government often lacks the capacity to monitor seriously. The result is that organizations become adept at manipulating definitions, budgets, and procedures, and even the most important requirements are commonly subverted. The proliferation of trivia often takes attention from the really important issues.

Although it might be argued that the United States has followed a middle course between the harsh realities of a private medical marketplace and the bureaucratic consequences of a rationally planned system of care, this is more illusion than reality. The middle course is costly and inefficient in its administrative demands, while offering little real protection to consumers to ensure access or adequate care once they enter the system. As each new problem surfaces, resulting in public alarm, new rules are designed to confront the problem. In any individual case, the rules, although often indirect to deflate strong opposition among those being regulated, have some rationale and justification. The total pattern of regulatory activity, however, is a crazy quilt of rules that often operate at cross-purposes, require considerable resources of time and money, and undermine morale and vitality. Within institutions, it shifts power from those who provide care to financial and administrative personnel whose responsibility it is to ensure compliance and who monitor activities consistent with existing legislation and procedures. Although this may be an advantage from an economic perspective, its consequences for patient care are more dubious.

It is clear that regulation is an essential aspect of large-scale organization, and its importance increases in an environment of multiple and competing interests. Rules are attempts to specify how activities are to be carried out and are intended to substitute for protracted and acrimonious interpersonal negotiation. One approach to rule-making is to establish standards as each problem arises, on the assumption that direction is needed. An alternative is to view the regulation as an activity carrying both potential benefits and potential costs. Before new rules are imposed, it becomes necessary to calculate the trade-offs between what one achieves with a rule and the costs of imposing it on the various parties affected.

A related issue is the level at which it is most appropriate for administrative authority to be applied. Certainly central government has the informational resources to make economic and organizational calculations to define broad principles and necessary constraints. Centralized authority, however, has great difficulty in successfully monitoring, or even understanding, the complexities and contingencies at the service level, and intrusions into these areas often have perverse consequences. Moreover, when the inflexibility and inappropriateness of specific guidelines are perceived by those who must apply them, the result is often not only a subversion of central authority but also, and even more important, a loss of its legitimacy. Effective regulation, thus, tends to be restrained. It sets constraints but delegates more specific decisions to those who are responsible for delivering the necessary services. If it does not undertake responsibilities that it cannot monitor or enforce, it is more likely to protect its credibility.

Alternatives to the Regulatory Muddle

There are basically two radical alternatives to the proliferation of government rule-making. The first truly allows a private sector to exist within some specified boundaries but with minimal detailed interference. The second grants total funding to medical providers to take responsibility for the needs of defined populations and, although the range of services and coverage is mandated, the health care unit itself has great discretion in the establishment of procedures, priorities, resource allocations, or whatever. In each case, government sets the value framework but remains detached from the day-to-day operations of medical care.

The private marketplace is a radical alternative, because such a marketplace is at present almost nonexistent and would be difficult to establish (Mechanic, 1978). Although the price and responsiveness of some types of medical programs and services might be favorably affected—e.g., the structure of medical insurance plans, the cost of drugs and medical devices, or even the fees for particular surgical procedures—the core aspect of medical care, involving the physician's assessment of patients' complaints and the sequence of decision-making and treatment, is not likely to be much affected. Yet this is the essence of the medical care process, and the aspect of care of greatest concern to both patients and physicians.

Proponents of the marketplace approach see it as the best means of maximizing allocative efficiency and believe that any major problems of equity can be approached through selective subsidy or income redistribution. Stimulating the marketplace, they believe, requires considerable deregulation of professional controls and exclusive practice domains, encouragement of advertising, and stimulation of consumer power in deciding the allocations of their medical dollars. Government subsidy, thus, would come in the form of economic entitlements that the consumer could exchange for varying types of insurance plans or service mixes. Thus incentives would exist to encourage economical decision-making; patients would share in the costs or benefits when they selected more or less expensive medical alternatives. While government might set boundaries and constraints on what trade-offs take place in the system to avoid catastrophic situations that consumers fail to anticipate, consumers would have considerable discretion as to the type and amount of services they purchase, and thus what the cost would be to them. Under the proposal by Enthoven (1978), for example, consumers would have a minimum acceptable level of subsidy to which they could add amenities or not, depending on their personal inclinations and circumstances.

The marketplace models assume responsiveness of the institutional sector (including health insurance plans, hospitals, and professionals) to the new economic climate in which consumers have incentives to economize, but there is little evidence that the types of responsiveness envisioned could actually occur. One must assume that consumers would make informed economic choices on the basis of economic interests rather than habit, inertia, or psychological considerations, and that large providers would feel pressured to compete in offering more economical and efficient plans. One must also assume that such providers have and could use their institutional powers to effectively constrain physician decision-making. Although the theory has a certain plausibility, it depends on many uncertain assumptions and a radical restructuring of existing institutional arrangements and practice patterns. It would certainly require a great deal of momentum to get there from where we are at present. Also, the model requires too many changes from many actors to enlist strong political support.

The alternative approach, more consistent with existing organizational forms if not with prevalent social ideologies, is to put increasing economic constraints on the medical sector, creating pressures for professionals and organizational providers to reestablish priorities and operating procedures. Under this approach, government could deal with basic equity issues by extending entitlements to consumers but would deal with cost problems by budgeting decisions, and not by more direct interventions. Payments could come in the form of capitation or negotiated budgets. In contrast to explicit mandates on how funds could be expended and for what purposes, each medical unit would be encouraged to assess its responsibilities and priorities for meeting them. In short, autonomy would be protected but in a constraining environment in which efficiencies would be required.

From the perspective of needed regulation, however, how is the public to be assured that their needs will be met? How can one ensure access to entitlements, sensitive and responsive care, and a willingness to treat patients equitably? Only the naive would assume that medical institutions and professionals under pressure would necessarily come to decisions in the public's interest, particularly when the public interest may be in opposition to their own. Yet, we know from present experience how difficult it is to regulate relationships between medical institutions, professionals, and patients, and what a costly burden these regulatory activities can be for all concerned.

There is no obvious solution to such issues, only some possible options. The alternatives are not optimal, but they may be satisfactory compromises that can be modified over time and may work better than current regulatory approaches. First, any system in which patients are linked with particular providers on a capitation or budgetary basis should make it simple for patients to shift providers easily on the basis of relatively short notice. While this may create some administrative burdens and instability of budgeting, the organizations and providers most affected would be those with the most dissatisfied patients. Such structural support for consumer choice increases the possibilities for countervailing influence relative to the power of professionals. Such influence is maximized when information about providers is readily available and can be disseminated easily. Individual consumers do not have the resources to obtain adequate information, but representatives of consumers such as union welfare funds, consumer organizations, or even official groups such as health systems agencies and state insurance departments might be encouraged to play a larger role in bringing pertinent considerations and performance data to the attention of constituents. As such organizations become more expert in monitoring medical services, they might develop considerable bargaining power to affect provider priorities.

At the level of professional work, the absence of direct regulation leaves many possibilities for abuse. We have few guarantees that physicians remunerated within a capitation structure would not devote less effort to patients, shorten their hours, concentrate their attention on more "attractive" and more "interesting" patients, or give unequal care to patients from different ethnic or social groups. Indeed, we have research findings suggesting that all these results might well occur (Mechanic, 1979b). In addition to countervailing pressures already noted, other incentives toward good performance are possible. For example, the fact that institutions, clinics, or medical groups are paid on a capitation basis does not require that professionals need be. Any of a great variety of options exist to reward productivity, professional commitment, and patient responsiveness through remuneration or other means. I believe we require serious study of how best to reward physicians and other professionals within a capitation reimbursement system.

Realistically, only professionals in the same settings are likely to be acceptable arbiters of institutional rewards; thus rewards must be allocated by peers or by administrative officers of the plan, the medical group, or the hospital. The controls of colleagues or peer groups among physicians have not been found to be particularly effective (Freidson, 1975), but the conditions for such control may change. Colleague control is likely to depend on three factors: 1) goodwill among professionals and a desire to improve professional practice; 2) some reasonable degree of agreement as to what is unacceptable practice; and 3) situational or structural pressures to undertake peer regulation within the colleague group. I am inclined to believe that the first condition generally exists in most settings and, although there are substantial disagreements on quality standards, a consensus concerning unacceptable standards can be reached in a general sense. What has been most problematic in the past, and may be in the future, is the unwillingness of peers to sanction one another. However, if and when medical units are required to function within more constrained budgets, the actions of the wasteful begin to affect the options of all. Such circumstances may be more conducive to peer or even administrative controls than in the climate of the past where there has been enough fat for all.

In sum, it is difficult to be very optimistic about the possibilities of constructive change in a context so complicated, so fettered with entrenched traditions and deeply felt interests, and so perverse in its incentives. Pressure on the dollar, however, has produced a need for readjustment and provides an opportunity to reshape some of the conditions affecting practice. The process is, of course, fiercely political, with strong contenders. Serious dangers exist that, in the readjustment process, poor and minority groups will lose some of the ground gained in the 1960s and 1970s, and advocates of these groups must remain vigilant.

There is a consensus on two points: that there is a formidable cost problem and that regulation is a growing burden. Perhaps a constructive compromise is possible by reducing regulatory pressures as the health sector demonstrates a willingness to work within a more controllable reimbursement policy and to take responsibility for developing internal processes of accountability consistent with concern for reasonable access, quality, and equity.

References

Alford, R.R. 1975. *Health Care Politics: Ideological and Interest Group Barriers to Reform.* Chicago: University of Chicago Press.

Enthoven, A.C. 1978. Consumer-Choice Health Plan. A National Health Insurance Proposal Based on Regulated Competition in the Private Sector. *New England Journal of Medicine* 298: 709–720.

Congressional Budget Office. 1979. *The Effect of PSRO's on Health Care Costs: Current Findings and Future Evaluations.* Washington, D.C.: Government Printing Office.

Freidson, E. 1970. *Profession of Medicine: A Study of the Sociology of Applied Knowledge.* New York: Dodd, Mead.

———. 1975. *Doctoring Together: A Study of Professional Social Control.* New York: Elsevier.

Fuchs, V.R. 1974. *Who Shall Live? Health, Economics and Social Choice.* New York: Basic Books.

Mechanic, D. 1978. The Medical Marketplace and Public Interest Law: Part I. The Medical Marketplace and Its Delivery Failures. In Weisbrod, B.A., in collaboration with Handler, J.F., and Komesar, N.K., *Public Interest Law: An Economic and Institutional Analysis,* 350–374. Berkeley: University of California Press.

———. 1979a. Changing Conceptions of the Physician and Medical Care. Prepared for Conference on Public Views of Law and Medicine, Annenberg School of Communications, University of Pennsylvania, October. To be published by the Annenberg School of Communications.

———. 1979b. *Future Issues in Health Care: Social Policy and the Rationing of Medical Services.* New York: Free Press.

Powles, J. 1974. On the Limitations of Modern Medicine. In Kane, R., ed., *The Challenges of Community Medicine,* 89–122. New York: Springer.

Salkever, D., and Bice, T. 1976. The Impact of Certificate-of-Need Controls on Hospital Investment. *Milbank Memorial Fund Quarterly/Health and Society* 54: 185–214.

Waitzkin, H. 1979. A Marxian Interpretation of the Growth and Development of Coronary Care Technology. *American Journal of Public Health* 69: 1260–1268.

This work was supported, in part, by a grant from the Robert Wood Johnson Foundation. An earlier version of the paper was presented at the meetings of the American Sociological Association, August 31, 1980, New York City.

Address correspondence to: David Mechanic, Ph.D., Acting Dean, Faculty of Arts and Sciences, Rutgers University, 18 Bishop Place, New Brunswick, NJ 08903.

20

POLICY SHIFTS AND THEIR IMPACT ON HEALTH CARE FOR ELDERLY PERSONS

Carroll L. Estes and Philip R. Lee

Three major shifts in federal policy have been initiated recently that will directly affect the medical care of the elderly: (1) A significant reduction in federal expenditures for domestic social programs; (2) decentralization of program authority and responsibility to states, particularly through block grants; (3) deregulation and greater emphasis on market forces and competition to address the problem of continuing increase in the costs of medical care.

The federal policy shifts come at a time when many state and local governments are experiencing fiscal strain or fiscal crisis due, in part, to the rapid rise in expenditures for medical care for the poor and the imposition of limitations on, and even reductions in, tax revenues.

In the short term, changes at the state level, particularly limitations on Medicaid expenditures, are likely to have the most profound effect on medical care for the elderly. These changes will most likely include reductions in Medicaid eligibility and in scope of benefits as well as tight controls on hospital, nursing home and physician reimbursement.

NOT SINCE the debate on Medicare has federal policy affecting the elderly attracted so much attention. The changes in federal domestic social policy have been described as "massive," "revolutionary" and "drastic." Although the changes may seem to be dramatic and of very recent origin, they are, in fact, rooted in changes in the economy and public policy that began more than a decade ago.[1] In examining the potential effects of changes in the economy on physicians, on medical care, and on research and teaching, Fuchs observed that the likely impact of current trends will be a reduced flow of funds for patient care, research and training in the 1980's.[2] Blendon and co-workers stated that the decreased rate of economic growth in the 1980's will have a disproportionate impact on public expenditures, including those for health care, and they predicted an era "of challenge and stress for America's health institutions."[3] Geiger, who observed that conditions for the elderly have grown worse since the mid-1970's, noted that "social policy currently portends a decade of disaster for the health of older Americans, regardless of our ultimate actions in the area of medical care."[4]

The impact of changes in the economy and changes in federal policies that are attracting so

Refer to: Estes CL, Lee PR: Policy shifts and their impact on health care for elderly persons, In Geriatric Medicine. West J Med 135:511-518, Dec 1981

Dr. Estes is Professor of Sociology and Director, Aging Health Policy Center, School of Nursing, University of California, San Francisco, and Dr. Lee is Professor of Social Medicine and Director, Institute for Health Policy Studies, School of Medicine, University of California, San Francisco.

Reprint requests to: Carroll L. Estes, PhD, Aging Health Policy Center, School of Nursing, University of California, San Francisco, N 631 Y, San Francisco, CA 94143.

From Carroll L. Estes and Philip R. Lee, "Policy Shifts and Their Impact on Health Care for Elderly Persons," 135(6) *Western Journal of Medicine* 511-518 (1982). Copyright 1982 by the Western Journal of Medicine. Reprinted by permission of the California Medical Association.

> **ABBREVIATIONS USED IN TEXT**
> AFDC = Aid to Families With Dependent Children (program)
> FY = fiscal year
> GNP = gross national product
> HMO's = health maintenance organizations
> SSI = Supplemental Security Income (program)

much attention can be viewed from the standpoint of individual persons or groups of persons who are affected, programs and institutions, local and state governments, or areas of the country (for example, the Northeast may be more severely affected than the Southwest).

Although many policymakers, policy analysts and health professionals view the shifts—particularly the budget cuts in domestic social programs—as essential to combat inflation, they seem less certain about the impact of these shifts on services for those who are largely dependent on public programs and institutions that provide those services. This uncertainty exists because there have not been detailed analyses of the federal policy shifts in relation to the growing fiscal problems in many state and local jurisdictions.

Our own studies in health and aging policies during the past decade have convinced us that the next few years will be difficult, challenging and troubled times for the elderly and for those who provide medical care for this population. The problems arise mainly because of the continued rapid increase in the cost of medical care, particularly hospital care, and the fiscal crisis that is affecting local, state and, now, the federal government.

In this paper we will discuss three major federal policy shifts that will affect medical services, including long-term care for the elderly. We will examine these policy shifts in relation to the concepts of fiscal crisis and decentralization. Not only will access of older persons to medical care be affected by the changing policies, but physician-patient relationships and the capacity of the independent sector (nonprofit), public and profit-making institutions to provide necessary services may be vitally affected as well.

The three major shifts in federal policy that will directly affect the medical care of the elderly are (1) a significant reduction in federal expenditures for domestic social programs; (2) decentralization of program authority and responsibility to the states, particularly through block grants; and (3) deregulation and greater emphasis on market forces and competition to address the problem of the continuing increase in the cost of medical care.

A fourth policy development of major importance, the Economic Recovery Tax Act, may have many indirect effects on health care for the elderly, but these will be mediated largely through philanthropic contributions to independent (nonprofit) sector institutions. These are difficult to gauge at present. Two of the policy initiatives have already been adopted by congress in the Omnibus Budget Reconciliation Act of 1981 and signed into law by the President. The cuts in federal spending and the decentralization of program authority to the states spelled out in the act respond to problems (for example, fiscal crisis) and build on policies (such as new federalism) that began to emerge in the early 1970's. We believe that the fiscal constraints at the state and local levels will have a more dramatic effect on medical care for elderly people who are poor than will the federal policy shifts.

The Concept of Fiscal Crisis and Reduced Federal Expenditures

Fiscal crisis is a concept that has had a major impact on the policies of local and state governments. In the past the term fiscal crisis had been used to describe the problems of a local government that could not service its debts (for example, New York City and Cleveland) or of a state whose expenditures exceeded its revenues. The term fiscal crisis is now being applied to federal expenditures for social programs.

Since 1975 there has been a decline in federal, state and local expenditures as a percent of the gross national product (GNP) and a decline in per capita expenditures in constant dollars.[5(p4)] After intergovernmental transfers (such as federal and state to local, or federal to local), the most significant declines are at the local level.[5(p6)] Since 1975 state and local expenditures have declined from 15.1 percent to 13.5 percent of the GNP, while federal expenditures have decreased from 12.3 percent to 11.9 percent of the GNP.

The fiscal problems are further compounded by the fact that there are five different classes of local governments competing for increasingly limited funds: counties, municipalities, townships, school districts and special districts. In most states, the counties and municipalities are primarily responsible for health and hospital services, but in some states, special hospital districts also play an important role. Competing for these limited funds are education, public welfare, highways, police, fire, corrections, sewage and other sanitation services, housing and urban renewal, parks and recreation, government administration and, increasingly important, interest on government borrowing.

Fiscal crisis at the local level will be exacerbated because of the severe cutbacks in direct local federal aid. The community development block grants and the comprehensive employment and training block grants have been eliminated, and others have been significantly reduced.[6]

Two issues link fiscal crisis and health care for the aged: (1) the escalation in expenditures for medical services for the elderly, partly due to increased access and increased numbers of older people, but primarily due to the rising cost of medical services, and (2) the imposition of limitations on, and even reductions in, revenues for such services at the state and local levels.[7,8] While costs are escalating there are definite limits on funding for health and social services.

From above there are (1) federal limits on Medicaid expenditures and (2) major block grant initiatives with a 25 percent reduction in the funding level of the prior categorical programs that the block grants replace. Both of these conditions are shifting medical care costs to the states, to local governments and to the elderly themselves.

From below there are fiscal crises and tax revolts at the state and local levels. Caught in the squeeze, health and social services are involved in a "fiscal crisis" of their own. During the 1980's all levels of government will seek to cut costs and shift expenditures to other jurisdictions. For example, at least half of the states were planning Medicaid cuts before the enactment of the Omnibus Budget Reconciliation Act of 1981. Many more will follow suit as a result of the limits that the act placed on the federal share of Medicaid costs.

These fiscal pressures at multiple government levels pose a particular problem for Medicaid-funded services because of the magnitude and rapid increases in these expenditures, now outrunning the capacity of states to raise the necessary revenue.[9] In view of the Medicaid expenditure escalation (Medicaid costs have risen more than 500 percent between 1968 and 1978, from $3.5 billion to $18 billion), and the fact that 20 percent of the elderly receive Medicaid and 39 percent of Medicaid expenditures are for the elderly, the cost-containing policy changes at the state level are likely to affect the elderly directly. The federal Medicaid expenditure limitation* and the difficulty that many states face in funding Medicaid will require (1) a major effort by the states to contain costs in the Medicaid program itself and (2) policy modifications in other state benefits that could directly and adversely affect health care for the elderly.

Long-term care services for the elderly will be affected in several ways: reductions in supplementary income support—such as reductions or elimination of state supplementation or cost of living increases in Supplemental Security Income (SSI) benefits for the poor elderly; and reductions in such social services as state supplementation of vitally needed homemaker, home health and adult day health services under Title XX of the Social Security Act (this has been cut 25 percent, from $2.9 billion to $2.4 billion, under the Social Services block grant).

The Omnibus Budget Reconciliation Act includes a number of provisions related to Medicare and Medicaid that are expected to reduce federal expenditures for these programs in fiscal year (FY) 1982 by $2.5 billion. The 3 percent reduction in the federal share of Medicaid expenses is only one of these policy changes. Among the more important Medicaid policy changes are (1) states are given greater flexibility with respect to coverage of and services for the medically needy, (2) states no longer need to reimburse hospitals at the Medicare rate, (3) the freedom of choice provision of the state Medicaid plan can be waived by the Secretary of Health and Human Services and (4) participation in health maintenance organizations (HMO's) is encouraged.

The Medicare policy changes in the Omnibus Budget Reconciliation Act of 1981 increase significantly the copayments and deductibles paid by older persons. The Part B deductible was raised from $60 to $75 per year. The Part A deductible for those admitted to hospital was increased from $204 to $250 (it had been scheduled to rise to $228); in 1984 it will be $328. The coinsurance for extended care in hospitals and skilled nursing facilities was also raised.

Although appearing to be small, these increases

---

*In fiscal year (FY) 1982 the federal Medicaid expenditure limitation will be 3 percent below the FY 1981 formula requirement; in FY 1983 it will be 4 percent below and in FY 1984 it will be 4.5 percent below the present formula.

become significant when viewed in the context of the rapidly rising out-of-pocket costs that are already borne directly by the elderly, estimated to be in excess of $1,000 per capita in 1979, and the increasing rate of poverty among this population. The other major changes in Medicare and Medicaid are primarily in hospital reimbursement. These changes will reduce current levels of Medicare and Medicaid reimbursement for hospitals.

In attempting to contain Medicaid costs, at least six options are available to state governments: (1) reducing Medicaid eligibility, (2) reducing the scope of benefits, (3) holding reimbursement for hospitals, nursing homes or physicians at current levels as costs rise, (4) improving program management to reduce fraud and abuse, to reduce use, particularly of hospital services, and to eliminate inappropriate payments, (5) initiating delivery system reforms (for example, HMO's and vouchers) and (6) initiating program restructuring (such as long-term care block grants).

Our own and others' research indicates that several states have already begun to reduce the level of benefits and to restrict Medicaid eligibility. Two of the biggest items (and most likely targets) for Medicaid cost cutting are (1) reducing or eliminating eligibility for the "medically needy" and (2) reducing optional benefits, including intermediate care nursing home benefits. At the same time, hard-pressed cities and counties have been closing neighborhood clinics, hospital outpatient departments and other services, as well as restricting eligibility for city- or county-provided services.

If the medically needy Medicaid category now established by many states were limited in eligibility, many older persons would be removed from eligibility and would not be able to obtain needed services such as nursing homes, home care, and hospital and physician services or they would be forced to pay for these services out of pocket. Many of these elderly patients are in nursing homes at the time they become eligible for Medicaid. They have "spent down" their income and assets to a level that qualifies them for Medicaid. Reducing the income and asset requirements even further will shift the costs to the elderly and their families—many of them hard pressed or unable to meet the costs of such care.

Another approach to reducing Medicaid eligibility, which the states might initiate, would be to hold requirements to the level established for the previous years, while inflation continues to increase costs for food, housing and medical care. Spitz and Holahan and many others have advised that cutting back on Medicaid eligibility as a cost containment strategy may have unanticipated negative cost implications, such as shifting costs from one program to another or transferring costs from state to local government.[10,11] Although such a strategy may save the federal or state governments money, local governments may not be able to meet these demands. During recent years, the number of Medicaid eligibles has declined by almost 3 million, largely due to the failure of states to adjust Aid to Families With Dependent Children (AFDC) eligibility (thus Medicaid eligibility) to inflation.

Another likely method for states to control Medicaid costs would be to reduce or eliminate optional benefits (such as prescription drugs, intermediate care facilities, dentistry, physical therapy, prosthetics or optometry). There is little evidence that cutoff of certain optional benefits, such as prescription drugs, will reduce costs because some patients may have to be admitted to hospital to receive the necessary drug treatment. In such cases, the impact of eliminating some optional benefits may be to increase the overall program costs. Because the optional benefits of prescription drugs, dentistry and prosthetics constitute a minor portion of the overall budget and the cost increases of the Medicaid program, eliminating such programs may not reduce the Medicaid budget. And most important, the cutoff of optional benefits will affect those with the most chronic illnesses disproportionately, making them suffer the greatest hardships.[10,11]

Among the other alternatives, the most likely to have an immediate impact are reducing hospital, nursing home and physician reimbursement as well as further restricting Medicaid patients in their choice of private practitioner, community hospital and nursing home. These changes may be the ones most strongly resisted by the medical lobbies because the American Medical Association has indicated its preference for cuts in eligibility rather than cuts in reimbursement.[12]

Improved program management, including prior authorization for elective hospital admissions, utilization review, fraud and abuse control, audits and other management techniques have already been adopted in many state Medicaid programs. It is unlikely, in our view, that these will produce sufficient short-term savings to compensate for the rising costs of medical care and the reductions in the federal share of expenditures. Delivery system reforms are also unlikely to be initiated soon enough to have a substantial impact on Medicaid expenditures in the next few years. They are much more likely to be encouraged for patients with private health insurance or Medicare coverage. Finally, program reforms, such as long-term care block grants, are likely to be considered but are unlikely to deal with the fiscal crisis in the short run.

The largest problem with the federal Medicaid spending limitation is that, in itself, it does nothing to address the source of rising medical care costs, particularly the increase in hospital costs. It merely shifts to the states the difficult and politically treacherous decisions about how to deal with those costs and the resultant public expenditures. Further, there has been little consideration of the possible cost shifts that the new Medicaid expenditure policy will generate—for Medicare or for programs funded by the state (such as SSI supplements and social services for the elderly).

There has been no published analysis of the possible consequences of the federal limitation on Medicaid for the Medicare program. Such an expenditure shift could occur, for example, if patients who are no longer eligible for nursing home coverage (because of Medicaid spending limits) are kept (at Medicare expense) for longer hospital stays than would occur if Medicaid nursing home coverage were available.

Decentralization and Block Grants

Budget cuts have also been made in the block grants, which represented the second major element in President Reagan's domestic social program proposals. In the 1970's this policy concept emerged under the banner of "new federalism," which converted several categorical programs to block grant type revenue-sharing programs (for example, Title XX of the Social Security Act). Designed to decentralize responsibility for domestic social programs to state and local governments through block grant type funding and to limit federal involvement in those programs, new federalism boosted the fiscal and political responsibility of state and local governments for multiple programs, including those affecting health care.[13]

Both the block grants of the 1970's and those created in the Omnibus Budget Reconciliation Act of 1981 ease the constraints of categorical funding and of federal requirements, resulting in increased discretion for state government decision-making in multiple programs that affect the elderly, including such health programs as community mental health centers, home health services, emergency medical services and hypertension control.

An important consequence of the block grants is that the wide discretion that they provide the individual states fosters great inequities in the same program across the states. This, in turn, makes it impossible to assure uniform benefits for the same target population (for example, the aged) across jurisdictions or to maintain accountability with so many varying state approaches. Finally, because the most disadvantaged are heavily dependent on state-determined benefits, they are extremely vulnerable in this period of economic flux.

The net result of the large-scale shift to block grants in health and social services, combined with the across-the-board 25 percent reduction in FY 1982 federal expenditures for the block-granted programs, is increased pressure on state and local governments to underwrite program costs at the same time that many states, cities and counties are under great pressure to curb rising expenditures. The result is likely to be serious for elderly poor people in many communities.

Deregulation and Stimulation of Procompetition Market Forces

The third major policy initiative is deregulation and stimulation of procompetition market forces. These strategies are based on the assumption that market forces can produce an effective competitive medical care system and that the present system is not competitive except in ways that increase costs. Two distinct market structures have been proposed to meet the requirements of a competitive system: (1) the cost-sharing approach (large front-end deductibles and coinsurance) based on provider price competition over service price and (2) the health plan approach (such as health maintenance organizations and other plans that provide specified benefits for a population at a fixed premium through various practice arrangements). Although physicians, hospitals and others involved in medical care favor deregulation, there is growing concern about and opposition to some of the procompetition proposals that are likely to be advocated by the Reagan administration. The writings of Enthoven and others give a clue to what these policy proposals will include.[11,16] The "competition strategy" described by Enthoven refers to the proposed application of the following four principles in health care financing: (1) multiple choice—each consumer would be offered the opportunity to enroll each year for the coming year in any of the qualified plans for health care offered in the area; (2) fixed dollar subsidy—each consumer would receive a fixed dollar subsidy (by his or her employer) toward the purchase of a health plan membership; (3) use of the same rules for all competitors would govern premium setting practices, minimum benefit packages, catastrophic expense protection and so on, and (4) organization of physicians into competing economic units, which could include group practices or other organizational arrangements, would be required.

Several procompetitive proposals have been introduced in the 97th Congress, including H.R. 850—National Health Reform Act of 1981 (Representative Gephardt); S. 433—Health Incentives Reform Act (Senator Durenberger), and S. 139—Comprehensive Health Care Reform Act (Senator Hatch). The Reagan administration has also indicated its intention to propose procompetitive legislation during this congress.

Although the bills differ in detail, there are several elements that characterize the procompetitive approach. These are (1) changes in tax treatment, for employers, employees or both, regarding employer contributions to health insurance plans; (2) establishment of incentives or requirements for employers to offer employees multiple choice of health insurance plans subject to certain limitations with respect to coverage of services and cost sharing, including catastrophic benefits and preventive care, and (3) establishment of Medicare and Medicaid voucher systems under which elderly, disabled, blind and AFDC-eligible persons would receive a fixed value voucher that could be used toward the purchase of a qualified health insurance plan.

One proposal being considered by the Reagan administration would provide Medicare-eligible persons with a voucher—initially worth perhaps $1,700 (average Medicare cost at present)—with which they could purchase private health insurance. The voucher plan may also include the provision that beneficiaries may opt to retain current Medicare coverage and that no voucher-eligible private plan can provide less coverage than Medicare itself. It is impossible to predict or provide an analysis of the likely consequences of this voucher proposal because few details of the administration's proposal have been made available. The voucher is, potentially, a mechanism for capping federal Medicare expenditures and shifting the financial risk to the individual patient. These elderly people might control expenditures by selecting a health insurance plan with the minimum required benefits.

The voucher may be a viable alternative for relatively healthly older people, particularly those who do not have chronic illnesses that require extensive medical and hospital care. However, for those with serious chronic illnesses and disability, particularly the poor, the picture is different. They may not be able to enroll individually in a plan that can meet the high costs that their care may entail. This is particularly true for the medically needy elderly who are in skilled nursing facilities or intermediate care facilities.

Much of the impetus for the procompetitive proposals comes from the success of health maintenance organizations in reducing costs for their controlled populations and for stimulating competition among providers in the fee-for-service sector. The picture is not that simple, as our colleague Harold Luft has pointed out.[17,18] It is clear that medical care costs for HMO enrollees are 10 percent to 40 percent lower than those in conventional plans. The factors that account for this reduced cost are less clear. It is evident that HMO's dramatically reduce hospital admissions, and for those in hospital, the length of stay and the use of services are slightly reduced. It is not clear whether part of the reduction in hospital use is due to (1) the particular consumers who select HMO's, (2) the group practice organization, (3) the lack of financial incentives for physicians to admit patients to hospital or (4) the more conservative practices of HMO physicians. A recent study comparing utilization patterns in a large multispecialty, primarily fee-for-service group practice and a prepaid group practice suggests that the group practice organization itself may be a critical factor in reducing hospital admissions.[19]

In analyzing the limited role that HMO's have

played in the care of the elderly, Harper, Butler and Newacheck[20] examined the factors that may influence HMO efforts to attract older patients, the factors that may stimulate older persons to consider joining HMO's, and the formidable obstacles to HMO enrollment of the elderly, particularly Medicare reimbursement of hospitals, the relationship of elderly patients to fee-for-service physicians, and people's reluctance to change to a new form of care. The authors concluded that without any change in Medicare policy, HMO growth in serving the elderly will take place slowly. This is an area that has been explored in only a few policy studies.

Two other approaches to cost containment strategies—also labeled procompetitive—have been proposed during the past decade. One of these approaches resembles Enthoven's strategy in that it attributes a large share of increases in health care cost to the spread of third-party coverage for the costs of care. This theory, which has been advanced by Feldstein,[21] Pauly and Seidman,[22] has been increasingly accepted as a major factor contributing to rising costs. The lack of incentives for provider and consumer restraint led Feldstein to propose that third-party coverage should be limited to catastrophic costs and that transactions between patients and physicians in day-to-day care should be subject to normal competitive market forces.

The other procompetition strategy, advocated by Havighurst and the Federal Trade Commission, is basically an antitrust strategy aimed at providers.[23] Advertising would be encouraged, and collusion among providers and other forms of illegal behavior would be prohibited. Again, the stress is on the market and on permitting it to function in a traditional fashion.

In view of the procompetitive proposals—particularly those using vouchers and changes in tax policy—that are likely to emerge as public policy in the coming months, the best strategy would appear to be one of well-designed experiments coupled with careful monitoring of the medical care market to analyze the effects of alternative approaches on access, quality and cost, and reduction of disincentives to competition (such as tax subsidies to employers who purchase expensive health insurance plans for employees or current Medicare reimbursement policies); most informed observers believe that increased regulation will also be needed to stimulate competition.

It is paradoxical that to stimulate competition, which may actually control cost increases, regulation must be increased.

In view of the recent federal policy shifts affecting health care for the elderly—particularly expenditure reductions, block grants and deregulation-procompetition proposals—we believe several steps are necessary. First, we believe it is necessary to initiate federal and state policy monitoring and policy analysis, as well as health services evaluation at the local level to assess the impact of the policy shifts on state and local governments, on providers, on the elderly and on other groups dependent on public programs and institutions for needed services. Because of the importance of independent sector (nonprofit) institutions in providing services for the elderly, we believe it is particularly important to assess the impact of federal and state policy changes on these institutions and on the elderly whom they serve.

These are indeed times of change and challenge for physicians and health care institutions and for the elderly they serve. To meet the formidable challenges ahead, physicians must be better informed about the impact of public policies on health care for the elderly; further, they must examine more critically what can be done within medicine to meet the health care needs of those with chronic illnesses and disability, particularly elderly patients. We believe, as do many others, that the resources devoted to health care are ample to meet the needs, but they will not be if we continue down the path that medicine has followed for the past 30 years.

REFERENCES

1. Estes CL: The Aging Enterprise. San Francisco, Jossey-Bass, 1979
2. Fuchs VR: The coming challenge to American physicians. N Engl J Med 304:1487-1490, Jun 11, 1981
3. Blendon RJ, Schramm CJ, Moloney TW, et al: An era of stress for health institutions—The 1980s. JAMA 245:1843-1845, May 8, 1981
4. Geiger HJ: Elder health and social policies: Prelude to a decade of disaster. Generations IV:11-12, 52, May 1980
5. Significant Features of Fiscal Federalism—1979-80 Ed. Washington, DC, Advisory Commission on Intergovernmental Relations, Oct 1980
6. Recent Trends in Federal and State Aid to Local Governments. Washington, DC, Advisory Commission on Intergovernmental Relations, Jul 1980
7. Gibson RM: National health expenditures, 1979. Health Care Financing Rev 2:1-36, Summer 1980
8. Fisher CR: Differences by age groups in health care spending. Health Care Financing Rev 1:65-90, Spring 1980
9. Estes CL, Lee PR, Harrington C, et al: Public Policies and Long-term Care for the Elderly—A Multibillion Dollar Dilemma. San Francisco, Aging Health Policy Center, School of Nursing, University of California, San Francisco, Jan 1981
10. Spitz B, Holahan J: Modifying Medicaid Eligibility and Benefits. Washington DC, The Urban Institute, 1977
11. Estes CL, Lee PR, Harrington C, et al: A Federal Cap on Medicaid Expenditures: Impact on the Elderly. San Francisco, Aging Health Policy Center, School of Nursing, University of California, San Francisco, Mar 1981

12. Peterson HN: Changing federal and state relationships—A new era in health? JAMA 245:2169-2170, Jun 5, 1981
13. Lee PR, Estes CL: Eighty federal programs for the elderly, chap 5 *In* Estes CL: The Aging Enterprise. San Francisco, Jossey-Bass, 1979, pp 76-117
14. Enthoven AC: Health Plan—The Only Practical Solution to the Soaring Cost of Medical Care. Reading, MA, Addison-Wesley Publishing Company, 1980
15. Enthoven AC: The competition strategy: Status and prospects. N Engl J Med 304:109-112, Jan 8, 1981
16. Ginzberg E: The competitive solution: Two views—Competition and cost containment (Sounding Boards). N Engl J Med 303:1112-1115, Nov 6, 1980
17. Luft HS: How do health maintenance organizations achieve their "savings"? N Engl J Med 298:1336-1343, Jun 15, 1978
18. Luft HS: Health Maintenance Organizations: Dimensions of Performance. New York, John Wiley & Sons, 1981
19. Scitovsky AS: The Use of Medical Services Under Prepaid and Fee-for-Service Group Practice. San Francisco, Institute for Health Policy Studies, University of California, San Francisco, School of Medicine, Nov 1980
20. Harper A, Butler LH, Newacheck PW: Health maintenance organizations and the elderly. Home Health Care Services Q 1: 81-97, Winter 1980
21. Feldstein PJ: Health Care Economics. New York, John Wiley & Sons, 1979, pp 279-302
22. Seidman LS: Income-related consumer cost sharing: A strategy for the health sector, *In* Pauly MV (Ed): National Health Insurance—What Now, What Later, What Never? Washington DC, American Enterprise Institute for Public Policy Research, 1980, pp 307-328
23. Havighurst CC: Prospects for competition under health planning-cum-regulation, *In* Pauly MV (Ed): National Health Insurance—What Now, What Later, What Never? Washington DC, American Enterprise Institute for Public Policy Research, 1980, pp 329-359

FUTURE RESEARCH AND POLICY DIRECTIONS IN PHYSICIAN REIMBURSEMENT

Peter McMenamin

Payments to physicians absorb the second largest share of the health care dollar in the United States. In 1979, the share was 19 percent of the total, or $40.6 billion (Gibson, 1980). The Health Care Financing Administration (HCFA) alone spent $8.6 billion for physician services, representing approximately 16 percent of all public funds disbursed under HCFA programs.

This paper presents an overview of various issues concerning physician reimbursement. Several major areas have been identified (access, cost, quality, and improving or refining the Office of Research, Demonstrations, and Statistics' [ORDS] research techniques for analyzing topics concerning physician reimbursement). Each area is introduced with a brief discussion of some of the problems associated with the physician reimbursement systems relating to that area. Selected results are then presented from the previous research in each area, along with descriptions of continuing studies currently underway. Each section concludes with a discussion of potential future directions for new research or data development.

Introduction

Payments to physicians absorb the second largest share of the health care dollar in the United States. In 1979, that share was 19 percent of the total, or $40.6 billion. (Gibson, 1980). The Health Care Financing Administration (HCFA) alone spent $8.6 billion for physician services, representing approximately 16 percent of all public funds disbursed under HCFA programs. This total also amounted to 22 percent of all payments to physicians in the United States. Hence, it is true that HCFA payments are a large part of physicians' budgets, and physician payments are a large part of the HCFA budget. (When one further considers physician influence on the use of other health services, physician reimbursement affects a considerably larger share of the HCFA budget.)

Accordingly, physician reimbursement issues are intertwined with HCFA's ability to accomplish its basic missions:

- To promote the timely, cost effective delivery of appropriate, quality health care services to its beneficiaries;

- To make beneficiaries aware of the services for which they are eligible, and to make those services accessible to them in the most effective manner; and

- To ensure that its policies and actions promote efficiency and quality within the total health delivery system which serves all Americans (*HCFA Administrators Report*, 1979).

Therefore, the Office of Research, Demonstrations, and Statistics (ORDS) has designated physician reimbursement as a priority area within its research and demonstrations programs. Both internal and external research are conducted in this area. Under the revised 1981 budget ORDS will spend $2.1 million on extramural research with respect to physician reimbursement.

This paper presents an overview of the various issues concerning physician reimbursement. Several major issue areas have been identified, and each area is introduced with a brief discussion of some of the problems associated with the physician reimbursement systems relating to that area. Selected results are then presented from the previous research in each area, along with descriptions of the continuing studies currently underway. Finally, each section concludes with a discussion of potential future directions for new research or data development.

Three major areas have been identified from the statements of HCFA's mission. These areas involve the issues of access, cost, and quality. In addition, since the ORDS research and demonstration program exists to support HCFA's objectives, a fourth issue area also merits attention. This area involves improving or refining ORDS research techniques to analyze various aspects of physician reimbursement.

It is common practice to separate access, cost, and quality in discussions of health care issues. (Holahan, 1980). However, all three issues are interrelated. For example, enhancing the quality of care rendered to HCFA beneficiaries is likely to lead to increasing costs; efforts to reduce costs may also result in reduced access to care for some beneficiaries. It is the purpose of

---

From Peter McMenamin, "Future Research and Policy Directions in Physician Reimbursement," 2(4) *Health Care Financing Review* 61-75 (Spring 1981). Reprinted by permission.

Enhancing Beneficiary Access to Physician Services

HCFA Physician Reimbursement Methods

The Medicare and Medicaid programs were established in 1965 and 1966, respectively, to subsidize the purchases of health care services by the aged and the poor. A "pure" financing approach was taken; no attempt was made to guarantee the direct provision of health care services through, for example, a national health service. The private market for health care services was assumed adequate to supply sufficient services for potential beneficiaries of the Medicare and Medicaid programs.

Because the private market is relied upon to supply physician services, beneficiaries' access to medical services is highly dependent on the willingness of providers to participate in the HCFA programs. Further, because the physician reimbursement systems used in HCFA programs establish the terms under which physicians participate, most of the external analyses have focused on the relations between reimbursement policies and physician participation. There also exists a considerable body of internal research on variations in use of physicians' services under Part B of Medicare, which provides a context for drawing inferences about the impact of reimbursement policy (Ferry, et al., 1980; Gornick, et al., 1980).

Although Medicare and Medicaid use different reimbursement systems (with corresponding differences in nomenclature) there are some basic similarities in their physician payment systems. Both have a system under which a maximum allowable reimbursement rate is determined. Also, in both programs the physician makes the decision whether or not he will formally participate on a case-by-case basis.

Reimbursement rates are usually determined through the use of one of two types of fee determination systems: fee schedules or the customary, prevailing, and reasonable (CPR) charge determination process. Approximately half the States under Medicaid use a fee schedule. Under this type of system, each service a physician may render has a set fee and, with few exceptions, this fee is identical for all physicians. Revisions of the fee schedules are made by the State Medicaid programs as is found warranted.

Medicare uses the CPR charge determination process. Approximately half the States under Medicaid, and most Blue Shield plans also use this type of system. Under the CPR system, a physician's reasonable charge is established by comparing his actual charge to the charges he and his peers submitted in a previous year.

Under the CPR system, reimbursement is limited to whichever is lowest: the actual charge, the physician's customary charge, or the prevailing charge. A physician's customary charge for a particular procedure is defined as his median charge for that procedure in the previous year. The prevailing charge is a measure of the charges of all "peer" physicians in a particular "locality." (The responsibility for defining "peer" and "locality" has been delegated to the Medicare Part B carriers, the private organizations that receive, process, and reimburse physician claims. Some carriers develop different prevailing charges for each specialty; others define all physicians as peers for developing charge screens. Localities have been identified as single counties, groups of counties, or an entire State). The "unadjusted" prevailing charge is defined as the lowest customary charge which is greater than 75 percent of all customary charges weighted by their volume—"the seventyfifth percentile." The "adjusted" prevailing charge is defined as the lower of the unadjusted prevailing, or the product of the unadjusted prevailing in effect from July 1972—June 1973, multiplied by the Medicare Economic Index (MEI). The MEI is an index which reflects changes in the costs of physicians' practices and changes in general earnings levels. The MEI limitation was added to the reasonable charge process in 1972 by Public Law 92-603 to assure that physician reimbursement under Medicare would follow rather than lead inflation.

Physician Participation

For Medicaid, a physician's participation depends on whether the physician accepts a Medicaid eligible as a patient for billing purposes. If he does accept the patient, he must also accept the Medicaid determined reasonable charge as payment in full. (Alternatively, the physician may provide "free" health care and not bill Medicaid.) Again, the decision is made on a case-by-case basis. The physician may accept all Medicaid eligibles who come to him as patients or he may accept only some, (for example, previous patients). He may also accept a Medicaid eligible as a patient on one occasion, and not accept him as a patient at some later date.

Under Medicare, physician participation is a somewhat more involved concept. A Medicare enrollee who receives a covered physician service is entitled to a reimbursement benefit. That benefit is equal to 80 percent of the reasonable charge for that service once the enrollee has exceeded his deductible. Instead of being reimbursed directly, the beneficiary may elect to assign the benefit to the physician who provided the service. If the physician accepts assignment, he must accept the reasonable charge as payment in full (and he must bill the beneficiary for the 20 percent coinsurance and any remaining deductible.) If he does not accept assignment, the physician is not bound by the reasonable charge process when he bills the beneficiary, and the beneficiary is liable for any difference between the physician's actual charge and the reasonable charge, in addition to the coinsurance and deductibles. The Medicare determined reasonable charge is independent of assignment. (In cases where a physician elects to treat a patient who is eligible for both Medicare and Medicaid, accepting assignment is mandatory.)

Physician Participation and Beneficiary Access

Beneficiary access to services depends on physician participation in HCFA programs. For Medicare beneficiaries the lower the assignment rates, the greater the beneficiary's expected financial liability. This higher cost can act as a financial barrier to care. For Medicaid beneficiaries, only physicians who participate in the program are viable sources of care. For both programs a low participation rate for a particular specialty may erode beneficiary access to specific kinds of health care services.

This section will present some general statistics on physician participation in HCFA programs. In the succeeding sections current research on physician participation will be described, and potential new areas for research on participation will be enumerated.

In 1977 46.0 percent of physician services provided under Medicare Part B were billed on claims where the physician accepted assignment (McMillan, 1980). For the same year 47.3 percent of charges were accepted on assignment. These assignment rates are lower than the rates observed in the late 1960's and early 1970's, but are somewhat higher than those observed in the mid-1970's.

Considerable variation in these rates exists across beneficiaries, States, and physician specialties (Ferry, et al., 1980). In 1975 almost 70 percent of all Medicare eligibles had at least one unassigned claim. This statistic ranged from a low of 48.5 percent in Mississippi to a high of 93.3 percent in Oregon. The average assignment rate for the aged in 1975 was 45.8 percent for services and 47.2 percent for charges. Assignment rates for the Medicare disabled populations are consistently higher than those for the aged. The assignment rate for the aged for services varied by State, from 18.0 to 80.6 percent; for charges the range was 19.8 to 81.6 percent. Nationally, general surgeons had the highest assignment rates among office-based physicians: 49.9 percent for services and 55.3 percent of charges. Among the medical specialties, otolaryngologists had the lowest assignment rates—35.4 percent and 43.2 percent for services and charges, respectively.

No comparable national participation statistics are available for the Medicaid program. However, a 1975 survey of physicians (Sloan, et al., 1977, p. 16) provided some initial estimates of physician participation in Medicaid. Just over 70 percent of those responding to the survey reported that they saw some Medicaid patients. The distribution of responses, however, was quite skewed. While Medicaid patients accounted for 10 percent of all physicians' visits on the average, 5 percent of the physicians reported that over 50 percent of their patients were Medicaid recipients, and nearly 30 percent of the physicians reported that less than 1 percent of their practice consisted of Medicaid patients.

This kind of participation pattern may create a real personal and economic burden on the poor. Many beneficiaries may have to bear substantial transportation costs in getting to and from the offices of physicians who do accept a significant number of Medicaid patients. Alternatively, Medicaid patients who perceive reduced access to private physicians' offices may elect to use hospital outpatient departments and emergency rooms as their regular source of care. Unfortunately, this may result in the lack of continuity of their care and higher costs to the Medicaid program.

Previous and Current Research on Beneficiary Access

Virtually all of the HCFA sponsored external research in this area has focused on what factors influence physician participation in HCFA programs. Physician characteristics such as medical school and specialty have been examined; aspects of the reimbursement system, such as payment lags and perceived red tape burdens, have been considered; and, of course, the role of price has been investigated.

HCFA sponsored research has developed the most commonly used economic model of physician participation in public programs. The physician is modeled as a price discriminating monopolist who can participate in each of the following markets: the private market, a Medicare nonassigned market, the Medicare assigned market, and the market for Medicaid. The relative reimbursement level declines in each succeeding market: the private market is the highest and the Medicaid market is the lowest. Physician participation in each market will depend on the relationship between the cost of producing medical services and the relative reimbursement level.

A study by Abt Associates (Sloan, et al., 1977, pp. 18-20) examined physician participation in Medicaid. Relative price was found to be important: a 10 percent increase in Medicaid fees, holding private fees constant, would increase physician participation in Medicaid by 7 percent. In addition, Abt Associates found administrative problems such as "the red tape burden" and payment delays to be negatively related to physician participation in Medicaid. The study reported that physician participation was more responsive to price than to these administrative features. However, the report suggested that administrative changes might be more efficient than raising fees as a means to increase participation, because the administrative changes would require a one-time investment while fee increases would probably remain forever.

Abt Associates also found that participation in Medicaid was quite sensitive to physicians' costs of practice. In particular, the wage elasticity of Medicaid participation was estimated at -1.88. (A 10 percent increase in staff wages would lead to an 18.8 percent decline in Medicaid participation). Hence, Federal policies which constrained hospital costs and wages—and, by extension, wages of physician office personnel—might have the unintended side-effect of stabilizing Medicaid participation rates.

Finally, foreign medical graduates (FMGs) were found to have higher Medicaid participation rates than American medical graduates, and General Practitioners (GPs) had higher rates than internists. (A follow-up study discussed below, (Mitchell, 1980) also found that medical practices with a high proportion of patients eligible for Medicaid were more likely to have FMGs as staff members than were practices with relatively smaller Medicaid volumes.) As FMGs become a smaller proportion of the number of physicians in the United States, Medicaid beneficiaries' access to medical services may be diminished, but this situation may be improved if newer physicians continue to elect the specialties of family practice and general practice.

Economists at the Urban Institute have examined both physician participation in Medicaid (Hadley, 1978) and physician assignment acceptance under Medicare (Paringer, 1980) using California data from a sample of 3,000 GP's, general surgeons, and internists. Their Medicaid results are consistent with those found from the national survey. For example, the California results indicated that, other things being equal, a 10 percent increase in Medicaid fees would increase physician participation in Medicaid by 7 percent, the same result found in the national study. In addition, a 10 percent increase in Medicaid fees would increase the number of Medicaid patients per participating physician by 18 percent. However, a 10 percent increase in the private market price would lead to a 9 percent decline in participation and a 22 percent decline in average Medicaid case load. These results indicate that equal percentage increases in both the Medicaid and private market prices would lead to net reductions in Medicaid participation.

Analyses of Medicare assignment rates are somewhat more complicated because physicians who participate in both Medicare and Medicaid can be expected to behave differently from those who participate in Medicare alone (Paringer, 1980). Empirical estimates suggest that a 10 percent increase in Medicare reasonable fees would increase assignment rates by 14 percent for those doctors who do not participate in Medicaid. The same increase would not significantly increase the total assignment rates of physicians who participated in both Medicare and Medicaid. Similarly a 10 percent increase in private market fees would reduce assignment rates by 20 percent for doctors participating in Medicare only, and 6 percent for doctors participating in both Medicare and Medicaid.

An inference from these results is that anything that results in lower average Medicare reasonable charges relative to private fees should tend to reduce assignment rates. The Medicare Economic Index (MEI), designed to restrain the growth of Medicare prevailing charges, is of particular concern in this regard. Studies of the MEI, including its impact on assignment rates, will be discussed in the next section.

The results obtained from the analyses of factors affecting Medicare assignment rates are consistent with the results from the studies of Medicaid participation rates. For example, GPs were found to be more likely to accept assignment than were internists or surgeons. FMGs were also found to be more likely to accept assignment than were American graduates, although this result was statistically significant only for physicians who also participated in Medicaid.

A consistent result from all of the economic studies is that attempts to increase fees under HCFA programs will also lead to spillover fee increases in the private market. The Urban Institute studies (Hadley and Lee, 1978) examined this question from both a theoretical and an empirical perspective. In theory, an increase in Medicare reasonable charges would be interpreted by physicians as an increase in the marginal revenue available in the Medicare market. Their optimal response would be to seek an equal increase in marginal revenue in the private market, hence there would be an increase in private fees. Since Medicaid reimbursement levels are lower than Medicare levels, the impact of increasing Medicaid fees is less clear, although it was presumed to also act to increase private fees. These theoretical results were confirmed in the estimations of private fee equations. The Medicare reasonable charge coefficients were positive and significant. The Medicaid fee coefficients were smaller in value, but still positive and significant. The specifications used may have yielded estimates that were biased upward, but the authors still concluded that the evidence supported the notion of a positive spillover impact on private fees. To the extent that this is correct, it will tend to reduce the positive impact on participation rates that might be caused by increased HCFA fees.

Several studies currently under development are examining other factors that may influence physician participation in HCFA programs. For example, SRI, International is conducting a study (HCFA Grant 95-P-97516/9) which will examine whether physicians are more reluctant to accept assignment for a beneficiary who has a Medigap policy. A study conducted by the American Academy of Pediatrics (HCFA Grant 18-P-97159/2) is examining some noneconomic factors that may influence pediatricians' participation in Medicaid. In addition to practice cost and fee information, data on attitudes and knowledge of the provisions of their State's Medicaid program have been collected from a sample of 814 pediatricians. This sample data will be compared to the actual Medicaid provisions to examine the role of better information in determining physician participation in Medicaid. Results from this type of analysis may aid the HCFA in assisting the States in their efforts to improve Medicaid participation rates.

A solicitation for demonstrations to improve Medicare assignment rates was recently issued (Maletz, 1980). Four types of demonstrations were requested: Health Credit Card, Prospective Interim Payments, Negotiated Fee Schedules, and "Other" Innovations. A Health Credit Card demonstration would involve a simplification of billing for physicians who elect to participate. Under the current system, a physician must bill his patient for the coinsurance and any deductibles owed by the patient, regardless of whether the services were provided on assignment. Under the Health Credit Card demonstration, a physician would accept assignment for all services, but he would bill the carrier for 100% of his reasonable charges, and he would be relieved of the responsibility of billing his patient for coinsurance or deductibles. The carrier will be responsible for collecting the cost sharing amounts from the beneficiary. The premise of this demonstration is that the simplification in billing will be attractive enough to physicians that they will agree to accept assignment on all of their claims, thus reducing potential beneficiary burden. The demonstration will also assess the feasibility of various mechanisms the carriers will develop to collect beneficiary cost sharing amounts. The evaluations of such demonstrations will include a focus on any negative impacts caused by carrier collection practices.

A Prospective Interim Payments (PIP) demonstration would also involve a change in billing. Under this type of demonstration, participating physicians, again, would agree to accept assignment on all claims. In return, such a physician would receive a quarterly advance based on his anticipated Medicare volume. At the end of the quarter, the actual accrued claims would be compared with the amount prospectively advanced, and any differences would be carried over to the succeeding quarter as an adjustment to the prospective payment. The PIP approach would benefit the supplier by ensuring a more regular cash flow in addition to potential interest on advanced monies. These benefits could be of particular advantage to those physicians with a high proportion of Medicare patients.

Fee schedules have certain advantages over the reasonable charge process because there would be no need to maintain and apply charge profiles for individual physicians, and there would be less uncertainty to both physician and beneficiary about the allowed charge for any service. The particular demonstrations solicited would have several specific objectives. The first objective is to develop a method of *negotiating* fee schedules with representatives of the professional sector without violating conflict of interest principles or price fixing prohibitions. The second objective is to achieve fee schedules, at least for certain procedures, that will not generate an increase in the aggregate level of benefit payouts. This type of experiment is expected to generate physician interest and provide some initial information about the impact of a fee schedule on assignment rates.

Finally, an "Other Innovations" category has been included in the solicitation to allow the carriers to use their own ingenuity and experience to suggest other means to improve assignment rates. Suggested possibilities include physician directories, expedited handling of assigned claims, and enhanced carrier public relations and professional relations.

One other more direct access problem may be more fundamental than the participation question. This problem involves access to physician services in areas where there are few or no physicians. These are primarily rural areas although there are also inner-city areas which are underserved. HCFA has no direct influence on physician placements in underserved areas, although the pattern of allowed charges developed through the Medicare and Medicaid programs can create location incentives. In fact, previous internal research on fee variations has found that there are location incentives in HCFA reimbursements which favor urban areas (Burney and Gabel, 1980). In metropolitan areas, Medicare prevailing charges during 1975 were 23 percent higher than in non-metropolitan areas. (Medicaid fee levels did not show a marked difference between metropolitan and non-metropolitan areas, probably because of the extensive use of uniform Statewide fee schedules.) In addition to the location incentives, the effective increase in aggregate demand for physicians due to the existence of Medicare and Medicaid may also have aggravated access problems in rural areas (Cantwell, 1979). Without these programs the potential excess supply of physicians might have led to a more even distribution of physicians across geographic areas. Unfortunately, however, there exist no estimates of the responsiveness of physician supply at either the micro level of relative prices or the macro level with respect to aggregate demand.

Access: Future Research

Four issues in this area warrant consideration in the next few years. These issues involve the general question of potential oversupply of physician services, and more specific questions about access to particular kinds of health services, particular kinds of health care institutions, and particular kinds of health care practitioners.

Because of the vast expansion of medical school classes in recent years, a very significant increase in the supply of physicians will occur in the next decade. The coming tide of new physicians heightens the need to understand more thoroughly the nature of competition for patients in the market for physician's services. The increased supply of physicians might lead to improved patient access or enhanced patient amenities or it might lead only to more doctoring. Teknekron, Inc. (HCFA Contract 500-78-0052) has initiated some preliminary projections about this question, but a whole host of studies could be carried out to monitor these events.

In addition, the relation between physician participation in HCFA programs and beneficiary access to services needs to be more thoroughly explored. The theory linking participation and access is a plausible one, but a more fundamental examination of the question is needed. A potential data development effort in this regard will be discussed in the last section of this paper (Future Data and Research Needs).

The effects of physician reimbursement on access to primary care services and preventive health care services is another important potential focus of future research. If HCFA beneficiaries' access to these services can be enhanced, both improvements in beneficiary well-being and decreases in costs to both beneficiaries and HCFA should result. Current HCFA reimbursement levels, however, create long run incentives which would tend to reduce access to these services. Relative reimbursements are higher for specialists than for general or family practitioners (Burney and Gabel, 1980); and relative reimbursements are higher for "high technology" procedures than for more primary services (Hsiao and Stason, 1979).

ORDS has begun to solicit grant applications in the area of child health for specific demonstrations of methods to improve access to primary health care services. An alternative focus of research would be to examine the responsiveness of physicians to changes in the relative price of primary care or preventive health care services, or both. The Institute of Medicine (1978), for example, has recommended that the relative fees of primary care services be increased to give additional incentives to physicians to provide such services. One Urban Institute study (HCFA Grant 95-P-97516/3) now in the development stage should yield some initial results on the effects of reimbursement policy on access to ambulatory care. This study will analyze three years of California Medicaid data, covering periods both before and after a change in the California reimbursement system, that changed relative fees in favor of primary care services. Other potential examinations of the impacts of relative prices on physicians' treatment choices also will be discussed later in this paper.

Several relatively new types of institutions—organized ambulatory care centers—will change beneficiary options for obtaining health care services. These institutions include former hospital facilities which have been sold, leased, or operated under contract by physicians as well as freestanding surgicenters, dialysis facilities, and satellite clinics. Very little is known about the placement, operation, or impact of these facilities, although the American Hospital Association has noted that they have already had a significant effect on the measurement of hospital outpatient visits.

A multifaceted approach should be used to anticipate the impacts of these developments. First, surveys should be conducted to identify and enumerate these new sources of care. The American Hospital Association was awarded a grant in 1981 to develop and implement an initial survey of hospital outpatient departments (HCFA Grant #18-P-97880). Second, research might examine the reasons for the development and growth of these new centers. Third, the impact of these centers on beneficiary access to care should be measured. Ultimately, studies could also be initiated to examine the effects of these centers on the performance of competing office-based physicians and remaining hospital outpatient departments.

In spite of the increases in the number of physicians over the next several years, certain communities or populations could still be relatively underserved by physicians. Hence, non-physician alternatives for providing health care services may still be needed to assure beneficiary access to services. Another vehicle for increasing the provision of such health care services might be direct payments to physician extenders such as nurse-practitioners, physician assistants, midwives, and so forth. It is generally accepted that appropriately trained physician extenders can perform many tasks that were formerly performed solely by physicians. For the most part, these extenders can work only under the direction of a physician, but if they could establish their own practices they might prove to be another option for improving beneficiary access to health care services in areas which are currently underserved.

The recent Rural Health Act does allow direct reimbursement to physician extenders for Medicare and Medicaid. However, to investigate this option, research should be conducted to determine if States' regulatory environments might restrict the development of these practices. Further, one would need to study whether beneficiaries and the general public would accept and patronize these practices so they might remain financially viable. Finally, the issue of appropriate payment levels would need to be addressed as well as the question of the appropriateness of retaining the existing payment levels for services which can be performed by an extender but which might still be provided by a physician.

Restraining the Rate of Growth of Expenditures for Physician Services

Background

Between 1976 and 1979, HCFA expenditures for physician services increased at a rate of 15.5 percent per year (Gibson, 1980). During the same period, total expenditures for physician services in the United States increased 13.6 percent per year. Not only have HCFA physician payments been growing faster than the nation's physician expenditures as a whole, they have been growing at a faster rate than the HCFA budget as a whole. Although one must be aware of the inverse relation between payment levels and physician participation in HCFA programs, it seems appropriate to examine these increases in costs to identify potential means for reducing the growth rates of expenditures.

Several different factors are involved in the growth of expenditures. Changes in prices, changes in the use of services, and changes in the number of beneficiaries all contribute to the increase in expenditures. For example, although the growth of Medicare expenditures for physician services exceeded total expenditure growth of the United States by 5 percent, the Part B enrollee population growth exceeded the total U.S. population growth by almost 3 percent. As a result of these many sources of change, research studies on rising costs become more complicated, because all of these factors are changing simultaneously.

Another set of problems makes studies of rising costs more difficult. Only a small amount of useful disaggregated information is available on variations in cost increases that might be used to analyze why costs are increasing for one service faster than another. For example, the national Medicaid program has been "successful" in holding the rate of growth of physician expenditures to less than the rate of growth of physician prices (8.1 percent vs. 9.0 percent from 1976-1979). Yet no single national Medicaid data base exists that would allow the comprehensive examination of changes in physician expenditures (and the likely changes in participation and beneficiary access). The differing channels of payments sometimes tend to frustrate attempts to understand cost differences. Pathology services for Medicare beneficiaries may be billed fee-for-service under Part B or they may result in hospital charges under Part A. A similar situation can occur for payments to teaching hospital physicians. As a result, simple data collection and data display efforts—Uwe Reinhardt's "bean counting"—will continue to play a significant role in the development of research on physician costs.

Finally, achievement of HCFA's objectives will require that physicians be remunerated appropriately for the services they provide to Medicare and Medicaid beneficiaries. This means that the levels of payment should approximate the costs of efficiently providing any given service, as well as the value to the beneficiary. Physicians should not be paid at arbitrarily low rates nor at levels which are beyond some standard of reasonableness.

Previous and Current Research on Costs

Five sub-issues have been identified in the cost area. Each relates to either an avenue or an obstacle to cost control. The first sub-issue involves the appropriateness of the fee being charged to identify whether it is too high (or too low). The next sub-issue is an obvious and probably noncontroversial means of reducing cost: improving productivity and efficiency. Third is a most problematic issue and a real potential obstacle. This sub-issue involves the role of physician demand for income. To the extent that physicians can control demand for their services they may be able to frustrate attempts to control medical expenditures. The fourth sub-issue involves regulation as a means to cost control. The final sub-issue deals with alternative reimbursement arrangements that might either directly lead to lower costs or provide incentives that indirectly result in lower costs.

Empirical research related to the question of appropriateness of physician reimbursement levels has been conducted with respect to time and effort differences and differences in physician training levels. A Harvard University project (Hsiao and Stason, 1979) has examined the relation between differences in payment levels and differences in amounts of physician time per service. For half of the surgical procedures studied, the relation between relative physician resource time and relative reimbursement rates was quite close. (Both the California Relative Value Study and local Medicare prevailing charges were used to estimate relative reimbursements). However, there were significant disparities between relative effort and relative reimbursement for the other half of the surgical procedures. Also, very significant differences were found when surgeries were compared to office visits. For example, specialist fees for an initial office visit yield estimates of reimbursement of $68 per hour. The minimum estimate for cataract lens extractions was $473 per hour.

The Institute for Demographic and Economic Studies (Dresch, 1980) compared returns (earnings) to investments in physician training (cost of schooling) in an initial assessment of the appropriateness of reimbursement levels. Earnings functions were estimated for physicians and 15 other professional occupation groups. The findings of the study suggest that medicine is an extremely profitable career and that it would remain profitable even if medical students were charged tuition at the full cost of medical training. Hence, a substantial element of pure economic rent is found in physicians' lifetime earnings.

In the productivity-efficiency area, several general results have become fairly well accepted. There are at least modest economies of scale to group practice (although dilution of cost consciousness occurs as practice size increases, vitiating the scale economies). Physician extenders can and do make a physician more productive. On the latter point new data suggest encouraging progress. It had been long accepted that physicians underemploy aids (Reinhardt, 1972). A recent HCFA study has concluded that physicians' employment of aids is at or near optimal efficiency levels (Brown, 1980).

A Northwestern University study has recently examined the effect of hospital resources on physician productivity (Pauly, 1980). By estimating the effects of the availability of hospital employees per bed in the hospitals that individual physicians identified as their primary hospital, the study concluded that those employees have a significant positive effect on physician productivity, and a possible negative effect on physician prices. The net impact on costs is uncertain, since the use of hospital resources will be reflected in hospital charges. However, it is plausible, for example, that diagnostic tests done in a hospital should be less costly than those done in a physician's office. Hence, a physician's efficient use of hospital services as complements to his own resources may result in reduced costs.

A major area of controversy in health economics involves the influence of physicians on prices paid and quantities of service demanded in the medical market. One school of thought contends that physicians behave as any other economic entity, that they respond to prices determined by the market. Another school of thought contends that physicians can induce demand for their own services, that physicians can set fees with little regard to market conditions, or that they make price and output decisions to achieve some target level of income. If the former school be correct, the coming increases in the number of physicians will be accompanied by relatively lower costs or improved access, or both. If the latter school be correct, there may be a significant increase in expenditures for physician services without necessarily an increase in health of equal value. Evidence supporting both sides is available from previous research. For example, several studies have identified significant inter- and intra-area differences in physician fees which could not be explained by cost of living differences.[1] Relatively high fees were found to occur in areas which had an abundance of physicians. These variations are not consistent with a perfectly competitive market for physicians. Recently, an examination of 1976 data from the HCFA Survey of Physician Practice Costs and Incomes could not refute the physician induced demand hypotheses (Woodward, 1980). Finally, a HCFA study at the Boston University School of Medicine (Mitchell and Cromwell, 1981) examined variations in the incidence of surgery using Health Interview Survey data from 1969—1976. Holding other factors constant, surgical supply was found to induce demand: a 10 percent increase in surgeons *per capita* resulted in a 1 percent increase in total surgery rates and a 1.3 percent increase in elective surgery rates.

On the other hand, researchers at City University of New York (CUNY) (Muller and Otelsberg) and at the Urban Institute (Lee and Holahan, 1978) have found some evidence of a negative correlation between fees and physician density, a result more consistent with competitive theory. In addition, a consistent result from several studies of paid claims is that physicians do not appear to discriminate between payors when *billing* for specific services.[2] Price discrimination behavior would be evidence that a market was not competitive. (A form of passive price discrimination does exist when the different payors use different rules to determine allowed charges, giving rise to different transaction prices.) Finally, a recent study conducted at the National Center for Health Services Research (Willensky and Rossiter, 1980) suggests that the effects of physician inducement on utilization are not large and may not be significant.

Research on this question continues. Economists at Vanderbilt University are developing new models that might lead to unambiguous tests of the competing hypotheses in this area (HCFA Contract 500-78-0018). A new study being conducted by Michigan Blue Shield (HCFA Grant 18-P-97619/5) will attempt to use a large paid claims file to provide more evidence on this question. Finally, a related study at the University of California, San Francisco (HCFA Grant #18-P-97556) is examining the competitive effects of HMOs. To the extent that such competitive effects exist, the opportunities for physician induced demand may be inhibited.

---

[1]For more information, refer to the following studies: Institute of Medicine, *Medicare and Medicaid Reimbursement Policies* (Washington, D.C.: National Academy of Sciences), March 1976; Schieber, George, *et al.*, "Physician Fee Patterns under Medicare: A Descriptive Analysis," *New England Journal of Medicine* (May 13, 1976) 294: 1089-1093; Redisch, Michael, *et al.*, "Physician Pricing, Costs, and Income." Paper presented at the Western Economic Association Meetings, June 20, 1977; and Burney, Ira and Jon Gabel, "Reimbursement Patterns Under Medicare and Medicaid," in Jon Gabel, *et al.*, (eds), *Physicians and Financial Incentives*, 1980.

[2]The studies include: Urban Institute, Grant 95-P-97178/3, ORDS, HCFA, DHHS, 1976; Pennsylvania Blue Shield Contract 600-76-0146, ORDS, HCFA, DHHS, 1976; and University of Southern California, Contract 600-76-0160, ORDS, HCFA, DHHS, 1976.

The third research area directed toward cost control involves analyses of regulatory programs to control fees or expenditures, or both. For the most part these analyses have included examinations of the experiences under the Economic Stabilization Program (ESP, August 1971-April 1974). More recently, studies have been initiated to examine the rationale and impact of the Medicare Economic Index (MEI).

Urban Institute economists (Holahan and Scanlon, 1978) studied data on physician services in Northern California during the ESP. They found that even though fees for individual services were held to ESP guidelines, the average intensity and volume of services billed by physicians increased substantially. As a result there was a more rapid increase in Medicare expenditures during the ESP years than in non-ESP years. Additional evidence on the impact of ESP is also expected from paid claims studies being conducted by Pennsylvania Blue Shield (HCFA Grant 95-P-97156; Contract 600-76-0146) and the University of Southern California (HCFA Contract 600-76-0160).

The MEI is an additional limitation added to the reasonable charge determination process by the Social Security Act Amendments of 1972. The MEI places a cap on prevailing charges. (A prevailing charge is the maximum allowed charge for a particular procedure.) Although the MEI may result in program savings, to the extent that this constraint is binding, it may reduce Part B reasonable charges relative to private market fees, and hence reduce assignment rates. Several studies have begun to examine the various features of the MEI.

Price increases allowed through the use of the MEI have been shown to be consistent with the price increases which would be observed in a perfectly competitive market in the long run (McMenamin, 1980, pp. 21-23). Hence, the use of this kind of index to determine price increases may represent an improvement on the reasonable charge process. (This may not be an unambiguous improvement for the Medicare beneficiaries if the non-Medicare market is not competetive, and if private fees rise relative to Medicare reimbursements.) Empirical analysis, however, suggests that use of a single index for all specialties may not be equitable. Teknekron, Inc. (Berry, 1980) examined the average cost shares of various specialties in 1976. This single cross section of data suggests that surgeons' cost increases may be underestimated by a single index compared to the estimated cost increases of medical specialties (which, in turn, are low compared to general practitioners and family practitioners.) The magnitude of these differences, however, is quite small. Work done at Vanderbilt University (Steinwald, 1980) suggests that cost increases of hospital based physicians are overestimated by a single index because of their relatively low practice expenses compared to office based physicians.

A preliminary examination of the impact of the MEI on allowed charges was conducted by CUNY (Muller and Otelsberg). This report suggested that the MEI had its widest impact on reasonable charges for surgical procedures performed by specialists. Charges for laboratory services for specialists were the least affected by the MEI. Between 1976 and 1978, an increasing number of procedures were affected by the MEI, according to researchers.

Research on the MEI continues. Using their large California data base, an Urban Institute research project (HCFA Grant 95-P-97178/3) is examining the magnitude and incidence of the price constraints imposed by the MEI. An ongoing series of HCFA internal beneficiary studies (Ferry, et al., 1980; Gornick, et al., 1980) will examine changes in assignment rates that can be observed in data since the advent of the MEI. The Teknekron study will continue to investigate changes in cost shares over time. And HCFA may initiate a national data solicitation to get more direct measures of variations in MEI impact. Finally, estimates will also be calculated with respect to the reduction in general revenue contributions to the Part B Trust Fund as a result of the impact of the MEI.

A second section of the legislation mandating the MEI established a price limit program for laboratory tests and durable medical equipment. These "Lowest Charge Limitations" (LCL) were initiated by regulations issued in January 1979. To the extent possible, the LCL impact analyses will follow the types of analyses conducted on the MEI. The Urban Institute (HCFA Grant 95-P-97178/3) will begin an analysis of the impact of the LCL constraints in their MEI project, and the Bureau of Program Policy has solicited data from the Regional Offices (Newman, Howard, 1980) to support an evaluation.

A final vein of research involves examinations of alternative reimbursement systems. This research includes studies of both new systems and the current systems. With respect to the latter, several studies have examined the consequences of using a CPR approach to determining allowed charges. One of the primary disadvantages of this system is that physicians whose actual charges exceed their customary charge limits will be rewarded with higher customary limits in the next year. Hence, the CPR system encourages billing patterns that may aggravate any pre-existing inflation. In fact the inherent inflationary bias to the CPR approach has been demonstrated both theoretically (Frech and Ginsburg, 1975) and empirically (Hadley et al., 1979).

The effects of relatively minor variations in (or modifications to) the reasonable charge process have also been studied. The CUNY project (Muller and Otelsberg) examined the effect of carrier discretionary practices on fee levels. Some of the practices for establishing a physician's allowed charges in the absence of previous claims experience had a slight downward effect on fees but, in general, no significant aggregate impact due to carrier practices was found.

Several studies are currently examining the impacts of changes that have occurred in locality designations.[3] In addition, a variety of simulations are being conducted to examine the effects of both locality consolidations and specialty screen consolidations (Health Care Financing Administration, 1980).

One other important change within the CPR framework involves the use of coding classifications for identifying medical procedures on claims forms. In the past, each carrier was allowed its own choice of a procedural terminology and coding (PTC) system for processing claims. To simplify present administrative arrangements and to encourage as much uniformity as possible in the

---

[3]One of these studies is being conducted by SRI, International, Grant 95-P-97156/9, ORDS, HCFA, DHHS, 1977. Evaluation projects have also been initiated to examine locality changes which occured in South Carolina and Arkansas.)

physician reimbursement systems for Medicare and Medicaid, a common PTC system is being sought. In the past, however, changes between systems were accompanied by increases in benefit payments. Internal research has found that the average intensity of services reimbursed under Medicare increased when the California carriers switched from using the 1964 California Relative Value Study (CRVS) coding system to the 1969 version (Sobaski, 1975). A similar result was found in a study of a change from a Blue Shield coding system to an American Medical Association coding system which occurred in Virginia in 1973 (Newman, A., 1980).

Related HCFA research by Moshman Associates, Inc. has shown that the evolution of coding systems has been accompanied by greater opportunities for increased itemization in billing (or "unpackaging") for services. This greatly enhances the potential for a "taxonomic inflation." (A taxonomic inflation is said to occur over time when health care billing claims show an increase in the number or complexity of services rendered, while the services actually provided remain the same.) A solicitation for further studies of the packaging issue was issued in February 1981.

Although most physicians participate in HCFA programs on a fee-for-service basis, a variety of other reimbursement arrangements are currently employed throughout the health care system. There are also variations in fee-for-service payments which might be introduced into HCFA programs. These alternatives include fee schedules, salary arrangements, and risk sharing arrangements (including modified capitation payments).

Due to the apparent success of many Health Maintenance Organizations (HMO) in reducing hospital use, a great deal of interest exists in the question of how physicians (singly or in groups) would perform under risk sharing agreements. One major focus of interest is on the United Healthcare (Safeco) system in Seattle (Moore, et al., 1980). Under this system primary care physicians become the financial managers for their patients' costs of care. When such a physician achieves a case load of 200 or more patients in the plan he goes on a capitation reimbursement scheme in which his payment is based on the age and sex composition of his patient load. (For fewer than 200 patients he is paid on a fee-for-service basis.) He is also given charge of a capitation account which is used to pay for all services he himself does not provide. The physician gets a monthly listing of all charges against this account and must approve the payment before any reimbursements are made by the plan. Because the physician is required to share (with some limits) 50 percent of the deficit or surplus against his account at the end of a year, he has an incentive to be more efficient in ordering services.

HCFA has a grant with the University of Washington (Grant 18-P-97144/0) to conduct a large-scale evaluation of this system which will compare the Safeco experience with that of competing systems in the Seattle area—Blue Cross and Group Health Cooperative in Puget Sound. It will focus on the effectiveness of the Safeco model in controlling the use and costs of medical care, and will examine the following questions:

- What type of patients choose United Healthcare?
- Why do doctors participate or refuse to participate, and what are the impacts of the plan on their practices?
- What is the impact of risk-sharing by primary care physicians on cost containment within the Safeco system? and,
- How does the United Healthcare Plan in Washington compare to the United Healthcare Plan in California?

Solicitations for additional risk sharing demonstrations will be issued in fiscal years 1981 and 1982. One type of demonstration sought in FY 1982 will be Safeco replications involving Medicare and Medicaid populations in other geographic areas. A second type of demonstration will involve area-wide risk sharing. Under this type of proposal all participating physicians in a geographic area would share in the savings (or loss) due to aggregate, prospectively determined utilization goals. The solicitation for area-wide projects should be issued in fiscal year 1981 with the expectation of funding the proposed demonstrations to implement operational projects in 1982.

The HCFA has also sponsored seven capitation demonstrations which are examining a variety of systems for providing health services to Medicare and Medicaid beneficiaries through HMOs. Under most of these projects, risks are shared by an organization rather than a physician. However, in the Marshfield Medical Foundation Plan (HCFA Contract 500-78-0084) private physicians who treat patients from the Plan will be reimbursed at 85-90 percent of submitted charges. If physician reimbursements under the Plan are less than expected, additional incentive bonuses will be paid to physicians who participated, up to 100 per of their charges.

A modified capitation method is currently available as an option under the End Stage Renal Disease Program (ESRD.) Under this "Alternative Method" participating physicians agree to become the primary medical provider for an individual ESRD patient. That is, in return for a monthly reimbursement per patient they agree to provide all routine medical services occasioned by their patient's renal disease. The other alternative, "the Initial Method," is fee-for-service.

The Center for Health Services and Policy Research at Northwestern (Held and Pauly, 1979) has examined the incentives created by these two reimbursement schemes. Their analyses suggested that the two methods should be compared in terms of their impact on total patient costs (for a given level of quality) rather than simply in terms of the total physician costs under each of the options.

A follow-up study (Held and Pauly, 1980) of production and costs of in-center maintenance dialysis treatments found that facilities where physicians were reimbursed on the alternate method appeared to be more efficient than initial method facilities. A direct comparison of program costs under the two systems is anticipated in 1981 with the procurement of a data base on ESRD patients, characteristics of their facilities, and Medicare reimbursements on their behalf.

Several reimbursement arrangements exist for physicians who are considered primarily hospital based: radiologists, anesthesiologists, and pathologists. Arthur Anderson and Company conducted a preliminary study of these reimbursement arrangements (HCFA Contract 600-76-0055). This study found that radiology, anesthesiology, and pathology practices were very remunerative; considerable economic rents accrued to physicians in these specialties under certain reimbursement arrangements. Physicians in these specialties who were paid on a percentage of gross billings from their departments received the highest full time equivalent earnings. Salaried physicians earned the least amounts (Anesthesiologists' average earnings were the lowest of the three specialties, since most anesthesiologists were in salaried positions). The Vanderbilt University project (Steinwald, 1980) will follow up this study with a more detailed examination of alternative reimbursement arrangements currently available to hospital based physicians. These alternate arrangements include percentage of gross and net billings, salaried, and mixed reimbursement arrangements. Initial findings to date suggest that percentage of gross arrangements are becoming less common. However, on the average, physicians in these specialties still earn higher net incomes than office based specialists.

As was indicated previously, there is interest in fee schedules, as opposed to the CPR system, because of their administrative simplicity. There is also some empirical evidence (Holahan, 1974) that those State Medicaid programs which use fee schedules have had lower cost increases than those on CPR systems. (There is no clear evidence about the resulting—presumably negative—impacts on physician participation and beneficiary access.) As a result, considerable interest exists in the development and implementation of fee schedules. One of the Urban Institute projects (HCFA Grant 95-P-97178/3) is examining the initial reimbursement consequences of switching Medicare payments to a fee schedule system.

Cost Control: Future Research

Several areas are targeted for new or expanded research efforts. These areas include: examination of the potential to improve competition in the health care market to reduce medical care expenditures; identification of strategies for rational development of fee schedules or relative value studies; investigations of the impact of new technologies and newly available capital equipment on physician costs and total health care expenditures; and an examination of the impacts of cost containment curricula in medical education programs.

The study of health economics has long been a challenge to economists because of the absence of many of the features associated with competitive markets. Recently, however, a great deal of interest has been expressed in trying to improve competition in health care markets to achieve the economies that result from perfect competition.

As noted earlier, the focus on the supply side of the market has involved the question of physician induced demand. However, potential increased competition among physicians and between physicians and alternative sources of ambulatory care has also been noted given the coming increases in the numbers of physicians and in the emergence of new institutions providing ambulatory care. Future research in this area should identify the circumstances under which providers do compete with one another and whether the competition occurs (1) on prices; (2) in increased availability (such as weekend or evening office hours), or (3) in increases in quality or other amenities.

On the demand side of the market there is interest in enhancing the competitive position of consumers. For example, as a result of recent court decisions and actions by the Federal Trade Commission, considerable attention has been devoted to methods to improve consumer information about health care prices. These methods include advertising in general and physician directories, in particular. Unfortunately, health insurance and health subsidy programs such as Medicare and Medicaid tend to weaken the monetary incentives of beneficiaries to search for low prices. For example, ESRD beneficiaries who are on home dialysis have the option of purchasing a new dialyzer for each maintenance treatment or they can reuse their dialyzer two or more times. The total cost of a dialyzer is $25, of which the beneficiary pays $5. Hence, dialyzer reuse saves the beneficiary only $5 while it costs time, and attention, and perhaps some anxiety in assuring that the used dialyzer is properly sterilized for its next use. Since the beneficiary does not partake of the potential $20 savings to Medicare, he may elect not to reuse dialyzers. Similarly, since Medicare and Medicaid beneficiaries share little or no part of the savings that might result from "shopping" for relatively inexpensive physicians, they have little incentive to change their health care purchasing habits, even if they do become informed through physician advertising.

Future research and demonstrations in this area might focus on ways to enhance these incentives without increasing beneficiary burden. These methods might include reducing the costs of obtaining price and assignment information, such as through the use of physician directories. Demonstrations might also be undertaken to assess the impact of beneficiary bonuses for reduced health care expenditures. One possibility would be modifying a physician risk sharing experiment to allow beneficiaries to share the rewards of better than average claims experience.

Some initial work has already begun on the mechanics of negotiations to establish fee schedules. An effort at the University Health Policy Consortium (HCFA Grant 18-P-97138/1) is examining basic U.S. labor law principles to identify representative groups that might participate in the process of fee schedule negotiations. This work will continue, and will address such issues as: the best frameworks for negotiations; which parties should participate; and whether negotiations should attempt to develop entire schedules or focus on specific fees.

Princeton University (HCFA Grant 95-P-97309/2) will examine various aspects of the role of fee schedules in physician reimbursement under third party systems. This study will include a review of fee schedules and relative value systems that have been developed in West Germany, France, and Canada. A second survey of a sample of general practitioners in Quebec, and an analysis of their responses to fee schedules will also be conducted. A descriptive analysis of fee screens and relative price structures in the United States will then be performed. Finally, the researchers will develop a framework for assessing changes in fee schedules.

A new solicitation for a study of relative value systems was issued in FY 1981. This study will examine the conceptual bases for establishing relative value studies such as: existing fee distributions; time and motion studies; societal and individual benefits from various procedures; how to set a value for new procedures; and whether to revalue the old.

Another relatively new focus of attention involves the role of rapidly changing medical technology and its impact on the costs of health care. For the most part new technology involving capital has remained in hospitals, but two forces exist which may tend to bring new capital investment opportunities for physicians in their offices. The first stems from technological innovations involving miniaturization and computerization. These innovations will reduce both the size of diagnostic testing equipment and the time needed to develop and interpret results. These improvements will make such equipment more practical, hence more attractive for physicians' offices. At the same time, Certificate of Need regulations and other hospital capital acquisition review requirements may shift innovation and demand for new technology out of the hospital sector and into the physician sector.

Research in this area would identify the determinants of physicians' investments in office capital. This research could include estimation of expenditure functions for practice inputs. (An expenditure function would relate optimal purchases of particular kinds of inputs to changes in the level of outputs.) Another question involves the impact of investments in physicians' office capital on total expenditures for physicians' services. A related capital investment issue involves both new and not-so-new technology. This involves the investment decisions of physicians who are establishing their practices for the first time. If the new physicians entering the market are not judicious in their purchases of equipment, considerable upward pressure on health care costs could arise. Hence, research in the near future should examine the patterns of practice development by new physicians to identify efficient modes of organization, and to discourage the inefficient ones.

Finally, a new slant on cost control is emerging in terms of raising the cost consciousness of physicians. While once a doctor could say "Cost is not a professional concern of physicians,"[4] in recent years both former HEW Secretary Califano[5] and the AMA sponsored National Commission on the Cost of Health Care have referred to the need to bring cost consciousness into medical school curricula. The number and variety of these medical economics courses keep expanding and may form a virtual "Physicians' Voluntary Effort" of the future. But as yet there exists no comprehensive assessment of the scope or prevalence of such courses and no strategy for evaluating their impact on the cost of care. This evaluation would require a survey of the spectrum of educational activities from undergraduate medical education to continuing medical education, and from modules on health care costs in, for example, community medicine courses to practice cost seminars to full blown courses on health economics. An evaluation of the impact of these endeavors might require a very long frame of follow up surveys to compare the cost experience of physicians who receive this kind of training to those who do no not receive formal cost training or consciousness-raising.

---

[4]Comments made by Robert B. Hunter, M.D. at the PSRO Evaluation Subcommittee Meeting, Bethesda, Md. August 26, 1973. Dr. Hunter became President of the American Medical Association in 1980.

[5]Comments made by Joseph Califano in an address presented to the Association of American Medical Colleges, October 1978.

Assuring Quality and Appropriateness

Background

The Medicare and Medicaid programs attempt not merely to facilitate beneficiary access to health care but to facilitate access to "mainstream" health care. In particular, there is a desire that a two class system of health care should not develop (in which Medicare and Medicaid beneficiaries would receive lower class health care). The quality of health care services provided to these beneficiaries should equal that available to private market patients.

Quality of care has been addressed in previous research and regulatory programs, but it usually has been treated as a topic completely separate from costs or compensation methods. Similarly, most previous reimbursement research has not included any well developed consideration of quality. Treatment of the issues of quality and appropriateness consisted solely of ritual allusions to "other things being equal." However, in the evaluation (or design) of a physician *reimbursement* system the quality of service and the appropriateness of the service are important considerations.

In particular, the reimbursement system should contain incentives which encourage the appropriate type or level of care (for example, primary care versus subspeciality care, and inpatient care versus outpatient care). These incentives should discourage physicians from performing unnecessary surgery, ordering inappropriate or unnecessary diagnostic tests, hospitalizing patients who can be treated as effectively on an ambulatory basis, or providing medical care of low quality.

The interest in the interaction between physician reimbursement and health care quality is a relatively new focus of the research program. However, studies have been done which are related to this issue. Results from these studies will be cited in the next section (Research on Physician Reimbursement and Quality). A discussion of potential future studies on quality and physician reimbursement will conclude the section on quality. (As a prefatory note, any discussion of quality and appropriateness will include the topics of quality assurance regulations and enforcement of regulations designed to prevent fraud and abuse. Although both kinds of regulations establish a setting in which physicians' decisions are constrained, for the purpose of this discussion that setting is taken as a given. The question at hand involves the relation between physician reimbursement and quality or appropriateness within those constraints.)

Research on Physician Reimbursement and Quality

Some of the problems in this area have already been referred to with respect to access to primary care services and costs of physician induced demand. Regarding access to primary care services, the value of relatively high technology services is increasing compared to more physician intensive services such as history taking (Hsiao and Stason, 1979). As a result, the process of determining a diagnosis may become more skewed toward highly technological ancillary services, even though this may not necessarily improve the quality of the diagnosis. Concerning physician induced demand, studies have shown extraordinary variations in surgical rates *per capita* (Wennberg, 1980) that raise questions about the appropriateness of some of the surgery being performed. However, Dr. Wennberg contends that the variations in surgery rates reflect physician uncertainty rather than physician-induced demand. Similarly, studies of Second Surgical Opinion programs have found significant numbers of proposed surgeries not confirmed by consulting physicians (McCarthy, 1980). (ORDS is funding a major evaluation of Second Opinion Demonstration Programs through Abt Associates, Inc., Contract 500-780047.)

For the most part, evidence about quality problems consists of anecdotes or horror stories. Most prominent, perhaps, are the reports from former Senator Frank Moss on Medicaid mills (1979). These mills featured low quality, high volumes, unnecessary testing, and high markups over costs. Although Medicaid mills may very well exist, a recent HCFA study has shown that not all large Medicaid practices are the mills of Senator Moss's horror stories. The research was conducted at Boston University (Mitchell, 1980) and examined data from the HCFA Survey of Physician Practice Costs and Incomes. The Large Medicaid Practices (LMPs) studied were those that reported that at least 30 percent of their patients were Medicaid eligibles. A comparison of quality of care, as measured by length of visit, showed little difference between LMPs and all other practices. In addition, there were few differences in markups for ancillary services. Physicians' incomes in the large Medicaid practices were often roughly equal to those in other practices, and, in some instances, they were less. In terms of the caliber of those physicians, however, LMP physicians tended to be older, to be trained in foreign medical schools, and to have fewer credentials such as board certification. Two additional studies have been initiated as a result of these findings. The initial analysis will be duplicated using more recent data to examine the stability of these results over time. The Center for Health Economics Research has received a grant (HCFA Grant 95-P-97723/1) to examine the characteristics of Large *Medicare* Practices to determine how they compare to all other practices.

Quality: Future Research

Future research in this area should address three specific topics: identifying incentives which inappropriately influence treatment choices; assessing physicians' behavioral responses to differences in prices paid for medical services; and identifying the relationship between quality of care and the costs of health care services.

Within the current system of physician reimbursement there may be incentives which lead to inappropriate choices between competing forms of treatment. The system of fees currently in place should be examined to assess both the extent and magnitude of any potential inappropriate incentives. For example, do current reimbursements favor inpatient (or emergency room) care rather than office care? Does the system produce incentives which inappropriately influence physicians' decisions about the quality of care? Are there incentives which lead to unnecessary diagnostic testing or unnecessary surgery?

Although previous research has documented the existence of potential incentives in the reimbursement system, very little work has been performed to assess physicians' behavioral responses to these incentives. In fact, there exists a need for both (1) theoretical work establishing the basis (if any) for paying different prices for different services, and (2) empirical work identifying differences in physician performance (if any) with respect to such price differentials. The need for the theoretical research was discussed in the cost section. However, the empirical question remains: Do relative prices make a difference? The research to date has focused on identifying incentives without pulling together behavioral models that can test physician responsiveness to those incentives. This problem should begin to be remedied by a solicitation for a study of the impact of relative prices to be issued in FY 1982.

In fact, the initial studies of physician responsiveness will only begin to scratch at the surface of some very deep research questions. They will likely be able to examine only fee-for-service patterns among fairly well defined methods of care. The behaviors of salaried physicians, hospital-based physicians, teaching physicians and even interns and residents all have an impact on quality and cost. But here the reimbursement channels are ill-defined and a host of nonfinancial constraints and incentives also cloud the possibilities for obtaining unambiguous results.

The remaining issue is probably the most difficult—that of explicitly measuring the tradeoffs between quality and cost. Quality and cost are commonly believed to be inversely related, but there are no available estimates of this relation. This research area is the most speculative of any of those discussed, and planning for studies in this area is still in a formative stage. However, in conjunction with the PSRO Evaluation, ORDS has funded a benefit-cost analysis of medical care evaluation studies through the Rockburn Institute (Contract 500-78-0050). The methodologies developed in this study may lead to future work more directly focused on the cost-quality tradeoff.

Improving Data and Statistical Methods

Background

The final research area involves data development and meta-research, that is, research about research. This focus is specific to ORDS since it only indirectly relates to the accomplishment of the HCFA mission. However, since it is an ORDS mission to identify ways to improve the methods available to achieve HCFA's objectives, the ORDS must also consider these activities which can enhance the performance of the research and demonstrations programs.

Although activities in this area may arise from an examination of a particular problem about access, cost, or quality, often a new data set or research technique will have broad application. Current activities in the data area assist the ORDS staff in keeping abreast of trends and developments in all of the areas of physician reimbursement. Very often the acts of "bean counting" or "naming of parts" will lead to new research hypotheses and future evaluations. On the meta-research side, very often a particular research technique yields an ambiguous result or no result. Sometimes a new technique or a new way to manipulate the data is required before the research can proceed.

Current Data and Research Studies

The ORDS has several paid claims data collection efforts currently being conducted through the external research program. The Urban Institute's California data bases have been frequently cited already in this report. Pennsylvania Blue Shield is assembling a 10 year data base of private and Medicare data from Pennsylvania. South Carolina, New Hampshire, Vermont, and Colorado. The University of Southern California contract (HCFA Contract 600-76-0160) was initiated to try to develop a nearly national data base with data from Blue Shield plans across the country. A relatively small data base from Maine has been assembled by the Codman Research Group, Inc. (HCFA Contract 600-77-0039). This data base has been merged from Medicare, Medicaid, and Blue Shield files.

These data on claims will be used to document trends in intensity of care, quantities of service, and physician pricing patterns and, where possible, to compare Medicare and Medicaid reimbursement levels to those in the private market. Pricing pattern data will also be contrasted with Bureau of Labor Statistics data to assess the accuracy of the physician component of the Consumer Price Index. In addition, the Codman Research Group program will examine whether physician-patient market areas are the same for Medicare, Medicaid and the private market. More refined analyses, such as the aforementioned Michigan Blue Shield project on induced demand, also will be conducted using these data sets.

Another data base derives from the HCFA Survey of Physician Practice Costs and Incomes. This survey was conducted by the National Opinion Research Center (HCFA Contract 600-77-0077). Telephone interviews were conducted with approximately 5,000 physicians each year to elicit data from calendar years 1976, 1977, and 1978. (Two smaller surveys were conducted for 1975.) These data have been used in several studies of variations in costs, practice arrangements, productivity and so forth.

Future Data and Research Needs

In the future, inhouse physician oriented data bases from Medicare and Medicaid would be useful. Neither Medicare nor Medicaid currently has this data, which hampers the ability to conduct physician reimbursement research with respect to HCFA's own programs. For example, a Medicare Part B physician oriented data base would significantly improve the possibility of directly evaluating the impacts of the Medicare Economic Index (As indicated previously, several internal studies have examined variations in Part B assignment rates and reimbursements. The data for these studies came from a beneficiary oriented sample of records. In the future these records may also be sorted by provider number to allow additional studies of physician responses to reimbursement policy).

Under Medicaid, a physician oriented, patient ordered data base could allow the examination of physician performance across all health services for particular patients—physician provided and ordered services, hospital services, and prescriptions. This type of data base would be a much richer source for assessing the impact of relative prices on treatment choice because more of the treatment data would be available.

The discussion of future research on access indicated the need for another potential data development effort. This effort would involve a data set that would allow a more direct examination of the relation between physician participation in HCFA programs and beneficiary access to health care service. Previous research results suggest that increased physician reimbursement levels would increase physician participation. However, no clear inferences exist about whether such increases would result in (1) physician services being provided to more beneficiaries than at present or (2) simply more physicians providing services to current beneficiaries with few access problems, without affecting beneficiaries who currently have limited access to care. Such data might be developed from a survey of beneficiaries and their sources of care. This type of information might then be examined in terms of correlations between beneficiary access measures and the number or percent of physicians with significant participation in HCFA programs. (Data from such a survey might support analyses of beneficiary access to the complete spectrum of health care services.)

Another data need alluded to in the cost section involves reimbursement flows in and around the hospital. Because hospital claims and physician claims are often processed by different systems—for example, Medicare Parts A and B or Blue Cross versus Blue Shield—payments for services which may be billed under either system are very difficult to study. As a result, problems in such payments may be impossible to resolve and myths about problems may be impossible to refute. A large data collection effort might be useful in this regard if data could be collected from several hospitals in a specific area (or from several areas) to be merged with the corresponding physician payment data. This process could allow the examination of differences in either total costs or in the costs of specific kinds of services where such differences derive from accouting or billing differences rather than from differences in treatments. If the data set had abundant information, one might also examine the question of whether there were differences in treatment that might be due to the differences in billing method.

The potential for research using claims data leads to a future meta-research question. Claims data are potentially very detailed about patterns of physician performance, treatment decisions by diagnosis, billing behavior with respect to different reimbursement mechanisms, and so forth. In fact, the data are too detailed. They must be analytically reduced to be amenable even for multivariate analyses. This type of reduction typically is performed on an *ad hoc* basis, involving calculations of means and standard deviations. Additional research will have to be conducted in the future to identify reduction techniques which do not suppress all of the details.[6] Failing that, further research should identify any unambiguous biases that might be introduced by using selected data elements to construct indices of physician performance.

Finally, another meta-research question arises from the lack of complete data sets for all of a physician's patients. Most often a claims based data set will derive from a specific patient population and will include data only from that population, such as Medicare only or Medicaid only. Since physicians can provide services to patients under a wide variety of payments options, use of a single "incomplete" data set may introduce bias into the results. Unfortunately, creation of complete data sets would be very costly and, as suggested, might be very difficult to manipulate. Therefore, it might be useful to construct a small number of such complete data sets to assess the robustness of estimates produced by the use of a single population subset. The existence of one or more complete data sets might allow the estimation of general equilibrium models of physician fees, which might take into account the effects of all the different markets in which a physician might participate.

Conclusion

The research conducted to date has had significant impacts on the operating reimbursement programs and has provided useful insights for future work. For example, in light of the analyses of the impacts of changing coding systems, a regulation has been issued prohibiting Medicare carriers from changing procedural coding and terminology systems used for Medicare processing unless a net advantage can be demonstrated. The results of the Arthur Anderson study were reflected in HCFA's FY 1980 budget, which contained a proposal to change the way hospital-based physicians are reimbursed. Regulations to support these changes are now pending due to litigation by the groups that would be affected. The Medicare Economic Index has been refined through the use of data collected in the HCFA Survey of Physician Practice Costs and Incomes.

No single result in and of itself is likely to lead to a vast improvement in HCFA's ability to accomplish its mission. But to the extent that this research plan anticipates the challenges created by an increasing number of physicians, an increasing beneficiary population, and increased opportunities for providing more sophisticated health services, HCFA's operations have that much better a chance at success.

---

[6]Factor analysis was used to reduce the HCFA Survey of Physician Practice Costs and Incomes to produce five medical practice "styles." Anthony Boardman, *et al.*, presented a paper "Physicians' Styles of Practices," on this subject at a research conference on Studies of Micro Survey Data on Physician Practice Costs and Incomes, Washington, D.C., February 27-28, 1980.

References

Berry, Robert, "Development of an Equitable Medicare Economic Index: An Analysis of Variation in Practice Costs Among Specialties." Paper presented at a research conference on Studies of Micro Survey Data on Physician Practice Costs and Incomes, Washington, D.C., Feburary 27-28, 1980.

Brown, Douglas, "Are Auxiliary Inputs Underutilized?" Paper presented at a research conference on Studies of Micro Survey Data on Physician Practice Costs and Incomes, Washington, D.C., February 27-28, 1980.

Burney, Ira and Jon Gabel, "Reimbursement Patterns Under Medicare and Medicaid," in Jon Gabel, *et al.* (eds.), *Physicians and Financial Incentives*, 1980.

Cantwell, James R., "Implications of Reimbursement Policies for the Locations of Physicians," *Agricultural Economics Research* (April 1979), 31(2): pp. 25-35.

Dresch, Stephen, "Physician Earnings and Returns to Medical Training and Specialization," Paper presented at a research conference on Studies of Micro Survey Data on Physician Practice Costs and Incomes, Washington, D.C., February 27-28, 1980.

Ferry, Thomas P., *et al.*, "Physicians' Charges Under Medicare Assignment Rates and Beneficiary Liability," *Health Care Financing Review*, Winter 1980, 1(3) pp. 49-74.

Frech, H.E., and Paul B. Ginsburg, "Imposed Health Insurance in Monopolistic Markets: A Theoretical Analysis," *Economic Inquiry* (March 1975) 13: pp. 55-70.

Gibson, Robert M., "National Health Expenditures, 1979," *Health Care Financing Review*, Summer 1980, pp. 1-36.

Gornick, Marian, *et al.*, "Factors Affecting Differences in Medicare Reimbursements for Physicians' Services," *Health Care Financing Review*, Spring 1980, pp. 15-38.

Hadley, Jack, "An Econometric Analysis of Physician Participation in the Medicaid Program, Urban Institute Working Paper No 998-9, April 1978.

Hadley, Jack, and Robert Lee, "Physicians' Price and Output Decisions Theory and Evidence," Urban Institute Working Paper No 998-8, April 1978.

Hadley, Jack, *et al.*, "Can Fee-for-Service Reimbursement Coexist with Demand Creation?" *Inquiry* (Fall 1979) 16: pp. 247.

HCFA Administrator's Report, No. 17, August 27, 1979.

Health Care Financing Administration, *Research and Demonstrations in Health Care Financing, 1978-1979*, 1980, p. 59.

Held, Philip J., and Mark V. Pauly, "An Economic Analysis of the Production and Cost of Renal Dialysis Treatments," Center for Health Services and Policy Research, Northwestern University, June 19, 1980.

Held, Philip J., and Mark V. Pauly, "Compensation of Physicians in the End Stage Renal Disease Program," Working Paper #25, Center for Health Services and Policy Research, Northwestern University, March 10, 1979.

Holahan, John. "An Economic Analysis of the Medicaid Program." Urban Institute Working Paper 976-05. December, 1974

Holahan, John. "Physician Reimbursement." in Judith Feder et al. (eds). National Health Insurance. Conflicting Goals and Policy Choices. (Washington, D.C. The Urban Institute). 1980. p 73

Holahan, John and William Scanlon. "Price Controls Physician Fees, and Physician Income from Medicare and Medicaid Urban Institute Working Paper No 998-5. January 1978

Hsiao, William C., and William B Stason. "Toward Developing a Relative Value Scale for Medical and Surgical Services." Health Care Financing Review, Fall 1979, 1(2) pp 23-38

Institute of Medicine, A Manpower Policy for Primary Health Care (Washington, D.C. National Academy of Sciences). May 1978.

Institute of Medicine, Medicare and Medicaid Reimbursement Policies (Washington, D.C. National Academy of Sciences). March 1976

Lee, Robert, and John Holahan. "Variations Among Urban and Rural Areas in Levels and Rates of Changes in Fees A Descriptive Analysis." Urban Institute Working Paper No 998-7. January 1978

McMillan, Alma. Preliminary estimates of 1977 assignment rates. Division of Beneficiary Studies. ORDS. 1980. (Unpublished)

Maletz, David. Overview of assignment rate improvement demonstrations. Division of Health Systems and Special Studies. ORDS. 1980

McCarthy, Eugene. "Second Surgical Opinion Solution or Sham?" in Jon Gabel, et al. (eds). Physicians and Financial Incentives. 1980

McMenamin, Peter. "On the Welfare Economics of Government Subsidized Demand for Health Care." ORDS Internal Working Paper #OR-1. July 1980. pp 21-23

Mitchell, Janet B. "Large Medicaid Practices Are They Medicaid Mills?" Health Care Financing Grants and Contracts Report. DHHS. HCFA. ORDS. March 1980

Moore, Stephen H., et al. "Cost Containment Through Risk-Sharing by Primary Care Physicians A History of the Development of United Healthcare." Health Care Financing Review. Spring 1980, 1(4), pp. 1-14

Moshman Associates, Inc. Medical Procedural Terminology Systems Development and Characteristics of Three Major Systems for Third Party Payment," Health Care Financing Research and Development Series, Report No. 4. DHEW. HCFA, OPPR, no date

Moss, Frank E. "Through the Medicaid Mills." in Allan D Spiegel, (ed.). The Medicaid Experience (Germantown, Md Aspen Systems) 1979

Muller, Charlotte F., and Johan Otelsberg. "Study of Physician Reimbursement under Medicare and Medicaid." Health Care Financing Grants and Contracts Report. USDHHS. HCFA. ORDS (Washington, D.C. no date)

National Commission on the Cost of Medical Care. Summary Report (Chicago, Ill American Medical Association) December 1977

Newman, A. "Virginia Physician Responses to Changes in Coding Terminology." in Jon Gabel, et al. (eds.). Physicians and Financial Incentives. 1980

Newman, Howard. Regional Letter Medicare. Transmittal No 80-36. HCFA. DHHS. August 1980

Paringer, Lynn. "Medicare Assignment Rates of Physicians Their Responses to Changes in Reimbursement Policy." Health Care Financing Review. Winter 1980, 1(3) pp 75-90

Pauly, Mark. "The Relationship Between Hospitals and Physician Costs. Outputs, Prices, and Incomes." Paper presented at a research conference on Studies of Micro Survey Data on Physician Practice Costs and Incomes. Washington, D.C. February 27-28, 1980

Redisch, Michael et al. Physician Pricing, Costs, and Income. Paper presented at the Western Economic Association Meetings. June 20, 1977

Reinhardt, Uwe. "A Production Function for Physicians Services." Review of Economics and Statistics (February 1972) 15 pp 55-66

Schieber, George, et al. "Physician Fee Patterns Under Medicare A Descriptive Analysis" New England Journal of Medicine (May 13, 1976) 294 1089-1093

Sloan, Frank, et al. A Study of Administrative Costs in Physicians Offices (Cambridge, Mass Abt Associates, Inc). 1977

Sobaski, William J. "Effects of the 1969 California Relative Value Studies on Costs of Physician Services Under SMI." Health Insurance Statistics HI-69. ORS. SSA. DHEW, June 20, 1975

Steinwald, Bruce. "Hospital-Based Physicians Current Issues and Descriptive Evidence." Health Care Financing Review. Summer 1980

Wennberg, John, al. "Small Area Analysis of Surgery Rates." in Jon Gabel, et al. (eds). Physicians and Financial Incentives. 1980

Wilensky, G R, and L F Rossiter. "The Magnitude and Determinants of Physician Induced Demand." 1980

Woodward, Robert. "Physician Productivity, Remuneration Method, and Supplier-Induced Demand." Paper presented at a research conference on Studies of Micro Survey Data on Physician Practice Costs and Incomes. Washington, D.C., February 27-28, 1980

HEALTH INSURANCE AND HEALTH POLICY IN THE FEDERAL REPUBLIC OF GERMANY

Uwe E. Reinhardt

This paper presents a structured survey of the West German health care and health insurance system. The West German health insurance system is very comprehensive and generous. The scheme provides full coverage for all medically necessary services, including ambulatory and inpatient care, prescription drugs, dental care, medical appliances and even prolonged rehabilitation in the so called Kurorten (localities with health spas). Typically, patients do not bear any copayment at the point of service, or only very modest ones. Physicians are paid on a fee-for-service basis (according to negotiated fee schedules), hospitals are reimbursed on the basis of prospectively negotiated per diems, and the suppliers of drugs and appliances are reimbursed at what is referred to as "market prices" (that is, at prices set by suppliers with only mild indirect control from the public sector or third-party payors). This extraordinarily liberal insurance system causes West Germany to devote no greater a proportion of their Gross National Product (GNP) to health care than does the United States. Using the American definition of "national health care expenditures," both nations currently devote about 9.4 percent of their GNP to health care.

Introduction

Most modern societies view certain basic health care services as commodities to which every member of society should be guaranteed access regardless of ability to pay. This general proposition seems widely shared among nations, whatever their cultural and political complexion. Vastly different approaches, however, have been adopted to act on that precept. Some nations have proceeded on the assumption that the desired guarantee requires the nationalization of both the *production* and the *financing* of health services. This approach has been favored in the United Kingdom and in the Socialist nations. The overall capacity of the delivery systems in these nations is determined by a political algorithm, and available capacity is distributed regionally on the basis of explicit planning. It is rationed among individual consumers on some basis other than monetary charges—usually on the basis of time prices or on the basis of the providers' medical judgment. The time prices faced by individual patients are, of course, also set indirectly by some provider's assessment of the patient's "need" for health services.

At the other end of the spectrum are nations that seek to provide the desired guarantees with a minimum of public-sector intrusion into the production and financing of health services. These nations would prefer, in principle, to effect the guarantee simply by redistributing appropriate amounts of general purchasing power—for example, through negative-income tax schemes. Upon making the necessary transfers one could, in principle, rely on the price mechanism to determine the system's overall capacity and to distribute the resources among members of society. In practice, however, this ideal approach has typically been found infeasible because the necessary transfers of general purchasing power tend to exceed the political tolerance for such transfers. Consequently, one observes, even in these nations, varying degrees of public-sector intrusions into at least the *financing* of health-care services. The *production* of health services, however, has remained more or less completely in the private sector.

From the perspective of health policy in the United States, the second approach is clearly the more interesting. The nationalized and centrally planned health systems can—and do—claim for themselves certain advantages. In the United States, however, it is not generally believed that the advantages of centrally planned, publicly owned health systems compensate adequately for the rigidities inherent in them. Should

---

Research for this paper has been supported by the Health Care Financing Administration of the Department of Health and Human Services under Grant No. 95-P97309/2-01. That support is gratefully acknowledged.

From Uwe E. Reinhardt, "Health Insurance and Health Policy in the Federal Republic of Germany," 3(2) *Health Care Financing Review* 1-14 (December 1981). Reprinted by permission.

Americans ever wish to copy other nations' approaches to national health insurance, they would more probably look to contexts in which at least the production of health-care services remains in the private sector.

Even that confined scope, however, presents one with a remarkable variety of mechanisms used to provide the desired guarantees. Some nations (for example, Canada) have chosen to nationalize the financing of health services completely. Other nations (for example, Australia) seem to view complete nationalization of the financing mechanism as unnecessary and, indeed, undesirable. Still other nations (for example, France) have sought to have the best of both worlds. Although the financing of health services in France is accomplished through nongovernmental insurance funds—so-called *caisses d'assurance maladie*—these insurance funds operate under close supervision of the central government's ministry of health. So close is this supervision on a day-to-day basis that the insurance funds have, in effect, become the central government's arm in the implementation of national health policy.

In this paper I shall focus almost exclusively on the health insurance system of West Germany. That system is interesting because: (1) the delivery system resembles in important respects those found on the North American continent; (2) virtually the entire West German population is now covered by the most comprehensive health insurance imaginable, and (3) the public sector's role in the production and financing of health care is merely to provide a statutory framework, to occasionally provide compulsory arbitration, and to finance capital expenditures by hospitals (and with it, to participate in the planning of inpatient capacity).

The remainder of the paper is organized as follows. The next section presents a brief description of the West German health care delivery system, of its health insurance system and of recent trends in health care expenditures. In the section entitled "Control of Cost and Expenditures Under the Statutory Health Insurance System" the focus shifts to current issues in West German health policy, especially approaches to the control of health care costs and expenditures. The paper concludes with some general remarks on the arbitration of social conflicts concerning the allocation of health care resources.

Description of The West German Health Care System

Health Care Resources and Their Use

West Germany currently has a population of about 61.5 million. As Table 1 indicates, this population is served by roughly 1.7 million health workers, a term defined to include any person employed by the health care sector, in whatever capacity. Only about 700,000 of this total are health professionals as that term is used in the United States. Of these, roughly 120,000 are physicians.

TABLE 1
Employment in The West German Health Care Sector, 1976

Category	Number	Per 100,000 Population	
Total Employment	1,710,000	2,780	
Health Professionals			
Physicians —Inpatient	54,648	89	
—Ambulatory	56,969	93	182
—Other	12,949	21	
Dentists	31,858	51	
Pharmacists	25,885	42	
Other Health Professionals²	487,709	793	
Other Persons Employed in Health Care³	1,039,982	1,691	

¹Includes physicians in the public health departments, in administration and in industry.
²Includes nursing personnel and physicians in training.
³Includes workers in the industries producing supplies, medical equipment and drugs.

Source: Wissenschaftliches Institut der Ortskrankenkassen (1978), p. 33.

The labor force in the health care sector is complemented by about 3,500 hospitals with a capacity of about 11.6 beds per 1,000 population. As Table 2 shows, slightly over 54 percent of all hospital beds are in publicly owned facilities (mainly municipal hospitals), 35 percent are in hospitals founded and administered by private organizations (churches or foundations) on a non-profit basis, and 10.5 percent are in other private hospitals, some of which are operated on a for-profit basis. Only about 7.9 beds per 1,000 population are allocated to general acute care. The remaining beds are in long-term or special care facilities.

TABLE 2
Hospitals, Hospital Beds and Hospital Use in West Germany, 1974

Number of Hospitals, All Types	3,483	100%
Public	1,309	38%
Private, Non-profit	1,200	34%
Other private	974	28%
Number of Hospital Beds	716,530	100%
in Public Hospitals	387,590	54%
in Private, Non-profit Hospitals	253,949	35%
in Other Private Hospitals	74,991	11%
Number of Beds Per 100,000 Population		
All Hospitals		11.56
Acute-care Hospitals		7.85
Special Hospitals		3.71
Number of Admissions Per 100,000 Population		159
Acute-Care Hospitals		140
Special Hospitals		19
Average Length of Stay		
Acute-care Hospitals		17 Days
Special Hospitals		63 Days
Average Utilization Rate		
Acute Care Hospitals		84%
Special Hospitals		89%
Number of Patient Days Per 1,000 Population		
Acute-care Hospitals		2,405
Special Hospitals		1,206

Source: Bundesminister fur Jugend, Familie und Gesundheit (1977), pp. 239-249.

American or Canadian physicans typically treat their patients in their own practices and in the hospital(s) with which they are affiliated. Only about 6 percent of the West German physican population—typically, hospital chiefs of staff—enjoys similar hospital privileges. Other West German physicians work fulltime either in their own private practice or in the hospital. Physicians in private practice (Niedergelassene Ärzte) typically treat their patients on a fee-for-service basis, with the bulk of the fees (about 85 percent) coming directly from third-party payors. Physicians in hospitals (Krankenhausärzte), on the other hand, are salaried, and only the chiefs of staff enjoy the privilege of treating private patients on the hospital's premises, for a fee.

The dichotomy between the ambulatory and inpatient physician practice is statutory and strictly enforced, and has a number of peculiar consequences. First, most hospitals are prohibited from operating outpatient departments, because the provision of ambulatory care is the preserve of the Niedergelassen Arzte—that is, of physicians in private practice. Hospitals may intrude on this monopoly only if they are affiliated with a medical school and their outpatient clinic serves a teaching function. Second, a private physician sending a patient to a hospital loses both medical and economic control over the patient during the latter's hospital stay (although hospitals may and often do report back to the patient's private physician). A corollary is that, although West German patients have the right to choose their own physician for ambulatory health services, freedom of choice does not extend to treatment within the hospital, unless the patient is treated, on a private basis, by one of the chiefs of medicine. Finally, the strict division between ambulatory and inpatient care contributes to an excessive application of diagnostic tests, because hospital physicians do not invariably accept the diagnosis determined by the private practitioner and prefer to conduct their own tests, at the risk of repeating some tests. While this practice may enhance the accuracy of the diagnosis, it is expensive.

As Tables 2 and 3 show, West Germans rely rather more heavily on the hospital than do Americans. Although the West German admission rate is below the comparable rate in the United States, the average length of stay per admission in West Germany is roughly double the comparable rate in the United States. Case mix differentials may distort this comparison to some extent. On the other hand, the average length of stay for specific illnesses in West Germany tends to be much higher than that for identical illnesses in the United States. As a result of this differential, the number of patient days per 1,000 population is substantially higher in West Germany than it is in the United States.

TABLE 3
Hospital Use in The United States, 1974

	General and Special Hospitals	Psychiatric and Tuberculosis Hospitals
Admissions per 1,000 population	165	4.2
Total Days in Hospital per 1,000 Population	1,432	662
Average Length of Stay	8.7 days	N.A.
Occupancy Rate, Percent	76%	N.A.

Source: U.S. Statistical Abstract 1978, Table 168, p. 110.

Unfortunately, similar data on the use of ambulatory services are not publicly available in West Germany, as they are in the United States. Evidence exists that West German physicians see far more patients per office-hour than do their American counterparts and that they place heavy emphasis on diagnostic and other technical procedures in the composition of treatment packages. In this respect, West German physicians appear to respond to fee schedules that tend to reward technical procedures relatively more generously than face-to-face contact with patients, at least in comparison with the typical structure of fees in the United States.

The Health Insurance System

Institutional and Historical Background

The onset of national health insurance in Germany is usually dated to 1883 when low-income industrial workers and their families were compelled by law to become members of sickness funds, many of which had already been in existence throughout the nineteenth century. At that time, the statutory system covered only about one sixth of the population. The benefit package included mainly sickness cash payments and only a modest range of medical benefits in kind. In the ensuing decades, the system evolved in predictable directions: coverage was extended across both population groups and medical services. Today the system covers the bulk of the population and offers a remarkably comprehensive benefit package. Expenditures on benefits in kind now dwarf sickness cash payments.

From 1883 to the 1930's the sickness funds negotiated contracts privately with individual physicians and had the right to limit the number of physicians participating in their program. In 1931, the statutory basis was laid for collective contracts between regional associations of sickness funds and newly created professional associations of sickness fund physicians—the so-called *Kassenaerztlichen Vereinigungen* (KV's). These physician associations were originally chartered on a *Land* (that is, State) basis, but they eventually formed national associations as well. Under the 1931 statute, the sickness funds collectively transferred agreed-upon lump sums per insured patient to the physician associations, which in turn agreed to have their members render the insured all medically necessary services and disburse the lump sum to their members, typically on a capitation basis. The sickness fund associations have always negotiated separate contracts with individual hospitals, usually on the basis of agreed-upon per diem charges.

After World War II, West German physicians won the right to establish themselves as sickness-fund physicians without the funds' prior approval. The distribution of funds from the physician associations to individual physicians began to proceed more and more on a fee-for-service basis, according to fee schedules negotiated between the sickness funds and the professional associations. Until very recently, this system was open-ended. The sickness funds paid for whatever billings were submitted by physicians to their physician associations. Since 1976, attempts have been made to place a cap on overall physician reimbursement, although the success of this approach is not assured. These attempts, culminating in a formal cost-containment act in 1977, will be described in the section "Control of Cost and Expenditures. . .").

The so-called *Ersatzkassen* (literally, "substitute funds"), whose membership includes primarily white collar workers, developed parallel to the compulsory insurance system. For the most part these funds have not been accessible to blue collar workers.[1] In competing with the compulsory sickness funds for voluntary[2] members, these *Ersatzkassen* have frequently sought to attract patients by offering their physicians better financial terms. It is sometimes alleged that the *Ersatzkassen* can do this because of an ability to select among risks. Evidence does exist that the role of the *Ersatzkassen* had shifted the evolution of the West German health insurance system in directions favored by physicians. The shift from capitation to fee-for-service reimbursement is one example. That shift was spearheaded by the *Ersatzkassen* sometime during the 1960's.

Administration and Financing of the Current System

The West German health insurance system is actually a mosaic of roughly 1,500 autonomous sickness funds organized on the basis of geography (the *Ortskrankenkassen*), of enterprise (the *Betriebskassen*), or of trade *(Innungskassen)*. About half of the insured population has membership in the *Ortskrankenkassen*. Another one quarter of those insured are members of the *Ersatzkassen* (the substitute funds). Tables 4 and 5 provide further detail on the insurance status of the West German population and the distribution of insured "members" across sickness funds. The term "member" means the insured employee or retired person. Membership in a sickness fund automatically extends full coverage to all of the member's dependents as well. The number of persons insured by a sickness fund thus tends to exceed the number of its "members" significantly (see Table 4, item I).

---

[1] In 1974, only 3.9 percent of the members of the *Ersatzkassen* were blue collar workers (see Reinhart Schmidt [1978], Table 17 p. 59).

[2] As I will describe later, individuals not mandated by law to join a sickness fund often enjoy the right to join a fund voluntarily

TABLE 4
Percentage Breakdown of the West German Population by Health-Insurance Status, 1974

Insurance Status	Percent of the Population
I. Insured Under the Statutory System:	90.15%
Mandatory "Members"	30.75%
Voluntary "Members"	7.53%
Retired Person who are "Members"	11.82%
Dependents of "Members" Who are Automatically Covered	37.04%
II. Covered by Private Health Insurance	7.20%
III. Covered by Special Insurance Schemes:	2.36%
Policemen	1.00%
Person on Public Assistance	1.07%
Students	0.29%
IV. Not Insured	0.29%
Total Population	100%

Source: Reinhart Schmidt (1978), Table 15, p. 57.

TABLE 5
Membership in the Statutory Health Insurance System, 1974

	Percentage of All Insured "Members"
Local Sickness Funds (Ortskrankenkassen)	48.5%
Enterprise Funds (Betriebskrankenkassen)	12.9%
Other Funds[1]	11.0%
Substitute Funds (Ersatzkassen):	27.6%
Blue Collar Workers	1.1%
White Collar Workers	26.5%
Total: 31.64 Million Members	100%

[1]Funds organized around a trade or craft: for example, funds for sailors, for miners and for farmers and agricultural workers.
Source: Reinhart Schmidt (1978), Table 18.

Depending on the member's economic status, he or she is either a voluntary member of a sickness fund or must join on a mandatory basis. Included in the group of mandatorily insured are:
- All blue collar workers;
- White-collar workers with incomes below a certain level;
- White-collar workers with incomes below a certain level;
- Retired persons;
- Virtually all farmers;
- Students and apprentices; and
- Sundry other groups of modest economic status

Over three quarters of the persons insured under the statutory system now are mandated to be insured. Persons not mandated to seek coverage have the right to join sickness funds on a voluntary basis.

About 7 percent of the population obtains private insurance coverage. This group includes civil servants who receive a cash supplement from the government in case of illness and obtain private supplemental insurance to cover costs not covered by the government indemnity.

The sickness funds are governed by boards composed of members representing employers and employees. The individual funds are members of associations at the level of the *Land* (State) which, in turn, form the national associations. The *Land* and national associations negotiate with their counterpart associations of health care providers.

In principle, each individual fund is expected to be fiscally autonomous. Its financial affairs are supervised, however, at the level of the *Land*. Overall supervisory authority over the statutory insurance system rests with the Federal government's Ministry of Labor and Social Affairs. Since the sickness funds must operate within statutory guidelines that prescribe, among other things, the benefit package that must be offered the insured under Statutory Health Insurance, the funds are actually fairly similar to one another. Broadly speaking, membership in a sickness fund entitles members and their families to all necessary medical and hospital services in case of illness, to certain types of preventive care, to prescribed drugs, and to cash benefits to cover loss of income due to illness.[1] Maternity benefits, the services of health workers in patients' homes, medical appliances, dental care (including dentures), eyeglasses, stays in rest homes, and rehabilitative services are also included in the typical benefit package. Indeed, it is hard to think of medical services that are not covered by the statutory health insurance scheme.

West Germans insured under the statutory system usually enjoy first-dollar coverage for insured items. There is a modest copayment on prescription drugs (currently one Deutsche Mark, or about 50 U.S. cents, per item) and a 20 percent coinsurance rate on dentures. A wide range of medical supplies are fully covered, but only for certain basic models. Thus, the insurance funds will fully cover the cost of a basic type of eyeglass, leaving the cost of a more attractive frame fully to the consumer. A valid generalization, however, would be that cost-sharing by patients in West Germany is rare and insignificant in both absolute and relative amounts.

---

[1] Since 1970, employers have been mandated to provide such cash payments (*Lohnfortzahlung*, that is, continuation of wages) directly, at least for some weeks. As a result, the percentage of such cash payments in total disbursements by the funds shrank from 21 percent in 1969 to 10.7 percent in 1978. It was 7.1 percent in 1979.

Tables 6 to 8 provide information on the financing of the Statutory Insurance System. The system is almost wholly financed by employers and employees. Contributions for insured members are raised in the form of a flat payroll tax, with employers and employees each paying an equal share. Contributions for members who are retired are made by their respective pension funds. The public sector itself makes only modest contributions to the system (Table 6) and mainly indirectly through pension funds.

TABLE 6
Direct and Indirect Sources of Finance for the Statutory Health Insurance System in West Germany, 1974

Employers	39.0%
Private Households (Mainly Employees)	48.8%
Federal Government (Bund)	7.2%
States (Länder)	1.7%
Municipalities	1.9%
Other	1.4%
Total, in Deutsche Marks	DM 51.705 billion

Source: Reinhart Schmidt (1978), Table 20, p. 96.

TABLE 7
Secular Change in Contribution Rates to the Statutory Health Insurance System, 1974-1978

Year	Local Sickness Funds	Enterprise Funds	Other Funds	Substitute Funds for:		All Funds in the System
				Blue Collar Workers	White Collar Workers	
	Percentages of Gross Earnings¹					
1-1-74	9.35%	8.63%	8.95%	9.38%	9.81%	9.36%
1-1-76	11.34%	10.20%	11.10%	11.09%	11.85%	11.30%
1-1-78	11.51%	10.61%	11.34%	11.47%	11.82%	N.A.

¹Shared equally by employers and employees.
Source: Bundesverband der Ortskrankenkassen, *Die Ortskrankenkassen im Jahre 1977*, (mimeographed, 1978), Table II.

TABLE 8
Variation in Contribution Rates to the Statutory Health Insurance System, 1975

Contribution Rate, In Percent¹	Local Sickness Funds	Enterprise Funds	Other Funds	Substitute Funds	All Funds
	Number of Sickness Funds				
0-6%	-	12	-	-	12
6.1-7%	-	56	1	-	57
7.1-8%	7	155	8	-	170
8.1-9%	34	299	30	1	364
9.1-10%	84	318	53	2	457
10.1-11%	134	113	60	8	315
11.1-12%	49	12	12	4	77
12.1-13%	6	-	-	-	77
					6
Total	314	965	164	15	1458

¹Percentage of gross earnings, shared equally by employer and employee.
Source: Reinhart Schmidt (1978), Table 43.

Contributions to the sickness funds are made on the so-called "solidarity principle" which means that members should contribute according to their ability to pay, regardless of the number of dependents or their health status. No attempt has ever been made to set contributions for individual members within a fund on actuarial principles. A fund as a whole, however, must set its overall contribution rate strictly on the basis of the actuarial cost of serving the entire membership (and dependents). Because the actuarial cost per member depends on the demographic mix of members, and the latter can and does vary among sickness funds, one observes a rather striking variability in the contribution rates imposed by the various funds (see Table 8). In recent years, this disparity in contribution rates has become, quite understandably, an increasingly controversial issue. The disparity has so far persisted because there is actually little effective competition for members among the numerous funds. By and large, an employee's or retired person's membership is dictated by his or her employment, geographic location, or both.

Expenditures

Table 9 presents details on the pattern of expenditures under West Germany's Statutory Insurance System. To provide a basis of comparison, gross national product data are shown as well.

TABLE 9
Total Expenditures Under the Statutory Health Insurance System by Type of Service, 1978¹

Category	Billions of DM	Percent of Total
Ambulatory Medical Services	13.2	19.1%
Dental Services and Dentures	10.6	15.3%
Drugs	10.6	15.3%
Hospital Services	21.8	31.6%
All Other Expenditures (Medicinal Aids, Maternity Benefits, Preventive Care, etc.)	9.6	13.9%
Administration	3.3	4.8%
Total Expenditures, Excluding Cash Benefits and Administration	69.1	100.0%
Cash Benefits	5.3	7.7%
Gross National Product	1,278.0	

¹Preliminary data
Source: Federal Department of Labor and Social Affairs, cited in Ulrich Geissler (1978), Table 4

Total expenditures by the Statutory System (excluding cash benefits) amounted to about 5.4 percent of West Germany's gross national product in 1978. This figure is, of course, not directly comparable to the national health care expenditure series published in the United States. The West German figure excludes expenditures by private households for non-prescription drugs, public-sector expenditures for capital investments in hospitals, medical schools, and medical research, as well as expenditures made by the private insurance carriers. It is difficult to estimate an exact counterpart of the U. S. figure from the available West German data. A reasonable approximation, however, can be developed from data published by West Germany's Federal Ministry of Labor and Social Affairs (See Bundesminister für Arbeit und Sozialordnung, 1978). According to these data, total national expenditures from all sources for inpatient care, ambulatory care, drugs, supplies and dentures, medical research and public health services amounted to 97 billion Deutche Marks (DM) in 1975, a figure that includes 6 billion DM for administrative costs. Gross national product in 1975 amounted to 1,030 billion DM (Geissler, 1978, Table 4). Using the more comprehensive U. S. definition of health expenditures, then, West Germans appeared to spend roughly 9.4 percent of their gross national product on health care in 1975. In other words, the total expenditure figure of 69.1 billion DM attributed to the Statutory Health Insurance System in Table 9 represents only about 71 percent of the total that approximates the American concept of national health expenditures. This ratio should always be kept in mind in reacting to data strictly on the Statutory System.

Table 10 presents the distribution of expenditures by the Statutory System (including 4.2 billion DM cash-benefits payments) over the various categories of sickness funds in 1974. The table also indicates the

TABLE 10
Distribution of Expenditures Over Categories of Sickness Funds, and Expenditures Per Member by Category of Sickness Funds, 1974

	Percentage of Total Expenditures Paid by Funds	Expenditure Per Member¹
Local Sickness Funds	47.7%	DM 1,446
Substitute Funds for White Collar Workers	26.7%	1,467
Enterprise Funds	13.3%	1,529
Funds for Miners	4.2%	1,902
Funds for Trade Guides	4.1%	1,306
Funds for Rural Workers	2.7%	1,368
Substitute Funds for Blue Collar Workers	1.1%	1,488
Funds for Seamen	0.2%	1,396
Total	100.0%	1,469¹

¹Standard deviation of category means about overall mean is DM 182
Source: Adapted from Reinhart Schmidt (1978), Tables 34 and 35

variability of expenditures per insured "member." This number is not to be confused with expenditures *per capita*, because membership in a sickness fund automatically extends full coverage to all of the insured "member's" dependents. The interfund variability in expenditures per member, therefore, reflects to some extent mere differences in the demographic mix of the funds' membership, including differences in the number of dependents per "member."

Table 11 exhibits the secular growth in health care expenditures by the Statutory System. Although all categories of these expenditures increased more rapidly than gross national product during the 1960's, that differential in growth rates reached remarkable proportions during the first half of the 1970's. Overall expenditures during that period grew at more than twice the rate of growth of the gross national product. The pattern received widespread and highly critical comment in the media and eventually triggered public intervention in the form of a Federal cost containment law. This law and its impact so far are examined in the next section.

Reimbursement of Providers

Hospitals are reimbursed by the sickness funds on the basis of negotiated *per diems*. These *per diems* cover all operating costs incurred in connection with inpatient physician care, including the cost of drugs and supplies. The *per diems* do not cover capital costs which are, since 1972, supplied from State and Federal sources in conjunction with regional planning. The negotiated *per diems* are unique to each hospital; but they are subject to approval by a State authority. As already noted, hospital physicians are salaried, and only chief medical officers are permitted to deliver health care to private patients on a fee-for-service basis.

The sickness funds pay pharmacists for drugs and supplies furnished to patients against prescriptions obtained from ambulatory-care physicians. Payment is at so-called "market prices." The latter are the sum of wholesale prices paid by pharmacists to the producers of pharmaceuticals or to wholesalers, plus a mark-up *(Handelsspanne)* fixed by law and not subject to any influence by the sickness funds. Precisely what countervailing power makes this retail price a "market price" is an intriguing question. In principle, the individual physician is to prescribe the lowest-priced drug within any set of drugs of comparable bio-availability and effectiveness. In practice, this mandate had been widely circumvented for lack of information on drug equivalence.

A recently established commission of physicians, pharmacists and representatives of the pharmaceutical industry has been charged with the task of devising an officially accepted list of bio-equivalencies and associated drug prices. That list is expected to contribute toward greater economy in the prescription of drugs. Furthermore, experiments have been done—notably in the state of Bavaria—with reimbursement methods that hold the individual physician fiscally responsible for excessive prescribing of drugs.

The reimbursement of ambulatory physicians and dentists is somewhat complicated, as Figure 1 shows.

TABLE 11
Average Annual Growth Rates in Selected Expenditures Under the Statutory Health Insurance System, 1960-1978

Category	Average Annual Percentage Growth					
	1960-1965	1965-1970	1970-1975	1976	1977	1978'
Ambulatory Medical Care	11.3%	11.4%	15.6%	5.9%	4.6%	5.7%
Dental Services and Dentures	13.1%	13.8%	26.8%	15.6%	3.4%	6.2%
Drugs	13.1%	15.9%	16.1%	8.3%	1.5%	8.7%
Hospital Services	13.5%	15.3%	23.9%	9.8%	5.7%	7.1%
Total Expenditures Excluding Cash Benefits for Sickness and Administration	12.3%	13.8%	20.1%	10.0%	4.3%	7.2%
Gross National Product	8.8%	8.3%	8.5%	9.1%	6.2%	7.1%

'Preliminary data
Source: Federal Department of Labor and Social Affairs, cited in Ulrich Geissler (1978) Table 5

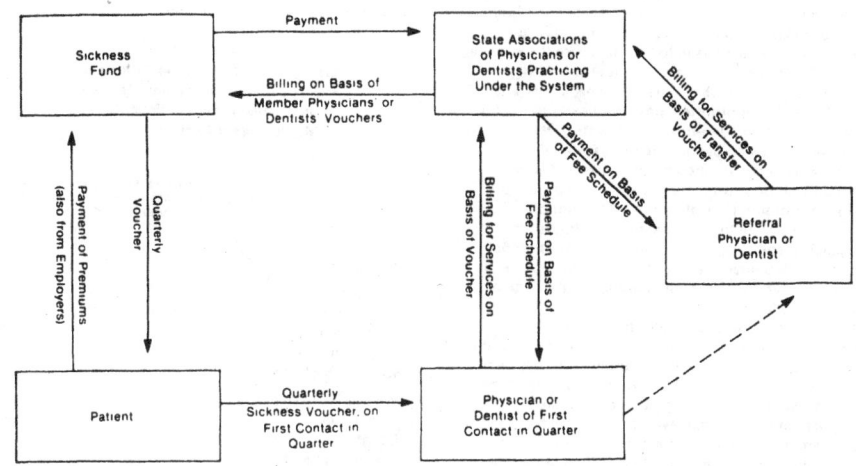

FIGURE 1
Reimbursement of Physicians and Dentists Under the Statutory Health Insurance System

Each insured person in Germany receives from his or her sickness fund a so-called *sickness-voucher* every quarter. The patient surrenders this voucher to his or her physician on the first contact in a quarter. Referrals to specialists proceed on a transfer certificate issued by the referring physician, although patients may go directly to a specialist as initial contact with the medical system. The physician notes individual services rendered on the voucher (or transfer certificate) and submits it to the appropriate physician association for reimbursement on a fee-for-service basis. If the association faces an overall cap on distributable funds—as is being attempted now—then individual fees are scaled up or down by the association to meet the budget constraint. Utilization review to control overservicing is, in the first instance, in the hands of the physician associations, although the sickness funds have recently gained the right to participate actively in utilization reviews. The reimbursement system for dentists parallels that of physicians.

The fee schedules used under the statutory system are negotiated periodically between associations of the sickness funds on the one hand, and the professional associations on the other. The overall structure of the fee schedule (that is, relative value points) are negotiated at the national level. The original basis for these negotiations is a Federal fee schedule issued by the Ministry of Economics in 1965.[4] The national negotiations take the form of amendments to this schedule.

The money value of the relative value points is negotiated between sickness funds and professional associations at the level of the *Land* (State). Although fee levels vary across the States, such variations are small compared to regional variations of fees in the United States. (In 1976, for example, the highest level was only 6 percent above the lowest level of fees). Minor variations in the fee levels also occur among the various types of sickness funds, but, once again, they are in no way comparable to the variations in fees one observes in the United States.

For patients insured under the statutory scheme, physicians (and dentists) must accept the negotiated fees as payment in full. They may, and invariably do, charge private patients considerably higher fees. Indeed, it is not uncommon for physicians to divide their day into practice hours for statutorily insured and privately insured patients, and to adopt different practice styles for the two types of patients. Table 12 presents data from a recent study of practice styles in the city of Munich. These data suggest that practice styles are sensitive to differences in insurance coverage. Patients covered by the *Allgemeine Ortskrankenkasse* (local sickness fund), which generally offers physicians

[4] This is the so-called Gebuhrenordnung fur Ärzte (fee schedule for physicians). The annual amendments to the relative-value structure in this basic schedule are called *Bundesmantelvertrage* (Federal envelop contracts).

the least generous terms, tended to spend considerably more time in the waiting room than private patients (who paid relatively higher fees). Private patients also spent more time per visit with the physician than did patients under the statutory system.

TABLE 12
Average Wait Time in the Office and
Average Length of Patient Visits by
Insurance Status of Patients
Munich, West Germany, 1979

	Patients Insured by		Local Sickness Fund
	Local Sickness Fund	Private Insurance	Private Insurance
Men Age 18-55:			
Wait time in the office (minutes)	45.2	28.9	1.56
Length of Patient visit (minutes)	10.5	11.9	0.88
Women Age 18-55:			
Wait time in the office (minutes)	47.0	28.0	1.68
Length of patient visit (minutes)	10.5	13.5	0.78

Source: Neubauer and Birkner (1980), Figures 1 and 2, pp. 155-156

Control of Cost and Expenditures Under the Statutory Health Insurance System

Under the Statutory Health Insurance System of West Germany, providers and patients are mandated to economize in the use of health-care resources. That mandate, however, is not really compatible with the financial incentives built into the system. With few exceptions, all insured services and supplies are received by patients free of charge at the point of delivery.

Physicians are reimbursed on a fee-for-service basis, and hospitals are reimbursed for the number of patient days they report. Both face a fiscal incentive to service their patients generously. In the wake of a rapid expansion of health-care resources—both facilities and manpower—the sharp secular increase in expenditures during the 1970's is not surprising.

The system has always been equipped with formal cost control mechanisms. The prices of drugs, for example, are reviewed and authorized by the Ministry of Economics. The fees for physician's services are negotiated between sickness funds and physician associations. The use of physician services and the prescription of drugs are monitored by the physician associations themselves and, in principle, controlled by them. The funds flowing to the hospital sector are controlled, at least in part, through negotiated *per diems* on the basis of approved cost sheets. Finally, since 1972, the physical capacity of the hospital sector has come under the influence of regional planners whose approval is required for State and Federal financing of capital expenditures by hospitals.

As Table 11 shows, these various controls either failed to work during the early 1970's or they were not applied. Because the secular growth during this period led to successive increases in the premium rates (see Table 7), both organized labor and employers pressed for more overt forms of cost control. In that climate the Federal government succeeded in enacting its Health-Care Cost-Containment Act of 1977, an act that seems in keeping with West Germany's penchant for policy by consensus.

The overall thrust of the Cost-Containment Act is to constrain the growth of expenditures to the growth of gross national product. The basic mechanism is an annually negotiated agreement of overall health-care budgets at the Federal and State level. To accomplish this the Act mandates the establishment of a National Health Conference *(Konzertierte Aktion)* embracing all major interest groups active in the health-care sector, including the sickness funds, the associations of sickness funds' physicians, hospitals, the pharmaceutical industry, unions (representing consumers), associations of employers, the State *(Land)* governments and the Federal government (Geissler, 1978). The Conference is mandated to develop annually a consensus on guidelines for the economic development of the statutory health-insurance system, including the growth of total expenditures by type of service and, indirectly, increases in fees and prices. To illustrate, during its first sessions in December 1977 and March 1978, chaired by the Federal Minister of Labor, the Conference reached a consensus on the following recommendations for July 1, 1978 to June 30, 1979:

1. Expenditures per insured member for ambulatory physician services are to increase by not more than 5.5 percent above the previous fiscal year. Of this total, 2.5 percent is allocated to increases in fees, and 3.0 percent to increases in use.
2. Similarly, expenditures per member for dental services (excluding materials and laboratory costs) from July 1, 1978-June 30, 1979 may exceed the previous year's expenditures by only 2.5 percent.
3. Drug expenditures per insured member in the second half of 1978 may exceed average expenditures during 1977 by only 3.5 percent.

Physicians, pharmacists, the pharmaceutical industry, and the sickness funds agreed on recommendations 1 and 3. These recommendations, therefore, had force. Because the dental association dissented from recommendation 2, the reimbursement of dentists was left for further negotiations between dentists and the sickness funds. An explicit recommendation for the hospital sector could not be offered because that sector is not covered by the Cost-Containment Act.[5]

To implement the recommended guidelines, the Act mandated the sickness funds and physician associations to establish so-called Economic Monitoring Committees at the State level, with equal representation of both parties and rotating chairmanship. The Committee's monitoring system screens the charge profile of every physician. Physicians whose average number of services or prescriptions per case (voucher) exceed their class average by 30 percent are selected for further examination. If the observed deviations are not justified the physicians' reimbursements are cut accordingly. Under this system, the individual physician can, therefore, be held fiscally liable for excessive prescribing of drugs.

A remarkable feature of the West German approach to cost containment is that the guidelines recommended by the Conference are reached by consensus and they are not binding upon the negotiating parties. Although the guidelines may thus appear as a toothless tiger, they are nevertheless thought to influence the direction of negotiations, especially the compulsory arbitration that is triggered whenever negotiations between the sickness funds and providers break down. In effect, the law represents an attempt to replace the vacuum left by the secular erosion of market forces with a new type of market—one in which professional and economic interest groups bargain collectively toward a national consensus within a set of constraints provided by statute.

By contrast, the thrust of public policy in the United States has been, by and large, to replace the eroding market forces in health care by direct and often unilateral regulation of the health-care sector.

How successful the West German approach to cost containment will be in the long run remains to be seen. As Table 11 shows, the growth of expenditures under West Germany's statutory health insurance system has abated markedly since 1975, although the most dramatic decline in the growth rate actually preceded the introduction of the Cost-Containment Act of 1977. The explanation generally given for this early decline is that health-care providers agreed to a stringent voluntary cost containment effort in anticipation of Federal legislation, to demonstrate its redundancy.

---

[5] The hospital sector was excluded from the Act, because some of the States—notably the city State of Hamburg—were reluctant to relinquish their control over hospitals to the Conference. At the time of this writing, the hospital sector still remains outside the Act and has not been subject to any separate cost-containment legislation. For more information, see "Kostendampfung und Strukturverbesserung im Gesundheitswesen" (1978).

Also, the relative harmony prevailing at the early sessions of the Conference has given way to more open dissention in subsequent sessions. Some observers of the West German health system—policymakers among them—appear increasingly disillusioned with the approach.[6] One reaction to this sense of frustration may be stronger government interference in the health sector. A provision in the Cost-Containment Act, for example, mandates the Federal executive to report, in 1981, to Parliament on the effectiveness of the Act and to assess the need for more potent policies.

An alternative reaction might be to subject the delivery and financing of health care more extensively to classical market mechanisms—for example, to significant cost-sharing among patients. Some economists (for example, Henke and Metze, 1978) have advocated this approach, as has organized medicine in West Germany. On the other hand, neither policymakers nor politicians in West Germany seem to have shown any inclination to employ cost-sharing by patients as a cost containment strategy.

The economist's case for coinsurance rests on a well known body of theory which assumes that patients are: 1) well informed; and 2) capable of rational action on accurate information concerning their health status and alternative approaches to treating given medical conditions. Also, it is assumed that even if patients were not well informed or were incapable of choosing rationally among treatment alternatives, physicians would keep the patient's financial interest in mind when choosing treatment on their patient's behalf.

Why physicians would favor cost-sharing by patients is not as clearly evident. When physicians do make the case for cost-sharing they typically do so on the argument that it would: 1) elicit more responsible conduct on the part of patients; 2) free medical practice from trivial cases, and 3) contribute toward expenditure-containment. The first argument, and possibly the second, may have merit. One doubts, however, that physicians seriously believe the third. Organized medicine is not known to favor policies that reduce the aggregate flow of funds to physicians. As M. L. Barer et al., (1979), have recently argued, a more plausible explanation for the profession's posture is that cost-sharing, coupled with third-party coverage, is believed by physicians to draw more money overall to the physician sector than could otherwise be had from third-party payers under universal first dollar coverage, because it is usually more difficult to maintain an overview of and control over fiscal flows from many spigots than to control a single source.

In West Germany, the discovery of additional sources of revenue for physicians has a particular urgency. Current prognoses put the number of active physicians per 100,000 population in the year 2000 at 406 to 485, (Lefelmann and Geissler, 1979) depending on the assumptions embodied in the forecast. Because the hospital sector is not likely to expand significantly, the bulk of this projected increase in physician density will spill over into the ambulatory-care sector where physicians are free to establish a private practice without the approval of an intervening institution, such as a hospital. Table 13 indicates the effect of this expected spill-over. In reacting to these projections, one should keep in mind that the physicians included in the table will cater solely to the population's need for *ambulatory* physician services. Just how, in the face of these numbers, West Germany proposes to keep the growth of total physician remuneration roughly in line with the growth of gross national product—the apparent goal of cost-containment policy in that country—is an interesting question. From the American vantage point, the resolution of this question may yield instructive lessons.

---

[6] For more information, see, for example, Jonathan Spivak, (1979)

[7] Article 2, paragraph 6 of the Cost-Containment Act. For more information, see Ulrich Geissler (1978), p. 13

TABLE 13
Actual and Projected Number of Active Physicians in West Germany, 1975-2000

Category	1975	1980	1990	2000
		—Year—		
Total Number of Active Physicians	118,007	136,900	190,400	256,600
—in Research and Administration	11,819	13,100	18,900	24,200
—Primarily in the Hospital	52,340	57,000	60,000	62,000
—in Private, Ambulatory Practice	53,848	66,800	111,500	170,400
Number of Physicians in Private Ambulatory Practice, per 100,000 Population				
—Number	87	110	191	306
—Index, 1975 = 100	(100)	(126)	(220)	(351)

Source: Adapted from Gerd Lefelmann and Ulrich Geissler (1978), Tables 2 and 3, pp. 16 and 17.

Concluding Remarks

In the Western democracies, conflicts over the allocation of real resources among members of society are usually arbitrated by private-market forces. Ideally, this process takes the form of competitive bidding with purchasing power that is distributed among individuals on the basis of a mixture of merit, lineage and luck. In general the resource-allocative verdicts of this arbitration process tend to be accepted with remarkable equanimity as long as the bidding process itself has been reasonably fair, this is, competitive. Almost invariably the impersonal, though often harsh, verdicts of private markets are accepted more tranquilly than possibly less harsh verdicts by identifiable individuals, for example, by public servants.

For many decades—indeed, centuries—this form of arbitration was accepted also in conflicts over the allocation of health-care resources. As I have asserted in the introduction, however, one cannot think of a modern society that still favors this process. Many societies—for example, the United States and Australia—wish to guarantee their members access to at least a *minimally adequate set of health services*, regardless of the distribution of purchasing power, although not necessarily on an equal footing.[8] Other societies—for example, Canada, the United Kingdom, the Continental European nations and the socialist nations—profess as a basic tenet that all members of society ought to have unfettered access to *all technically available and medically justifiable health care* on an equal footing. Although these nations have not so far been able to implement this tenet fully in practice, at the very least they pretend to structure their health-care and health-insurance systems on this fundamental principle.

Whatever particular ethical principle various societies posit for their health systems, all of them have found it necessary to replace the classicial process of free-market arbitration at least partially with some alternative, collective process of arbitration over resource conflicts in health care. A widely shared belief among American health economists—and some European ones as well—is that one ought to move cautiously in this direction and never more than is absolutely necessary for the sake of equity.

Many policymakers in the United States and, apparently, most policymakers elsewhere, seem to have despaired long ago of the economist's favored strategy. In particular, little credence is given to the notion that consumers could participate sensibly in resource-allocative decisions in health care, even if they were given the basic information for such decisions—information health-care providers sometimes withhold from them.[9] Lacking any faith in the consumer's competence, the thrust of public health policy almost everywhere has been to replace market mechanisms altogether with something else, in piecemeal or wholesale fashion.

In the United States this tendency has manifested itself in a penchant for centrally directed planning and direct regulation of individual's behavior—for example, Professional Standards Review Organization (PSRO's) or Certificates of Needs (CON's) for hospital capacity. In West Germany, the thrust of public health policy so far has been not to move sharply towards either planning or direct regulation,[10] nor to resurrect the long moribund play of free-market forces. Instead, public policy has attempted to create novel, quasi-economic, quasi-political markets that fall somewhere between the extreme of classical markets and central planning.[11] The ideal decision-making units in these quasi-markets are freestanding associations of the individuals and organizations active in these markets (for example, association of providers, of insurers, of the insured, and so on). The process of reaching equilibrium through the myriad of independent bids, as envisioned for classical markets, give way to collective bargaining among these freestanding associations, all within a statutory framework that guards the rights of weaker parties and provides for compulsory arbitration of inconclusive negotiations. The so-called Health Care Conference (*Konzertierte Aktion*) provided for in the Health Care Cost-Containment Act of 1977 can be interpreted as an attempt to refine this type of "market" mechanism.

---

[8]Practically, equal footing in health care means that two patients falling victim to the same medical condition in a given locality would receive the same treatment regardless of their socioeconomic position.

[9]This asymmetric management of information in health care is often justified, by physicians, as part of a good therapy. As it happens, however, the asymmetry bestows both medical and market power on the provider. The motives behind it may, therefore, be questioned.

[10]The exception here is the application of planning in the hospital sector as part of the financing of capital expenditures.

[11]A clear exposition of this strategy can be found in Philipp Herder-Dornreich (1977).

It can be asked whether, at this time, anyone can seriously claim to know the superior, universally applicable form of arbitration in health care—or even the clearly superior mechanism for the United States.

During the 1960's and early 1970's, when economic growth was rapid everywhere and resources plentiful, almost any chosen form of conflict-arbitration in health care seemed to work, after a fashion. Potential conflicts over real resources were simply smothered in funds and resolved by muddling through with what was thought to be only temporarily fixed physical capacity. In the meantime the very nature of the allocation problem has changed. Plenty of physical capacity exists but there is widespread unwillingness to allocate *budgets* for the use and longrun maintenance of this capacity. All of the Western industrialized nations find themselves in the midst of this new problem and all of them are seeking to develop civilized and acceptable rules to solve it. Just what set of rules other nations—for example, West Germany—will develop and how they work shall be of more than mere academic interest to American observers.

Acknowledgments

The author is indebted to Professor Klaus-Dirk Henke, Technische Universitat, Hannover, West Germany and to Dr. Peter McMenamin of the Health Care Financing Administration of the Department of Health and Human Services for their careful review of the manuscript and for their many helpful comments.

References

Barer, M. L., R G. Evans, and G. L. Stoddart *Controlling Health Care Costs by Direct Charges to Patients: Snare or Delusion?* Ontario Economic Council, Occasional Paper No 10, Toronto, Canada, 1979

Bundesminister fur Arbeit und Sozialordnung, *Die Struktur der Ausgaben im Gesundheitsbereich und ihre Entwicklung seit 1970.* Gesundheitsforschung Series, Vol. 7, Bonn, September, 1978.

Bundesminster fur Jugend, Familie und Gesundheit, *Daten des Gesundheitswesens—Ausgabe 1977,* Bonn-Bad Godesburg, July 1977

Bundesverband der Ortskrankenkassen, *Die Ortskrankenkassen im Jahre 1977,* (mimeographed), 1978.

Geissler, Ulrich, *Health Care Cost Containment in the Federal Republic of Germany,* (mimeographed), November 1978

Henke, Klaus Dirk and Ingolf Metze, "Selbstbeteiligung und Kostenentwicklung," in *Medizin Mensch Gesellschaft,* Vol. 4, 1979, pp. 34-40.

Herder-Dornreich, Philipp, *Strukturwandel und Soziale Ordnungspolitik,* Cologne, 1977.

"Kostendampfung und Strukturverbesserung im Gesundheitswesen," Part A. III of *Sozialbericht 1978 der Bundesregierung,* BT-Drucksache 8/1805, December 12, 1978, pp. 26-32.

Lefelmann, Gerd and Ulrich Geissler, "Die Entwicklung des Arzteangebotes bix zum Hahre 2000: Analyse, Bewertungsgesicht-punkte, Massnahmen," in Wissenschaftliches Institut der Ortskrankenkassen, *Gesundheitsokonomische Aspekte der Vergutungspolitik,* Bonn-Bad Godesberg, 1979; pp. 9-24.

Neubauer, Grunter and Barbara Birkner, "Beeinflusst die Krankenversicherungsart das Verhalten von Arzt und Patient?" *Sozialer Fortschritt,* Vol. 29 (July/August, 1980), pp. 153-60.

Schmidt, Reinhart, *Strukturanalyse des Gesundheitswesens in Schleswig-Holstein,* Vol. 8, Kiel, 1978.

Spivak, Jonathan, "Health Cost Controls in Germany," *The Wall Street Journal,* December 19, 1979, p. 81.

U. S. Department of Commerce, *Statistical Abstract of the United States 1978,* Washington, D. C. 1979.

Wissenschaftliches Institut der Ortskrankenkassen, *Personalentwicklung im Gesundheitswesen in Vergangenheit und Zukunft;* Bonn-Bad Godesberg, January, 1978.

Youth Unemployment and Training

Youth unemployment in the United States has been aptly described as a "lingering crisis." Indeed, growing evidence suggests that youth unemployment does not respond in the same manner as does adult unemployment to changes in the economy. For black youth in particular, the unemployment figures over the past fifteen years have steadily grown worse, and their employment opportunities have also deteriorated steadily, regardless of whether the economy in general was expanding or contracting. Youth unemployment tends, overall, to be approximately two to three times greater than that for adults, while black youth unemployment is five times greater.

Youth account for only 10 percent of the labor force but 25 percent of the unemployed. Various policy and program initiatives have attempted to respond, and these initiatives, broadly sketched, have tended to stress either education and employment-skill training or public-sector work opportunities. The former—in focusing on the supply side of the supply-versus-demand equation and in emphasizing the upgrading of the education and skills of youth—has presumed to better equip them to enter the labor market. Much of the underlying rationale behind this approach is that youth are unemployed because they do not possess the skill, motivation, and resolve to obtain employment successfully. Programs abound that aim at developing these attributes in youth.

Critics of this approach argue that the issue is not the absence of skills in the young, but rather the absence of employment opportunities. In short, there is simply no demand for the labor of the young. Analysts who hold to this view suggest that what is needed is systematic and widespread attention to job creation. In the absence of jobs, it is argued, all the supply-side services one might provide will be for naught. Viable transition services presume that job opportunities do exist, but in the absence of jobs the rationale for such services is severely weakened.

The articles in this section take up various aspects of the youth unemployment situation, with a number of pieces focusing especially on the supply-versus-demand argument. The Levin chapter draws important cross-national comparisons between youth unemployment in Australia and in the United States. Having examined four quite distinct explanations for youth unemployment in the two countries, Levin concludes that for both, the lack of jobs (that is, the lack of demand) is the most appropriate analytic framework for understanding current conditions. While not denying the role that job creation must play in any comprehensive attack on youth unemployment, Barton stresses the supply-side necessities of education and job training. Arguing for a coherent national policy in the 1980s regarding vocational education, he examines the various aspects of this overall policy and addresses seven specific federal policy initiatives. Barton argues for a strong federal role, focusing on the means to bring education and industry closer together to create viable transition strategies.

One effort sponsored by the federal government to build linkages between education and industry is assessed by Rist. The 1977 Youth Employment and Demonstration Projects Act (YEDPA)—introduced as an amendment to the 1973 Comprehensive

Employment and Training Act (CETA)—stipulated various requirements for linkages between education, employment, and training institutions. Of particular concern were those linkages that sought to enhance the transition opportunities for in-school youth. Data from more than forty programs studied by Rist indicated that creating and sustaining such linkages was an extremely difficult process. Barriers to implementation were immense and thwarted any number of potential linkages. Further, without local commitments to such linkages, the federal government did not have the fiscal resources to purchase them.

The final article by Hamilton and Claus challenges much of the conventional policy thinking on youth unemployment. The authors suggest that regardless of whether one focuses on either the supply or the demand, the underlying racial and social class inequalities persist. Stated differently, the programs that seek to put youth to work or give them skill training in classrooms are programs that reinforce existing social class inequities. They argue that youth unemployment is not a matter of being young per se, but of being young, low-income, and minority. They posit two quite different policy approaches to the current situation: to create youth entrepreneurial projects, and to encourage high levels of youth participator democracy throughout all youth employment programs.

23

YOUTH UNEMPLOYMENT AND ITS EDUCATIONAL CONSEQUENCES

Henry M. Levin

Introduction

The problem of youth unemployment has become a serious dilemma throughout the western industrialized societies (Melvyn and Freedman, 1979). In this paper, I will focus specifically on youth unemployment in two countries, Australia and the United States, with particular emphasis on the relations between education and youth unemployment. To at least some politicians, the problem is essentially rooted in the alleged failures of the educational system. For example, the Prime Minister of Australia, Malcolm Fraser, has charged on several occasions that the Australian educational system simply does not qualify many youth for the substantial job vacancies that exist in that country (Colless, 1980; Fraser, 1980; Hoare, 1980). But there are several competing explanations for youth unemployment, and each of these has profoundly different implications for policy. The purpose of this inquiry is to explore the rather different histories of youth unemployment in Australia and the United States and to evaluate the causes of the problem as well as some possible solutions.[1]

Before proceeding with these analyses, it is important to present the recent experiences of the two countries with respect to youth unemployment. In general, youth unemployment refers to the situation of persons below the age of 25 who are in the labour force, but lack productive work.[2] A component of youth that is particularly susceptible to unemployment is that of teenagers, so a separate evaluation is often made for persons between the ages 15 and 19 in Australia and 16 and 19 in the US. The seriousness of the youth unemployment problem in both countries as well as its increasing gravity in recent years is displayed in the table which shows unemployment rates for selected years and age groups.

Until 1974, Australia had a very low rate of overall unemployment at 2 per cent or below, and youth unemployment was only slightly higher,

---

From Henry M. Levin, "Youth Unemployment and Its Educational Consequences," in P. Karmel (ed.) *Education, Change and Society*. Copyright 1981 by The Australian Council for Educational Research Limited. Reprinted by permission.

Unemployment Rates for Selected Years and Age Groups — Australia and United States
(Unemployed as Percentage of Civilian Labour Force)

Australia	Age			
Year	15-19	20-24	25 and over	All ages
1965	2.8	1.5	0.9	1.2
1974	4.2	2.4	1.1	1.6
1975	10.1	5.6	2.5	3.9
1979	17.0	9.3	3.7	6.2

United States	Age			
Year	16-19	20-24	25 and over	All ages
1955	11.0	7.0	3.6	4.0
1965	14.8	6.7	3.2	4.5
1973	14.5	7.8	3.1	4.9
1979	16.1	9.0	3.9	5.8

Source: Australian data are taken from Australian Bureau of Statistics, *The Labour Force*, Canberra: various dates. US data for 1955-73 are taken from Norman Bowers, Young and marginal: An overview of youth unemployment, in United States Department of Labor, Bureau of Labor Statistics, *Young Workers and Families: A Special Section*, (Special Labor Force Report 233), Washington, DC: 1979, p. 5. 1979 data are calculated from United States Department of Labor, Bureau of Labor Statistics, *Employment and Unemployment during 1979: An Analysis*, (Special Labor Force Report 234), Washington, DC: 1980, Table 4.

with teenage unemployment of 3-4 per cent, and unemployment of those 20-24 years of age between 1.5 and 3 per cent. Between 1974 and 1975, the overall unemployment rate in Australia more than doubled, with an even greater absolute and proportionate increase in youth unemployment. All of these rates have continued to rise until, by 1979, teenage unemployment had risen to 17 per cent, that of 20- to 24-year-olds to over 9 per cent, and the overall rate of unemployment to over 6 per cent. In summary, there has been a precipitous rise in both overall Australian unemployment rates and those of youth in the latter part of the decade of the seventies.

In contrast, the United States has had consistently higher unemployment rates than Australia for all groups until very recently. Even in 1955, teenage unemployment in the US was 11 per cent and overall unemployment was 4 per cent. Over the last quarter century, the overall unemployment rate has increased from 4 per cent to just below 6 per cent with large fluctuations over the business cycle. Teenage unemployment has increased over this period by about the same proportionate change, an increase from 11 per cent to 16 per cent, and the unemployment rates of 20- to 24-year-olds have increased from 7 to 9 per cent.

The patterns in the two countries show both similarities and differences. For both countries, youth unemployment has generally moved in the same direction as adult unemployment, only the former has become more serious relative to the latter in recent years. In 1965, the teenage unemployment rate was about three and one half times as great as that for persons 25 and over in the US and about three times as great in Australia. By 1979, these ratios had increased to about four for the US to over four and one half for Australia, suggesting a tendency for the teenage unemployment rate to rise at an even faster rate than that of adults. There is also evidence of relatively greater deterioration in unemployment rates for 20- to 24-year-olds when compared with those 25 and over.

Indeed a related similarity is the remarkably low level of adult unemployment in both countries. As youth gets older, the probability of their facing unemployment declines considerably, a matter that we will return to when we consider why youth unemployment is a problem. Despite these similarities in youth unemployment patterns between the two countries, there is one major difference. Problems of high overall unemployment and youth unemployment are relatively recent phenomena in Australia in comparison with the US. For example, in 1965 the US overall unemployment rate was 4.5 per cent and that of teenagers was almost 15 per cent. In the same year, the corresponding rates for Australia were only 1.6 per cent and 4.2 per cent. But, by 1979, Australia had unemployment rates in both categories that exceeded those of the US.

Why is youth unemployment considered to be such a serious problem? After all, it is just a matter of time before youth reach the age where the probability of unemployment reaches the national average, generally five or six years at the most. There are several reasons for social concern. At the very least, youth unemployment rates are high in relation to any reasonable standard, and there is good reason to believe that the situation is getting worse. But there are other aspects that tend to underline the gravity of the youth situation.

First, it is feared that youth unemployment may have profound effects on altering values and attitudes of the affected persons and make it increasingly difficult to integrate them into both social and economic institutions. Historically, the western industralized nations like the US and Australia have had relatively high rates of employment with jobs available for almost all who sought work. Clearly this has been less true for the US than for Australia, but now both countries are confronting youth with an increasing probability of unemployment. Even the present rates of unemployment understate the true situation because they do not include the so-called discouraged worker who has given up looking for work because of poor employment prospects.

Youth who face a situation of unemployment for prolonged periods are likely to be angry and frustrated at their inability to find productive employment. This frustration may undermine their respect for traditional social values in a society that cannot provide employment to those who desire and need jobs. Such cynicism may contribute to various forms of antisocial behaviour such as vandalism, crime, drug use, and alcoholism. Indeed there is a danger that a sub-culture of cynical and destructive youth could become a major by-product of massive youth unemployment.

Second, even though the probability of unemployment falls very rapidly as youth approach their mid-twenties, there is a concern that periods of youth unemployment may have longer-term consequences on earnings and job performance. For example, some persons may become so accustomed to working irregularly or not at all that they may develop anti-work attitudes. Others will lack the early experiences in the labour market that provide the background for later career mobility, and they may be relegated to lower level positions for their entire careers. Others yet will simply never catch up to their colleagues who were more fortunate in obtaining jobs at the time of leaving school. There is at least some evidence of the long-run damage of youth unemployment in the US where statistical studies of workers show that earlier periods of unemployment for black youth are associated with lower earnings in later years when regular employment patterns are established (Becker and Hills, 1980; Ellwood, 1980; Corcoran, 1980).

A third aspect of youth unemployment is that it has important implications for equity among races, sexes, and persons drawn from different social classes. The probability of unemployment among youth is hardly a random event that affects all social groups equally. In the US, it is heavily concentrated among the black people and persons drawn from the least advantaged educational and social backgrounds. For example, although about 14 per cent of white males and females in the 16- to 19-year-old category were unemployed in 1979, black males and females in this age range faced unemployment rates of 36 per cent and 39 per cent respectively (US Department of Labor, 1980: A-6–A-7; Mangum and Seninger, 1978; Newman, 1979). Likewise those with the lowest educational attainments and whose parents have low incomes and occupational status are more likely to be victims of the youth unemployment phenomenon than those with more education and from more advantaged families (Rees and Gray, 1980). Indeed 50 per cent of all teenage unemployment in the US seems to be concentrated among only 10 per cent of teenagers, and these are predominantly those with the least education and other resources (Freeman and Wise, 1979:8; Clark and Summers, 1980). In Australia, too, it is recognized that the early school leaver is especially subject to unemployment (Williams, 1979), and that such persons are typically concentrated among the lower socioeconomic groups (Karmel, 1979:6). Thus basic patterns of economic and social inequity are mirrored in the patterns of unemployment among youth, where those who derive from the least advantaged circumstances are also those who are most susceptible to youth unemployment.

A final reason for social concern is the effect that youth unemployment has on the schooling process itself.[3] To the degree that one of the principal reasons for pursuing secondary schooling conscientiously is the expectation that it will lead to reasonable employment prospects, high rates of unemployment are likely to have an impact on the behaviour of students. At the very least, it may be difficult to keep such students motivated to undertake educational experiences that are not intrinsically interesting to them. Problems of student discipline may rise in response to a frustration with both the educational process and its falling currency as a ticket to employment. Under certain circumstances, high youth unemployment may also lead to reduced incentives for secondary school completion.[4] In Australia, in particular, there is evidence in recent years of declining rates of secondary school completion among males (Karmel, 1979:5).

In summary, high levels of youth unemployment are troubling for Australia, the US, and other industrialized societies for several reasons. First, the phenomenon undermines a traditional expectation and implicit right of youth that jobs will be available to all who wish to work. This means that many youth will suffer through protracted periods in which they are unable to find productive work, and these experiences may create a cynicism and anti-social set of attitudes and behaviour among those who are affected. Second, youth who experience substantial unemployment may also experience lower future wages and career mobility as a consequence, even when they are able to obtain regular employment as they reach adulthood. Third, there are important equity implications in that persons from the least advantaged social backgrounds are most heavily impacted by youth unemployment. Finally, substantial prospects of unemployment among youth may affect schooling patterns by reducing the incentives of youth to adapt to the demands of the educational system and to complete secondary school.

Causes of Youth Unemployment

As with so many complex social phenomena, there are many explanations for youth unemployment. Each view competes for adherents with the others, and each suggests a rather different policy approach to addressing the problem. In this section, we will review the four main explanations for youth unemployment. Before proceeding with this comparison, it is important to mention two aspects of youth unemployment which are often sources of analytic confusion in trying to assess the phenomenon.

The first source of confusion on evaluating the major causes and cures of youth unemployment is the rather common difficulty of mixing analyses at two different levels of social aggregation. Most of the literature that addresses youth unemployment views it as a macro-level phenomenon in which the concerns are expressed on a societal level. That is, they ask what are the causes of the *overall* magnitude of youth unemployment, and how can it be reduced? But, it is also possible to ask why certain youth are more susceptible to unemployment than others and to explain differences in the likelihood of unemployment among individuals. That is, one can ask why certain types of *individuals* are more likely to be unemployed than others, and what can be done about it.

The major error that arises when the two levels of analysis are confused is the application of findings on the determinants of unemployment among individuals to solutions for alleviating the overall problem of youth unemployment. For example, it is clear that individual youth with low educational accomplishments are the ones most likely to suffer from unemployment, while persons with higher educational attainments suffer the least. Therefore, from the perspective of the individual young person, obtaining more education will reduce his or her probability of unemployment. However, it does not follow from this that when everyone obtains more education than the average the amount of youth unemployment will be diminished or that the level of employment for the labour force will rise.

The individual who obtains more schooling is simply likely to displace one with less schooling in the overall job queue. In this case, the understanding of differences in employment prospects among individuals cannot be used to address employment prospects for large groups (Thurow, 1975). Improving the prospect of one individual may simply serve to displace another from the existing pool of jobs. Without an aggregate increase in the size of the job pool itself, increasing the probability of employment of one individual cannot be done without jeopardizing that of another. Thus, the employment solution for an individual youth is not an appropriate basis for addressing the overall problem of youth unemployment.

A second area of potential confusion in evaluating the causes of youth unemployment is that most of the evidence is based upon comparing the trend of youth unemployment over time with the trends of various potential determinants. Over the past decade and one half, there have been increases in the population of youth, aggregate unemployment, minimum wages, and unemployment compensation and decreases in measurable educational standards. Since all of these are considered to be factors that may affect the magnitude of youth unemployment, it is possible to construct a case for any one of them by just asserting the coincidence of time trends. That is, it can be argued that it was an increase in the minimum wage or in the demography of youth or a fall in educational standards that explains the rise in youth unemployment by virtue of the fact that changes in each of these tend to coincide with changes in youth unemployment.

But such an interpretation may be quite erroneous. First, since all of the potential determinants have followed a similar time trend, it may be difficult to separate their unique impacts on youth unemployment.5 Second, it is possible that a common set of forces has influenced the behaviour over time of both the potential determinants and youth unemployment, so that there is no causal pattern at all. In this case, any inference about causality becomes hazardous, since a common time trend will have affected all of the data. The main conclusion that can be drawn from this discussion is that the precise timing of the trends as well as supportive evidence that is drawn from other sources must be used to determine the validity of any causal inference. The fact that the general time trend between a potential explanatory factor coincides with rises in youth unemployment is not sufficient evidence in itself to support a causal relation.

There are four leading causes of youth employment that are asserted in the literature: the demographic bulge of youth entering the labour market in recent years; minimum wages for youth that exceed the value of their productivity or make them non-competitive with adults; a deterioration in education and training in recent years; and poor economic conditions under which youth suffer more than their older peers. All of these may have some basis, but it is important to ascertain which are the dominant causes from a policy perspective. That is, if some of the explanations account for only a small portion of the increase in youth unemployment and others account for most of the increase, the policy solutions should focus on the implications of the major explanatory factors rather than give them all equal weight.

In what follows, an attempt will be made to review each explanation in three parts. First, a presentation and analysis of the explanation will be made. That is, what is the causal link between a particular phenomenon and youth unemployment? Second, the appropriate policy solution that follows from the explanation will be delineated. That is, how can public policy be used to intervene to improve the situation? Finally, a presentation will be made of the evidence supporting the particular explanation as well as an evaluation of that evidence. By reviewing systematically each of the four explanations, it is possible to draw some tentative conclusions about both the causes of and possible solutions for youth unemployment.

Youth Demography

One of the most popular explanations for the deteriorating situation of youth in labour markets is that the sheer number of young persons entering the workforce tended to increase at a much faster rate than they could be absorbed. Especially important in this respect was the effect of the baby boom that followed World War II. The sixties and seventies were characterized by rather large increases in the number of persons in the 16- to 24-year-old age range. Although the increase in such persons could normally be handled by the labour force over the long run, it has not been possible to absorb them over the short run. Accordingly, youth unemployment rates have risen dramatically in the seventies.

The main policy solution that is associated with this explanation is that of patience. That is, although there has been a temporary bulge in the number of youth seeking work, it will fall as the youth population declines in both absolute and relative terms. Thus, if we wait long enough to get over the effects of the baby boom on the labour market, unemployment rates for youth will decline. In addition, any policy that can delay youth from entering the labour market at such times can also be helpful. Education and training programs and expansion of the military that will reduce the supply of youth searching for jobs can have such an effect.

The evidence supporting the view that youth demography is a principal cause of youth unemployment is singularly unimpressive. In the case of Australia, the population aged 15-19 grew dramatically from 9.2 per cent of the population aged 15 and over in 1954 to almost 13 per cent in 1966.[6] By 1971 the population aged 15-19 had fallen to 12.2 per cent, and continued to fall in the latter seventies when youth unemployment experienced its most marked increases (Burke, 1980: 9, Table 4). The highest levels of increase of the youth population were associated with the lowest levels of youth unemployment.

For the US, the explanation is equally unconvincing as a dominant one. First, a pure demographic effect would have resulted in poorer employment prospects for all youth. Yet, despite large increases in the number of white youths in the population, the percentage of that group that was employed actually increased between 1969 and 1977, while the employment rates of black youth as a percentage of their population decreased profoundly (Freeman and Wise, 1979:6; Ginzberg, 1980; Bowers, 1979; Newman, 1979). That is, to a large degree it was the employment opportunities of black youth that deteriorated rather than all youth. This suggests that there was no 'pure' demographic effect, since by at least one measure (employment as a proportion of population) the situation of white youth actually improved. Second, by the latter seventies, the youth population had begun to stabilize as a proportion of the population with a forecast for a relative decline in the eighties. Yet there was no evidence of improvement in employment prospects during this period.

In summary, while the demographic situation may have accounted for some increase in youth unemployment, it does not appear to be a major cause. The time patterns of increase in the youth population do not coincide well with the levels of youth unemployment in either Australia or the US. Indeed youth unemployment had been high in the US over all phases of the demographic cycle, and in Australia the demographic bulge preceded the present youth unemployment crisis.[7] Further, the fact that there is a distinct racial pattern to the increase in youth employment and unemployment in the US, in which employment/population ratios of white youth have actually improved while those of nonwhites have deteriorated, suggests that the demographic explanation has little generalizable power. That is, the explanation requires assumptions about racial separability of labour markets to be even moderately plausible.

Minimum Wages

A second explanation is that minimum wages for youth have tended to price them out of jobs, since their productivity is not adequate to justify such wages. This explanation is based upon the assumption of perfectly competitive labour markets in which it is assumed that workers are paid the value of their contribution to production. Given high minimum wages for youth who are not productive enough to earn such wages, employers will tend to hire older workers and provide more capital investment in plant and equipment in place of youth who might otherwise have been hired at a lower wage. The solution that follows from this explanation is to reduce the minimum wage for youth by creating a two-tiered minimum wage system (Coleman et al., 1974:168). Under this system, employers would provide a lower minimum wage for youth than for adults. Presumably, more youth would be hired, and they would receive the lower minimum wage only while receiving job experience and training. By the time their productivities had risen to a level commensurate with higher wages, they would be eligible for the higher adult minimum wage or market forces would have caused their remuneration to rise to a level above the minimum wage.

The effect of minimum wages on youth unemployment is difficult to assess, since there are a number of possible relationships. First, if the minimum wage rises, it is possible that 'more productive' adults will be preferred to youth so that youth will lose jobs to adults. Second, if the minimum wage rises, it is possible that employers will substitute more capital-intensive methods of production for all employees. Third, there is the possibility that the effects of the minimum wage will not be felt immediately, because it takes a while for employers to make adjustments. Even so, the view that youth unemployment has been largely attributable to rises in the minimum wages seems unlikely for both Australia and the US.

In Australia, the best evidence to support the effects of a rising minimum wage are that, between 1971 and 1974, the relative weekly earnings of junior males (under 21) rose from 52.4 to 55.9 per cent of that of adult males (Burke, 1980:Table 3). Beginning in 1975, there was a precipitous increase in unemployment rates of youth, possibly stimulated by the earlier rises in youth earnings. However the pattern tends to be contradictory. For example, after 1977, the ratio of junior to adult earnings declined slightly, but unemployment of 15- to 19-year-olds rose from 15.2 per cent to the 18 per cent range by the beginning of 1980 (Burke, 1980:Table 2; ABS, 1980:3). Further, the earnings of female juniors relative to female adults had changed scarcely at all between 1966 and 1978 (Burke, 1980:Table 3). Yet female unemployment among 15- to 19-year-olds has followed the same pattern as that for males, rising from about 4 per cent in 1966 to over 20 per cent in 1979 (Burke, 1980:Table 2).

For the US, the evidence is equally anomalous. Most important is the fact that the earnings of young males relative to adult ones *declined* rather substantially between 1967 and 1977, regardless of rises in the minimum wages (Freeman and Wise, 1979:12). That is, the poor labour market conditions faced by the young seemed to have their effects not only on unemployment rates, but on the relative earnings of youth as well. Further, the rapid increase in prices in the seventies meant that the minimum wage was no higher relative to the median wage than it was in the preceding two decades (Gamlich, 1976). Finally, even the largest estimate of the effects of minimum wages on youth unemployment is rather small, given the magnitude of such employment.[8] Taken together, these findings suggest that minimum wages in both Australia and the US do not seem to be dominant factors in explaining youth unemployment in recent years.

Education and Training

A third explanation for the rise in youth unemployment is the view that the quality of the youth labour pool has declined in recent years by virtue of a deterioration in education and training. According to this explanation, youth are increasingly lacking in the skills that are required for productive work. As the Prime Minister of Australia explained in a speech given in August 1980, there is a rather straightforward explanation for the 'paradox of high youth unemployment co-existing with the growing shortage of skilled labour' (Hoare, 1980). If the educational system were to do its job in creating a more qualified youth population, such youth would not face unemployment (Hoare, 1980).

If youth unemployment were a function of the low skills of the unemployed, the policy solution would be straightforward. Schools would need to be improved to make certain that they met the standards of employers, and training programs would have to be established and/or refurbished to address directly the types of skills that were needed in labour markets. That is, just as the US War on Poverty of the sixties was largely fought on the beachheads of schools and training sites by an infantry of educators and training supervisors, the enemy of youth unemployment would be vanquished by a similar policy onslaught. The answer to youth unemployment and training would be to improve the effectiveness of the education and training system.

Three types of evidence seem to be used as a basis for the assertion that youth unemployment has risen in response to a deterioration in the education and training of youth. First, it is pointed out that the job situation is worse for persons with low educational attainments than for those with greater ones. That is, jobs are available for those with better education. Second, employers have complained about the performance of young workers (Williams, 1979:Vol. 1, 618). Finally, there is widespread discussion and some data that suggest that educational standards have been declining (Wirtz et al., 1977).

It is generally true that more educated youth are less likely to face unemployment than less educated ones. It has also been claimed that jobs are becoming more and more complex and are requiring ever increasing skill levels.[9] When these two are taken together, it is only a small step to conclude that youth unemployment is simply a function of an increasing number of young persons who lack the education for work in an increasingly sophisticated work place. This view rests on the premise that more jobs are available than qualified young persons to fill them.

Virtually all of the available evidence for both Australia and the US suggests that this is not the case. In order to explore claims of a shortage of skilled labour, the landmark Williams inquiry did a special survey of the Australian labour market for 1977/78 (Williams, 1979:Vol. 2, Appendix M). In the middle of 1977, it found that for every unfilled vacancy in the skilled trades, there were five adult males registered as unemployed in those trades (Williams, 1979:458). Further, the pattern was similar in all major trade areas. To the degree that there were openings, they were attributable primarily to a regional mismatch of demand and supply, and even these amounted to only 1.3 per cent of all jobs (Williams, 1979:468, 474–97). Further, the vast majority of these unemployed lacked work because it was unavailable rather than because they lacked qualifications for the jobs that they sought (Williams, 1979:493).

In addition to the shortage of jobs, it is highly doubtful that existing entry-level jobs are too advanced for the young. There is considerable evidence that one of the major effects of automation has been the constant deskilling of jobs, and particularly ones where computerization has replaced human judgment.[10] Indeed, the job behaviour of youth and the high quit rates may be a response to the lack of challenge represented by the routinization of so many jobs as well as the lack of a career ladder (Brown, 1980). Thus, if the skill requirements of jobs that have been filled traditionally by youth are declining and the opportunities for advancement and higher wages are also diminishing with technological change, it would not be surprising to find that the response by youth was a deterioration in job performance. But, paradoxically, this phenomenon may result from education and skill levels of youth that are too high for available jobs rather than too low (Rumberger, forthcoming).

In any event, data on the determinants of unemployment for individuals cannot be generalized to that of all of the unemployed as we stated above. Although a person with more education is less likely to be unemployed, it does not follow that a high-enough level of education for all youth will eliminate unemployment. That is, one must not confuse the factors that explain the distribution of unemployment with its causes. It must also be shown that enough jobs will be forthcoming to employ all job seekers, and this assurance is noticeably absent from such analysis.

Finally, there is the rather widespread view and some evidence to show that educational standards have fallen. Although this view is found in both Australia and the US, the data are widely available in the US (Wirtz et al., 1977). Indeed the Australian case is immediately suspect when one considers that the youth unemployment explosion began rather suddenly in 1975 rather than developing over a longer period of time in response to a longer-term education deterioration. Since there is no evidence in Australia of a sudden decline in educational standards over a one- or two-year period preceding the 1975 rise in youth unemployment, the relationship seems implausible.

However, in the US, there is evidence that student performance on standardized tests administered at the secondary level has shown a continuous decline since the late sixties (Wirtz et al., 1977). To the degree that these test scores serve to reflect student job skills, it might be argued that a larger and larger group of students leave secondary schools without the skill to obtain productive work. Of course, there is a great deal of debate about what the test score declines actually mean.[11] However, even if we accept this evidence as reflecting a true decline in the job skills of the young, there is the larger issue of cause or effect. That is, are the declining test scores a response to the deteriorating employment prospects or are they the cause of it? It is probably reasonable to assume that most students in secondary school pursue their studies, not because of the intrinsic value of the educational experience, but because of compulsory attendance laws and the expectation that what is learned will have value in the labour market. This is the principal reason that many students are willing to tolerate the boredom of the classroom and the discipline of the school. It is expected that at least a tolerable level of effort is necessary to succeed well enough in school to have access to a decent job.

Thus, a rather different interpretation of the relation between youth unemployment and falling test score performances of youth is that youth are devoting less effort to the traditional requirements of secondary education as the payoffs to such schooling decline. In the US, this phenomenon may be exacerbated by the increasingly relaxed admissions policies of colleges and universities as they scramble for a relatively smaller number of students in the aftermath of the record enrolments created by the baby boom generation. College admission is no longer as competitive a phenomenon as it was in the sixties, as students are successful in gaining access to institutions of similar status with lower test scores and poorer achievement in traditional academic subjects. Under such conditions, the incentives to devote long hours to study and to pursue some of the more difficult elective courses have subsided.

In summary, the view that a decline in education and training standards relative to skill requirements of jobs is responsible for youth unemployment seems to have little support. The sheer scarcity of jobs for both youth and adults suggests that, at best, education may be used as a rationing device to determine who has greatest access to available employment. But this does not mean that more jobs would be forthcoming for all youth or adults with higher educational attainments. Moreover, falling test scores seem to be more of a response to the depressed job market for youth than a cause of it.

Poor Overall Economic Conditions

This brings us to the fourth explanation of youth unemployment, that of poor aggregate economic conditions. This explanation suggests that as unemployment rises generally in the economy, youth are particularly vulnerable because of their lack of training and experience. Firms tend to be more willing to retain their experienced workers than to keep ones with low seniority or to hire new ones with no experience. Further, a lack of hiring will mean that those persons just entering the labour market will be most affected by the paucity of new opportunities. Thus youth can be expected to suffer more from aggregate unemployment, with rates that exceed considerably the average level of unemployment. Under such a situation, there will simply be far more persons seeking jobs than available positions, and youth will have the least access to the openings that do exist.

The policy solution for high levels of general unemployment is to stimulate the economy through monetary and fiscal policies. More specifically, expansion of the money supply and planned deficits in the public budget have been used in the period since World War II to increase the level of national income and employment in virtually all of the western industrialized societies. In addition, specific programs for creating jobs for young persons through public employment and subsidies of jobs in the private sector would be used to augment the macro-economic solution for stimulating the economy (Palmer, 1978; US Congressional Budget Office, 1977). These policies are, themselves, fraught with problems which will be discussed in the next section. But, if unemployment results from an economy which is operating below capacity, policies to stimulate the economy should increase employment along with those designed to augment particularly the job demand for youth.

The evidence that poor aggregate economic conditions and overall unemployment comprise the primary determinant of youth unemployment seems to be the most convincing single explanation. It is clearly the only explanation that fits closely the timing of changes in youth unemployment and its magnitude. As the overall unemployment rates for the two economies have varied, so have rates of youth unemployment. That is, youth seem to be the principal victims of the aggregate economic situation as reflected in the table, Unemployment Rates for Selected Years and Age Groups, and the more detailed time series describing the age composition of unemployment. For the US a one percentage point rise in the adult male unemployment rate is associated with a 4-6 per cent decrease in the proportion of males in the 16- to 19-year-old group who are unemployed (Clark and Summers, 1980:4). That is, youth tend to bear a disproportionate share of increase in unemployment.

This finding is further buttressed by a study of employment rates of young males in major metropolitan areas of the US for 1970. In that study, an attempt was made to explore the relationship between adult unemployment in metropolitan areas and teenage employment patterns. With each one percentage point rise in adult male unemployment among metropolitan areas, there was a fall in the proportion of youth who were employed of 3-5 per cent with the largest negative impacts on teenage unemployment (Freeman and Wise, 1979:10).

The evidence on this point is so compelling that a recent analytic report on the youth labour market by the US Department of Labor concluded:

> Perhaps the most significant fact about the youth labor market from a policy viewpoint is the severe disruption brought about by declining aggregate economic conditions. The initial job is more difficult to procure, young workers are more likely to be pushed out of their jobs, the duration of unemployment is extended, and wage growth is depressed. (US Department of Labor, 1979: 163-4)

In summary, although four principal causes were posited for explaining the rise of youth unemployment in Australia and the US, the deterioration in overall economic conditions in the two countries seems to be the most important determinant of the phenomenon. The increase in the relative numbers of youth in the labour market, minimum wages, and declining educational standards may have had some impact, although the evidence on each tends to be contradictory. However, the state of the economy has shown a consistent and substantial relationship to youth unemployment, and it can be concluded that it is the key factor.[12]

Policy Directions and Education

According to the preceding analysis, the problem of youth unemployment is unlikely to yield to an educational solution for the reason that it is not primarily an educational dilemma. Rather, it is attributable in large measure to an economy that has provided fewer jobs than there are jobseekers. In this section, we will explore possible policy directions with respect to how to address youth unemployment, with special emphasis on the possible educational aspects. An underlying aspect of the discussion is the assumption that educational and training programs can only be a part of the overall solution, not the central solution.

Aggregate Economic Policies

The usual response to unemployment and low economic growth in societies like Australia and the US is to stimulate the economy through both fiscal and monetary policy. By increasing the effective demand for goods and services through reducing taxes and raising government expenditures as well as by expanding the availability of credit and the money supply, the output and employment of the economy are expected to rise. Since youth unemployment is closely related to overall economic conditions and the rate of unemployment, the unemployment of youth could be expected to fall as general economic conditions improved.

But, in recent years, there have been limits to the ability to stimulate the economy through monetary and fiscal devices. Perhaps the most important obstacle has been that of high levels of inflation. Expansionary policies tend to trigger higher price levels by increasing both demand for goods and services and by creating tighter labour markets that enable workers to obtain higher wages. Even in the absence of expansionary policies in the US and Australia, increases in the price level have been substantial and troublesome.[13] There has been a reluctance to push for expansionary policies that will increase imports and raise prices of exports at a time of chronic deficits in the balance of trade. Further, monopoly concentration in both economies has meant that the responses to rising demand may be bottlenecks and shortages in some sectors with continuing problems of overcapacity in others, while multinational firms ignore national priorities by pursuing an international rationalization of production that will maximize their profits.

A fuller response is to combine monetary and fiscal policy with the active labour market approach that has been developed most fully in Sweden, but has been emulated in most of the industrialized countries including Australia and the US. Such an approach acknowledges that aggregate economic policies in themselves will not work appropriately to address unemployment and low economic growth, unless they are augmented by other policies that will address structural problems in the economy (Rehn, 1980). Thus monetary and fiscal policies are supplemented by subsidies to particular industries and firms in depressed regions, by substantial investment in training and retraining programs, by public employment programs and public subsidies for private sector jobs[14], by substantial public assistance for the unemployed, by tax incentives and other promotional assistance for export industries, and by possible trade barriers on a selective basis against imports that threaten national industries.

For the foreseeable future, policies like these will be used to address unemployment in Australia and the US with clear limits to their potential success. In part the limits derive from the fear of inflationary effects, and in part from the political realities that constrain such policies. Increases in public spending must come from either higher taxes or greater public debt. The former response invites taxpayer opposition and revolt, and the latter tends to fuel inflation. Further, it is difficult to pursue national labour market policies, if substantial numbers of the firms that participate are multinational in nature. The latter firms have not only the options available to them in a given society, but also potential options around the world. This means that they may seek subsidies as a form of blackmail to maintain their production facilities in a particular country or set governments against each other in the competition to provide incentives for plant location or expansion.

Further, job-subsidy programs for the private sector may simply provide support for those firms that were already expanding employment. That is, at any given time some sectors will be expanding and others receding, and the same is true for firms. To a large degree, subsidies that are provided for 'new' jobs will simply support jobs that would have been forthcoming in any case. In addition, the political realities are that the large corporate firms are more likely to receive subsidies, loans, and other incentives than small businesses. The reasons for this are not only the greater political power of the larger firms, but also the relatively substantial employment or unemployment effects of changes in such entities. Relatively speaking, the employment intensity of small businesses is generally far greater than larger ones, and an equal subsidy to the small business sector is likely to absorb more of the unemployed than one to large businesses (World Bank, 1978). But small businesses lack the political power of the multinational corporate behemoths.

In summary, to the degree that active labour policies are used to promote economic growth and full employment, they are limited by their inflationary potential and a political process which supports certain industries and sectors at the expense of others. Although investment in the less capital-intensive small business sector is likely to create more jobs than investment in the corporate sector, political realities favour the largest entities. Moreover, active labour market policies are limited by their relatively high tax requirements; for, when economies are suffering from low economic growth and underemployment, there is likely to be a large resistance to rising taxes. Thus the future of active labour market policies for substantially reducing youth unemployment can hardly be viewed as an optimistic one.

Education and Youth Unemployment

Given this general background on aggregate economic policies to address unemployment, it is appropriate to return to the specific policies for reducing youth unemployment with special emphasis on educational concerns. However, it is important to point out the two major choices before us. Given a dearth of available jobs, many job seekers will be unemployed at any one time. As some get jobs, others will be displaced from work. In both Australia and the US, such unemployment is not distributed randomly among different social groups. Rather its burden is vested heavily among youth, and in the US among non-white youth.

There are two ways to reduce youth unemployment. The first is to improve overall economic conditions so that all groups, including youth, benefit. The second is to create programs exclusively for youth, often at the expense of older workers. Most concrete suggestions for improving the employment situation of youth tend to follow the latter strategy; that is, to redistribute the burden of unemployment from youth to adults. For example, it has been suggested that the employment of youth would be more attractive in Australia (Corden, 1979) and the US (Coleman et al., 1974:168) if youth were eligible for a lower minimum wage.

It is true that the provision of a lower minimum wage for youth is likely to shift jobs from low-wage adults to lower-wage youths. But, in the US, even the present minimum wage for full-time adult workers is not adequate to provide a standard of living for supporting a small family above poverty levels. Yet a dual minimum wage would reduce employment among such adults to provide more jobs for youth. Further, when public employment and subsidized jobs in the private sector are targeted for youth, this is necessarily done at the expense of adults who might have received those benefits. Even more to the point, education and training programs that give youth a greater competitive edge in the labour market will ultimately have the effect of displacing adults who would have received these jobs.

In fact, the most distressing aspect of youth employment programs is that, if they are successful at getting youth employed, they must necessarily create unemployment for other groups. Whether this is good public policy is obviously a normative issue. That is, one could argue that the terrible dilemma of youth unemployment requires that, at the very least, other parts of the population share the burden of inadequate employment.[15] Therefore, by equalizing the burden among all groups, there is a fairer outcome. However, the counter view is that, as bad as the situation is for youth, it is even worse when adults are unemployed. Youth typically have few financial responsibilities beyond their own personal needs, and they are often able to obtain room and board and other types of assistance from their parents. In contrast, adults have heavy financial obligations and other responsibilities associated with the support of other family members and health problems that arise as one gets older.

Given a movement towards a more pro-youth policy, targeted education and training programs for youth will certainly have some effect on improving the position of youth in labour markets. While such educational and training programs have not shown notable success in the past — often because training has taken place in fields where there is already a surplus of job-seekers — it certainly would seem possible to improve their performances.[16] Foremost in improving these programs would be more careful attention to matching the actual needs of the labour market with the training required to perform well in those jobs. Even better would be a job-contracting approach between training centres and employers, that committed employers to take a minimum number of trained youth who met particular skill requirements. However, even these gains by youth would tend to be at the expense of older workers who had not received the training.

A second type of educational approach is that of using educational leave programs as ways of increasing the number of labour market openings. A number of countries in western Europe have initiated programs of paid educational leave, where workers have a right to a periodic period of study that is paid for out of a fund that is financed by a payroll tax on employers and employees (Von Moltke and Schneevoight, 1976). Presumably, educational leaves provide a means to upgrade the skills of workers while creating openings for new workers to replace those who are taking such leave. Indeed, in Holland, this approach is seen as an important tool for actively promoting a reduction in unemployment (Emmerij, 1979). Since the plan is based upon a voluntary rotation of the labour force in which those on leave improve their own skills, it tends to increase the welfare of both the persons on leave as well as those who gain employment by these policies. The biggest obstacles from a social perspective are matching the needs of employers with the available supply of unemployed workers as well as finding new positions that will use the training of those who return from educational leave.

Another voluntary approach to increasing employment opportunities for youth through education would be to promote, to a greater extent, careers that enable part-time employment in combination with part-time study. The advantage of such a plan would be that a larger number of youth would be able to obtain job experiences through job sharing, while still enabling further training and education on a part-time basis. In both Australia and the US, the incentives tend to be patterned in the direction of full-time work or full-time employment. On the employment side, many employers seek full-time workers for jobs rather than considering the sharing of jobs among two workers. Further, student subsidies and scholarships are typically limited primarily to full-time students on the basis that the part-time student already has adequate financial support from his or her work. By designing public policies to encourage more part-time opportunities in both public and private employment and the provision of student subsidies for part-time study, it is possible to increase the number of youth in both the work place and schools.

Finally, the gravity of the youth unemployment situation calls for bold new approaches to both job creation and training. One possibility would be the establishment of youth producer co-operatives, firms that would be both owned and democratically managed by their workers. Such establishments would cater for young persons by requiring that half or two-thirds of their positions be allotted to workers under the age of 25. The reason for including older workers would be to provide a core of experienced workers to create stability in the firm and guidance for those with less experience. The fact that these firms would be owned and democratically operated by their workers would create strong attachments of workers to the work process because all would share in the success of the enterprise. Further, the shape of the work environment would be determined by the workers themselves.

Producer co-operatives have typically devoted themselves to extensive on-the-job training and job rotation so that workers obtain skills in a variety of areas. Further, they have been shown to have relatively low capital requirements and high productivity in contrast to more conventional firms (Levin, 1980; Jackall and Levin, forthcoming). The government could assist with financing, organization, and initial training with the same funds that would otherwise be used for public employment or private sector job subsidies. However, ultimately the youth producer co-operatives should be self-sustaining. Such firms would be developed in areas of social needs for which the private sector is not responding adequately. For example, the production of energy-saving products or manufacture and installation of solar-heating devices are prospective areas of continued market growth.

These firms could also be linked to secondary schools, training institutes, and universities by providing opportunities for part-time members and more limited ownership and voting rights. Thus some individuals could advance to full-time status upon graduation, while others would leave for full-time positions elsewhere. The firms would also benefit youth by emphasizing co-operative training and problem solving in the production and marketing spheres. Such firms would have the advantages of both creating jobs and continuing training in a flexible way that connected secondary and tertiary educational institutions to labour markets.

Summary

Since youth unemployment is not primarily an educational problem, education and training must be viewed as a part of the solution rather than its core. Rather, job creation and increased employment for the economy as a whole are the necessary conditions for addressing youth unemployment. However, various educational and training programs can give youth a greater competitive advantage relative to adults than they presently have, increasing youth employment at the expense of their older colleagues. Further, systems of paid educational leave and the encouragement of part-time work and part-time schooling combinations can rotate existing job opportunities among a larger number of persons. Finally, bold new approaches that can create jobs at relatively low cost and combine them with further training while connecting schools to the overall labour market would have the most promise. One possibility that appears particularly promising is the youth producer co-operative, but no educational or training device should be viewed, in itself, as a major onslaught on youth unemployment.

It is important to emphasize that, in both the US and in Australia, the attack on youth unemployment has largely been a war of words. When educators and others talk of career education and the need to develop an institutional transition from school to work, there is a certain futility to their rhetoric; for, whatever the justification is of providing additional knowledge about the working world and further work experience or training, these devices do not address the fundamental issue of inadequate employment opportunities. There will be no solution to the problem of youth unemployment without more jobs, and little improvement is likely in the relatively high turnover of youth among existing jobs without greater job challenges and more opportunities for career growth rather than dead-end jobs.

Although education and training policies can be used to support the necessary preparation required for new jobs and ones with greater challenge for youth, the strategies of job creation and enrichment must come first. The persistent failure of economies that are dominated by a relatively small number of powerful, multinational, corporate entities to provide full employment and price stability has raised a much larger issue for the eighties. Can social objectives in the economic sphere be obtained without democratic control of the economy; that is, a movement towards economic democracy? (Carnoy and Shearer, 1980) Or should we continue to leave these crucial decisions to a relatively few and powerful enterprises operating on a global basis with the hope that their quest for profits is compatible with our basic societal needs for full employment, stable prices, economic growth, and social equity?

Notes

[1] There are substantial publications for each country on the general issue of youth unemployment and on its specific aspects. This literature is so voluminous that no attempt will be made to summarize it here, although pertinent citations are made in different parts of this paper. For Australia, a good summary of the situation is found in Karmel (1979). For the US, summaries are found in Freeman and Wise (1979), Adams and Mangum (1978), and Newman (1979). Societies like Australia and the US are different enough in so many aspects of their economies and educational systems that comparative studies of the causes and solutions for youth unemployment are risky. Accordingly this paper will attempt to explore general patterns for the two societies rather than make detailed comparisons. An attempt to carry out a more rigorous comparative endeavour and its hazards is found in Layard (1980) which contrasts the US and UK. See especially the criticisms of his work that follow the presentation.

[2] One issue that will not be addressed in this paper is the accuracy of unemployment rates

in reflecting unemployment. The numbers reflect only those persons who did not have employment and were looking for work at the time of the survey. Thus, they are not adjusted for persons who withdrew from the labour force because of poor prospects or persons working part-time who desired full-time work. A discussion of some of these issues across major surveys in the US is found in Freeman and Medoff (1980). Further, if youth increase their length of job search over time to obtain better jobs or take and leave jobs in relatively rapid succession to search for better employment, the effect on the unemployment rate and its interpretation become even more open to controversy. See, for example, Leighton and Mincer (1980), Hall (1980), and the comments following both articles that present critiques of their interpretations.

[3] I am indebted to Professor R.W. Connell of Macquarie University for this point.

[4] Obviously the incentives for completion of any level of schooling are related to both the opportunities for early leavers and those for graduates. If the economic returns to graduates are very high relative to those for leavers, the incentives to complete school are high. For a technical analysis of these relations, see Becker (1964).

[5] For an example of how even the most sophisticated analyses of statistical time series can lead to ambiguous results, see Wachter and Kim (1980). Analyses of the effects of federal minimum wages in the US on the employment of youth tend to lead to different conclusions, depending on whether measures of the changes in youth demography that paralleled rises in the minimum wage are included in the analysis. Thus studies that find a negative impact of rises in the minimum wage on youth employment omit a measure of increases in youth cohorts, and those that find no impact include such a measure. See US Congressional Budget Office (1976:33–39).

[6] According to the Australian Bureau of Statistics, the absolute number of 15- to 19-year-olds is declining at present, with no obvious impact on unemployment rates. See Australia. Committee of Inquiry into Education and Training (1979:Vol. 1, 587).

[7] It is also noteworthy that the US labour market has been able to deal with a tripling in the proportion of the population that has been seeking work in the summer for the first time, without an appreciable increase in unemployment rates. See Wachter and Kim (1980:16–21).

[8] See note [5] on the varying estimates of effects of minimum wages on unemployment. Even if it is assumed that the largest estimated effects are valid (a dubious assumption), they would explain only a small proportion of youth unemployment. For example, Ragan (1977) estimated that the increase of the minimum wage in 1966 in the US caused unemployment rates for white teenagers to be almost four percentage points higher and for black teenagers about three percentage points higher in 1972 than in the absence of that rise in the minimum wage. This estimate would have left over 70 per cent of the unemployment rate of white teenagers and almost 90 per cent of the unemployment rate of black teenagers to be explained by other factors. See also Lovell (1972).

[9] The assumption that skill levels for satisfactory performance in an occupation are rising is highly controversial. What empirical evidence does exist tends to support the opposite conclusion. See, for example, Bright (1966), Rumberger (1981), Braverman (1974), and Berg, Freedman, and Freeman (1978).

[10] ibid.

[11] For example, even when test scores are found to be related statistically to employment success and earnings, the relation seems rather trivial. For example, a recent US study found that an increase in student test scores of one standard deviation (from the 50th percentile to the 84th percentile) was associated with a wage rate that was about 3 per cent higher and about one additional week of employment annually. See Meyer and Wise (1980).

[12] This is clearly the conclusion of studies on the overall youth labour market such as Clark and Summers (1980) and US Department of Labor (1979).

[13] The average increases in price levels between 1970-78 for Australia and the US were 12.8 and 6.8 per cent respectively. See World Bank (1980:111).

¹⁴ For analyses of both expansion of public sector jobs and subsidized jobs in the private sector see the essays in Palmer (1978) and Bishop and Haveman (1978).

¹⁵ Possibly the shifting of the unduly high unemployment burden of non-whites to whites might be desirable, even if an overall reduction in unemployment cannot be attained. It should be noted that since non-whites are a smaller proportion of the population than whites, a large reduction in non-white unemployment in the US could be done with only a small increase in white unemployment. The absurdity of all this is in its debate over how to share the shortage of jobs, where the shortage itself is taken for granted.

¹⁶ It is remarkable how much the public-policy solution for youth is still focused on education and training programs, given their relatively dismal past and the fact that, even if they are successful, they are likely only to redistribute the unemployment from youth to adults. For present initiatives in Australia, see Carrick and Viner (1979) and their proposal, A Comprehensive Policy for Transition from School to Work. For the US, see the Youth Employment Act that was wending its way through Congress in Autumn 1980. The latest version at the time that this paper was being drafted was printed in *Congressional Record*, 27 September 1980. The rather depressing record of educational and training programs for the disadvantaged with respect to improving their economic status for the first ten years of the War on Poverty are reviewed in Levin (1977).

¹⁷ This tends to be recognized by many policy makers, but the political attractiveness of training and education tend to push public policy in that direction. See, for example, the options set out by the US Congressional Budget Office (1976). The education and training solution has certain attractive qualities, such as the ideological one of helping youth to help themselves and implicitly placing the blame on youth for their own failure to find work until they are properly trained. In contrast, policies of job creation are expensive, interfere with the private market, and tend to place blame on the society and its economic system for not creating enough jobs for all who wish to work at reasonable wages. See Harrington (1980) and Thurow (1980). A more optimistic view is given in National Council on Employment Policy (1980).

References

Adams, V. and Mangum, G.L. *The Lingering Crisis of Youth Unemployment*. Kalamazoo, MI: W.E. Upjohn Institute for Employment Research, 1978.
Australia. Committee of Inquiry into Education and Training. *Education, Training, and Employment*. (Chairman: B.R. Williams). 2 vols. Canberra: AGPS, 1979.
Australian Bureau of Statistics (ABS). *Social Indicators*. (No. 2–1978). Canberra: 1978.
———. Table 1, Unemployed persons (a). *Unemployment Australia . . . Preliminary Estimates*, (ABS Catalogue No. 6201.0), 1980, (March), 3.
Becker, B.E. and Hills, S.N. Teenage unemployment: Some evidence of the long-run effects on wages, *Journal of Human Resources*, 1980, 15 (3), 354–72.
Becker, G. *Human Capital*. New York: Columbia University Press, 1974.
Berg, I., Freedman, M. and Freeman, M. *Managers and Work Reform*. New York: Free Press, 1978.
Bishop, J. and Haveman, R. *Targeted Employment Subsidies: Issues of Structure and Design*. (Special Report Series, SR 24). Madison, WI: University of Wisconsin, Institute for Research on Poverty, 1978.
Bowers, N. Young and marginal: An overview of youth unemployment. In US Department of Labor, Bureau of Labor Statistics, *Young Workers and Families: A Special Section*. (Special Labor Force Report 233). Washington, DC: 1979, 4–18.
Braverman, H. *Labor and Monopoly Capital*, New York: Monthly Review Press, 1974.
Bright, J. The relationship of increasing automation and skill requirements. In United States, National Commission on Technology, Automation, and Economic Progress, *The Employment Impact of Technological Change:* The Report . . . Appendix Volume II. Washington, DC: Government Printing Office, 1966, II-207-21.

Brown, C. Dead-end Jobs and Youth Unemployment. (NBER Conference Paper No. 31). Cambridge, MA: National Bureau of Economic Research, 1980. To be published in Freeman and Wise, op. cit.

Burke, G. Teenage Unemployment and Educational Participation. Presentation to 50th ANZAAS Jubilee Congress, Adelaide, 12-16 May 1980. Clayton, Vic.: Monash University, Faculty of Education, 1980.

Carnoy, M. and Shearer, D. *Economic Democracy: The Challenge of the 1980s.* White Plains, NY: M.E. Sharpe Inc., 1980.

Carrick, J.L. and Viner, I. A Comprehensive Policy for Transition from School to Work. Statement by the Minister for Education and the Minister for Employment and Youth Affairs, 22 November 1979. Canberra, 1979.

Clark, K.B. and Summers, L.H. The Dynamics of Youth Unemployment. (NBER Conference Paper No. 26). Cambridge, MA: National Bureau of Economic Research, 1980. To be published in Freeman and Wise, op. cit.

Coleman, J.S. et al. *Youth: Transition to Adulthood.* Chicago: University of Chicago Press, 1974.

Colless, M. PM slams schools for youth job problems. *The Australian,* 15 January 1980, p. 2.

Corcoran, M. The Employment and Wage Consequences of Teenage Women's Nonemployment. (NBER Conference Paper No. 30), Cambridge, MA: National Bureau of Economic Research, 1980. To be published in Freeman and Wise, op. cit.

Corden, W.M. Wages and unemployment in Australia. *Economic Record,* 1979, **55,** 1–19.

Ellwood, D.T. Teenage Unemployment: Permanent Scars or Temporary Blemishes. (NBER Conference Paper No. 29). Cambridge, MA: National Bureau of Economic Research, 1980. To be published in Freeman and Wise, op. cit.

Emmerij, L. Paid Educational Leave with Particular Emphasis on its Financial Aspects. Paper prepared for Project on Financing Recurrent Education. Paris: OECD, 1979.

Fraser, M. Extract from Address to the National Convention of the Young Liberal Movement. Bundoora, Vic.: La Trobe University, 1980.

Freeman, R.B. and Medoff, J.L. Why Does the Rate of Youth Labor Force Activity Differ across Surveys? (NBER Conference Paper No. 23). Cambridge, MA: National Bureau of Economic Research, 1980). To be published in Freeman and Wise, forthcoming, op. cit.

Freeman, R.B. and Wise, D.A. Youth Unemployment. (NBER Summary Report). Cambridge, MA: National Bureau of Economic Research, 1979.

——. (Eds). *The Youth Employment Problem: Its Nature, Causes and Consequences.* Chicago: University of Chicago Press, forthcoming.

Ginzberg, E. Youth unemployment. *Scientific American,* 1980, **242** (5), 43–9.

Gamlich, E.M. Impact of minimum wages on other wages, employment and family incomes. *Brookings Papers on Economic Activity,* 1976, **2,** 409–51.

Hall, E. The Minimum Wage and Job Turnover in Markets for Young Workers. (NBER Conference Paper No. 33). Cambridge, MA: National Bureau of Economic Research, 1980). To be published in Freeman and Wise, forthcoming, op. cit.

Harrington, M. *Decade of Decision.* New York: Simon & Schuster, 1980.

Hoare, J. Fraser gives the schools a serve. *Financial Review,* 26 August 1980, p. 7.

Jackall, R. and Levin, H.M. (Eds). *Producer Cooperatives in the US* (forthcoming).

Karmel, P. *Youth, Education and Employment.* Hawthorn, Vic.: Australian Council for Educational Research, 1979.

Layard, R. Youth Unemployment in Britain and the U.S. Compared, (NBER Conference Paper No. 34). Cambridge, MA: National Bureau of Economic Research, 1980. To be published in Freeman and Wise, forthcoming, op. cit.

Leighton, L. and Mincer, J. Labor Turnover and Youth Unemployment. (NBER Conference Paper No. 27). Cambridge, MA: National Bureau of Economic Research, 1980. To be published in Freeman and Wise, forthcoming, op. cit.

———. A decade of policy development in improving education and training of low income populations. In R. Haveman, (Ed.), *A Decade of Federal Antipoverty Programs: Achievements, Failures, and Lessons.* New York: Academic Press, 1977, Ch. 4.

Levin, H.M. Improving the Creative Potential of Human Resources with Producer Cooperatives. Invited paper for Sixth World Congress of International Economic Association, Mexico City, August 1980.

Lovell, M. The minimum wage, teenage unemployment, and the business cycle. *Western Economic Journal,* December 1972, pp. 414-27.

Mangum, G.L. and Seninger, S.F. *Coming of Age in the Ghetto: A Dilemma of Youth Unemployment.* Baltimore, MD: Johns Hopkins Press, 1978.

Melvyn, P. and Freedman, D.H. Youth unemployment: A worsening situation. In D.H. Freedman (Ed.), *Employment Outlook and Insights.* Geneva: International Labour Office, 1979, 81–92.

Meyer, A. and Wise, D.A. High School Preparation and Early Labor Force Experience. (NBER Conference Paper No. 28). Cambridge, MA: National Bureau of Economic Research, 1980. To be published in Freeman and Wise, forthcoming, op. cit.

National Council on Employment Policy. *An Employment Policy to Fight Recession and Inflation.* Washington, DC: National Council on Employment Policy, 1980.

Newman, M.J. The Labor Market Experience of Black Youth, 1954–78. In US Department of Labor, Bureau of Labor Statistics, *Young Workers and Families: A Special Section,* (Special Labor Force Report 233). Washington DC: 1979, 19–27.

Palmer, J.L. (Ed.). *Creating Jobs.* Washington, DC: Brookings Institution, 1978.

Ragan, J.F. Jr. Minimum wages and the youth labor market, *Review of Economics and Statistics,* 1977, **59** (2), 129–36.

Rees, A. and Gray, W. Family Effects in Youth Unemployment. (NBER Conference Paper No. 32). Cambridge, MA: National Bureau of Economic Research, 1980). To be published in Freeman and Wise, forthcoming, op. cit.

Rehn, G. Expansion against stagflation — some unorthodox reflections based on the Swedish experience. *Working Life in Sweden,* 1980, No. 18. Available from the Swedish Information Service, Swedish Consulate General.

Rumberger, R. *Overeducation in the U.S. Labor Market.* New York: Praeger Publishers, 1981.

Thurow, L. *Generating Inequality.* New York: Basic Books, 1975.

———. *The Zero-Sum Society.* New York: Basic Books, Inc., 1980.

United States. Congressional Budget Office. *Budget Options for the Youth Employment Problem.* (Background Paper No. 20). Washington, DC: 1977.

———. *Policy Options for the Teenage Unemployment Problem.* (Background Paper No. 13). Washington, DC: 1976.

United States. Department of Labor. *Employment and Unemployment during 1979: An Analysis.* (Special Labor Force Report 234). Washington, DC: 1980.

———. Bureau of Labor Statistics. *The Youth Labor Market: A Dynamic Overview.* (BLS Staff Paper 11). Washington DC: 1979.

Von Moltke, K. and Schneevoight, N. *Educational Leaves for Employees: European Experience for American Consideration.* San Francisco: Jossey-Bass Publishers, 1976.

Wachter, M.L. and Kim, C. Time Series in Youth Joblessness. (NBER Conference Paper No. 26). Cambridge, MA: National Bureau of Economic Research, 1980. To be published in Freeman and Wise, forthcoming, op. cit.

Williams, B.R. *See* Australia. Committee of Inquiry into Education and Training.

Wirtz, W. et al. *On Further Examination: Report of the Advisory Panel on the Scholastic Aptitude Test Score Decline.* New York: College Entrance Examination Board, 1977.

World Bank. *Employment and Development of Small Enterprises.* (Sector Policy Paper). Washington, DC: 1978.

———. *World Development Report, 1980.* New York: Oxford University Press, 1980.

24

VOCATIONAL EDUCATION
Federal Policies for the 1980s

Paul E. Barton

The federal government played a key role in 1917 in creating a new segment of education at the high school level—vocational education. This federal initiative, the Smith Hughes Act, was successful in stimulating state and local activity. From time to time, the federal government has attempted to chart the course for this system, with recent significant legislation in 1963, 1968, and 1976. Given this strong role played by the federal partner, what policies are most appropriate for this decade, considering the central tendencies in the pattern for development of vocational education; and considering the needs of the economy in this period of inflation, declining productivity and the competitive position of our products in foreign markets?

This article posits seven policies for vocational education, policies desirable for the system and appropriate for pursuit by the federal partner, given the role it has chosen to play in this segment of the public education system.

> *Policy 1. Increasing collaboration among educators, employers, and union leaders in achieving the objectives of vocational education.*

The Vocational Education Act of 1917 was the product of a collaborative effort. We now think of education legislation

---

AUTHOR'S NOTE: *The article is drawn from a much longer document entitled* Vocations and Education Policy: A Federal Perspective, *by Paul E. Barton, forthcoming from the National Institute of Education.*

emerging from intensive lobbying from education bureaucracies, but vocational education legislation emerged after a combined campaign waged by the National Association of Manufacturers, the AFL-CIO, and educators intent on broadening high school education for youth going directly into employment.[1] In fact, the forerunner of the present American Vocational Association, the National Society for the Promotion of Industrial Education, brought into its membership a wide array of persons from agriculture, business, industry, government, and the public at large.

The principal actors in the 1917 drama assembled into a coalition because they had a common interest. Industry had skill needs. Enough educators believed the education system could supply them. Unions thought prospective workers should receive useful educations.

These perspectives are as valid today as they were in 1917. Yet the collaboration which started vocational education has seriously eroded. Business people talk about vocational education and, from their perspective, its inadequacies, rather than talk to—or work with—the people who run the system. Unions often slip into a protective stance, understandably worried about the effect of youth programs on adult employment. Vocational educators, part of a large bureaucracy, tend to get too isolated from the real world of business and industry. The result, too frequently, is that the work world changes and vocational education fails to change with it.

If the idea of vocational education as part of the public school system is going to realize its full promise, the kind of collaboration that invented it in the first place is going to have to be restored. There have been, from time to time, a number of laws and regulations designed to require participation in planning vocational education. But it is usually possible to comply with the forms of these laws without achieving their substance. The usual perception of the vocational education advisory committees that result from these planning requirements is that they *generally* achieve more the form than the substance of participation, although there are advisory committees that have contributed immensely to exemplary vocational education systems and schools.

New efforts to achieve a more collaborative effort are needed. If vocational education is developing skills for the employment system, the whole system has to become involved in it if this mode of imparting skills is to become a leading actor rather than just a supporting player. What is needed is a system in which the public (meaning public education), the employers, and the unions (where they are a significant factor in a business or industry) collaborate to (1) provide occupational training, (2) provide on-the-job work experience settings, and (3) provide access to relevant jobs after the skills are acquired. All of this should be done in a system in which goals in the area of *basic* education are also met.

A longer-range objective for achieving this collaboration would be to involve employers and unions more in the actual governance of vocational education. The best start in this direction would be the creation of a working party comprised of government, employer, and union representatives to work out a system whereby vocational education could become more a joint undertaking.

But while this longer-range approach is being planned, there are some practical immediate steps that could broaden participation and create models for the future. Some portion of vocational education funds could be earmarked for administration through existing collaborative councils comprised of education, employer, and union representatives, much in the fashion that a portion of funds of the Comprehensive Employment and Training Act have been earmarked in Title VII for control through the new Private Industry Councils.[2]

> *Policy 2. Recognizing the educational objectives of the vocational education approach, rather than a fixed focus on immediate placement outcomes, and striving for a system open to all who want it.*

While it is essential to involve industry in the vocational education enterprise, it is also essential to recognize that vocational education is a system of *education*, not a job *training* system. To be sure, the distinctions sometimes get a bit fine, but they are nonetheless real and important.

The first priority is that vocational education be good education—in reading, in writing, in computing, in listening, in problem solving. A single evaluation yardstick of the percentage of graduates immediately placed in "jobs for which they are trained," to use the common expression, is much too short a measure to apply. We must also ask how well they are educated. For one reason, employers need people with good basic educations. For another reason, in the United States we want to keep all options open for young people as long as possible, and this means keeping options open to pursue postsecondary education as well as immediate employment. You can't get into college if you can't read.

It is a matter of achieving a proper balance. To serve its students, vocational education has to equip them in light of what works in the marketplace, and this means being responsive to industry needs. But educational institutions are responsible as well for making independent judgments about what constitutes an education and in no way should become subservient to *narrowly* defined needs of individual employers. Its aim is vocational preparation to launch a lifetime of work and living, not to shape a worker for a narrow set of skills good for only one employer. There should be some tension between educators and industry, but in a climate where both recognize that their larger objectives are complementary. The head and hand debate in education will continue, and should. As Horowitz (1975) said, "the historic split between head work and hand work characterizes the teaching and learning processes since antiquity."

If the basic education is of high quality, there is no reason why vocational education graduates should not have a wide range of choices for postsecondary education. For it to be any other way would mean that tracking begins after junior high school, and that vocational education is known and expected to be a track that does not go past high school but goes only to lower, entry-level jobs (and if these high school graduates don't have high school level basic educations, they won't go to decent entry-level jobs either).[3]

In the beginning, federal policy encouraged a separation between vocational education and general education, through the Federal Board of Vocational Education, abolished in 1933. It is said of Charles Prosser, the first executive director of that board, that "in his brief tenure there, his passion for separate vocational schools and specific-task training of students for existing jobs produced policy directives, articles, and advice to thousands of like-minded advocates across the country" (see Cuban, 1981).

In the intervening decades, there have been cycles of separate schools and of integration of vocational education into comprehensive high schools.[4] Achieving an appropriate balance depends on achieving maximum integration of basic education and occupational preparation, wherever vocational programs are housed. Federal policy should encourage the maximum integration possible between occupational and general education.

Another approach that is needed is broadening the dimensions of the standards used to evaluate vocational education outcomes. We need to know the *educational* progress of all students. The recognized system for doing this is the National Assessment of Educational Progress (NAEP). However, NAEP does not separately identify vocational education students among the national sample of 17-year-olds being assessed for educational progress. The necessary background information should be collected in the examinations of 17-year-olds to identify students enrolled in vocational education, under what arrangements, and to what degree. This would enable a comparison over time of achievements in reading, writing, and mathematics, by region of the country and by socioeconomic level of the student. Such identification would recognize the dual objectives of vocational education—the providing of an education and preparation for a specific vocation.

> Policy 3. *Moving toward joint school-employer occupational instruction, with the burden of proof shifting to justify a solely classroom approach.*

Integration between occupational education and general education is not, by itself, enough. Occupational education itself generally needs both school and employer effort. Integration is required between schools and employers.

There has been a trend under way for some time in the direction of blending schooling and working together, at both the secondary and postsecondary levels of education. This has complemented a trend during that same period of time in which more adults have gone back to school on a part-time basis. Most of the work at the secondary level is work arranged by young people, although there has been some growth in cooperative education programs in vocational education, as well as in work study programs for the disadvantaged.

According to Evans and Herr (1978), "Despite strong opposition from vocational educators in the forties and early fifties, the program [of cooperative education] grew in secondary school enrollment from zero in 1930 to 117,000 in 1965-66 and to 312,000 in 1971-72.... The number is certainly higher now, but no one knows how much higher." They also report that "studies of the economics of vocational education have shown higher rates of return on investment in cooperative programs than in other types of vocational education." The 1968 amendments to the Vocational Education Act had a special section to encourage the development of cooperative programs.

One clear finding from national-level studies is the correlation between working part-time while still in high school and the unemployment rate after high school. The most comprehensive set of data (although not the only set) on this comes

TABLE 1

Hours Worked Per Week Senior Year	Average Unemployment Rate (%) (4¼ years after high school)
0	12
1-5	11
6-10	9
11-15	9
16-25	7
More than 25	6

SOURCE: Harrell and Wirtz, 1980.

from the National Longitudinal Survey of the high school class of 1972 (data for those who did not enroll full-time in postsecondary education) (see Table 1). This relationship holds irrespective of race or sex.

The experience basis for learning gets its clearest expression in education philosophy in the work of John Dewey, writing at the turn of the century, who said: "As formal teaching and training grow in extent, there is the danger of creating an undesirable split between the experience gained in more direct asociations, and what is required in school" (Dewey, 1916).

There are, however, a number of practical considerations and observations based on common sense. Together, they make a strong case for steadily enlarging the proportion of youth who have a combined work-learning option.

(1) Actual experience in real work settings is an aid to learning an occupational skill ... the reason industry relies so heavily on on-the-job training.
(2) In cooperative education, the school and employer work together to correct deficiencies.
(3) Joint work-study programs provide a job connection for after graduation.
(4) A market test is applied at all times; to interest employers in such joint efforts, the occupational areas must be ones in which demand is reasonably strong.
(5) Cooperative style education reduces the problem of having adequate equipment in the schools.

(6) In general, such joint ventures require the schools and employers to stay in communication.

Unfortunately, however, such joint school/employer programs command only a small portion of vocational education funds. Only 2.0% of federal funding (from the basic grant) goes for cooperative education, and 2.2% of nonfederal funds (Interim Report, 1980).

The burden of proof should now shift to showing why a particular occupational area should *not* be approached on a cooperative basis, before federal money is spent on teaching occupational skills. This would move toward a system in which continued adjustments would have to be made to market shifts and in which educators and employers would find it necessary to work together.

Policy 4. Better development and coordination of market information at the local level, both to keep vocational education offerings current with the market and to help in expanding employer use of vocational graduates.

There has been improvement in the availability of labor market information for vocational education planning, the results of a combination of events. One was the passage of the 1968 Vocational Education Amendments providing for transfer of money to the Labor Department to purchase better information. The efforts of the Labor Department culminated in guidebooks to states showing them how to translate national projections into state and metropolitan-area projections (1969); the merger of BLS economic growth modeling, using input matrices; and the creation of the BLS Occupation Employment Statistics program, getting occupational statistics directly from employers. Most important, from the point of view of process as well as advancement of technique, were the education amendments creating the National Occupational Information Coordinating Committee (NOICC) and the co-operating State Occupational Information Coordinating Committees (SOICCs), to bring the education and labor market agencies together.[5]

The developing view, often expressed, is that occupational projections should be a principal basis for curriculum planning. The view expressed here is that while they are important, their usefulness has to be kept in perspective, and the problem of an adequate information base for planning and decision making is more complex than just projecting occupational trends.[6]

Three recommendations are advanced to improve the information base.

1. The steps taken to coordinate development and use of labor market information through NOICC and the SOICCs have been important but do not reach down to the local level. The local counterpart should be created: *Community* Occupational Information Coordinating Committees, to bring local developers and users together.

2. There is a need, at the local level, to go beyond the occupational projections prepared by statisticians to get information directly from an area's employers to find out what hiring they are doing and what preparation they want their prospective employees to have.[7] In order to do this, the use of account managers is recommended. They would be on the staff of the school system and would make systematic visits to the area's employers.

3. The account manager approach would not be a passive one of collecting information and always adjusting to existing employer practices, but would also provide the vocational education system with the opportunity to convince employers to use more of its graduates.

> *Policy 5. Recognizing that it is facilitating the youth transition to work that is important, that classroom occupational education is only one element in the transition, and that federal policy should encourage states and localities to deal with all elements of the transition.*

The interest of the promoters of vocational education was in serving that large portion of youth going directly into the job market, as well as meeting the skill needs of industry. In the meantime, institutions have become larger—education institutions, employment institutions, and union institutions. The range of job offerings and occupational specializations has enlarged greatly. A geographic factor has come into the picture as metropolitan areas have grown. All this means that information needs to be better, more choices need to be made about vocations, brokers are often needed to help youth make the job connection, and young people need to be taught how to negotiate this complex labor market in order to land on their feet. None of this is being done very well in most places, although there are outstanding efforts that could serve as a guide for more general application.

Federal policy successfully encouraged the creation of classroom occupational training. But it has not made consistent efforts to effect the other activities that would deal with the *whole* of the youth transition to work. It is here proposed that federal policy now concentrate on these neglected matters, neglect which prompted this observation in a *Washington Post* editorial of December 28, 1980:

> In no other industrialized country are the transitions from school to work and from one job to another left so much to chance as in the United States.

There are three areas in which the transition to work needs improvement, beyond classroom occupational training.

Job placement. While there are good job placement systems in some school systems, their availability to in-school youth and recent graduates is a hit-or-miss proposition. The recommendation is that a portion of federal funds, matched by state and local funds, be provided for placement services that are available to all vocational *and* general track students, and that the state plan address the provisions of such services with the same seriousness as it now addresses occupational education.

Toward this end, there should be available at the national level (though not necessarily in the federal government) modest technical assistance and training to assist states to establish quality services and to provide them with successful models.

Job search education. While there should be regular placement assistance available for students on a routine basis, the person with the primary responsibility for finding jobs, throughout working life, is the individual job seeker. Even when assistance is provided in breaking into the market, there will be a number of job changes during working life. The teaching of an occupational skill does not, itself, provide the necessary instruction for how to navigate in complex labor markets and how to approach employers in ways that will be successful. When interviewed two and a half years after graduation, 47% of the high school class of 1972 reported having gotten their jobs by applying directly to employers and 36% through leads from friends and relatives. Only 6% got jobs through formal means such as the public employment service, 8.6% through school placement services and 4.2% through private agencies (National Center for Educational Statistics, 1975).

We put them on their own; we should teach them how to do it. In the last few years, experience has been gained in teaching "job search skills" under various CETA programs for the disadvantaged and under career education banners. Federal policy should encourage states and localities to provide young people with basic knowledge about the operation of the job market and how to conduct themselves in it—education that is practical and experiential, rather than abstract and theoretical.

Employment assistance officers. There is a growing recognition that we have come to rely on professional "counseling and guidance personnel" for too many things, particularly in view of the fact that their numbers have been inadequate in high schools. Whether for good or bad, the evolution of that profession has been away from assisting high school graduates with immediate postschool and in-school job choice and job finding to counseling built on the treatment model of psychology and psychiatry, giving the counselor an ever larger number of duties to perform.

It is time to be inventive and create a small cadre of personnel in schools and in communities who are equipped to tell all young people leaving high school without immediate college plans what is out there, what they have to do to be prepared, and what employers offer that fits their interests. These people do not have to be professional counselors; their base of knowledge is in the job market. They might well work, however, under the general supervision of a counseling department.

Policy 6. Aiding in occupational adjustments and aiding employers upgrading their labor force.

It should not be forgotten that the vocational education of adults is an important objective of the vocational education system. To specify exactly how large that enterprise currently is would require agreement on definitions and choices among several ways of doing the counting. The NCES survey of participation in adult education shows enrollments in 1978 of 711,000 full-time vocational students over 24 years of age. The Bureau of Occupational and Adult Education showed total enrollments of 3.5 million adults in occupational education.

Expansion of adult occupational training has been dramatic over the last decade, particularly in part-time enrollments in junior and community colleges. The vocational education system is involved to varying extents in these developments, depending on the funding patterns and organizational arrangements in individual states.

The successful transition from school to work is important. But so is the ability of adults to make transitions back to education. A principal reason why adults go back to school is occupational, in one form or another—to advance in a job, to change jobs, or to adjust to another occupation when they have been dislocated from their employment.

Only a few priority matters with regard to adult learning will be treated here which are of particular relevance to the vocational education system and the federal role in it.[8] One is the need to help workers dislocated from jobs prepare for new ones. Another is the need for vocational education to work cooperatively with industry both in skill upgrading and in working collaboratively to help workers take advantage of the tuition aid benefits available to them from their employers or unions or under collective bargaining agreements.

OCCUPATIONAL ADJUSTMENT ASSISTANCE

A dynamic economy based on principles of free enterprise requires adjustments on the part of all participants in it. A most remarkable attribute of American workers is that they have been very enterprising in making the transitions required. Hundreds of thousands are doing so every year, out of their own resources, and using their own initiative and ingenuity. However, not all are successful, and not all can do it without help. There are those who find that they need to change to a wholly different occupation and that it requires further education or retraining to do so.

The use of occupational education/training as a means of facilitating the adjustment of dislocated workers has dwindled, and what is left of the effort is almost wholly targeted on people who meet a means test. I argue that such retraining as a measure to prevent people dislocated by economic shifts from being thrown into poverty is also a worthy public objective, and one that contributes to the ability of the economic system to remain vital. I also argue that the benefits of free and unfettered adjustments of business enterprises to shifts in markets and new market opportunities accrue to all, and that the hardships imposed on the relatively few workers who must be dislocated because of these necessary shifts should soon be borne by all, not just the dislocated workers. The Federal Vocational Education Act should stimulate the expansion of retraining opportunities for displaced workers.

A PUBLIC-PRIVATE SECTOR RELATIONSHIP

Moving forward with the adult learning enterprise involves adults who want to both work and go to school. The tremendous growth in adult learning in the last decade has been in part-time students. In order to serve adults, many of the traditional practices used for young and full-time students must be abandoned. In the adult learner enterprise there are several potential beneficiaries, all of whom must work together if that potential is to be realized. Employers want career advancement. Unions advocate educational opportunity for their members. Educational institutions are more and more turning to adult learners to compensate for the loss of young learners.

The first fact of interest to all these potential beneficiaries is the growing availability of funds in the private sector for education and training. One element of this growth is the large expenditure of business enterprises for internal education and training directly related to a production objective. The other is the increasing use of "tuition-aid" arrangements through which employers (and sometimes unions) pay the costs of part-time education outside of working hours.

These tuition-aid benefits are growing in availability, but only a small proportion of employees are taking advantage of them. Only four to five percent avail themselves of these benefits, and only one or two percent of blue-collar workers use them.[9] While a number of reasons explain this limited use, experimental work by the National Manpower Institute (now the National Institute for Work and Learning) established that increasing information to workers about these plans, providing educational counseling services, helping them deal with educational institutions, and getting educational institutions to tailor their offerings more to workers' needs (in content, time, and place) will increase workers' use of these benefits and enlarge enrollments in education institutions.

From the standpoint of federal policy, enrollments can be enlarged through this avenue with much less expenditure of public funds than would otherwise be the case. What is involved is the exercise of some leadership to get communities and the vocational/technical schools in them to maximize these opportunities.

This leadership could be exercised through the funding of a number of experimental and demonstration projects through educational institutions in order to perfect approaches to this opportunity and create models for other institutions to learn from. Recommended is a series of tuition aid pilot programs to create a base of experience in education and employment institutions working together in this area.

The pilot programs would involve

- collaborative arrangements between schools and employment institutions;
- the provision of information and brokering services;
- identifying what workers want and where they are comfortable getting further education; and
- experimenting with the ways to deal with the problem that these plans usually reimburse the employee after completion of the course, and many are not able to pay "up front."

Tuition aid arrangements are by no means the only basis for joint efforts between employers and educators, but they might be a good place to start and might lead to other joint efforts to develop the skills needs of industry and aid the career mobility of workers.

Policy 7. Meeting national skill shortages and promoting entrepreneurship.

While the whole of this article is about federal involvement in vocational education policy, there are some particular interests and responsibilities that merit separate attention, either because of overriding national interest, because of wholly new initiatives on the youth unemployment front, or because the federal partner in this whole venture of human resource development has approached its task on an *ad hoc* and uncoordinated basis.

National Skill Shortages: Directing federal resources toward meeting clearly recognized economic needs.

Adequate development of the human resource is increasingly recognized as playing an important role in economic wellbeing, along with such other important factors as the availability of natural resources and an adequate level of investment in plants and equipment. The pioneering work in this area was done by Denison (1974), although more specific and more explicit estimates have been made recently (drawing on Denison's data) by Kendrick. Kendrick (1979) concludes that .7% of the 1.3% productivity rate (over half of it) from 1966 to 1977 was due to education and training.

There arise from time to time skill shortages of national importance, and when they exist it is critical that the technical institutes and other skill-producing institutions take steps to relieve these skill shortages. Currently there are severe shortages in various categories of computer skills, some of which can be alleviated through the output of two-year postsecondary vocational education institutions.

Such critical skill shortages can be of considerable detriment to individual firms, as well as exacerbating national economic problems. The development of a skill bottleneck can slow down production and affect a large number of other workers. A skill shortage can lead to the use of inadequately trained personnel and to quality problems in the product or service. The existence of skill shortages of sufficient magnitude to affect production have potential for contributing to inflation.

There is, I believe, sufficient argument for earmarking a portion of federal funds appropriate for vocational education for use as a reserve for allocation to local vocational and technical institutions to help them meet specifically identified national skill shortages. These funds should be kept outside the regular formula allocation to the states and released only when there is a bona fide skill shortage, identified by some process that provides confidence that the shortage in fact exists.

Entrepreneurship: Teaching skills necessary to run very small businesses, and developing youth-operated enterprises from the base of the school system.

There is one prime candidate for federal stimulus to broaden the mission of the vocational education system beyond basic education, occupational education, and employment transition services.

There are a number of developments that make it important that vocational education expand its efforts to help young people create and enter small business enterprises. While we have an economic system that has relied on risk taking and entrepreneurship, public education has supposed that preparation for work means preparation to be hired in ongoing organizations.

It is not likely that the individualism inherent in creating one's own business can be factored into a standard curriculum. On the other hand, much of the job growth in recent years has been in very small businesses. The service sector is loaded with opportunity to create small enterprises, from dry cleaning establishments to appliance repair shop to typing services.

Time was when this was relatively simple. But small business attempts frequently run aground on the shoals of inadequate bookkeeping, inadequate tax records, inadequate knowledge in purchasing, and so on. Those barriers can be eased, if not removed, if some of the basics are combined with training in delivering the service itself. Teaching appliance repair can be combined with teaching basics of how to sell the service and open a small shop and how to go about securing funding. Teaching about the risks of opening a small business should be included. The failure rate is high. Some people fail several times before they establish a "going concern."

The federal government has chosen to exercise a responsibility for vocational education far beyond that of any other segment of public education, and it played a key role in 1917 in its creation as a nationwide institution. It has, after finding some problems unattended, reassumed a responsibility for modernizing and expanding this system in the legislations of 1963, 1968, and 1976.

The case for a federal role remains strong, but it is time for that role to change, bringing industry and education closer together, getting more of the occupational training component taught jointly by schools and employers, putting more of a spotlight on the basic education component of the system, smoothing the whole of the youth transition to work rather than concentrating resources on classroom occupational education, helping adult workers adjust to occupational shifts forced on them by a dynamic and churning free economy, working with industry in the tuition aid system now growing in the private sector, paying attention to national skill shortages and the human resource needs of the economy, helping more people with the knowledge required for starting and running small businesses, and achieving a better integration of scattered federal efforts in the area of human resource development.

NOTES

1. For one account, see Barlow (1976).
2. There are now about 150 such collaborative councils, with varying names, including Industry, Education, Labor Councils and Community Education Work Councils. See National Institute for Work and Learning (forthcoming).
3. For an excellent analysis of all possible elements of vocational education, see Silberman (1980).
4. These cycles are well described in Evans and Herr (1978).
5. For a review of these developments, and useful instruction in how to use occupational projections, see Goldstein (1980).
6. Not dealt with here is the problem of forecasting, of being able to project very far into the future. For one review of the official projections, and an alternate scenario to them, see Froomkin (1980).
7. For one reason, employers may not hire people under 21, even in a growing occupation. For a discussion of age of hiring, see Barton (1975).
8. For an extensive treatment of the whole of adult learning, from a worklife perspective, see Barton and the National Institute for Work and Learning (forthcoming).
9. For a full description of these programs, their use, and the barriers to their use, see Charner et al. (1978).

REFERENCES

BARLOW, M. L. (1976) The Unconquerable Senator Page. Washington, DC: American Vocational Association.

BARTON, P. E. (1975) "Youth employment and career entry," in S. Wolfheim (ed.) Labor Market Information for Youths. Philadelphia: Temple University School of Business Administration.

——— and National Institute for Work and Learning (forthcoming) Work-Life Transitions: The Adult Learning Connection. New York: McGraw-Hill.

CHARNER, I. et al. (1978) An Untapped Resource. Washington, DC: National Manpower Institute.

CUBAN, L. (1981) "Enduring resiliency: enacting and implementing federal vocational education legislation. Draft paper.

DENISON, E. F. (1974) Accounting for United States Economic Growth, 1929-1969. Washington, DC: Brookings Institution.

DEWEY, J. (1916) Democracy and Education. New York: Macmillan.

EVANS, R. N. and E. L. HERR (1978) Foundations of Vocational Education. Columbus, OH: Charles E. Merrill.

FROOMKIN, J. (1980) "The future role of vocational education." Prepared for the National Institute of Education, November.

GOLDSTEIN, H. (1980) "Future labor market demand and vocational education." Prepared for the National Institute of Education, September.

HARRELL, A. V. and P. W. WIRTZ (1980) Social and Educational Antecedents to Youth Unemployment. Washington, DC: Social Research Group, George Washington University.

HOROWITZ, I. L. (1975) "Head and hand in education: vocationalism versus professionalism." School Rev. (May).

Interim Report of the Vocational Education Study (1980) Washington, DC: National Institute of Education, September.

KENDRICK, J. W. (1979) "Increasing productivity," in C. C. Walton (ed.) Inflation and National Survival. The Academy of Political Science.

National Center for Educational Statistics (1975) Class of '72. National Longitudinal Survey. #75-208. Washington, DC: Government Printing Office.

National Institute for Work and Learning (forthcoming) Industry-Education-Labor Collaboration: A Directory of Local Collaborative Councils. Prepared under contract with U.S. Department of Education. Washington, DC: Government Printing Office.

SILBERMAN, H. F. (1980) "The intrinsic benefits: non-economic returns of vocational education." Vocational Education (September).

25

MANDATING COLLABORATION THROUGH FEDERAL LEGISLATION
YEDPA and the CETA-School Linkage

Ray C. Rist

INTRODUCTION

The Youth Employment and Demonstration Projects Act (YEDPA) became law on August 5, 1977. It amended the 1973 Comprehensive Employment and Training Act (CETA) so as to provide the initiative for an expanded effort to address the problems of youth unemployment. YEDPA added several new programs to improve employment and training opportunities for young people in their late teens and early twenties, particularly those from low-income families. It has sought to emphasize more experimentation and innovation on the part of the local CETA prime sponsor than has been the case with programs developed for unemployed adults.

From Ray C. Rist, "Mandating Collaboration Through Federal Legislation: YEDPA and the CETA-School Linkage," in *Research in Sociology of Education and Socialization,* Vol. 3 (1982). Copyright 1982 by JAI Press, Inc. Reprinted by permission of the author.

The act is particularly concerned with overcoming the barriers between school and work by more closely linking education, employment, and training institutions. It seeks to forge new relationships. One of the four programs authorized by YEDPA was the Youth Employment and Training Program (YETP). This program was designed to provide a full range of work experiences and skills necessary for future employment, especially for those low-income youth, sixteen to twenty-one years of age, who are in school or out of school and unemployed or underemployed (see U.S. Department of Labor, 1977:18-34). Certain YETP provisions also allow designated forms of participation by youth fourteen and fifteen years old, as well as by youth who are not economically disadvantaged.

What provides a sense of urgency to this effort is that there is a desperate need both to improve the education of low-income minority youth and to find the means by which to create more employment for them. The evidence on this point is both conclusive and sobering: the situation for poor minority youth, as compared with white middle-class youth, has steadily deteriorated since the mid-1960s. Whether one measures employment rates or labor force participation rates, the disparities have grown and continue to do so. This is in spite of all the education, employment, and training programs initiated since the mid-1960s and carried on to the present (see Adams and Mangum, 1978:19-34).

The spending level for YEDPA for both fiscal years 1979 and 1980 was approximately $1.1 billion. The first priority for these funds was to generate in the vicinity of three hundred thousand employment opportunities for youth. As such, they have become an integral component of efforts by the administration to reduce the present levels of youth unemployment.

YEDPA AND KNOWLEDGE DEVELOPMENT

Although the direct support for youth employment programs commands the bulk of YEDPA appropriations, improved knowledge development is of high priority. Indeed, the Congress authorized in the legislation that up to a full 20 percent of the YEDPA funding could be used for demonstration projects seeking innovative means by which to address the problem of youth employment. The first general principle of the YEDPA Planning Charter of August 1977 stated (U.S. Department of Labor, 1977:5):

> Knowledge development is a primary aim of the new youth programs. At every decision-making level, an effort must be made to try out promising ideas, to support on-going innovation and to assess performance as rigorously as possible. Resources should be concentrated and structured so that the underlying ideas can be given a reasonable test. Hypotheses and questions should be determined at the outset, with an evaluation methodology built in.

This emphasis upon new approaches and new strategies for addressing the persistence of youth unemployment came none too soon. As Mangum and Walsh (1978) have cogently stated, little or no systematic effort has been made over the past years to learn from previous efforts, either positive or negative. The decisions on what programs to instigate, what policies to pursue, and what objectives to seek have heretofore not been made. Their rather somber assessment includes much of what they understand to be in the YEDPA initiatives as well. They note (Mangum and Walsh, 1978:11):

> It is ironic that after 17 years of experimentation with employment and training programs for youth, Congress found it necessary to legislate activities and programs aimed at discovering the causes of youth unemployment and its potential solutions. It seems fair to ask whether the assumptions upon which past youth programs were based were faulty, or whether the programs themselves were poorly designed or mismanaged. Yet, aside from the research provisions of the Youth Employment and Demonstration Projects Act (YEDPA), the programs authorized by the Act are the same as those which have been implemented over the past 17 years—work experience on community improvement and conservation projects, institutional and on-the-job training, counseling, placement and other kinds of supportive services.... Congress undoubtedly hoped that programs initiated under YEDPA would be innovative and would unearth heretofore untried techniques, but one of the criticisms of past programs has been that they have been almost exclusively experimental. Experiment has been piled upon experiment, but a concerted, overall policy for treating youth unemployment and transitional problems has never emerged.

If Mangum and Walsh are correct in this assessment that "aside from the research provisions" little new or innovative could be anticipated from the YEDPA effort, then, of necessity, attention should focus on what the research sponsored by YEDPA might yield in the way of new insights or programmatic initiatives.

With the first phase of YEDPA funding in fiscal year 1978, an ambitious agenda of demonstration, research, and assessment activities was implemented. The *Knowledge Development Plan* structured an array of discretionary efforts to address a number of the most pressing questions facing national policymakers (U.S. Department of Labor, 1978). Within this 1978 plan were eight "first-order" questions which needed to be answered to both design and implement the national priorities regarding youth unemployment. The eight questions were as follows (U.S. Department of Labor, 1978:3-4):

1. Does school retention and completion increase the future employability of potential dropouts and the disadvantaged, and are employment and training services linked to education an effective mechanism for increasing school retention and completion?
2. Can the school-to-work transition process be improved? Are new institutional arrangements feasible and warranted? Can new transition routes be created?

3. Given the fact that work experience has become the primary emphasis of youth programs, are the jobs productive, which ones are most "meaningful" and how can they be improved?
4. Does structured, disciplined work experience have as much or more impact on future employability than other human resource development services or a combination of services and employment, i.e., should public policy emphasize straight work experience, combinations of work and training and other services, or should training, education and supportive services be emphasized?
5. Are there better approaches and delivery mechanisms for the types of career development, employment and training services which are currently being offered?
6. To what extent are short-run interventions and outcomes related to longer-term impacts on employability during adulthood? Put in another way, how much can public interventions redirect the developmental process?
7. What works best for whom? What performance or outcome standards are best to determine what does and does not work for youth? Which youth with what characteristics benefit from which programs and approaches?
8. What is the universe of need for youth programs? What is the cost of fully employing youth? How many would take jobs if they were available and how many hours of employment do they require?

It became apparent as YEDPA moved into its second fiscal year (1979) that a number of "second-order" questions also deserved attention. For the most part, these questions were refinements and further clarifications of the original eight. They focused more specifically, for example, on targeting for subpopulations of youth, on isolating the effects of specific service components, and on comparing alternative delivery approaches. Seven such second-order questions were posed for the fiscal year 1979 effort. They are (U.S. Department of Labor, 1978:4-5) as follows:

1. What approaches and procedures can be used to involve the private sector in employment and training efforts and to increase the placement of the participants in private sector jobs? How effective are these approaches in accessing new jobs and providing better career tracks for youth?
2. How can youth programs be better integrated to improve adminstration and to provide more comprehensive services to youth? To what extent are the programs already integrated at the local level?
3. How can the lessons from knowledge development activities best be transferred to improve existing youth programs? How can the institutional change process be promoted?

4. What is the best mix of enrollees in terms of age and income status? Will poor youth benefit from interaction with nondisadvantaged youth or with older persons? Is targeting achieved and is it a worthwhile notion?
5. What arrangements can be made to increase the duration of employment and training interventions and to assure that participants realize lifetime benefits? Will youth demonstrate the commitment and consistency to make these long-term investments pay off?
6. What strategies are most important at different points in the lives of youth? Must training be delayed until greater maturity is achieved? Are employment and training programs a way of inducing maturity?
7. How do the problems of significant youth segments differ, including those of migrants, rural youth, the handicapped, offenders, young women with children, runaways and the like? Are special need groups and special problems better handled by mainstreaming or by separate programs for these groups?

THE "EXEMPLARY IN-SCHOOL DEMONSTRATION PROJECTS"

In recognition that present approaches to reduce youth unemployment are imperfect, both in design and implementation, the act has authorized the secretary of labor to allocate up to one-fifth of YEDPA funds on demonstration projects to support knowledge development. The mandate from the Congress was clear:

> Sec. 321. It is the purpose of this part to establish a variety of employment, training, and demonstation programs to explore methods of dealing with the structural unemployment problems of the nation's youth. The basic purpose of the demonstration programs shall be to test the relative efficacy of the different ways of dealing with these problems in different local contexts.
>
> Sec. 348. . . . to carry out innovative and experimental programs, to test new approaches for dealing with the unemployment problems of youth, and to enable eligible participants to prepare for, enhance their prospects for, or secure employment in occupations through which they may reasonably be expected to advance to productive working lives. Such programs shall include, where appropriate, cooperative arrangements with educational agencies to provide special programs and services.

The monies that were to be distributed according to formula among the local sponsors of programs for youth would alleviate some unemployment and "buy time." Yet there was little confidence that, in the end, these projects would either address the long-term needs of the youth or provide new insights into how programs might be more effectively organized and implemented so as to have a greater impact. New ideas, new aproaches, and new actors would have to be on the scene if innovative and pathbreaking approaches were to be found.[1] And while it was not explicit in the legislation, it can be surmised that if successful projects could be located where jobs were created and the youth were prepared to assume them, then perhaps cities and states would be encouraged to redirect portions of the 80 percent formula funds toward projects of this kind. Thus, the discretionary funds projects could achieve a ripple effect throughout the infrastructure of youth employment and training programs.

To learn more about one aspect of the complex set of relations between education and present/future employment opportunities, the Department of Labor set aside in fiscal year (FY) 1979 and again in FY 1980 from the discretionary funds within YETP approximately $15 million for "Exemplary In-School Demonstration Projects." These grants were to explore the dynamics of in-school projects and their effectiveness. They also would be awarded to promote cooperation between the education and the employment and training systems.

As a result of a five-tier evaluation process designed to select from among the more than 520 submitted proposals, 48 projects were chosen. The first contracts were signed and projects began operation in September 1978. Forty-seven of the projects did become operational. Programs were funded in one of four substantive areas: Academic Credit for Work Experience, Expanded Private Sector Involvement, Career Awareness, and Job Creation Through Youth-Operated Projects (see Rist et al., 1980a).

The individual local programs selected for this demonstration project were slated to operate from between nine and eighteen months, specifically, between September 1978 and March 1980. Programs could include summer activities in 1979 if those activities were shown to be a logical extension of the school year program. The projected size of the youth populations to be served in the programs varied from a low of 35 to a high of 10,000. Sites were located across the nation in thirty-one states and in locations that ranged from rural to metropolitan areas. Individual grants ranged from approximately $175,000 to $400,000 with the average being near $300,000. Additional funding during FY 1980 from the Department of Labor enabled twenty-five of the sites to continue beyond their original termination dates.

A national cross-site comparative evaluation employing qualitative data collection strategies was undertaken by a group of researchers at the College of Human Ecology, Cornell University. Trained observers at each of the project sites gathered data for up to two academic years on selected key policy issues. These data were in turn analyzed and used by the Cornell staff as the basis for reports and for the development of national policy recommendations (Rist, 1980b).

Data for this present analysis have been gathered by trained on-site observers at a subsample of twenty-four projects in nineteen states. These sites were selected because they represented that group with the longest continuous period of on-site data collection. The data have taken the forms of intensive and in-depth interviews, participant observations, the use of written materials, and statistics gathered by each site for the purpose of reporting to the Department of Labor.

PATTERNS OF COLLABORATION: DEFINING THE ISSUES

Even before the present economic recession made all the more in vogue such buzz words as *interinstitutional interface* and *institutional linkages*, there was a growing recognition that any realistic attempt to address the nation's unemployment problems would necessitate the collaborative efforts of multiple sectors and institutions in the society. To provide training without cognizance of labor market demands and projects (Berg, 1971), to seek economic development in a community without recognition of established businesses and how they might be affected (Pressman and Wildavsky, 1979), or to assume that work experience can be gained vicariously through classroom instruction (Carnegie Council on Policy Studies, 1979) are but three documented examples of unsuccessful efforts "to go it alone."

The alternative approach would be to seek linkages, patterns of collaboration, and incentives for cooperation. As Wurzburg has noted (1980:1):

> YEDPA is not maintenance legislation designed to sustain existing policies and service levels. More than anything else, it is legislation intended to produce change. The purpose of these changes has been to rationalize service systems and better articulate the relationships between institutions that are in a position to improve the abilities of youth to function in job markets for the purpose of providing more comprehensive and higher quality services than have been provided in the past.

As Taggart and Ganzglass (1980:46) have noted in much the same view:

> YEDPA was not just "more of the same." It sought to change ways of doing business particlarly in the relationship between the education and employment and training activities, and between local education agencies and prime sponsors.
>
> The provision most directly aimed at bringing this change was the requirement that 22% of the Youth Employment and Training Program (YETP) funds provided to State and local prime sponsors be spent on in-school programs under agreement between the prime sponsors and local education agencies.

Though not stated explicitly, the assumptions of policymakers evident from the approach taken in the YEDPA legislation are several: (1) the education and employment/training sectors had not effectively collaborated in the past; (2) each was less than fully successful in its mandate as a result of its practices; and (3) the complexity and growing enormity of the youth unemployment problem necessitated new approaches that bridged the schism between these two delivery systems. Each of these can be briefly discussed in turn.

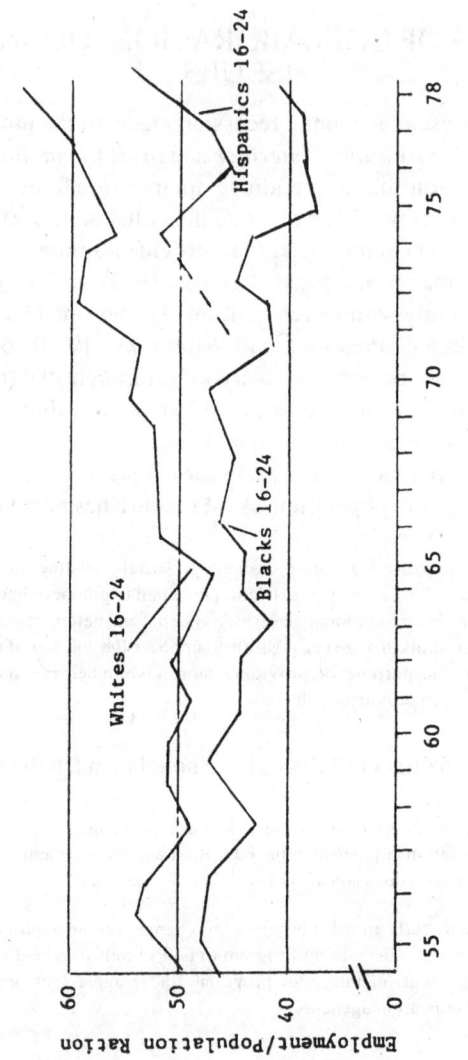

Figure 1. Employment/Population Ratios Over 25 Years 1954-1978

Source: Testimony of Shirley M. Hufstedler, Secretary of Education, before the Subcommittee on Elementary, Secondary, and Vocational Education of the House Education and Labor Committee, February 25, 1980.

It is neither new or startling to note that the education and employment/training systems have not worked cooperatively to address youth unemployment problems. A long list of studies, ranging from those of presidential commissions and national evaluations to those of academics and social critics, have first noted and then judged (positively or negatively) the presence of this hiatus. As far back as the work of John Dewey (1938), there have been calls for closing the gap between education and preparation for the world of work. Increasingly, the assumption (and at present it is only an assumption) has been accepted that an important means by which to address youth unemployment is to bring these two systems into an ongoing relation. Much of the current research sponsored by the YEDPA legislation appears to be a test not of whether this assumption proves correct, but only of the best means by which to operationalize it (Rist et al., 1980b).

The second assumption, that each of the two systems is less than successful in its efforts to accomplish its objectives, is also one that is widely held. Whether one examines the illiteracy and dropout rates among minority youth from the nation's schools or the declining labor force participation rates for these same youth, the outcomes are highly similar: sizable numbers of minority youth are increasingly distanced from the institutions of the society. The consequences are known. The unemployment rates for all youth are aproximately 20 percent, and those for minority youth are nearly double that figure (Westcott, 1979:87-100). What gives particular saliency to these findings is that they are indicative, particularly for black youth, of a trend in labor force participation that dates back more than a decade. Figure 1 provides graphic evidence of these trends.

Third, the juxtaposition of these two sets of assumptions suggested to those who drew up the YEDPA legislation that new initiatives could not take a "business as usual" approach to the matter of youth unemployment. New initiatives, new actors, and new relations would have to be forged if anything other than "more of the same" was to be done. Both the enormity and complexity of the current situation made apparent that the consolidation and collaboration of several institutional sectors would be necessary if any new initiative was to have even the remote opportunity to succeed.

There is a fourth, and perhaps no less obvious, justification for bringing together the education and employment/training systems to address the matter of school-to-work transition and the future employability of American youth. If one examines the data available from the federal budget for the fiscal year 1979, it is immediately evident that the federal government has spent considerably less on secondary school poor youth in comparison to poor youth in either elementary or postsecondary education. The data are in several forms: $3.2 billion was spent for poor children in grades K-6, while $1.2 billion was spent on poor youth in grades 7-12. For those low-income young persons who went on to higher education, the federal government spent, on an average, $3046 per

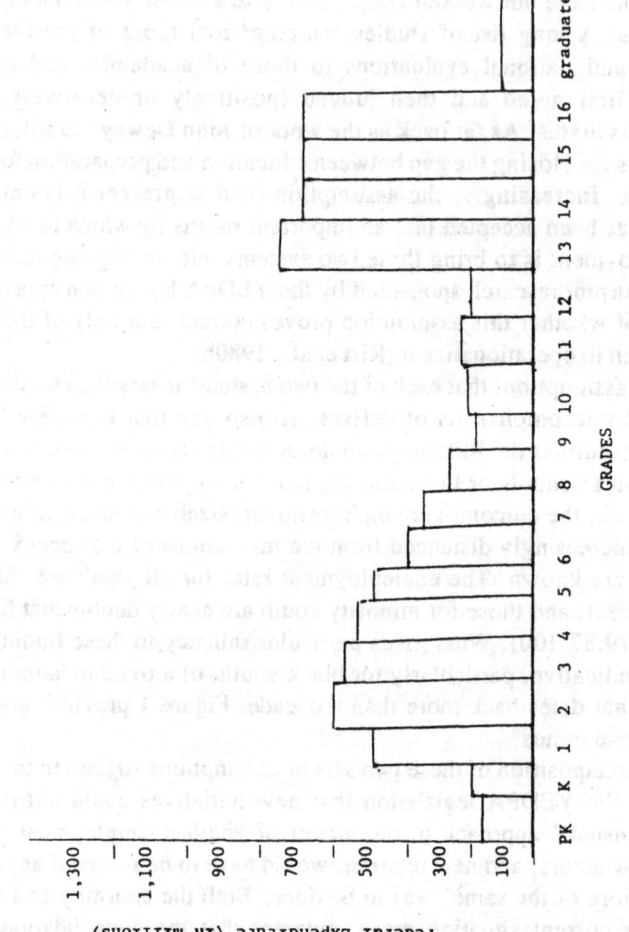

Figure 2. Federal Education Expenditures For Young People With Special Needs—FY 1979

Source: Testimony of Shirley M. Hufstedler, Secretary of Education, before the Subcommittee on Elementary, Secondary, and Vocational Education of the House Education and Labor Committee. February 25, 1980.

student, but only $231 on each low-income high school student. The data are portrayed in Figure 2. For those low-income students who did graduate from high school but did not go to college, the average expenditure on additional education and training was $161.

The point can be simply made: so long as a substitution of dollars does not take place, any collaboration between institutions ought to increase the total amount spent on low-income youth in grades 7-12. Given the extremely low level from which current support begins (as evidenced above for the education sector), the concentration of resources to better assist these youth is highly desirable. The evidence is building that the rather sizable expenditure of funds on low-income youth in the elementary grades has had a positive effect on their academic achievement (Hufstedler, 1980). Whether the same could be said for secondary school youth is premature, as such funds have not been expended. Yet collaboration between the education and employment/training sectors appears necessary to generate the "critical mass" of funds necessary for making any change in the current condition of low-income youth, whether in their academic performance on basic skills, or on their knowledge, interest, and motivation to participate in the world of work.

Parenthetically, this approach appears now to have been institutionalized within the proposed Youth Act of 1980. Additional funds for youth education and employment training above the $825 million currently allocated to Title IV of CETA (the youth programs title) would be split evenly between the Department of Education and the Department of Labor for their respective programs. While such a stipulation at present is written into only the version of the legislation passed by the House Labor and Education Committee, the precedent of establishing fiscal incentives that encourage cooperation is set. This is especially so, given that the bill proposes a 22 percent set-aside for both education and CETA efforts. Thus 44 percent of the monies available each for prime sponsors and LEAs are earmarked for collaborative efforts. With increased appropriations, the impact of this set-aside grows proportionately. The sum total of funds that are to be spent according to an agreement between a CETA prime sponsor and the LEA approximates one-third of all monies authorized by the new act (see Byrne, 1980:14).

THE ISSUE OF IMPLEMENTATION

If the general consensus is that collaboration *ought* to exist between the education and employment/training sectors so as to enhance the opportunities of American youth, then the matter of *how* this is to be accomplished must be addressed. In short, what is necessary is an understanding of the mechanisms by which one moves from establishing goals to achieving them. What has been documented time and again is that little systematic study or attention has been paid to the process of implementation (Hargrove, 1975). Indeed, Hargrove sees it as the "missing link" between policy formation and program operation.

What further complicates the goals of planners is that seldom are programs implemented as they were designed. As the recent (and massive) Rand Corporation study of implementation of federal programs has made clear, the implementation process must itself be treated as an independent variable that profoundly affects what kind of program ultimately emerges (Berman and McLaughlin, 1978). Little is known about the processes of implementation and about the strategies that are most appropriate to achieve successful program operation. The twenty-four YEDPA projects reported upon in this present analysis have essentially had to rely either on previous experience or "best guesses" as to how to proceed. The development of linkages in these projects was essential to the goals the projects had stated for themselves. The route to developing these linkages, however, was difficult and uncharted (Rist, 1980a).

A critical difficulty in effecting viable linkages between the education and employment/training sectors comes from neither one having an articulated understanding of what linkages should consist. The goal for the Exemplary In-School Projects reported here was to enhance linkages in order to enhance services to youth. But the rationale and methodology were not clear. As Pressman and Wildavsky have stated in this regard (1979:xxi):

> Policies imply theories. Whether stated explicitly or not, policies point to a chain of causation between initial conditions and future consequences. If X, then Y. Policies become programs when, by authoritative action, the initial conditions are created. X now exists. Programs make the theories operational by forging the first link in the causal chain connecting actions to objectives. Given X, we act to obtain Y. Implementation, then, is the ability to forge subsequent links in the causal chain so as to obtain the desired results.

Given that the projects were to be "demonstrated projects," i.e., trying new and different ways of addressing the needs of in-school youth, it is perhaps not surprising that prior to the beginning of the programs, there was little sense of how to "forge subsequent links in the causal chain so as to obtain the desired results." The consequence was an ongoing set of improvisations—some of which were successful and more of which were not.

But again, this is to be expected. Failure, rather than success, is the more likely outcome of social change. Quoting again from Pressman and Wildavsky (1979:109):

> Our normal expectation should be that new programs will fail to get off the ground and that, at best, they will take considerable time to get started. The cards in this world are stacked against things happening, as so much effort is required to make them move. The remarkable thing is that new programs work at all.

Key to our understanding of when these new programs "do work at all" in terms of forging new relations is that the *linkages were made between institutions with comparable or compatible organizational features.* The work of

Elmore (1978) has been particularly informative in this regard. Elmore (1978:185) suggests that "understanding organizations is essential to the analysis of implementation."[2] He posits not one, but four distinct models of organizational life, each of which approaches the matter of implementation differently. His four analytic models are systems management, bureaucratic process, organizational development, and conflict and bargaining. What is critical about these differentiations, as Elmore (1978:188) notes, is:

> Viewing the implementation process through a number of different organizational models allows us to be specific about the organizational assumptions we make when we offer prescriptions for improving implementation. Different models, we will see, lead to quite different perceptions and conclusions.

Neither the CETA prime sponsors nor the LEAs involved in the Exemplary In-School Demonstration Projects exhibited the organization structure that Elmore would categorize as *systems management*. More appropriate to this present analysis is the fact that among the twenty-four sites represented in this study, examples of all three remaining organizational models were present. Elmore describes the *bureaucratic process model* as one that represents the sociological model of organizations. It takes as its point of departure that "the essential feature of organizations is the interaction between routine and discretion." The *organizational development model*, blending sociological and psychological theory, focuses "on the conflict between the needs of individuals and the demands of organizational life." Finally, the *conflict and bargaining model* "addresses the problem of how people with divergent interests coalesce around a common task. It starts from the assumption that conflct, arising out of the pursuit of relative advantage in a bargaining relationship, is the dominant feature of organizational life."

Each of these models stresses a different aspect of and vantage point from which to study the process of implementation. Comparing the manner in which the different Exemplary Projects operationalized their implementation strategies leads to a better understanding of why it was that many linkages failed and why others existed in only the most tenuous of terms. Conversely, those linkages that grew stronger during the first two years of program implementation existed in those instances where there were similar compatible organizational structures.

The theoretical work of Elmore leads to an examination of different organizational models and the modes of their implementation. The findings suggest that a mismatch between organizational types made exceedingly difficult the establishment of successful linkages. As but one example, when an LEA functioned on the bureaucratic process model and the project saw itself as a change agent in constant conflict with the larger system (i.e., functioning within the conflict and bargaining model), successful linkages were few. The project termed the LEA obstructionist, while the school system saw the project as refusing to follow established guidelines, constantly interested in procedural shortcuts, and generally unwilling to accept the present routine as the way in which business was to be accomplished. The instances could be multiplied, but the point is made: implementation across organizational types presents significant obstacles in achieving interinstitutional collabortion. This finding is central to several of the conclusions drawn in the following section of this chapter.

BUILDING COLLABORATION

A consistent finding across all four approaches is that linkages work best in those settings where enlightened self-interest and reciprocity are evident. This is stated as the first general finding because it appears to be such a consistent and critical determinant of whether linkages can first be created and then sustained between two or more organizations. Further, given that a number of forces are grouped against any such successful linkage, those factors that do enhance collaboration must be clearly articulated. In noting how current institutional arrangements make for difficulty in establishing new relations, Wurzburg (1980:x) has written:

> There is one important problem with federal policy encouraging institutional collaboration uder CETA as YEDPA does: In the prime sponsor-education relationship, only the CETA prime sponsor is accountable to Washington. Even the most forceful federal policy makers cannot convert reluctant unions, schools, local government agencies, or private employers to the CETA religion. Furthermore, uncertainties about the level and availability of funding force local programming decisions to be delayed to the last moment. These conditions make it extremely difficult for CETA sponsors to develop working partnerships.

Data from the six sites exploring means of "Expanded Private Sector Involvement" lend particular weight in support of this conclusion. The incentives for the private sector to become involved with in-school programs are basically few and far between. When they have worked, the involvement has frequently been because the private sector employer recognizes certain benefits, e.g., particularly the ability to screen for potential long-term employees and to be relieved of a significant portion of the early wage costs through a wage subsidy. Though aspects of the reciprocity may change when one moves from private to public sector employment, data from other projects also suggest that linkages are not as likely to be initiated or to be sustained when no exchange of benefits occurs.

What is implied by this analysis is that greater attention ought to be paid to the various obstacles that are placed in the path of collaboration—be these obstacles of (1) overly restrictive regulations and guidelines; (2) continually changing policy signals which eventuate in local programs doing less and less as they wait for the inevitable memo dictating new modifications; (3) not providing sufficient program money to allow efforts to be done as they ought; or (4) not providing sufficient wage subsidies for both private and public sector employers to compensate them for their involvement. It should be stressed that time and again in interviews with potential private and public sector employers, the belief was that involvement with CETA programs was simply "not worth the hassle." So long as that continues to be a general perception and little is done concretely to change it, the disincentives for both public and private sector participation and collabortion will remain (see Johnson, 1980).

A second general finding of this study of collaboration is that the greater the number of organizations involved, the greater the complexity of the linkage system and the greater the amount of time invested in maintaining these linkages. Stated alternatively, there is a point (range?) of diminishing returns for projects as they link themselves to other organizations and agencies. A full quarter of this sample (six sites) gave evidence of having been overextended through the number of liaison groups, organizations, agencies, and advisory committees with which they had one or more collaborative relations.

What further exacerbated this situation for many sites was that beyond the linkages that were collaborative, there were those that necessitated participation, but seemingly had little relevance or utility to the project itself. The countless hours spent on boards, committees, citywide coordinating councils of all types, and the like, took up a large proportion of the working hours of the top administrators. This is not to say that such participation should not have occurred, but only that with a scarce commodity like time, the allocation of it to these activities left other more program-specific activities unattended and unaccomplished (see Pressman and Wildavsky, 1979:121). This overextension of senior staff had a direct impact upon the long-time lag that many projects experienced in becoming operational.

A final factor related to the matter of complexity in linkages is that more than half of the programs found themselves within a network wherein the number of decisions to be made and the number of participants involved meant an increasing accumulation of delays in implementation. Again, to state it differently, the more decisions to be made, the less the likelihood of program success. Many of the Exemplary In-School programs required dozens of clearance actions by a wide range of organizations and agencies, ranging from the Department of Labor at the federal level through the decisions of local school boards in rural communities. Pressman and Wildavsky (1979:107) have calculated that when there are multiple actors involved, each with the right and obligation to participate in a decision-making process, an agreement level of 80 percent among these actors means that with just four decision points, the likelihood of successful implementation drops to less than 50 percent.

Linkages that were generated as a result of a "crisis atmosphere" or because of the sudden availability of resources were not initially stable. They were not likely to endure unless modified to reflect long-term benefits for the organizations involved. That such were the origins of nineteen of the Exemplary projects and that only eleven successfully transformed their linkages into more permanent and beneficial patterns of collaboration suggest the difficulty in establishing such collaborative relations. In the remaining eight programs, a slow (or not so slow) dissolution of agreement occurred. Delay enhanced the loss of momentum, the loss of consensus, and the increased likelihood of competing perspectives gaining in adherents and intensity.

A final general assessment to emerge from this study is that there is an essential need for technical assistance to local projects—technical assistance that not only addresses the problems of program implementation, but that also allows local programs to ascertain just what precisely it is that they have implemented. While all the projects have in one manner or another implemented a school-to-work transition effort, it is also the case that, almost without exception, what now is in place is not entirely what was anticipated nor promised when the grant application was made. The process of improvisation and of continually readjusting the goals of the program to changing political, economic, and social condition resulted in efforts dissimilar to those initially envisioned.

The work of Goldberg and Prager (1979) as well as of Hall and Loucks (1977) suggests that technical assistance is absolutely essential to successful program implementation. This is so not only for the reasons of sharing experiences and procedures that might not be known, particularly at a new project, but also to continue to push the local project to clarify its objectives, its goals, and its assumptions to the translation of policy into program. Technical assistance is warranted for local program personnel to sharpen their understanding of the consequences of accumulated decisions. That so little "history" existed at the Exemplary Projects resulted in successive waves of staff repeating the same behaviors—and often to little avail.

There is another dimension to the providing of technical assistance. It concerns equipping local projects to sort out what organizational system they are employing for their own project and what systems are in place for the organizations and agencies around them. Such understanding has important and concrete implications for the form and content of linkages that can or cannot be developed. Data from this present study suggest that building linkages and collaborative relations across organizational types such as the four detailed by Elmore (1978) is exceedingly difficult. Equipping projects better to understand the ecology of their organizational network could have considerable impact upon their ability to effect the linkages and collaborative ties that would be both reciprocal and sustaining.

POSTSCRIPT

As Wurzburg (1980), Taggart and Ganzglass (1980), and others have all noted, the YEDPA legislation was not intended to reinforce the status quo, but to promote change in the manner by which the education and employment/training systems related to each other, *specifically at the local level*. The carrot of federal dollars was to induce local change. But moving the policy down through the various levels of government invariably transforms and mutates the initial design and intention (Porter, 1980). Tracing down just one of the various channels of decision making, specifically, between the federal CETA system and the local prime sponsor office, Wurzburg (1980:ix) has written:

> Uncertainty about funding levels, regulations and the law itself is a distinguishing characteristic of the entire CETA federal/prime sponsor partnership. Habitual as such uncertainties are, and continue to be under YEDPA, they still exact an enormous toll. Changing signals regarding funding levels caused sponsors to accelerate enrollments and then back-off; some were forced to lay off enrollees and staff. Doubts about what Congress would do with CETA reauthorization in the Fall of 1978 strained relations sponsors had newly established with local schools. These factors have reduced the planning and development time for new programs, and hurt the credibility of sponsors with other local agencies. They have also created a difficult work climate and seriously undermined prime sponsor staff stability. In the end, they have almost certainly lessened the effectiveness of the programs.

The very manner in which the federal government planned through YEDPA to influence local behavior gives every indication in some instances of having produced nearly the opposite. Local programs and organizational boundaries became more defined and less permeable as a reaction against confusion, conflicting guidelines, and mixed messages as to the goals of the federal initiatives. The federal government was relying on the creation of linkages through fiscal incentives as the means to generate the necessary change. That the funds, in and of themselves, have not put this infrastructure in place is a point not to be missed. The infrastructure occurred when there were viable local reasons for having it so.

ACKNOWLEDGMENT

The views expressed here are those of the author and no endorsement by the U.S. General Accounting Office or the United States Congress is intended or should be inferred.

NOTES

1. As but one indication of the disenchantment with current approaches, witness the efforts of the Carter administration to cut by almost $200 million the funding during fiscal year 1979-1980 for vocational educational programs. Then-Secretary Califano called vocational education one of HEW's "least effective" programs (Carnegie Council on Policy Studies, 1979:146).
2. See chapter by Karen S. Louis in this volume.

REFERENCES

Adams, A., and G.L. Mangum
  1978   The Lingering Crisis of Youth Unemployment. Kalamazoo, Mich.; Upjohn Institute.
Berg, I.
  1971   Education and Jobs: the Great Training Robbery. Boston: Beacon Press.
Berman, P., and M.W. McLaughlin
  1978   Federal Programs Supporting Educational Change. Vol. VIII. Santa Monica, Ca.: The Rand Corporation.
Byrne, J.S.
  1980   "School-CETA cooperation: something money can buy." Jobs Watch 1(3):13-15.
Carnegie Council on Policy Studies in Higher Education
  1979   Giving Youth a Better Chance. San Francisco: Jossey-Bass.
Dewey, J.
  1938   Experience and Education. New York: Macmillan (Collier Books); paperback edition, 1963.
Elmore, R.F.
  1978   "Organizational models of social program implementation." Public Policy 26 (2):185-228.
Goldberg, J.F., and A. Prager
  1979   Policy Implications of Preliminary Findings of the Study of Education and Work Councils. Cambridge, Mass.: Abt Associates.
Hall, G.E., and S.F. Loucks
  1977   "A developmental model for determining whether the treatment is actually implemented." American Educational Research Journal 14(3)263-76.
Hargrove, E.C.
  1975   The Missing Link: The Study of the Implementation of Social Policy. Washington, D.C.: Urban Institute.
Hufstedler, S.M.
  1980   Testimony before the Subcommittee on Elementary, Secondary and Vocational Education of the House Education and Labor Committee. Washington, D.C., Feb. 25.
Johnson, S.D.
  1980   Employer Involvement: a Study of Public and Private Sector Linkages to Youth Programs. Ithaca, Youthwork National Policy Study, Cornell University.
Mangum, G., and J. Walsh
  1978   Employment and Training Programs for Youth: What Works Best for Whom? Office of Youth Programs, Employment and Training Administration, Washington, D.C.
Porter, P.
  1980   "Policy perspectives on the study of educational innovations." Educational Evaluation and Policy Analysis 2(4):73-84.
Pressman, J.L., and A. Wildavsky
  1979   Implementation; 2nd ed. Berkeley, Calif.: University of California Press.
Rist, R.C.
  1980a   "Confronting youth unemployment in the 1980s: sorting out the issues and tends." In R. Rist (ed.), Confronting Youth Unemployment in the 1980s. Elmsford, N.Y.: Pergamon Press.
  1980b   "Qualitative policy analysis: a case study of an emergent methodology." A paper presented to the American Sociological Association, New York, Aug.
Rist, R.C., et al.
  1980a   Targeting on In-School Youth: Four Strategies for Coordinating Education and

Employment Training. Ithaca, N.Y.: Youthwork National Policy Study, Cornell University.

1980b   Patterns of Collaboration: The CETA/School Linkage. Ithaca, N.Y.: Youthwork National Policy Study, Cornell University.

Taggart, R., and E. Ganzglass
 1980   "Youth employment: a challenge for the 1980s." In R. Rist (ed.), Confronting Youth Unemployment in the 1980s. Elmsford, N.Y.: Pergamon Press.

U.S. Department of Labor
 1977   A Knowledge Development Plan for the Youth Employment and Demonstration Projects Act of 1977. Washington, D.C.: U.S. Government Printing Office.
 1978   A Knowledge Development Plan for the Youth Employment and Demonstration Projects Act of 1977. Office of Youth Programs, Employment and Training Administration. Washington, D.C.: U.S. Government Printing Office.
 1979   A Knowledge Development Plan for Youth Initiatives, Fiscal 1979. Office of :Youth Programs, Employment and Training Administration. Washington, D.C.: U.S. Government Printing Office.

Westcott, D.
 1979   "The nation's youth: an employment perspective." Children and Youth Services Review 1(1):87-100.

Wurzburg, G.
 1980   Youth and Local Employment Agenda. Washington, D.C.: National Council on Employment Policy.

26

INEQUALITY AND YOUTH UNEMPLOYMENT
Can Work Programs Work?

Stephen F. Hamilton and John F. Claus

Most youth employment programs attempt to remedy perceived deficiencies in disadvantaged youth, to expand a limited job market, or to do both. While programs with these aims can reduce unemployment among disadvantaged youth, they cannot substantially alter racial and social class inequalities that are built into the structure of opportunity in our society. Radical critics of education in the United States have, over the past decade, forced a reexamination of what education can and cannot do to reduce inequality. The same critique applies equally well to youth employment programs.

However, to take seriously the idea that youth unemployment results from structural inequality implies that only large-scale changes in the social and economic structure can solve the problem. Although we believe this is ultimately true, we also believe that ameliorative steps can be taken that will simultaneously reduce the extent and consequences of unemployment among disadvantaged youth and contribute to a broader movement toward greater equality. Two recommended steps are to emphasize entrepreneurial activities and to promote high levels of participatory democracy in youth employment programs.

Unemployment rates are high among all youth, but the problem is not one of youthfulness; it is one of race and class. Being young is associated with a particular pattern of labor

From Stephen F. Hamilton and John F. Claus, "Inequality and Youth Unemployment: Can Work Programs Work?" 14(1) *Education and Urban Society* 103–126 (November 1981). Copyright 1981 by Sage Publications, Inc.

force experience: low-skill, low-paid, short-term, part-time, and sporadic work (Barton, 1975). Most young people outgrow this pattern with advancing age and the completion of higher levels of education. However, a disproportionate number of low-income and minority youth get trapped in this kind of labor market experience for the long term (Feldstein and Ellwood, 1979). They remain in the "secondary" labor market with its high turnover, low pay, and absence of career ladders, while their more fortunate age mates complete technical school, college, and training programs and move into the "primary" labor market where prospects for gradual increases in status, responsibility and income are reasonably good. A large proportion of youth unemployment can be attributed to the "friction" of frequent movement in and out of the labor market and from job to job (Smith and Vanski, 1979). But frictional unemployment is not as serious a problem for a white, middle-class high school student hoping to earn some spending or college money as it is for a poor black dropout trying to earn a living and gain work experience. The opportunities of the black male dropout are more significantly linked to this unemployment than are those of the white, middle-class student (Adams et al., 1978).

Compounding this problem is the stark reality that unemployment rates for minority youth are much higher than those for other youth. A review of the trend data from 1955 to 1978 indicates, for example, that the unemployment rate of young white males has remained between 10% and 15% while the nonwhite male unemployment rate has jumped from 16% to 40% (Ginzberg, 1980). Moreover, labor force participation rates have been climbing steadily for white youth while they have been gradually declining for black youth.

PERSPECTIVES ON YOUTH UNEMPLOYMENT

Employment and training programs for low-income minority youth are an attempt to address these problems. An assumption underlying such programs is that deficiencies in low-income minority youth cause their unemployment difficulties. These youth are far more likely to have dropped out of high school. Serious drug abuse is more widespread and more debilitating among them. And the males are more likely to have criminal records while the females are more likely to have borne children out of wedlock. Assuming that such characteristics precede and contribute to a lack of entry into the primary labor market, employment programs address the unemployment of poor minority youth by reducing or compensating for the "deficiencies" in knowledge, skills, and attitudes associated with these behaviors. In general, programs attempt to change these youth in order to make them more employable; they do this by taking an individualist perspective, meaning that their locus of change is the individual.

This way of thinking about youth unemployment is consistent with prevailing explanations of and responses to other social and economic problems in the United States (Ryan, 1976). Nevertheless, there is an alternative, although not mutually exclusive, way of thinking that has at least as much empirical support. According to this view, unemployment is a consequence of the structure of the economy rather than of the "deficiencies" of the unemployed. Mainstream proponents of the structural explanation emphasize job scarcity as the principal cause of unemployment. If there were enough jobs to go around, the unemployment problem would be solved; as long as there are too few jobs, the least experienced are sure to suffer the greatest unemployment (Levitan, 1976). A more radical version of the structural explanation accepts that job scarcity is at the root of unemployment but attributes the scarcity to the very nature of a capitalist economy rather than to cyclical variations in the demand for labor.

According to this view, a pool of unemployed persons assures employers of a steady supply of workers willing to occupy the relatively low-paying and undesirable jobs so functional to owners' profits. In other words, a certain amount of unemployment is seen to depress wage rates to the advantage of owners and employers. Thus, the economy, which is driven by owners' profit motivations, is believed to do best when jobs are scarce. And as long as the economy is structured in this way, there will be chronically unemployed people who will transmit to future generations many of the attitudes and behaviors associated with their disadvantaged position. This means that employment and training programs aimed at individual "deficiencies" can, at best, help some disadvantaged young people win over others in the competition for jobs; they cannot eliminate unemployment or the transmission of low skill levels and negative work attitudes often associated with unemployment. It also suggests that to attribute the unemployment of low-income minority youth solely to a lack of education, experience, or proper attitudes is to "blame the victim," for if the economy really needed the labor of these people they would be hired and trained by employers despite the symptoms of their disadvantaged condition.

Ginzberg (1979) has pointed out that both the individualist and the job scarcity interpretations underestimate the flexibility of the labor market. The former, which assumes that unemployment is caused by deficiencies in the unemployed, assumes a rigid standard of employability that strictly limits employer hiring. While some employers do complain that they could increase their activity if more qualified workers were available, the standard response to increased demand for goods and services is to hire what would, under less favorable conditions, be considered unqualified workers and to train them. The fact that unemployment varies with economic conditions over time and from place to place is strong evidence for this flexibility.

The second interpretation, that unemployment results primarily from a shortage of jobs, assumes that the number of jobs in the economy is fixed. The same fact of systematic variation in employment as a function of economic conditions that indicates flexibility in employability standards also challenges this assumption. Furthermore, economic interdependence results in a ripple or multiplier effect, such that when additional workers become sufficiently qualified to enter the labor force, their earnings and production stimulate the creation of new jobs. This phenomenon is attended to most closely when it operates in the opposite direction. When an automobile plant closes and several thousand workers are thrown out of work, the loss of their income leads to additional unemployment as supermarket clerks, barbers, teachers, and others are laid off in the community and tire builders, steel workers, car radio assemblers, and others lose their jobs in far-flung locations.

Without doubt, both the individual and the structural positions contain some truth. Because we believe youth employment and training programs currently achieve only limited impact by creating some new jobs and by addressing the deficiencies in the unemployed, we shall argue the radical structural position and then develop some of the implications of this point of view for employment programs. One purpose of this article is to apply the insights of the "radical critique" of U.S. education to employment and training programs. In so doing we shall attempt to avoid the implication many have drawn from that critique when applying it to schools: that schools have no impact at all. Consistent with our recognition that neither the individual nor the structural explanation of the causes of unemployment is wholly adequate, we will argue that employment and training programs can have a beneficial impact on the employment prospects of disadvantaged youth, but that in order to have the greatest effect these programs must be designed to contribute not only to the employability of participants, but to the alteration of the structure of the economy as well.

THE RADICAL CRITIQUE

The radical explanation for the high unemployment rate of poor, minority youth begins with the assumption that in a corporate capitalist economy one's class, status, and level of opportunity are, to a significant degree, inherited. High unemployment among low-income minority groups is held to result not from individual character flaws or cultural group inadequacies, but from a lack of opportunity which persists from one generation to the next. And this disadvantage is seen as structurally imposed by the unequal profit and authority relations of the traditional capitalist workplace and economy.

In this view the socioeconomic structure of the capitalist economy constitutes a relatively fixed hierarchy rather than a ladder that people ascend according to their personal merit. At the top of the hierarchy, where decisions are made, jobs are high in autonomy, flexibility, and substantive complexity. Workers at this level exert substantial control over the flow of investments, the labor process, and the physical means of production, and their pay and status are high. Close to the bottom, where decisions are carried out and directions followed, jobs are low in control, flexibility, self-direction, and complexity. Workers at this level have little or no effect on the investment or capital process, and they have no formal voice in how things get produced. Their tasks are often highly fragmented and repetitive while their pay and status are low (Braverman, 1974; Kohn, 1977).

Finally, at the very bottom of the hierarchy are the chronically unemployed. Their economic and social situation is overwhelmingly negative. In a society where one's work is a fundamental source of status and power, chronic unemployment means not only a lack of money but a considerable undermining of self-respect and an inability to manipulate the social environment.

The radical perspective challenges the American myth of equal opportunity, highlighting the self-perpetuating nature of class distinctions. Evidence supporting this position includes the high probability that children will attain occupational and socioeconomic positions similar to those of their parents. This is especially true of low-income, minority groups in our society

(Blau and Duncan, 1967; Brittain, 1977). The radical literature suggests that this occurs by way of a process of socialization which takes place in two primary youth environments—the home and the school. Both of these settings are significantly influenced by the profit and authority relations of the economy.

With regard to schools, Bowles and Gintis (1976), propound the "correspondence principle," which states that the socioeconomic relations of capitalist work are reproduced in the schools, thus providing preliminary socialization of potential workers to the competences expected of them in the segment of the labor market to which their family's socioeconomic position consigns them. Other writers argue that the pedagogy and curriculum of schools promote an ideology and culture which obscure and rationalize the unequal structure of capitalist social and economic relationships (Apple 1979; Bourdieu and Passeron, 1977). Moreover, the language and communication patterns considered appropriate in the classroom and implied by the organization of the curriculum are shown to be rooted in linguistic "codes" employed by the upper classes (Bernstein, 1977). And the social relations of the educative process are held to reinforce the unequal distribution of those social and intellectual competences associated with economically dominant groups (Bourdieu and Passeron, 1977).

With regard to the home, it is argued that parents socialize their children in accordance with their own work experiences and the opportunities they perceive to exist for their children in the occupational structure. As deLone (1979) explains, individuals and groups have "probable futures" which influence parents' values and child-rearing behavior. Upper-middle-class children, for example, are encouraged in the home to be creative and independent, just as their parents' jobs demand these qualities. Lower-class children, on the other hand, are trained to be compliant (Ogbu, 1979; Kohn, 1977; Kohn and Schooler, 1978). Thus, according to this view, the differences in children's attitudes toward and achievement in school and educational programs may result from an interaction between parental values rooted in work experiences and the organization of the schools as a preparation for different roles in the labor hierarchy.

This is important in understanding the radical explanation for high rates of school and job market failure among poor, minority youth. Ogbu (1978, 1979), for instance, suggests that the poor school performance and negative work orientations that inhibit the employability of disadvantaged youth are functional adaptations to reality. He points out that for poor blacks there is a "job ceiling" based on a long history of discrimination and adaptation. Moreover, he argues that minority perceptions of this unequal "opportunity structure" influence poor minority youths' behavior and aspirations. Parents in these groups, albeit unconsciously, may rear their children in accordance with their perceptions of this ceiling. They may socialize their children the way they do because the competences and attitudes they themselves have developed are the ones children will require in their future low-status social, occupational, and political roles. In this way they prepare their children for the statistical likelihood of experiencing a disadvantaged life. Thus, when a low-income minority youth adopts behaviors detrimental to success in school and the competition for jobs, he or she may do so not out of weakness but as a logical adaptation to real conditions. What Bourdieu and Passeron (1977) call the "causality of the probable" may make a willingness to participate in socialization to middle-class values and behaviors appear irrational to these youth. As Metz has written about schools,

> a child must believe there is some purpose for himself in learning what is presented him in school or he will not learn it. ... So long as the society appears stratified on a largely ascriptive basis ... the students who think they are bound to lose will not embrace its representatives in the public schools [1978: 243, 254].

Ogbu makes a convincing argument that the perception of a limited opportunity structure by the disadvantaged is accurate and that only real changes in that structure will make it rational for such youth to strive for academic achievement and stable employment. We believe recent experience with federal youth work programs supports such a contention.

The radical perspective on youth unemployment is illuminating, though we do not wish to deny that some low-income and minority people achieve upward mobility or that educational programs can succeed in making some such people more employable than they would otherwise be. It is not that personal characteristics are irrelevant, but that the structure of the economy is more responsible for unemployment than is typically acknowledged in either the rhetoric or the design of employment and training programs. If this position is correct, we would expect to find that employment and training programs do not solve the problems of youth unemployment but that they are capable of a greater impact than that being currently achieved. This, we think, is precisely what numerous evaluations of such programs suggest.

RECENT WORK PROGRAM EVALUATIONS

The reports and reviews of evaluations of youth employment and training programs we have read tend to be optimistic about the value of such programs and constructively critical about how they might be improved. Adams et al. (1978) find that education and training are positively correlated with employment and earnings. Barton and Fraser (1978) summarize numerous evaluations of employment and training programs for youth, many of them showing positive results. Especially noteworthy among these is Somers and Warlick's (1975) creative study matching social security numbers of subjects in the National Longitudinal Survey with those recorded in Manpower Administration programs. Program completers are shown to have better records than either nonparticipants or dropouts. Goodwin (1980) tempers this optimism by pointing out that although participants in youth work programs typically demonstrate a sharp increase in employment shortly after completing the programs, this increase does not last.

Robert Taggart, former administrator of the Office of Youth Programs, U.S. Department of Labor, in a remarkably candid assessment of the effects of youth employment and training programs (1980), distinguishes intensive programs for older youth and young adults—the Job Corps being the prime example—from short-term, low-intensity programs for people under 21. The former he finds to be quite effective in improving the employability of severely disadvantaged young people. Effectiveness, it should be noted, increases with length of participation, and Job Corps centers typically experience a 50% dropout rate over the first three months (p. 122). With respect to short-term programs, he has this to say:

> Part-time school year and summer jobs for students plus year-round "aging vat" or "bridge" jobs for high school dropouts or graduates not ready for career entry constitute the primary activity in CETA for persons 21 and under. These ... jobs are generally temporary and of limited intensity. . . . There is no evidence of substantial short-term post-program employment and earnings gains resulting from such limited duration work experiences. Available measurement tools cannot isolate the modest expected impacts of such activities. Also, the immediate results may not be indicative [p. 1].

Taggart goes on to suggest that work programs of this type, like the part-time employment of youth not in federal programs, contribute to a cumulative work experience that can, over several years, improve employability. In further support of these programs, he cites benefit-cost studies demonstrating that the value of the work produced in well-run youth employment programs approaches or surpasses the wages paid.

The theme we find running through evaluations of these programs and syntheses of evaluation studies is modest accomplishment: Many programs have no measurable effects; those that do move some participants a bit higher on the scale of employment and earnings. Summaries of new reports just emerging from the massive "knowledge development" effort funded by the Youth Employment and Demonstration Projects Act (YEDPA) seem to bear out this theme (Youth Programs, 1981). Three explanations tend to recur for the modesty of measured program effects: design problems, implementation problems, and the magnitude of the resocialization task.

One design problem that has been noted is the attempt to teach specific job skills. Too often, critics say, such skills are quickly outdated or are suited for occupations in low-growth areas of the economy. Furthermore, numerous assessments of employers' needs have indicated that "coping skills" such as problem-solving, control of aggression, and ability to learn new tasks are far more important in gaining and keeping employment than specific job skills, which can in most cases be taught in a short time. A second design problem involves the focus of federal youth employment programs on disadvantaged youth and the resulting concentration in such programs of large homogeneous groups of youth with the poorest employment prospects. This practice can lead to problems when participants reinforce each other's negative behavior and employers come to view applicants' experience in the program as a stigma rather than a credential. Among those who have noted these difficulties are Lynton et al. (1978), Mangum and Walsh (1978), and Rogers (1973).

The most brilliantly conceived program is no better than its implementation. Too often the gap between a program's design and the actual practice that determines the day-to-day experience of participants has rendered programs less effective than they might be. The General Accounting Office (1979) severely criticized the quality of work and supervision provided in the 1978 Summer Youth Employment Programs (with apparently beneficial results: U.S. Department of Labor, 1980). Hersher (1978) argues that Comprehensive Employment and Training Act (CETA) programs were not accurately targeted to those most in need. Rist et al. (1978, 1980a, 1980b) report both strengths and weaknesses in the links between programs and other agencies, schools, and employers, which constitute a major element in the implementation of YEDPA.

The third explanation for the modesty of program accomplishments emphasizes the conflicts between the attitudes and behavior prevelant among disadvantaged youth and those required for successful participation in the primary labor market. Walther (1976) noted this problem and labeled it (after Caplan) "competing competencies," stating that employment and training programs force disadvantaged youth to choose between "street skills" and behavioral styles appropriate to a work setting. Given that youth spend more time in settings that encourage street skills and gain more support for those skills from their peers, employment and training programs offer only a weak countervailing force, particularly in a labor market that offers minimal opportunities. According to Walther, this problem becomes most visible at the point of transition from the program to either school or a regular job, a point at which many participants revert to their former behavior. This is consistent with Goodwin's (1980) interpretation of the absence of long-term program effects.

We see merit in these arguments and support many of the recommendations flowing from them. However, we wish to point out that a radical view of the U.S. economy yields a somewhat different explanation of the finding that employment and training programs have modest effects and has substantially different implications than the more conventional one. While the conventional interpretation calls for improvements in the design and implementation of programs like those now in place—improvements that will make those programs more powerful resocialization agents—the radical interpretation questions the potential of programs to have more than marginal effects on the extent and distribution of unemployment and underemployment. The most dramatic implication of the radical perspective is that the solution to the problem of youth unemployment awaits the restructuring of the economy. This is an inescapable conclusion once the argument has been accepted that the structure of the economy is the principal explanation for youth unemployment. That is one of the reasons why the radical perspective has not been widely accepted: to do so can make us feel powerless to affect the problem at hand because we are aware of the difficulties of radical change.

We are persuaded by the logic of the radical perspective and believe that an acceptable level of social and economic equality ultimately requires radical change in the U.S. economy. However, ultimate goals should not prevent us from taking immediate steps to alleviate current problems. Those steps should be in the direction of ultimate goals, though, while they relieve the immediate problem. Our recommendations follow for some ways in which youth employment programs could continue to address the individual aspects of youth unemployment while simultaneously contributing to making structural change in the economy.

These recommendations grow out of a reinterpretation of the modest effects of work programs. We would argue not only that conventional youth employment and training programs are flawed in design and implementation and are insufficiently powerful resocializing agents but that they can inadvertently reinforce the inheritability of disadvantage. Just as schools reproduce the social relations of work and therefore tend to confine lower-class children to the same socioeconomic stratum occupied by their parents (Bowles and Gintis, 1976), so youth employment and training programs, even when they are successful, teach poor and minority youth to function at the lower levels of the labor market. These programs can offer some individuals the chance to move from unemployment to employment, but they cannot substantially alter the socioeconomic hierarchy. More concretely, an effective program may provide a vehicle for one disadvantaged youth to avoid abject poverty, but, taking the structural view, his success is at the expense of another disadvantaged person; it does not place him in competition with middle-class youth whose cultural and educational credentials ease them into much higher levels of the labor market.

The broad conclusion is, then, that training programs are insufficient. What is required is reform of the structural inequality extant in the workplace and the society at large. On at least an abstract level we take this to be true. However, this kind of sweeping social and economic reform is neither imminent nor likely under current political and economic conditions. Thus, as a practical measure for the immediate future, we suggest that work programs for disadvantaged youth be designed in accordance with the radical perspective. We believe these programs can take into account the radical explanation for the academic and job market failure of poor minority youth, such that these youth will be more willing to engage in some of the resocialization required of them for success in current job market competition. We also believe such a redesign of employment programs promises, at least on a small scale, to promote the broad social and economic reform seemingly so fundamental to achieving increased opportunity for the disadvantaged.

ENTREPRENEURIAL DEMOCRATIC PROGRAMS

The central recommendation we have for redesigning programs is to concentrate on entrepreneurial projects that are democratically operated. The most thorough and thoughtful treatment of youth entreprenuership we have seen is McArthur's (1980) report on YEDPA-funded programs testing this approach. His study of five demonstration programs at 17 different sites led him to conclude that youth entrepreneurship is an excellent idea that has not yet been tried.

> A large majority of programs developed under this initiative have little if anything to do with entrepreneurship; those that do are held hostage to demands and expectations which are irrelevant and often contradictory with entrepreneurship goals [p. 1].

The barriers he identifies to truly entrepreneurial youth projects include contradictions between the traditional goal of improving youths' employability and the innovative goal of creating viable youth-operated businesses, and a pervasive lack of confidence among adults that youth are actually capable of establishing and operating profitable enterprises.

Recognizing these barriers and the complexity of using public funds to initiate private profit-making enterprises, the Department of Labor has adopted the term "limited entrepreneurial projects" to efforts such as these. We see potential benefits from both limited and true entrepreneurial projects, benefits that meet some of the needs highlighted by the radical perspective.

We would define as a limited entrepreneurial project any youth employment program that produces and markets goods and services and in which youth are actively engaged in management. This definition allows for projects in which little capital is required, profit is not essential, and adults make the most important decisions. Even with these limitations, entrepreneurial projects have some important advantages. First, producing goods and services that people are willing to pay for can be more demanding, more satisfying, and better preparation for subsequent employment than the performance of "make work." Not all public service employment is "make work" by any means, but some of it is and young people generally know and care when what they are doing has little lasting value (Hamilton and Stewart, 1980). Second, the range of knowledge and skills required for participation in the management of a limited entrepreneurial project exceed the range normally found in subsidized jobs in either the public or private sector. Low-income and minority youth placed in adult workplaces typically perform only low-level tasks. Those who are fortunate will observe and learn about what their superiors do, but they will not be responsible for keeping the books or deciding whether to bring out a new product line. Third, even limited entrepreneurial projects can give their participants a better understanding of how the economy functions and a broader range of options for fitting into it than most work experiences in adult-dominated workplaces.

One of the most daunting challenges in creating entrepreneurial projects is that even mature, talented, and experienced adults fail more often than they succeed at founding profit-making businesses. However, if the need to subsidize the employment of disadvantaged youth is accepted, the above arguments favor using at least some of that subsidy to pay wages and supervisors in youth-operated enterprises even when those enterprises are unlikely to prove self-sustaining.

McArthur's criteria for entrepreneurial projects are much more stringent. They define a nearly ideal situation in which the benefits cited above would still accrue and others would be added. His criteria are that true entrepreneurial programs have as explicit objectives:

I. Establishing a revenue-generating enterprise;
II. The establishment of a viable business venture that provides new unsubsidized jobs for youth;
III. Youth ownership of the venture [pp. 20-23].

These criteria place heavy demands on youth employment programs, but programs meeting them could have substantially greater impact on reducing inequality than conventional programs. The jobs created by such programs could last longer than those created solely on the basis of a subsidy, thus reducing the incidence of unemployment much longer. Furthermore, those new jobs would include technical and managerial positions that would be filled by disadvantaged youth, opening to those youth places in the occupational hierarchy well above what they would otherwise be likely to achieve. Such enterprises could provide real upward mobility instead of just protecting some disadvantaged youth from chronic unemployment. At least some of the jobs created could yield well above subsistence income and a degree of occupational status not usually attainable by disadvantaged people. Even if the businesses initiated by true entrepreneurial projects sometimes fail, and that is inevitable, the experience of taking responsibility, learning to make decisions, and developing technical and managerial skills would serve disadvantaged youth well, not only directly as qualifications for subsequent employment but indirectly by transforming those young people's perceptions of themselves and their capacities.

We have made the point that subsidized employment in low-paid, low-status, low-responsibility jobs may unintentionally confirm the subordinate status of disadvantaged youth because it is continuous with their experience at home and in school and with the experiences of their friends, neighbors, and relatives. Being an owner and manager of a small business thus also promises to alter disadvantaged youth's perceptions of themselves and of the opportunities open to them, giving them incentive to develop capacities that are not needed in the secondary labor market. In terms borrowed from cognitive psychology, they would experience "psychological disequilibrium," which, according to Piaget (1948) and Kohlberg and Gilligan (1971), is a prerequisite to the development of new, more sophisticated ways of thinking.

This leads to the second part of our recommendation: that youth employment programs can be democratically operated.

Entrepreneurial programs lend themselves to democratic control, but it is possible for them to be designed and controlled either by adults or by one or a few youth. By democratic control we mean that all participants engage in group decision making, that work tasks are rotated to provide diversity and flexibility, and that profits are collectively controlled. We do not mean that all participants are always equal, since length of service and talent can justify differences in the degree of power participants exercise. Democratic programs can prepare youth to function effectively in current and future job markets, they can be a powerful positive influence on disadvantaged youth's ways of thinking about their environment and themselves, and they can foster the skills and attitudes needed to make workplaces more democratic in the future.

Employers' concerns about the "coping skills" of youth are too often limited to youths' tractability. While all of us have to be able to respond appropriately to legitimate authority, the implication of adopting "coping skills" as a program objective is that disadvantaged youth need primarily to be obedient in order to hold jobs. This is probably true in the secondary labor market, but to train disadvantaged youth only to fit into that sector of the economy is perpetuating inequality. Compliance is not enough.

Social scientists, social critics, and even some employers have become convinced that the hierarchical structure of authority in the workplace is increasingly dysfunctional, not only because it often leaves workers frustrated and apathetic, with serious personal consequences, but for the dollars and cents reason that it impedes productivity (Blumberg, 1973; Work in America, 1973; O'Toole, 1979; Zwerdling, 1980). If worker participation in management becomes more common, then disadvantaged youth need to be prepared for that opportunity rather than for docility.

Most experiments in workplace democratization have been conducted in the industrial sector of the economy, but the kinds of skills fostered by experience in a democratic workplace would seem to be especially suited to the growing service sector. Cooperation, communication, and an ability to understand diverse points of view are all essential to many service jobs, especially at the highest levels of pay and prestige, but also at the lower end of the hierarchy. Dewey (1916) and many others since (for example, Newmann, 1975) have urged democratic education to develop precisely these skills. Democratic work experience would be an excellent method of teaching the skills required in the most rapidly growing sector of the U.S. economy.

Although reliability and respect for authority will continue to be needed in the workplaces of the near future, the submissive assembly line operative will no longer be the ideal employee. In O'Toole's words:

> What will be required is humane individuals with analytical and entrepreneurial skills, people who know how to work in groups, people who know how to solve problems, and people who will not panic when something untoward starts to occur [1979: 19].

A second benefit of democratically operated programs is that they are likely to be distinctly different from the previous experiences of disadvantaged youth, or "discontinuous." As such they can be powerful motivators for change. (See Hamilton and Crouter, 1980, for an argument in favor of "discontinuous" work experience for disadvantaged youth.) Two related types of change are important. One is in young people's structures of thinking; the other, in their perceptions of themselves. Effective functioning in a democratic program requires and fosters abstract thinking, thinking that is also functional in technical and managerial jobs where principles must be articulated and applied, relationships perceived, and new conceptions weighed and tested. Merely following orders does not encourage this type of thinking. Neither does it encourage young people to see themselves as active and powerful. Being part of a group that makes serious decisions, the consequences of which can be seen and are important to other people, can give young people the sense of efficacy they need to aspire to and achieve higher occupational levels than their parents occupy.

This prospective benefit of democratic programs is subject to the same challenge that can be made to conventional programs seeking to improve the employability of individual youth: if all attain greater self-confidence and higher aspirations, these qualities will be devalued in the same way that diplomas have been devalued as more and more people obtain them. Our answer to that challenge involves a third benefit of democratic programs. When substantial numbers of youth have experienced this form of work organization, additional pressure will accumulate to reform workplaces in the direction of greater democracy. Furthermore, these reform efforts are more likely to be successful precisely because a larger proportion of workers will have acquired the skills and attitudes needed to make them work. Providing democratic work experiences to disadvantaged youth, in other words, can add to the impetus toward workplace democratization that currently comes primarily from disaffected priviledged youth (Yankelovich, 1974).

Although we have presented entrepreneurship and democracy separately, we view them as interdependent. Both are critical to fostering disadvantaged young people's ability to engage in rewarding and demanding jobs, to establishing perceptions of themselves as being able to hold those kinds of jobs, and to altering the structure of the labor market, which currently restricts both the numbers of such jobs and the proportion of disadvantaged youth who are allowed access to them. Programs that are both democratic and entrepreneurial will have sufficient impact on the "opportunity structure" that disadvantaged youth will have greater motivation to participate in and complete them. There will be rational motivation in the probable returns for their investment of time and energy.

CONCLUSION

Our primary purpose has been to challenge the assumption upon which conventional youth employment programs are based, that youth unemployment is caused by deficiencies in disadvantaged youth and by occasional job scarcity. We argue instead that the concentration of unemployment among low-income minority youth is a direct consequence of the current economic and social structure. We propose that democratic entrepreneurial work programs are more likely than conventional youth employment programs to have a substantial impact on the racial and social inequality that underlie youth unemployment. Entrepreneurship can give disadvantaged youth experiences that are closer to those found in private sector employment than most currently found in subsidized employment programs. A democratic form of organization assures youth access to positions of greater authority and responsibility than they would be likely to achieve elsewhere. It also prepares them for the kind of workplace many experts predict will become more common in the near future, and it contributes to the fulfillment of that prophecy by fostering a commitment to democratic work organization in a substantial number of workers who also have the skills required to function in such organizations.

There is, of course, some irony in our recommending democracy and entrepreneurship while claiming a radical perspective. And yet, when programs for disadvantaged people are paternalistic and bureaucratic, democracy is radical. When the economy is dominated by large corporations, entrepreneurship is radical. When both democracy and entrepreneurship are practiced by the disadvantaged, they can contribute to reducing the inequality that is at the root of the problem of youth unemployment.

REFERENCES

ADAMS, A. V., G. L. MANGUM, W. STEVENSON, S. F. SENINGER, and S. MANGUM (1978) The Lingering Crisis of Youth Unemployment. Kalamazoo, MI: W.E. Upjohn Institute for Employment Research.
APPLE, M. (1979) Ideology and Curriculum. London: Routledge & Kegan Paul.
BARTON, P. E. (1975) "Youth employment and career entry," in S. L. Wolfbein (ed.) Labor Market Information for Youths. Philadelphia: Temple University.
—— and B. S. FRASER (1978) Between Two Worlds: Youth Transition from School to Work, Vol. 2. Washington, DC: Center for Education and Work, National Manpower Institute.
BERNSTEIN, B. (1977) Class, Codes and Control, Vol. 3: Towards a Theory of Educational Transmissions. London: Routledge & Kegan Paul.
BLAU, P. M. and O. D. DUNCAN (1967) The American Occupational Structure. New York: John Wiley.
BLUMBERG, P. (1973) Industrial Democracy: The Sociology of Participation. New York: Schocken Books.
BOURDIEU, P. and J. PASSERON (1977) Reproduction: In Education, Society and Culture. Beverly Hills, CA: Sage.
BOWLES, S. and H. GINTIS (1976) Schooling in Capitalist America. New York: Basic Books.
BRAVERMAN, H. (1974) Labor and Monopoly Capital: The Degradation of Work in the Twentieth Century. New York: Monthly Review Press.
BRITTAIN, J. A. (1977) The Inheritance of Economic Status. Washington, DC: Brookings Institution.
deLONE, R. (1979) Small Futures: Children, Inequality and the Limits of Liberal Reform. New York: Harcourt Brace Jovanovich.
DEWEY, J. (1916) Democracy and Education. New York: Macmillan.
FELDSTEIN, M. and D. ELLWOOD (1979) Teenage Unemployment: What is the Problem? Working Paper No. 393. Cambridge, MA: National Bureau of Economic Research.
General Accounting Office (1979) More Effective Management Is Needed to Improve the Quality of SYEP. Washington, DC: Government Printing Office.
GINZBERG, E. (1980) "Youth unemployment." Scientific American 242: 43-49.
—— (1979) Good Jobs, Bad Jobs, No Jobs. Cambridge, MA: Harvard University Press.
GOODWIN, L. (1980) "Poor youth and employment: a social psychological perspective." Youth and Society 11: 311-351.

HAMILTON, S. F. and A. C. CROUTER (1980) "Work and growth: a review of research on the impact of work experience on adolescent development." J. of Youth and Adolescence 9: 323-338.

HAMILTON, S. F. and S. K. STEWART (1980) "A multi-method approach to research on youth employment programs: a case study of the Youth Conservation Corps." Children and Youth Services Rev. 2: 187-210.

HERSHER, J. (1978) "CETA's $11 billion." Civil Rights Digest 10, 3: 3-9.

KOHLBERG, L. and C. GILLIGAN (1971) "The adolescent as a philosopher: the discovery of the self in a postconventional world." Daedalus 100: 1051-1086.

KOHN, M. (1977) Class and Conformity: A Study in Values. Chicago: University of Chicago Press.

——— and C. SCHOOLER (1978) "The reciprocal effects of the substantive complexity of work and intellectual flexibility: a longitudinal analysis." Amer. J. of Sociology 84: 24-52.

LEVITAN, S. A. (1976) "Coping with teenage unemployment," in The Teenage Unemployment Problem: What are the Options? Washington, DC: Government Printing Office.

LYNTON, E., J. R. SELDIN, and S. GRUHIN (1978) Employers' Views on Hiring and Training. New York: Labor Market Information Network.

McARTHUR, V. (1980) Youth Entrepreneurship Demonstration Project: Interim Report #2. Manchester, NH: New England Institute of Human Services.

MANGUM, G. and J. WALSH (1978) Employment and Training Programs for Youth: What Works Best for Whom? Washington, DC: U.S. Department of Labor.

METZ, C. (1978) Classrooms and Corridors. Berkeley: Univ. of California Press.

NEWMANN, F. (1975) Education for Citizen Action. Berkeley: McCutchan.

OGBU, J. (1979) "Social stratification and the socialization of competence." Anthropology and Education Q. 10, 1: 3-20.

——— (1978) Minority Education and Caste: The American System in Cross-Cultural Perspective. New York: Academic Press.

O'TOOLE, J. (1979) "Education is education and work is work—shall ever the twain meet?" Teachers College Record 81: 6-21.

PIAGET, J. (1948) The Moral Judgement of the Child. New York: Free Press.

RIST, R., M. HAMILTON, W. HOLLOWAY, S. JOHNSON, and H. WILTBERGER (1980a) Targeting on In-School Youth: Four Strategies for Coordinating Education and Employment Training. Ithaca, NY: Youthwork National Policy Study.

——— (1980b) Patterns of Collaboration: The CETA/School Linkage. Ithaca, NY: Youthwork National Policy Study.

——— (1978) Forging New Relationships: The CETA/School Nexus. Ithaca, NY: Youthwork National Policy Study.

ROGERS, D. (1973) "Vocational and career education: a critique and some new directions." Teachers College Record 74: 471-511.

RYAN, W. (1976) Blaming the Victim. New York: Random House.

SMITH, R. and J. VANSKI (1979) "The volatile teenage labor market: labor force entry, exit and unemployment flows." Youth and Society 11: 3-31.

SOMERS, G. G. and J. L. WARLICK (1975) An Evaluation of Manpower Programs for Young Men, 1964-1972. Madison: Department of Economics, University of Wisconsin.

TAGGART, R. (1980) "Lessons from program experience," in B. Linder and R. Taggart (eds.) A Review of Youth Employment Problems, Programs and Policies; Vol. 3: Program Experience. Washington, DC: U.S. Department of Labor.

U.S. Department of Labor, Employment and Training Administration (1980) A Report on Monitoring and Corrective Action Efforts for the 1979 SYEP. Washington, DC: Government Printing Office.

WALTHER, R. H. (1976) Analysis and Synthesis of DOL Experience in Youth Transition to Work Programs. Springfield, VA: National Technical Information Service.

Work in America: Report of a Special Task Force to the Secretary of Health, Education, and Welfare (1973) Washington, DC: Government Printing Office.

YANKELOVICH, D. (1974) The New Morality: A Profile of American Youth in the 70's. New York: McGraw-Hill.

Youth Programs (1981) Waltham, MA: Center for Employment and Income Studies (Spring).

ZWERDLING, D. (1980) Workplace Democracy. New York: Harper & Row.

Social Welfare Policy

Social welfare policies are presently undergoing a reexamination and challenge to their basic assumptions regarding who is to be served, how these services are to be delivered, and the extent of services to be offered. As the country continues in a period of little or no economic growth (as of April 1982, the industrial sector was operating at 70.3 percent of capacity), serious questions are being asked about government ability to sustain the present level of support for welfare programs. The "politics of scarcity" necessitates a different orientation and approach to social welfare issues. No longer can we presume to "throw programs at problems" in the hope that somewhere amidst this near-random behavior we will find a strategy that is successful.

Several aspects of this change are particularly important. First, there is the matter of reassessing the role of the marketplace and the private sector. For the past three decades, the broad consensus has been that the primary sector of the society to respond to welfare issues was to be government at all levels. Private sector initiatives were welcomed but thought to be secondary to the dominant position of government. This consensus is now being challenged vigorously by those who argue that the private sector ought to play a major if not dominant role. This approach is especially prevalent in the present policies of the Reagan administration. The articles by Cochran, on the role of the private-for-profit sector in child care services, and by Khadduri and Struyk, on housing vouchers for the poor, both address aspects of "public versus private" sector responsibilities in providing welfare services.

A second of the basic assumptions of current social welfare policies now being reexamined is the extent of coverage under one or another program. Heretofore, as close to universal coverage as possible has been defined as a desirable social goal. The alternative thesis is that universal coverage is seldom desirable because it builds disincentives for private economic activity and because the costs exceed the capacity of the system to absorb them. The argument, then, is for the targeting of services to those defined as eligible by relatively narrow criteria. This strategy is being applied with some energy by the present administration. Increasing restrictions and limitations are being placed, for example, on eligibility for such programs as food stamps, income support under social security, student loans, and subsidies for home heating fuel. Targeting strives to ensure that those narrowly defined do, in fact, receive the services, and that those no longer eligible seek out the private sector and the market place. The effort is to constrict the range of services from government that individuals think they are entitled to receive. All four articles here address this issue.

Third, programs increasingly must account for their performance adequately and accurately. Scarce funds demand that public sector initiatives justify themselves and that programs be implemented as proposed. While it has been common knowledge that many social welfare programs have emerged from start-up with little resemblance to what was promised or originally funded, the message now is that lack of adherence to originally established goals and procedures will make that program vulnerable to extinction.

Yet many of the originally established goals for programs were not clear, or were so ambitious in their objectives that successful implementation was not possible. Rodgers demonstrates this with the program to demand work tests for welfare recipients, and Erie documents the consequences of conflicting government goals on the economic well-being of the black community. The end result is that existing programs are difficult to justify, and pressure is generated for alternatives. Rodgers in particular makes clear that issues of implementation will confront not only those programs developed by liberals but those created by conservatives as well.

27

PROFITS AND POLICY
Child Care in America

Moncrieff Cochran

The nonmedical care of human beings by salaried professionals and paraprofessionals has become a major industry in the United States, as it has in most Western, industrialized countries. This care is provided primarily to individuals at the beginning and at the end of their lives; to the elderly in nursing homes and to very young children in day care centers and other preschool programs. What distinguishes the U.S. scene from those abroad is the use in this country of profit making as an economic incentive for the provision of such services.[1] The economic dimensions of the policy debate surrounding care of the elderly have been one aspect of the nursing home scandals spotlighted in the popular press during the 1970s and examined in policy and analyses during that same period.[2] Much less visible, but equally extraordinary from an international perspective, has been the gradual movement of entrepreneurial interests into the field of child day care.[3] Although overshadowed in public child-care debates by reassessments of the Head Start program and national evaluations of center- and family-based child care arrangements, group care for profit has, over the past 10 years, become an increasingly recognized member of the child care community. Visibility for the profit-making approach probably reached its zenith in the 1970s when, in 1974, President Gerald Ford seriously considered the appointment of Joyce Hatton, owner of a day-care center chain in Michigan called Young World, Inc., as Director of the Office of Child Development, HEW.[4]

Exerting their influence on the social policies of the 1980s are a set of demographic and political forces that are likely to give added impetus to private-sector involvement with day care for children. On the demographic front, mothers are entering the paid labor force in unprecedented numbers, continuing what the U.S. Census Bureau has recently referred to as "the most significant demographic shift of the 1970's."[5] This shift to work outside the home is most pronounced among mothers with children of preschool age,[6] and can only be accelerated by the current economic downturn. One consequence of this movement is increased demand for child care from a set of community resources that is already stretched to capacity in most locales.

The political dimension contains two related aspects likely to encourage private-sector involvement with child day care. First, the Reagan administration has repeatedly stated its commitment to greater involvement by the private and voluntary sectors in the provision of services hitherto thought of as primarily in

---

From Moncrieff Cochran, "Profits and Policy: Child Care in America," original manuscript. Copyright © 1982 by Sage Publications, Inc.

the public domain. Second, the federal government has sharply reduced its contribution to the costs of providing child care services at state and local levels, as a part of the administration's attempts to balance the federal budget and reduce the federal role in the affairs of local communities.[7] So the national leadership is calling for greater involvement by profit-making concerns in the care of young children, at a time when the public demand for such care has never been higher, while simultaneously reducing support from the federal coffers for public and nonprofit child care programs. Within such a climate it becomes appropriate, and even essential, to assess the probable impacts of these general economic policies upon social programs *as they are experienced by those receiving them.* In this chapter the focus is on day care centers for young children as instruments of social policy. The central thesis of the chapter is that the validity of one or another economic approach to the provision of day care services should be measured by the impacts of that approach upon the quality of services provided to child, family, and community. Data in support of this theme are drawn from cross-cultural comparisons of the ideologies surrounding child day care as social policy, from studies of the factors contributing to the quality of care provided by day care centers, and from an examination of how allocations within the day care budget might affect that quality. The chapter concludes with a discussion of ways to ensure a "balance of power" among the several constituencies with interest in the policy through appropriate regulation and public education.

THE IDEOLOGICAL CONTEXT

The historically rooted values of a culture, its economic underpinnings, and the characteristics of its political system are all reflected in its social policies. These forces combine to produce a prevailing system of beliefs that help to explain both the broad outlines and the particular details of how a society cares for its poeole. The child day care services available to and utilized by American parents are shaped by a largely implicit set of beliefs about privacy, child rearing, work, and employment. These beliefs are not easily combined; a tension is created by their simultaneous application. For instance, there is a strong feeling that child rearing is a family affair, to be carried out by the mother, with help from the father, separate from public life. A national commitment to pluralism, stimulated by successive waves of immigration, has carried with it an agreement that different people rear their children differently, and has reinforced the belief that child-rearing practices are the private province of family members. At the same time, the value of work, and the economic independence associated with it, has been promoted by both church and state since the colonizing of the continent. When the industrial revolution drew fathers into jobs away from their homes, work as a valued undertaking increasingly came to mean employment outside the home. Dishwashers and vacuum cleaners, while a relief to the homemaker, also carried with them the implication that such work was more fitted to machinery than to the human hand. Increasingly women as well as men are responding to a society that has long preached the virtues of work as the key to maximization of human potential—work that, to be fulfilling, increasingly must consist of employment in the marketplace.

The creation of a middle class in American society provided the potential for mass consumption of goods beyond that required by subsistence. This economic opportunity led in turn to the definition of consumption as a value in itself, and the conviction that economic growth was (and is) dependent upon high levels of consumption. Thus materialism, as a value, is inextricably bound up in the economics of our society. The costs of consuming have reached the point where they cannot be supported by a single income. Now the economics of participation in American society combine with the belief that human potential is realized through paid work to draw mothers into the labor market. Adding to this movement is a realization by employers that women are "good" workers—eager to please and satisfied with a wage that frees them from the isolation of the home.

The tension created by combining the belief that child rearing is a private affair, to be carried out primarily by the mother, with a desire to maximize human potential, individual freedom, and socioeconomic participation through work for pay is being felt both inside the family and at every other level of American society. One visible manifestation of that tension can be seen in our systems of day care for young children. They too are considered a private affair, consisting primarily of informal family-based arrangements.[8] Parents would like to accomplish the impossible—to work full time while simultaneously caring for their preschool children themselves.[9] Some couples are able to do both by working nonoverlapping shifts, but at significant cost to their own relationships. When others outside the immediate family are called upon to provide day care, they are likely to be relatives and neighbors.[10] The majority of such family day care is not regulated in any way by federal, state, or local authorities. Each arrangement is a private one, negotiated directly between parent and caregiver.

Another characteristic of U.S. day care programs that can arguably be considered a product of the tension between the value of caring for one's own child and the value of working outside the home is the "parent involvement" aspect of those services. In comparing day care in the United States with programs abroad, Kamerman and Kahn note that "participation ideology is at the 'maximum' end of the continuum and much more than is called for in 'requirements' for parental participation."[11] Part of the reason for an emphasis on participation in the day care program could be parents' desires to work outside the home without giving up too much control over the activities of their children during the hours when they are apart. This concern may be exacerbated in a multiethnic, multicultural society, where parents cannot assume that the child-rearing practices of nonrelatives will parallel their own.

The number of preschool children who receive day care in centers, while still smaller than those in family-based day care, has increased steadily over the past decade.[12] That increase has been absorbed primarily by private rather than public programs. Kamerman and Kahn point out that "the public-private ratio of centers caring for children under age three is one to three," and that "more than half of the private centers are proprietary-organized to make a profit."[13] This acceptance of profit as a motive for providing day care to young children distinguishes U.S. child care programming from its European counterparts, including programs in demonstrably capitalistic countries such as West Germany, France, England, Norway, and Sweden.

The ideological context for child day care in the United States is composed, then, of beliefs about privacy, child rearing, work, and employment, which, when examined side by side, contain some inherent contradictions. These contradictions produce a dynamic tension that is manifested in the particular characteristics of American day care programs. The predominance of home-based care arrangements, the heavy emphasis on parent involvement, and the emergence of day care centers organized for profit are all aspects of the day care scene in the United States that can arguably be attributed to the conflict between wanting to raise one's own children and the necessity or desire to participate in the marketplace provided by a capitalistic society. The right to engage in profit-making activities in such a society goes virtually unchallenged; it is considered a natural extension of the individual freedoms guaranteed by a democratic political system. The making of profit requires, however, satisfaction by the consumer with a product provided at the lowest possible cost to the producer. Little attention has been paid to whether the quality of care to human beings can be, or should be, assessed with the criteria used by private enterprise in general. It is to the identification of criteria for assessing the impacts of profit-making and nonprofit day care services that we now turn our attention, after briefly defining profit making in the day care center.

A DEFINITION OF PROFIT MAKING

Profit making, in this discussion, refers to income derived by a person over and above any salary paid to her or him for work performed in the direct provision of child care services. The definition becomes very important when applied to the range of day care services provided across the country, because it distinguishes women providing day care in their own homes ("day care mothers") and couples running small, local center programs ("mom and pop" centers) from entrepreneurs owning several or a chain of large, private centers. Day care mothers and moms/pops charge the parents they serve enough to cover costs and to pay themselves a salary for their labors. Entrepreneurs collect a percentage of the revenues taken in by each of the centers they own independent of any salary that they might receive for services rendered to parents and children.[14] Only this income beyond salary is considered profit for the purposes of this chapter.

CRITERIA FOR IMPACT ASSESSMENT

The first criterion that comes to mind for assessing the impact of child care programs, or any program involving the care of human beings, is program quality. Unlike the situation in the marketing of some goods, where lower quality can be compensated for by lower price, there are sharp limits to how much the quality of a child care program can be lowered without seriously damaging the consumer. Human beings are not like disposable containers, to be used once and then discarded. Research by Skeels and others[15] demonstrated many years ago that mechanical, "assembly-line" approaches to the care of young children seriously retard their development. It is also important to understand the fact that the day care program serves the entire family, not just the child, and so assessment of the quality of the program must take into consideration the needs of other family members.

A second measure of impact that can be applied to comparisons of different economic approaches to the provision of child day care is cost effectiveness. How expensive is the service to provide and to purchase? Of course, the issue of quality quickly enters into a discussion of cost, because if the consumer finds the quality of the product unacceptable, then it will not be purchased even at the lowest possible price.

A third way to assess child day care programs is in terms of their accountability. One kind of accountability is financial: Is the consumer getting the best possible buy for his or her money? In order for the economic marketplace to work freely, it is assumed that there must be unrestricted competition among producers (service providers). Another kind of accountability has policymaking and the consumer as its primary orientation. How accountable is the provider to consumers when deciding how to design or alter the service provided? It is accountability in these terms that has been of particular interest to the human services community during the past two decades.

The fourth dimension of child day care services especially deserving of attention in the assessment of those programs is parent involvement. Parent involvement can vary in type and magnitude, from chats with the caregiver at the beginning or end of the day to work as a part-time staff volunteer and participation on a policymaking board. This assessment criterion is clearly justified by the presence of the value conflicts involving parental participation in the rearing of their children versus involvement in the labor market discussed earlier.

Four basic criteria have been identified for the making of comparisons between child day care programs, or groups of programs: quality of care, cost effectiveness, accountability, and parent involvement. Each of these ways of assessing the overall value of the service provided can be applied to the profit-nonprofit question. We turn now to those discussions.

The Quality of Care

Staff/child ratio, groups size and caregiver qualifications have long been considered key determinants of quality in center care; all have been central factors in both state licensing requirements and federal fiscal regulations. Taken together these regulable center characteristics have been widely assumed to influence the nature and number of contacts between caregiver and child and among children on a day-to-day basis within the day care center.[16]

The National Day Care Study (NDCS), completed in 1978, was a study of center-based child day care carried out over a 4-year period. The purpose of the study was to determine the impact on the development of preschool children of variations in group size, number of caregivers, adult/child ratio, and staff qualification. In the process of data collection the study's staff observed and tested 1800 children, interviewed 1100 parents, observed and interviewed caregivers in 129 classroom groups, and gathered program and cost data from 57 centers located in Atlanta, Detroit, and Seattle. Child outcome measures were tests focused on knowledge of language, colors, shapes, and spatial relationships, which had demonstrated value for predicting success in elementary school.

Two findings from this study deserve particular attention. First, NDCS results show that positive outcomes for children are associated with small groupings of children and adults. That is, groups of 15 or fewer children were "associated with higher frequencies of desirable child and caregiver behavior and higher gains on the (child development scales) than groups of 25 or more children."[17]

The second important finding from the NDCS was that caregiver qualifications, and especially amount of specialization in child-related fields (developmental psychology, early childhood education, special education), were also associated with higher test scores by the children under their care. Such caregivers engaged in more social interaction with children (questioning, responding, instructing, praising, and comforting), and spent less time than other caregivers interacting with other adults. When the researchers looked at training together with group size, they concluded that "all caregivers, with and without specialization, are more effective with smaller groups, and that caregivers with specialization are more effective than others with groups of any size."[18]

There are other dimensions of the day care center that can have real significance for program quality but are less easily measured than group size and caregiver qualifications. One such dimension is the caregiver-parent relationship.[19] This relationship represents the bridge between center and home for the child, and how well the two settings fit together as regards the boundaries, support, understanding, and love given the child depends to a considerable degree upon this bridge. Two elements essential to the building of this link between parent and caregiver are time and accessibility. The caregiver must have time to spend with parents, especially at the beginning and end of the day. That time is only available if he or she is sharing care of the group with another adult. Even a few minutes of relaxed chatting are impossible if eight to ten children are constantly clamoring for your attention.

Time to spend with the caregiver often translates into a question of geographic location and accessibility for the parent. If the center is neighborhood-based, and thus nearby, she or he can afford to linger a few more minutes chatting with the caregiver and even having a cup of coffee, knowing that the trip home will be quick and easy. The parent is also more likely to drop by for an evening get-together at the center if it is close to home than if such an activity requires 15-20 minutes of driving each way after a long day's work.

Being neighborhood-based has another effect that can influence the quality of life for the family using day care center services. If a large proportion of the families using a center live in the same neighborhood, there is a good possibility that those families will encounter each other outside the center as they use a local park, shop at a local store, or simply walk the streets of the neighborhood. Thus having the center in common may serve as a reason to become acquainted and participate together in other activities. These social links are helpful to both parent and child. For the parent they mean a helping hand in an emergency, someone to talk to about a problem, or a ride to work. For the child it becomes another link between home and center when a playmate in the neighborhood is also a friend in day care.

Still another complex issue affecting quality in day care involves the relationships among caregivers working in the same center. One hopes that such a group can work as a team, respecting and supporting each other and sharing common values and goals. A staff larger than 10-15 people is probably too big to permit the building of a real sense of community among caregivers, and the absence of such a community has a negative impact on the daily functioning of everyone involved, including parents and children.

Several consistent themes run through this discussion of quality in day care. Those themes are human linkages and mutual support. The caregiver-child connection is enhanced by small groups and by the presence of enough well-trained caregivers to provide each child with one-to-one care and attention. Links between caregiver and parent, generated by provision of time and accessibility, contribute to a mutually supportive atmosphere and more assurance in the parent-child relationship. Small program size (15-40 children) and a neighborhood orientation can strengthen ties between caregivers within the center, and serve as a basis for more enduring contacts among parents and children from different families in the neighborhood served by the day care program.

Cost Effectiveness

> The bottom line of the delivery of service is who can do best within the money constraints. In other words, who can do best for the most reasonable amount of money. There is no reason that proprietary or profit-making organizations should not have the opportunity to compete. We feel one of the reasons, if for no other reason, is that it will keep all programs.
>
> There is this element of competition. All programs will constantly strive to develop the best service for the most cost-effective means and that is one of our basic reasons for having the profit-making organizations [Owen Preagler, Dean, Pace University School of Continuing Education].

The quality-related dimensions of the day care center mentioned earlier—number and skills of caregivers, size of groups and of total program, and neighborhood orientation—interact as an ecological whole to produce benefits for children, parents, and caregivers. How are these benefits translated into financial costs and are those costs reasonable? First, there are the salaries of the caregivers staffing the center. More and better qualified caregivers means a greater number of salaries at a somewhat higher wage level.

Second, there is the size of the total program, and groups within the program. Size, in economic terms, has been often associated with the concept of economies of scale. Applied to the day care center this concept suggests that larger groups of children, without increase in the number of caregivers, is more economical than smaller groups of children, other things being equal. But other things are not equal, according to the National Day Care Study. Larger groups of children were associated with care of lower quality than were smaller groups of children. The issue of economies of scale versus program quality can also arise at the level of the entire program. Meal preparation is a good example. If the cook has the capacity to prepare meals for 75 children and adults (a larger center), why run a smaller program that must pay her the same salary for feeding fewer people? Again, the answer lies in a careful assessment of program quality. The cook who has 35 instead of 75 mouths to feed may find time to let some of the children make the spaghetti sauce, and is more likely to pay attention to parental suggestions about foods their children especially like or dislike.

When the focus is shifted from caregiver-child relationships to those involving caregiver and parents the economic issue continues to be caregiver salaries. Enough caregivers must be hired to make possible *both* the care of children and good communication with parents. Good communications take time; parents cannot be shunted in and out of the day care center on an assembly line. In fact, it may be necessary to conclude that a certain amount of economic inefficiency is a necesssary prerequisite to provision of day care services that are truly supportive of family life.

It appears, then, that most of the variation in the quality of the day care services provided to preschool children and their parents can be traced to the personnel providing the services, and is likely to be reflected in the amount of money invested in that component of the service. Just what portion of the day care budget is made up of wages and salaries? The budget of a small day care center with which the author has been associated as a board member is presented below for illustrative purposes. Total annual cost of running the program is just over $50,000.00.

salaries (director, teachers, part-time accountant, including payroll taxes)	71.0%
rent	6.6%
food	5.3%
supplies	3.4%
insurance	2.6%
equipment	2.2%
utilities	1.6%
transportation	.8%
miscellaneous (outdoor play equipment, photocopying, etc.)	6.5%
total	100%

The item "profit" does not appear in the budget presented above because the center has nonprofit status. The question is, where would the profit come from if it were to be extracted from these expenditures? In testimony before congressional subcommittees in 1975, proprietary operators expressed the conviction that they must clear 10 percent to 15 percent per year to make day care "worth the investment."[21] A report prepared by the Bank of America analyzing the costs of proprietary (profit-making) day care centers indicates where those cuts must be made.[22] In that report they permit 65 percent of total expenditures for "salaries" in a budget providing a 10 percent profit. So the bulk of the profit, should one be taken from the income of the center used above as an illustration, would have to come straight from where the quality is in the program—the caregivers. Bank of America also presents a budget calculated to show a 20 percent profit. There the percentage of total budget paid to salaries drops to 55 percent. Use of that percentage in the budget presented earlier would mean taking about $1000 out of the annual salaries of each of the 5 caregivers in the program, none of whom is currently earning more than $8000 per year.

Profit-making centers that are linked together as a "chain" are a part of a franchise, and must pay a fee to the owner of the franchise. That fee is 10 percent to 12 percent of gross income, and is in addition to profit taken by the center operator.[23] Where can the additional fee come from? Salaries must be considered the prime candidates for cuts. The food budget would appear to be another likely source of reduction.

The available evidence indicates that profits, whether to a franchiser or to an operator, are drawn almost exclusively from staff salaries, salaries that even in the nonprofit context are barely above minimum wage. When the salary pool shrinks, fewer caregivers are hired and the size of the program is increased to achieve "economies of scale." Yet there is reason to believe that larger programs with smaller staffs bring a marked drop in the quality of child care provided by a center, and reductions in caregiver-parent communication. In his Senate testimony (quoted earlier), Owen Preagler argues that "the bottom line of the delivery of service is who can do best within the money constraints." To "do best" is to provide service of high quality. This issue of quality is at the core of cost effectiveness, and must not be lost sight of when comparing programs. No service, whether profit-making or nonprofit in nature, is cost effective if it is delivering an inferior product. Quality is to be found in caregiver qualifications, group size, and caregiver-child ratios, all of which are reflected in the amount of the total budget devoted to wages and salaries.

Accountability

> Where in this bill is the motivation to provide quality, excitement, instill values to be accountable? Where is the opportunity for the market to work? For bad programs to fail? [Joyce V. Hatton, President, Young World, Inc. (day care franchise)].[24]

Ms. Hatton, like Owen Preagler, implies that there is some mechanism built into proper use of free-enterprise capitalism that ensures that the resulting product will be of high quality. Accountability, to her, refers to competition in the economic marketplace. Hatton and others testified against the proposed Child and Family Services Act in 1975 because they were afraid that such legislation would provide nonprofit service providers with a competitive edge. Nowhere in their testimony do those involved with proprietary programs address the question of what makes up a day care service of high quality. It is now clear from the results of the National Day Care Study that it is possible to define the elements of a high-quality program. It is also reasonable to believe that some public subsidy to day care programs will increase their capacity to provide services of high quality, because that capacity is so dependent upon the ability to pay decent salaries. Thus accountability to a standard of excellence would seem to this author more appropriate than automatic subservience to an abstract economic principle. Service providers have both rights and responsibilities. With the right to participate in the marketplace must come the responsibility to provide services of high quality. If the taking of profit interferes with that quality to any significant degree, then the legitimacy of such an approach to the provision of service can be seriously questioned.

A third object of accountability is the consumer. In the case of child day care services the consumers are children and their parents. Accountability to parent users, and through them to their children, requires the involvement of those parents in development of the policies governing center operations. Parent involvement takes on an added dimension within the American context, where many parents' belief systems lead them to feel ambivalent about giving up any responsibility for the care of their children. This ambivalence can be alleviated to some degree through active participation in the affairs of the child's day care center. Because of its uniquely American properties, parent participation deserves special attention as a criterion for comparing day care centers.

Parent Involvement

> Our problem with the bill in parent involvement is that the way the bill is written now is you are going to ask these mothers, especially the mothers, to play a very active role in deciding on what groups should get the money and make other judgments when they don't even have time to worry about their child in one individual center. . . .
>
> I think . . . that the practicality of the matter is that you are not going to get them involved because of their obligation to their job and their obligation to their other homemaking chores [Wayne Smith, President, National Association for Child Development and Education].[25]

The National Association for Child Development and Education is a national lobbying organization for the interests of those owning profit-making child day care centers. Its president, Mr. Smith, testified against the parent involvement provisions of the proposed Child and Family Services Act (1975) by simply claiming that working parents could not be expected to get involved in center policies and activities after a hard day on the job. Yet there are many day care centers in the United States in which working parents are very actively involved.

So the question becomes, is the amount of parental participation in center affairs a function of parental capacities and interests, or a reflection of the attitudes of center owners and staffs toward the involvement of parents?

Kammerman and Kahn report that "participation rates are low for U.S. private, profit-making centers. They are higher in non-profit centers, especially in those with federal financial subsidization."[26] From a financial standpoint these differences are understandable; close scrutiny by parents of how financial resources are being allocated could interfere with the protection of some income for profit-making purposes. It is hard to imagine parents who would willingly dispense with more qualified caregivers or better food for their children to protect the profit margin of the center owner or franchise. Yet it is precisely this kind of scrutiny that can go far in ensuring that any day care program, whether profit-making or nonprofit in character, makes the needs of the child and parents the primary focus of fiscal decision making.

Lobbying against the parent involvement provisions of a family services bill is an oddly defensive reaction to what would appear to be a family-strengthening aspect of day care programming. Such a negative response raises questions about how active a role the promoters of day care for profit want parents to play in the rearing of their own children, and just how much they would permit parents to know about what their programs look like from the inside.

A BALANCE OF POWER

> To exclude private enterprise is against our way of life. Private enterprise is what makes our country the great country that it is. Think and think hard. Are you ready to have our children face your future of regimentation? [Bonny Albano, Administrator, Playhouse Day Care Centers, Inc.][27]

When the advocates of profit-making child day care services testified before the Senate Subcommittee on Children and Youth in 1975, their basic complaint was that the proposed legislation did not include federal support for proprietary day care programs. They called forth, in support of their position, the "American Way." Yet information presented earlier indicates that the profit motive can compete with the provision of quality care and support to children and their parents. What policies might be adopted at the local, state, or federal levels that would ensure that parents can have some control over the quality of care provided their children during the working week?

First and foremost, it is the parents themselves who are in the best position to assess the quality of the services provided by the day care centers to them and to their children. The states can, through regulation and information dissemination, ensure that parents have the opportunity and the knowledge needed to ask the questions about salary levels, group size, adult-child ratios, caregiver qualifications, and daily routine the answers to which will permit accurate assessment of program quality. State regulations can require as a condition of licensing that center programs include an active parent-participation component, and that day care teacher certification programs include training in how to involve parents effectively in center affairs. The states can require center directors to provide parents with financial information about each program detailed enough to assess the amount of income being devoted to wages and salaries, and can provide the parents with information explaining how to analyze those financial statements. This examination could be greatly facilitated by local day care coordinating bodies, such as day care councils or local government child development committees. Such an examination of budget information should be carried out for both nonprofit and profit-making programs, to ensure accountability and examine cost effectiveness. Only by comparing different programs can parents and others understand the potential impacts of poor planning, sloppy financial management, or the removal of some percentage of income from the operation of the center for profit.

There is now evidence that policy-manipulable aspects of a day care center do indeed affect the quality of care provided to children. Those data should be the basis for regulations requiring that centers meet the necessary standards for the provision of quality care before receiving licenses or license renewals. Standards should be established at the federal level, and therefore should apply to any day care programs receiving federal financial support. States should be required to include equivalent regulations in state licensing standards before being eligible for federal day care funds. These standards should be applied to all day care center programs, whether organized for profit or with nonprofit status.

Finally, after examining the unavoidable conflict existing between the desire to provide high-quality care and the need to show a profit, this author has concluded that support for proprietary programs should continue to come only from private sources. Parents should be free to express their preferences by purchasing care from profit-making programs, but not with funds provided from public coffers. Nor should federal, state, or local tax revenues be invested directly into profit-making day care programs. Such use of public funds has never been possible in the past, but the New Federalism of the Reagan administration carries with it a new set of assumptions about the relationships between the public and the private sectors of our economy. The current attempt by that administration to provide federal subsidy to private schools is one reflection of those new assumptions.

An effort has been made in this chapter to demonstrate that the economic approaches applied to the provision of child day care services can be evaluated in terms of their impacts upon the quality of care provided to children and families. Analyses of this sort need not be restricted to child care services; they could illuminate our understanding of the interaction between expenditures and services in nursing home services to the elderly, and perhaps even in hospital care. Most consumers of human services are highly dependent upon the assistance they receive; they are not active, questioning participants in a marketplace filled with available alternatives. Analyses such as the one carried out here, and the policies that accrue from them, redress the balance of power somewhat, emphasizing the quality of services provided and accountability to the consumer.

NOTES

1. S. Kamerman and A. Kahn, *Child Care, Family Benefits and Working Parents* (New York: Columbia University Press, 1981), p. 110.
2. Special Committee on Aging, Subcommittee on Long-Term Care, U.S. Senate, *Nursing Home Care in the United States: Failure in Public Policy* (Washington, DC: Government Printing Office, 1975); see especially Supporting Paper 9, Profits and the Nursing Home: Incentives in Favor of Poor Care." See also C. C. Pegels, *Health Care and the Elderly* (Rockville, MD: Aspen Systems Corp., 1981), and M. A. Mendelson, *Tender Loving Greed* (New York: Alfred A. Knopf, 1974).
3. W. Pierce, "Power, Profits, and the Preschool 'Market.' *American Teacher* (supplement, "Changing Education"), December 1971, pp. 11-14.
4. *Day Care and Child Development Reports* 3, no. 21 (October 14, 1975): p. 5.
5. U.S. Department of Commerce, Bureau of the Census, *Current Population Reports*, "Population Characteristics," Series P-20, No. 366 (September 1981) and No. 367 (October 1981).
6. U.S. Dept. of Labor, Bureau of Labor Statistics, *News USDL* 81-522, November 15, 1981.
7. *C.D.F. Reports* 3, no. 2 (April 1981) p. 1; (Children's Defense Fund).
8. Kamerman and Kahn, *Child Care*, p. 107.
9. H. Weiss, "Work," in *Contexts for Childrearing: The Ecology of Family Life in Syracuse, N.Y.*, M. Cochran et al. Final Report to the National Institute of Education. July 1981.
10. Kamerman and Kahn, *Child Care*, p. 108.
11. Ibid., p. 165.
12. Ibid., p. 106.
13. Ibid. p. 110.
14. Joint Hearings on the Child and Family Services Act, 1975, before the Sub-committee on Children and Youth and the Subcommittee on Employment, Poverty and Migratory Labor of the Committee on Labor and Public Welfare, U.S. Senate, and the Subcommittee on Select Education of the Committee on Education and Labor, U.S. House of Representatives, 94th Congress, 1st Session Senate Bill S626 and House Bill 2966, Part 2, February 21, 1975. Washington, DC: Government Printing Office, 1976), p. 262.
15. H. Skeels and H. Dye, "A Study of the Effects of Differential Stimulation on Mentally Retarded Children." *Proceedings of American Association of Mental Deficiency* 44: (1939) 114-136; W. Dennis and P. Najarian "Infant Development Under Environmental Handicap." *Psychological Monographs* 71, no. 7 (1957).
16. J. Travers and R. Roupp *The National Day Care Study: Preliminary Findings and Their Implications.* (Cambridge, MA: Abt Associates, Inc., 1978), p. 8.
17. Ibid., p. 35.
18. Ibid., p. 42.
19. See D. Powell, "Day Care and the Family: A Study of Interactions and Congruency." Final report of the Parent-Caregiver Project, Merrill Palmer Institute, July 1977.
20. Quoted in Joint Hearings, Child and Family Services Act, Part 9, June 20 and July 15, 1975, p. 2051.
21. Ibid., Part 5, p. 810.
22. Ibid., p. 812.
23. Ibid., Part 2, p. 262.
24. Quoted in Ibid., Part 9, p. 1989.
25. Quoted in Ibid., Part 5, p. 824.
26. Kamerman and Kahn, *Child Care*, p. 164.
27. Joint Hearings, Child and Family Services Act, Part 5, p. 787.

28

HOUSING VOUCHERS FOR THE POOR

Jill Khadduri and Raymond J. Struyk

Abstract Can the nation's social programs survive the push toward leaner appropriations, a greater use of the market, and a narrower definition of the needy? A program to provide housing assistance for the poor is proposed that fills all these requirements. Housing vouchers are found to be cheaper than other housing programs and more satisfactory for participants. Moreover, the political climate augers well for the new approach.

If the first year of the Reagan administration is any guide, the social programs of the U.S. government in the years ahead will be dominated by three ideas: be frugal; use the market; target the benefits to the truly needy. For some social programs, these admonitions may prove to be impossible constraints, sharply limiting their effectiveness. In other cases, however, the new requirements could lead to a radical recasting of the program, perhaps preserving and even enlarging its benefits. Housing assistance to the poor is one of those programs in which such a creative response may be possible. The direction of that reform may offer hints for creative shifts in the directions of the other programs as well.

OLD DIRECTIONS AND NEW Housing assistance for poor people is one of the social programs that survived the administration's first year, albeit with some budget cuts. Commitments to subsidize additional households were reduced from $27.6 billion in the 1982 Carter budget proposal to $18.2 billion in the Reagan proposal. Thus, the Reagan administration has shown a willingness to continue to devote substantial resources to help lower-income people with their housing.

If the present administration spends the $18.2 billion in the usual way, that sum will be used partly to build more public housing units of the traditional kind, partly to subsidize the building of structures by the private sector, and partly to subsidize

---

From Jill Khadduri and Raymond J. Struyk, "Housing Vouchers for the Poor," 1(2) *Journal of Policy Analysis and Management* 196-208 (1982). Copyright © 1982 by the Association for Public Policy Analysis and Management. Reprinted by permission of John Wiley & Sons, Inc.

the rents of low-income households who live in adequate existing dwellings. However, there is an alternative use of the $18.2 billion which, as we intend to demonstrate, would make a substantially greater contribution to the housing of the lower-income groups who correspond roughly to the "truly needy" in the housing field.

We define our target group as renters with incomes below 50 percent of median family income for the geographic area in which they live. For the country as a whole, this group of households numbers about 9 million, roughly 11 percent of all U.S. households. Of the 9 million poor renters, about 2.7 million are helped in current housing assistance programs: 1 million in the traditional public housing units that are owned by local housing authorities; 300,000 in units that were constructed under interest subsidy programs extant in the late 1960s and early 1970s, the largest dubbed Section 236 housing; and 1.4 million in units provided by a subsidy program begun in the mid-1970s, so-called Section 8 housing, which makes up the difference between the rent of a unit and 25 percent of the household's income. (Section 8 subsidies can be used to rent existing units or to guarantee rents to developers of new or rebuilt units.) This leaves approximately 6.3 million in the class of poor renters without assistance in housing. The $18.2 billion expended in housing vouchers would be sufficient to help about 2.5 million households in that unaided group. As we propose to demonstrate below, the $18.2 billion could be spent with far greater efficiency than any like sum spent on new construction or reconstruction, such as public housing, Section 236 housing, or the Section 8 approach.

The housing voucher idea, which has been discussed for a considerable period of time, led to various experiments during the 1970s, under the general title of the Experimental Housing Allowance Program (EHAP). Together they provide a firm basis that permits us to predict what the effects of a voucher system might be. One experiment, the Demand Experiment, laid the basis for measuring the effects of vouchers on the housing consumption of participating households, and for comparing the effects of vouchers and other forms of housing assistance in two metropolitan areas, Phoenix and Pittsburgh.

In two other metropolitan areas, South Bend and Green Bay, the Supply Experiment was open to all households that met an eligibility test. As a result of the open enrollment feature in these areas, policymakers now have very good estimates of the number of households that would actually exploit the opportunity to participate in a housing voucher program. Moreover, this experiment served to answer one crucial question that has to be faced in connection with any general voucher scheme, namely, whether the scheme would do no more than elevate the rentals in the area where it applied, without increasing housing facilities for the poor. Inasmuch as such a scheme does not generate directly an increase in the supply of housing in the market, many were concerned that its introduction would simply raise the rents on the existing supply without providing better housing for the poor. Contrary to widely held expectations, however, the voucher program did not cause rent increases above those that could be attributed to increased costs.[1]

In addition to EHAP, the voucher idea was put into practice in the 1970s in a program of national scope—one component of the Section 8 housing assistance program mentioned earlier. Nearly 1 million households will be subsidized under Section 8 in 1982 through vouchers similar to those involved in the test programs. As a result, we can estimate the costs per household of a national voucher program quite accurately, and identify ways of keeping those costs under control.

The key to being able to offer housing assistance to 2.5 million households in addition to those already served within the administration's $18.2 billion budget authority is to use all the funds to rent adequate existing units rather than to divert some to new construction or to the rebuilding of existing housing stock. Almost three-fourths of the 3.7 million units provided under current programs were newly constructed (or virtually rebuilt) as subsidized housing. What the figures below suggest, however, is that public funds can be used more effectively to enlarge the supply of housing available to the poor by improving the ability of the poor to bid for such housing.

VOUCHERS AND OTHER PROGRAMS

Over the past 20 years, the poor have been offered increasing latitude in the form in which they receive public assistance. Numerous examples reflect this trend. Food aid was once provided from a limited set of commodities, which were distributed to recipients from fixed locations; eventually, however, the nation shifted to food stamps that can be spent on a wide range of items at regular retail food stores. Similarly, the provision of medical services to the needy has been evolving from a system of clinic-based agencies to systems under Medicare that offer poor patients a much broader choice of doctors and associated facilities. To be sure, the country has not been prepared to take the next major step, under which the poor would simply receive cash transfers to spend on their needs as they define them; but the trend has been there nevertheless.

The reasons for allowing recipients greater choice in allocating the resources provided by government are substantial. Economists theorize that recipients value each dollar of a subsidy more highly than they value a fixed amount of goods or services of equivalent cost. Some economists also argue that the market is a more efficient producer of services than government because of government's "red tape," restrictive conditions, and the like.

The counterarguments are also formidable. Some economists have argued that the level of satisfaction that taxpayers receive depends on how the poor are helped; if the assistance is for goods and services that the taxpayers view as appropriate, then taxpayers will be more supportive of assistance in general.[2] For this reason restricting services to accord with the perceptions of taxpayers is desirable. Political scientists, for their part, have observed that the committee structure of the Congress strongly militates in favor of a piecemeal approach. Since each comittee will fight to maximize the size of the programs and funding levels under its jurisdiction, the total resources going to the poor are larger than they would be if the appropriate level of aid were examined *en bloc*, as would be the case under a purely cash transfer system.

In acknowledgment of the arguments that some restrictions are undesirable, the housing vouchers that have been used in the various test programs in the past and the vouchers proposed here are restricted in various ways. Most important is the fact that the housing occupied by the voucher recipients must pass a quality test. The experimental studies mentioned earlier demonstrate, however, that this restriction does not greatly affect the value of the vouchers; according to these studies, the value of the vouchers to recipients is close to the cost of such vouchers to the government. Moreover, the vouchers score better than the government outlays under other housing programs. This "consumption efficiency," in the economist's jargon, is demonstrated in Table 1. Total benefits—the rental value of the housing as assessed by the

Table 1. Composition of tenant's monthly benefits per household in selected housing programs in 1975.

	Public housing	Section 236	EHAP
Pittsburgh			
Total benefit[a]	$ 79	$28	$ 77
Benefit in housing[b]	25	31	16
Benefit in disposable income	54	−3	60
Housing as share of total benefit	.32	1.11	.21
Cash equivalent value of subsidy	$ 67	$13	$ 67
Deadweight loss	12	15	10
Phoenix			
Total benefit[a]	$113	$72	$107
Benefit in housing[b]	41	43	27
Benefit in disposable income	72	30	80
Housing as share of total benefit	.36	.60	.25
Cash equivalent value of subsidy	$ 91	$52	$ 86
Deadweight loss	22	21	21

Source: Stephen K. Mayo, Shirley Mansfield, W. David Warner, and Richard Zwetchkenbaum, *Housing Allowances and Other Rental Assistance Programs: A Comparison Based on the Housing Allowances Demand Experiment* (Cambridge, MA: Abt Associates, Inc., 1980), Parts 1 and 2, Tables 3–9.
[a]Market rents minus tenant contributions to rent.
[b]Estimates based on a comparison of market values of units occupied by program participants with market values of units of similar control households.

market minus the tenant's contribution—are shown in the first row. In some cases, the existence of government housing assistance leads tenants to acquire better housing; in other cases, however, it leads the tenant to increase the household's disposable income, while leaving its housing facilities unchanged; and in still other cases, a little of both takes place. Table 1 presents estimates of the outcome for the average tenant in two of the U.S. government's traditional housing programs mentioned earlier, as well as in the Demand Experiment of EHAP, an experimental government voucher program. Because these data were collected in 1975, the analysis does not include projects constructed under the Section 8 program, which was legislated in the Housing and Community Development Act of 1974.

Total benefits per household vary sharply among the programs, being the largest in public housing and the smallest in Section 236 housing. Even in the Section 236 case, however, benefits amount to $50 per month for the average household, equivalent to 11 percent of the income that was regarded as the poverty threshold for a family of four in 1975. In the public housing program and in the housing voucher experiments, there were only small improvements in the housing facilities of the participants, as tenants took most of the benefits in the form of increased disposable income; only in the relatively small Section 236 program were the benefits fully absorbed in improved housing.

The benefits to the household can be calculated more precisely, however, by estimating the size of a cash grant that the tenant would consider equivalent to the benefits received under the program. As one would expect, the rank order of the program's "cash equivalent value," shown in Table 1, is the same as the ordering of benefits in disposable income. Wherever the tenant's cash equivalent estimate is less than the total benefit, the difference can be construed as representing added housing facilities which the tenant valued at less than their market value. That difference can be thought of as a waste of government resources, dubbed in the table as "deadweight loss." The amount of resources so wasted is generally modest—on the order of 15-20 percent. The exception again is Section 236 where the loss ranges to over 50 percent in Pittsburgh.

How do the programs compare in terms of the costs incurred to produce the housing services that each program generated? This question can be addressed by comparing the estimated resource cost of providing the housing services in the program with the market rental value of the units involved. The resulting ratios appear in Table 2.

The lowest ratios appear in the housing allowance program. Thus, on efficiency grounds, housing vouchers appear to be the best vehicle for delivering housing services. Still, even vouchers entail a wastage of resources on the order of 25-30 percent. The wastage occurs because the housing consumed under the program costs the government more than it would cost the tenant if he operated alone in the market, and because the tenant values the increased housing at a little less than its market value. (This, in

Table 2. Estimated ratio of total costs to market rental value for units in 1975.

Program	Pittsburgh	Phoenix
Public housing	2.20	1.79
Section 236	2.01	1.47
Housing voucher experiment	1.15	1.09

Source: Stephen K. Mayo, Shirley Mansfield, W. David Warner, and Richard Zwetchkenbaum, *Housing Allowances and Other Rental Assistance Programs: A Comparison Based on the Housing Allowances Demand Experiment* (Cambridge, MA: Abt Associates, Inc., 1980), Parts 1 and 2, Tables 3-9.

other words, is the sum of the losses from production and consumption inefficiencies.) Balanced against this wastage of resources are the arguments in favor of earmarking assistance for housing consumption: greater satisfaction to taxpayers and the greater likelihood of adequate levels of total assistance to the poor.

THE POLITICS OF HOUSING

Housing vouchers have been proposed at various times since 1935; accordingly, the urge to provide housing with fewer restrictions on tenants has a long history.[3] The difference today is that evidence exists for the economic advantage of vouchers over other housing programs. Moreover, the political environment may at last be right for the adoption of vouchers on a wide scale.

Both the relevant congressional committees and the Office of Management and Budget in the executive branch are acutely aware of the inefficiency of new construction programs. Moreover, both are uneasy about the inescapable need to make long-term subsidy commitments under existing programs that support new construction or the rebuilding of dwellings.

The federal budget for housing programs takes into account both single-year contract authority and multiyear budget authority. Contract authority for a unit is the maximum subsidy payable for that unit in the first year the subsidy is paid. Budget authority is the contract authority for that unit multiplied by the number of years for which the government plans to pay the subsidy.[4] For programs that entail construction, the number of years is fixed by the term of the contract the government signs with the entities that are providing the subsidized housing, such as local housing authorities. The term ranges from 20 to 40 years, but generally is 30 years. For existing units, the government signs a five-year contract with the local agency that administers the voucher program; but to minimize the need for additional appropriations actions, the term of budget authority for existing housing has been set at 15 years.

The budget for fiscal year 1982 shows that twice as much contract authority is needed for each new unit as for each existing unit. Since, in addition, the term of years that budget authority covers for new units is typically twice as long as the term for existing units (30 years compared with 15), budget authority for new units is about four times as great as budget authority for existing units. For a Congress that is deeply concerned over the building up of budgetary authority with its implications for the mortgaging of future budgets, this difference is an important one.

Nevertheless, a voucher program which is open to all households that pass an eligibility test may be opposed in both the executive branch and the Congress because of the explosive growth in coverage that occurred in other programs in the past, especially in the Aid for Dependent Children and food stamp programs. The experiments in Green Bay and South Bend, however, provide reassuring data on this score, data that are summarized in a later section of this article. Assuming that the available data are adequate to allay fears that the program may grow out of control, the prospects for an open enrollment program would depend on its acceptability on other grounds to groups inside and outside the U.S. government.

The Office of Management and Budget, for instance, would probably be favorably disposed. With its objectives for cost-cutting and improved equity, it would clearly favor the program over one that entailed the construction of rental housing.

Among the outside interest groups, various views are likely to be encountered. Housing developers represent a key constituency. In each community, only a handful benefit from HUD projects that require new construction. Not surprisingly, therefore, the strength of developers' interest in lobbying for these programs has been low compared with programs for the building of single-family units. Moreover, community acceptance of exclusively low-income projects is becoming increasingly difficult to secure in light of the management problems for many existing projects, reflected in their high rate of defaults.[5] Thus, developers may not be vociferous opponents to a voucher program, especially if they feel that traditional construction projects were the likely alternatives.

Local governments, public housing authorities, and tenants that are already being subsidized through existing programs may prove resistant to a major innovation such as housing vouchers. Giving up well-established construction programs that serve the poor for a relatively untried voucher program might appear too great a risk. On the other hand, in the face of dwindling housing appropriations, the voucher program may prove attractive for its ability to serve more households. As a straw in the wind, an organization representing the poor before the Congress on such issues—the National Low-Income Housing Coalition—has already come out for a voucher program, complemented with some new construction.

Capitol Hill is harder to judge. As with OMB, cost-cutting and equity goals are close to the hearts of many members of Congress. However, as will be shown below, a voucher program of the kind proposed here would require an increase in spending in the short run, despite a reduction in long-term spending commitments, that is to say, in budget authority. The prospect of higher outlays in the short run could prevent favorable consideration, unless Congress could be made to recognize the savings that would be realized in later years by avoiding the obligation of constructing expensive new housing units. Adding to the possibility of congressional difficulties is the fact that a voucher program would simplify legislation in the housing field and therefore reduce the amount of annual legislative activity under the authorizing committee's purview. On the other hand, housing programs are especially vulnerable to budget-cutting exercises in the present move against federal spending on domestic programs; without a program that automatically generates its own spending levels, the authorizing subcommittees might well preside over ever-eroding domains.

HOW A VOUCHER PROGRAM WOULD WORK

The type of voucher that has been tested extensively in EHAP and that has the most desired effects is called a "housing gap minimum standards" voucher. Its amount is based on a comparison between the income of each household in a given size category and an estimate of the cost of standard housing for such a household in the locality; some fraction of the difference is provided by the housing voucher. The household can rent any private market unit, including units above or below the official estimate of the cost of housing, so long as the housing unit passes an inspection that shows it to be structurally sound and free of health and safety hazards.[6]

For many years, it has been assumed that a low-income household can afford to pay 25 percent of its income for housing; this standard was used in EHAP and is used in the Section 8 programs.[7] In recent years, however, the fraction of income spent for housing by poor and near-poor households has increased dramatically, so that at the present time over half of the 9 million households that we classified earlier as our target group are paying more than 50 percent.[8]

Clearly, there has been a shift in the overall relationship between the cost of housing and the cost of other basic needs, and that shift should be reflected in housing program rules. A shift to a 30-percent standard for housing payments would still provide subsidized households with substantial assistance, while making it possible to subsidize a larger number of households than is covered in existing programs.

In concept, it may not appear necessary to limit a housing voucher of this type explicitly to recipients below a specified income; according to the formula, entitlements decline as incomes rise, reaching zero at a given income level. In fact, however, the formula works in such a way that the subsidy does not reach zero until relatively high income levels are reached. To enable the most needy households to be served with the available resources, therefore, it makes sense to have an upper income limit.

In contrast to other major programs supporting the living standard of the poor, such as food stamps, income limits for housing assistance vary by geographic areas and are set as a percentage of the median income of each such area. The current limit for the Section 8 program is 80 percent of median income of the area. A drop to 50 percent of median income appears desirable. Recent work on the relationship between income and housing needs suggests that households below 50 percent of median income are much more likely to have severe housing problems than households in the income range immediately above that level; the group under the 50-percent line are more likely to live in substandard housing, to pay more than two-fifths of their incomes for rent, or both.[9] An estimate based on data from the Annual Housing Survey suggests that 24 percent of the housing units occupied by families with incomes below the 50 percent of median level do not measure up to minimally standard housing as defined by the Department of Housing and Urban Development, a standard that is much less strict than the Section 8 standards. By contrast, of the families that would be excluded from the program because of the tightening of the Section 8 definition, only 14 percent occupy housing that fails to pass the HUD standard.[10]

Tightening the income limit would reduce the cost of an open enrollment program by rendering about 4.7 million households ineligible to participate. According to our estimate, about 12 percent of these households—some 500,000 households—would participate if they were eligible. Some of this savings is lost, however, because the average subsidy of those to be served will be greater when these higher income households are excluded.[11] Nevertheless, the sum saved from excluding these 500,000 families—a sum amounting to at least $.75 billion—would cover the cost of subsidizing poorer households with even greater needs.

THE CRITICAL QUESTION: HOW MANY PARTICIPANTS? We now have five years of experience with open enrollment programs in Green Bay and South Bend, which provide a basis for estimating the number of households that would actually request and receive assistance from a voucher program. Table 3 provides an estimate of the number of eligible renter households, so far unserved by any of relevant federal programs, who would join a voucher program if the program were available nationally to households with income below 50 percent of the area median.[12] Rates for specific types of families—instead of a composite rate—are used here because HUD programs already serve different types at different rates and because the groups have sharply differing expected participation rates.

The figures show that from 2.3 to 2.8 million households would likely participate. At that point, the coverage for many types of households—particularly those likely to have long-term needs for assistance—would be quite high. For example, about 80 percent of elderly renters living alone and about the same percentage of single-parent families that rent would be assisted. The cost of serving an additional 2.5 million households through a voucher program would be about $4.4 billion or $1,770 per subsidized household in 1979 dollars.[13] In Table 4, we present estimates of the budget authority and outlays for an additional 2.5 million units

Table 3. U.S. households eligible for and likely to participate in a proposed voucher program (numbers in millions).

Household type	Eligible households[a]	Estimated participants Based on South Bend experience	Estimated participants Based on Green Bay experience
Elderly singles	1.35	0.57	1.00
Elderly couples	0.80	0.21	0.30
Single parent with children	0.87	0.43	0.57
Two parents with children	1.74	0.61	0.36
Nonelderly couples	1.09	0.49	0.55
Totals	6.44	2.31	2.77

[a]Defined as renter households not so far served by any of the relevant federal programs with incomes below 50 percent of the area median.

over an eight-year period starting in 1982.[14] The estimates are based on the assumption that it would take six years to add the 2.5 million additional households to those already served,[15] a rate somewhat slower than that experienced in analogous EHAP experiments.[16]

The average time a household is in an allowance program is between two and three years,[17] but new households take the place of those that leave the program. We know from the open enrollment experimental program that, after start-up, the number of recipients in the program at any time is more or less constant, although some variations in cost may still occur.[18]

How do vouchers stack up against other alternatives? Compared with a program like that in the Reagan budget for fiscal year 1982—80,000 newly constructed units plus 100,000 leased existing

Table 4. Budget authority and outlays for an additional 2.5 million units of housing provided by a voucher program.

	Units added to program		Financial data (in constant 1982 dollars)	
	In year indicated	Cumulatively	Added budgetary authority	Outlays
1982	500,000	500,000	18.2	0.5
1983	400,000	900,000	14.8	1.2
1984	400,000	1,300,000	15.1	2.8
1985	400,000	1,700,000	15.3	3.8
1986	400,000	2,100,000	15.5	4.8
1987	400,000	2,500,000	15.8	5.9
1988	—	2,500,000	0.5	6.4
1989	—	2,500,000	0.5	6.5

units—vouchers entail much lower budget authority. After the phase-in period of six years, the added budget authority each year amounts to about $500 million versus the $18.2 billion that would be entailed in a continuation of the Reagan program. This is an especially important difference given the concern of many in the administration and Congress about controlling the cumulative, long-term commitments already on the books for housing—over $200 billion.

On the other hand, vouchers entail higher outlays for the first decade. Whereas the Reagan program, repeated every year between 1982 and 1989, would entail only $4.7 billion of expenditures (in constant 1982 dollars) to serve 1.44 million households, the voucher program over the same years would require $6.5 billion to serve 2.5 million households. Of course, with a longer phase-in period for the voucher programs, outlays entailed in the two alternatives could be equalized. However, the equalization would be purchased at real cost. Whereas the proposed program could make the claim of being available to any household that could meet the income test, a curtailed program could not. Housing programs would again take on the characteristics that they have exhibited in the past, a picture of moving inexorably at great cost to some ill-defined destination.

Housing policy in this country, as in some other domestic areas, stands at a crossroads of potentially great significance. With a sharp turn in direction, housing assistance can be better targeted to those most in need, can assist its clients at a lower cost per household, and at the same time can actually provide equivalent benefits to households by permitting them to follow their preferences. Pursuing our present policies, on the other hand, will place the country on an expensive and seemingly endless trek, until a confused and irate body of taxpayers finally ends the federal government's support for housing the poor.

JILL KHADDURI is a staff analyst in the Office of Policy Development and Research at the U.S. Department of Housing and Urban Development.

RAYMOND J. STRUYK, Senior Research Associate, is Director of the Center for Housing, Community Development, and Energy Policy Research at the Urban Institute.

NOTES
1. Barnett, C. Lance, "Expected and Actual Effects of Housing Allowances on Housing Prices," *AREUEA Journal*, 7(3): 277–297.
2. Hochman, H. H., and Rodgers, J. D., "Pareto Optimal Distribution," *American Economic Review*, 59(4) (1969).
3. Struyk, Raymond J., and Bendick, Jr., Marc, *Housing Vouchers for the Poor* (Washington, DC: The Urban Institute Press, 1981), Chap. 2.
4. Increases in subsidy costs over time as a result of inflation are supposed to be provided for by this system. The actual subsidy paid in the first year is almost always less than the maximum subsidy, that is, the subsidy paid for a household with zero income. The excess contract

authority for each of the early years becomes part of a reserve account used to pay for increased subsidies in future years. There is no inherent reason why these reserves should be sufficient to cover the full subsidy costs in later years, and it has been estimated that in most cases the reserves will prove inadequate for new construction programs. See Congressional Budget Office, *The Long-Term Costs of Lower Income Housing Assistance Programs* (Washington, DC: U.S. GPO, 1979).

5. U.S. Department of Housing and Urban Development, *1979 Statistical Yearbook* (Washington, DC: U.S. GPO, 1981), pp. 106–112.

6. The Section 8 subsidy referred to earlier differs somewhat. In that program, as currently structured, the household does not have an incentive to rent units below the program estimate of the cost of housing, since it receives a correspondingly lower subsidy if it does so. The household also may not rent a unit above the estimated rent of the cost of a typical local unit that meets the physical standards. These rules both restrict the housing available to the program and permit above-market rents to be charged.

7. For a history and assessment of the 25-percent rule, see Lane, Terry S., *Origin and Uses of the Conventional Rules of Thumb* (Cambridge, MA: Abt Associates, Inc., 1977).

8. Estimate by Joseph Riley, reported in *Supplement to the May 20, 1980 Report to the Congress on Section 212 of the Housing and Community Development Act of 1979* (Washington, DC: U.S. Department of Housing and Urban Development, November 1980).

9. Studies of the relationship were actually conducted in terms of "poverty" levels as defined by U.S. Department of Health, Education, and Welfare. A level of 125 percent of poverty, however, is roughly equivalent to 50 percent of the area median income. Results of the study appear in Budding, David, *Housing Deprivation Among Enrollees in the Housing Allowance Demand Experiment* (Cambridge, MA: Abt Associates, Inc., 1980).

10. Tabulation from 1977 Annual Housing Survey, based on definition of substandard housing similar to that used in U.S. Department of Housing and Urban Development, *How Well Are We Housed?* (Washington, DC: U.S. GPO, 1980), Vols. 1–6.

11. Wallace, James, et al., *Participation and Benefits in the Urban Section 8 Program* (Cambridge, MA: Abt Associates, Inc., January 1981); U.S. Department of Housing and Urban Development, *Lower Income Housing Assistance (Section 8): Nationwide Evaluation of the Existing Housing Program, Part I* (Washington, DC: U.S. GPO, 1978).

12. The source for household types already served is internal HUD computations based on HUD occupancy data. Sources for those now being served are U.S. Department of Housing and Urban Development, *op. cit.* (1978); and Wallace et al., *op. cit.* Participation rates by household type for households with incomes below 50 percent of area median are from special tabulations by the Rand Corporation, October 1980.

13. Subsidy cost is $1,517 and administrative cost $253. These estimates assume that households consisting of a single person below the age of 62 would not be eligible. They are eligible for current HUD programs only if other households cannot be found to fill the housing units.

14. The distribution of household types in the current program is from the analyses cited in note 9. Household types in the additional 2.5 million units are from our analysis based on Supply Experiment data. Differences in per-unit subsidy costs for lower-income, very-low-income, and different household types are from U.S. Department of Housing and Urban Development, *op. cit.* (1978), p. 87. This figure is based on

the current Section 8 program but assumes that all households served have incomes below 50 percent of the area median income and that a larger proportion of those who remain to be served will be single-person elderly households and a smaller proportion will be single parents with children than in the current program.
15. The Housing Allowance Supply Experiment found it could control the rate of enrollment fairly well through the active recruitment of applicants. A national implementation might have to be slower than one confined to two cities. Although the Section 8 program is in place in most large and many small jurisdictions, current staff could not handle a tenfold increase in new unit allocations in a single year, which is what we are proposing. We have used the Office of Management and Budget's estimates of inflation rates and growth in incomes for the difference between the inflation rates of rents and of incomes of participating households. For other details of these calculations, see J. Khadduri and R. Struyk, *The Case for Housing Vouchers in a Time of Fiscal Austerity* (Washington, DC: The Urban Institute, 1981).
16. *Sixth Annual Report of the Housing Allowance Supply Experiment* (Santa Monica, CA: The Rand Corporation, 1980), p. 18.
17. See Struyk, Raymond J., and Bendick, Jr., Marc, *op. cit.*, Chap. 4.
18. See *Sixth Annual Report of the Housing Allowance Supply Experiment*, *op. cit.*, p. 17.

29

WORK TESTS FOR WELFARE RECIPIENTS
The Gap Between the Goal and the Reality

Charles S. Rodgers

Abstract *In the past, work tests have largely failed to reduce the rising cost of welfare programs. Part of the reason has been a slippage between the objective and the way it has been implemented. The slippage, according to one major study, has been due to a number of causes: a failure to translate the objective into operating rules consistent with the objective; the difficulties of enforcing the requirement in the field; and the unwillingness to penalize innocent dependents of uncooperative welfare recipients. But more effective implementation may be possible through a number of measures.*

Practically everyone agrees that able-bodied recipients on public welfare should be obliged to look for and accept employment as a condition of receiving benefits. Nearly all the major income maintenance programs serving persons who are not old or disabled, including Unemployment Insurance (UI), Aid to Families with Dependent Children (AFDC), and the Food Stamp Program, contain provisions to this end. While the societal goals which underlie these provisions are straightforward, the task of translating them into a set of workable administrative procedures is fraught with problems. The problems are poorly understood, and the remedies are even more unclear.

Work tests, as these provisions are generally known, have their origin in European social programs which date back at least to the enactment of the Elizabethan Poor Laws of the sixteenth century. Recently, there has been increasing emphasis on such requirements in many of our major public assistance programs. In January 1981, for instance, the work test was considerably strengthened in the Food Stamp Program by requiring employable recipients to search intensively for a job over an eight-week period, including mandatory visits to the local employment service office and mandatory contacts with a minimum number of prospective employers.[1] Various demonstration programs have been launched

---

From Charles S. Rodgers, "Work Tests for Welfare Recipients: The Gap Between the Goal and the Reality," 1(1) *Journal of Policy Analysis and Management* 5-17 (1981). Copyright © 1981 by the Association for Public Policy Analysis and Management. Reprinted by permission of John Wiley & Sons, Inc.

which require Food Stamp and welfare recipients to accept a subsidized job in order to maintain their eligibility, or to work off the benefits they received in unpaid employment. The emphasis on work requirements and their effective implementation, moreover, is increasing under the Reagan administration. When President Reagan was Governor of California, his approach to welfare reform stressed such policies, including the possibility that recipients work off their benefits in public service jobs.[2] President Reagan's proposal for national welfare reform envisions a workfare program for AFDC recipients in which nearly 800,000 individuals would be assigned to community jobs for which they would receive no pay beyond the amount of their monthly welfare grant.[3]

The best example of the increased emphasis on work requirements is in the AFDC program. The goal of the program, as originally specified in the Social Security Act of 1935, was to provide income support to widowed mothers of dependent children so that they would not have to enter the labor market. The number of families eligible for AFDC was expected to decrease as the Survivors Insurance program was added in 1939. The caseload increased, however, with the dramatic rise in the number of single parent families resulting from rising rates of divorce and family dissolution. Partly in response to the change in the types and circumstances of families receiving AFDC, a series of legislative amendments to the Social Security Act sought to encourage the participation of female household heads in the job market. This change culminated in the enactment of the Work Incentive Program (WIN) in 1967. The reasons underlying this shift in policy were the considerable expansion of the welfare rolls during the 1950s and 1960s and the attendant costs to the federal and state governments. A similar shift has occurred in both the Unemployment Insurance and Food Stamp programs.

In spite of this increasing emphasis on work requirements, there is very little direct evidence of the effects of these requirements on program participants and very little is known of the difficulties involved in implementing and administering the requirements. The few studies that have examined such issues indicate that work tests as administered in the past have had little effect on inducing clients to obtain employment and that there have been substantial difficulties in implementing the requirements.[4]

This article examines the difficulties that have been inherent in implementing work requirements, identifying the major reasons why slippage has occurred between the policy objective and its ultimate implementation. The slippage has arisen at a number of different stages, beginning with the confusion surrounding the stated objectives and continuing through to the application stage at the local level. While each point of slippage has been minor by itself, the cumulative effect has been overwhelming. A key question for the future, therefore, is: How can this type of slippage be reduced?

WHAT ARE WORK TESTS? Work requirements are often presented as if they consisted simply of making recipients accept employment and of removing them from welfare if they refused. In the AFDC and Food Stamp programs, however, the requirements have applied in practice to only a small percentage of recipients. Work has not been required as a condition of eligibility for receiving benefits. All that has been demanded of those recipients is that they look for or accept suitable work when offered. What the current regulations stipulate in terms of work effort is not a prescription for moving recipients from welfare to employment on any large scale.

Moreover, the work requirement for AFDC recipients is embedded in a complex body of rules and procedures governing the conditions of the client's participation in the program. In fact, it is probably more accurate to speak of a "participation" requirement than a work requirement. Most of the mandatory provisions pertain to clients' *participation* in all phases of program activities from registration to counseling and training sessions. Failure to participate in the program is supposed to result in a reduction or loss of welfare benefits.[5]

Moreover, in the AFDC program, even a participation requirement has applied only to a minority of the recipients. Nationally, nearly two-thirds of all adult recipients have been exempt under the statutory criteria. For instance, recipients with children under age 6, and those who are ill or physically remote from a WIN office, have not been required to participate. A secondary screening occurs when the recipients who must participate are appraised by the employment program staff. Those determined to be "job ready" are expected to participate with the staff in a search for employment and to accept referrals to "suitable" work and training. Those not determined to be "job ready" are expected only to participate in counseling or other support activities; for many, none of these support activities actually have taken place.

Registrants may be removed from the program not only because they have rejected a suitable job, but for other reasons as well. The principal ones are: not appearing for a job interview with agency staff; not participating in program appointments, classes, or other activities; disrupting a program activity; failing to utilize skills and experience; failing to make a bona fide application for employment when requested to do so by WIN staff; and being fired, or voluntarily leaving a job without cause, during the initial 90 days of employment.[6]

Decisions regarding whether registrants have, in fact, failed to comply according to the criteria listed above must take mitigating circumstances into consideration. For instance, staff members must determine if failure to participate was the result of such factors as illness, a breakdown in transportation arrangements, or lack of child care. If so, the failure is "for cause" and is to be excused.

In the WIN Program, an adjudication system has been used to

resolve disputes and to assure registrants the protection of due process. Before initiating the adjudication process, program staff have been directed to use informal means to resolve the problem. The steps in the adjudication process have included a conciliation meeting between registrant and staff, a notice of intent to remove the registrant from the program, the right to a hearing, an appeals process, and ultimately separation from the program. The amount of time between the initial refusal to cooperate without cause and the ultimate resolution of the issue has varied according to the decision the registrant makes regarding hearings and appeals. A registrant who exercises the right to a hearing and an appeal (short of appeal to a National Review Panel) can extend the process for over 150 days.

Added to this complicated set of regulations and determinations is the bureaucratic complexity that surrounds the administration of work requirements. In most states, the administration of the work requirement in the AFDC program is shared by two separate agencies. The principal responsibility lies with the WIN agency (usually a division of the State Employment Service), which must determine whether registrants are complying with program rules governing participation. The responsibility for applying penalties for noncooperation after notification by the Employment Service, however, lies with the local welfare agency. The employment agency's finding of noncompliance is without effect unless the welfare agency acts to reduce or terminate benefits. This division of labor applies also in the Unemployment Insurance and Food Stamp programs.

As the preceding discussion shows, many of the sources of the slippage have been built into the regulations that specify how the requirements are to be administered. The attempt to distinguish the recipients who are "job ready" results in exempting large numbers of recipients from any exposure to work or participation requirements. Due process procedures add to the length and complexity of the process of administering the requirement. The involvement of two separate agencies creates conditions for still more slippage. The net effect of this slippage is to reduce the coercive power of the state and minimize the impact of the requirements.

CLIENT AND STAFF BEHAVIOR The Minnesota Work Equity Project and various WIN studies provide valuable data on the behavior of both staff and registrants in the application of these requirements.[7] A major objective of the Minnesota project was to test the feasibility of more rigorous work requirements. Those in the program were not only to look for work; they were to be required to accept a subsidized job or training position if they could not find a job on their own. (This represents a significant change from the WIN program where lack of funds has severely limited the number of subsidized jobs that is available.) The guarantee of a job at the end of the job search period was intended to greatly strengthen the work requirement by directly testing the willingness of each participant to work.

What our study demonstrates, however, is that the more stringent provisions were never implemented. For a variety of reasons—some of which we examine in the following sections—the guarantee of a job never materialized and the work requirement proved to be not significantly different from the usual requirement of the WIN Program. The resistance of the staff at all levels to apply the new provisions thwarted its implementation. Even the less rigorous requirements of the WIN Program have been enforced in a highly selective fashion, and have been applied only to the most blatant forms of noncompliance. In a study of a workfare program for male heads of AFDC households in Massachusetts, a similar failure to implement more stringent requirements was detected. Out of a potential population of 5228 male WIN registrants, only 256 were actually referred to work.[8]

Data from the Minnesota project corroborate the view that the work requirements have been poorly enforced. Staff members estimated that at least 25 percent of the registrants failed to participate or comply with the rules at one time or another. However, very few registrants were ever formally declared to be out of compliance with program rules and fewer still for reasons having to do with refusal to accept employment. As can be seen in Table 1, only 4.6 percent of the registrants in the WIN and Work Equity sites were submitted to the adjudication system for failure

Table 1. Incidence of adjudication in Work Equity and WIN.

	Work Equity sites	WIN Program comparison sites[a]	Combined
Total registrants as of July 1979	2463	1920	4383
Clients adjudicated[b]	120	83	203
Assistance type:			
AFDC	99	83	182
General Assistance	19		19
Food Stamp	2		2
Hearing requested	6	14	20
Number deregistered	62	47	109
Percent in adjudication	4.9	4.3	4.6
Percent deregistered	2.5	2.4	2.5
Cases in progress	20	13	33

Source: Manual record search of the files of clients who were involved in the formal adjudication process. The files of 203 clients in the St. Paul, St. Cloud, and Mora Work Equity offices, and in the Minneapolis WIN office, are included in this record search. These files cover all adjudication activity in the study sites between October 1978 and June 1979.
[a]The WIN Program in Minneapolis serves as the comparison site in the Work Equity evaluation.
[b]Adjudicated clients are those who have received a so-called "Notice of Intended Deregistration."

to comply with the program rules, and only 2.5 percent were actually dropped from the WIN or Work Equity programs due to noncompliance. This is consistent with data collected in interviews with program staff which indicate that only a fraction of the violations of program rules were acted upon.

Agency procedures regarding the call-in of registrants reflect the magnitude of the problem. In one location, WIN staff routinely called in 60 registrants for an initial group orientation session in order to get about 20 registrants to actually appear.[9] Moreover, few registrants who were formally threatened with separation from the programs requested a hearing: Only 5 percent of those who reached the adjudication stage in Work Equity and only 17 percent in WIN did so.

In Minnesota, of those registrants who are terminated by the employment program staff for failure to participate, one-quarter did not experience any reduction in the amount of their welfare grants.[10] Thus, a substantial number of registrants who did not want to participate in the WIN or Work Equity program may have been "rewarded" for their noncompliance by being removed from the program while experiencing no reduction in welfare benefits.

Table 2 presents information on those registrants who have been involved in the adjudication process. In a very few cases, the

Table 2. Reasons given for adjudications in the Work Equity and WIN Programs.[a]

	Frequency cited		
Reason	Work Equity	WIN	Combined total
Failure to appear for appraisal interview	3	1	4
Refusal of job referrals or offers	5	—	5
Failure to show up for program appointments or activities	100	79	179
Failure to make effort to benefit from program activity[b]	2	79	81
Quit job or fired for cause	19	1	20
Refusal to accept child care or other services	2	—	2
Failure to submit required medical forms	2	1	3

Source: Manual record search of files of clients who were involved in the formal adjudication process. The files of 203 clients in the St. Paul, St. Cloud, and Mora Work Equity offices, and in the Minneapolis WIN office, are included in this record search. These files cover all adjudication activity in the study sites between October 1978 and June 1979.

[a] Column totals may exceed total number of adjudications since more than one reason may be cited in the "Notice of Intended Deregistration."

[b] This catch-all category is checked automatically in addition to a more specific issue; hence the number reported has no special significance.

registrant was charged with refusing to accept job referrals or to keep a job. In the overwhelming majority of cases, however, the accusation was that the registrant had failed to show up for an appointment with program staff or had committed some other breach not directly related to employment. This supports the notion that the program rules constitute a test of participation, rather than a test of willingness to work. The conclusion is reinforced by the reports of the staff on their conciliation activities. Less than half of the scheduled conciliation meetings required by adjudication rules actually took place. When registrants did come to scheduled meetings, however, the outcomes of these meetings were nearly always "positive" in the sense that the registrant was persuaded (or coerced) to participate.

Instances of noncooperation occur most commonly (in nearly 90 percent of the cases) at the early stages of program participation, usually in failure to appear for an initial counseling or orientation session. As noted earlier, failure to attend scheduled appointments is only a violation of program rules if the registrant does not provide an acceptable excuse. One can only speculate as to the full explanation for this passive noncooperation. Failure to keep such appointments may be a deliberate refusal to cooperate, or it may reflect a general passivity that is unrelated to the requirements of the program.

THE GAP BETWEEN GOAL AND IMPLEMENTATION What the evidence suggests, then, is that the staff resisted the application of work requirements, that few clients were ever penalized for violations of the rules, and that most of the penalties applied for noncompliance involved a failure to appear for interviews with the staff. The reality of the work requirement in the AFDC program appears to have stopped well short of the stated goal of requiring work of welfare recipients. Several factors have accounted for the slippage between policy and performance.

Clarification of Program Goals A large part of the difficulty in implementing work tests must be attributed to the underlying confusion regarding the focus of the AFDC program. As was noted earlier, the original goal of the AFDC program was to enable female heads of households to remain out of the labor force in order to protect the integrity of the family. The introduction of the WIN Program in 1967 marked a significant change in this goal; in that program, the emphasis was on moving recipients from welfare to employment, in order to hold down welfare costs. Yet it has never been clear just how big a change the government intended to bring about. First, the new requirements for "participation" incorporated in the WIN Program applied to only about 30 percent of all welfare recipients. Of that group, only a fraction has been subject to any of the job-related services, such as counseling and job-search assistance. Nationally, over one-half of the WIN caseload has been assigned to what is essentially a holding category in which few services or no services at all are provided.

Second, as noted above, WIN regulations require "participation" rather than actual work; to regard the WIN Program as having a "work requirement" is misleading. This confusion exacerbates the perception of the gap between the policy goal of substituting work for welfare and what the program has actually been designed to accomplish.

Most importantly, the Government's strategy of moving recipients from welfare dependence to employment has vacillated considerably over the years. A tension has existed between a cooperative effort aimed at enhancing recipients' employability and a punitive approach aimed at requiring acceptance of any job that meets the definitions of "suitable" employment. Without doubt, this tension has reflected a failure to come to terms with the diverse needs and circumstances of welfare recipients and to identify the most appropriate service interventions.

Another factor in the failure to implement program goals has been the vagueness of the criteria governing the conditions of participation in the program. Key program definitions such as "available for work," "job ready," or "failure to utilize skills to benefit from the program" are grossly imprecise. It is axiomatic that a mandatory program that relies on terms which have little operational content will not be fully implemented. Any imprecision in the guidelines leads not only to the wide use of staff discretion but also to the likelihood of legal challenges. In a context in which clients can easily avail themselves of a hearing and appeals process, it is not surprising that the staff has failed to pursue a large number of cases of apparent noncompliance.

Incentives for Staff A second major source of the slippage in implementation has been the failure to provide any incentive to staff members to enforce the requirements. Staff members are reluctant to refer recalcitrant or unwilling registrants to employers for job interviews. Aware that such interviews are unlikely to produce job placements, staff members see only negative results from such an interview, including the refusal of the employers to continue to list their jobs with the WIN agency. The allocation of funds to the WIN Program and the assessment of staff performance rest, in part, on the number and quality of placements. If the cooperation of employers is lost, the program suffers. This reward structure leads the staff to "cream" registrants for job placement, and it militates against applying the work requirement uniformly across all types of program registrants.

Part of the reluctance to apply the work requirement may also be the knowledge that, when enforcement leads to a reduction in the welfare benefit, the consequences fall on the recalcitrant registrant's family.[11] It is impossible to impose any penalty on the noncooperator without adversely affecting the children.

Incentives for Agency Cooperation Another complicating factor in implementing work requirements is the distribution of responsibilities among three different organizational units: an employment and training agency (in most states the Employment Service), which has the major responsibilities in administering the WIN Program; the so-called Separate Administrative Unit (SAU), which, as part of the state welfare agency, provides needed social services to WIN clients; and an Income Maintenance Unit (IMU), also within the welfare agency, which makes the initial referral of clients to WIN and is responsible for adjusting grant amounts as a result of noncompliance with the work requirement.

This diffusion of control over the process has substantially reduced the effectiveness of the work requirement. If the SAU fails to maintain close ties with the employment agency and to agree upon strategies for handling uncooperative registrants, the two units may develop conflicting judgments about the same individual. The employment and training staff have often complained that their efforts to deal with recalcitrant registrants were undone by the willingness of SAU staff to accept the most tentative signs of compliance as evidence of agreement to cooperate.

Meanwhile, the IMU—although organizationally remote from WIN—plays a critical role in the application of a work requirement. The only penalty in the system operates through the IMU, when it reduces the recalcitrant registrant's welfare payments. But for many reasons the IMU may not act: the administrative burden of processing short-term changes in grant amounts; a failure of communication between the employment and training staff and the IMU; or a lack of enthusiasm in the IMU for mandatory requirements. The separation of the enforcement function commonly subverts the policy's bite by removing the certainty of penalties.[12]

Difficulties in Monitoring An additional reason for the slippage in implementing the work tests has been that monitoring is so difficult. The behavior being monitored in the application of work requirements is often nearly impossible to observe. Registrants are to be available for work and are to participate in job search. But as one authority has noted, availability for work is a condition, not an act.[13] Whether a registrant responds to a specific job referral and appears for an interview may be easily determined. It is not easy, however, to determine whether the registrant pursued the opportunity in good faith. A registrant may, for instance, behave in a job interview in a way calculated to ensure that no job offer is made; but establishing that fact may be close to impossible. While such behavior does not constitute a search effort made in good faith, it is almost impossible to detect, short of accompanying the client to interviews. This difficulty in making determinations about the behavior of clients, added to the difficulty of defining "suitable" employment, probably helps to explain why the most easily monitored types of noncompliance—missed appointments and quitting—have figured so prominently among the reasons for initiating the adjudication process. Even the detection of people who quit of their own accord, thereby violating WIN rules, is not easy. Employers have no incentive to cooperate in helping to make such a determination and their cooperation is essential to a finding of noncompliance.

A final difficulty is that if a registrant breaks an appointment for reasons reportedly beyond the registrant's control, no penalty is likely to be imposed. Verifying the client's excuses, such as a breakdown in transportation arrangements or an illness, is difficult and costly. Understandably, it takes a blatant or consistent pattern of noncooperation to elicit some reaction from the staff.

TOWARD MORE EFFECTIVE IMPLEMENTATION The most evident flaw in the work requirements has been that they are so different from what the public perceived them to be. Given the fact that basic intent was never clarified in WIN, it is understandable that staff behavior undermined the enforcement of the work requirements. Provided the choice of working with cooperative registrants or attempting to detect and sanction the uncooperative registrants, local staff members chose the former. The program design failed to provide incentives to do otherwise.

The notion of incorporating incentives for agencies and individual staff members to implement new policies is quite foreign to the public sector. It is expected that institutions will assume new, even conflicting, functions simply because they are stipulated in regulations. When a new program or policy is promulgated, however, it is not enough to think only of the development of regulations. The barriers to implementation at the local agency level as well as the strategies for building incentives for agency and staff compliance must be carefully studied. The interests, the incentive structure, and the other missions an agency performs are also important ingredients in a plan to assure faithful execution of new policies. It is only at this level of analysis that the potential conflicts and problems can be identified and solutions offered.

We have already reviewed the substantial difficulties that exist in translating the objective of self-support for welfare recipients into a set of procedures that can be effectively executed at the local level. Some positive steps are, however, feasible.

One obvious step is to reconsider the methods that will move welfare recipients into employment. The policy objective implicit in work requirements rests in part on erroneous ideas of the behavior and motivations of welfare recipients. Recent research has indicated that many on welfare regularly move in and out of employment without any government intervention.[14] Using government resources to make recipients accept the type of employment they customarily locate on their own does not seem an appropriate policy, especially if the policy merely reinforces an unstable pattern of movement in and out of the labor market.

Moreover, a punitive approach is relevant only if the intent of public policy is to compel large numbers of recipients to accept low wage jobs. With AFDC benefits at or near the wages that can be earned from such jobs, there is no strong monetary incentive for welfare recipients to switch. While many recipients want to work and do so, it is not clear that they will want to work at any wage level in any type of job. Unfortunately, no one has explicitly confronted the issue of the wage level at which recipients would voluntarily choose employment. On the other hand, some recipients with no prior work history or substantial barriers to employment may require a degree of coercion to accept jobs at almost any wage rate.

Once recipients have been appropriately sorted according to their needs, the administration of the punitive provisions has to be considered. For those individuals who willfully resist the work requirement, it may be advisable to have specialized staff equipped with investigative skills to document noncompliance; this is currently done in the Unemployment Insurance program. Leaving compliance in the hands of a staff whose primary function is to work cooperatively with the registrants dampens the likelihood of effective enforcement.

To develop realistic expectations of how much the welfare or Food Stamp caseload can be reduced through work requirements, one must first of all be able to identify the portion of the population that can be expected to work. It also seems reasonable to develop a mechanism for testing whether recipients will accept work which does not depend upon the good offices of local employers. One way in which this could be done would be to subsidize a number of job slots to which recalcitrant individuals or those with little possibility of obtaining employment on their own could be referred. This option would allow the staff to test in a concrete situation the willingness of certain recipients to work and would provide useful work experience to those recipients who want to work but cannot otherwise be placed.

Beyond this step, the current exemptions from WIN participation deserves reexamination. For example, with 46 percent of mothers of preschool children now working, is it justifiable to automatically exempt from participation mothers of children under 6? This issue is even more important in the Food Stamp Program where "caretakers" of children under 12 are exempted. To be sure, as the cost of child care increases, women who work must assume those increasing costs. But women who take a 6-year absence from the labor force after each child find reentry much more difficult. In terms of equitable treatment, there is little reason to continue this exemption, notwithstanding the contrary objective in the original version of the AFDC program.

If large numbers of individuals are ultimately confronted with the requirement to accept a job (as opposed simply to register or participate in other program activities such as job search or counseling), it is likely that the incidence of noncooperation will increase. This will be true especially if individuals who are just barely employable are required to participate. If a larger proportion of the recipients fail to cooperate—either by refusing to accept jobs, by quitting their jobs, or by inviting themselves to be fired—the resources that would be consumed in enforcing a work requirement might rise dramatically. At that point, it is a real question whether society will be willing to bear the economic and political costs of enforcement.

While the concept of work requirements is widely supported, an array of evidence is beginning to suggest that there are substantial limits to the degree to which they can be effectively implemented and enforced, given current institutional arrangements and attitudes. Proposals to strengthen the requirements highlight the reality of these constraints. In the current welfare system it is all too easy for the costs of effectively monitoring and enforcing these requirements to outstrip the potential benefits. But continuing or strengthening the requirements without facing up to their enforcement is not a solution to that problem.

CHARLES S. RODGERS is a senior analyst at Abt Associates, Inc., in Cambridge, Massachusetts.

Research for this article was supported by the U.S. Department of Labor, Employment and Training Administration, under Contract No. 20-25-77-15. Interpretations and viewpoints contained in this article are the author's own, and do not necessarily represent the official opinion or policy of the Department of Labor. I would like to thank Ernst Stromsdorfer for his helpful comments on early drafts.

NOTES
1. Department of Agriculture, Food and Nutrition Service, and Department of Labor, Office of the Secretary, "Final Rules, Food Stamp Program, Work Registration and Job Search," *Federal Register* (January 16, 1981), pp. 4622–4632.
2. California Department of Employment Development, *Community Work Experience Program—Third Year and Final Report*, April 1976.
3. *New York Times*, March 11, 1981, p. 1.
4. See for instance, Camil Associates, *Services to Applicants Required to be Registered with the U.S. Employment Service*, final report submitted to the U.S. Department of Labor, Employment and Training Administration under Contract No. 20-42-75-42 (Philadelphia, PA: Camil Associates, 1979); Robert Evans, Jr., Barry Friedman, and Leonard Hausman, *The Impact of Work Tests on the Employment Behavior of Welfare Recipients*, research monograph submitted to the U.S. Department of Labor, Employment and Training Administration, prepared under Grant No. 53-25-73-03, 1976; David W. Stevens and V. Christine Austermann, *Equity and Efficiency Considerations in the Unemployment Insurance Work Test: An Analysis of Local Office Administrative Practice*, research monograph submitted to the U.S. Department of Labor, Employment and Training Administration, prepared under Grant No. USDL-L-73-119, 1975; U.S. General Accounting Office, *Food Stamp Work Requirements—Ineffective Paperwork or Effective Tool*, CED 78-60 (Washington, DC: General Accounting Office, 1978); and U.S. Department of Labor, *Final Report: Pilot Evaluation of the Work Registration Activity Under the Food Stamp Program*, DSS Report No. 36 (Washington, DC: Manpower Administration, Division of Special Studies, 1974). A discussion of the administrative feasibility of work requirements in the context of large-scale job creation can be found in Barry Friedman and Leonard Hausman, *Is Compulsory Work for Welfare Recipients Manageable?* (research paper prepared for the 1978 meetings of the Industrial Relations Research Association and American Economics Association in Chicago, IL, 1978). See also Charles S. Rodgers, *The Administration of the Work and Training*

Requirement in the Work Equity Project, interim research report submitted to the U.S. Department of Labor under Contract No. 20-25-77-15 (Cambridge, MA: Abt Associates, 1979).

5. Recently, the provisions governing the duration of the loss of benefits were changed as a result of a court decision [*McLean v. Califano*, 458 F.Supp.285 (S.D.N.Y. 1977)]. Prior to the decision, failure to comply resulted in a loss of eligibility for welfare benefits for a three-month period; a subsequent failure to participate results in a six-month loss of benefits. Under the new regulations effective April 1980, registrants failing to participate in WIN are to be deregistered and ineligible for benefits only for so long as they have failed or refused to participate. The procedures that establish the period of noncooperation, however, are such that the maximum duration of the sanction period cannot exceed 42 days.
6. U.S. Department of Labor and U.S. Department of Health, Education and Welfare, *WIN Handbook,* 3rd ed. (Washington, DC: U.S. GPO, 1979), Chap. XI, pp. 3–4.
7. The Minnesota Work Equity Project is a welfare reform demonstration funded by the U.S. Department of Labor (ETA/OPER) operated in the City of St. Paul and in seven rural central Minnesota counties between September 1978 and March 1981. The project served employable AFDC recipients and, in the seven counties, also served employable Food Stamp and General Assistance recipients.
8. Barry Friedman, Barbara Davenport, Robert Evans, Andrew Hahn, Leonard Hausman, and Cecile Papirno, *An Evaluation of the Massachusetts Work Experience Program,* final research report submitted to the U.S. Department of Labor under Contract No. 51-25-78-02 (Waltham, MA: Brandeis University, 1980).
9. These data were obtained in interviews with staff in each site of the Minnesota project during the summer of 1980. Interviews with WIN staff in other states corroborate this impression.
10. This estimate comes from a record search of over 200 Minnesota Department of Public Welfare files in June 1980. There is considerable variation across county welfare departments in the extent to which sanctions are imposed.
11. In the regular AFDC program, the grant is reduced by the share of the mother; for the AFDC-Unemployed Parent Program (where both parents are present) the entire grant is taken away. For regular AFDC, the reduced benefits are provided to the dependent children via vendors.
12. The welfare IMU staff can also reduce the application of the rules by other means. For instance, in Massachusetts 12.7 percent of all errors in the AFDC program involved the failure of the staff to require recipients to register for WIN (Massachusetts Senate Committee on Ways and Means, *Excerpts from the Fiscal 1981 Budget Narrative,* May 15, 1980, pp. 12–18).
13. Stevens and Austermann, note 4, p. 11.
14. See, for instance, Barry Friedman and Leonard Hausman, *Work and Welfare Patterns in Low Income Families,* final research report submitted to the U.S. Department of Labor under Grant No. 51-25-73-03 (Waltham, MA: Brandeis University, 1975), Chap. II.

30

PUBLIC POLICY AND
BLACK ECONOMIC POLARIZATION

Steven P. Erie

Black economic development since the mid-1960s has been polarized, with an urban underclass developing alongside a fledgling middle class. The author appraises how government policies—specifically, public employment, public assistance, and worker training—may cause or perpetuate this polarization, and considers the possible political consequences of simultaneous economic progress and growing dependence on government assistance.

That the economic development of black Americans since the mid-1960s has been polarized is a now-familiar observation. This era has featured both the rise of a fledgling black middle class and the development of a near-permanent black underclass in the nation's ghettos.[1]

The economic well-being of blacks also has become, at least ostensibly, a major public policy concern during this period. Yet very little inquiry has been made into the extent to which public policy has fashioned or reinforced the polarization of black economic de-

---

1. For example, see Andrew F. Brimmer, "The Economic Progress of Negroes in the United States," a speech delivered at Tuskegee Institute in 1970, cited in Daniel Patrick Moynihan, "The Schism in Black America," *Public Interest* 27 (Spring 1972): 3–24, at 12–13. The proportion of black families with incomes greater than $15,000 (in constant 1977 prices) grew from 22 percent in 1967 to 30 percent in 1977. The proportion of black families with incomes less than $7,000, however, stabilized: 37 percent in 1977, compared with 39 percent in 1967—down from 76 percent in 1947. The proportion of black families in the middle-income bracket declined from 39 percent in 1967 to 33 percent in 1977. See U.S., Bureau of the Census, *Current Population Reports*, Series P–60, no. 116 (Washington, D.C.: Government Printing Office, 1978), table 3, p. 10.

© 1980 by The Regents of the University of California. Reprinted from POLICY ANALYSIS 6:3 (Summer 1980), pp. 305-317, by permission of The Regents.

velopment. With rare exceptions, studies of the economic impacts of public policy on blacks have focused narrowly on the effects of particular government programs—affirmative action, employment, worker training, contract compliance, education, and public assistance. As a result, gauging the interrelated effects of various governmental policies has been a difficult task.

This study represents a modest effort to make such an assessment. It appraises the combined effects of public employment, worker training, and public assistance policies on black economic development from 1940 to 1976. Previous studies of black occupational mobility since 1940 have highlighted impressionistically the important role of white-collar and skilled blue-collar job opportunities in the public sector.[2] Other research has suggested that public assistance and worker training programs have reinforced (although not necessarily created) a peripheral labor market, largely composed of ethnic minorities, in the nation's economy.[3] (I make no attempt to assess the significant impacts of macroeconomic and educational policies on the evolution of the black class structure.)

This inquiry raises even larger economic and political questions. First, it allows us to determine whether public policy, the national labor market, and the black labor market have developed new interrelationships. Previously, economists such as Bennett Harrison argued that welfare and worker training programs maintained a

2. Daniel Price, comparing the number of blacks in various occupations in the 1940–1960 censuses, found that most of the twenty-year increase in black skilled blue-collar and white-collar workers occurred in occupations where government was a major employer (*Changing Characteristics of the Negro Population* [Washington, D.C.: Government Printing Office, 1969], pp. 163–64, 183). Andrew Brimmer and others have suggested that a large share of black occupational progress in the 1960s resulted from expanding public employment opportunities and from federal prodding of government contractors ("Economic Situation of Blacks in the United States," *Review of Black Political Economy* 2 [Summer 1972]: 34–54; and "Widening Horizons: Prospects for Black Employment," *Review of Black Political Economy* 4 [Summer 1974]: 91–116). See also Reynolds Farley and Albert Hermalin, "The 1960s: A Decade of Progress for Blacks?," *Demography* 9 (August 1972): 353–70.

3. See, for example, Bennett Harrison, "Public Employment and the Theory of the Dual Economy," in *The Political Economy of Public Service Employment*, ed. Harold L. Sheppard et al. (Lexington, Mass.: D. C. Heath, 1972), pp. 61–64; and Harold M. Baron and Bennett Hymer, "The Dynamics of the Dual Labor Market," in *Problems in Political Economy: An Urban Perspective*, ed. David M. Gordon (Lexington, Mass.: D. C. Heath, 1971), pp. 94–101.

national dual labor market segregated along racial lines.[4] Have expanding public employment opportunities for blacks created a bifurcated labor market *within* the black work force? Second, the extent to which government is underwriting both black progress *and* poverty may serve as a plausible hypothesis partially explaining the political quiescence of blacks in the 1970s.

While the schismatic pattern of black economic development has been most apparent since the mid-1960s, my analysis adopts 1940 as a baseline because many of the relationships between these and related public policies and black economic development have their roots in the New Deal as well as in the Great Society of the 1960s. Government efforts at nondiscriminatory employment practices, although initially limited in scope, can be traced back to the federal Fair Employment Practices Committee, created by executive order in 1941. Yet, as Edna Bonacich has argued, chronically high black unemployment and underemployment rates also can be traced to the New Deal, as the aftermath of protective labor legislation neutralizing employers' incentive to use cheap black labor.[5]

My analysis addresses the following questions: (1) To what extent has black economic progress from 1940 to 1976 depended upon public employment? (2) To what extent have public assistance and worker training programs institutionalized ghetto poverty? (3) What have been the likely political consequences of this pattern of simultaneous economic progress and dependence on government?

BLACK ECONOMIC PROGRESS: THE ROLE OF PUBLIC EMPLOYMENT

Before World War II, black economic life remained rooted in postbellum sharecropping and wage labor arrangements in the poorest states of the South. The limited gains for this period could be traced largely to northern industrial opportunities created by World War I, because migrating blacks exchanged low-paying agricultural jobs for better-paying manufacturing positions.[6]

4. Harrison, "Dual Economy."
5. Edna Bonacich, "Advanced Capitalism and Black/White Race Relations in the United States: A Split Labor Market Interpretation," *American Sociological Review* 41 (February 1976): 34–51.
6. For analyses of the pre-1940 period, see Dale L. Hiestand, *Economic Growth and Employment Opportunities for Minorities* (New York: Columbia University Press, 1964), pp. 41–57; and John F. Kain, ed., *Race and Poverty: The Economics of Discrimination* (Englewood Cliffs, N.J.: Prentice-Hall, 1969), pp. 5–12.

Progress occurred after 1940 with the massive movement of blacks into the northern metropolitan labor force. Between 1939 and 1975, the ratio of black to white median family income rose from 37 to 61 percent.[7] By 1971 the proportion of blacks in white-collar and skilled blue-collar jobs had risen from 10 to 37 percent; among whites, from 48 to 75 percent.[8]

To what extent has government employment contributed to this development? Why has the public labor market been so attractive to blacks?

First, since the 1940s, job discrimination (at entry level and in terms of promotion) has generally been less prevalent in government employment than in private employment. Efforts to promote equal opportunity in public employment, although initially limited in scope and enforcement power, clearly predate similar efforts at reducing employment discrimination by private employers, such as Title VII of the 1964 Civil Rights Act. As a result, salary differences between black and white public employees were reduced sooner than those between black and white private employees. By 1949, for example, black government workers earned 76 percent of the median income of their white counterparts, while among private wage and salary workers, blacks earned only 51 percent of the median for whites. In 1970, after the implementation of Title VII, the median income for blacks in public employment was 83 percent of that for whites. Among the experienced civilian labor force as a whole, the ratio was 64 percent.[9]

Second, the salaries, fringe benefits, pensions, and job security of black government workers have been better than those of blacks employed elsewhere. Contrary to popular impression, government workers historically have enjoyed greater financial benefits than

---

7. The ratio closely followed the business cycle, rising during the war-induced expansionary periods of 1941–47, 1950–52, and 1966–70, and falling during the recessionary periods of 1957–58 and 1971–73. The ratio peaked at 64 percent in 1970. The relative deterioration in the position of blacks in the 1970s is due to recession-induced layoffs and hiring freezes, which affect blacks more than they do whites. See Lester C. Thurow, "The Economic Progress of Minority Groups," *Challenge* 19 (March/April 1976): 21–2.

8. U.S., Bureau of the Census, *The Social and Economic Status of the Black Population, 1971* (Washington, D.C.: Government Printing Office, 1972), p. 66.

9. U.S., Bureau of the Census, *Census of Population: 1950* (Washington, D.C.: Government Printing Office, 1950), vol. 2, pt. 1, table 142, pp. 311–13; and idem, *1970 Census of Population* (Washington, D.C.: Government Printing Office, 1973), vol. 1, pt. 1, sec. 2, table 256, pp. 951–52.

their privately employed counterparts. Throughout the entire post–World War II era, the median income for government workers has been at least 10 percent greater than that for other workers. Some of this difference in median salaries can of course be traced to government's proportionally greater demand for professional and technical workers. In 1970, for example, these two job categories accounted for 35 percent of total public employment, compared with 10 percent of private employment. Furthermore, although exceptions increased in the 1970s, civil service systems historically have shielded public employees from short-term fluctuations in the business cycle. As a result, a much greater proportion of public employees than of private employees work the entire year. In 1970, for example, 86 percent of all men and 70 percent of all women in the public service worked at least fifty weeks. The comparable proportions in private employment were 73 and 53 percent, respectively.[10]

Third, government employment has grown enormously since the 1930s. The fact that blacks entered the urban labor force during the "takeoff" period in governmental responsibilities has been little appreciated. These responsibilities took such varied forms as New Deal relief, recovery, and reform measures in the 1930s, an augmented defense and national security posture from the 1940s onward, and sharply expanded state and local services after World War II, particularly in the fields of health, education, welfare, and transportation, to meet the needs of a growing urban and suburban population. Government employment increased commensurately. In 1930, federal, state, and local government employed 4 percent of the civilian labor force, roughly the same proportion as in 1900. By 1975, however, government directly employed 17 percent of the civilian labor force; and, an additional 5 percent in private employment provided goods and services to public agencies. Of all civilian jobs created since 1930, nearly one-third have been in public employment.[11]

What has been the impact upon the black work force of expand-

10. U.S., Bureau of the Census, *1970 Census*, vol. 1, pt. 1, sec. 1, table 229, pp. 778–9 (weeks worked), and sec. 2, table 225, pp. 749–57 (occupations).

11. See Alba M. Edwards, *Comparative Occupational Statistics for the United States, 1870 to 1940* (Washington, D.C.: Government Printing Office, 1943), pp. 59–62, 104–112; U.S., Department of Labor, *1976 Employment and Training Report of the President* (Washington, D.C.: Government Printing Office, 1976), table A–17, p. 238; and U.S., Bureau of the Census, *Public Employment in 1975* (Washington, D.C.: Government Printing Office, 1976).

ing public employment opportunities? Between 1940 and 1975, 43 percent of the 5.2 million increase in the number of jobs held by blacks occurred in public employment; among whites, 23 percent of the 50.3 million increase occurred in government jobs.[12] The role of government employment in the expansion of the black work force was most dramatic during the politically turbulent 1960s, a period of tremendous growth in state and local public employment as well. Between 1960 and 1970 the proportion of blacks working for government spiraled upward from 12 to 21 percent, with more than one-half of the decade's overall black employment increase occurring in public occupations.

What has been the effect of public employment opportunities on the development of the black middle class? Between 1960 and 1970, fully 60 percent of the increase in black professional and managerial employment (compared with 40 percent for whites) occurred in the rapidly expanding public sector. By 1970, over one-half of all black professionals and managers were directly employed by government, compared with slightly over one-quarter of similarly situated whites. Countless other black professionals and managers, ostensibly privately employed, worked for government-funded, community-based organizations dispensing health and social services.[13]

The new middle-class black public servants, unlike other less-skilled and less-educated black government employees, generally functioned as providers of social welfare services, primarily to the disadvantaged. As of 1975, nearly 60 percent of all black professionals and administrators (compared with 40 percent of their white counterparts) employed by state and local governments outside the field of education worked in the areas of welfare, health and hospitals, public housing, and community development. At the federal level, over 40 percent of all blacks working at General Schedule (GS) 9 or above (compared with one-quarter of their white counter-

12. See U.S., Bureau of the Census, *Sixteenth Census of the United States: 1940* (Washington, D.C.: Government Printing Office, 1943), vol. 3, pt. 1, table 76, pp. 188–89; U.S., Department of Labor, *1976 Employment and Training Report* (Washington, D.C., 1977), pp. 219, 223, 238.

13. See U.S., Bureau of the Census, *Census of Population:1960, Subject Reports, Occupational Characteristics* (Washington, D.C.: Government Printing Office, 1963), pp. 277–90; idem, *Census of Population: 1970, Subject Reports, Occupational Characteristics* (Washington, D.C.: Government Printing Office, 1973), pp. 693–706, 715–35.

parts) outside the U.S. Department of Defense and the U.S. Postal Service were employed by the four major agencies implementing social welfare policy: the U.S. Departments of Health, Education, and Welfare; Labor; Housing and Urban Development; and the Veterans Administration.[14]

The large-scale movement of blacks into the public labor market since 1940 (and especially since 1960) thus has accounted for a significant share of black economic progress, particularly for the fledgling middle class. While occupational and income disparities between blacks and whites have narrowed since 1940, significant differences remain, in public as well as private employment.[15]

DO WELFARE AND WORKER TRAINING PROGRAMS INSTITUTIONALIZE BLACK POVERTY?

Prior to the 1960s, black poverty had primarily reflected low agricultural wages in the South. It had not been associated with either unemployment, the breakup of the family, or massive dependence upon public assistance. Yet by the late 1960s a new form of black poverty was seriously challenging the old. More than one-half of all low-income black families now lived outside the rural South. Among the urban poor, more than one-half of the families were headed by women. In the rural South, however, three-quarters of all impoverished black families were headed by men.

14. See U.S., Equal Employment Opportunity Commission, *Minorities and Women in State and Local Government, 1975* (Washington, D.C.: Government Printing Office, 1977); and U.S., Civil Service Commission, *Minority Group Employment in the Federal Government, 1975* (Washington, D.C.: Government Printing Office, 1977).

15. The U.S. Civil Service Commission's study of minority group employment in the federal government reveals that blacks are overrepresented in wage-system (blue-collar) ranks and underrepresented among participants of General Schedule and similar better-paying salary plans, and that blacks are under-represented in grades GS 9 and above. The U.S. Equal Employment Opportunity Commission's study of the status of minorities in state and local government (excluding public school systems) reveals that over two-thirds of all blacks are crowded into the three job categories with the lowest median salaries—service/maintenance, office/clerical, and paraprofessional. Over one-half of all black state and local employees are concentrated in the four functions of government with the lowest median salaries—hospitals, streets and highways, sanitation and sewage, and public welfare. As a consequence, the median government salary for blacks was only 83 percent of that for whites. See Civil Service Commission, *Minority Group Employment in the Federal Government*; and Equal Employment Opportunity Commission, *Minorities and Women in State and Local Government.*

What has been the overall effect since the mid-1960s of welfare policies aimed at alleviating the condition of the new urban black poor? Some reduction in black poverty has occurred in the post–Great Society era, especially where in-kind transfers (food stamps, public housing, Medicare, and Medicaid) are added to cash transfers (public assistance and social insurance). The Congressional Budget Office has estimated that for fiscal year 1976 44 percent of all nonwhite families, compared with 25 percent of white families, were below the poverty level on the basis of their pretransfer income.

When cash and in-kind transfers were included, only 16 percent of the nonwhite families and seven percent of the white families remained below the poverty level. Social insurance and in-kind transfers, rather than public welfare cash transfers, were responsible for lifting three-quarters of the non-white poor above the poverty threshold and into the low-income category.[16]

While public transfers clearly sustain the black poor at a higher economic equilibrium, Richard Perlman and others have pointed out that much cash and in-kind transfer assistance is income-conditioned, and hence discourages the search for work and higher earnings.[17] Despite the massive increase in the scale of welfare cash transfers since the late 1960s, the proportion of blacks below the poverty level remains the same: 31 percent in 1976, compared with 32 percent in 1969, and down from 55 percent in 1959. The *dependence* of the black poor on public cash transfers—public aid and social insurance—has dramatically increased, however. Table 1 displays income sources in 1969 and 1976 for black families and unrelated individuals below the poverty level. The growth in reliance upon public income-maintenance payments (particularly

---

16. U.S., Congressional Budget Office, *Poverty Status of Families under Alternative Definitions of Income*, Background Paper no. 17, rev. (Washington, D.C.: Government Printing Office, 1977), table 5, p. 11. For other assessments of the poverty-reducing effects of transfer payments, see Benjamin A. Okner, "Transfer Payments: Their Distribution and Role in Reducing Poverty," in *Redistribution to the Rich and the Poor*, ed. Kenneth E. Boulding and Martin Pfaff (Belmont, Calif.: Wadsworth, 1972), pp. 62–77; and Anita B. Pfaff, "Transfer Payments to Large Metropolitan Areas: Their Distribution and Poverty-Reducing Effects," in *Transfers in an Urbanized Economy*, ed. Kenneth E. Boulding (Belmont, Calif.: Wadsworth, 1973), pp. 93–130.

17. Richard Perlman, *The Economics of Poverty* (New York: McGraw-Hill, 1976), pp. 198–203. Also see Daniel R. Fusfeld, "Transfer Payments and the Ghetto Economy," in Boulding and Pfaff, *Redistribution*, pp. 78–92.

TABLE 1. THE DEPENDENCE OF THE BLACK POOR UPON GOVERNMENT TRANSFER PAYMENTS HAS INCREASED DRAMATICALLY SINCE THE LATE 1960s

	Percent of Aggregate Income by Source for Blacks below Poverty Level			
	Families		Unrelated Individuals	
Sources of Income	1969	1976	1969	1976
Earnings	62.8	34.9	33.7	21.2
Income other than earnings	37.2	65.1	66.3	78.8
Government transfer payments[1]	33.7	62.3	59.0	74.4
Social insurance[2]	11.7	18.0	35.0	45.7
Public aid[3]	22.0	44.3	24.0	28.7
Other income[4]	3.5	2.9	7.4	4.3
Total	100.0	100.0	100.0	100.0

SOURCES: U.S., Bureau of the Census, *Census of Population: 1970, Subject Reports, Low Income Population* (Washington, D.C.: Government Printing Office, 1973), pp. 313–21; idem, *Current Population Reports*, Series P–60, no. 115 (Washington, D.C.: Government Printing Office, 1978), pp. 164–69.

[1] Excludes government employee pensions.
[2] Includes social security, unemployment compensation, workman's compensation, and veterans payments.
[3] Includes public assistance and, for 1976, Supplemental Security Income.
[4] Includes dividends, interest, rent, private pensions, government employee pensions, alimony, annuities.

welfare) was quite evident among poor black families: cash transfers accounted for one-third of their aggregate income in 1969 and for nearly two-thirds by 1976. Much of this increase was due to the expansion of a single program, Aid to Families with Dependent Children. While income-conditioned cash and in-kind transfers thus have raised the economic level of the black poor, in the long run welfare policies may be institutionalizing a government subsidized underclass.

The Great Society's War on Poverty programs and subsequent federal worker training programs have represented alternatives to welfare cash and in-kind transfers for alleviating ghetto poverty. Plagued by chronically inadequate funding and by a focus on the most employable, these programs have only marginally reduced black underemployment and hard-core unemployment.

Are worker training programs, in tandem with welfare programs, also functioning in the long run to institutionalize black poverty? One labor market theory, the dual labor market hypothesis, suggests that this may be the case. The worker training programs of the 1960s reflected the neoclassical assumption of many labor economists that ghetto blacks did not possess the requisite investments in human capital—such as education and training—to respond adequately to the demand for more skilled labor. This approach was based upon two critical premises: that there was a single or integrated labor market, and that structural unemployment and underemployment were more problems of labor supply than of labor demand.

When the War on Poverty programs, fashioned on neoclassical principles, did little to eradicate ghetto poverty, two different interpretations resulted. Neoclassicists moved increasingly to the demand side, incorporating discrimination as a preference for which some employers were willing to pay. Other economists, however, questioned the assumption that a single labor market existed.[18] Studying both the operation of ghetto economies and the effects of the War on Poverty programs, the critics discovered that the movement of ghetto blacks among worker training and welfare programs, illicit economic activities, and low-paying blue collar and service jobs increased at a far greater rate than the rate of upward mobility into better-paying, more secure, skilled blue-collar and white-collar positions.[19]

This finding suggested that government worker training and welfare programs essentially serviced a secondary labor market, characterized by low skill requirements, low productivity, high sensitivity to competitive market pressures, low wages, and high job turnover rates. Furthermore, by maintaining a peripheral market, antipoverty and public assistance programs were buttressing the unionized, oligopolistic core of the nation's economy. This primary labor market was characterized by substantial human and capital investments, high productivity, high wages, and low job turnover.

The critics soon realized that government was even more inti-

18. For the development of a "dual" labor market interpretation, see Michael J. Piore, "The Dual Labor Market: Theory and Implications," in *Problems in Political Economy: An Urban Perspective*, ed. David M. Gordon (Lexington, Mass.: D. C. Heath, 1971), pp. 90–94. For evaluations of neoclassical and dual interpretations of the labor market, see Glen G. Cain, "The Challenge of Dual and Radical Theories of the Labor Market to Orthodox Theory: A Survey," *Journal of Economic Literature* 14 (December 1976): 1215–57.

19. Harrison, "Dual Economy," p. 61–64. For analyses of the nature and functions of ghetto economies, see William K. Tabb, *The Political Economy of the Black Ghetto* (New York: W. W. Norton, 1970); and Thomas Vietorisz and Bennett Harrison, *The Economic Development of Harlem* (New York: Praeger, 1970).

mately involved in the development and maintenance of a dual labor market, for public employment represented a large and growing component of the primary labor market. While some thus argued that public service jobs afforded an important route out of ghetto poverty, less sanguine observers pointed out that this mobility strategy was checked by restrictive civil service entrance requirements, such as educational credentials and competitive examinations, and by public unions wedded to existing civil service systems.[20]

Because dual labor market theorists were more concerned with the impact of public policy on the black poor than on blacks per se, they did not assess whether recent black middle-class gains largely were due to expanding public employment opportunities. Consequently, the critics were unable to explore an important implication of their argument: public policy might be furthering the tendency toward an economic schism *within* the black community.

The economic polarization most evident among blacks since the late 1960s may indeed have public policy antecedents. On the one hand, public employment has been responsible for a major portion of blacks' recent economic gains, especially for the middle class. On the other hand, if the dual labor market theorists are correct, welfare and training programs may be institutionalizing more than significantly reducing the black underclass.

AN EMERGING POLITICAL SCHISM?

Because of substantial dependence upon both public employment and welfare, a majority of urban blacks now comprise a "public sector community."[21] Yet it is a community in an economic double

---

20. For a more optimistic assessment, see Samuel Krislov, "Government and Equal Employment Opportunity," in *Employment, Race, and Poverty*, ed. Arthur M. Ross and Herbert Hill (New York: Harcourt, Brace and World, 1967), pp. 337–64. For more sober analyses of the obstacles to using public employment as a route out of poverty, see the National Civil Service League, "Overcoming Civil Service Barriers to Employment in the Public Sector: the Case of Model Cities," in Sheppard et al., *Public Service Employment*, pp. 215–30; and Marilyn Gittell, "Public Employment and the Public Service," in *Public Service Employment: An Analysis of Its History, Problems and Prospects*, ed. Alan Gartner et al. (New York: Praeger, 1973), pp. 121–42.

21. Charles V. Hamilton, "Public Policy and Some Political Consequences," in *Public Policy for the Black Community: Strategies and Perspectives*, ed. Marguerite Ross Barnett and James A. Hefner (New York: Alfred, 1976), pp. 242–44. As for the magnitude of the black community's reliance

bind: impoverished welfare recipients *and* middle-class service providers. This economic schism in the black community may have a political corollary, expressed in terms of differences in political participation rather than in terms of ideology. On the one hand, recipients of welfare services, especially the urban young and unemployed, are withdrawing from political participation. Between 1964 and 1976 the voting rate for blacks under the age of twenty-four who lived outside the South dropped sharply, from 56 to 29 percent, while the voting rate of young whites dipped slightly, from 52 to 45 percent. The voting rate for unemployed blacks plummeted from 62 to 37 percent during these years. Among unemployed whites, however, the rate only dropped from 57 to 46 percent.[22]

On the other hand, the providers of public services display high rates of political participation. In 1976 nearly 70 percent of black government employees voted, compared to 46 percent of all other blacks. Participation rates were even higher for black professionals and administrators, a majority of whom were publicly employed. Over three-quarters of them voted in 1976, a proportion similar to their white counterparts.[23]

Politically, blacks in the 1970s seemed trapped by a shift from nongovernmental to governmental ways of organizing the polity. As the welfare state has grown in scale, specialization, and complexity, governments have shown an increasingly independent capacity to generate and structure political responses.[24] Compared with earlier

---

upon the public sector, the following observation by Los Angeles City Councilman David Cunningham, offered in the wake of Proposition 13's passage, is unusually revealing: "Seventy percent of the population in districts 8, 9 and 10 (South-Central Los Angeles, downtown, Watts and Crenshaw) is in some way dependent on government—federal, state or local—for their resources, either for jobs, or work with companies that do business with the government, or welfare" (*Los Angeles Times*, 20 June 1978).

22. U.S., Bureau of the Census, *Population Characteristics: Voter Participation in the National Election, November, 1964*, Current Population Reports, Series P-20, no. 143 (Washington, D.C.: Government Printing Office, 1965), pp. 11–13, 21–22; and idem, *Population Characteristics: Voting and Registration in the Election of November, 1976*, Current Population Reports, Series P-20, no. 322 (Washington, D.C.: Government Printing Office, 1977), pp. 14–23, 61–62.

23. Bureau of the Census, *Election, 1976*, pp. 61–64.

24. For an elaboration of this argument, see Samuel H. Beer, "The Adoption of General Revenue Sharing: A Case Study in Public Sector Politics," *Public Policy* 24 (Spring 1976): 127–29.

generations of white immigrants, blacks face a new, more complicated, and even contradictory set of political rewards and sanctions, related more to the dynamics of governmental institutions—especially the service delivery bureaucracies of the welfare state—than to the extragovernmental processes of party machine and pressure group.[25]

Thus, on the one hand, the precipitous decline in political participation by black urban young people and unemployed flows from the declining strength of urban parties and organized labor over the past fifteen years. The decline is further compounded by welfare and unemployment eligibility requirements, which encourage recipients to adopt a general strategy of low visibility vis-à-vis government. On the other hand, the growing cadre of public employees has strong economic incentive to participate in the electoral process. In 1976, for example, public employees voted at a considerably higher rate than the rest of the population—77 versus 58 percent. Yet the political activities of civil servants are restricted by the Hatch Act and similar legislation. Such limitations, needless to say, strike the black community with particular force. Middle-class black public servants, liberal and interventionist by any standard, find their hands tied when trying to mobilize an inert constituency.[26]

Public employment and welfare related policies, then, may be promoting, albeit unintentionally, the polarization of black economic and political development.

25. For a comparison of the Irish experience with the urban machine and the black experience with public social welfare bureaucracies, see Steven P. Erie, "Two Faces of Ethnic Power: Comparing the Irish and Black Experience," *Polity* (forthcoming).
26. For evidence of how antipoverty programs have politicized black service providers and depoliticized black service recipients in New York City, see Charles V. Hamilton, "The Patron-Recipient Relationship and Minority Politics in New York City," *Political Science Quarterly* 95 (Summer 1979): 211–27. For a more conspiratorial view of the depoliticizing consequences of welfare programs for the poor, see Frances Fox Piven and Richard A. Cloward, *Regulating the Poor* (New York: Vintage, 1971), pp. 256–82.

Education and Equity: Policy Considerations

Few areas of domestic social policy generate the intense scrutiny and controversy that education does. Endemic to educational systems are conflicts over what is to be taught, who is to teach and how, who is to be taught with whom, who is to finance what, and who decides what. Frequently, a close examination of these controversies reveals not only educational issues, but also cleavages and schisms inherent in the American social system. This relation of education and broader social issues is reflected, for example, in the policy debates over school desegregation, bilingual education, sex education, the mainstreaming of handicapped children, provision of aid to private and parochial schools, allowance of tax exemptions for racially segregated schools, the issue of prayer in classrooms, and the teaching of different theories on the origins of the universe. There is no way (nor perhaps should there be) to isolate the schools from controversy.

One area in which the policy controversies are especially heated is that of how the schools should promote equity in the society. Promoting change or sustaining stability in present arrangements is not an irrelevant consideration for school policymakers. The equity issue confronts the realities of race, social class, ethnicity, geography, gender, language, and more. The development of educational programs that respond to these factors necessarily involves judgment of several kinds: pedagogical, political, and moral. There are no absolute answers, only tentative responses. The struggle comes in finding means that one hopes are consonant with democratic principles and reflect a commitment to educating all children justly and to their potential.

The three chapters in this section address the themes of equity. The chapter by Hill is an insider's account of how policy-relevant research on providing compensatory services to low-income children was conducted over a period of several years at the National Institute of Education. Hill was the study director for a congressionally mandated study of the impacts of Title I of the Elementary and Secondary Education Act (ESEA). Title I was providing millions of dollars each year to school districts to enable them to give special services to the target population of low-income youth. The analysis of pressures on the study team from special interest groups, and from the conflicts between the Congress and the administration, provides illuminating insights into the politics of policy research in the area of educational equity.

Berne and Stiefel take up a crucial but widely neglected aspect of previous work on policymaking, demonstrating the central role that value judgments play in the policy process and the very real consequences such judgments have on the formulation of public policy. The authors develop their analysis from a study of school financing and link alternative measures of financial support to varying judgmental decisions. They call for policy analysts to be more explicit in their treatment of values and to trace out the implications of these judgments for resulting programs.

Finally, Coleman addresses the matter of public barriers to private education. He argues that the high cost of tuition creates barriers that inhibit the access of low-income and minority groups to private education—education he believes superior in quality to the public education poor youth now receive. Coleman argues that current restrictions on support for private education are unnecessary. Further, he urges consideration of policy options to provide tuition tax credits or tuition vouchers so that more youth may have access to private education.

31

EVALUATING EDUCATION PROGRAMS FOR FEDERAL POLICYMAKERS
Lessons from the NIE Compensatory Education Study

Paul T. Hill

INTRODUCTION

This essay distills what the author learned about the problems of evaluating federal education programs during three years as Director of the National Institute of Education (NIE) Compensatory Education Study.[1] NIE's was the first of what now appear to be a number of studies mandated by Congress for its own use in reauthorizing federal education programs. This account of the author's experience may therefore be useful to other federal research managers who conduct evaluation studies for Congress; and because virtually all federal program evaluations are at least partly intended for Congressional use, this essay may also help private scholars, research contractors, and federal managers who plan and execute evaluation studies.

The essay is in three parts. The first sketches the background of the NIE study and identifies problems that NIE faced—problems that appear to be common to evaluations of federal education programs. The second part describes how the NIE staff coped with those problems; and because the essay aspires to be more than an interesting collection of "war stories," the concluding section presents the most important lessons to be drawn from the NIE experience.[2]

---

[1] The essay also draws on the shared experience of several NIE researchers. Iris Rotberg and Alison Wolf laid the foundation of the research plan even before the study was mandated by Congress. Iris Rotberg, as deputy director of the study, shared every task, from negotiating with Congress to editing final reports. James Harvey made fundamental contributions to every aspect of the study, and Joy Frechtling, Margot Nyitray, Don Burnes, Ann Milne, and Charles Troob made important contributions to the overall strategy and managed the key projects. They, and many others, are in some sense the coauthors of this paper.

Sue Berryman, Tom Glennan, and John Pincus of Rand, and Jerry Fletcher of the Office of the Assistant Secretary for Education, made valuable comments and suggestions on earlier drafts of this essay.

[2] The following reports are available from the National Institute of Education, 1200 19th Street, N.W., Washington, D.C., 20208:
  Evaluating Compensatory Education: An Interim Report on the NIE Compensatory Education Study, December 1976;
  Compensatory Education Services, June 1977;
  Administration of Compensatory Education, September 1977;
  Title I Funds Allocation: The Current Formula, September 1977;
  Using Achievement Test Scores to Allocate Title I Funds, September 1977;
  Demonstration Studies of Funds Allocation Within School Districts, September 1977;
  The Effects of Services on Student Development, September 1977.

From Paul T. Hill, "Evaluating Education Programs for Federal Policymakers: Lessons from the NIE Compensatory Education Study," in J. Pincus (ed.) *Educational Evaluation in the Public Policy Setting*, Rand Corporation publication R-2502-RC (May 1980). Reprinted by permission of the Rand Corporation.

THE NIE STUDY AND THE PROBLEMS IT FACED

The NIE Compensatory Education Study was established by Section 821 of PL 93-380, the statute that reauthorized Title I of the Elementary and Secondary Education Act (ESEA) in 1974. That law required NIE to conduct a broad study of ESEA Title I and similar compensatory education programs conducted by several states. The legislative mandate identified social problems for study, required NIE to submit an official research plan for Congressional review, established deadlines for interim and final reports to Congress, and provided a budget of $15 million for the three-year study. Finally, the mandate required NIE to submit its reports directly to Congress without any prior outside review.

By requiring reports in time for the next Title I reauthorization hearings, Congress showed that it wanted to use the results in legislative deliberations. By making Congress the sole judge of NIE's research plan, and the first recipient of its results, Congress stressed that its own interests were to dominate the study.

The mandate also identified some topics for special attention. In particular, it directed NIE to investigate Representative Albert Quie's 1974 proposal to change the statute so as to allocate Title I funds on the basis of counts of low-achieving children rather than low-income ones. Congress defeated that proposal in 1974, but many key members of the House Education Committee felt some sympathy for it. As the ranking member of the House Committee, Mr. Quie was thus able to gain support for measures, such as the NIE study, that would keep his idea alive.

The mandate also asked for "an examination of the fundamental purposes of [compensatory education] programs and the effectiveness of such programs in attaining such purposes," and for an analysis of how well individualized instructional plans worked in the schools.

When the mandate was signed into law in August 1974, it presented a number of unfamiliar problems for NIE. Until then, NIE had never done a study at the behest of Congress, nor had it ever evaluated a major public program. Some researchers on the NIE staff had experience in evaluating compensatory education, but none of them had worked on the noninstructional aspects of a national program.

NIE also had political problems. The Institute was struggling for its life after a series of devastating reverses dealt by the Senate Appropriations Committee. Some NIE supporters in Congress saw the mandated study as NIE's chance to redeem itself; an unspoken implication was that failure of the study might be fatal to the Institute. Other federal agencies had found research on compensatory education to be a minefield. Evaluations of Head Start, Follow Through, and ESEA Title I had produced intense methodological disputes in the research community. These evaluations had generally drawn discouraging conclusions about the effectiveness of compensatory instruction, leading supporters of the program to oppose the whole idea of evaluation. Congressmen interested in education programs did not know what to make of these evaluations, and were disturbed by the resulting controversy. Conducting evaluations had been a major source of political trouble for the U.S. Office of Education. In turning toward NIE for a major evaluation, Congress had imposed some important new political risks on the Institute.

The significance of all this was not lost on the management of NIE. NIE established a special unit to conduct the study, and agreed to give the unit's leaders a free hand in dealing with Congress, interest groups, and researchers. This group, called the NIE study staff, was to plan and manage the research and write the reports to Congress. Thus, for the purpose of the study, the "Institute" was to be the study staff. The rest of NIE might contribute people and ideas at the request of the study director, but they were not involved in routine management.

Once responsibility for the study was clearly delegated, the staff faced five major technical and tactical problems:

1. *How to move from the broad research objectives set by Congress to specific statements of researchable problems.* Only a few of Congress's objectives had implied specific focus and conduct of particular research projects. Most of the objectives required interpretation and refinement in order to be specified as problems suitable for formal research.

2. *How to guarantee that the research made a fair assessment of the strengths and weaknesses of the Title I program.* It was clear that the results of the Title I study could affect how Congress saw the program, and thus its prospects for reauthorization and funding. The only guidance available to NIE at first was the negative example of an evaluation strategy that was widely regarded as incomplete and biased against the program. The outcome measure previously used—student achievement test scores—was under criticism. People believed that it failed to take account of the program's social objectives, and was technically inadequate, even for estimating the program's effects on children. The challenge facing the study staff was to find a way of evaluating Title I that was equally sensitive to the program's accomplishments and failures.

3. *How to overcome Congress's distrust of researchers.* At the beginning of the study, senior Congressional staff members were openly skeptical about the utility of any further research on Title I. They believed that most researchers do not take legislators' information needs seriously, and do not understand the policy process well enough to produce relevant information. This meant that, above all, the staff had to gain the professional respect of the members and staffs of the education committees at the outset.

4. *How to resist pressures from the contending parties in policy disputes.* The study mandate was originally formulated by Congressional staff members, whose principals disagreed about the merits of the Quie bill. Thus, the study's chief Congressional supporters were also strongly committed to antagonistic positions about one of the most important questions NIE had to investigate. In addition, interest groups hoped that the study results would support their positions. The study staff, under political pressure from all sides, had to gain a reputation for complete impartiality if its work were to be accepted.

5. *How to make the reports of research results useful to Congress.* Congress's dissatisfaction with prior evaluations arose partly from the reports' poor timing for legislative use, and their inaccessible language and format. Congress therefore seldom used research reports except as advocacy tools in the hands of particular members. The authors of the Title I study legislation intended the results to be a general resource to Congress, and the NIE staff knew that its work would not be considered a success unless Congress could use it that way.

The next part discusses these problems in more detail and the way NIE tried to cope with them. Some of the problems, such as advocacy pressures, are inevitable for a major program evaluation; they can be kept at bay but never eliminated.

Others may be solvable in theory, but are too complex for anyone to solve on the first try.

THE PROBLEMS AND HOW NIE DEALT WITH THEM

How to Build a Strategy of Research in Response to the Mandate

We began trying to build the research strategy months before the mandate became law, and continued to work on it for nearly two years, until long after the first research projects started. We tried to start with the obvious research projects, and the ones that would take longest to complete, but we continued trying to understand the mandate's implications as long as we had time and money available for research.

The effort had two main features. The first was to consult with researchers and interest group representatives, soliciting their advice about topics to be studied and avoided. We conducted these consultations early, and they helped shape the broad outlines of our research strategy. The second feature was continual consultation with Congressional staff in order to understand their priorities, identify information needs that were not clearly stated in the mandate, and obtain their support for projects that we wanted to include.

Consultation with Researchers and Interest Groups. During the summer and early fall of 1974, when we were writing first drafts of the research plan, some of our staff held formal meetings with researchers, representatives of state and local practitioners, and minority group leaders. When full drafts of the research plan were available, we met again with selected interest group representatives to hear their criticisms and suggestions.

Researchers mostly offered general advice, but did not suggest specific projects. Many of them had become discouraged from their own efforts to quantify the relationships between education program inputs and student achievement. They urged us to ask simpler, more fundamental questions, and to avoid sophisticated causal modeling until we understood more about program operations. Researchers associated with state departments of education and local school districts were more concrete, urging us to conduct simple descriptive studies and to employ familiar and proven research methods. They recommended that we set modest goals, especially for studies of the effects of Title I services on student achievement: These studies should acknowledge the diversity of instructional programs, and judge the effectiveness of instruction only when its characteristics are well understood. The study should pay attention to the problems of day-to-day program implementation, and try to understand the effects of federal and state regulations on local education practice.

Interest groups were concerned with protecting the future of the Title I program and their own stake in it. Their most common theme was a demand that they be consulted throughout the study. Minority groups also asked that their members be well represented on the NIE staff and among research contractors. There was no distinctive practitioner or minority group position on the problems to be studied.

The consultations with researchers and interest groups did not help much in defining research problems. Our discussions with Congressional staff, however, defined much of the research agenda.

Consultations with Congressional Staff. We began our consultations with Congressional staff by trying to make sure that we understood the language of the mandate. We knew that we had to investigate Representative Quie's proposal, to study different ways of allocating funds, and to study the effectiveness of individualized instruction. But our early discussions with authors of the statute revealed that the mandate did not include many of the questions most important to them. Congressional staffers wanted NIE to think beyond the written mandate, and to present them with a richer menu than either the mandate or their direct questions encompassed. They expected us to use creatively the great sums they had given us, to respond to their concerns and to a broader range of questions that we would develop together.

We therefore decided to take our planning orientation from discussions with Congressional staff. In our discussions, we first reached agreement about how to respond to the requirements expressly contained in the mandate; second, we asked them to identify important topics that they thought the mandate had left out; and third, we did our own analyses of Congress's information needs and proposed additional research.

Responding to the Express Requirements of the Mandate. From the statute it was apparent that Congress wanted the study to provide a clear account of how Title I—including the statute itself, the actions of federal, state, and local administrators, and the services finally delivered to children—was then operating; and to help them anticipate how changes in the statute would affect funding, administrative arrangements, and services.

Description of a program is a necessary first step toward understanding it, but entails far more than compiling a mountain of facts. Programs like Title I involve at least two, and usually three, levels of government. The federal government has many bureaucratic compartments, negotiations among which can profoundly affect the way a Congressional decision is implemented. The states and localities also have internal divisions with different functions, goals, and points of view. All of these facts affect the program's operations, and no single research project can encompass them all, nor could Congress ever hope to assimilate them. But researchers can try to explain at least the broad outlines of the program and the generic relationships among Congressional actions, management decisions by the federal bureaucracy, and the operation of the program by state and local governments.

We resolved to do that, but first we had to find a simple, intuitively satisfying conceptual framework. We saw two basic choices. One was to construct a framework based on the different levels of government that have administrative responsibilities. That approach would have led to a study that focused separately on federal, state, and local activities. The other possible framework would cut across the levels of government, through the chain of administrative actions by which the program is implemented. It would lead to a study organized around the sequential functions of funds allocation, administrative decisionmaking, and delivery of services to children. We chose the latter option because we thought a dynamic conception of the program would make it easier to anticipate the likely effects of changes in the statute. Consequently, we planned and managed the whole study around four broad topics:

- Allocation and distribution of funds;
- Relationships of federal, state, and local education agencies (school districts) in regulating and managing program activities;
- Delivery of services by school districts; and
- Changes in abilities and performance of participating students.

This framework of four topics became the organizing principle for the original research plan. When members of the House and Senate Education Committees accepted it, we decided also to build the research staff and our reports to Congress around it. The framework affected our work profoundly. It may have been one of our most important products, because it emphasized the fact that Title I is a program with many features, all of which had to be understood. It treated changes in student achievement as an important but not dominant topic. By regarding student achievement as only one element of the program, we hoped to play it down as an evaluation criterion and to make the point that a program's effects on student achievement can derive from funding and administrative arrangements as well as from the quality of instruction.

Working with Congressional Staff to Identify Important Topics Not Included in the Written Mandate. In our early negotiations with Congressional staff members, they made it clear that they regarded the written mandate as merely an illustrative list of possible research topics. Our discussions about the implications of the mandate cemented our relations with Congressional staff; they also gave us a real opportunity for leadership. Congressional staff members asked us to conduct several studies that were not expressly mentioned in the statute. Their requests, however, were very general: They identified general topics to be investigated, but left it to us to formulate research problems and propose particular projects. We took care to formulate reasonable research problems, and to present Congressional staff members with options that both bore on the topics they had identified and would lead to interesting research.

One example concerns the research on subcounty allocation of Title I funds that was reported in Chap. 6 of the NIE report, *The Title I Funds Allocation System*. That study began with a request from a senior House committee staff member for "a close look at subcounty allocation." The federal funding formula did not control the allocation of funds within counties, and regulations were very loose; the staff member had the impression that the process in some places was based on negotiation, not standard data, and might be working to the disadvantage of central city districts. He wanted to know more about the topic, but was not prepared to formulate a specific question about it. An NIE staff member was assigned to read up on subcounty allocation. He concluded that the regulations were indeed very loose, but the various allocation methods used were not necessarily creating very different patterns of funds allocation. We therefore proposed a study that would describe the range of subcounty allocation procedures then in use, describe the effects on actual allocation, and analyze possible ways of standardizing the process. Congressional staff accepted the proposal. Though all of this took place after Congress had accepted NIE's formal research plan, the new project was carried out as part of the mandated study. Several of our other projects were started in the same way.

Proposing Additional Research that We Thought Would Be Useful to Congress. Most of our consultation with Congressional staff was about research projects identified through NIE's own analysis of Congress's likely information needs. The projects were presented to Congressional staff, to find out whether they would be useful to Congress and to elicit a clear statement of interest so that they could thereafter be regarded as "mandated." Once a study was so "mandated," we could use study funds for it, and could cite Congressional interest in requesting cooperation from federal, state, and local agencies. That process continued throughout the study. The formal research plan submitted in December 1975 contained many such proposals, but others were defined thereafter.

Two papers written for us by Jim Harvey, a former Congressional staff member who had been a key participant in the 1974 House-Senate Conference negotiations on ESEA, made major contributions to that process. The first paper reviewed the legislative history of the study mandate, identified the members of Congress who expressed interest in the study, and analyzed the sources of support and opposition for the study. That paper both identified topics that were "musts" for the study, and warned about areas of Congressional conflict in which the study should operate very carefully.

The second paper discussed the political environment of Title I. It identified the long-term political commitments of key members of Congress and discussed the customary positions of important educational, minority, and public interest pressure groups. After drawing a rough "map" of such political pressures and commitments, the paper drew inferences about the political possibility of changes in the program.

The two papers identified some things that had to be done or avoided, but they could not provide a general framework for thinking about Congress's information needs. For that, we tried to think systematically about the kinds of choices that Congress as an institution is able to make. We found that it was not enough to say that we wanted to focus on "policy relevant" research. Congress's range of policy-making is narrower than the whole set of questions that could be asked about the operation of Title I. Congress can make policy in some areas (the appropriation of federal funds for example) where others have no standing, but others may make policy in some areas (such as the selection of teachers and day-to-day delivery of instruction) that are beyond Congress's control.

To understand Congress's information needs, we identified the ways that Congress can affect the operation of Title I; we then used the list of Congress's policy "tools" to identify possible research questions. Congress performs the following functions:

- Controlling the appropriations of federal funds among programs;
- Establishing formulas for the distribution of program funds among jurisdictions;
- Specifying the broad classes of purposes for which funds may be spent;
- Reviewing the regulations under which programs are administered;
- Determining the gross amounts to be spent on program administration; and
- Reviewing federal administrative performance.

Those tools are powerful, but very crude. Together they might enable Congress to exert a fine day-to-day control over events, but only with far more sustained attention to each program than individual members, or Congress as an institution, are able to give.

The simple exercise of listing Congress's policy tools made it clear that we should emphasize questions about the effects of funding formulas, regulations, and administrative arrangements, rather than questions beyond Congress's control, such as the effects of alternative teaching methods. We could not adhere to these limits rigorously, because neither we nor Congress fully understood them. Further, Congress itself had written some questions into the formal mandate about such topics as the effectiveness of individualized instruction that could bear only indirectly on any concrete decisions about the statute, regulations, or funding. Still, the focus on Congress's policy tools strongly affected our selection of research problems. For example, we did not have to include difficult—and politically problematic—basic research on the cognitive processes of disadvantaged children, and our attention was directed toward problems within the Title I program. Descriptive information, to provide Congress with a coherent picture of how the program affected the actions of federal, state, and local education agencies, was indispensable. Consequently, most of our research was primarily descriptive, especially that reported in *Compensatory Education Services, The Administration of Compensatory Education,* and *Title I Funds Allocation: The Current Formula.*

Congress also wanted information about the possibility of some narrowly circumscribed changes in the Title I program, particularly about the costs and feasibility of Mr. Quie's proposal to base funding on student achievement measures, but it did not want an exhaustive review of possible funding systems. Similarly, Congress wanted to know whether Title I regulations and management could be adjusted or strengthened with marginal commitments of new resources, but it did not want to consider a major change in the respective roles of the federal, state, and local governments.

In general, Congress was content to know about the likely effects of making marginal changes in its use of familiar policy instruments, and did not need speculative research on more fundamental or unlikely changes. The goal of most of NIE's research was therefore to understand the Title I program—how it worked, where changes were technically possible, and what their effects might be.

It is impossible to overestimate the importance of our good luck in being able to work with experienced and interested Congressional staff. The principal staff members of the House and Senate Education Committees (Jack Jennings and Chris Cross in the House, Jean Frolicher and Greg Fusco in the Senate) knew they needed more information about Title I, and were willng to work with us to get it. In the beginning, most of them were openly skeptical about whether our demands on their time could be worthwhile. We learned quickly that we should contact Congressional staff only when we had a sharply defined question or piece of information, and that they were always on the alert for signs of political bias or obscurantism on our part. We tried not to contact any Congressional staff member more often than twice a month, and prepared our agendas carefully. After enduring several months of testing—and a few rebuffs—we gained relatively easy access to key staff members. Had they been less willing to talk with us, discuss the plans, and respond to drafts and proposals, our study would not have been responsive.

The necessary discussions could not have taken place in the formal atmosphere of hearings. In such hearings, Congressional staff have time only to probe for weaknesses or make charges. Researchers need to be on their guard, and have reason to give as little information and attract as little attention as possible. Our Congressional clients never let such an adversary relationship develop.

Our experience demonstrates that researchers can do a great deal to turn difficult mandates into researchable problems, but there clearly are some impossible situations. In Chap. 5 of this report, Daniel Weiler and Marian Stearns discuss the problems that arise when legislators make unrealistic demands or provide inadequate resources. In those situations, researchers may feel compelled—by the desire to please policymakers or by competition for the opportunity to study an interesting problem—to make promises they cannot keep. With such promises, researchers can buy a brief honeymoon for themselves and their clients, but the aftermath is sure to be bitter. We were fortunate to have both a feasible mandate and a reasonable set of clients.

Ensuring that the Research Made a Fair Assessment of the Strengths and Weaknesses of Title I. Though most of Congress's questions concerned the operation of Title I and the effects of possible changes in the program, the mandate also included the term "evaluation." It instructed us to examine the "fundamental purposes of [compensatory education] programs and the effectiveness of such programs in attaining such purposes." From our early discussions with Congressional staff, it was clear that the term "fundamental purposes" was not intended to force us to produce a definitive statement about the value of Title I. But we could not pretend that the mandate was free of references to evaluation. We also knew that the original writers of the mandate could not hope to control the way that the study results were used. Because the debate about whether compensatory education had failed was then at a peak, we knew that disputants on both sides would use our results for ammunition. Whether we or the mandate writers liked it or not, our results would be seen as an evaluation of Title I.

We decided to take the "fundamental purposes" language seriously and to use it as the core of our evaluation strategy. In search of "fundamental purposes," we traced the legislative history of the program back to Adam Clayton Powell's early speeches and committee reports. Those sources confirmed that the authors' conceptions of the purposes of Title I were extremely diverse. The program was meant to establish the principle of federal aid to education, help out needy school districts, provide a symbol of federal concern for the poor, provide employment in low-income areas, revolutionize educational practice, and provide children with everything from clothing and pocket money to better instructional services. Title I, like most other major federal programs, was established through a complex legislative process that required the formation of broad coalitions of supporters. The legislative history shows that support for the program came from diverse sources. Congress was not united behind any single version of the program's goals.

The diversity of legislative purposes made it clear to us that the existing research models for evaluating federal education programs were inappropriate. Prior evaluations conducted by people who wanted to be objective about compensatory education had tried to measure the effectiveness of the program in terms of its effects on participating students' achievement test scores. As Berryman and Glennan explain in Chap. 2, earlier evaluators assumed that the Title I program was a single intervention, like a treatment in a psychological experiment, whose effects could be summarized by a simple measurement. That assumption made it possible to use readily available standard methods to evaluate the Title I program, but it did not correspond to the program's purposes. The program's goals are not limited to instructional outcomes. An evaluation that draws unfavorable conclusions about the program on the basis of student achievement outcomes ignores objectives that the Congressional supporters of Title I had in mind.

We thus had a clear mandate to evaluate the program, but no model of how to conduct such an evaluation. We tried to use our early discussions with Congressional staff to define Congress's expectations and to try out different possible responses to the evaluation requirement. It soon became clear that we did not have to produce a single "bottom line" measure of the worth of Title I. Our results might be used in evaluating the program, but Congress had no intention of delegating final judgment to us.

Perhaps our most important discovery was that Congress, not researchers, evaluates federal programs. Some of our research results might prove germane and useful in its debates, but no piece of research was likely to be conclusive. The experience with evaluations of Title I bears this out. From 1965 to the present, most researchers have drawn dire conclusions about the effectiveness of Title I, yet Congress has continued to reauthorize and expand it. Much the same is true for programs in bilingual education and Follow Through.

Congressional reluctance to act directly on the results of evaluations can be taken to mean that politicians are not wise or brave enough to act on the results of rational analysis—a conclusion that is satisfying to researchers whose findings have been ignored. Unfortunately, the opposite is far more plausible: Many research results are inadequate for evaluating federal education programs as then understood by Congress.

Because our purpose was to help Congress do its own evaluation, we had to identify Congress's main objectives for Title I. We had to present information about how closely Title I was meeting each of the objectives Congress had set for it. Naturally, everyone hoped the program would enhance student achievement, but that was not necessarily the one *fundamental* objective against which the program should be judged. Members of Congress, individually and together, had to decide what weight to give each of the objectives in judging the program.

Our solution to the problem of providing information that Congress could use in evaluating the program was summarized in the 1976 Interim Report of the NIE study:

> To identify the fundamental purpose of compensatory education, NIE studied the provisions of Title I and its various amendments, accompanying House and Senate reports, and Congressional debates. Those sources indicated that Title I of the Elementary and Secondary Education Act had three fundamental purposes:
>
> - To provide financial assistance to school districts in relation to their numbers of low-income children and, within those school districts, to schools with the greatest numbers of low-income students.
> - To fund special services for low-achieving children in the poorest schools.
> - To contribute to the cognitive, emotional, social, or physical development of participating students.

NIE's strategy for assessing compensatory education programs begins with the recognition that the program has several purposes ... these fundamental purposes of Title I are consistent with one another, but each is not equally important to all Members of Congress. Congressional debates, and even the language of different parts of committee and conference reports, suggest that members of Congress differ over the relative importance of the respective purposes. Although some Congressional statements imply that the purposes form a hierarchy in which Title I delivers funds and services only to increase children's academic achievement (thus making the third fundamental purpose the most important), other statements make it clear that the allocation of funds and delivery of services are important ends in themselves.

The early national evaluations of Title I considered only the third fundamental purpose—contributing to children's development—and often judged program efficacy without accounting for the diverse ways in which school districts had implemented it. Those evaluations overlooked some important truths about Title I: It has several objectives, and under it school districts deliver a range of services with a variety of aims and emphases to a diverse set of beneficiaries. In contrast to earlier evaluations, therefore, NIE's strategy is designed to (1) provide clear information about what Title I is accomplishing toward achievement of each fundamental purpose, and (2) examine the implications of alternative ways of organizing the efforts of the federal, state, and local governments to achieve these purposes.

We took care to re-state the "three fundamental purposes" concept at every opportunity. By the time Congressional hearings started in the fall of 1977, it was familiar to the key staff members in the House and Senate. Congress apparently understood and accepted this approach. Despite our apprehensions, there was no further pressure on NIE to return to student achievement as the sole criterion.

Overcoming Congressional Distrust

Congressional staff members who wrote the NIE study mandate apparently did so with ambivalence. They needed research information to improve their future decisions and to help resolve political conflicts, but they had grave doubts about whether the mandate they had written would lead to anything worthwhile. Some of their misgivings concerned social scientists' ability to produce clear, comprehensible conclusions (discussed below under "Producing Usable Results"). Many of their doubts, however, stemmed from a real distrust of the motives of social scientists. They apparently believed that researchers do not take politicians seriously, and are secretly activists with their own axes to grind.

The impression that researchers do not take politicians seriously is rooted in an accurate perception of the attitudes that many researchers adopt in dealing with politicians. As we discovered in trying to adapt to the demands of the Congressional mandate, our research training strongly disposed us to consider practical politics an essentially nonintellectual activity. It was natural to draw a sharp distinction between "rational analysis" and the decision process of politicians. The distinction implies that politicians do not care about the relationship of means and ends, and are either uninterested in or incapable of fine logical analysis. As we learned in our contacts with senior Congressional staff, that implication may be correct for some politicians, but it is probably no more true of politicians in general than of professional researchers or any other group.

Many members of the NIE staff were trained as political scientists. We found it useful to think back to our early training, which taught that politicians, especially good ones, are intensely conscious of the connections between means and ends, and of the need to accomplish objectives without wasting financial or political resources. They are seldom free, however, to pursue one end to the disregard of all others, or to denominate all costs according to a simple uniform measure such as dollars of public expenditure. The essential role of a politician is to reach accommodations among people who are seeking contrary ends. To enlist support for a program with a goal he or she wishes to achieve, a politician often has to incorporate additional goals that other politicians want. The problem is to construct a program that maximizes the attainment of two or more goals, within the constraint that both (or all) of them must be served by the same instrument.[3] This requires rational analysis of a very high order, but to a naive observer the results can look thoroughly irrational. Researchers' intellectual contempt for politicians is often based on the *researchers'* failure to understand how programs are created. Congressional staff members are aware of that contempt, which plays no small part in Congress's distrust of researchers.

In dealing with Congressional staff, we genuinely believed that serving the decisionmaking process was a worthy professional activity. Some, including many other researchers, found that hard to believe. The present author once discussed the study with the May 12 Group, an informal group of distinguished educational researchers. Some members of the audience simply could not accept that description of our orientation. One member opined that our ostensible professional commitment to serving the decisionmaking process was a way of maintaining credibility while we built a case for our own policy preferences. He noted that one way to buy time for grinding an axe is to keep the axe out of sight as long as possible.

Another listener observed that the author, if sincere, was failing to do the researcher's most fundamental job, that of challenging the assumptions made by legislators and other politicians. He said that serving the decisionmaking process by providing the information most likely to be used by Congress in its deliberations limits the scope of research: It rules out fundamental questions, such as whether any level of government should have the power over people's minds that comes with controlling education.

The author had to agree with him, and observed that his attitude validated the very distrust we were trying to overcome. It is true that providing information for a specific decisionmaking process limits a researcher's scope for revolutionary thinking. It makes him a collaborator with the regime: Providing information to

---

[3]One clever way that politicians have discovered for meeting this challenge is to delegate the engineering of programs to bureaucracies. ESEA Title I is a good example. Once Congress had agreed to spend federal money on aid to education, program design was left to the Office of Education. USOE thus had to execute the compromises and live with the internal tensions that had been written into the statute. The fact that OE bureaucrats have often looked bungling and confused in the administration of Title I may very well testify that they have faithfully implemented the political accommodations reached by Congress in 1965.

facilitate its decisionmaking processes implies an acceptance of its right to act in a particular area. It is important to remember, however, that no one is forced to undertake such a study, and researchers can decline to do so if they disagree with the regime's premise. In the case of compensatory education, the NIE staff accepted the legitimacy of the basic program and therefore agreed that it was worth helping Congress to define it. We did not feel morally obliged to be gadflies or adversaries to the state. Because the Congressional staff members we were dealing with disagreed among themselves about how particular decisions should be made, we hoped to avoid any pressures to produce biased reports. But we were indeed content to point our work toward the coming reauthorization of Title I and to provide evidence that others could use in making policy decisions.

Neither the author nor the critics at the May 12 Group meeting recognized a third possibility: that research problems could be identified from the current academic literature, without reference to the information needs of policymakers. Adopting that recourse would have relieved us of any choice between opposing or supporting the existing regime; if there were any political biases in our work, we would at least be spared from knowing about them. Political advocates might find ways of using our results, but as far as we would have been concerned that would be accidental.

We did not follow this third course because we were excited about the professional challenge of finding ways to make research useful in the coming Title I debates. Had the mandate been hopelessly ambiguous, internally contradictory, or technically infeasible, we would have turned to the professional literature for guidance in defining the research problems. But we had accepted an explicit and technically feasible contract from Congress, and saw no reason to violate it.

After a while, Congressional staff did come to believe that we were professionally committed to a detached service of the decisionmaking process, which made us more credible to Congress, as well as to the federal and state managers of the Title I program.

Managing Advocacy Pressure. Studies of major federal programs take place in an atmosphere of advocacy pressure. By undertaking a study of a major federal program, the researcher enters an arena where important things are at stake. Other participants will strive to protect their interests; they will be alert for any signs of hostile intent on the researcher's part and will do all they can to ensure that the research results help their own causes. We quickly found ourselves subject to advocacy pressures from Congress, interest groups, and the Executive Branch.

Pressures from Congress. Advocacy pressures from Congress were acute because the study originated in a Congressional conflict over Representative Quie's proposal to allocate Title I funds according to student achievement measures instead of according to measures of poverty then in use.

Though the mandate had several parts and a variety of Congressional supporters, its one indispensable purpose was to guarantee that the Quie proposal would be thoroughly investigated. That fact exposed the study to political conflict in two ways: First, Quie's opponents begrudged the publicity his proposal would receive by being exhaustively studied and reported, and therefore pressed NIE to hold its work on the Quie proposal to a minimum. Second, both Quie and his opponents wanted to guarantee that NIE's findings would support their positions. The mandate required

An exploration of alternative methods, including the use of procedure to assess educational disadvantage, for distributing funds ... to States, to State educational agencies, and to local educational agencies in a ... manner which will ... insure that such funds reach the areas of greatest current need ... (P.L. 93-380, Sec. 821(a)(2)); and

An analysis of means to identify accurately the children who have the greatest need for such programs ... (P.L. 93-380, Sec. 821(a)(2)).

That placed us in the center of the conflict, where we had to manage, rather than evade, the advocacy pressures on us. We did that in three ways. The first and most important was to make it clear that research could not settle a conflict that was fundamentally political. We did so by forthrightly acknowledging that our research could not prove that low-achieving children, regardless of their income, deserved or needed special services more than low-income children. NIE's 1976 Interim Report to Congress echoed the message that we delivered in every informal conversation on the issue:

The choice between allocation using achievement scores and allocation using poverty counts cannot be made on the basis of research results alone. It depends ultimately on a political choice about the characteristics of places and persons who are to benefit from funds the program provides. NIE's research can illuminate the practical consequences of a change in methods of funds allocation, but it cannot determine which method is "best" in a philosophical or ethical sense (p. II-14).

The second method was to make advocates on each side of the issue aware of the pressures we were receiving from the other side. Those pressures were apparent at the joint meetings we held from time to time with Congressional staff. They were underscored in private communication by vividly phrased acknowledgments of NIE's delicate position, such as "I know perfectly well that you would kill us if we biased things in Quie's favor, but so would [Quie's supporters] if we were to be biased in your way."

The third method was to avoid any hint of personal preference or bias on the part of NIE staff. We made it clear that we intended to conduct the extensive study of Quie's proposal that the mandate expressly required—but that in doing so we were fulfilling a professional obligation, and not advocating any particular conclusion.

The message was clear to Congress. The strategy of letting both sides see the conflicting pressures on the research made it possible for NIE to operate. Those methods worked in part because we were consistent in applying them. But success ultimately relied on the professionalism of the Congressional staff members who planned to use our results. Both sides recognized that results tainted by bias would be of no use to them. They understood that they had an important stake in maintaining our independence and respectability. This realization did not exempt us from scrutiny and criticism; both sides continued to apply gentle pressure, lest we forget they were there. That pressure had a benign effect because it reinforced our objectivity.

Pressures from Interest Groups. The Quie proposal was the most important source of advocacy pressure on NIE, but not the only one. A great deal of pressure came from interest groups outside Congress that had stakes in the Title I program. These included minority groups, state education agencies, teachers' unions, school board associations, and Catholics. Few of these groups had definite agendas; their main concern was to ensure that the results of our study would not weaken their positions. A few, notably parent groups and parochial school interests, wanted to make sure that we recognized the importance of their own place in the Title I program, and were content once we mounted small studies of their problems. Most simply wanted to frighten us away from saying anything critical about them.

Interest group pressures were never subtle, and generally came in the form of attacks on our honesty or professionalism. We resolved not to give in to them. We decided that appearing to be easily swayed by attacks would cause more suspicion than would mounting a stout defense. We chose the means of our defense carefully, however. We seldom engaged in direct confrontation with groups that attacked us. When under attack, our main concern was to ensure that we would not lose the support of the key Congressional staff members who were the study's main clients. In response to written attacks, we drafted very careful, balanced replies, which we delivered to Congress first and the attackers later.

The most serious attack was launched by the National Advisory Council on the Education of Disadvantaged Children in January 1975. The Council demanded that the study be halted until a new director of NIE could root out the biases in the research plan. We did not respond directly, but gave drafts of our response to Republican and Democratic committee staff members some days before we sent it to the National Advisory Council. Our concern always was to ensure that the attacks did not endanger our Congressional support. In a few cases, when the attacks were persistent or very strong, Congressional staff members would contact the attackers directly to express support for us. In one case, Mr. Quie made some remarks on the House floor that shut off an attack.

Having Congressional support did not remove the need to deal fairly with interest groups. We could not hope to maintain Congress's sympathy if we failed to take due account of interest group concerns. We therefore tried to understand and avoid aggravating the special sensitivities of the major interest groups. Our consultations during the planning phase of the study had helped us to identify "loaded" words and phrases that could elicit suspicion and opposition whenever they were used. As relative newcomers to the politics of compensatory education, we were at first unaware of the histories associated with particular terms and the freight they could carry. We soon learned, for example, that the term "district need," when used to refer to a possible criterion for allocating Title I funds, was associated in the minds of big-city education interests with an earlier New York State plan that would have reduced funding for cities. Minority group interests were also vigilant for any word or phrase that might reveal that we were operating from a "deficit model," i.e., an assumption that the failures of education are caused by the habits or abilities of minority students or their communities. We also learned that using the term "educationally disadvantaged student" could mark one as a supporter of the Quie bill, because Mr. Quie had taken care to define it to refer to students whose performance on formal achievement tests was low.

We learned to avoid such terms, and were generally able to avoid attack by inventing neutral synonyms. With one exception—the decision not to investigate aggregate "district need" indicators as possible Title I funding criteria—sensitivity over terms did not cause us to make substantive changes in the study.

These examples may appear trivial, but they underline the political sensitivity of our task. Without some degree of toleration from the interest groups, the study staff could have been forced to spend most of its time responding to attacks. In the unlikely event that the study could have been done at all in those circumstances, the reports would have been condemned by the interest groups, and would have lost much of their value as authoritative general sources of information. We therefore took great care to avoid any use of words that could incite suspicion or confer a rhetorical advantage on any of the contending sides. As one NIE staff member observed, all of us were becoming experts in propaganda through the effort to avoid rather than to create it. Taking these precautions was difficult, but it was the only way to ensure that our work could be understood for what it was rather than according to a system of political symbols that we did not understand.

None of these methods succeeded in heading off attacks from interest groups, which continued—though at a steadily declining pace—throughout the study; but we were able to keep operating.

Pressure from the Executive Branch. Throughout the study, we were able to avoid what every government program manager fears most: the imposition of review and clearance boards to diffuse the pressure on a controversial activity. Because of the short and firm deadlines for our reports, the delays caused by formal governmental or public reviews would have been disastrous. Support from the Hill was an important factor: Nobody wanted to take responsibility for delaying or derailing a study that Congress clearly wanted. Our short life span was also an asset: Since the study staff was a temporary unit with no bureaucratic future (and an untouchable budget), we were exempted from most of the pressures for review that permanent units always experience.

There was pressure on us from within the government, however. Unlike the pressures from Congress and interest groups, the pressures from the Executive Branch were not for conclusions favorable to a particular idea; they were for early release of data that could be used as private resources by officials in the Executive Branch, either for internal negotiations or to capture the initiative from Congress. We concluded the study within HEW at a time when the Department was trying to formulate its own policy about Title I. HEW wanted to improve the program and, at the same time, ensure that the Administration, rather than Congress or the interest groups, kept the initiative. Data from our studies could have been important ammunition, both for contending factions within HEW and for the Department as a whole in dealing with Congress. As a result, there was always pressure on us to provide preliminary results, do special tabulations, and contribute to internal HEW staff work. Those pressures became especially strong in the summer of 1977, when we were writing our final reports and HEW was trying to work out the Administration's proposals.

We were therefore in the middle between Congressional staff members who had initiated, negotiated, and funded the study and therefore felt that it was theirs, and HEW, especially the offices of the Assistant Secretary for Planning and Evaluation (ASPE) and the Assistant Secretary for Education (ASE), who reminded us that we were part of the Department and therefore had to act as good staff members first and contractors to Congress second. Both sides wanted the reports first, so that they could announce what they meant for policy. The relationship between the Hill and the Department was essentially competitive, and the fact that both were controlled by the same political party meant little.

Congress had protected its first access to our data by a provision in the mandate which read:

> Any provision of law, rule, or regulation to the contrary notwithstanding, such reports shall not be submitted to any review outside of the Institute before their transmittal to the Congress ... (P.L. 93-380, Sec. 811(c)).

That language controlled our behavior effectively, but it did not set well with the Department. Iris Rotberg, the deputy director of the study, had a confrontation with HEW Secretary Caspar Weinberger, who held that such an arrangement was unthinkable and therefore moot. Near the end of the study we were under constant pressure from the Department. A friend of the present author had the relevant section of the mandate photoenlarged and framed, to be hung on the wall for display to visitors who needed a reminder.

We received further help from the Hill in the form of a threat from the staff of the House Subcommittee. A member of NIE's external relations office had a copy of one of our drafts for purposes of internal review. While on a trip to the West Coast, he let a reporter take a peek at a couple of tables; they became the subject of an AP news story, and Congressional staff learned about one of our findings from the newspapers. They were mightily displeased, and threatened to rake NIE over the coals in public if it ever happened again.

We made some preliminary oral reports to HEW, taking care to talk to Congressional staff members at least a few hours beforehand. They were usually glad to get the preliminary information, but HEW staff were dissatisfied with it. They were convinced that we were sitting on mountains of useful material, holding it back until we got the reports all assembled. In one sense they were right: We had piles of computer printouts and unrelated facts that could have been used, along with some clever argumentation, to support any point an advocate wanted to make. But we were trying desperately to make a clear and defensible use of it, and we did not want to be forced by premature publicity into defending someone else's interpretation.

Much to our surprise, the part of the Department we encountered the least trouble with was the Title I program staff itself. We expected them to resist the evaluation, out of fear that it would damage Congressional support for the program or bring about criticism of their own conduct. Had they resisted, we would have found it difficult to obtain needed information about the program or to get state and local education agencies to cooperate with our data collection.

The Title I program staff dealt with us stiffly in the beginning, but it became clear that they were willing to cooperate with the study. After reading our research plan they were reassured that the study was not biased against the program. It took them longer to be convinced that we were not interested in evaluating the performance of particular administrators.

Our study of federal administration of Title I (reported in Chaps. 1-3 of *The Administration of Compensatory Education*) was the severest test of their cooperation. The Title I staff was reluctant, but willing to cooperate; other parts of the

Bureau of Elementary and Secondary Education (the OE unit that includes Title I) put up some resistance. We were able to overcome their resistance only after we had presented the plan for that project to Congress and received strong statements of interest. That made the project a "mandated" part of the study, and BESE then gave its full cooperation.

Our report writing was not a stately process. We were making major changes in the drafts until the day they were printed, and most reports went to the Hill less than ten days after we finished writing. So we were not hoarding valuable information; as soon as we knew what to make of research results, we published them.

The study staff clearly had the resources to resist pressures from the rest of the Department, and to retain control over the publication of our results. That was a unique privilege, due in part to the mandate, in part to constant pressures from Congress, and in part to the fact that our research organization was temporary, with no other projects and no bureaucratic future to protect. A permanent organization, such as the Office of Planning, Budgeting, and Evaluation (OPBE) in the Office of Education, would need to worry about its future funding and the fate of other less protected projects. Even with a similar mandate and active Congressional interest, OPBE would have found it hard to avoid responding to the Administration before it did to Congress.

While the main reports of the study were being written, the pressures within the Department made life especially difficult for the Director of NIE. Although the NIE study staff was able to rely on Congressional support to fend off attacks from the rest of the Department, the Director had to be concerned about a broader set of relations with the Commissioner of Education, the Assistant Secretary for Education, and the Secretary's office. Other NIE projects (or the Institute's budget) could be affected by their displeasure. The Director resisted those pressures and supported our determination to avoid sharing our report drafts inside the Department before they were transmitted to Congress. That required a great deal of personal courage on the Director's part; it was made only slightly easier by the fact that Congressional staff members had contacted her directly to urge that the reports be sent directly to Congress as the mandate required.

Making the Results Useful to Congress

From the beginning of the study, it was clear that Congress would consider the study a success only if the results were reported in time for use in the Title I reauthorization hearings, and in a form that Congressional staff members could readily understand. Meeting those requirements demanded intense management effort throughout the study, as well as great care in drafting the reports. It will help to distinguish the measures we took to assure punctuality from those we took to present the reports in a clear and understandable form.

Meeting the Deadlines. The mandate had established two deadlines: December 31, 1976, for an interim report and September 30, 1977, for the final products. The latter date was dictated by the reauthorization schedule for Title I.[4] Schedules

---

[4]A second "final" report was added later, for September 30, 1978, to permit a full report on demonstration projects that would not end until June 1978.

for reauthorizing Title I are fixed by statute, and little can be done to relax them. If our research was to be useful for reauthorization, its results had to be available when Congress and the Administration were ready to start their review. Regardless of its quality, research that became available after decisions were made—or even after the main lines of debate had been drawn—was not going to be useful.

The question of when research is on time is not always easy to answer. A Congressional mandate can answer the question by setting a date, but even that may not cause the research to be available at the right moment. If the House had started its hearings on ESEA in the early summer of 1977, our reports would have come too late, even if we had faithfully met the statutory deadline of September 30. Happily, the Counsel of the Elementary and Secondary Education Subcommittee was interested in our reports, and got the hearings delayed until October.

For research to be used by Congress, results must be available at least a month before hearings are to begin—before witnesses are scheduled and blocks of time are assigned to particular topics. That gives the committee staff time to read the reports and decide how to use them. After receiving the NIE reports, the House decided to build the whole hearings process around them, holding approximately one week's hearings on each of the major topics we addressed. That forced everyone to pay attention to the results; it would not have been possible if our results came later. If reports become available during the hearings, they become part of a flood of information that cannot all be assimilated. After the hearings, Congress is busy with bargaining, not assimilating facts; it is then too late for research to be useful.

It is much harder to say when reports are "on time" for Executive Branch use. The Administration is able to assign staff to work on reauthorization issues for years before the hearings begin. The planning offices in HEW always want results before they can be produced: There is no one best time. From that, one may conclude that the Congressional process gives the best cues about when research should be completed.

To fit the cycle for reauthorizing Title I, the NIE study had to be completed in almost exactly three years. The mandate was enacted on August 24, 1974, and the reports to be used in Congressional hearings were due on September 30, 1977. The first six months were spent writing a research plan and making it available for Congressional review. As a result, the first Requests for Proposals (RFPs) for the study were issued in April 1975, and the first research projects started in late May of that year. They all had to be finished in about two years, by the summer of 1977, so that we could write our formal reports to Congress.

Our main response to the deadlines was to live by them. That required both political and managerial determination. On the political side, we had to resist heavy pressure from the National Advisory Council on the Education of Disadvantaged Children, which wanted us to do a several-year longitudinal study of the effects of compensatory instruction. When we pointed out that such a study would take more time than the mandate allowed, and therefore miss the reauthorization deadline, they insisted that we stand up to Congress on behalf of the imperatives of good research. We did not do that, both because we thought Congress had given us enough time to do what was necessary, and because USOE was starting the very longitudinal study (the Sustaining Effects Study) that the Council had suggested.

On the managerial side, the key to living within the deadlines was to attempt only what could be accomplished on time. That is not a profound thought, but it is an important one. It meant that we had to select our problems and methods very carefully, and we had to be sure that the interested members and staff in Congress knew the limits of what we could produce. We could not answer questions about the long-term development of children who receive compensatory services, and if we wanted to trace the development of instructional or administrative practices, we had to do it retrospectively.

The deadlines also forced us to define simple projects that could be designed, put into the field, and reported quickly. We mounted a large number of small projects, each designed to accomplish a simple objective, rather than a few complex, multipurpose studies.

That practice had several advantages. It meant that each project was simple enough for one NIE staff member, rather than a team, to monitor. Iris Rotberg and the author, as directors of the overall study, were thus able to get reliable and complete information on each study from a single staff member. Similarly, because our contractors did not need vast interdisciplinary teams of researchers, they experienced fewer managerial problems. Because projects were relatively self-contained, a problem or failure in one did not threaten the whole study. Had one project failed, we would have had a hole somewhere in our final report, but we would still have been able to give Congress most of what it needed.

We were, finally, able to conduct backup studies to protect ourselves against the possible failure of very crucial or difficult efforts. We knew, for example, that our study would be a failure if we could not produce a good report on the effects of changing the criterion for allocating Title I funds from poverty to student achievement (that is, adopting Mr. Quie's proposal). Producing such a report required some risky and difficult analysis of existing achievement test files. To protect ourselves, we mounted three different studies to produce that information. Happily, the best and most technically ambitious project—the one conducted by David Wiley and Annegret Harnischfeger of CEMREL, Inc.—produced very good results that Margot Nyitray of NIE was able to use as the basis for our report, *Using Achievement Test Scores to Allocate Title I Funds*. (We note in passing that it is politically risky for a government agency to conduct redundant research projects. Most outside reviewers point to "overlap and duplication" as evidence of bad research management. To the contrary, it is argued here that redundant research on the core problems of a mandated study can be essential to the study's success.)

Our reliance on a large number of simple studies did impose a special management burden. Each of the many small projects continually threatened to assume a life of its own. It was easy for members of the NIE research team to make decisions on particular projects without reference to the rest of the study. It was therefore necessary to Iris Rotberg and the author, as managers of the whole study, to keep the goal in view for all the members of the research team.

We accomplished that through the planning of the final report. Early in 1976, nearly two years before the main reports to Congress were due, we started outlining elements of the reports. Original drafts of those outlines were written by James Harvey, who was designated "report coordinator." These outlines included statements of the problems to be addressed, examples of the data to be provided, and identification of the projects that would provide the data. The researchers whose projects were to provide data then suggested better ways to formulate research questions and commented on whether the data required could be made available. When there were discrepancies between the report outline and the projects on which it relied, we then either revised the report outline or made changes in the relevant research projects.

By February 1977, eight months before the final reports were due, we had decided to issue the six separate reports identified in the Introduction to this essay. A senior staff member was then designated "drafter" for each of the six reports. The "drafters" produced detailed outlines, including expected table shells and figures. These were discussed in formal planning meetings, and appropriate changes were made in the outlines or research projects, or both.

The report plans changed significantly every time, and the eventual products were often quite unlike any of the plans. Report planning was an important tool for keeping the study integrated, however. There was always a working outline, which we could use as a framework for describing our work to Congress, NIE management, and the public.

From September 1976 until the main reports were due a year later, the senior NIE study staff devoted virtually full time to the preparation of reports. The mandate required an interim report to Congress at the end of December 1976. We used that report to lay out the research strategy in detail, give examples of early findings from the research on compensatory education services, and present previews of the objectives and logic of each of the six reports due the following September. Writing the interim report (*Evaluating Compensatory Education, An Interim Report on the NIE Compensatory Eduction Study, 1976*) was, for the staff, the most difficult and exhausting part of the whole study. We were forced to make explicit the heretofore loose connections between different studies, and had to settle important disagreements within the staff that we had been able to ignore previously.

The interim report also gave clear notice to Congress about what to expect. That helped Congressional staff to organize their own ideas and reduced our risk of being criticized by Congress for producing unpleasant surprises the following September.

Making the Reports Clear and Understandable. After years of trying to use the results of educational evaluations, Congressional staff members have developed an active distaste for the reporting conventions of social science. That distaste was expressed to us very early by a senior House committee staff member, who warned that Congress would ignore our reports if they were laborious or jargonized, or failed to draw conclusions. His advice to us was to be clear, brief, and definitive; not to fear arriving at a conclusion; but, of course, to be technically unassailable.

That injunction was formidable, but useful. The written mandate and our early discussions with Congressional staff members made it evident that the reports could not be simplistic. The study's sponsors had a great variety of questions, and they knew enough to distrust pat answers. They also intended to ask other researchers to comment on the technical quality of our research and the appropriateness of our conclusions. Thus, the reports could not be slick, trivial, or even very brief. We had to present a substantial body of material without either boring or overwhelming the readers. The reports had to use simple and direct language, but more important, they had to address topics of intrinsic interest to Congress and provide information that would help members of the Congress in their work.

The two most important things we did toward that end have already been discussed: focusing the study on understanding how the elements of the Title I program work together; and selecting research projects in collaboration with Congress, to ensure that the results would be germane to Congressional decisions about Title I.

These efforts pointed us in the right direction, but did not guarantee that the reports would be readable, of course. To render them so, we resolved on two further measures.

The first was to make the reports as direct and readable as possible. Clarity in this case, we decided, entailed more than avoiding arcane language and professional jargon. Above all, the writer should keep the audience in mind, and give first consideration to the audience's needs and interests, not the writer's. Accordingly, we resolved to concentrate on communicating findings and to resist the reseacher's natural inclination to recount a blow-by-blow history of the research. Policymakers need to know research results; they are less interested in the details of the research process. That may be what distinguishes a report for policymakers from one for scientists, who are interested equally in method and results. Still, because research is not likely to be useful to Congress if the scientific community condemns it, the reports must be buttressed by thoughtful and professional analysis. One solution is to relegate the professional credentials of research —compendious backup data, accounts of methodology, and the like—to appendixes or separate reports, where they are available to scientists but do not encumber the policymaker.

Our second measure was to present information in a strong interpretive framework. We assumed that policymakers are too busy for intellectual puzzles—for going over material again and again and teasing out its implications. If so, it would be a disservice to the reader if we left it up to the reader to integrate an assortment of disparate findings. Doing that for the reader, we concluded, was our most important intellectual task: finding how things fit together and explaining why data were important, thus enabling Congress to make informed decisions on changes in policy or practice. That task was far from easy. We found that it was impossible both to call attention to every finding of every project and to combine the results of all the projects into a logical whole. Selectivity therefore became necessary. We emphasized those results that bore on the questions Congress had asked us, or that we had woven into the original research strategy; we were able to accommodate new or unanticipated information only when it related to the mandate or the research strategy. That left a fair amount of data on the cutting-room floor (some of which may be reported independently by contractors or members of the NIE study staff).

In general, the need to synthesize our 35 studies put a premium on deciding what our data meant, instead of on reporting research results as if they were valuable for their own sake. Doing that made the whole exceed the sum of its parts. Important people in Congress read and understood our reports; they surely would not have read or understood the reports of 35 separate studies.

This effort was agonizing. Some of the reports went through as many as ten drafts before we were confident that the readers would know why we were presenting particular bits of information, but the effort was worthwhile. Perhaps the best thing about our reports is that they gave the staffs and senior members of the House and Senate authorizing committees a command of the issues brought before them. The House in particular used the topics of our reports as the organizing principle of its hearings on Title I in the fall of 1977. Each week of the hearings was focused on the topic of one of our reports. NIE's testimony—an oral summary of the relevant reports, with an opportunity for questions and answers—opened the hearings.[5] The Committee was able to confine subsequent witnesses to the topics of the hearings and to use the reports as checks against witnesses' statements. On occasion, Congress asked for special memoranda from NIE commenting on claims or problems raised by witnesses. Congress is seldom able to organize and discipline its flow of information in this way. Witnesses are often free to discuss whatever they like, and are able to make assertions with little fear of immediate contradiction by a generally trusted outside source.

HEW apparently had good reason to be concerned about our reporting directly to Congress. As Christopher Cross (then minority counsel of the House Education and Labor Committee) has recently written,

> By the time the Administration finally got around to formulating their position and formulating that into a bill, the results of the NIE and DECIMA studies had so thoroughly shaped the nature and content of the hearings that there were not many areas left in which the Administration could have a clear shot at shaping policy.[6]

To appreciate the institutional advantages conferred on Congress by our reports, it is important to remember that Congress received our reports hours, not days or weeks, before HEW.

Congress did not receive private advance reports, but did receive an organized body of information that could be read and assimilated before the hearings began. In the past, Congress has had to wait until the Administration gave its testimony to get the benefit of research conducted by the Executive Branch. NIE's reports may in this instance have changed the balance of power between Congress and the Executive, but they did so simply by giving Congress information in time for staff to use, and in a form that was not orchestrated to support particular proposals.

We took the precaution of avoiding making recommendations in our reports. One good reason for doing so was that few, if any, of our results led to unambiguous prescriptions. We could make "if ... then" statements, in which the "if" was an assumption about policymakers' objectives; but we had reason to believe that policymakers were divided about objectives, and it was not in our province to make political judgments.

We had another very important reason for refraining from recommendations. We wanted to avoid the appearance of being merely another advocate or claimant. The main public role of members of Congress and their staffs is to receive demands and listen to self-interested versions of the facts. When a researcher couches his or her research findings in the form of a recommendation—which can be considered a mild form of demand—the researcher's objectivity is immediately suspect. But we could be a source of disinterested information, thereby helping members of Con-

---

[5]See *Hearings before the Subcommittee on Elementary, Secondary, and Vocational Education of the Committee on Education and Labor,* U.S. House of Representatives, 95th Con., 1st sess., on H.R. 15, parts 13, 18, and 19.

[6]Christopher T. Cross, *Compensatory Education: A Congressional Perspective,* paper prepared for the National Conference on Urban Education, CEMREL, Inc., St. Louis, Missouri, July 13, 1978.

gress and their staffs understand and control their own world, instead of our trying to control them.

After we submitted the formal reports, Congress requested our comments on several questions. Many of the requests were for more detailed reports on findings that had caught their attention, or for analyses of problems that witnesses had identified in the reauthorization hearings. Some of the questions could be answered from data we already had. Our responses, usually in the form of letters to the Chairmen of the House and Senate Committees, were incorporated into the hearing records. Other requests required small new studies, which we conducted quickly and submitted as supplementary reports, for example, a study of the effects of school desegregation on the delivery of Title I services to children. NIE's supplementay report on that study resolved a number of disputes that had previously impeded Congressional decisionmaking about rules for the targeting of Title I funds.[7]

Congress made its most important request after the hearings were over. The Chairman and ranking minority members of the House Education Committee, Representatives Perkins and Quie, formally asked NIE to analyze the entire Title I statute in light of the study findings. They wanted a technical review of the internal logic and clarity of the statute, and other recommendations, in the form of proposed legislative language, that reflected what NIE had learned about ways to improve the program.

The request amounted to an invitation to make the kinds of recommendations that we had avoided making in the formal reports. We were heartened by the request, but it proved difficult to handle. It threatened to put the study staff, and the Institute as a whole, in an untenable position between Congress and the Administration. Because our formal reports had now been submitted, we were no longer able to decline requests for special help from the HEW Secretary's Office. On the one hand, the Secretary's staff was then conducting a department-wide effort to draft the Administration's proposals for reauthorization of Title I, and NIE was expected to participate without reservation. On the other hand, the House committee had expressly requested our recommendations as supplements to our formal reports. Like those reports, our recommendations were to be submitted to Congress without prior review in the Executive Branch. The dilemma was obvious: Our recommendations might conflict with the Secretary's, yet NIE was clearly expected to support Department policy.

Unlike most of the problems we had encountered earlier, this dilemma admitted of no direct solution. We had to find a reasonable way of serving two masters.

We first arranged to respond to Congress's request indirectly, by hiring a contractor to do the work. The contractor selected was Robert Silverstein of the Lawyer's Committee for Civil Rights Under Law. Silverstein, who had analyzed the Title I legal framework for our report, *The Administration of Title I,* by then knew more than anyone else about the inner workings of the Title I statute. His first task was to propose ways of resolving ambiguities in the law and consolidating related provisions that had previously been scattered throughout the Elementary and Secondary Education Act. He was to recommend technical improvements in the

---

[7]These included "Implications of Follow-the-Child Proposals," "Indirect Costs of Administering Title I," and "Title I Funding and the Largest Cities—The Changes Since 1974."

legal drafting of the statute, not substantive changes in the program. His second task was more sensitive. He was to draft amendments to the law that would correct problems in program operation identified by any of the NIE reports. Silverstein worked with NIE staff to comb the reports for possible recommendations and draft the appropriate legislative language. His third task was to draft amendments requested jointly by the Democratic and Republican staff of the House committee. The results were to be published by the Lawyer's Committee, without endorsement by NIE.

That arrangement provided Congress with the information it needed, and it took the framing of explicit recommendations out of our hands. It was obviously not a perfect arrangement, because the Secretary's office knew about the request we had received from Congress and was aware of NIE's part in producing the Lawyer's Committee's report.

At the same time, we participated fully in the Secretary's task force. Our chief contribution was to answer questions and provide data requested by the task force. We took the initiative only to call attention to the lines of analyses that we knew would be reflected in the Lawyer's Committee report.

The arrangement appeared to work at first. There were no major conflicts between the Lawyer's Committee report and the Department's recommendations. Silverstein's redrafting of the statute was technically straightforward and uncontroversial. Soon after the reauthorization was complete, however, it became evident that the Department had been stung by NIE's working expressly for Congress. Senior officials in the Secretary's Office and USOE lobbied hard against a mandate that some members of the House had proposed for NIE to conduct a broad study of elementary and secondary school finance. As a result of HEW's lobbying, the 1978 Education Amendment assigned the mandate to the Secretary, not NIE. Congress made it evident that NIE was to have some role in the study, but left the exact arrangements to the Secretary. The intradepartmental negotiations about NIE's role proved so difficult that the whole study was delayed for several months. The study could not be done without NIE's research capabilities, but the Secretary's office was determined to prevent the development of another independent research staff. It is now apparent that a special Congressionally oriented study like ours is a foreign body in the Executive Branch and that Congress can have such studies only if it provides explicit legal and political support. Once that special relationship has expired, the organization responsible for the research is vulnerable to Executive Branch reprisals.

In the end, NIE's findings were repeatedly cited as authority for conclusions drawn in the House and Senate committee reports. The study succeeded in providing policymakers with trusted information and a common ground for discussion. It called attention to problems in the program's structure and operation, many of which were addressed in the reauthorization process. The results were not used, either by NIE or Congress, to support recommendations for fundamental changes in the program's objectives or levels of funding. They were used, however, to sharpen Congress's understanding of the Title I program and the options available for improving it.

SUMMARY AND CONCLUSION

One dual theme unites all of our responses to the five problems discussed above: Our essential strategy was to acknowledge Congress as the chief client for our work; our one irreducible goal was to give Congress the information it needed, when it was needed, and in an immediately usable form. Having Congress as a client helped us deal with each of the five problems in the following ways:

1. *Building a strategy of research in response to the mandate.* Though we put a great deal of energy into our early consultations with interest groups and researchers, the advice we got was diffuse and general. Those discussions did not provide much concrete guidance. In contrast, our discussions with Congress provided both a general conceptual framework for the study and helped us identify particular problems for research. Those discussions led us to think systematically about the political context in which Congress must work and about the tools it has for influencing policy. We were thus able to explain the study's objectives in terms that people in Congress understood and to propose studies that they thought would be helpful to them.

2. *Ensuring that the research made a fair assessment of the strengths and weaknesses of Title I.* At the beginning of the study, even though the mandate required us to evaluate the effectiveness of Title I, we had little confidence in the methods of evaluation then available in the research literature. Our early discussions with Congressional staff helped us define an alternative strategy. We learned that Congress never intended to delegate judgment on the worth of the program to a group of researchers. They knew that legislative politics had produced a diverse set of objectives for Title I, and that some members of Congress would evaluate the program on different grounds from others. That led us to define our role in evaluation in a new way: We identified the sets of objectives most often cited by Congress, and planned research to estimate the program's performance according to each. We then presented the results for each major objective, so that members of Congress could apply their own values and draw their own conclusions. We did not select among the objectives or apply our own weighting schemes. In effect, we used our research skills to supply facts that would help our Congressional clients conduct their own evaluation.

3. *Overcoming Congressional distrust.* Congressional staff members expected that we would have little respect for their needs and would try to formulate research problems to serve our own personal and professional interests. They were frankly surprised when we showed that we took their needs seriously and were not trying to advocate our own policy preferences. Adopting the client relationship with Congress was the specific antidote to Congressional distrust.

4. *Managing advocacy pressure.* The study was founded on a conflict between powerful adversaries in Congress, and its likely effect on the future of Title I made the study salient to the operators, beneficiaries, and opponents of the program. Advocacy pressures could have made the study impossible to conduct. However, it soon became obvious that both NIE and our Congressional sponsors needed the study to have a reputation for objectivity. Our Congressional sponsors were themselves in the ranks of those for and against the Quie bill, and needed us to serve as a trustworthy source of background information for their debates.

Our Congressional sponsors were also united about the desirability of improving Title I operations. Our research could help them in that effort only if it appeared fair and balanced to all of the interest groups involved. Finally, Congress had an institutional interest in guaranteeing that our results were not censored to fit the policy preferences of the Executive Branch.

Even before the study mandate was written into law, we discussed these facts with interested Congressmen and other staffs. As a result, they were careful to avoid imposing strong advocacy pressures themselves. They expected us to deal fairly with interest groups, but protected us against any partisan attacks, and they gave us the resources to resist any efforts at clearance or censorship by our superiors in the Executive Branch.

5. *Making the results understandable and useful to Congress.* Our effort to devise a responsive research strategy was an important first step toward ensuring that Congress would find our reports useful. Further, our discussions with Congressional staff helped us understand how the findings should be presented. Congress being our primary audience, our reports had to be readily understandable to the staff, written in terms Congress would find clear and familiar, and ready for use when issues were being formulated. Congress needed a synthesis of what we had learned about the program's current operation and about the effects of possible changes in it. Nothing else was germane. Methodological exposition was not helpful, nor was a litany of the blind alleys we had gone down. The reports had to be crisp and factual, and illuminate the relationships between facts. We accordingly presented our reports as syntheses of several studies, not study-by-study accounts of research procedures and data.

We also knew that members of Congress and their staffs wanted to use our results to define the important issues for future debate and evaluate the claims made by interest groups in public testimony. They did not want us to preempt their opportunity to define the issues by advancing our own prescriptions. We therefore provided facts and analyses of widely recognized alternatives, but did not present recommendations.

The value of a client relationship with policymakers is the most important lesson that we learned. Evaluators need policymaking clients, both to clarify the research problems they face, and to provide support against inevitable political pressures. In return, policymakers who are willing to act as clients increase their chances of getting useful evaluation results.

The relationship may not always be easy to establish. Ours was ready-made, because Congress had designed a far more explicit study mandate than its previous ones. Although most previous evaluations of Title I were technically based on statutory language (e.g., Section 151 of Title I, which requires the Office of Education to conduct periodic evaluations of ESEA programs), the statute contained few hints about Congress's information needs, and no clear requirements for a close working relationship with Congressional staff. Those evaluations had several audiences, including educational researchers, practitioners, federal program managers, and policymakers in HEW and Congress, but no single client. They were beset by the same technical and political problems that we faced, and had none of the advantages conferred by the client relationship.

This is not to imply that only Congress can be an appropriate governmental client for evaluation. Evaluations can certainly be done for Executive Branch policymakers, or even for program managers at the federal, state, and local levels.

However, it is difficult to imagine how an evaluation can be done well for more than one client. Because each set of policymakers has its own unique schedule for making decisions about a program, and its own policymaking tools, an evaluation tailored for one is unlikely to fit others.

Congress can be a particularly rewarding client for research, however, as much of the above discussion shows. The research results are likely to be used in decisions because Congress (in particular, the authorizing committees in the House and Senate) is the most important single institution in setting federal education policy. Congress can be a sophisticated consumer of research because key Congressional staff have a long professional commitment to education policy. Researchers can hope to maintain independence on the big issues because the Congressional clients are themselves likely to differ. Finally, members of Congress have long time horizons; if the evidence on a particular proposal is hopelessly mixed or if debate becomes acrimonious, they are often willing to defer decisions until the next reauthorization.

The Executive Branch can be a more difficult client. Its leaders are ultimately the bosses of government-employed researchers. They are thus able to censor or withhold research results (as the Secretary of HEW recently did in the case of the OE Sustaining Effects Study), and to take reprisals against researchers or agencies that do not support their own policy proposals. Because the structure of the Executive Branch is always changing, the agency that requests a study may not exist when research is completed. Even when structures are stable, personnel are not: During the life of the NIE study, there were three Secretaries of Education (and two acting assistant secretaries), three Commissioners of Education (and three acting commissioners), and three Directors of NIE. Meanwhile, none of the principal authors of the NIE mandate left the Hill. Consequently, leaders in the Executive Branch are eager to affect policy quickly, and are unlikely to wait for researchers to refine and reshape their reports. Executive Branch leaders are able to set Departmental policy and to report research results selectively in support of it.

Like the Congress, however, the Executive Branch has urgent needs for information and will still do its own evaluations, with or without special Congressional mandates. The primary client for those evaluations will be the Secretary's office (rather than the Secretary personally, whose name will not be known years in advance). When the research is planned, it should anticipate Secretarial information needs. That process should rely in part on the experience of the Department's legislative and program staffs and in part on an analysis of the issues that Congress is likely to force the Secretary to attend to.

Some evaluators may still find it impossible to establish a firm client relationship with any set of policymakers. The statutory mandate for a study may subject the research to coordination at several levels in the Executive Branch as well as require approval by Congress. In such cases, the researchers cannot focus on any one set of information needs, and cannot hope for the kind of political protection we received. For evaluators in that position, the most important lesson of the NIE study is that evaluation results are useful when they provide information relevant to a specific decisionmaking process. Since most, if not all, evaluations bear on the reauthorization of particular statutes, the decisionmaking process will be easy to identify. The nature of the reauthorization decision can imply a great deal about who will be the participants and what decisions they will have power to make. The record of past decisions on the same problem can provide information about perennial issues and topics of particular controversy.

Evaluators cannot hope to be completely insulated from politics. To conduct useful evaluations of national programs, researchers need some taste for political analysis and some respect for politicians. Although evaluation results are essentially technical, their ultimate use is political. Without some appreciation for the politics of a decision, evaluators are unlikely to serve the decisionmaking process well. They may produce irrelevant information and neglect research on topics that will be hotly debated; worse, they may fall into the hands of one side in a political dispute by unwittingly presenting results in terms that have assumed a special political coloration.

Being aware of the political context is not the same thing as being a political activist or advocate. Advocacy for either side in a debate, or for another position favored by the researcher, is professionally irresponsible, and the researcher who indulges in it is likely to reap well-deserved criticism or rejection. Political awareness—understanding the goals and strategies of the politicians who are likely to use evaluation results—is necessary and perfectly consistent with professional detachment.

MEASURING THE EQUITY OF SCHOOL FINANCE POLICIES
A Conceptual and Empirical Analysis

Robert Berne and Leanna Stiefel

To measure the equity of school finance policies, numerous choices among alternative equity concepts and statistical techniques must be made. The authors develop a framework for equity analysis that highlights choices and interprets the choices as value judgments. Elementary and secondary school finance data are used to show that the selection of different value judgments can have an effect on equity findings. The authors conclude with observations on the policy implications of conflicting evaluations of school finance equity.

Issues of equity have always been considered in the public policy process. The development of standard and widely agreed-upon ways to measure equity has not yet occurred, however, primarily because of professional fears of making value judgments and the lack of a proper analytical apparatus. There are some exceptions to the underdevelopment of quantitative equity analysis, namely in the areas of income distribution, tax incidence, and elementary and secondary school finance. The latter is emphasized here. As a result of the numerous *Serrano*-type court cases during the 1970s and the legislative responses to them, more analytical work has been devoted to developing standards and measurements of equity in school finance

The research on which this paper is based was carried out at the Public Policy Research Institute, Graduate School of Public Administration, New York

© 1981 by The Regents of the University of California. Reprinted from POLICY ANALYSIS 7:1 (Winter 1981), pp. 47-69, by permission of The Regents.

than in most other policy areas.[1] In addition, Congress has recently legislated a requirement for equity measurement in school finance. The Education Amendments of 1978 include a mandate for the U.S. Department of Education to publish biennial profiles of each state showing the degree to which equalization of resources has been attained among the state's school districts.[2]

The broad purpose of this paper is to illustrate how value judgments, embedded in statistical measures of equity, influence evaluations of the equity of school finance policies. The paper is divided into two parts: (1) a framework describing four components of an equity standard that can be characterized as answering the questions, Who, What? How? and How much? (2) presentation of data on the distribution of education revenues per pupil from twenty-two states in order to answer the question, Do differences in the choice of an equity standard matter empirically? The method used to assess the empirical differences between any two standards of equity is based on comparisons of the equity rankings from 1 (most equitable) to 22 (least equitable) that result when each standard is applied to the distribution of education revenues in the twenty-two states. The degree of difference in the rankings is quantified with the help of two techniques described herein, the concordance measure and a technique called unambiguous rankings.

The analysis of equity in school finance is related to a large number of issues, some of which we do not discuss in this paper. For

---

University. The effort was fully collaborative and the authors' names are in conventional alphabetical order. Funds were provided by the Ford Foundation and by the Education Commission of the States through a grant from the National Institute of Education. We would especially like to thank Herbert Klarman for his generous assistance in clarifying our ideas and our writing. Elizabeth Durbin, Peter Keen, Peter Stowe, Emanuel Tobier, and two anonymous referees for *Policy Analysis* also contributed many insightful comments. None of these people is in any way responsible for what appears, however. We would also like to thank Chris Hakusa for excellent computer programming assistance and Karen Gruhn for fine secretarial assistance.

1. For an analysis of court cases in school finance, including *Serrano* v. *Priest* (1971), see Joel S. Berke, *Answers to Inequity* (Berkeley, Calif.: McCutchen, 1974).

2. For a discussion of the state profiles required by the 1978 Education Amendments in the House bill, see U.S., Congress, House, Committee on Education and Labor, *Excerpts of House Report 95-1137 on the Education Amendments of 1978, H.R. 15* (Washington, D.C.: Government Printing Office, 1978), esp. pp. 130-34.

example, while we emphasize the choices that are available in the development of an equity standard, we do not analyze how a specific choice is or should be made. We also refrain from discussing the causes of equity and inequity. Clearly most people interested in school finance equity evaluation are also interested in knowing how greater equity can be achieved. Our goal is the more modest one of emphasizing the effect of different standards on equity rankings.

A FRAMEWORK FOR THE ANALYSIS OF EQUITY IN SCHOOL FINANCE

An evaluation of equity in school finance policies must begin with a definition of the standard of equity against which a policy will be judged. We here develop a framework to describe the choices that are made when a quantifiable equity standard for school finance is specified. The equity framework is organized around four questions. First, from whose *perspective* is equity to be assessed? Second, what is the *object* of concern—that is, what is to be equitably distributed? Third, what is the *principle* that determines whether the distribution of the object across the group is equitable? Fourth, for a specific group, object, and equity principle, how is the empirical *measure* of equity formulated? All four questions must be answered, explicitly or implicitly, in order to formulate a standard of equity.

In school finance equity, children and households are the main contenders for an answer to the question of whose perspective will dominate. In this paper, we focus on children, but this is a value judgment, and households are no less plausible as a group.[3] Table 1 illustrates the application of the four-question framework to the analysis of school finance equity for children. We also describe the last three questions in the equity framework—what, how and how much—from the children's viewpoint.

What? The Choice of an Object to be Distributed

There are three different kinds of objects related to school finance policy whose distribution among children can be analyzed.

Schooling inputs are the resources used to produce education in schools. Inputs can be defined as revenues or expenditures per child,

---

3. For an analysis of the household perspective, see Robert Berne and Leanna Stiefel, "Taxpayer Equity in School Finance Reform: The School Finance and the Public Finance Perspectives," *Journal of Education Finance* 5 (Summer 1979): 36–54.

TABLE 1. STANDARDS OF CHILDREN'S EQUITY IN SCHOOL FINANCE INVOLVE NUMEROUS CHOICES BASED ON VALUE JUDGMENTS

Component of Equity Standard	Alternatives For Each Component		
Who? The Group	*Children*		
What? The Object	*Inputs* Dollars; price-adjusted dollars; resources and quality-adjusted resources	*Outputs* Cognitive skills measures; behavioral output measures	*Outcomes* Earning potential; income; satisfaction
How to Define? The Principle	*Horizontal Equity* Equal treatment of equals: minimize spread in distribution	*Vertical Equity* Differential needs (or other factors) taken into account: more of the object to the neediest	*Equal Opportunity* No discrimination on the basis of property wealth in school district or other arbitrary categories; minimize undesirable systematic relationships
How to Measure? The Summary Statistic	*Univariate/Dispersion** RANGE; VAR; COEF VAR; GINI; LOG SD; REL MN DEV; RES RANGE; FED R R; PERM VAR	*Relationship** SIM CORR; SLOPE W; SLOPE W2; SLOPE W3; ELAST W; ELAST W2; ELAST W3	

* See the text for an explanation of the abbreviations.

price-adjusted or cost-adjusted revenues or expenditures per child, or real resources per child, such as teachers, professionals, and supplies.

Schooling outputs are the immediate products of schooling and can be represented by such things as achievement test scores, competency levels, and graduation rates. Outputs can be characterized as absolute levels, changes, or changes per unit of input.

Schooling outcomes represent the longer-term influences of school, such as earning potential, actual income, and personal satisfaction in life.

We will not elaborate further on the choice of an object, but our basic point should be clear. There is a selection to be made and any selection incorporates different value judgments.

How? The Choice of an Equity Principle

Three equity principles can be used to assess whether the distribution of the above objects is fair.

Horizontal equity is defined as equal treatment of equals. This principle states that when children are all alike, each should receive the same share of objects distributed. Inequity is measured by the dispersion in the distribution of objects, where no dispersion represents perfect equity.

Vertical equity recognizes that students are different, and requires that unequals receive appropriately unequal treatment. Defining unequals involves a specification of "legitimate" differences, such as handicapping conditions, poverty background, non-English speaking, as well as the nature and extent of the appropriate unequal treatment. In terms of the above kinds of differences among children, this principle would require more of the object for the handicapped, low-income, and bilingual child.

Equal opportunity is a negative principle, which states that there should not be differences according to characteristics that are considered "illegitimate" (or unconstitutional), such as property wealth per child, household income, race, or sex. For example, this principle could require that there be no relationship between objects and the property wealth per child of a school district.

How Much? The Choice of a Numerical Summary Measure

The ideas of horizontal equity, vertical equity, and equal opportunity are broad equity principles. They can be applied in a specific study using a variety of dispersion-type or relationship-type measures. Much scholarly attention has been devoted to the identification of value judgments inherent in alternative statistical measures of equity, and we now draw on that literature for an analysis of statistical measures used in school finance equity standards.[4]

Value Judgments Inherent in Univariate Dispersion Measures—Studies of school finance equity commonly utilize one or more of nine dispersion measures to capture the extent to which horizontal equity has been achieved.[5] The measures are all concerned with the degree of spread or variation in a distribution, and greater equity is usually represented by lower values of the measure.[6] These nine measures are listed below, along with an abbreviation that will be employed throughout the paper, and a short description that uses revenues per child (R_i) to represent the value of the object received by each child.

1. The range (RANGE): The difference between the highest and lowest value of R_i in the distribution.
2. The variance (VAR): The average of the sum of the squared deviation of R_i from its mean.
3. The coefficient of variation (COEF VAR): The square root of the variance divided by the mean.
4. The Gini coefficient (GINI): The ratio of the area between the Lorenz curve and the 45° line to the area below the 45° line.
5. The standard deviation of logarithms (LOG SD): The square root of the variance of the natural logarithm of R_i.

4. See Robert Berne and Leanna Stiefel, "The Equity of School Finance Systems Over Time: The Value Judgments Inherent in Evaluation," *Educational Administration Quarterly* 15 (Spring 1979): 14–34; Amartya Sen, *On Economic Inequality* (New York: W.W. Norton, 1973); Anthony Atkinson, "On the Measurement of Inequality," *Journal of Economic Theory* 2 (1970): 244–63.

5. Univariate dispersion measures can also be used to characterize vertical equity, if the children are weighted differently according to their handicaps or needs. For examples of empirical work on vertical equity, see Robert Berne, Allan Odden, and Leanna Stiefel, *Equity in School Finance* (Denver, Colo.: Education Commission of the States, 1979), ch. 4. This publication also contains mathematical formulas for all the measures described in this article.

6. For one measure, the permissible variance, higher values represent greater equity.

6. The relative mean deviation (REL MN DEV): The ratio of the sum of the absolute value of the deviations of R_i from its mean to the sum of R_i.
7. The restricted range (RES RANGE): The difference between the value of R_i below which five percent of the children fall and the value of R_i above which five percent of the children fall.
8. The federal range ratio (FED R R): The restricted range divided by the value of R_i below which five percent of the children fall.
9. The permissible variance (PERM VAR): The ratio of the actual sum of R_i for children below the median to the sum of R_i that would be required if all children were at the median level.

Many of the nine measures are familiar. For example, the range, variance, coefficient of variation, Gini coefficient, and standard deviation of logarithms are frequently used in studies that describe dispersion in a distribution. Some of the other measures are more esoteric because they are unique to the school finance literature (the restricted range, federal range ratio and permissible variance). We include them all because each incorporates different value judgments and has been used by different analysts of school finance.

One way to illustrate the nature of these value judgments inherent in the measures is to state them as a series of questions. For expositional purposes these questions assume that revenues per child are the chosen object. It should be recalled that, except for the permissible variance, lower values of each measure represent more equity.

1. Are all children taken into account by the measure?
2. Does the measure always show an increase in equity when revenues are transferred from a child higher in the distribution to one lower in the distribution, without reversing the ranking of the children? (This transfer is one that preserves the mean of revenues and is called "mean preserving.")
3. Does the measure always show an increase in equity when a constant amount of revenues is added to each child's revenues?
4. Does the measure always show an increase in equity when each child's revenues are increased by a proportional amount?
5. Does the measure record revenue changes at different levels of the distribution in the same way?
6. Is the mean level used as a basis of comparison?

7. Is the median level used as a basis of comparison?
8. Are all levels compared to one another as a basis of comparison?

Table 2 provides answers to the eight questions for each of the nine measures. Three of the questions and answers (numbers 1, 2, and 4) are used to illustrate more fully how the measures are differentiated by the value judgments.

The first question asks whether all children are included in the measure. Some people's values are better represented by measures that exclude some of the available data. For example, a policymaker may be concerned only with raising the bottom of the distribution (leveling up), in which case a measure such as the permissible variance is appropriate. Other policymakers may wish to have most children at or near the average, without caring about either tail of the distribution. If so, the federal range ratio is useful. As a final example, a policymaker may want to see no larger than a $100 difference between any two children, in which case the range would be an appropriate measure.[7]

Question 2 is concerned with what happens to the measure when there is a transfer of revenues from a child higher in the distribution to one lower in the distribution. Such a transfer does not affect the value of the mean nor does it change the relative positions of children involved in the transfer. Many people think that such a transfer should increase the equity rating. Figure 2 shows that about half of the measures do exhibit such an increase in equity, while half do not. In particular, the most commonly used measures in studies of income distribution—the variance, coefficient of variation, and Gini coefficient—all exhibit the increase in equity.

Question 4 asks how the measure responds to equal proportional changes in the revenues associated with each child. There are alternative views on how an equity measure should respond to such proportional changes. On the one hand, since there are more revenues to be distributed, some may think that equity has diminished if the dispersion stays relatively the same. The range, variance, and restricted range are the only three measures that are consistent with this value judgment because they are the only three that show *less*

---

7. The $100 difference as it relates to the *Serrano* decision is discussed in Lee Friedman, "The Ambiguity of *Serrano*: Two Concepts of Wealth Neutrality," *Hastings Constitutional Law Quarterly* 4 (Summer 1977): 487–503.

TABLE 2. DISPERSION MEASURES THAT REPRESENT HORIZONTAL EQUITY CONTAIN DIFFERENT VALUE JUDGMENTS

VALUE JUDGMENTS	RANGE	VAR	COEF VAR	GINI	LOG SD	REL MN DEV	RES RANGE	FED R R	PERM VAR
1. All children taken into account	No	Yes	Yes	Yes	Yes	Yes	No	No	No
2. Increase in equity for mean preserving transfers?	No	Yes	Yes	Yes	Almost Always*	No	No	No	No
3. Sensitive to equal additions?	No	No	Yes	Yes	Yes	No	No	Yes	Yes
4. Sensitive to equal percentage increases?	Yes	Yes	No	No	No	No	Yes	No	No
5. Changes at different levels recorded identically?	No	Yes	Yes	No	Yes	No	No	No	No
6. Mean for comparison?	No	Yes	Yes	No	No	Yes	No	No	No
7. Median for comparison?	No	No	No	No	Yes	No	Yes	No	Yes
8. All levels for comparison?	No	No	No	No	No	No	No	No	No

* Not always true for very high end of distribution.

equity after proportional increases. Others may think that because each child's level has increased by the same proportion, that each child is as well off in relation to every other child as before and that therefore the equity of the distribution has not changed. The six remaining measures are all consistent with this second value judgment because they do *not* change with proportional increases.

In general only the range and the restricted range respond identically to all questions. All the other measures differ on at least one question, which means that the choice of a univariate measure cannot be value free.

Value Judgments Inherent in Bivariate and Multivariate Relationship-Type Measures—Relationship-type measures are used to represent the vertical equity and equal opportunity principles. In the case of vertical equity, a position relationship between the object and, for example, a handicapping condition, is more equitable. In the case of equal opportunity, no systematic relationship between the object and, for example, property wealth per child, is more equitable. Conclusions in school finance studies rely heavily on bivariate or multivariate relationship measures such as correlations, slopes, and elasticities. We have identified the following seven commonly used measures and, as with the univariate measures, an abbreviation and a brief description follow each measure. For expositional purposes, it is assumed for each measure that we are concerned with the relationship between revenues per child (R_i) as the dependent variable, and property wealth per child (W_i) as the independent variable. Since the measures are representing the equal opportunity principle, equity is improved as the measures show less of a relationship or approach zero in value.

1. The simple correlation (SIM CORR): The Pearson correlation coefficient between R_i and W_i.
2. The slope from the simple regression (SLOPE W): The slope coefficient which equals dR_i/dW_i from $R_i = a + b_1 W_i$.
3. The slope from the quadratic regression (SLOPE W2): The slope coefficient which equals dR_i/dW_i from $R_i = a + b_1 W_i^2$, calculated at mean W_i, W^*.
4. The slope from the cubic regression (SLOPE W3): The slope coefficient which equals dR_i/dW_i from $R_i = a + b_1 W_i + b_2 W_i^2 + b_3 W_i^3$, calculated at W^*.

5. The elasticity from the simple regression (ELAST W): The elasticity from the regression of R_i on W_i, which equals (SLOPE W) x (W^*/R^*) where W^* is mean W and R^* is mean R.
6. The elasticity from the quadratic regression (ELAST W2): The elasticity from the regression of R_i on W_i and W_i^2, which equals (SLOPE W2) x (W^*/R^*).
7. The elasticity from the cubic regression (ELAST W3): The elasticity from the regression of R_i on W_i, W_i^2 and W_i^3, which equals (SLOPE W3) x (W^*/R^*).

Each of these seven measures is associated with a unique set of value judgments, which can again be presented as a series of questions. The questions parallel the ones for the univariate dispersion measures, but they are reformulated in a bivariate or multivariate context so that both a dependent variable (R_i) and an independent variable (W_i) can be given attention.

1. Are all children taken into account by the measure?
2. Does the measure always show an increase in equity when revenues (dependent variable) are transferred from one child to another with lower revenues per child and lower wealth per child without reversing the ranking of the children? (This kind of transfer is one that preserves the mean of revenues and is labelled "mean preserving.")
3. Is the measure sensitive to equal additions to revenues per child (dependent variable)?
4. Is the measure sensitive to equal percentage changes in revenues per child (dependent variable)?
5. Is the measure sensitive to equal additions to wealth per child (independent variable)?
6. Is the measure sensitive to equal percentage increases in wealth per child (independent variable)?

Table 3 provides answers to each question for the above seven measures. The answers tend to separate the measures roughly into three groups composed of the simple correlation, the slopes, and the elasticities. The simple correlation is insensitive to most kinds of changes in either the independent or the dependent variables. In general, the slopes are sensitive to equal percentage changes but not to equal addition changes, while the elasticities are just the opposite and respond to equal addition changes but not to equal percentage changes.

TABLE 3. RELATIONSHIP MEASURES THAT REPRESENT VERTICAL EQUITY AND EQUAL OPPORTUNITY ALSO CONTAIN DIFFERENT VALUE JUDGMENTS

VALUE JUDGMENTS	SIM CORR	SLOPE W	SLOPE W2	SLOPE W3	ELAST W	ELAST W2	ELAST W3
1. All children taken into account?	Yes	Yes	Yes	Yes	Yes	Yes	Yes
2. Increase in equity for mean preserving transfers?	Not Necessarily	Yes	Not Necessarily	Not Necessarily	Yes	Not Necessarily	Not Necessarily
3. Sensitive to equal additions to dependent?	No	No	No	No	Yes	Yes	Yes
4. Sensitive to equal percentage increases in dependent?	No	Yes	Yes	Yes	No	No	No
5. Sensitive to equal additions to independent?	No	No	No	No	Yes	Yes	Yes
6. Sensitive to equal percentage increases in independent?	No	Yes	Yes	Yes	No	No	No

The development of standards of children's equity in school finance involves a series of value judgments. Often these are implicit, but we have tried to make the alternatives explicit. We now demonstrate an empirical application of the children's equity standards. One would hope that in the real world most seemingly technical choices make no difference with respect to the final evaluation of equity. The empirical data serve as a case study of the conditions under which that hope is likely to materialize.

EMPIRICAL ASSESSMENT OF CONTRADICTIONS AMONG STANDARDS OF EQUITY

In school finance, equity standards are often used to rank a set of states from most to least equitable, at a given point in time. If identical or nearly identical rankings do not occur when alternative equity standards are employed, then there is empirical justification for a concern over different value judgments built into the equity standards. In this section we utilize data from a number of states to measure empirically the contradictions among a subset of equity standards discussed in the last section.

As stated above, the empirical analyses are confined to equity standards with children, rather than households, as the group of concern. To carry out these empirical illustrations, certain choices concerning the group, object, and principal have been made. These are expositional and are not intended to indicate a preference for some values over others.[8] First, we examine the contradictions among alternative children's univariate dispersion measures, where the group (children), object (revenues), and principle (horizontal equity) are held constant and the measures are varied. For horizontal equity measures, the absence of any dispersion in the distribution represents perfect equity and equity decreases as the dispersion increases. Second, we examine the contradiction among alternative children's relationship measures, and once again the group (children), object (revenues) and principle (equal opportunity) are held constant and the measures are varied. In this case, we examine

---

8. It is likely that alternative choices about the group, object, and principle will result in larger contradictions among rankings of states than will choices of a statistical measure. Without wishing to minimize the importance of these first three choices, we think that the differences resulting from a choice of statistical measures are large enough to warrant the attention of policy analysts in education finance as well as other areas.

the relationship between revenues per pupil and property value per pupil. The absence of a relationship represents perfect equity and equity decreases as the strength of the relationship increases. Before presenting the two analyses, we discuss how the degree of contradictions among two or more measures of equity can be quantified and also briefly describe the data used in the analyses.

While the univariate dispersion and relationship measures can be used cardinally (as interval scales), in this analysis we use them only ordinally, to rank order the twenty states from most to least equitable.[9] Given our interest in assessing the contradictions among ordinal ranks when two or more measures of equity are used to rank the states, the Spearman rank correlation coefficient may seem to be the appropriate statistic to use. However, we do not use the Spearman rank correlation coefficient because two more descriptive techniques are available.

One is the concordance measure, which is a more appropriate statistic because, unlike the Spearman rank correlation, the concordance measure can assess the agreement among *more* than two rankings. The formula for the concordance measure is analogous to that for the Spearman rank correlation, and when the agreement among only two rankings is being assessed they are equivalent.[10] The concordance measure can range from zero (complete disagreement among all rankings) to one (complete agreement among all rankings).

The other technique we employ to assess the extent of agreement among numerous rankings is a technique we call unambiguous rankings. For policy purposes, it is often desirable to combine alternative rankings into one summary ranking in order to draw conclusions about the relative positions of the items, in our case states, being ranked. If the summary ranking is formed by averaging the various rankings, then the summary ranking will possibly contain states that are out of order compared to the individual rankings. Therefore, if the values inherent in each of the individual rankings are to be maintained in the summary ranking, an alternative to

---

9. In the study of income distributions as well, equality measures are used ordinally to rank units, usually nations. See, for example Atkinson, "Measurement of Inequality," pp. 244–63; and Sen, *Economic Inequality*.

10. See Maurice Kendell, *Rank Correlation Methods*, 4th ed. (London: Griffith, 1970), ch. 6, for an in-depth discussion of the concordance measure. We are indebted to Richard Schramm for calling this statistic to our attention.

averaging must be utilized. The number of unambiguous rankings is such a technique, since it can be used to assess the degree to which a summary ranking can be formed without including any rankings that are out of order compared to the individual rankings.

The problems inherent in forming a summary ranking by averaging the ranks can be seen with a simple example. Table 4 shows the

TABLE 4. UNAMBIGUOUS RANKINGS DO NOT VIOLATE VALUE JUDGMENTS IN INDIVIDUAL COMPONENT RANKINGS

	Sample Data				
State	Equity Measure X	Rank (X) (1 = Most Equitable)	Equity Measure Y	Rank (Y) (1 = Most Equitable)	Summary Ranking Achieved by Averaging Ranks
A	0.1100	1	0.0110	1	1.0
B	0.1200	2	0.0120	3	2.5
C	0.1300	3	0.0124	4	3.5
D	0.1400	4	0.0115	2	3.0
	Calculation of Unambiguous Rankings				
State	Rank (X)		Rank (Y)		Unambiguous Rankings
A	1		1		1
B	2		3		
C	3		4		2
D	4		2		

values of two equity measures (X and Y) computed for four states (A, B, C, and D) and the resulting rankings labelled RANK(X) and RANK(Y). The summary ranking formed by averaging RANK(X) and RANK(Y) violates or disagrees with each of the individual component rankings. The summary ranking places D more equitable than C, which violates RANK(X), and the summary ranking places B more equitable than D, which violates RANK(Y).

The number of unambiguous rankings can be defined as the maximum number of rankings that results when a summary ranking is formed that does not violate any of the individual component rankings. When unambiguous rankings are used to form a summary ranking, the following condition holds: any conflict in ranking among the individual component rankings results in a smaller number of unambiguous rankings than the number of rankings in the individual components. The number of unambiguous rankings can be used to record the contradiction among the individual equity measures since, when all measures agree (without ties), the number of unambiguous rankings equals the number of states being ranked. Thus, the maximum number of unambiguous rankings equals the number of states being ranked. The minimum number of unambiguous rankings is one and the minimum will appear when the rankings are jumbled or exactly opposite. In the example illustrated in table 4, only state A can be ranked unambiguously more equitable then states B, C, and D based on equity measures X and Y. No further unambiguous rankings are possible. Thus, for these four states there are two unambiguous rankings.

One characteristic of the unambiguous ranking technique that sets it apart from the concordance measure is that a small number of states, if ranked substantially differently by individual equity measures, can force the number of unambiguous rankings to the minimum number, one. To take an extreme case, if one state in a set is ranked first by one measure and last by another, then any unambiguous rankings for the states that includes these two measures will always be equal to one. Thus, in a sense, the unambiguous ranking ignores the presence of some agreement among the measures. Since the concordance measure and the number of unambiguous rankings are very different ways to assess the agreement among a set of rankings, both are used in the analyses to follow.

The data used in the empirical analyses were generated by a loose federation of researchers and policy analysts known (to themselves) as the School Finance Cooperative.[11] Cooperative members are doing research in various states. Since a national data base for all school districts in all states does not currently exist, the cooperative members pooled their data to form the data set used here. Included in the data set are univariate dispersion measures computed for twenty-two states using the 1975–76 school year and relationship measures for eighteen of these states in the same year.[12]

---

11. The work of the cooperative is funded by the Ford Foundation and the National Institute of Education. The following cooperative members contributed data: Center for Study of Educational Finance at Illinois State University, Education Commission of the States, Education Policy Research Institute, Intercultural Development Research Institute (in cooperation with Professor Walter Garms, University of Rochester), Lawyers Committee for Civil Rights Under Law, National Conference of State Legislatures, and the Rand Corporation.

12. A pooled data set of this type is not perfectly comparable across states. The problems of comparability are such, however, that they do not affect conclusions of a methodological nature—that is conclusions about the con-

Several additional characteristics of the data can be identified. The number of children is a pupil count for each kindergarten-through-twelfth-grade school district in the state, measured in terms of average daily membership. The object is local and state revenues per pupil, excluding local and state revenues for capital and debt service. The wealth variable used as the independent variable in the relationship measures is state equalized assessed value of property per pupil for each district. The dispersion and relationship measures used in the analyses are those listed in tables 2 and 3, respectively. All the equity measures are computed using the pupil unit of analysis. Since data are available only at district level, however, each pupil in a district is assigned the district level average revenue figure. Another way of viewing the pupil unit of analysis is as district-level data, weighted by the number of pupils in the district.[13]

Children-Dollar-Univariate Dispersion Equity Measures

The first empirical analysis examines the contradictions among the children-dollar-univariate dispersion equity measures, using data from twenty-two states. An example of the rankings yielded by two of the univariate measures, the coefficient of variation and Gini coefficient, is displayed in table 5. The lines and resultant five groups drawn on the summary ranking matrix indicate that the number of unambiguous rankings equals five. The concordance measure, which in this case equals 0.9712, is also shown in the table. For this pair of rankings the number of unambiguous rankings is low (five out of a possible twenty-two) relative to the concordance measure because certain states, Maine and New Hampshire in particular, are ranked rather differently by the two univariate measures. This example shows that the number of unambiguous rankings and the concordance measure do not assess the level of agreement between the univariate measures in the same way.

---

tradictions among the measures. Nevertheless, there are some differences among the states, so that precise statements concerning the equity of a particular state must await a national data base. For a more in-depth assessment of the data see Robert Berne and Leanna Stiefel, *A Methodological Assessment of Education Equity and Wealth Neutrality Measures,* Papers in Education Finance, no. 17 (Denver, Colo.: Education Commission of the States, 1978).

13. For an analysis of the equity measures using the district unit of analysis and a comparison between the district and pupil units of analysis, see Berne and Stiefel, "Methodological Assessment."

TABLE 5. THE NUMBER OF AMBIGUOUS RANKINGS AND THE CONCORDANCE MEASURE PROVIDE DIFFERENT ASSESSMENTS OF THE AGREEMENT BETWEEN TWO UNIVARIATE MEASURES

Measure—COEF VAR			Measure—GINI			Summary Ranking Matrix			
Rank	State	Value	Rank	State	Value	State			Sum
1	La.	0.09594	1	N.M.	0.05236	La.	1	2	3
2	Fla.	0.09774	2	La.	0.05342	Fla.	2	3	5
3	W. Va.	0.10293	3	Fla.	0.05507	W. Va.	3	4	7
4	N.C.	0.10758	4	W. Va.	0.05520	N.M.	7	1	8
5	Ala.	0.12071	5	N.C.	0.05792	N.C.	4	5	9
6	Minn.	0.12531	6	Ala.	0.06569	Ala.	5	6	11
7	N.M.	0.13699	7	Minn.	0.06959	Minn.	6	7	13
8	Miss.	0.15400	8	Miss.	0.07856	Miss.	8	8	16
9	Vt.	0.17316	9	S.D.	0.08762	Vt.	9	10	19
10	Conn.	0.17840	10	Vt.	0.09100	S.D.	11	9	20
11	S.D.	0.17863	11	Mo.	0.09163	Mo.	12	11	23
12	Mo.	0.18223	12	N.H.	0.09500	Conn.	10	13	23
13	Maine	0.18319	13	Conn.	0.09800	Maine	13	14	27
14	N.J.	0.19078	14	Maine	0.09820	N.H.	17	12	29
15	Ore.	0.19407	15	Ore.	0.10256	Ore.	15	15	30
16	S.C.	0.20878	16	N.J.	0.10300	N.J.	14	16	30
17	N.H.	0.22056	17	Tex.	0.10395	S.C.	16	19	35
18	Mass.	0.22374	18	Mass.	0.11200	Mass.	18	18	36
19	Tex.	0.22451	19	S.C.	0.11322	Tex.	19	17	36
20	Ky.	0.23779	20	N.Y.	0.12200	Ky.	20	21	41
21	N.Y.	0.24382	21	Ky.	0.12463	N.Y.	21	20	41
22	Ga.	0.33620	22	Ga.	0.15680	Ga.	22	22	44

NOTE: Concordance measure (C) = 0.9712. Number of unambiguous rankings (UR) = 5.

The number of unambiguous rankings and the concordance measure for all pairs of univariate measures are displayed in table 6. These data show that the concordance measures (C) are rather high (all are statistically significant at the 1 percent level) while the number of unambiguous rankings (UR) are rather low. This reinforces the point that the two techniques differ in their definition of agreement. However, both techniques show that certain measures are more in agreement than others. One way of seeing this is to use the criteria C >0.9000 *and* UR >1 to define the pairs most in agreement. These two criteria isolate a group of eleven pairs. The six pairs formed by the Gini coefficient, relative mean deviation, coefficient of variation, and federal range ratio are *all* in this group of eleven pairs. On the other hand, the permissible variance and standard deviation of logarithms are in none of the pairs, while the range is in one. Thus, certain univariate dispersion measures appear to

TABLE 6: THE NUMBER OF UNAMBIGUOUS RANKINGS AND THE CONCORDANCE MEASURE REVEAL THAT SOME GROUPS OF UNIVARIATE MEASURES ARE MORE SIMILAR THAN OTHERS

	RES RANGE	FED RR	REL MN DEV	PERM VAR	VAR	COEF VAR	LOG SD	GINI
RANGE	0.8893	0.8295	0.8346	0.8340	*0.9407	0.8972	0.8334	0.8402 C
	1	1	1	1	2	1	1	2 UR
RES RANGE	X	*0.9215	*0.9401	0.8735	*0.9678	0.9136	0.8862	*0.9328 C
		2	2	1	7	1	1	2 UR
FED RR		X	*0.9497	0.8600	0.8617	*0.9458	0.8363	*0.9622 C
			3	1	1	5	5	2 UR
REL MN DEV			X	0.8673	0.9091	*0.9622	0.8775	*0.9955 C
				2	1	5	5	17 UR
PERM VAR				X	0.8385	0.8312	0.8351	0.8600 C
					1	1	1	2 UR
VAR					X	0.9238	0.8865	0.9001 C
						1	1	1 UR
COEF VAR						X	0.8735	*0.9712 C
							7	5 UR
LOG SD							X	0.8713 C
								1 UR

NOTE: C = concordance measure. UR = unambiguous rankings.
* Pairs of measures where C > 0.9 and UR > 1.

cluster together, while others are less in agreement. The measures that cluster together—the Gini coefficient, relative mean deviation, coefficient of variation, and federal range ratio—are insensitive to equal percentage increases and do not stress the lower end of the distribution. On the other hand, the measures that display relative disagreement are either sensitive to equal percentage increases (for example, the range) or emphasize the lower end of the distribution (that is, the permissible variance and standard deviation of logarithms). To a certain degree, the clustering of the univariate measures parallels the value judgments identified in the previous section.

The same pattern of agreement among the univariate measures occurs when groups of three and four univariate measures are compared. The groups of univariate measures that have the highest concordance measures include three or four from the group of measures that agreed most among themselves in the pairwise comparisons: the coefficient of variation, relative mean deviation, Gini coefficient, federal range ratio. Also, groups that include two or more measures from among the permissible variance, standard deviation of logarithms, and restricted range tend to show more contradictions than the other groups of three or four measures, whether judged by the concordance measure or number of unambiguous rankings. For example, when the rankings from the relative mean deviation, coefficient of variation, and Gini coefficient are compared, the concordance measure is 0.9684 and the number of unambiguous rankings equals five. However, when the federal range ratio, permissible variance, and coefficient of variation are compared, the concordance measure is 0.8386 and there is only one unambiguous ranking.

The analyses of the univariate dispersion measures demonstrate that, by the criterion of unambiguous rankings, considerable disagreement exists among the measures. Furthermore, the concordance measures and number of unambiguous rankings indicate that certain of the univariate dispersion measures tend to cluster together more than others. Finally, the clustering of the univariate measures is consistent with several of the value judgments that are inherent in the measures.

Children-Dollar-Relationship Equity Measures

Using data from eighteen states for the 1975–76 school year, we now examine the seven relationship measures listed in table 3, which relate dollars of education revenues per pupil to equalized assessed value per pupil.[14] When the concordance measures and number of unambiguous rankings are calculated for the twenty-one pairs of rankings generated by the seven relationship measures, a rather striking pattern emerges. For the three pairs formed by the group of three slope measures (SLOPE W, SLOPE W2, and SLOPE W3) and the three pairs formed by the group of three elasticity measures (ELAST W, ELAST W2, and ELAST W3), the number of unambiguous rankings and concordance measures are quite high. For these six pairs, the concordance measures range from 0.9752 to 0.9948 and the number of unambiguous rankings range from nine to fourteen, out of a possible eighteen. The remaining fifteen pairs of relationship measures exhibit considerably less agreement. For these fifteen pairs, where the relationship measures are not from the same group (either slopes or elasticities), the concordance measures range from 0.6522 to 0.8349 and there are one or two unambiguous rankings.

When the relationship measures are grouped in pairs, the agreement is closely aligned with the value judgments built into the individual measures. Specifically, relatively high agreement occurs among the three slope measures and among the three elasticity measures, where within both groups, the sensitivity to changes in the revenue and wealth variables is the same. There is substantially less agreement across the three general types: correlation, slopes, and elasticities.

These conclusions are supported further when the rankings produced by three measures are examined (see table 7). When the three elasticity measures and slope measures are grouped together, the

TABLE 7: PATTERNS OF AGREEMENT AMONG GROUPS OF THREE RELATIONSHIP MEASURES IS CONSISTENT WITH VALUE JUDGMENTS INHERENT IN MEASURES

SIM CORR	SLOPE W	SLOPE W2	SLOPE W3	ELAST W	ELAST W2	ELAST W3	C	UR
				X	X	X	0.9821	8
	X	X	X				0.9761	9
X	X			X			0.6886	1
X		X			X		0.6468	1
X			X			X	0.6427	1

NOTE: C = concordance measure. UR = number of unambiguous rankings.

14. The seven bivariate measures were not calculated for four states analyzed in the prior section because property wealth data was unavailable.

concordance measures are very high and the number of unambiguous rankings is eight or nine for the eighteen states. However, when the simple correlation is matched with one slope measure and one elasticity measure, the concordance measures drop considerably and there is only one unambiguous ranking.

The empirical analysis has demonstrated that there can be differences among the seven relationship measures and that these differences are consistent with the value judgments embedded in the measures. Even if there is agreement that children-dollar-relationship measures with wealth as the independent variable are an appropriate way to assess equity, the selection of a relationship measure can still have a substantial impact on the findings of a particular equity analysis.

CONCLUSIONS

The measurement of equity in school finance should not be treated as a technical issue. Two findings from this paper support this conclusion. First, equity standards in school finance can be devised from a series of choices that are value judgments. Even the choice of a statistical summary measure reflects such a value judgment. Second, the empirical analyses show that the value judgments embedded in equity standards do make a difference empirically. Several issues that deserve serious attention by school finance policy analysts follow from our findings.

First, policy analysts should be urged to describe complex goals, such as equity, in ways that clarify the implicit value judgments. The four-part equity framework developed here will hopefully stimulate others to think and write about equity in a manner that highlights values.

Second, the findings on empirical differences among the standards of equity should encourage others to use multiple standards of equity in policy analysis. The empirical differences documented in this paper only concentrate on differences in the statistical measures of equity. It is almost certain that greater empirical differences will emerge when other dimensions of equity, such as the group or the principle, are varied as well. Policy analysts in school finance need to be clear about which equity conceptions are included in their analyses and which are excluded.

Third, since school finance analysts are likely to use multiple measures of equity to rank states from most to least equitable, more attention should be devoted to ways of combining disparate rankings, when they occur. Averaging the disparate rankings is a popular solution since one single clear-cut ranking results. If the value judgments inherent in the different equity measures are to be preserved, however, then alternatives to averages are necessary. The use of unambiguous rankings, as described in this paper, commences to deal with the methodology of combining different rankings, but more thought on this issue is certainly desirable.

Although the focus in this paper has been on school finance, several of the issues raised have broader applications. For example, the equity framework may be applicable to concerns beyond school finance, and the problem of combining rankings is faced by other analysts, such as those who work with indicators of urban fiscal health. Finally, this paper emphasizes the point that, regardless of the policy area, policy analysis is not value free.

33

PUBLIC SCHOOLS, PRIVATE SCHOOLS, AND THE PUBLIC INTEREST

James Coleman

THERE is not one private school policy issue today, there are two. Certain proposed policies would expand the role of private schools in American education or at least make it easier to attend them; other policies would inhibit their use. Thus, there is the unusual situation in which conflict is so strong that support exists for policies that would go in exactly opposite directions. The principal examples of policies that would aid private schooling are tuition tax-credit legislation at the federal level, such as the Moynihan-Packwood bill currently in the Senate, and tuition vouchers at the state level, such as the proposal designed for California by John Coons, Professor of Law at Berkeley. The principal examples of policies that would restrict private schooling are attempts by the Internal Revenue Service to impose some form of racial-balance criterion on private schools in order for them to maintain tax exempt status. Opponents of the first set of policies argue that those policies would destroy the public school system; opponents of the second set argue that those other policies would destroy the private school alternative to the public system.

Another unusual aspect of the private-public education conflict, especially in its voucher incarnation, is that it cuts across traditional liberal-conservative lines. John Coons, for instance, was also the principal moving force behind the Serrano case in California, which brought equal financing to schools in California and elsewhere. Vouchers have been supported or proposed by conservatives like Milton Friedman and liberals like Christopher Jencks. Still another curious aspect is that the conflict separates action from advocacy for a number of persons: There are many who vigorously oppose making private school attendance easier and at the same time have their own children enrolled in private schools; and there are many who support private schools and still have their children in public schools.

The principal arguments of those who favor aid to private schools are that: (a) private schools provide better education; (b) attendance at private schools is available only to those who can afford it; therefore, (c) reducing costs of private schooling will make the better education of private schools more equally available to families of different incomes. What may be questioned in this argument is the assumption that private schools provide a better education. This assumption is one of the two central questions studied in the research to be summarized here.

The principal argument of those who support constraints upon private schooling, or oppose making it easier to attend them, is that private schools segregate different segments of the population, due to the "self-selective" character of these schools. The specific arguments differ. One, the oldest, is that private schools draw off the most economically affluent from the public school system, and then engage in further economic stratification among schools within the private sector, resulting in economic elitism in the schools. Another argument, the most recent, is that private schools segregate racially by drawing off whites from the public sector, and then further segregate among schools within the private sector as whites choose certain schools and blacks others. The only solution is for students to be assigned to particular private schools, as is ordinarily done in the public sector. One final argument is somewhat different. This argument says that assisting private schooling, by any public means, constitutes "establishment" of a church and thereby violates the church-state separation provision of the Constitution.

What is subject to test in these arguments, except the last, is the fundamental assumption that private schools do segregate different segments of the population. The truth of this assumption appears at first self-evident, but the matter turns out to be more complex: Public schools are themselves not perfectly integrated on these economic and racial dimensions, and there is already social self-selection within the public sector when people choose where to live. The question is whether the education system as it now stands, containing private schools, is more segregated along income, racial, or religious grounds than would be a system without private schools. Or to put it differently: Does the choice which results from the existence of private schools lead to greater segregation than the choice that exists within the public sector?

A study of school differences

To help address these important questions about private-public school differences, the National Center for Education Statistics held a conference in April 1981 at which the first reports of its "High School and Beyond" study of high school sophomores and seniors were presented and criticized. Both analyses had to do with comparisons of public and private schools, but the first one, conducted by Andrew Greeley, was focused mainly on the role of Catholic schools in the education of blacks and Hispanics. The second analysis ranged more broadly over the issues of achievement and segregation that I discussed above, and was conducted by Thomas Hoffer, Sally Kilgore, and me.[1]

As has become evident from the intensity of the response to these reports, the issues they addressed touched some very sensitive points—more sensitive than was anticipated by any of the authors, and certainly more than was anticipated when the reports were initially planned in the Spring of 1980. For this reason, it is useful to briefly review the results of the Coleman-Hoffer-Kilgore report here—an action which may also help to dispel the confusion created by what has appeared in the media—and to suggest something about the deeper and more sensitive questions which this report touched.

First of all, it is useful to give a sense of how schools in the public and private sectors differ. Public high schools (grades nine through twelve) enroll over 90 percent of the total high school population and have an average of 750 students, while the Catholic schools enroll about 6 percent and average about 500 in size, and the other private schools enroll between 3 and 4 percent and aver-

---

[1] The Coleman-Hoffer-Kilgore report was written in August 1980, and initially planned for release in the Fall of 1980. However, delays in the reviewing-and-revision process led NCES to defer its release until April 1981. The Greeley report was written in early Fall 1980, and also initially intended to be released in Fall 1980. A fuller outline of overall study is given in the research note at the end of this article.

age only about 150 in size. The pupil-teacher ratios in Catholic and public schools are very similar but in the other private schools they are less than half as large.

Students and principals in Catholic schools are much more likely than students and principals in public schools to report that their schools have rules about student dress and that students are held responsible for damage to school property; students and principals in the other private schools report this more frequently than in public schools but less than in Catholic schools. Students in Catholic schools are much more likely than public school students to report that discipline in their school is effective, with the other private schools again in between. And both Catholic and the other private school students are somewhat more likely than public school students to say that school discipline is fair. Overall, *the evidence shows that discipline in the Catholic and other private schools is both stronger and fairer than in the public schools,* with discipline in the Catholic schools being strongest and that in the other private schools most fair (as perceived by the students).

Students in Catholic schools are much less likely to be absent or to cut classes than are those in public schools (again with the other private schools in between and closer to the Catholic schools) and public school principals are much more likely to report that absenteeism constitutes a problem in their school than are either Catholic or other private school principals. On other measures of student behavior as well, *students in the Catholic and the other private schools show far fewer "problems"—as reported either by the students themselves or the principals—than do those in the public schools.* Catholic school students do about half again as much homework as do public school students, and students in the other private schools do even more.

In all the above respects, Catholic schools are the most homogeneous, differing least from one another, while the other private schools are most heterogeneous, showing greatest variation in discipline and student behavior.

Achievement—public and private

This sketch of the differences between schools in the public, Catholic, and other-private sectors gives an indication of how these schools differ in their everyday activities. But it says nothing about the central policy questions. The question of whether there is higher average achievement in the private sector than in the public sector is answered very simply through a comparision of scores on standardized tests in the two sectors. The answer is that in the areas in which both sophomores and seniors were tested (in reading, vocabulary, and mathematics), students in Catholic schools and students in other private schools scored about two grade-levels higher than did students in the public sector. But this is not the question asked by the parent choosing between a public and private school, or legislators deciding whether to support a bill assisting attendance at private schools. They ask a question asked of me by a colleague shortly after the report had been released. He asked, "How can you determine whether the *same* child would achieve more highly in the private school? Couldn't the achievement difference be solely due to selection?"

This question—which asks whether the school itself really makes a difference, and if so, how much—is as difficult to answer as the first one is simple. But it is not impossible. An extreme way would be illustrated by pairs of identical twins with one twin from each pair assigned to School A, and the other to School B. If the achievement of the twin assigned to School A was consistently higher, this would be strong evidence that School A brings about greater achievement.

A study of identical twins assigned to different schools, or even a study of non-twins assigned randomly to different schools, could test the effect of the schools on achievement. With random assignment of non-twins, a larger number of children would be necessary for statistical reasons—but the conclusions could be just as strong. Absent this kind of evidence—a problem which is characteristic of research in the social sciences because of ethical constraints on "arbitrary" assignment (and random assignment is certainly arbitrary) to different settings which might have long-term consequences—other methods must be used to separate the effects of selection from the effects of the school itself.

We used three methods in our study. The first was to "control" the background characteristics of students through multiple regression analysis, in effect comparing achievement for students who have similar background characteristics. Seventeen background characteristics were used (including some which might be consequences rather than causes of achievement) in order to control as fully as possible, even to the extent of overcompensating, for selection into the schools. These background characteristics ranged from things like family income, to each parent's education, to ownership of a pocket calculator, to each parent's aspirations for the child's education. The result of this analysis showed that about half of the original difference in achievement is due to selection, and about half the original difference remains. Less remains in reading and more in mathematics, and slightly less remains in the other private schools than in the Catholic schools.

A second method of analysis examined differences between the sophomore and senior groups (adjusting for dropouts) and used the two groups to measure gains and learning rates between sophomore and senior year. *This method showed higher learning rates in the other private schools than in public schools in all three achievement areas, higher rates in the Catholic schools than in the public schools in vocabulary and mathematics, and equal Catholic and public rates in reading comprehension.* Learning rates in the other private schools were higher than those in Catholic schools in reading comprehension and mathematics, but the two sectors were alike in vocabulary.

This second method roughly confirms the public-private differences in the first analysis, though it shows achievement growth in the other private schools to be somewhat higher than that in the Catholic schools, while the first analysis showed the sophomore achievement levels to be slightly higher in the Catholic schools.

Better schools do better

Both of these methods for discovering differences among schools in their effects on achievement contain a potential flaw: There may be some *other* uncontrolled background factor which determines whether, even among students alike in all the characteristics that are statistically controlled, the better-performing students are selected into the private sector and the less-well-performing students remain in the public sector. This seems possible or even likely for those private schools which select entrants using admissions tests, but these constitute only a handful of schools, a tiny fraction of the more than 6,000 private schools with secondary grades in the country. It seems less likely for the vast majority of private schools in which admission depends on the parents' ability to pay.

Despite the improbability of selection accounting for the remaining differences, we carried out a third analysis. And it is this analysis which carries special implications for public education. The argument is as follows: *If* Catholic or other private schools bring about higher achievement for comparable students, and *if* they do so through those attributes measured in the research which distinguish

Catholic and other private schools from public schools, *then* we should find achievement differences among schools within any sector, public or private. In other words, those schools within any sector which are like the Catholic and other private schools should have students performing at levels comparable to those in the Catholic and other private schools, while those schools in any sector that are like the public schools should have students performing at the public school levels.

The major measured differences between the public and private sectors, other than size, are those described earlier: differences in disciplinary climate, in academic demands, and in student behavior. Further, even when the backgrounds of students are statistically controlled, much of these differences remains—differences in homework, in student attendance and in-school behavior, and differences in the disciplinary climate perceived by students. These differences can reasonably be attributed to differences in school policy rather than student background.

When we examined, wholly within the public sector, the performance of students similar to the average public school sophomore, but with the levels of homework and attendance attributable to school policy in the Catholic or other private schools, and those levels of disciplinary climate and student behavior attributable to school policy in the Catholic or other private schools, the levels of achievement are approximately the same as those found in the Catholic and other-private sectors.

The first implication of these results is that they strongly confirm the school-effect results found by the other two methods. For the selection hypothesis necessary to account for these differences must be especially tortured, operating not only between sectors but also to the same degree within sectors, and operating to select students, on the behavior variables indicated above, into schools with particular disciplinary climates. Thus, the validity of the private-sector effects is strongly confirmed by these results.

A broader implication holds as well: that *these attributes described above are in fact those which make a difference in achievement in all American high schools no matter what sector they are in*. Schools which impose strong academic demands, schools which make demands on attendance and on behavior of students while they are in school are, according to these results, schools which bring about higher achievement. This is not to say that such policies are easy to institute in all schools. Public schools have greater constraints on suspending or expelling students than do private schools, for example, and quite beyond that, a public school principal may have less autonomy from the district in establishing a particular educational and disciplinary philosophy than does a private school principal. Rather, it may be said that in those schools where these policies *do* exist, students achieve more on average than in schools where these policies do not exist.[2]

Besides the overall difference between the public sector and the private sector in effects on achievement, there is another strong achievement-related difference—this time between the Catholic schools on the one hand, and the public schools and other private schools on the other. This is in the *homogeneity* of achievement: Catholic schoolchildren of college-educated and high-school-only parents achieve about the same, as do whites and blacks in those schools, even after other background characteristics are statistically controlled. This means that Catholic schools in general do less for students from the most advantaged backgrounds, and more for students from the most disadvantaged backgrounds, than do schools in the other-private sector. In both the public sector and the other-private sector there is a wide range of schools from the benighted to the elite; there is far less variance in the Catholic sector.

Do the private schools segregate?

The second major policy-relevant question examined in the report is whether private schools increase segregation. Segregation operates as the consequence of two different mechanisms: first, the segregation *between* sectors (that is, through high-income or white students going to the private sector), and second, through internal segregation within each sector. The segregation in American secondary education as a whole is a result of both between-sector and within-sector segregation.

As it turns out, the impact of the private sector on segregation differs in the religious, economic, and racial dimensions. Examining only segregation between Catholics and non-Catholics, the proportion of Catholics is, of course, sharply different in the Catholic, public, and other-private sectors—about 90, 30, and 17 percent,

---

[2] Nor is this to imply that the same factors would be critical in other settings or at other times in American schools when discipline would be taken as given. Results of the sort discussed here, while they point to factors that affect achievement in a given population of schools, will not hold in a population of schools which varies much less on the factors found to be important, or more on others. Twenty-five years ago, when discipline in American public schools was far less problematic than it is now, the results found here might very well not hold.

respectively. This means that the between-sector segregation is very high. Within each of the three sectors, *given* the proportion of Catholics in the sector, the within-sector segregation is quite low. Taking together the high between-sector segregation and the low within-sector segregation, *the overall effect of the private sector is to increase somewhat the degree of religious segregation in American secondary schools*, relative to that which would exist if Catholic and non-Catholic students from the private sector were distributed into the public schools as Catholics and non-Catholics are now distributed in those schools.[3]

The impact of the private sector on economic segregation is somewhat different. Both the Catholic and other private schools have somewhat higher proportions of high-income students than do the public schools, and smaller proportions of the lowest-income students. The economic differences between sectors are not, however, especially high, with median incomes reported as $18,200 in the public sector, $22,700 in the Catholic sector, and $24,300 in the other-private sector. The economic segregation within each sector is also low, though there is more economic segregation in the public sector than in either of the private sectors or in both taken together. *The combined result of the between-sector and within-sector economic segregation is to give a degree of overall economic segregation that is not high, but is slightly higher than is found in the public sector.* In other words, it is slightly higher than would exist if private school students were redistributed among the public schools.

The impact of the private sector on black-white segregation is still different.[4] There is a substantial difference between the proportion of blacks in the public sector, the Catholic sector, and the other-private sector: about 14, 6, and 3 percent, respectively. *Within the public sector, segregation is much higher than the black-white segregation in either of the private sectors or in the total private sector combined. The joint result of the substantial between-sector segregation and the substantially lower private within-sector segregation is that there is no overall impact of the private sector on black-white segregation.* If whites and blacks now in private schools

---

[3] The results of such a "redistribution" are obtained very simply, merely by assuming that the public sector was expanded to cover all students, maintaining the same level of religious segregation now found in the public sector.

[4] There is no effect on the Hispanic/non-Hispanic segregation because the private sector has about the same proportion of Hispanics as does the public sector, and the degree of segregation within public and private sectors is about the same.

were redistributed into the public sector in just the way whites and blacks are now distributed in that sector, there would be no greater and no less segregation than currently exists. This result may go against intuition, which sees the private sector as a haven used by whites when desegregation rulings are passed; but intuition overlooks the fact that suburban schools within the public sector are used as a haven to a much greater extent than is the private sector. Eliminating the private sector would hardly deposit whites back in the public schools they were attending, even those who had used a private school as a haven in the first place. It is probably less true to say that private schools increase the degree of racial segregation in education than to say that private schools permit a greater degree of residential integration by race than would exist in their absence.

Tuition as "tariff"

The results of this report, as I have described them above, are generally favorable to private schools. Further results in the report not described here are also generally favorable to private schools. A common response of some people, when confronted with these results, is the question, "But is the public interest served by assisting enrollment at private schools?" This is a question that merits serious attention, for private schooling on its face negates the classic American ideal of the public school.

I believe the matter can be usefully examined by viewing private school tuition as a protective tariff relative to tax support for free public schools. Just as a protective tariff on automobiles would protect the American automobile industry from foreign competition, private school tuition, measured against the free tuition at public schools, protects the public schools from competition by private schools. As students in first-year economics have learned, protective tariffs are generally inimical to the public interest. They benefit producers at the expense of consumers, but the producers they benefit most are those that would fail without the tariff—that is, the least efficient firms and industries. Protective tariffs keep resources employed inefficiently, lowering the general level of welfare, and opposing the general public interest. Furthermore, protective tariffs harm the interests of the least well-off, for the increase in prices relative to incomes (which is what protective tariffs bring about) hurts most those with the fewest dollars.

The effect of private school tuition and other barriers to attendance at private schools is very much the same. It protects the public schools to which students are assigned, and it protects most the worst public schools, those public schools that would be most depopulated by families' freedom to choose. It harms the consumers of education (the children and their families) and it harms most those to whom the price of tuition or the choice of school by moving residence is the greatest barrier—that is, the low-income family that is least able to leave a bad public school, and the black family that confronts the greatest barriers to moving elsewhere. (The evidence that this has occurred in American high schools is most fully seen in Greeley's report, which I have not discussed here.[5])

There are some conditions under which protective tariffs can be beneficial to the public interest—though as economists are quick to point out, these are rare, far less numerous than the arguments of certain producers would lead one to believe. In the same way that one must be suspicious of these arguments, one should be suspicious of public school arguments for maintaining their protective tariff. The most frequent condition under which protection is beneficial is when "infant industries" need a period of protection to get started.

Public schooling is not an infant industry, but a somewhat different argument could be made: There is a public interest (or perhaps a community interest or a national interest) in broad participation in common institutions. The same kind of argument could be (and sometimes is) made for the military draft, or for non-military national service. The same kind of argument could be made against "private schools in the public sector"—that is, homogenous elite public schools in homogenous suburbs. But there are two points of importance about this argument as it applies to private schools. One is that the public schools are no longer a "common" institution. Residential mobility has brought about a high degree of racial segregation in education, as well as segregation by income. The second point is that the public interest in common institutions is not an *overriding* public interest. It is a relatively weak public interest when measured against the public interest in helping all children, particularly those of the disadvantaged, receive a better education. It is a relatively weak public

---

[5] An interesting proposal that would give tuition vouchers, but only to children who do badly for a period of time in public schools, has recently been made by Barbara Lerner in *Minimum Competence, Maximum Choice: Second Chance Legislation*. This would eliminate the tuition tariff barrier in those schools which are doing worst for those students who are most harmed by the barrier.

interest when measured against the interests of children who are being directly and manifestly harmed by the school environment in which they find themselves, but who are unable to escape that environment. That plight is a poor family's plight, not one that policy-makers find themselves in. It takes sympathetic identification beyond their own experience to recognize this plight.

Some part of the plight is of very recent origin, for it is only very recently that control of a community's schools has been taken largely out of the community's hands by federal (and to a lesser extent, state) intervention. Public schools have become an over-regulated industry, with regulations and mandates ranging from draconian desegregation to mainstreaming of emotionally disturbed children, to athletic activities that are blind to sex differences. It is in part these regulations, imposed on the community and the school, which are responsible for the slackening of academic demands and the breakdown of disciplinary climate that many public schools have experienced in recent years. And it is the disadvantaged who are least able to select a school, in the public or private sector, that continues to function reasonably well.

There may be a rationale for some protective barriers to encourage participation in the public schools, but certainly not those that exist now, which harm most the interests of those least well-off and protect most those public schools that are worst. In short, the tuition barrier to private schooling as it exists now is almost certainly harmful to the public interest, and especially harmful to the interests of those least well-off.

RESEARCH NOTE

The study from which these data were taken, titled "High School and Beyond," is designed as a longitudinal study of a national sample of high school seniors and sophomores of 1980. The study is sponsored by the National Center for Education Statistics of the U.S. Department of Education, and has been conducted by the National Opinion Research Center of the University of Chicago. The first wave of data, on which the results described in the article are based, was collected in the Spring of 1980. The sample of schools consists of 1,015 high schools, the sample of seniors in these schools (randomly drawn from the list of seniors in each school) consists of 28,465 students, and the sample of sophomores, drawn in the same way, consists of 30,263 students. The study is designed for examining a number of policy questions, perhaps the most central of which are those involving the transition of youth from secondary education to a variety of post-secondary activities and into adulthood. The data set, which will be augmented by subsequent waves of questionnaires at approximately two-year intervals, is publicly available for analysis from NCES. The two reports which have been released to date are "Minority Students in Catholic Secondary Schools" by Professor Andrew Greeley of the University of Arizona and NORC, and "Public and Private Schools" by James Coleman, Thomas Hoffer, and Sally Kilgore at the University of Chicago and NORC.

Urban Housing Policy

The relations between the availability, cost, and condition of urban housing and government policy have been both complex and of long duration. Direct fiscal subsidization, tax deductions, manipulation of interest rates, restrictions on public sector competition with the private sector, and stipulations on where and how housing may be constructed are but a few of the means by which government policy has directly affected and frequently dominated the housing sector in Western industrial societies.

The range of influence of urban housing policy has not been restricted to any one segment of the housing market or to any one component of the population. Policies have affected, for example, the rich and the poor, choices to purchase a home in the city or in the suburbs, the choice of housing available to those who are white and those who are not, and whether one finds financing for housing in the public or private sectors of the lending market. A clear theme that emerges in this collection of articles is that it is government policy that shapes, controls, and determines the availability of and access to housing.

The study of housing policy, as articles on both the United States and Britain suggest, is the study of a web of often conflicting societal concerns, monetary strategies, and political agendas. It is in housing policy that many of the schisms and cross-currents in the society become readily apparent. The study of housing brings to the fore concerns of social class stratification, racial segregation, ethnicity, urban tax policy, mass home ownership, protection of personal investment, entrepreneurship, and both public- and private-sector lending policies. For each aspect of this issue, there are frequently competing claims and objectives. Further, different levels of government can find themselves in conflict over goals and policies. These concerns cannot all be accommodated simultaneously. Resolution takes on "zero-sum" characteristics. The articles here are especially important in detailing this tension among competing goals and objectives.

Taggart and Smith have examined the mortgage activity of financial institutions in the Boston metropolitan area to access patterns of disinvestment in the urban area. This process of "redlining," whereby lending institutions ostensibly refuse to lend money for housing mortgages or commercial investment in particular urban neighborhoods or commercial districts, is critical to an understanding of urban decline. Redlining, in the final analysis, is a process of disinvestment (funding from urban investors being used to subsidize and finance suburban development) and discrimination (redlined areas being those with significant numbers of poor and minority persons). This study provides conclusive evidence on how pervasive this practice is in metropolitan Boston. It also indicates the linkages in this effort among financial, real estate, and municipal agencies.

A second case study in this section focuses on private neighborhood redevelopment and displacement in Washington, D.C. Goldfield systematically examines the phenomenon, one which many argue is critical to the revitalization of urban areas throughout the nation. According to the redevelopment argument, the future of the center city is doomed without middle- and upper-income residents. Private redevelopment is a means to attract such persons into the city, with their disposable income, higher tax revenues, and investment in the urban housing stock. Goldfield also assesses the displacement of poor persons resulting from this gentrification of urban areas. Here again, tensions in housing policy—between strengthening the urban tax base and housing the poor—are evident.

Creating and maintaining viable housing for the poor, the focus of an analysis at the Rand Corporation by Rydell, Mulford, and Helbers, has been the subject of various federal government initiatives. This chapter compares two approaches used to subsidize housing for the poor: housing allowances and "Section 8 assistance." Housing allowances provide direct financial subsidies to the poor to help cover rent. Participants in the program are allowed to live in any housing unit they wish so long as the unit meets particular program standards. Section 8 assistance, in contrast, provides the subsidy directly to the landlord, and the tenant makes up the difference between that subsidy and the total rent. Restrictions on where participants may live are more stringent for this program. A comparison of these two policy options suggests that the market approach far outperformed the regulation approach in controlling rental price escalations.

A comparative view of federal housing policy in Britain by Farmer and Barrell further illustrates the tensions inherent in developing housing policy. The argument here is a most provocative one. Specifically, so long as the federal government continues to subsidize the housing market, both directly and indirectly, a considerable percentage of available entrepreneurial funds in the society will go into the nonproductive but highly profitable housing sector, rather than into the business sector where they could stimulate economic activity. While private home buying remains profitable and highly subsidized, opportunities for other forms of entrepreneurial economic activity will be bypassed in favor of what can be gained in the housing market. Thus government intervention on behalf of one policy objective, housing ownership, conflicts directly with another objective, stimulation of entrepreneurship.

34

REDLINING
An Assessment of the Evidence of Disinvestment in Metropolitan Boston

Harriett Tee Taggart and Kevin W. Smith

The residential mortgage activity of financial institutions in metropolitan Boston was analyzed to identify and assess patterns of disinvestment. Data were obtained from most state-chartered institutions and larger national banks on the geographic breakdown of their mortgage portfolios, recent mortgage activities, and deposits. Additional information on home sales, population and housing characteristics, and homeowner interviews were used. The measures of disinvestment were (1) mortgage-to-deposit ratios, (2) number of bank mortgage applications compared to home sales, and (3) bank-financed home sales to total home sales. Results indicate that (1) the mortgage dollars invested relative to the savings dollars deposited by residents were disproportionately low in most urban neighborhoods; (2) the proportion of bank-financed home sales was substantially higher in suburban than in urban areas; and (3) bank home mortgage lending is disproportionately lower in minority and racially changing neighborhoods. These analytical techniques and results are compared with those of major redlining studies in other metropolitan areas.

"Redlining" has become a subject of increasing public concern in recent years. Originally used to refer to areas delineated on a map in red crayon where bankers would refuse to lend, the term is now applied to lending practices that may be less overt but that still arbitrarily discriminate against urban neighborhoods in favor of suburbs.

The fundamental issues underlying the redlining debate are disinvestment and discrimination. Members of the banking industry defend their practices by arguing that urban problems are essentially economic problems. From their perspective, loan policies and lending records have been the result, not a cause, of deteriorating urban housing stock and property owner disinvestment. Community groups, however,

---

From Harriett Tee Taggart and Kevin W. Smith, "Redlining: An Assessment of the Evidence of Disinvestment in Metropolitan Boston," 17(1) *Urban Affairs Quarterly* 91-107 (September 1981). Copyright 1981 by Sage Publications, Inc.

contend that antiurban lending standards often are based not on facts but, rather, on subjective perceptions of loan officers. They claim that many of these standards are insupportable when economic analyses of the loan and neighborhood viability are made.

As a public regulatory agency at the center of this controversy between community organizations and the lending industry, the Massachusetts Banking Department assumed responsibility for conducting analysis of mortgage lending practices and investment patterns in the Boston metropolitan area. The principal objectives of this analysis were (1) to generate a data base that could be used to assess lending practices within metropolitan Boston, (2) to develop further techniques to identify any disinvestment patterns, and (3) to examine some of the factors contributing to any observed patterns of disinvestment. This article summarizes the content of that work, compares the analytical techniques and results with those of other redlining studies, and critically evaluates the problem areas requiring further research that were identified in that analytical effort.[1]

INDICES OF BANK MORTGAGE INVESTMENT IN URBAN AND SUBURBAN AREAS

OVERVIEW

The literature on redlining has evolved through three generations of studies. The first generation was based on data obtained through property transfer records at local registries of deeds, census data, annual financial reports of individual banks, and case histories of mortgage application experiences of local residents. Among the more extensive studies of this series were analyses done on Baltimore (Home Ownership Development Program, 1973), Chicago (Bradford et al., 1975; Feins, 1976), Cincinnati (McKee, 1974), Los Angeles (Center for New Corporate Priorities, 1975), New York (Devine et al., 1973), Philadelphia (Northwest Community Housing Association, 1973) and Washington, D.C. (Public Interest Research Group, 1975).

The second generation of studies have been based on geographic breakdowns of mortgage loan activity. These data were publicly disclosed by each lending institution under recently enacted legal requirements of federal or state governments. In some cases, state regulators or a regional office of federal regulators also required corresponding deposit data. These studies included a survey of eight metropolitan areas (Pryzbyliski, 1978), an analysis of several cities in California (California Department of Savings and Loans, 1978), a study of each of the metropolitan areas in Connecticut (Gold, 1977), an analysis of mortgage and deposit disclosure data for metropolitan Boston (Taggart et al., 1977), and a preliminary report on each of the metropolitan areas in New York (New York State Banking Department, 1977).

A third, nascent generation of studies has been based on individual mortgage applicant and borrower data. These data have been developed through several different methods: through surveys developed by research personnel posing as applicants (U.S. Commission on Civil Rights, 1975); interviews conducted with homebuyers (Taggart et al., 1977); analyses from bank records of the disposition of written applications (Federal Home Loan Bank Board, 1975; Federal Reserve Board and Federal Deposit Insurance Corporation, 1975; U.S. Comptroller of the Currency, 1975; and Schafer, 1978); and risk studies designed to evaluate the loan experience of lenders in urban and suburban areas (Green and Von Furstenberg, 1975; Schafer, 1978; Von Furstenberg and Green, 1974; and Williams et al., 1975).

INDICES AND DATA BASES USED IN METROPOLITAN BOSTON ANALYSIS

This analysis of metropolitan Boston, which began as a second-generation study based on mortgage and deposit disclosure data, ultimately assessed bank investment in each urban and suburban community using indices developed from the types of data used in each generation of studies to obtain a more comprehensive assessment of the mortgage lending situation. The most useful of these indices were:

(1) mortgage-to-deposit ratios, which compared savings dollars deposited by neighborhood residents to mortgage dollars reinvested;
(2) number of bank loan applications filed compared with the total number of home sales in each area; and
(3) bank-financed home sales as a percentage of total residential sales.

These indices improved considerably upon those used in earlier studies. More detailed deposit disclosure data made possible analyses by type and size of bank in each neighborhood within the metropolitan area. First- and second-generation data were combined in the second and third indices so as accurately to assess bank loan activity in the context of market demand in each neighborhood.

The bank data on residential mortgages, savings deposits, and mortgage applications used in the first two indices were obtained under annual directives issued by the Massachusetts Banking Department in 1975, 1976, and 1977. The directives required all major financial institutions, state-chartered banks with deposits of $20 million or more, and those federally chartered institutions that were members of multibank holding companies to disclose the geographic distribution of their real estate loan portfolios, recent mortgage application and loan activities, and deposits by residence of depositor.[2]

Analyses of these bank disclosure data, however, indicated serious shortcomings inherent in this second-generation information. The principal shortcoming is that data obtained exclusively through mortgage lenders underestimated the market demand for loans, particularly in areas where redlining may be a problem. Although the Massachusetts directive did require banks to report applications received by geographic area, a number of factors may undermine the validity of these disclosure data as an indicator of demand. If banks have historically not made mortgage loans in an area, it is less likely that real estate brokers or homebuyers will approach those institutions for loans. Also, lenders may "prescreen" applicants and discourage those interested in purchasing homes in neighborhoods where they do not want to lend before a written application is even submitted for consideration.[3] Finally, in areas where bank credit has been difficult to obtain, alternative institutions such as mortgage companies have often located to originate and service loans that are ordinarily more costly than conventional loans available elsewhere. Since these lenders have not been regulated by the agencies administering disclosure data, their loan activity has generally not been reported in this type of data.

To develop better indicators of mortgage demand, data on home sales and the source of mortgage financing for each sale were obtained from a first-generation source, property transfer records reported by the *Real Estate Transfer Directory* for the period July 1, 1975, to June 30, 1977. The second and third indices were developed from these data.

Mortgage-to-Deposit Ratios

This measure was developed to resolve what has been a major debate between city residents and bankers. Bankers generally maintain that these ratios are higher in urban neighborhoods than in suburban areas, and that greater investment in risky urban areas would be a breach of their fiduciary responsibility to suburban depositors. Urban community leaders contend that, on the contrary, far more savings dollars are deposited by residents of their neighborhoods than are returned in mortgage dollars. Prior to the availability of bank disclosure data, the urban and suburban sources of a bank's deposits could only be estimated by a regulator or an outside researcher on the basis of the deposit size and location of its offices (Devine et al., 1973: Ch. V, 18-19, 41). However, once deposit disclosure data were available, the ratio results for the Boston area substantiated the perceptions of the urban residents, not the bankers, in considerably greater detail than the only two previous studies on Chicago (National Peoples Action on Housing, 1975) and on New York (New York State Banking Department, 1977).

Mortgage-to-deposit ratios were initially examined by each institution throughout the Boston metropolitan area. On the basis of this information, distinct patterns emerged relative to mortgage type, neighborhood type, and bank type.

First, a comparison of the most prevalent type of mortgage, conventional loans on one- to four-family homes, with savings by residence of depositor, indicated that, among neighborhood types, the core urban areas, those census tract and zip code areas in and adjacent to the central city, tend to receive the least reinvestment of their deposits.[4] Most core urban communities received only 3% to 33% reinvestment in mortgages of savings dollars deposited, while the outermost suburbs experienced reinvestment levels of 108% to 543%. These reinvestment ratios form a distinct pattern of concentric circles, with the inner-city communities at the center.

Second, analyses that included other types of mortgages, federally insured loans, larger residential and commercial real estate loans, and all types of deposits did not alter the reinvestment hierarchy between urban and suburban areas. During the three years, 1975 to 1977, for which mortgage and deposit ratios were analyzed, the mortgage activity of all banks increased, yet the relative position of urban to suburban neighborhoods did not change. The reinvestment levels to urban areas remained significantly below those of the suburbs.

Third, within the city of Boston there was considerable variation in reinvestment ratios among bank types. Larger thrift institutions (the largest savings banks and large cooperative banks) and commercial banks generally had reinvestment ratios lower than those of the neighborhood thrift institutions. While neighborhood thrift institutions reinvested from 26% to 50% of deposits, the larger thrifts reinvested only 12% to 16% and the commercial banks only 2%. Citywide, over the three-year period studied, the conventional mortgage reinvestment ratios of the larger thrifts remained relatively static, while the neighborhood thrifts significantly increased their investments (Table 1). On federally insured loans, which are usually 100% insured and thus involve little or no risk to the bank, and which are often more expensive for the consumer than conventional alternatives, the larger thrift institutions participated substantially more.

Fourth, within the city of Boston a three-way comparison of mortgage-to-deposit ratios by mortgage type, neighborhood type, and bank type was performed. Conventional home mortgage dollars relative to deposit dollars are considerably lower in minority neighborhoods than other areas for all types of institutions, particularly the larger thrifts. When federally insured mortgages are included, the reinvestment ratios of larger thrift institutions in minority neighborhoods increase substantially but still remain disproportionately lower than those in nonminority neighborhoods.

These analyses of mortgage portfolios and deposits document the existence of substantial capital export, but they do not address the principal argument of many bankers that there was no demand for mortgages in these urban areas. On viewing the mortgage-to-deposit ratios for metropolitan Boston, some bankers maintained that this investment pattern simply indicated the areas of residential growth and mortgage demand in the region. To test the strength of this argument, the authors designed a second and a third index, discussed below.

**Measures of Mortgage Demand
Relative to Supply of
Loans from Banks**

The second and third indices, the proportions of bank applications received and loans granted to home sales were developed as measures of

TABLE 1
Ratios of One- to Four-Family Mortgages to Regular Savings Deposits: City of Boston by Boston-Based Banks

Type of Institution	Conventional Mortgages Only			Conventional and Federally Insured Mortgages	
	1975	1976	1977	1976	1977
Largest Savings	.11	.10	.12	.27	.32
Large Thrifts	.17	.17	.17	.37	.30
Neighborhood Thrifts, South[b]	.19	.25	.26	.33	.36
Neighborhood Thrifts, West[b]	.22	.31	.50	.42	.59
Neighborhood Thrifts, North[b]	.21	.21	.27	.25	.30
THRIFTS INSTITUTIONS, TOTAL	.13	.13	.17	.29	.32
COMMERCIAL BANKS TOTAL	a	a	.02	a	.03

SOURCE: Massachusetts Banking Department, 1975, 1976, and 1977.
a. The banks in the Commercial Bank Group changed from 1975 to 1977, thus making comparable data for 1975 and 1976 unavailable.
b. Thrift institutions established in neighborhoods outside the central business district were grouped by location of main office—north, south, or west of the downtown financial district. Location of the main office is the criterion used by bank regulatory agencies to determine primary service area.

demand for residential mortgages relative to bank loans supplied in urban and suburban areas. Prior to the development of these indices, the authors had compared the percentage of bank applications to loans granted. In most urban and suburban areas, close to 100% of the applications received were granted. Bankers maintained that these percentages confirmed that there was no differential treatment between urban and suburban areas, as there was no shortfall in the supply of loans to meet the demand measured by their written applications. However, neighborhood organizations argued that as a result of both prescreening practices and historical patterns of disinvestment, written applications retained in the banks' records were not a bona fide measure of demand. Subsequently, data on residential sales in each area were compiled as a more complete indicator of homebuyer demand than mortgage applications on file at each bank.

A review of the second index indicated that bank applications relative to home sales were indeed disproportionately low in urban areas when compared to suburban areas. In most suburban communities, applications to banks generally numbered 85% or more of home sales; in those urban neighborhoods with a substantial minority population, applications averaged less than 50% of home sales. In sum, these results demonstrated differential patterns in the volume of bank mortgage applications relative to the volume of home sales between city and suburban housing markets.

In turn, the third index, which compared the number of home sales with the number of bank mortgages granted in each community, indicated that suburban areas received considerably more bank mortgages relative to the number of home sales than most urban areas. In some of the predominantly black or transitional neighborhoods, approximately 40% to 60% of the homes sales had no bank financing (Table 2). The fact that so many homes in these and other city neighborhoods were bought and financed by nonbank sources is a conservative indicator of potential markets for additional bank mortgages. On the basis of these data, low bank mortgage activity could not be dismissed by the claim that there is limited housing market activity in these areas.

In summary, the first of these indices, mortgage-to-deposit ratios, is a good measure of the flow of funds through financial intermediaries from urban to suburban areas. However, this first index is insufficient as a measure of disinvestment, since such capital export may be supportable where there is no further demand for funds in urban areas. Bank

TABLE 2
All Bank-Financed Home Sales as a Percentage of Total Residential Sales: Boston SMSA

Area	All Bank Mortgages as a Percent of Total Home Sales		Total Number of Bank Mortgages		Total Number of Home Sales	
	7/75-6/76	7/76-6/77	7/75-6/76	7/76-6/77	7/75-6/76	7/76-6/77
Boston Neighborhoods:						
40% + minority	42%	57%	748	657	1,795	1,159
10-39% minority	59	67	363	350	619	525
3-9% minority	64	74	657	637	1,023	861
2% or less minority	65	72	661	537	1,016	745
CITY OF BOSTON	55	63	2,429	2,181	4,453	3,438
BOSTON SMSA, EXCLUDING CITY OF BOSTON	81	83	20,728	20,519	25,483	24,648

SOURCE: Real Estate Transfer Directory, July 1975 to June 1977.

mortgage applications, used in the second index, proved to be an inadequate measure of demand. When compared with home sales in each area, mortgage applications received by the banks were disproportionately low in most urban neighborhoods. Finally, the third index, bank-financed home sales as a percentage of total residential sales, proved to be the best indicator of bank mortgages supplied relative to measurable housing demand in each market.

MARKET DYNAMICS ASSOCIATED WITH DISINVESTMENT PATTERNS

The low volume of mortgage applications generally and, more specifically, the geographic concentration of both nonbank mortgages and federally insured bank loans warranted further investigation. The fundamental question underlying each of these phenomena was the extent to which the market behavior of banks themselves and other representatives of the lending industry generated or dampened the demand for bank mortgages and fostered the development of often expensive nonbank sources of funds.

While all three measures discussed in the previous section indicated disproportionately low mortgage activity in urban areas, none offered explanations of why these patterns of disinvestment developed. The following sections explore two methods, homebuyer surveys and multivariate analyses, that may be used to identify the possible determinants of disinvestment.

Interviews With Homebuyers

A survey was conducted among homebuyers in those areas that had high concentrations of nonbank and federally insured mortgages. The first purpose of this survey was to ascertain why homebuyers in some urban neighborhoods frequently applied to mortgage companies instead of pursuing the same type of financing usually offered on less expensive terms at a bank. Had these same buyers initially applied to banks for mortgages and, only after being rejected, looked to nonbank sources? The second objective was to assess why, in each sample, homebuyers had sought federally insured mortgages. Had they needed low downpayment loans and, if so, were they informed about less costly alternatives offered by many banks in conjunction with private mortgage insurance companies?

The survey was thus designed to obtain data from two samples of homebuyers. The primary sample was made up of buyers who received a federally insured loan from a mortgage company. Since federally insured loans were the only type of financing available from nonbank lenders in the Boston area at that time, the survey was limited to federally insured borrowers. The second control sample of homebuyers was drawn from those who had obtained a federally insured mortgage from a bank during the same time period in the same geographic areas. A total of 106 homebuyers who had purchased their homes with federally insured loans were interviewed, 68 with mortgage company loans and the remaining 38 with bank mortgages.[5]

Regarding the first objective, the survey results indicated that real estate brokers, through whom buyers originally located the houses they wanted to purchase, played an instrumental role in directing a homebuyer to apply to a bank or to a mortgage company. The first group of homebuyers were never referred to a bank, even though many of them had savings accounts as regular customers at some of the local banks. In many cases, the broker actually made most of the financing arrangements with the mortgage company and informed the homebuyer only after these arrangements were made. Given that the broker's primary income is commissions received from successfully completed sales, regardless of the source and type of financing, both the growth in mortgage company business and the high percentage of federally insured mortgages may reflect bank disinterest in conventional financing. Racial minorities represented 93% of mortgage company borrowers but only 24% of the bank borrowers interviewed. The areas in which mortgage company activity was most pronounced tended to be racially transitional neighborhoods (10% to 39% minority) as opposed to those already predominantly black or Spanish-speaking (40% or more minority) where there was little institutional financing at all.

Regarding the second objective, the results of the survey indicated that 20% of the mortgage company homebuyers and 82% of the bank homebuyers actually made downpayments sufficient for private mortgage insurance, where premium costs over the life of the loan amount to less than those associated with federally insured mortgages. Some homebuyers had enough savings to make the downpayment required for conventional financing, and a few actually had put as much as 20% down on a FHA mortgage. Thus, it appeared that the decision to issue federally insured mortgages was, in many cases, not based on the borrowers' financial need but on other criteria, related to characteristics of the neighborhood where the borrowers were purchasing a home and possibly to racial characteristics of the borrowers themselves.

In the course of this survey work, the authors did uncover maps maintained by the major federal mortgage insurance agency, the Federal Housing Administration (FHA), which delineated predominantly minority neighborhoods in four central cities in Massachusetts as "high-risk areas" with "adverse environmental factors" and "questionable economic viability." In response to inquiries by the authors, FHA officials in the Boston Area Office stated that these maps were not used rigidly. Loans within the "high-risk" areas were not approved exclusively under the agency's special insurance fund. Nonetheless, data obtained from the central FHA office on loans in metropolitan Boston during the period covered by the survey data, July 1975 through December 1976, indicated that (1) of the total 694 loans made in the entire region, 330 or 48% were in the delineated high-risk area, and (2) of these 330 loans, 241 or 73% were approved only subject to the high-risk-area provision.

The importance of these maps extends beyond internal agency processing. Lenders originating loans with FHA insurance receive copies of the forms which indicate whether the loan was classified in the special "high-risk" insurance fund. If the public insurance fund of the U.S. Department of Housing and Urban Development considers these neighborhoods high-risk, it would be difficult for a private lending institution prudently to argue otherwise with its public regulatory agencies.

In sum, the survey data indicated that there are several key institutional factors that account for differential patterns of mortgage finance. The race of the homebuyer and the corresponding racial composition of the neighborhood appear to be influential in a real estate broker's decision to pursue mortgage company financing. White homebuyers in racially mixed or adjacent areas, both of which were encompassed by FHA's high-risk-area maps during the survey period, were often encouraged to pursue bank financing. In both cases, issuance of a federally insured loan apparently was not based on the perception of these homebuyers' financial circumstances as high-risk; rather, certain predominantly minority areas were perceived as high-risk neighborhoods by brokers, bankers, and public agencies such as the FHA.

Multivariate Analysis of Disinvestment Patterns

A serious shortcoming of first- and second-generation disinvestment-pattern indicators, and, hence, any subsequent analysis, is that they are based exclusively on aggregate data rather than on those individuals seeking home mortgages. For example, the authors conducted a multiple regression analysis using the proportion of bank-financed home sales, aggregated for 191 census tracts and zip codes in the Boston SMSA, as an index of disinvestment. After controlling for a number of socioeconomic, housing stock, and foreclosure rate variables, the racial composition of a neighborhood was found to be negatively related to the percentage of sales with bank financing. In any neighborhood, the greater the percentage of minority residents, the lower the proportion of bank-financed home sales (Taggart et al., 1977).

The problem with this analysis and others that use comparable data (e.g., California Department of Savings and Loans, 1978; Devine et al., 1973; New York State Banking Department, 1977) is that results based on aggregate data do not provide conclusive evidence of the determinants of disinvestment. A finding that predominantly minority neighborhoods have disproportionately low mortgages-to-sales ratios may mean that (1) the entire neighborhood has been "redlined," (2) certain racial or socioeconomic groups are discriminated against, or (3) the housing market in these areas comprises relatively weak prospective homebuyers of insufficient means to support the required mortgage financing and maintenance expenditures. Moreover, data aggregated at the neighborhood level, such as foreclosure rates, do not necessarily signal that investment in the neighborhood is inherently risky. High foreclosure rates, for example, may be more a function of the type of loan and the quality of lender services than an indicator that the areas in which these loans are concentrated are exceptionally risky (Bachman, 1977; Lefcoe and Toten, 1974).

More conclusive analyses of disinvestment patterns will require third-generation data on individual mortgage applicants and borrowers, including credit histories and debt-to-income ratios, as the unit of analysis. Individual applicant data and accepted and rejected loan files, thus far have been compiled and analyzed on New York State savings banks (Schafer, 1978), and those for California savings and loan associations have been analyzed by Schafer and Ladd (1980). As of March 1977, data on mortgage applications need to be compiled by federally chartered and federally insured institutions under the Equal Credit Opportunity Act. To date, these data have not been analyzed or disseminated.

Multivariate analyses of individual data on portfolio risk experience, at the neighborhood level, have been analyzed from New York savings banks (Schafer, 1978), 24 Connecticut banks (Morton, 1974), a few savings and loan associations in Pittsburgh (Green and Von Furstenberg, 1975; Von Furstenberg and Green, 1974; Williams et al., 1975) and California (Sandor and Sosin, 1975). Only the New York and Connecticut studies were based on data from a sufficient number of institutions to draw statistically valid conclusions regarding general bank experience. The results of both these studies were for the most part inconclusive and, thus, do not offer sufficient analytical insight on the issues of mortgage lending practices and patterns of disinvestment.

SUMMARY AND CONCLUSIONS

Analysis of metropolitan Boston data indicates (1) substantial savings of urban depositors are exported to suburban communities; (2) in many urban neighborhoods, particularly those with significant minority populations, both the number of bank applications received and the corresponding volume of loans granted are disproportionately low relative to the home sales activity in these areas; (3) real estate brokers and bank mortgage loan officers influence the demand for mortgages, particularly the types of loans applied for and the terms requested; and (4) public agencies such as the Federal Housing Administration may have had a pronounced influence in reinforcing private lenders' perceptions of minority neighborhoods as high-risk loan areas. These findings substantiate and expand on the research of several earlier studies in other metropolitan areas. While the indices used in this study are useful measures to identify patterns of disinvestment, further analyses of third-generation data at the individual applicant and mortgage borrower case level for individual institutions will be necessary to identify patterns of actual discrimination and to differentiate actual from perceived risks relative to mortgage lending in urban areas.

NOTES

1. The authors of this article were responsible for the public report, *Home Mortgage Lending Patterns in Metropolitan Boston*, which was issued by the Massachusetts Banking Department in December 1977.

2. Over three years, an average of 128 banks complied with the Disclosure Directive issued by the Banking Department for Boston SMSA banks. Approximately 75 small state-chartered savings and cooperative banks and 18 relatively small savings and loan associations, which are federally regulated, were not subject to this directive. All data were compiled by census tract for the cities of Boston and Lynn, and by zip code for all other communities in the Boston SMSA.

3. Some analyses, such as the one done in Rochester, New York, by George Benston (New York State Banking Department, 1977: Ch. V, 1-49) have overlooked these limitations of data obtained exclusively from bank files.

4. This analysis is based on 126 geographic areas, consisting of 15 Boston neighborhoods and 4 Lynn neighborhoods grouped by census tract and 107 zip areas in the surrounding communities. In subsequent multivariate analyses, these 15 neighborhoods were further disaggregated into 84 census tracts. Thus, in the latter analyses, 191 geocodes were used.

5. The first sample of 68 homebuyers represents one-third federally insured loans made by mortgage companies in these Boston neighborhoods between 1975 and 1977. The original sample was designed to be 100 homebuyers, or roughly one-half. Thirty-two homebuyers either could not be reached or did not make themselves available for an interview. The second control of 38 bank-financed borrowers was originally designed to obtain only one-half of the number of interviewees in the primary sample. These 50 interviewees represented 10% of the homebuyers receiving federally insured loans from banks in these Boston neighborhoods during this period. Twelve of these households either could not be reached or did not make themselves available for an interview. These homebuyers were selected by listing all such mortgagers in each of these two categories chronologically by date of property transfer, randomly selecting one, and subsequently taking every other one for the first sample and every tenth one for the second sample. Responses to the survey were tabulated in two- or three-way tables and tested with chi-square tests at a significance level of .01.

REFERENCES

BACHMAN, P. (1977) "An empirical investigation of the causes of mortgage default risk: a combined application of factor and cluster analysis." Prepared under contract with the U.S. Department of Housing and Urban Development. (unpublished)

BRADFORD, C., D. GROTHAUS, and L. RUBINOWITZ (1975) The Role of Mortgage Lending Practices in Older Urban Neighborhoods: Institutional Lenders, Regulatory Agencies and Their Community Impacts. Evanston, IL: Center for Urban Affairs and Policy Research, Northwestern University.

California Department of Savings and Loans (1978) Fair Lending Report. San Francisco: Author.

Center for New Corporate Priorities (1975) Where the Money Is: Mortgage Lending, Los Angeles County. Los Angeles: Author.

DEVINE, R. J., W. O. RENNIE, and N. B. SIMS (1973) Where the Lender Looks First: A Case Study of Mortgage Disinvestment in Bronx County, 1960-1970. New York: National Urban League.

Federal Home Loan Bank Board (1975) Fair Housing Information Survey: Form A Approach. Washington, DC: Government Printing Office.

Federal Reserve Board and Federal Deposit Insurance Corporation (1975) Fair Housing Survey: Form B Approach. Washington, DC: Government Printing Office.

FEINS, J. D. (1976) "Urban housing disinvestment and neighborhood decline: a study of public policy outcomes." Ph.D. dissertation, University of Chicago.

GOLD, A. S. (1977) A Report to the State Banking Commissioner Regarding Redlining and Home Mortgage Disclosure. Hartford, CT: Trinity College.

GREEN, R. J. and G. M. VON FURSTENBERG (1975) "The effects of race and age in housing on mortgage delinquency risk." Urban Studies 12, 1: 85-89.

Home Ownership Development Program (1973) Home Ownership and the Baltimore Mortgage Market. Baltimore: City of Baltimore.

LEFCOE, G. and E. F. TOTEN (1974) Causes of Defaults and Foreclosures in the FHA Single-Family Mortgage Insurance Programs. San Diego: University of Southern California.

McKEE, D. S. (1974) Housing Analysis in Oakley, Bond-Hill, and Evanston Financial Investment Patterns, January, 1960—April, 1974. Chicago: Coalition of Neighborhoods.

Massachusetts Banking Department (1975-1977) Mortgage and Deposit Disclosure Directive. Boston: Author.

MORTON, T. G. (1974) A Discriminant Function Analysis of Residential Mortgage Delinquency and Foreclosure. Hartford: Center for Real Estate Studies, University of Connecticut.

National Peoples Action on Housing (1975) "Mortgage patterns in Chicago." Exhibit B of Testimony, Hearings of the U.S. Senate Committee on Banking, Housing and Urban Affairs: The Home Mortgage Disclosure Act of 1975, 94th Congress, 1st Session (May): 191-200.

New York State Banking Department (1977) Mortgage Financing and Housing Markets in New York State: A Preliminary Report. New York: Author.

Northwest Community Housing Association (1973) Mortgage Disinvestment in Northwest Philadelphia. Philadelphia: Author.

PRYZBYLISKI, M. (1978) Perceptions of Mortgage Risk, The Bankers' Myth: An Eight-City Survey of Mortgage Disclosure Data. Chicago: National Training and Information Center.

Public Interest Research Group (1975) Redlining: Mortgage Disinvestment in the District of Columbia. Washington, DC: Author.

Real Estate Transfer Directory (1971-1977) Framingham, MA: Author.

SANDOR, R. L. and H. B. SOSIN (1975) "The determinants of mortgage risk premiums: a case study of the portfolio of a savings and loan association." J. of Business 48, 1: 27-38.

SCHAFER, R. (1978) Mortgage Lending Decisions: Criteria and Constraints. Cambridge: Joint Center for Urban Studies of the Massachusetts Institute of Technology and Harvard University.

SCHAFER, R. and H. F. LADD (1980) Equal Credit Opportunity: Accessibility to Mortgage Funds by Women and Minorities. Cambridge: Joint Center for Urban Studies of the Massachusetts Institute of Technology and Harvard University.

TAGGART, H. T., K. SMITH, and K. P. PHENIX (1977) Home Mortgage Lending Patterns in Metropolitan Boston. Boston: Massachusetts Banking Department.

U.S. Commission on Civil Rights (1975) Mortgage Money: Who Gets It? A Case Study in Mortgage Lending in Hartford, Connecticut. Washington, DC: Government Printing Office. (Publication 48)

U.S. Comptroller of the Currency (1975) Fair Housing Lending Practices Pilot Project: Form C Approach. Washington, DC: Government Printing Office.

VON FURSTENBERG, G. and R. J. GREEN (1974) "The effects of income and race on the quality of home mortgages: a case study for Pittsburgh," pp. 165-179 in G. B. Von Furstenberg et al. (eds.) Patterns of Racial Discrimination. Lexington, MA: D.C. Heath.

WILLIAMS, A. O., W. BERANEK, and J. KENKEL (1975) "Factors affecting mortgage credit risk in urban areas—a Pittsburgh prototype analysis." Hearing of the U.S. Senate Committee on Banking, Housing and Urban Affairs: The Home Mortgage Disclosure Act of 1975. 94th Congress, 1st Session (May): 674-698.

Harriett Tee Taggart is an urban planner, currently Regional Director of the New England Office of the National Consumer Cooperative Bank, a public development finance institution chartered by Congress to serve cooperatives. Her graduate degrees are a Ph.D. (urban studies and Planning, MIT, 1981) and an M.C.P. (city planning, Harvard University, 1973). The redlining and reinvestment study was conducted while Taggart was Director of Research at the Massachusetts State Banking Department. Her other research interests are in capital markets and economic development.

Kevin W. Smith is a statistician, currently Associate Research Scientist with American Institutes for Research. His graduate degree is an M.A. (sociology, Tufts University, 1981). Smith was a research assistant at the Banking Department at the time the research for this study was conducted. His research interests include program evaluation, evaluation methodology, mental health, and health care.

35

PRIVATE NEIGHBORHOOD REDEVELOPMENT AND DISPLACEMENT
The Case of Washington, D.C.

David R. Goldfield

As a result of various economic and demographic factors, Washington, D.C. is leading a national trend toward the private revitalization of inner city areas. It is not yet clear whether this trend represents a back-to-the-city movement or merely the shifting of population from one section of the city to another. Research to date is inconclusive both as to the extent of displacement and to the deposition of the displaced households. The local government had adopted, but not seriously enforced, several measures that would limit real estate speculation and protect the rights of the typically poor inhabitants.

Private neighborhood redevelopment has become a national phenomenon only within the last decade. Since 1968, nearly one-half of the cities with more than 50,000 people have experienced private rehabilitation (Black, 1975: 3-9). Even in cities like Detroit and Gary, the spark of private neighborhood revitalization has brought a ray of hope to an otherwise dark scene of decline.

Washington, D.C., deeply scarred by destructive riots more than a decade ago, where three out of every four residents are black and at least half that number are poor, and where local leaders are just beginning to enjoy a measure of home rule after generations of being a federal orphan, hardly seems to be a likely participant in the national trend of private redevelopment. Yet that very trend has become an epidemic. Washington, D.C. has become the national leader in private neighborhood revitalization—a laboratory in which to study both the successes and the excesses of that movement.

THE ATTRACTIONS OF
URBAN NEIGHBORHOODS

Housing is the most obvious attraction of District neighborhoods. With a two percent rental vacancy in the city and a median price of $75,000 for a home in the suburbs, the housing situation is critical. For those who can scrape enough money together to purchase a home, the phrase "house poor" frequently describes their lifestyle. The old yardstick of housing costs being one-quarter of a family's monthly income has stretched beyond 40% for some households (Daniel, 1977: 130-131).

The dream of suburban homeownership is becoming increasingly unlikely for thousands of Washington metropolitan-area residents. Prices on new homes and condominiums in the area rose by 18% during 1978. There are predictions that loans will be more difficult to obtain in the future, and interest rates are steadily rising (Washington *Post*, 1979a). The desperation of some homeseekers is reflected by the 600 applicants for 12 moderately priced ($35,490) townhouse units in suburban Montgomery County and by the all-night vigil of prospective buyers of 130, 30-year-old townhouses in suburban Alexandria selling for upwards of $45,000 (Washington *Post*, 1978d, 1977a).

The housing situation is more frustrating for the first-home buyer who lacks the equity and often the income to meet inflated housing costs. Washington, D.C. has an abundance of the young singles and adult-oriented couples who comprise an increasing portion of our population (Goldfield, 1976: 85-86). It is this population, in particular, that is turning to the city to fulfill its housing needs.

Although housing is a major attraction, employment is also a consideration. Cities with a mix of high-status, white-collar jobs seem to be most susceptible to the private redevelopment process (Lipton, 1977). Washington, D.C. is probably the prototypical example of a city with a high-status employment base. In addition, access to these employment opportunities becomes important in areas where commuting distances are lengthy, as in the Washington SMSA.

Finally, urban newcomers are attracted to city neighborhoods because of such traditional amenities of urban life as culture and entertainment. For some there is preference for high-density living and the satisfaction of conserving energy through reliance on public transportation. The city and its attractions are therefore convenient (that is, accessible); and access can be purchased with few of the technological supports necessary for suburban living.

THE NEW PIONEERS: PRIVATE REDEVELOPMENT IN THE DISTRICT

Profiles of individuals and families moving into the District's inner-city neighborhoods confirm the implications of the housing market. Capitol Hill, a deteriorating black slum nearly a generation ago, is among the District's oldest privately rehabilitated neighborhoods. Restoration is almost complete in the area, and fingers of redevelopment extend eastward and southward from the original neighborhood. The new households in the area are overwhelmingly white (94%) and affluent (75% above $25,000 incomes). While couples predominate (55%), there are substantial numbers of single (29%) and mixed-arrangement households (16%). Children are the exception. Nearly half of the new residents are in their early thirties (48%; see Gale, 1976, 1977).

Mount Pleasant, an area east of Rock Creek Park in Northwest Washington, is a relative newcomer to the private redevelopment process and is probably more typical of the newer redevelopment areas than is the more established Capitol Hill neighborhood. While whites predominate among "rehabbers" (77%), the ratio of whites to blacks is closer than in Capitol Hill. Couples (60%) and children (39%) are most characteristic of Mount Pleasant, although the same age group (30-34) accounted for the largest single proportion of newcomers (44%). The major differential occurred in the income category: The majority (55%) of Mount Pleasant newcomers earned less than $25,000 compared with the substantial (75%) proportion of Capitol Hill newcomers who earned more than $25,000. Private rehabilitation, at least in Mount Pleasant, is not necessarily a preserve of the wealthy (Gale, 1976: 1-12, 1977: 1-51). This may be changing, however, since the median price for a home in Mount Pleasant jumped by 27% during 1978 to $79,000 (Washington *Post,* 1979b).

Studies of people who have moved into renovated housing in Philadelphia and New York support the Mount Pleasant findings. In selected Manhattan and Brooklyn neighborhoods, the new residents, on average, were 31 years old, compared with a citywide average of 44; possessed an annual income of $21,781, considerably higher than the city average; and typically had earned at least one college degree (New York *Times,* 1977).

The residential origins of these primarily young householders indicate that both preference and necessity have combined to enhance the prospects of central-city living. In a study conducted by the Center for Municipal and Metropolitan Research (formerly the Washington Center for Metropolitan Studies) on 119,000 mover households in the District from 1970 to 1974, more than half (57%) of the mover households resided in the city prior to their move, while only six percent of all movers came from the Washington-area suburbs. Twenty-nine percent of the movers came from outside the Washington SMSA. Thus, it seems that private neighborhood revitalization in Washington, D.C. is a "stay in the city" rather than a "back to the city" movement (Grier, 1977). The scenario seems to be that of young renters, who probably prefer city living, purchasing their first homes in the District based on this preference plus the difficulty of finding an affordable home in the suburbs.

There is a qualification to this profile, however. In the specific areas of Mount Pleasant and Capitol Hill, most of the newcomers had indeed resided (usually rented) in other city neighborhoods (67% and 71%, respectively). Two-thirds of these movers, however, had grown up in the suburbs, indicating that while the origin of the most recent move was not usually the suburb, at one time there was a move back to the city. It is also apparent that the movement from suburb to city has increased since 1974. In one tract of Capitol Hill, for example, one out of every four newcomers had come from the suburbs (Gale, 1976: 7, 1977: 10).

The situation in other cities supports the back-to-the-city move. In Baltimore, housing administrator Jerry Doctorow has noticed that "older people in the suburbs aren't moving back in. But their children are buying in the city." Similarly, the New York City survey mentioned earlier counted 38% of the movers to renovated housing as suburbanites in their previous residences (New York *Times,* 1977). The question of origin is important to those who wish to see the private rehabilitation movement grow. The suburbs obviously include a significant reservoir of potential home-buyers that city realtors and political leaders are eager to tap, if in fact that reservoir is amenable to their advances. These figures suggest that they are.

DISPLACEMENT

The eagerness of urban economic and political leaders notwithstanding, private neighborhood redevelopment in Washington has generated a vicious side effect: the displacement of hundreds, perhaps thousands, of poor, black households by middle-income black and white newcomers. The extent of displacement can only be inferred from the extent and rapidity of the private redevelopment process. Speculators "case" prospective neighborhoods and offer to purchase properties from the owners. If the owners refuse, then the speculator may attempt a number of devices, including calling in building inspectors who invariably order extensive repairs on the typically decaying buildings. When speculators finally purchase the property, they frequently sell it (often on the same day) to a third party. This process is called "flipping"; often profits exceed 100%. Between October 1972 and September 1974, for example, one out of every five sales of homes in the District involved two or more sales of the same property, 80% within 10 months of each other. For those homeowners or tenants who manage to escape the initial wave of sales, inflated property taxes and higher rents brought on by the rapid increase in property values eventually force displacement (Richards and Rowe, 1977: 54).

The process is very rapid. It amounts to reverse blockbusting. When an area becomes a "hot" market, all properties are sold within two years or less. During that time, one socioeconomic class has totally replaced another—gentrification has occurred (Holman, 1977: 186-194).

The attractions of this "hot" market situation to speculators are apparent from some recent transactions in the Adams-Morgan section of the District, only a mile and a half from the White House. Ontario Road NW has been a particularly active street since early 1976. One speculator, for example, purchased eight single-family homes on the 2700 block for $20,000 each in 1976. The tenants were evicted and the homes boarded up until the following year. Then A&R Realty purchased the homes for $26,000 each. A few weeks later, A&R successfully marketed the homes for $65,000 each. No improvements had been made since the initial sale. Another realty firm, Kichko Associates, purchased 13 deteriorated row houses on Ontario Road and sold them for $80,000 each (New York *Times,* June 5, 1977).

The speculators and redevelopers do play a creative role with respect to the District's aging housing stock. When critics complain of reverse blockbusting, realtors retort: "It's not a choice between houses for poor people and houses for rich people. It's a choice between houses for rich people or no house at all" (Richards and Rowe, 1977: 55). While this statement obviously oversimplifies the process—the majority of new rehabbers in Mount Pleasant, for example, could hardly be termed "rich"—it underscores the importance of saving valuable housing stock when poverty and disinvestment threaten to remove increasing numbers of units from the tax rolls yearly.

Despite the positive elements of neighborhood reinvestment, it is difficult to balance its costs and benefits without knowing more about the extent of displacement. In addition, it is extremely difficult to determine the extent of displacement; it cannot be extrapolated directly from rehabilitation statistics. Abandoned units, for example, are likely rehabilitation candidates and they involve no displacement. In addition, it is necessary to separate those who would have moved from the neighborhood in any case—and 20% of American households move each year—and those who were forced out by the mechanisms of private rehabilitation. A recent study of 15 cities conducted by George and Eunice Grier concluded that private rehabilitation actually affected less than 200 households in each city. They revised their estimate later, however, by admitting that displacement probably involved at least 10 times that number in Washington, D.C. and San Francisco (Sumka, 1978: 134-167). Even without hard data on the extent of displacement, we do know that "this is not a major national phenomenon with huge proportions of the total poverty population being involved" (Washington Post, 1979c).

Knowing the extent of displacement does not fully define the problem, however. It is important to discover the destination of displaced households as well. The quality of the new housing, the extent to which old social ties are maintained or severed, and the proximity of services are some of the variables researchers must consider before defining the parameters of the displacement problem. It is becoming apparent that households displaced by private redevelopment tend to follow similar routes as households displaced by urban renewal a decade or two ago. The recent displaced residents will likely seek accommodation on another street in the neighborhood or in an adjacent area (Holman, 1977: 186-194). The major difference today, however, is that the household displaced by private redevelopment, if relocated in proximity to the old residence, must face the probability of successive displacement (James, 1977: 260). The problem of locating a new residence in the District is compounded by the low vacancy rate, rising assessments, and a rent control law that restricts the profitability of rental properties and encourages condominium conversions. Ironically, at a time of acute housing shortages, the supply of housing for the poor is decreasing.

It is the poor's very limited housing options, not necessarily displacement per se, that is the greatest aftershock of private redevelopment. Gentrification and destruction of housing stock have forced the poor to double- and triple-up in shoddy rooming houses and deteriorating private dwellings. Anacostia, perhaps the last refuge of the displaced poor in Washington, has recently been the subject of major townhouse development designed primarily for middle-class blacks. The suburbs currently offer few options for the poor and have, in fact, like the city, removed low-income housing stock from the market. "Old Town" Alexandria, a low-income black residential neighborhood two decades ago, is now a swank, restored community of well-to-do professionals. Prince George's County, the Maryland suburb with the only significant amount of low-income housing, is recoiling at the prospect of more poor. County Executive Winfield Kelly wanted to "close the county's gates to the poor" (Raspberry, 1978). Race is not necessarily the key to understanding the county's opposition to the further influx of poor households. Residents of a middle-class black development strongly protested plans for a low-income housing site next to their neighborhood (Raspberry, 1978).

The private rehab market in the District annually accommodates 15,000 to 20,000 households just from within the Washington SMSA. Assuming that most of the units that will be on the market were not abandoned when the speculation-rehabilitation cycle began, this could imply a displacement problem greater than earlier estimates. It must be added that we are discussing only that displacement which has occurred as a result of private redevelopment. A recent assessment by the Metropolitan Washington Council of Governments (COG) of the city's urban renewal efforts discovered that between 1974 and 1977 the District's own renewal policies in the downtown areas displaced over 4,000 households, 95% of which were renters. In 1977, 90% of all displaced households were low income. Besides adding to the displacement dilemma, such policies have removed hundreds of already scarce low-income rental units from the market (COG, 1977: 34-41).

Poor residents threatened with displacement have grown increasingly restive, and in some areas a potentially explosive situation exists. Some blacks claim that the private development effort is part of a white plot to regain political power in the city.

Others see it as a return to the early days of federal urban renewal and "black removal." Most threatened black residents, however, do not seem to view the situation in such stark racial terms. They are nonetheless angered, afraid, and occasionally violent. A group of low-income Adams-Morgan residents known as the Adams-Morgan Organization vandalized billboards in the area that announced luxury condominiums and stormed city council meetings to present their demands. Their targets were not the more affluent, predominantly white newcomers, but rather the speculators and the District government which made no effort to relocate or assist the displaced residents (Richards and Rowe, 1977: 56; Smith, 1977).

POLICIES FOR DISPLACEMENT

The perceived inaction of local government raises the question as to the role of government in devising a set of policies to deal with this elusive (but no less "real") problem. The Savannah (or Pittsburgh) Plan may be a promising model in mediating between private redevelopment and displacement. The Savannah Landmark Rehabilitation Project under the leadership of Leopold Adler II has been purchasing properties in the city's historic Victorian District with some federal aid, restoring the dilapidated structures, and renting them back to the original tenants at affordable rents. About half of this District has already undergone the gentrification process, so Adler's efforts are directed at preserving the low-income residents and the properties in the other part of the District (Peirce, 1977b).

Unfortunately, such a policy may be contrary to the dynamics of neighborhood life. Cosmetic and structural changes will do little to alleviate the poverty of the residents, and the neighborhood's market potential will not be enhanced. The commercial components of the neighborhood life will have little sustenance from the residents. Most important, such policies preclude neighborhood change which ultimately may be just as bad for the poor as for the wealthy who hope to purchase and rehabilitate homes in the area. While the policy will slow displacement, it creates a static environment that could, in some instances, perpetuate the patterns of segregation and poverty despite the enhancement of housing stock.

The Neighborhood Housing Services (NHS) program, pioneered in Pittsburgh and now under federal auspices, is another mixed-enterprise approach to neighborhood redevelopment. There is an NHS program already working in Anacostia. The NHS is designed to facilitate loans for and provide financial counseling to low- and moderate-income homeowners in target neighborhoods, including those homeowners who would not ordinarily qualify for conventional loans to renovate their homes (Washington *Post*, 1977d). While the NHS has been a positive element in an otherwise dreary Anacostia housing picture, however, most residents threatened by private development probably are neither homeowners nor qualified applicants for conventional or high-risk loans, nor do they live in neighborhoods appropriate for the NHS program. In fact, all mortgage schemes do not have much relevance for the low-income renter.

The District government acknowledges the mounting displacement problem, but seems reluctant to deal with it for fear of interrupting the private redevelopment of the city's neighborhoods. The government's wariness is understandable considering the widely acknowledged benefits accruing to the city as a result of private neighborhood revitalization. This is especially the case because of Washington's unique tax situation: The federal government accounts for more than one-third of the city's property. Over the past 40 years, taxable property in the District has shrunk by 24%. Not only the federal government, but the expansion of local government, embassies and chanceries for foreign governments, the increased number of streets, and the development of the subway system have served to reduce taxable property.

This tax situation has at least three effects on the urban economy: it has steadily eroded the city's tax base, diminished the already limited amount of land available for private development, and has driven up the price of homes. Local officials faced with these dim prospects have one of two choices: they can continue to raise taxes and thereby effectively make the city less attractive to businesses and residents, or they can limp along on a meager budget and depend on erratic congressional largess (Washington *Post*, 1978b).

In this context, the reluctance of the District government to tamper with the tax windfall that private redevelopment has become is predictable. Local officials are also aware that the revenue benefits from private redevelopment extend beyond the taxes derived from refurbished properties. James Banks, vice president of the Washington Board of Realtors, calculated that the multiplier effect of private redevelopment has created "30 million worth of purchases of services and materials each year and employs in excess of 5,000 persons" (Richards and Rowe, 1977: 55). In turn, of course, these jobs create others, and the ripple of rehabilitation spreads throughout the city's economy.

District officials have considered the displacement problem sporadically since 1976, but their efforts seem to lack impetus. The city council also established a commission in 1977 to devise policies for increasing homeownership among lower-income groups. The commission's report, released in April 1978, suggested the establishment of a loan program to facilitate repairs of deteriorating units. While this idea could help low-income homeowners fend off speculators, it would have little impact on fulfilling the council's original charge to the commission (Washington *Post*, 1978a). In any case, most displaced households are renters. A prohibitive tax on flipping introduced in the city council in 1977 passed in a watered-down version the following year. The legislation, the nation's first tax on real estate speculation, taxes the profits on the sale of residential property held for less than three years that does not comply with the housing code. If the residence is owner-occupied, and if the owner provides a two-year warranty for repairs, the property is exempt from the tax. In practice, owners falling outside the generous exemptions have ignored the law, and city officials complain about the "nightmare" of enforcement (Washington *Post*, 1979d).

The construction of more public housing in the District is another option available to city officials, but there is little enthusiasm for this alternative. Recent court rulings have questioned the legality of public housing units that perpetuate racial and income segregation, as such units constructed in the District invariably would. Also, under the fair-share housing plan drafted by COG, the city has more than its share of public housing. The suburbs are the underachievers with regard to low- and moderate-income housing, and these jurisdictions have demonstrated through zoning mechanisms, citizen pressure, and public pronouncements that residents displaced by private redevelopment in the District will find even fewer options in the suburbs.

Despite this opposition, the suburbs may, in time, hold at least a partial solution to the housing needs of displaced District households. Already, low-income blacks are filtering into Washington's inner suburbs. Prince George's County, Arlington, and Alexandria have the area's fastest-growing black populations. Most of these black newcomers are poor. This may be partially reflected by the 110% increase in aid to families with dependent children (AFDC) in Alexandria since 1973, and corresponding increases in 12% in Arlington and 42.5% in Fairfax County (Washington *Post*, 1977c).

Recent demographic data support these assumptions. In 1978, despite a decline in the District's total population, there was both a numerical and a percentage increase in the city's white residents (Jacob, 1979). This is evidence of the impact of private neighborhood redevelopment on the city's demographic structure.

The influx of poor blacks, displaced by private redevelopment, into the suburbs may be even greater in the future if HUD maintains its resolve to tie community development block grants to construction of low- and moderate-income housing in jurisdictions (that is, suburbs) where such units are uncommon. A recent decision in Fairfax County demonstrates the implications of such a policy. That wealthy northern Virginia suburb rejected the construction of a 100-unit subsidized housing project where 30% of the tenants would be low income. HUD threatened to withhold the county's block grant funds unless the county approved the project. Fairfax, faced with losing $3.7 million in federal funds or gaining 30 low-income families, chose the latter course and received the funds (Washington *Post,* 1977b, 1978). In short, federal policy may be a partial answer to the displacement problem in the future.

Private neighborhood redevelopment and the ensuing displacement of poor households can therefore have a significant impact on the area's future economy and demography. Robert Linowes, President of the Metropolitan Washington Board of Trade, depicts this future with obvious relish. He foresees the District as "solidly middle and upper class [and] racially balanced, . . . with the poor having been pushed to the suburbs" (Washington *Post,* 1978c). It is this vision that compels the reticence of the District government, the enthusiasm of the realtors, and the decisions of young middle-income singles and couples to become property-holders in central-city neighborhoods. Federal policy, apparently, will support this trend as well. For displaced households and some suburbs the vision is more like a frightening specter. They may wonder if this price for urban revitalization is worth paying.

It is possible that Washington's unique economic and demographic base intensifies the private redevelopment and displacement phenomena. Yet, it may also be that the situation in Washington may portend a national movement of extensive private neighborhood redevelopment and the accompanying displacement of low-income households. High-status employment, the extensive single population, and the extremely low vacancy rate are unique to Washington only in degree. Cities such as Boston, Chicago, and San Francisco have significant professional and administrative employment bases, and strong residential redevelopment markets as well. The trend toward smaller households, especially single-person households, is a nationwide phenomenon. Finally, although Washington's estimated vacancy rate is probably the lowest in the country, housing markets in Boston and San Francisco are almost as tight. It would not be the first time the Washington area has pioneered national economic and demographic movements. In the late

1950s and 1960s, Washington's suburbs led the nation in growth and affluence. Washington, D.C. was the first major city to have a majority of black residents. As urban analyst George Grier observed, the Washington area is a "leading indicator" of trends that will develop later in other regions (Washington *Post,* 1975).

In fact, private redevelopment, gentrification, and the possibility of displacement are common in many of the western world's major postindustrial cities. The situation of neighborhood dominoes in London, for example, rivals the pace of redevelopment in Washington. In the Birka district of central Stockholm, working-class residents comprised roughly three-quarters of the area's 6,000 residents fifteen years ago. Today, three-quarters of the population are white-collar—a trend becoming more common throughout the city. Both London and Stockholm have strong administrative and professional employment sectors, low vacancy rates, and a high proportion of single-person households. In some Stockholm neighborhoods, for example, two out of every three households is a single-person household (Stockholms Stads Statistiska Kontor, 1978: 215).

Research on private redevelopment in an international context could be helpful in coping with its domestic consequences. The objective, as Donna Shalala stated, is "to strengthen the tax base of the city and simultaneously protect poor people" (Washington *Post,* 1979c). This balance has not been achieved in Washington. In Stockholm, rent subsidies encourage private rehabilitation while limiting gentrification (Miller and Ahlgren, 1975; Roselius, 1979). Some Housing Action Areas in London are experimenting with subsidies to enable residents to purchase their dwellings as a hedge against speculative redevelopment (Scott, 1979). In Bologna, Italy, the Communist-controlled local government has avoided the inequities that private redevelopment has caused in Rome by renovating inner-city housing and maintaining the original residents at the old rents (Appleyard, 1975: 13-19). While all of these measures result in the improvement of the inner-city housing stock, they are all very expensive and, except for some instances in Stockholm, they have not resulted in a class, age, or income mix. The strategies do indicate a growing worldwide concern that the poor have a place in inner-city life and that equity is as appropriate as economic base in the consideration of public policy.

REFERENCES

APPLEYARD, D. (1975) "Introduction," pp. 4-43 in D. Appleyard (ed.) Urban Conservation in Europe and America. Rome: Fulbright Commission.
BLACK, T. J. (1975) "Private market housing renovation in central cities: a ULI Survey." Urban Land (November): 3-9.
COG [Metropolitan Washington Council of Governments] (1977) Residential Displacement in the Washington Metropolitan Area. Washington, DC.
DANIEL, E. C. (1977) "Housing is now beyond the reach of average family." J. of Housing (March): 130-131.
District of Columbia, Office of Planning and Development (1979) Provisional Population Estimates. Washington, DC: Office of Planning and Development.
GALE, D. (1977) The Back-to-the-City Movement Revisited. Washington, DC: George Washington University.
——— (1976) The Back-to-the-City Movement . . . or is it? Washington, DC: George Washington University.
GOLDFIELD, D. R. (1976) "The limits of suburban growth: the Washington, D.C. SMSA." Urban Affairs Q. 12 (September): 76-86.
GRIER, G. (1977) Movers to the City: New Data on the Housing Market for Washington, D.C. Washington, DC: Washington Center for Metropolitan Studies.
HOLMAN, C. (1977) Prepared Statement of Carl Holman, President, National Urban Coalition, Neighborhood Diversity. Hearing before U.S. Senate Committee on Banking, Housing, and Urban Affairs, 95th Congress, 1st session. Washington, DC: U.S. Government Printing Office.
JACOB, J. E. (1979) "The District: white in-migration, black exodus." Washington Post (May 2).
JAMES, F. J. (1977) Back to the City: An Appraisal of Housing Reinvestment and Population Change in Urban America. Washington, DC: The Urban Institute.
LIPTON, S. G. (1977) "Evidence of central city revival." J. of the American Institute of Planners 43 (April): 140-152.
MILLER, T. and B. AHLGREN (1975) "Conflict and participation in a renewal process in Stockholm: Birka," pp. 197-213 in D. Appleyard (ed.) Urban Conservation in Europe and America. Rome: Fulbright Commission.
New York Times (1977) "As housing prices rise, so do city renovations." (April 20)
PEIRCE, N. R. (1977a) "Savannah's human-scale renewal plan." Washington Post (November 22).
——— (1977b) "Cities make a comeback." Washington Post (July 7).
RASPBERRY, W. (1978) "Don't want no poor people 'round here." Washington Post (March 20).
RICHARDS, C. and J. ROWE (1977) "Restoring the city: who pays the price?" Working Papers for a New Society 4 (Winter): 54-60.

ROSELIUS, M. (1979) Interview at Regionplanekontoret. Stockholm (June 3).
SCOTT, M. (1979) Interview of Housing Action Area Director. London (August 16).
SMITH, F. (1977) Re-investment in Adams-Morgan. Washington, DC: AMO.
Stockholms Stads Statistiska Kontor (1978) Statistisk Årsbok för Stockholms Stad, 1977. Stockholm, SSK.
SUMKA, H. J. (1978) "Displacement in revitalizing neighborhoods: a review and research strategy." Occasional Papers in Housing and Community Affairs. Washington, DC: U.S. Department of Housing and Urban Development.
Washington Post (1979a) "Housing market throbbing despite 18% price boosts." (May 5)
——— (1979b) "Ten more D.C. neighborhoods move into $100,000 league." (February 17)
——— (1979c) "HUD finds little displacement of poor in inner city revivals." (February 14)
——— (1979d) "D.C. speculators' tax: few comply, fewer pay." (February 12)
——— (1978a) "New plan urged to aid district neighborhoods." (April 18)
——— (1978b) "Taxable property in district shrinks." (April 17)
——— (1978c) "New kind of city emerges out of ruins of '68 riot." (April 2)
——— (1978d) "600 compete to buy 12 homes." (March 22)
——— (1977a) "The all-night town house vigil." (November 23)
——— (1977b) "Fairfax lifts homes plan opposition: federal pressure aids rolling road public project." (November 22)
——— (1977c) "Families getting welfare rise 110% in Alexandria." (October 30)
——— (1977d) "Help for houses." (October 24)
——— (1975) "Surveying D.C.'s economy at a crossroads." (July 20)

David R. Goldfield is currently Fulbright-Hays Visiting Senior Lecturer at Stockholm University where he is pursuing research in comparative neighborhood redevelopment strategies. Dr. Goldfield's regular appointment is as Associate Professor of Environmental and Urban Systems, Virginia Polytechnic Institute and State University. His most recent book is Urban America: From Downtown to No Town *(Boston: Houghton Mifflin, 1979).*

36

PRICE INCREASES CAUSED BY HOUSING ASSISTANCE PROGRAMS

C. Peter Rydell, John E. Mulford, and Lawrence Helbers

SUMMARY

A major criticism of federal subsidies to privately owned housing for low-income households is that the subsidy accrues to landlords through price increases, rather than to tenants through increased housing consumption or reduced rent burdens. Two contrasting methods of subsidizing existing housing are "housing allowances," which rely on the discipline of the market to control price increases, and "Section 8 assistance" provided by Section 8 of the Housing and Community Development Act of 1974, which uses institutional regulations to control price increases. Contrary to preprogram predictions, evidence from actual program operations shows that the market outperforms regulation. Housing allowances cause a 1.2 percent increase, while Section 8 assistance causes a 26 percent increase, in the price participants pay for housing services. The housing allowance program shows how the Section 8 program could be revised to prevent the price increases: by restructuring the subsidy formula so that tenants pay the marginal rent dollar; by paying the subsidy directly to tenants so they know they are paying the marginal rent dollar; and by removing the rent ceiling so it can no longer act as a rent target. Restructuring the subsidy formula is the key change, because it alone would probably prevent most price increases.

From C. Peter Rydell et al., *Price Increases Caused by Housing Assistance Programs,* Rand Corporation publication R-2677-HUD (October 1980). Reprinted by permission of the Rand Corporation.

I. INTRODUCTION

Federal assistance to low-income housing used to be targeted primarily toward subsidizing construction and substantial rehabilitation. In the last decade, however, its application has shifted toward greater support of privately owned existing rental housing.[1] The purpose of the revised strategy is to distribute available funds more equitably, providing standard housing to many eligible households instead of above-standard housing to only a few households.

The government first displayed expanded interest in existing housing when it authorized the Experimental Housing Allowance Program (EHAP) through the Housing and Urban Development Act of 1970. Four years later, Section 8 of the Housing and Community Development Act of 1974 created a national program of similar intent.

One major criticism of the new approach focused on the expectation that the subsidies would benefit landlords through increased rents, rather than tenants by way of better housing and lower rent burdens.[2] Fears of rent inflation led the U.S. Department of Housing and Urban Development to sponsor preprogram studies to predict results before the actual effects of either program were observed. HUD also sponsored the Housing Assistance Supply Experiment as a part of EHAP to monitor rents under a full-scale housing allowance program, and established a project to evaluate the Section 8 Existing Housing Assistance Program on a nationwide scale for the same purpose.

This report compares the price increases attributable to the housing allowance and Section 8 programs in 1976. Comparable data exist only for that year. However, the housing allowance program has not changed since then, and the Section 8 program has changed only in minor ways (noted in the text), so the report's conclusions are not limited to that year. The report finds that differences in the two programs' rules caused markedly different price increases. Further, its findings strongly contradict the predictions of preprogram analytical studies.

DIFFERENCES BETWEEN HOUSING ALLOWANCES AND SECTION 8 ASSISTANCE

The two current methods of subsidizing existing privately owned housing address the rent inflation problem in radically different ways. The housing allowance program, currently subsidizing over 9,000 households in two north central metropolitan areas,[3] depends upon the

---

[1] In 1970 only 5 percent of subsidized rental units for low-income households were privately owned existing units not previously rehabilitated. By 1977 the percentage had risen to 25 percent. Of the 650,000 additional units subsidized between 1970 and 1977, 52 percent were privately owned existing housing. See *HUD Statistical Yearbook* (1971), Table 149; and (1977), Tables H85 and H125.

[2] Barnett and Lowry (1979) document the inflation concerns that housing policymakers and analysts expressed in the early 1970s, and review the assumptions underlying those concerns.

[3] Brown County, Wisconsin, containing the city of Green Bay, and St. Joseph County, Indiana, containing the city of South Bend, are served by the Housing Assistance Supply Experiment (HASE). Individuals in other cities were given housing allowances by the now completed Housing Allowance Demand Experiment (HADE) and Administrative Agency Experiment (AAE), although only the HASE counties received full-scale housing allowance programs. The three experiments together constitute the Experimental Housing Assistance Program (EHAP). Allowances began in 1974 for Brown County and in 1975 for St. Joseph County. They are funded by a ten-year annual contributions contract between HUD and the public housing authority in each location. The *Fourth Annual Report of the Housing Assistance Supply Experiment* (1978) reviews the Supply Experiment's purposes, scope, and preliminary conclusions. The count of 9,000 households was reached in February 1979.

discipline of the market to prevent price increases. The Section 8 Existing Housing Assistance Program, currently subsidizing over 520,000 renter households nationwide,[4] depends on institutional regulation to combat price increases. This report compares the effects of the housing allowance and Section 8 programs on prices of existing rental housing. The HASE housing allowance program also assists owner-occupied housing and other parts of the Section 8 program assist new construction and major rehabilitation. Zais, Goedert, and Trutko (1979, pp. 55-58) exhaustively compare the two programs. Table 1 outlines the specific differences relevant to this discussion.

Table 1

COMPARISON OF THE HOUSING ALLOWANCE
AND SECTION 8 PROGRAMS

Item	Housing Allowance Program	Section 8 Existing Housing Assistance Program
Subsidy	$S - .25Y$	$R - .25Y + (S - R)(.25Y/S)$
Payment	To tenant	To landlord
Maximum rent	No maximum	S

SOURCE: James P. Zais, Jeanne E. Goedert, and John W. Trutko, *Modifying Section 8: Implications from Experiments with Housing Allowances*, The Urban Institute, Washington, D.C., UI-240-10, January 1979, pp. 55-58.

NOTE: R = total actual rent, Y = adjusted gross household income, S = standard cost of adequate housing (denoted by R^* or C^* in the housing allowance program and by FMR, for "Fair Market Rent," in the Section 8 program).

In the housing allowance program, recipients get the difference between the standard cost of adequate housing[5] and one-fourth of their adjusted income. The housing allowance office pays the subsidy to the tenant, and the tenant pays the full rent to the landlord. Recipients can live in any unit that meets program standards.

In the Section 8 Existing Housing Assistance Program, recipients get the difference between the actual rent of their unit and one-fourth[6] of their adjusted income, plus a "Rent

---

[4]The Section 8 Existing Housing Assistance Program began in 1974 and is still expanding. The count of 520,000 units was reached in February 1979 (*Housing and Community Development Reporter*, 30 April 1979, p. 1094).

[5]"Adequate housing" is a dwelling that passes periodic evaluations by the housing allowance office to determine spaciousness, presence of essential facilities in good working order, and absence of hazards to health or safety. The specific standards were adapted from American Public Health Association standards and Building Officials and Code Administrators' model codes. "Standard costs" are estimates of the typical full market price of rental dwellings that meet the standards. The estimates are based on periodic surveys of local housing markets.

[6]For certain families (those very large in size or with very low incomes or exceptional medical expenses) the household contributed 15 percent instead of 25 percent (Zais, Goedert, and Trutko, 1979, p. 58). In October 1980 the minimum household contribution was raised from 15 to 20 percent (*Federal Register*, 1980, pp. 59309-59310).

Reduction Credit" if the actual rent is less than an administratively set rent ceiling called "Fair Market Rent" (see Table 1). The local public housing authority administering the Section 8 program pays the subsidy directly to the landlord and the tenant pays the landlord only the unsubsidized portion of rent. Recipients must live in a unit that not only meets program standards but whose rent is also no greater than the Fair Market Rent ceiling.[7]

In the housing allowance program, the rent does not affect the subsidy that the tenant receives.[8] If rent goes up a dollar, the subsidy remains unchanged. In other words, tenants pay the marginal rent dollar. Consequently, the usual market process of tenants bargaining with landlords determines rents.

In contrast, in the Section 8 program rent always affects the subsidy. If rent goes up a dollar, the subsidy increases by up to a dollar. Tenants pay only part of the marginal rent dollar; the public housing authority pays the rest.[9]

Consequently, the usual market process of tenants bargaining with landlords does not determine rents in the Section 8 program. Rather, institutional regulation of the negotiation between tenants and landlords determines rents. The process has three steps:[10] First, a tenant who has been certified to receive assistance has 60 days to find an acceptable unit. Second, the tenant and landlord submit the rent they have negotiated, together with a description of the unit, to the public housing authority for approval. Finally, the public housing authority must find the proposed rent "reasonable"[11] before it executes a Housing Assistance Payment (HAP) contract with the landlord for the subsidy it will pay on the unit.

The rent standards adopted by the two programs (HASE standard cost and Section 8 Fair Market Rent) have similar definitions. Both are "typical" costs of housing that meets the minimum requirements set by the assistance programs. Table 2 compares the two sets of rent standards (in the Brown and St. Joseph counties' housing markets in 1976) and shows that they are approximately the same.

However, the two programs use the rent standards very differently, and that use is the key to the different price impacts of the programs. The housing allowance program uses the standard cost of adequate housing to establish subsidy levels. Only indirectly, via increased housing consumption, does the standard cost affect program rents. In contrast, the Section 8 program uses the Fair Market Rent to establish permitted rent levels. Only indirectly, via the influence on housing prices, does the Fair Market Rent affect subsidy levels.

PREPROGRAM PREDICTIONS OF PRICE IMPACTS

The most comparable and carefully documented of the preprogram studies were carried out by The Urban Institute. For housing allowances, they concluded: "In seven of the eight cases

---

[7] In special cases units renting for 10 percent more than the Fair Market Rent may join the Section 8 program. See Drury, Lee, Springer, and Yap (1978), p. 29.

[8] Occasionally rent does affect the amount of the subsidy in the housing allowance program via a program rule requiring that the subsidy not exceed the rent. Less than 4 percent of the housing allowance program recipients are affected by this restriction.

[9] However, most tenants did not understand the Rent Reduction Credit. They believed that the public housing authority pays all of the marginal rent dollar. In October 1980, HUD eliminated the Rent Reduction Credit because a nationwide survey showed that no more than 14 percent of the tenants understood it (*Federal Register*, 1980, pp. 59308-59309). The public housing authority now pays the entire marginal rent dollar.

[10] Greenston, James, Yap, and Sadacca (1977), p. 8.

[11] The public housing authority must certify on a case-by-case basis that the rent being approved is reasonable in relation to comparable units in the private market and not in excess of rents being charged by the owner for similar units on the same property (*Public Housing Agency Administrative Practices Handbook for the Section 8 Existing Housing Program*, 1979, p. 6-9).

Table 2

RENT STANDARDS IN HOUSING ASSISTANCE PROGRAMS, 1976

Size of Unit (bedrooms)	Monthly Amount ($) per Housing Unit	
	Housing Allowance Program	Section 8 Existing Housing Program
Brown County, Wisconsin		
0	125	114
1	145	131
2	175	155
3	195	180
4	210	196
St. Joseph County, Indiana		
0	115	130
1	140	149
2	160	177
3	175	205
4	185	225

SOURCE: *Fifth Annual Report of the Housing Assistance Supply Experiment*, The Rand Corporation, R-2434-HUD, June 1979, p. 22; and *Federal Register*, Vol. 41, No. 1, 29 March 1976, p. 13042.

NOTE: In descriptions of the housing allowance program the rent standard is denoted by R^* or C^*, in descriptions of the Section 8 program it is denoted by FMR (for "Fair Market Rent"). The Section 8 program's rent standard also varies by the presence or absence of elevators, but since there are few elevator buildings in these housing markets, only the rent standards for non-elevator buildings are given in the table.

(simulations) . . . housing prices for recipients of the housing allowance rise. They rise by more than 10 percent in five of the eight cases. . . . The three cases in which prices rise by less than 10 percent are elastic supply cases, and the supply parameters in these cases are more conducive to an allowance without inflationary impacts than any of our empirical results suggest. The results thus do confirm the fear that a large-scale allowance program carries the danger of upward pressure on prices . . ." (de Leeuw and Struyk, 1975, p. 131).

For Section 8 assistance, they concluded that ". . . even a large-scale Section 8 program will, in general, cause only small market disruptions" (Struyk, Marshall, and Ozanne, 1978, p. 90). Only two out of their fifteen simulations of the Section 8 Existing Housing Assistance Program predicted price increases over 10 percent; and the average price increase forecast for recipients across all simulations was only 3.4 percent.[12]

However, we are no longer dependent on preprogram predictions. Actual operation of the programs now provides a clear-cut comparison of the discipline of the market vs. institutional regulation.

---

[12]Struyk, Marshall, and Ozanne (1978), p. 136. The predicted price effects are the ratio of the price indexes of estimated participant rents in the Section 8 Existing Housing Program to their rents before the program.

II. MARKET VS. REGULATION

The market wins handsomely over regulation in this instance: Housing allowances cause a short-run price inflation of no more than 1.2 percent, while Section 8 assistance causes 26 percent. Both numbers are average rent increases experienced upon joining the program by recipients who had not moved and whose dwellings did not require repairs to meet program standards. The first number comes from the Housing Assistance Supply Experiment, the second number comes from the nationwide evaluation of the Section 8 Existing Housing Assistance Program (see Table 3).

The "no-move, no repair" situation provides the sharpest possible evidence of price increases because the quantity of housing remains constant. The tenant does not move, but simply joins the program. The housing unit does not change because no repairs are needed to meet program standards. The entire rent increase is a price increase.

Table 3

AVERAGE PERCENTAGE RENT INCREASES UPON JOINING
A HOUSING ASSISTANCE PROGRAM

Situation	Housing Allowance Program			Section 8 Existing Housing Assistance Program
	Brown County	St. Joseph County	Average	
No move, no repair	1.6	.7	1.2	26
No move, repair	2.5	1.7	2.1	32
Move	34.0	45.0	40.0	71

SOURCE: Housing Allowance Program records for Brown and St. Joseph counties; Margaret Drury, Olsen Lee, Michael Springer, and Lorene Yap, *Lower Income Housing Assistance Program (Section 8): National Evaluation of the Existing Housing Program*, Office of Policy Development and Research, U.S. Department of Housing and Urban Development, Washington, D.C., November 1978, p. 66; and Lorene Yap, Peter Greenston, and Robert Sadacca, *Lower Income Housing Assistance Program (Section 8): National Evaluation of the Existing Housing Program--Technical Supplement*, Office of Policy Development and Research, U.S. Department of Housing and Urban Development, Washington, D.C., November 1978, p. 87.

NOTE: The table reports the percentage change from average preprogram gross rent (contract rent plus direct tenant payments for utilities) to average program gross rent. "No move" households did not change units when joining the program, and "no repair" units did not require repairs to meet program standards.

The other two situations in Table 3 provide less direct evidence because the quantity of housing does not remain constant. Housing consumption increases when households repair their units to meet the program's health and safety standards and it increases when they change units to meet the program's space standards. The rise in consumption accounts for some, possibly all, of the rent increase, obscuring any increase due to price alone. However, if we assume that the consumption increases are approximately the same in both programs, then we can determine the differential price increase caused by the programs. Note that the Section 8 rent increase exceeds the housing allowance rent increase by 29.9 percent in the repair situation and 31.0 percent in the move situation. Those differences are roughly of the same magnitude as the 24.8 percent gap in the no-repair situation, suggesting that the differential price increase caused by the Section 8 program is similar in all three situations.

DOES SECTION 8 CAUSE PRICE INCREASES?

The evidence in Table 3 establishes that substantial price increases occurred in the Section 8 program. However, that does not necessarily mean that the program caused the price increases.

Olsen and Reeder (1980) suggest that the differential price inflation under the program is caused by market forces removing price discounts, rather than the Section 8 program itself. Their argument has four steps: (a) At any given time in a housing market some units are underpriced and others are overpriced relative to the marketwide average. (b) The rent ceiling provision leads to a larger proportion of underpriced units joining the Section 8 program than the housing allowance program. (c) As new leases are signed (a requirement for joining either program) the rent of underpriced units goes up more than overpriced units. (d) Consequently, the Section 8 program has larger average price increases than the housing allowance program.

If the removal of price discounts were a major cause of the observed price increases, controlling for preprogram rent levels would show the percentage increases as similar. However, the increases categorized by level of preprogram rent are dramatically different.

Section 8's rent ceiling screens the units admitted to the program by allowing only those units whose preprogram rents are less than that amount to join. Consequently the preprogram rent of those units tends to be lower on average than those of units in the housing allowance program. For example, of the households receiving assistance who neither moved nor repaired, over 14 percent in the Section 8 program but less than 1 percent in the housing allowance program occupied units whose preprogram rents were below $50 per month (see Table 4).

Some of the low preprogram rents in both programs were due to price discounts (provided, for example, as private charity to relatives or elderly households).[1] In those cases, landlords might have raised rents to the market level when housing assistance became available to the tenants. However, most low rents presumably reflect the housing unit's quality relative to the rest of the market rather than landlord benevolence.

Whatever the reason for some very low preprogram rents, they were affected differently by the housing allowance and Section 8 programs. Table 5 shows that preprogram rents below $50 per month rose by an average of 11 percent under the allowance program and 267 percent

---

[1]About 9 percent of renters in the housing allowance program reported that they paid less than "full rent" before joining the program. Comparable information is not available for recipients of Section 8 assistance, but the screening argument suggests the Section 8 percentage is higher. By "price discounts" we mean both voluntary underpricing (landlords giving low rent to favored tenants) and involuntary underpricing (landlords setting rent below that of comparable units due to market imperfections).

Table 4

PERCENTAGE DISTRIBUTION BY PREPROGRAM RENT: NO-MOVE, NO-REPAIR UNITS

Preprogram Rent ($/Unit/Mo)	Housing Allowance Program			Section 8 Existing Housing Assistance Program
	Brown County	St. Joseph County	Average	
5-50	.9	.4	.7	14.4
51-150	35.9	50.7	43.3	43.1
More than 150	63.2	48.9	56.0	42.5
All rents	100.0	100.0	100.0	100.0

SOURCE: Housing Allowance Program records for Brown and St. Joseph counties; distribution calculated from information published in Margaret Drury, Olsen Lee, Michael Springer, and Lorene Yap, *Lower Income Housing Assistance Program (Section 8): National Evaluation of the Existing Housing Program*, Office of Policy Development and Research, U.S. Department of Housing and Urban Development, Washington, D.C., November 1978, p. 66; see Appendix B of this report.

under the Section 8 program. For preprogram rents between $51 and $150, the corresponding increases were 3 and 33 percent. Only preprogram rents which exceeded $150 received small increases in both programs.

Even if the housing allowance program had the same distribution of units by preprogram rents as the Section 8 program, the average rent increase under HASE would have been only 0.9 percent more than it was. Weighting the housing allowance program's rent increases according to that program's distribution of units shows an average rent increase of 1.2 percent (see Table 3). Weighting the same rent increases by the Section 8 program's distribution of units[2] yields an average increase of 2.1 percent. Consequently only 0.9 percent of the 24.8 percentage point gap between the price increases under the two programs can be attributed to the different mixtures of units the programs serve.

Only a very small part of the differential price increase under Section 8 is explained by market forces; the bulk of the increase must therefore be due to nonmarket forces—that is, to the program's regulations.

---

[2]It is also necessary, of course, to weight by the average preprogram rent in each preprogram rent category. The overall average rent increase equals

$$\sum_i n_i r_i f_i / \sum_i r_i f_i$$

where n_i is the average rent increase in category i, r_i is the average preprogram rent in category i, and f_i is the fraction of units in category i. The average preprogram rents in the three program rent categories for no-move, no-repair units in the housing allowance program were 43, 120, and 193 (see Tables B.1 and B.2 in Appendix B).

Table 5

AVERAGE PERCENTAGE RENT INCREASES BY PREPROGRAM RENT:
NO-MOVE, NO-REPAIR UNITS

Preprogram Rent ($/Unit/Mo)	Housing Allowance Program			Section 8 Existing Housing Assistance Program
	Brown County	St. Joseph County	Average	
5-50	9.6	11.9	10.8	267
51-150	3.4	1.5	2.5	33
More than 150	1.0	.1	.6	4
All rents	1.6	.7	1.2	26

SOURCE: Housing Allowance Program records for Brown and St. Joseph counties; and Margaret Drury, Olsen Lee, Michael Springer, and Lorene Yap, *Lower Income Housing Assistance Program (Section 8): National Evaluation of the Existing Housing Program*, Office of Policy Development and Research, U.S. Department of Housing and Urban Development, Washington, D.C., November 1978, p. 66.

ARE THE SECTION 8 PRICE INCREASES UNDESIRABLE?

Before either the housing allowance or the Section 8 programs had begun, there was wide agreement that program-induced price increases, if they occurred, would be extremely undesirable. The reason is that price increases divert subsidy dollars from their intended recipients—households with certified low incomes—to landlords. Moreover, the percentage of the subsidy that goes to the landlord is larger than the percentage increase in rent. For example, the average preprogram rent of Section 8 units is about $135, while the average subsidy per unit is $103. A 26 percent price increase means a rent increase of $35, which is 34 percent of the subsidy. The one-fourth price increase causes one-third of the subsidy to be diverted to landlords.

Nevertheless, after program experience showed that the Section 8 program caused a 26 percent price increase, some commentators offered reasons why the price increase might not be bad, after all. Drury et al. (1978, p. 65) suggest that additional services might be provided in the future in return for the price increases: "Though the initial upgrading of the low-income housing stock appears to be modest, future maintenance levels may be higher as a result of increased rents coupled with the change in the tenant-landlord relationship instilled by the program, and the oversight of the local PHA." Olsen and Rasmussen (1979, pp. 18-19) suggest that in spite of the price increases, "... the initial evidence suggests that Section 8 rents are reasonable for the quality of housing received ... there is little reason to expect Section 8 Existing units to rent for much more than comparable unsubsidized units." The argument, as elaborated by Olsen and Reeder (1980), is that the preprogram prices of units entering the Section 8 program may have been sufficiently below the marketwide average for program prices to be reasonable even after the 26 percent price increase.

However, neither of these arguments justifies the Section 8 rent increases. The Drury argument does not justify them because improved maintenance levels in the future, when and if they occur, only justify future price increases, not those of the present or past. The Olsen argument does not justify the increases because, however reasonable Section 8 rents are, they would have been more reasonable if the price increases had not occurred. A price increase is a price increase whether it starts from a low or a high level, and any price increase causes subsidy diversion.

WHY SECTION 8 CAUSES PRICE INCREASES

The Section 8 program causes price increases because it removes the tenants' incentive to bargain with landlords for market rents. Section 8 tenants know that they will pay no more than one-fourth of their income to the landlord, no matter how high the rent. They also know that the higher the rent, the greater the chance that the landlord will agree to join the Section 8 program. Consequently, the tenant-landlord interaction provides little restraint on Section 8 rent increases.[3]

The Section 8 program attempted to preserve the tenants' incentive to bargain for market rents by offering them a "Rent Reduction Credit." The credit reduced the tenant's rent payment by a fraction of the difference between actual gross rent and the official Fair Market Rent figure (see Appendix A).

However, the Rent Reduction Credit failed to restrain rent increases for three reasons. First, it was not adequately explained to tenants; although 46 percent of participating families received credits, only 14 percent understood the credit system (*Housing and Community Development Reporter*, 20 August 1979, p. 260). Second, it gave tenants too small a share of the rent saving (an average of only 40 percent) to motivate hard bargaining. Third, it gave the smallest shares of the rent saving to tenants with the lowest incomes, whose increases were therefore likely to be largest.[4] The nationwide evaluation of the Section 8 program concluded: "The Rent Reduction Credit has not functioned as planned. Very few certificate holders . . . made a specific effort to lower rents, and participants' understanding of it . . . was found to be very limited . . ." (Drury et al., 1978, p. 39).

With tenants indifferent to the rent charged, landlords are free to seek the maximum rent allowed by the local public housing authority. Moreover, the landlord knows the exact maximum rent allowed for a particular dwelling because the Fair Market Rent schedules are publicly available.[5]

Comparing the preprogram rents that rose by large amounts with the Fair Market Rent levels reported in Table 2 reveals that the larger the gap between preprogram rent and Fair Market Rent, the larger the Section 8 rent increases. Apparently, the Fair Market Rent acts as a rent ceiling only for landlords deciding what units they want subsidized by the Section

---

[3]The theoretical objection that an economically rational Section 8 household would simply move to a housing unit worth the Fair Market Rent overlooks the high cost of searching for any type of housing unit, let alone one that is exactly worth a given rent.
[4]See Appendix A for a detailed discussion of the three reasons.
[5]The Fair Market Rent for the unit size that fits a family's space requirements is written on the Certificate of Family Participation that tenants carry to prove they are eligible for Section 8 assistance (see Appendix A). Tenants almost certainly show that certificate to prospective landlords, but should they not do so the Fair Market Rent schedule is available from the housing authority and is also published in the *Federal Register*.

8 program. For units that are approved for the program, the Fair Market Rent becomes a target, rather than a ceiling.[6]

Nevertheless, the Section 8 program's encouragement of landlords to treat the rent ceiling as a target figure does not necessarily explain the program's rent increases. If the ceiling is truly a "fair market" price, why should preprogram rents differ from it? One explanation is that administrative formulas can state market rents correctly on average, but do not necessarily do so in specific cases.

The Section 8 program's Fair Market Rent for a given year and geographic area depends only on the number of bedrooms in a housing unit and whether it is in an elevator building. The Fair Market Rent does not depend upon the unit's quality (except that it must pass the program's minimum standards to be approved for the program). Landlords with high quality units whose rents exceed Fair Market Rent do not join the Section 8 program, because they can do better in the open market. However, landlords whose units are in poor enough condition for their market rents to be below Fair Market Rent (though good enough to meet minimum standards) will readily join the program because they can then raise those rents. The nationwide evaluation showed that 63.8 percent of program rents exceeded 90 percent of Fair Market Rent. Moreover, the reason given by 37.4 percent of landlords for their rent increases was "meeting the Fair Market Rent" (Yap, Greenston, and Sadacca, 1978, pp. 93 and 105).

The designers of the Section 8 program foresaw the possibility that the Fair Market Rent might become a rent target rather than a ceiling. To counter it, they required local public housing authorities to check for "rent reasonableness" as well as whether the rent was below the program's rent ceiling. However, in practice, the public housing authorities had great difficulties in defining and enforcing the rent reasonableness criterion.[7] In fact, they did not even always find it possible to require the clear-cut Fair Market Rent ceiling: 16.2 percent of program rents exceeded the ceiling (Yap et al., 1978, p. 105).

In a 1979 audit, HUD's Office of Inspector General found that at "21 percent of the projects reviewed, the PHAs did not make rent reasonableness determinations prior to approving the project rents . . . at 18 percent of the projects reviewed, PHAs allowed project rents to exceed the published Fair Market Rent limitations . . . at 6 percent of the projects reviewed, PHAs automatically increased rents *without* owner requests for rent increases . . . [and] at 4 percent of the projects reviewed, PHAs allowed owners to charge more rent for subsidized units than for similar unsubsidized units" (*Report on Special Operational Survey, Section 8*, 1979, p. 20). The nationwide review of the Section 8 program concluded: "It is highly unlikely that the rent reasonableness test has had a large effect on the units subsidized" (Drury et al., 1978, p. 38). Subsequent to the nationwide evaluation, a notice from HUD instructed local public housing authorities to exercise more care in determining rent reasonableness. Specifically, rent increases of over 10 percent must now be "fully documented" (*Housing and Community Development Reporter*, 9 February 1979, p. 897). There is as yet no evidence on how much the documentation requirement stiffens the rent reasonableness constraint on rent increases.

In short, implicit bargaining between the landlord and the local public housing authority establishes rents in the Section 8 program, and the landlord comes out ahead in that bargaining process. The only restriction on rent increases is the Fair Market Rent ceiling, but that constraint actually turns out to cause price increases by acting as a rent target for landlords

---

[6]Appendix A shows how HUD regulations signal the landlord that rent increases up to the Fair Market Rent ceiling are acceptable. Appendix C shows that the tendency of landlords to raise prices toward the FMR ceiling remained consistent from 1976 to 1979.

[7]Under Section 8, the public housing authorities apply to HUD for a specific number of housing units by type (Greenston et al., 1977, p. 40). This procedure provides no incentive for them to strictly enforce the rent reasonableness criterion because economizing provides no additional units.

who join the program. Landlords whose preprogram rents exceed the ceiling tend not to join the program, and landlords whose preprogram rents are less than the ceiling tend to join the program and raise their rents toward the maximum allowed.

WHY HOUSING ALLOWANCES DO NOT CAUSE PRICE INCREASES

The housing allowance program does not cause price increases because, unlike the Section 8 program, it preserves the tenants' incentive to bargain with landlords for market rents. The subsidy tenants receive depends on the standard cost of adequate housing rather than on the actual rent of the residence they occupy. Therefore, tenants pay the marginal rent dollar out of their own pockets and negotiate rent with their landlords just as they would without a subsidy.

However, even though design of the housing allowance program insures that recipients will pay market rents, critics of the program feared that the program would drive market rents up. They argued that the program would greatly increase the demand for standard housing services and that the supply of those services is inelastic. Consequently, rents would have to rise to equilibrate supply and demand, at least in the short run.

That fear has been proven groundless by the Housing Assistance Supply Experiment: No measurable increases in the price of housing services occurred.[8] Additional demand induced by the program is not as great and the supply of housing services is not as inelastic as the critics of housing allowances feared.

The demand shift caused by the program was not as great as many anticipated for two reasons. First, at any given time no more than half of the eligible households are in the allowance program; the dynamics of poverty create much movement in and out of program eligibility, and newly eligible households join the program at a slow pace.[9] Second, the income elasticity of housing demand is considerably less than 1.0, indicating a very modest added demand from the households that are in the program.[10]

Of course, the program's requirement that recipients live in standard housing does cause a significant increase in demand for that type of housing. However, the supply of standard housing services turns out to be very elastic, even in the short run. Much substandard housing can readily be upgraded to standard condition,[11] and the vacancy rate for standard housing services can decrease.[12] Those supply responses absorb additional demand for standard housing services, and prevent the housing allowance program from causing serious short-run price increases.

---

[8]See Barnett and Lowry (1979) for the evidence that the housing allowance program caused no significant price increases in either the tight (4 percent rental vacancy rate) Brown County housing market or the loose (9 percent rental vacancy rate) St. Joseph County housing market.
[9]Rydell, Mulford, and Kozimor (1979) show that the participation rate (fraction of eligibles that are in the allowance program) has risen gradually with time since the program began, reaching 40 percent at three years and 50 percent at equilibrium.
[10]Mulford (1979) estimates that the income elasticity of demand for rental housing is 0.2, which means that a 10 percent increase in household income results in a mere 2 percent increase in housing consumption.
[11]McDowell (1979, pp. 18-21) reports that three-quarters of renters who lived in substandard housing before joining the housing allowance program repaired their housing to standard condition (or persuaded their landlord to repair it) rather than move to find standard housing.
[12]The overall vacancy rate for housing services can decrease in either of two ways: First, existing households can move from small housing units into larger ones, and second, existing households can subdivide so that each new one consumes more housing services per capita. The vacancy rate for standard housing services also decreases when existing households move from substandard units to standard units.

Surveys of the two HASE counties provide dramatic evidence of the vacancy rate's[13] ability to absorb demand shocks and prevent short-run variation in the price of housing services. Table 6 compares market conditions, rents, and property values in the experimental sites before the allowance program began.[14] Because of rapid population growth, the 1973 vacancy loss rate was low in Brown County's rental market—about 4 percent. St. Joseph County has a segregated rental market; most of the county's black population lives in central South Bend.[15] The 1974 rental vacancy loss rate in central South Bend was 13 percent, compared to 6 percent in the rest of the county. The high rates resulted from declining job opportunities followed by population losses—especially from central South Bend—during the sixties and early seventies.

Table 6

EFFECT OF DEMAND SHIFTS ON RENT
AND CAPITAL VALUE

Location	Vacancy Loss Rate (%)	Rent ($/Unit/Yr)	Capital Value ($/Unit)
Central South Bend	13.2	1,727	6,862
Rest of St. Joseph County	6.1	1,732	9,315
Brown County	4.2	1,764	12,316

SOURCE: Housing Assistance Supply Experiment, rental housing in Brown County, Wisconsin, 1973, and St. Joseph County, Indiana, 1974. See C. Peter Rydell, *Shortrun Response of Housing Markets to Demand Shifts*, The Rand Corporation, R-2453-HUD, September 1979, p. 3.

NOTE: Rents and capital values have been adjusted to control for variation in building age and size, and the Brown County figures have been adjusted for price inflation during 1973-74.

The difference in vacancy loss rates between Brown County and central South Bend reflects about a 10 percent difference in demand, relative to the housing supply in each location. Rents differ by 2 percent, however, whereas the value of rental properties in St. Joseph County is 44 percent lower than in Brown County.

A theory of housing market behavior that explains the findings reported above (Rydell,

---

[13]"Vacancy rate" in this discussion is the fraction of housing services not used. It is measured operationally by the fraction of rent lost due to vacancies.

[14]The evidence was presented three years ago in Rydell (1977), and has since been sharpened by using the vacancy loss rate rather than the traditional vacancy rate to measure market condition (Rydell, 1979, pp. 2-4).

[15]Central South Bend includes all but the fringes of the city of South Bend. It has three-fourths of South Bend's rental units and one half of St. Joseph County's rental units.

1979) provides assurance that the minor price effects of the housing allowance program in Brown and St. Joseph counties would be replicated in other housing markets. Of course, the exact demand shift caused by such a program would depend on the proportion of low-income households in a given housing market. However, even doubling the demand shock caused in Brown and St. Joseph counties would result in very small price increases.

The salient points of the theory are that (a) landlords find it more profitable to accept vacancy losses than to cut prices enough to fill every unit, (b) therefore it is mostly changes in vacancy rates, rather than changes in rents, that bring supply and demand for rental housing into equilibrium, and (c) landlords do not escape the consequences of a demand shift because changes in vacancy losses are capitalized into changes in the value of rental properties. That is why, when market conditions change, rent changes little, relative to the change in capital value.

(text continued next page)

III. CONCLUSIONS

The experience gained from operating and studying the experimental housing allowance program and the national Section 8 Existing Housing Assistance Program provides an unambiguous answer to the two programs' effect on rent inflation. The discipline of the market held price increases to only 1.2 percent in the allowance program, while institutional regulation allowed prices to increase by 26 percent in the Section 8 program.

The housing allowance program prevents price increases by preserving tenants' incentive to bargain with landlords for market rents. Moreover, the Housing Assistance Supply Experiment has shown that the link between demand shifts and rent increases is weak enough so that even a full-scale allowance program does not drive up market rents.

The Section 8 Existing Housing Assistance Program causes price increases by removing the tenants' incentive to bargain, substituting regulations administered by the public housing authority. Those regulations take away the usual market link between tenant payments and rent, allowing price increases to occur. Moreover, the regulations establish a Fair Market Rent target which encourages landlords to raise their prices.

The crucial difference between the two programs is that housing allowance subsidy depends upon the standard cost of adequate housing while Section 8 subsidy depends upon the actual rent of recipients' housing. The first subsidy method makes the tenant pay the marginal rent dollar, so that the usual tenant-landlord bargaining process keeps rents at market levels. The second subsidy method makes the public housing authority pay the marginal rent dollar, and it turns out that the public housing authority does not bargain as hard with landlords as tenants do.

It is ironic that the housing allowance program has not been implemented nationally partly because of fears that it would cause price inflation; while the Section 8 program has been implemented nationally (and is being expanded) even though it does cause price inflation. From the perspective of this discussion, the two programs differ only in that housing allowances give subsidies exclusively to low-income tenants while Section 8 assistance gives a substantial portion of the subsidy to landlords.

These findings suggest two morals, one for analysis of housing policy and the other for housing policy itself. The first moral is that housing market theory does not always adequately support policy analysis. The preprogram simulation analyses were carefully constructed, state-of-the-art efforts, yet they concluded that housing allowances would cause substantial price increases and Section 8 assistance would not. Only when actual evidence on program operation became available from the housing allowance experiment and the national evaluation of Section 8 was it clear how the programs affect rent.

The other moral is that substituting regulation for market discipline, while it may sometimes be appropriate, does not always work well. The Section 8 program's regulations were designed to prevent price increases without having to trust the market. However, it turned out that not only was the market trustworthy, but the regulations were not.

This report should not be interpreted to mean that Section 8 is a bad housing program. A recent comprehensive evaluation of the program concluded: "Section 8 Existing is a fundamentally sound program. The program serves all the stated housing goals to a certain extent, but as with most new programs there exist opportunities to improve its performance" (Olsen and

Rasmussen, 1979, p. 27). We agree with that evaluation, and merely point out that one area where performance can be improved is in the prevention of price increases.

It may be feasible to improve the regulatory system so as to forestall the large price increases that now occur in the Section 8 program. For example, Khadduri (1979, pp. 49-50) suggests enforcing rent reasonableness tests more rigorously, by requiring documentation that justifies rent increases in terms of increased management or maintenance costs. She also recommends giving public housing authorities a positive incentive to prevent price increases by making rent savings (the difference between actual rents and Fair Market Rent) interchangeable with administrative costs. However, enlarging the regulatory system would surely entail more work for local housing authorities and HUD, and would therefore increase program costs. Moreover, there is no evidence that this approach would succeed in preventing the increases.

In contrast, the housing allowance program provides evidence that, without compromising program objectives, Section 8 rules could instead be revised to use market discipline as an administratively simple way to control unwarranted price increases. Comparison with the housing allowance program suggests that three changes would be sufficient: (a) *change the subsidy formula* to use the Fair Market Rent standard, rather than the actual rent of a recipient's unit, to compute the subsidy, (b) *pay the subsidy directly to the tenant* instead of to the landlord, and (c) *remove the rent ceiling*, allowing recipients to choose any unit that meets the program's housing standards (see Table 1 in the Introduction.) The first change would make the tenant pay the marginal rent dollar, restoring the usual tenant-landlord bargaining process. The second change would insure that tenants knew that they were paying the marginal rent dollar. The third change would remove the rent ceiling as a target toward which landlords are motivated to raise their prices.

The question remains whether all three changes are necessary to prevent price increases. That question cannot be answered with evidence from HASE because the housing allowance program differs from the Section 8 program in all three ways. Nevertheless, we suspect that the first change alone—simply altering the subsidy formula—would do the lion's share of the job. Tenants might well realize that they were paying the marginal rent dollar even if the subsidy were paid to the landlord by the public housing authority. Landlords would probably not be able to raise prices toward the Fair Market Rent target if tenants had to pay the marginal rent dollar.

Neither the second change (paying subsidy to the tenant) nor the third change (removing the rent ceiling) would help control price increases unless the first change was made, however. Changing the recipient of the subsidy payment without altering the subsidy formula would probably not affect price increases because tenant incentives would remain unchanged. Removing the rent ceiling without altering the subsidy formula would most likely make price increases larger because under the current subsidy formula the rent ceiling is the only control on price increases.

Hence, we judge that altering the subsidy formula is the key to preventing price increases in the Section 8 program. However, if the formula were modified, the other two changes could well be justified for reasons other than their effect on price increases. For example, paying subsidies directly to tenants would reduce administrative costs, and removing the rent ceiling would allow tenants to spend more of the subsidy on housing consumption. Those reasons and others are extensively discussed in Zais, Goedert, and Trutko (1979).

To sum up: Price increases caused by the current Section 8 program cause a diversion of a substantial portion of the program's subsidy dollars to landlords.[1] The housing allowance program shows how the Section 8 program could be revised to prevent the price increases: Structure the subsidy so tenants pay the marginal rent dollar; pay the subsidy directly to tenants so they know they pay the marginal rent dollar; and remove the rent ceiling so it can no longer act as a rent target. Restructuring the subsidy formula is the key change, because it alone would probably prevent most price increases. Adding the other two changes would insure that price increases were prevented, but neither would be helpful on its own. Paying the subsidy directly to the tenant while keeping the current subsidy formula would probably leave price increases unchanged, because tenant incentives would not be changed. Removing the rent ceiling while keeping the current subsidy formula would probably make price increases even larger, because under the present formula prices tend to increase until rents approach the rent ceiling.

---

[1] Roughly 34 percent of total subsidy payments are diverted to landlords because of the price increases (the 26 percent rent increase becomes a 34 percent subsidy diversion because subsidy payments are only about 76 percent of preprogram rent). At the February 1979 program level of 520,000 units (and using the 1976 average subsidy of $103 per unit per month), this diversion amounts to $218.5 million annually.

REFERENCES

Barnett, C. Lance, and Ira S. Lowry, *How Housing Allowances Affect Housing Prices*, The Rand Corporation, R-2452-HUD, September 1979.

De Leeuw, Frank, and Raymond J. Struyk, *The Web of Urban Housing: Analyzing Policy with a Market Simulation Model*, The Urban Institute, Washington, D.C., September 1975.

Drury, Margaret, Olsen Lee, Michael Springer, and Lorene Yap, *Lower Income Housing Assistance Program (Section 8): National Evaluation of the Existing Housing Program*, Office of Policy Development and Research, U.S. Department of Housing and Urban Development, Washington, D.C., November 1978.

Federal Register, Vol. 41, No. 1, 29 March 1976.

Federal Register, Vol. 45, No. 176, 9 September 1980.

Fifth Annual Report of the Housing Assistance Supply Experiment, The Rand Corporation, R-2434-HUD, June 1979.

Fourth Annual Report of the Housing Assistance Supply Experiment, The Rand Corporation, R-2302-HUD, May 1978.

Greenston, Peter M., Sarah James, Lorene Yap, and Robert Sadacca, *Experience in the Section 8 Existing Housing Program: FY 1975-1976*, The Urban Institute, Washington, D.C., WP-240-11, September 1977.

Housing and Community Development Reporter, Bureau of National Affairs, Inc., Washington, D.C., Vol. 6, No. 48, 30 April 1979.

Housing and Community Development Reporter, Bureau of National Affairs, Inc., Washington, D.C., Vol. 6, No. 38, 9 February 1979.

Housing and Community Development Reporter, Bureau of National Affairs, Inc., Washington, D.C., Vol. 7, No. 12, 20 August 1979.

HUD Statistical Yearbook, 1971, U.S. Department of Housing and Urban Development, Washington, D.C., HUD-338, 1972.

HUD Statistical Yearbook, 1977, U.S. Department of Housing and Urban Development, Washington, D.C., HUD-338, December 1978.

HUD Statistical Yearbook, 1978, U.S. Department of Housing and Urban Development, Washington, D.C., HUD-338-7-UD, March 1980.

Khadduri, Jill, "The Rent Reduction Credit Feature of the Section 8 Existing Housing Program," in *Occasional Papers in Housing and Community Affairs: Volume 6*, Office of Policy Development and Research, U.S. Department of Housing and Urban Development, Washington, D.C., December 1979.

McDowell, James L., *Housing Allowances and Housing Improvements: Early Findings*, The Rand Corporation, N-1198-HUD, September 1979.

Mulford, John, *Income Elasticity of Housing Demand*, The Rand Corporation, R-2449-HUD, July 1979.

Olsen, Edgar O., and David W. Rasmussen, "Section 8 Existing: A Program Evaluation," in *Occasional Papers in Housing and Community Affairs: Volume 6*, Office of Policy Development and Research, U.S. Department of Housing and Urban Development, Washington, D.C., December 1979.

Olsen, Edgar O., and William J. Reeder, *Does HUD Pay Too Much for Section 8 Existing Housing?* Department of Economics, University of Virginia, Charlottesville, Va., 1980.

Public Housing Agency Administrative Practices Handbook for the Section 8 Existing Housing Program, U.S. Department of Housing and Urban Development, Washington, D.C., No. 7420.7, November 1979.

Report on Special Operational Survey, Section 8 Leased Housing Program, Office of Inspector General, U.S. Department of Housing and Urban Development, Washington, D.C., July 1979.

Rydell, C. Peter, *Effects of Market Conditions on Prices and Profits of Rental Housing*, The Rand Corporation, P-6008, September 1977.

Rydell, C. Peter, John E. Mulford, and Lawrence W. Kozimor, "Participation Rates in Government Transfer Programs: Application to Housing Allowances," *Management Sciences*, Vol. 25, No. 5, May 1979.

Rydell, C. Peter, *Shortrun Response of Housing Markets to Demand Shifts*, The Rand Corporation, R-2453-HUD, September 1979.

Struyk, Raymond J., Sue A. Marshall, and Larry J. Ozanne, *Housing Policies for the Urban Poor*, The Urban Institute, Washington, D.C., September 1978.

Wallace, James E., Susan P. Bloom, William L. Holshouser, Shirley Mansfield, and Daniel H. Weinberg, *Participation and Benefits in the Urban Section 8 Program*, Abt Associates, Cambridge, Mass., AAI-80-135, forthcoming in 1981.

Yap, Lorene, Peter Greenston, and Robert Sadacca, *Lower Income Housing Assistance Program (Section 8): Nationwide Evaluation of the Existing Housing Program—Technical Supplement*, Office of Policy Development and Research, U.S. Department of Housing and Urban Development, Washington, D.C., November 1978.

Zais, James P., Jeanne E. Goedert, and John W. Trutko, *Modifying Section 8: Implications from Experiments with Housing Allowances*, The Urban Institute, Washington, D.C., UI-240-10, January 1979.

37

ENTREPRENEURSHIP AND GOVERNMENT POLICY
The Case of the Housing Market

Mary K. Farmer and Ray Barrell*

ABSTRACT

This article discusses the use made of the 'Austrian' concept of entrepreneurship in the present British government's policy discussions, and, using an 'Austrian' method of argument, demonstrates that there is a deep-seated inconsistency in its policies which suggests that it, along with the administrations of a number of other western democracies including the United States, has not fully understood the implications of the doctrines to which it appears to have committed itself. This inconsistency relates to its continued support for the existing structure of subsidies in the UK housing market which, it is argued, have made private home-buying so profitable an activity for entrepreneurial individuals as to substantially reduce the attractiveness of the option of setting up new businesses. Whether or not the government is right to believe that, in an economic environment with greater incentives, there would be a great expansion in individual entrepreneurial effort in 'productive' activities, this is not likely to happen whilst, amongst other things, the structure of housing subsidies remains substantially unchanged. We suggest, in the light of comparative international evidence, that a better alternative is available.

1. The government and the Austrian view of the economy

I am able to approach my task this afternoon on this one, crucially important piece of common ground: that the poor performance of the British economy in recent years has not been due to a shortage of demand. We are suffering from a growing series of failures on the supply side of the economy.

It is our belief that many of these failures are themselves the result of

---

* We would like to thank friends and ex-colleagues at Stirling University for a number of helpful discussions of these ideas, and especially Keith Glaister for constructive criticism of an earlier version of the paper. Donald Winch, Ray Robinson and Pete Saunders of Sussex University and Barry Smith of Manchester University have also helped us improve the argument, as have two anonymous referees for this journal. Errors and omissions remain our own responsibility.

Reprinted from "Entrepreneurship and Government Policy: The Case of the Housing Market," 1(3) *Journal of Public Policy* 307-332 (August 1981), by Mary K. Farmer and Ray Barrell, by permission of Cambridge University Press. © Cambridge University Press 1981.

actions and interventions by Government themselves – laws that stand in the way of change and stifle enterprise; and, as important as anything, a structure of taxation that might have been designed to discourage innovation and punish success... We need to strengthen incentives, by allowing people to keep more of what they earn, so that hard work, talent and ability are properly rewarded. (Sir Geoffrey Howe, Budget Speech, 12 June 1979)

The Conservative government which came to power in May 1979 has been greeted, by supporters and opponents alike, as one of the most theoretically doctrinaire British administrations of modern times. It shares with the Reagan administration in the United States (and to a greater or lesser extent with a significant number of other governments of western democracies) a commitment to a version of laissez-faire, free market economics, informed both by the thinking of recent monetarist economists, and the so-called Austrian economists such as von Mises, Schumpeter, and Friedrich von Hayek. With the intensely individualist, anti-interventionist 'Austrians' the Thatcher administration claim to believe,[1] as Sir Geoffrey Howe's first Budget Speech made clear, that government interference in the workings of the market is inherently disruptive. This is because they view the 'creaking semaphore' (Coddington, 1975) of the free market price system as the only really viable mechanism for conveying information between individuals about their respective tastes, abilities, wants and resources. Without reasonably reliable signals of this sort the economic activities of millions of separate individuals would fail to be co-ordinated.

With other proponents of laissez-faire, the Austrian economists stress that the special characteristic of a competitive market economy is that whilst allowing each individual to pursue their own interests by making mutually advantageous exchanges with other individuals, it would produce an allocation of society's resources to the places where they could be most efficiently used. Individuals maximising in their own interests will reach the positions which are optimal for them given the trades others are willing to make, and once all have achieved this end in a consistent way we may say that a state of equilibrium has been arrived at. In contrast to standard neo-classical economists, however, the Austrians have stressed that markets cannot be expected to reach an equilibrium state. Situations change, people's preferences change, and most importantly the world is uncertain and people must take risks in it. Thus although freely determined prices will tend to convey the best possible information about individual preferences over scarce resources, 'the best possible information' is not perfect information. Entrepreneurs are those who attempt to make profits by taking advantage of situations in which there is imperfect information, and for the Austrians these profits are the rewards for improving information. Entrepreneurs therefore play a crucial role in a healthy economy.

For Austrian writers entrepreneurship is simply the ability to see *potential* opportunities for gain and the willingness to take risks in their pursuit. Anybody who has a more than averagely optimistic expectation of the returns to some investment, for whatever reason, and acts on these expectations, is an entrepreneur. Thus as the major Austrian writer on this subject in recent years, Israel Kirzner, says:

> the entrepreneurial element in the economic behaviour of market participants consists... in their alertness to previously unnoticed changes in circumstances which may make it possible to get far more in exchange for whatever they have to offer than was hitherto possible (Kirzner, 1973, 15).[2]

Hence entrepreneurship is involved as much in an unemployed person moving to a region of the country which they expect soon to be suffering a shortage of labour, or a student teacher investing time in learning computing in the expectation that computer studies will in future years be an expanded subject in schools, as in a person deciding to set up in business by themselves to sell a new product. As we emphasised earlier, the Austrians stress that the economy is in general not in a state which can be characterised as equilibrium, and it is because of this belief that they place such importance on the role of entrepreneurial actions. Those who think they see potential profit for themselves in moving to an expanding region, acquiring skills which may be especially needed in the future, or setting up a company to sell a new product for which they think they see an untapped market, are all contributing to the movement of the economy towards equilibrium, towards a 'better' and more efficient use of its resources.

The Austrians stress that the entrepreneur does not need resources in the form of labour or especially capital ownership in order to operate, but they do have to make choices over the uses of their energy and time. They cannot buy any more entrepreneurial ability than they actually possess, and so their entrepreneurial activity has to be eked out, like (and with) their time. No being is omniscient, only *some* opportunities will be seen and only those thought to be the best, taken up. As Rothbard says about the law of diminishing marginal utility:

> It is a praxeological truth, derived from the nature of action, that the first unit of a good will be allocated to its most valuable use, the next unit to the next valuable, and so on (Rothbard in Dolan, 1976).

Like consumption, entrepreneurial action will be allocated to its most profitable use first then its next best use, and so on (see von Mises, 1949, 124). Like air, it has no opportunity cost on the market and cannot be sold, but unlike air it is not in unlimited supply. If entrepreneurship were in unlimited supply then there would be no economic problems of any consequence. Everything would be sorted out instantly.

Because entrepreneurial activity is thought by the Austrians to be so important for the functioning of the economy, and because they believe that there is not an unlimited stock of it available, they therefore put great emphasis on organising society in such a way that it is encouraged. Socialism and bureaucracy are deplored because their structures are such that the individual entrepreneurial effort they encourage is not productive, but is aimed at such objectives as individual advancement or avoidance of control. For a society, effective entrepreneurship is a scarce commodity, and the free market is believed to provide the most effective social environment for husbanding it.

The Austrians therefore place special emphasis on the dangers of government intervention in the economy. The imposition of a tax or a subsidy is not viewed as simply moving the economy to some new, less-than-optimal equilibrium position, but as upsetting the 'creaking semaphore' by falsifying the information conveyed from individual to individual about how much they subjectively value resources. The key effect of this is to mislead both potential and existing entrepreneurs about available opportunities and thus to retard economic growth.

Hayek stressed as early as 1931 in *Prices and Production* that once decisions have been taken at 'wrong' prices important investment decisions will have committed the economy to a particular pattern. (This trading at false prices is the major reason for the non-applicability of standard Paretian welfare economics.) He used this argument to explain the Great Depression: our task is more mundane. We hope to show that there is a simple Austrian explanation for the low level of new business activity in Britain today compared with most other western democracies. We believe our explanation also helps to account for the great variability in the scale and vitality of the small business sector across these economies.

2. *The enterprising individual and incentives in Britain*

The present British government shares with its predecessors the view that the UK economy is characterised by a worrying lack of entrepreneurial activity. As we show, there is evidence that their worries are well-founded. They believe that a healthy private sector is one in which there is a great deal of highly competitive new (and often small) business activity. As we have already stressed, Mrs Thatcher's administration believe that lack of such activity does not just lead to the higher prices and complacency and inefficiency in existing firms which worried the last Labour government, but is also a sign that opportunities for innovation and improvement are being missed and that the economy is therefore suffering serious dynamic distortion. The lack of businessmen willing to take risks is therefore seen by the government as a major cause of the poor performance of the British economy in recent years attacked by Sir Geoffrey Howe in his first Budget Speech.

One result of the lack of new businesses is that Britain now has the most attenuated small business sector amongst the industrialised nations. According to the Bolton Committee (1971) Britain has the lowest proportion of manufacturing employment in small establishments (less than 200 workers) of thirteen industrialised nations. It may, of course, be that technology is different in Britain, but this seems unlikely, especially as the number of small firms has halved in Britain in the last fifty years, whilst it has doubled in the USA. Small firms are on average much older in Britain than in the USA (three times as old), indicating that the small size of the sector is more the result of a decline in births than a rise in deaths.[3] It cannot be doubted that there has been a relative decline in the small business sector in the UK; we need to ask why.

A low level of new business activity naturally suggests to a government with an Austrian view of the world that the economy lacks opportunities for individuals to make positive gains from entrepreneurial ventures. Such a situation could of course indicate that the economy was already close to Kirzner's 'hypothetical equilibrium', with few opportunities left to be taken. This is an unconvincing picture of the present British economy, and the government naturally seeks an alternative explanation.

People no doubt set up in business by themselves for a wide variety of complex reasons. They may well get a great deal of satisfaction from being in control of their own work patterns, they may enjoy the challenge of a situation in which there is the chance of large gains along with the risk of bankruptcy, they may simply believe that they will be able to cash in on some opportunity for selling something profitably which others have failed to notice, or have not been so good at. Whatever the complexities of these reasons it is not very controversial to assert that in this society most people set up in business in order to make profits and accumulate wealth, and this is indeed what the present government believes.[4] If business profits and capital gains are heavily taxed it follows that fewer people will consider it worthwhile setting up small businesses. The government therefore believes that it can stimulate small businesses by reducing the tax burden.

But striving to increase one's wealth can obviously take place in any market. If individuals commit themselves to one market then they must, by the simple fact of their scarce resources, be less committed in others. For instance, profit opportunities will currently be bringing entrepreneurs into the market for oil saving devices, but these entrepreneurs must then necessarily be withdrawing their energies (as well as their capital) from other fields (see above). It should not matter to entrepreneurs whether the opportunities for gain which exist are in the so-called 'productive' or 'unproductive' sectors. Markets are interdependent, however, and if better opportunities for gain are seen to exist in an 'unproductive' area there will inevitably be less entrepreneurial energy available for application in other markets.

Subsidies have been offered in Britain in many markets, but the one which is fundamental to our argument is the housing market subsidy. Home ownership is heavily subsidised in Britain, and as we will show below, this subsidy has been increasing in size over recent years. The increases have produced large potential gans in this market, larger even than in the USA, and by the late 1960s the wise speculator will have realised this. Capital and effort have become increasingly tied up in own-home ownership, and have not therefore been available for 'productive', but possibly riskier (and less lucrative) purposes. Entrepreneurial ability has been sucked into the home-owning sector, not just because of the existence of the subsidy, but because of the *type* of subsidy given in the UK. We argue below that the form of subsidy distributes windfall gains throughout the population, and the alert entrepreneur has been able to make large gains in this market. To say that these gains were available, is, for an Austrian, to say that they were taken by some actors (see section 3.3 below).

3. Some evidence

3.1 Rising values and low interest rates

Our argument is based on a set of widely known facts. Between 1965 and 1979 (February) house prices in Britain rose by 559 per cent (this figure is the index for the price of new houses mortgaged by building societies), whereas the overall price level of consumer goods rose less than 360 per cent. This means that the real price of houses rose by over 50 per cent, and only a small part of this can be attributed to improvements in the stock of houses. This rise was not of course a regular one; the boom of 1971–3 accounted for a very large percentage of it, as can be seen from Table 1.

Such large changes in real values offer a great opportunity for profitable speculation. Those who owned houses outright in 1965 would have made a large capital gain simply by sitting in the house they owned. If they chose to sell their house and buy consumer goods they would have been able to buy a larger number of 1979 than in 1965 with the proceeds of the sale.

What about 'average' mortgage payers? Were they better off in 1979 as a result of the real change in house prices? It is widely believed that mortgagors have benefited, but it is important to show why they have, and who has paid for their good fortune.

During a period of inflation it is necessary to distinguish between real and nominal rates of interest. The real rate of interest is the rate paid after depreciation on the initial debt has been allowed for. A borrower pays the nominal rate of interest, and if inflation is fully taken account of in the

TABLE 1. *Real and nominal house prices*

	1965	1966	1967	1968	1969	1970	1971	1972	1973	1974	1975	1976	1977	1978	1979[4]
Nominal House Prices [1] 1970 = 100	73	79	84	88	94	100	113	144	198	221	242	261	287	346	408
Price index for goods [2] 1970 = 100	79.7	82.9	85	89.7	94.4	100	112.5	116	125.4	148.6	186.2	212.1	244.6	268.1	295.3
Real house prices [3] 1970 = 100	91.6	95.2	98.8	98.1	99.6	100	103.8	124.2	157.9	148.8	133.6	123	117.4	129	138

Notes: [1] New houses mortgaged by Building Societies. From *Housing and Construction Statistics*, HMSO.
[2] Consumer Expenditure Deflator. From Central Statistical Office Data Bank, available from *Monthly Digest of Statistics*.
[3] Row 1 ÷ Row 2.
[4] All 1979 figures are for February.

TABLE 2. *Hypothetical interest rates with positive real interest (3%)*

	1965	1966	1967	1968	1969	1970	1971	1972	1973	1974	1975	1976	1977	1978
	7.09	5.4	8.5	8.25	9.0	11.9	9.5	11.1	21.5	28.36	16.9	18.3	12.6	13.1

Source: These are the inflation rates calculated from Row 2 of Table 1 plus 3%.

TABLE 3. *Actual and real mortgage borrowing rates (pre- and post-tax)*

	1965	1966	1967	1968	1969	1970	1971	1972	1973	1974	1975	1976	1977	1978	1979[5]
Actual mortgage rate [1]	6.63	6.95	7.2	7.4	8.07	8.58	8.59	8.26	9.59	11.05	11.08	11.06	11.05	9.75	11.75
Real pre-tax rate of interest [2]	2.54	4.55	1.7	2.21	2.07	−0.32	2.09	0.16	−8.9	−14.31	−1.8	−4.2	1.4	−0.4	—
Actual post-tax rate of interest [3]	4.49	4.71	4.9	5.05	5.47	5.81	5.82	5.76	6.69	7.73	7.4	7.2	7.2	6.4	—
Real post-tax rate of interest [4]	0.4	2.3	−0.6	−0.2	−0.53	−3.1	−0.68	−2.34	−11.89	−17.64	−6.5	−8.1	−2.4	−3.7	—

Notes: [1] Source: Financial Statistics HMSO. Up to 1977 these are average rates paid, 1978–9 representative figures.
[2] Row 1 minus the inflation rate from Table 1, Row 2.
[3] Row 1 × (1 minus the standard tax rate). Tax rates from *Inland Revenue Statistics*, HMSO.
[4] Row 3 minus the rate of inflation from Row 2, Table 1.
[5] 1979 figures for February.

market for loans the nominal rate will be high enough to allow a positive real return to lenders. If mortgage borrowers had been paying a positive real rate of interest of say 3 per cent between 1965 and 1979 then their interest payments would have been as shown in Table 2. (Actuaries assume 3 per cent to be the underlying real rate of interest.) Even then they would have made capital gains (as outright owners did). But the *actual* real rate paid was much lower than 3 per cent; before allowing for tax relief on interest payments the real rate of interest on mortgages was actually negative in six out of the fourteen years. Own-home-buyers therefore made large capital gains in the period not only because of rises in the real prices of houses, but also because they were not having to pay a market rate of interest on their mortgages.

3.2 *The British housing subsidy system*

It has been said that those who complain that they don't understand housing policy would complain even more if they understood it (Robinson, 1978).

Why have house-buyers not been paying the opportunity cost of their money? The answer lies in the desire of successive governments to create a property-owning democracy (see section 5 below). Policies have been deliberately adopted to keep the mortgage rate down below the nominal rates of Table 2. In 1974–5, for instance, the government directly subsidised the building societies; in other years they have adopted policies that have kept interest rates down in general, at least in part to aid house-buyers. The serious long-run consequences of such actions should be obvious. Monetary expansion to keep interest rates low only leads to inflation, and higher rates in the future. Direct controls interfere with market efficiency and cause wealth to be redistributed from savers to borrowers. It is savers in building societies and other savings institutions, of course, who bear the costs of the low interest rates. They tend to be the old, the very young, and the hopeful. They are both poorer and more numerous than house-buyers. They pay for quite a large proportion of the buyer's house.

Governments have feared high interest rates, but have been unwilling to introduce alternative repayment rules which avoid the so-called front loading problem in mortgage payments during periods of inflation. To be forced to pay large portions of the value of a house early in the mortgage would be difficult if the individual was to pay the nominal rates outlined in Table 2. These rates would be crippling, but schemes can easily be devised to avoid onerous repayments.[5]

Who else pays? As is well-known, mortgagors receive tax relief on their interest payments. Table 3 gives the pre- and post-tax nominal and real rates of interest paid by a standard tax payer on an average mortgage. Only in the first two years was the real post-tax rate positive; since 1967 the post-tax rate of interest has been negative in real terms. As has been pointed out earlier, high nominal interest rates during inflationary periods will include some repayment of the initial loan. If the Government is giving a subsidy on nominal interest rates it is contributing to the repayment of the loan.

Government interference in the housing market takes one further form: it affects house prices via innovations in the rate of inflation. As is clear from the above argument (and from Tables 2 and 3), the higher the rate of inflation and consequently the higher the nominal interest rate, the higher will be the level of subsidy the individual receives. When the subsidy size is known the reactions of individuals will be reasonably certain; the larger the subsidy the more housing will be demanded. If inflation is rising (or is anticipated to rise) then the size of the subsidy will increase, and once people realise this the demand for houses will rise (as in 1971-3, and 1978-80). This forces the nominal and real prices of housing upwards. Paradoxically such a rise pushes housing beyond the reach of many first-time buyers: those whom the subsidy system was primarily intended to help. In this situation governments are of course forced to introduce subsidiary subsidies to provide further help for this group, thus pushing the market even further away from equilibrium. (Not all subsidy systems face this particular problem, as we shall see in section 4 below.)

It is the variability of the subsidy, owing to the variability of the rate of inflation in recent years which is at the heart of our argument. Each unexpected change in the rate of inflation causes unanticipated capital gains or losses to individuals involved in the housing market, and government induced changes in the rate of inflation have in fact had the unintended consequence of making available large capital gains in housing.

3.3 Method

In what follows we have attempted to restrict ourselves to forms of argument and evidence which would be methodologically acceptable to Austrian economists. This decision reflects our feeling that it is important to examine the present government's policies against the background of the economic philosophy from which its policies are in the main derived. Austrians would argue that we can never know exactly how the actions of individuals would have differed under different conditions. As Kirzner says: the two basic Austrian tenets are

that human action is purposeful, and, second, there is the insight that there is an indeterminacy and unpredictability inherent in human preferences, human expectations, human knowledge (Kirzner in Dolan, 1976, 41).

We cannot know, for example, what inventions and innovations would have been made by entrepreneurial individuals during the past two decades had they been facing a different structure of returns to various possible activities. To predict that an invention would have been made in different circumstances is, after all, to do the inventing oneself, and to be able to say that a market innovation would have been successful had the structure of prices been different, is to claim omniscient knowledge about choices consumers would have made, faced with goods which in fact never even saw the light of day. For these reasons Austrians claim that attempts at retrospective regression analyses using aggregate data are futile; we can only have knowledge of past economic events as individuals actually enacted them, subject to the constraints as they found them (von Mises, 1949, 55). This does not mean that statistics should not be used, but they are a tool of the economic historian. 'Statistical regularities can also be the starting point for a purely theoretical investigation...but the connection here is more suggestive than logical' (Rizzo in Spadaro, 1978, 52).

For the Austrians the fundamental *a priori* belief in the rationality of human action provides the only means of access to an understanding of past social events (von Mises, 1949; 1978). As Kirzner makes clear, the essence of praxeology is that people act in an instinctively unavoidable way. They are alert to opportunities available to them and act on them. This desire to act is radically different from the neo-classical description of the maximiser. The neo-classical individual is confronted with opportunities which are taken as constraints. The actor in Austrian works goes and *finds* opportunities: they are the instrument, not the constraint (Kirzner in Dolan, 1976, 119). Austrian economics is also distinct, in that:

The axioms of praxeology are:
1. So broadly based in common human experience they (are) self evident and hence do not meet the fashionable criterion of 'falsifiability'.
2. They rest on universal inner experience (Rothbard in Dolan, 1976, 25).

Thus we should ask what a rational typical individual would have done in some specified set of circumstances (for example, those which would have obtained had the government operated different policies), and thereby obtain some qualitative impression of the effect existing policies have had.

Our figures are not empirical in the sense that they claim to describe the real gain made by any real individuals: we have merely calculated the kinds of returns which have been available to typical individuals acting as rational wealth maximisers. It is on the assumption that individuals do act in this way that the present government bases its expectation that its policy of reducing taxation and state expenditure will give incentives to individuals to produce for themselves a healthier economy.

3.4 Housing speculation

The enterprising individual can consider three things when comparing alternative ways to make money. Firstly, will their income be at risk, or will it be reasonably secure? Secondly, what are the risks of actually going bankrupt? Thirdly, what are the chances of large capital gains and losses? House purchase for owner-occupation has provided the entrepreneur with an attractive package in recent years. Firstly, buying a house never means a safe job has to be sacrificed and there is therefore no risk of loss of income involved. Furthermore, unless the government engineers a massive deflation, without support for house-buyers, there is no bankruptcy risk. Only capital risks exist. If an entrepreneur has a taste for very large risks these will not be satisfied in housing, but as Table 4 shows, both gains and losses have been made in different years; some capital risk has therefore been involved. For a multitude of potential small businessmen, house-ownership has undoubtedly offered a more satisfactory combination of risk and return than they could possibly have got elsewhere. For many, ownership is just one of a number of entrepreneurial ventures, but for some at least it will be the only one. As we have stressed above, for the individual, the amount of possible entrepreneurial activity is limited. If it is more worthwhile spending effort on housing it will be less worthwhile spending it on other things. As Mises stresses, the actor does the best thing first, then the next best thing and so on. The entrepreneur does not have endless time and energy. It is of course possible to use a house as a source of collateral for a loan, a second mortgage, but this requires that sufficient of the house is 'uncovered', whilst paradoxically the entrepreneur in housing will try to have as little of his house uncovered as possible, to gain the maximum from the existing subsidy system. Other finance is always available if lenders can be persuaded of the soundness of the venture of course, but most individuals who are heavily mortgaged will face a steeply rising cost of borrowing, thus making other ventures seem even less desirable after the best has been done first.

What is the scale of the gains which have been available to the own-house speculator? In line with the Austrian method we have decided to adopt we will follow typical individuals through the market from 1965 (the period for which adequate figures are available). We have chosen as our reference individual someone with the average borrower's income in 1965; this was approximately 10 per cent above the average income of two-adult, two-children families at that date.

Given the size of the subsidy and the potential for capital gain it is obviously sensible for the wealth maximiser to stay 'borrowed up' by buying as large a house as possible. Because there are two parts to the subsidy, tax relief and low interest rates, this would entail regularly moving and re-borrowing on the basis of the higher income that inevitably results from

TABLE 4. *Equity and capital gains for a 'plunging mover with relative income growth'[2] in 1975 prices*

	1965	1966	1967	1968	1969	1970	1971	1972	1973	1974	1975	1976	1977	1978	1979[1]
Equity level	2,273	2,751	3,220	3,596	4,119	4,552	5,504	8,628	13,572	13,463	12,500	12,370	12,390	15,182	17,485
Equity change		478	469	376	523	433	952	3,124	4,944	−109	−963	−130	+20	2,792	2,303

Notes: [1] February 1979.
[2] This individual moves every three years (1968, 1971, 1974, 1977) and borrows to 'the limit' (see text).

inflation. Reborrowing does not in itself entail moving, and if there were only an interest rate subsidy, it might be thought that wealth maximisers would simply continually increase their mortgages. However, firstly, tax relief has not been available on remortgaging since 1974, and, more importantly, the government has tended to intervene to keep the interest rate low, and this has induced additional rises in the real capital values of houses. Since the more valuable the house, the larger the gains that can be made, it has therefore inadvertently provided an incentive for individuals to 'trade up the market' (and also of course to engage in home improvements they would not otherwise have chosen). The larger the potential gains from moving the more frequently will moves take place, although moving costs, which are hard to estimate but probably average 3–4 per cent of the cost of the new house, will inevitably temper this activity.

As entrepreneurial home-owners began to realise that there were large gains to be made from speculation we would have expected a decline in the length of life of mortgages and an increase in demand for mortgages from existing home-owners. Both have taken place over the last decade or so. Redemption rates for mortgages taken out in 1966 show that they had a median life of seven years.[8] Those taken out in 1973 had a median life of five and a half years. Over the 1970s there has also been increasing pressure from owner-occupiers wishing to move, and building society loans have shifted significantly towards movers, as can be seen from Table 5, which shows the ratio of loans to movers relative to those to first-time buyers. This gives some idea of pressure from movers which has obviously built up in the seventies (note the cyclical correlation with the rise in house prices). The evidence clearly supports our hypothesis.

TABLE 5. *Ratio of loans to movers to loans to first-time buyers*

1970	1971	1972	1973	1974	1975	1976	1977	1978	1979
0.64	0.66	0.73	0.93	0.97	1.12	1.01	1.08	1.12	1.21

Source: *Building Societies Association Bulletin*, 1980.

If entrepreneurial home-owners were trying to make gains from speculation we would also have expected the average distance moved to be short, because a move in the local area minimises dislocation costs and conserves precious information about relative valuations. The Nationwide Building Society Movers Survey (first quarter 1979) shows that 56.6 per cent of moves were of less than five miles, with only 23.4 per cent of moves being motivated by job considerations. These figures also strongly support our hypothesis that speculation has been taking place.

Inevitably the rational entrepreneur may choose to enjoy some of the fruits of speculation when moving, and there is some evidence of siphoning of funds out of the housing market by movers. The *Housing Policy Review Technical Volume II* (p. 109ff) presents evidence of the level of take-out in 1973. About £400m was taken out from gross advances of £3,540m; that is 11 per cent, or about £1,700 on average per move. It was assumed that £500 per move was paid in fees, so a net of about £250m was probably taken out, allowing the gainers to spend some of their proceeds as current income. Some of these gains will, of course, have been experienced as windfalls, but some will undoubtedly have been worked for by individuals acting entrepreneurially. Clearly the entrepreneurial individual has been able to raise both the value of the mortgage and the amount of deposit, and have money left over to spend immediately.

In our calculations we have assumed that our 'mover' moves every three years, so that the principal repaid will on average just cover the removal cost.[7] Not all house-owners will choose to (or even necessarily realise that they could) wealth-maximise by such a policy. It is not necessary to our argument that they should. All that is necessary is that some of the class of potential entrepreneurs see the opportunity for gain in such a pattern of action, and choose to invest their capital and their effort there, rather than elsewhere. As with most standard arguments in economics it is the marginal changes that matter.

We have calculated the nominal and real gains for five types of individual. First there is the non-mover. Then there are four types of mover, divided into 'plungers' and 'cautious individuals'. The plungers reborrow as much as possible. We assumed that would mean they would borrow the multiple of their income allowed on average to first-time buyers, which varied between 2.02 and 1.78 over the period.[8] Plungers obviously made the largest gains. Cautious individuals were assumed only to borrow the multiple of income previous home-owners actually borrowed on average. This varied between 1.63 and 1.81. Each of these two categories was then divided into those whose position in the income distribution stayed the same (i.e. 10 per cent above average income for a two-adult, two-child family) and those whose income grew 1 per cent per annum faster (i.e. someone in a safe job on an incremental scale: in the public sector perhaps?). The most likely entrepreneur is the plunger, especially the more able plunger who has relative income growth, and it is for such an individual that we will present the most detailed results.

In 1965 each of our representative house-buyers starts with an average house and a £1,000 deposit. The movers move every three years and buy a larger house. Their nominal gains by February 1979 are recorded in Table 6. The 1965 £1,000 would be worth £3,700 in 1979 prices, so Table 6 also reports their real gains in 1979 prices. The non-mover is obviously a special case because after fourteen years most of their debt is

TABLE 6. *Potential returns to moving* (£)

	Equity stake		Gains		Rates of return	
	1965	1979	Nominal	1979 Prices	Nominal	1979 Prices
Non-mover	1,000	17,400	16,400	13,700	22.6	11.7
Mover who is (a) Cautious (b) Has no income growth	1,000	25,100	24,100	21,400	25.9	14.7
Mover who is (a) Cautious (b) Has income growth	1,000	26,800	25,800	22,100	26.5	15.2
Mover who is (a) A 'plunger' (b) Has no income growth	1,000	26,900	25,900	23,200	26.5	15.2
Mover who is (a) A 'plunger' (b) Has income growth	1,000	28,500	27,500	24,800	27.0	15.7

Note: See text for further explanation. Figures have been rounded to the nearest 100 after calculation.

paid off. The mover's gains are almost all completely speculative, as very little of the principle is repaid in three years. The more entrepreneurial the individual's behaviour the larger the gains available. Not only has the plunger made over 15 per cent per annum in real terms over the period, he has also enjoyed the flow of services from progressively larger houses, and both these returns are completely free of tax.

Of course gains have been made only during some periods, as is obvious from Table 1. From 1974 to 1976 the speculator made real losses, but the thrill of very large gains at other times no doubt provided some compensation! The gains could be very large indeed, as can be seen from Table 4.

Could an entrepreneur have done better elsewhere? Only someone with a very special combination of good fortune and personal characteristics could have expected to do so.[9] Undoubtedly most could not. The average stockmarket speculator (another safer alternative to setting up in business on one's own) would not have done anywhere near as well (this holds even for more advantageous termination dates than February 1979). As Table 7 shows the All Share Index rose from 99.8 to 167.8 between 1965 and 1979, giving a capital gain of 68 per cent, and the pre-tax dividend yield varied between 3.10 per cent and 7.68 per cent. Taking an average yield of 5.0 per cent, plus the average capital gain of 3.8 per cent we get an annual average yield of 8.8 per cent. On this tax is payable, and you cannot live in a share portfolio! It is obviously difficult to obtain figures on the rate of return to new businesses, but the Bank of England has produced an economy-wide series of post-tax real returns. These (and Table 7) are indicative of the magnitude of returns that can be obtained from productive enterprise, and especially in the 1970s they are very low indeed. We have shown that there has been scope for entrepreneurial activity in the housing market. Profits have been available, and it is implausible that they have not been taken by many individuals. It is a tenet of what Austrian writers call praxeology, or the theory of action, that a change in price signals will change people's actions; in this case the direction of the effect is unambiguously clear, and we have been able to give some indication of the order of magnitude by considering some typical individuals whose actions, we believe, closely approximate those of large numbers of actual individuals. If opportunities for entrepreneurial activity in the housing market have been taken entrepreneurial effort will have been drained off from elsewhere. As Kay and King (1978, 65) point out, this favouring of 'civil servants' assets' will significantly reduce mobility between occupations and locations, so reducing effort for profit elsewhere.[10] The plungers of our analysis may indeed be those who choose safe but 'unproductive' public sector jobs from which to indulge their entrepreneurial housing market behaviour.

It seems unlikely that many ordinary new businessmen could have done better than the ordinary speculator in housing during the last decade and a

TABLE 7. *Returns from alternatives*

	1965	1966	1967	1968	1969	1970	1971	1972	1973	1974	1975	1976	1977	1978	1979
Stock index [1] (FT All Share)	99.08	100.46	107.32	151.01	148.82	134.9	164.49	212.26	184.61	106.75	133.11	153.04	191.91	216.68	167.79
Dividend yield [1]	5.35	5.47	5.02	3.62	3.82	4.39	3.76	3.10	3.83	7.68	6.43	6.10	5.52	5.54	5.19
Bank estimates of real returns [2]	7.0	5.7	6.3	5.9	5.0	4.1	4.5	5.0	7.2	4.0	3.0	3.0	3.6	3.8	

Notes: [1] *Financial Statistics.* Again 1979 figures differ, they are the observation for February.
[2] *Bank of England Quarterly Bulletin.* These are real, post-tax returns after depreciation, to non-North Sea Oil enterprises.

half. Some who were very lucky or very good at something might have made an annual return better than 15 per cent or so, but the returns from housing have been so good that many must have thought it not even worth trying to set up in business. There has been a decline in the provision of entrepreneurial funds supplied by relatives (Cmnd 7503, 1979). As a corollary to this the building societies have reported a rise in 'other lending' for mortgagors to make up the purchase price, and they presume this comes largely from relatives etc. (Aunt Agatha knows her funds are better placed in bricks and mortar, whether her own or a relative's.)

One implication of our argument may be found rather surprising. We have argued that the group from which small business proprietors are traditionally supposed to be drawn, those with some initial capital, a desire to increase it, and a taste for taking risks, will in general have been more sensible to continue to make their transfer earnings in their existing job, and speculate in the housing market. Who then *is* likely to have 'tried their hand' at entrepreneurship? Some unlikely groups of potential entrepreneurs come to mind: those with insufficient income to be able to get a mortgage, those too old to get a mortgage, and even those with a very strong aversion (for whatever reason) to living in a privately owned home. Casual empiricism does seem to produce a little evidence for this unlikely hypothesis: at a time when new business ventures are rare many towns sport new cooperatively run small wholefood cafés and shops, secondhand-clothes shops and junk stalls, tea shops run by retired couples, one-man van hire and taxi services, etc. Some of the sources of this sort of very small-time entrepreneurial activity will presumably also dry up as those not previously able to afford a home of their own and living in council houses are offered 'the right to purchase (their) own home at a substantial discount on the market price and with 100 per cent mortgages for those who need them' (Thatcher, 1979).

4. *Some international comparisons*

It is of course useful to compare the effects of a particular subsidy system with the alternative subsidy systems available. There are a large number of possible systems for subsidising home-ownership and they will have differential impacts on the economy. We can distinguish four basic ways of running housing subsidies (they are not exclusive):
(a) The building of houses for sale can be subsidised.
(b) The individual buying a house can be given a specific sum of money.
(c) The costs of buying and owning the house can be subsidised.
(d) Housing interest rates can be held below market levels.

There is a great variety of structures of savings institutions in housing sectors in different countries, but we shall not concentrate on these, because

it is the government treatment of actual purchases that matters. We need to answer a number of questions when looking at subsidy systems.
(a) Is the size of subsidy known, or can it be changed by the individual's actions over time?
(b) Is the size of the subsidy subject to unexpected variation because of variations in inflation rates?
(c) Does the subsidy system encourage trading-up?

Before giving country-specific answers we can make some general points. The interest paid on a loan may be fixed or variable, either at or below the market rate. If a fixed rate system is used the nominal size of any tax relief subsidy will be known, whereas a variable rate system will give a variable nominal subsidy. A fixed market rate will reflect inflation so that the real expected size of the subsidy will be known, in which case there will be less scope for entrepreneurial action than when it is not known. Any tax-relief-on-interest system will encourage trading-up to obtain a large subsidy. Individual subsidies obviously induce less speculative pressure (as do building subsidies), because they are known or fixed to incomes when purchase decisions are made, and individual subsidies can be much more directly channelled to first time buyers. Given these general principles we can compare subsidy system and their effects on entrepreneurship.

The only European country that appears to have a more generous policy than the UK is Ireland, where the system is the same as the UK's but also includes building subsidies. As a result the Irish have the highest level of home-ownership in Europe (75 per cent). The Danes and the Italians both have fixed interest loans markets with loans being made at the market rate reigning at the time. Both also allow interest against taxation, and so there is an interest subsidy, but it is fixed in nominal, and therefore in expected real terms. As evidence of less trading up the Building Societies Association reports much less home mobility in Denmark than the UK (*Building Societies Association Bulletin*, January 1980). A fixed interest bond will lead to unexpected gains (and losses) when inflation fluctuates, but it is exactly at the time when gains have been the largest (i.e. at or just after an inflationary peak), that it is most expensive to trade-up. Speculation is thus not encouraged by the Danish and Italian systems, and though their tax treatment is similar to the UK's we should expect the effects to be less.

The French had a fixed interest system, but have moved away from it since 1977 when the Barre reforms were introduced to combat 'subsidies to buildings not people'. Individuals get personal aid and subsidised loans depending on their means. Interest rates on housing loans are held down, but the tying of subsidies to individuals and scaling them to means cuts down the subsidy to speculative movers who are trading up. Higher subsidies come with higher income, and although this may seem inequitable it should lead to more enterprise and effort *outside* housing to increase the subsidy received. This sort of system can be (and is) heavily biased to first time buyers. It should induce a great deal less housing speculation.

The Dutch and the Germans appear to have the least generous and the least distortionary systems in Europe. The Dutch give person-specific subsidies (which decline over time), as well as assisting building, so there is little a person can do on the housing market to increase the subsidy received. The German system at first sight seems the least generous, and the Germans seldom move after they purchase their first home (on average rather late in life). Depreciation on a house is allowed against tax, and this subsidy is not subject to speculative or inflation-induced surges, so will not induce entrepreneurs to chase it. Very generous subsidies are given for two-family homes, and a common pattern is to rent half the house as a maisonette, then use it in the peak family size years, then rent out again in old age. This produces a much larger and healthier rented market than in the UK and obviously aids labour mobility; but the size of the subsidy is known, so there is little incentive for trading-up.

The US system has similarities to that in the United Kingdom, but trading-up on mortgages appears much more common, with the fraction of first of first time buyers varying between 18 per cent (1979) and 36 per cent (1977). Many mortgages in the USA are at a fixed rate, but this system has become much more flexible over the last ten years. Interest payments and property taxes (rates) are deductable from taxable income. As Anthony Downs (1980) stresses:

The really stupendous advantage of home-ownership results from...(not)... paying capital gains taxes on the proceeds (of a sale) as long as another home is purchased ($100,000 can be taken out after age 55).

Downs stresses the deleterious effects of housing subsidies on the economy during inflationary periods, especially their effects on small business. Despite these obvious drawbacks the Conservative Government of Joe Clark in Canada in 1979 was pledged to introduce mortgage interest relief for homeowners to bring Canada into line with the USA.

What implications do these differing subsidy systems have for the health of different national economies, and specifically their small business sectors? As the Interim Report of the Wilson Committee (Cmnd 7503, 1979) states, there are 'considerable difficulties in making reliable comparisons for the different countries' of the size of the small business sector. It is clear that the proportion of manufacturing employment in small firms is smallest in the UK for those countries where reliable data is available, and it is much higher in France, Belgium and the Netherlands where the housing subsidy system militates against entrepreneurial speculation. Table 8 indicates the relative magnitudes of the existing small business sectors.

TABLE 8. *Sizes of small business sectors and growth rates in seven countries*

Country	% Manufacturing in Small Firms* (Dates of Census etc. in brackets)		Growth in per capita GDP 1950-78
Italy	59%	(1971)	4.1
Belgium	45%	(1975)	3.4
Netherlands	42%	(1977)	3.3
France	38%	(1972)	3.8
USA	38%	(1972)	2.2
Germany	31%	(1976)	4.5
UK	29%	(1975)	2.1

Sources: Wilson Committee Interim Report (Cmnd 7503, 1973) and Bannock (1981, 52).
Note: *Generally small establishments (less than 200 employees) except for figures for UK and Netherlands, which refer to firms.

The atrophied small firm sector in Britain is attributed by the Bolton Committee (Cmnd 4811, 1971) to a low birth rate for enterprises in the UK compared to other countries, and this paper suggests a good reason for the low birth rate in Britain. It must be remembered when making international comparisons that it is not the level of subsidy that matters so much as the potential for individuals to increase the amount received by activity on the housing market. Growth has been low in the UK and the US, the most generous and most exploitable subsidisers. In France, Germany and the Netherlands, where it has been far more difficult to make entrepreneurial gains in housing, growth rates have been high. In Italy and Denmark, where the fixed rate system prevails, albeit with subsidies, there has been intermediate economic performance along with some possibilities for entrepreneurship in housing. We are not claiming that the exploitability of the housing subsidy system is the sole factor explaining differential performance, but the relationship is rather striking.

5. Why housing subsidies?

> I turn first to the question of choice in housing. Thousands of people in council houses and new towns came out to support us for the first time because they wanted a chance to buy their own homes. We will give every council tenant the right to purchase his own home at a substantial discount on the market price and with 100 per cent mortgages for those who need them. This will be a giant stride towards making a reality of Anthony Eden's dream of a property-owning democracy. It will do something else – it will give more of our people that freedom and mobility and that prospect of handing something on to their children and grandchildren which owner-occupation provides (Thatcher, 1979).

The rhetoric of this statement appears to be in tune with the fundamental social objectives of the new right both in Britain and elsewhere. Emphasis is put on the importance of freedom, mobility and wealth creation. On the other hand, these objectives are to be achieved by the offering of a substantial discount on the market price: not a policy usually approved of by those of this persuasion. The apparent inconsistency arises from an attempt to elide two quite distinct policy objectives: that of developing a vigorous free-market economy with as little government interference as possible, and that of guaranteeing the fundamental conditions for the existence of such an economy.

As far back as Adam Smith, advocates of the free market have stressed the necessity for certain well-defined functions to be fulfilled by the state. Smith confined the 'duties of the sovereign' to national defence, the administration of justice and 'erecting and maintaining those public institutions and those public works, which, though they may be in the highest degree advantageous to a great society, are, however, of such a nature, that the profit could never repay the expense to any individual of a small number of individuals' (Smith, 1976, 244). In this century many western governments seem to have added a fourth necessity to these: the necessity to extend property-ownership to as large a proportion of the population as possible. The necessity to expand home-ownership seems indeed to have come to be viewed (even perhaps by the British Labour Party) as a duty of government comparable to that to provide adequate defence of the realm, i.e. as necessary to guarantee the continued existence and stability of a democratic society.[11]

If this is the case then there is no necessary inconsistency in the Thatcher administration's advocacy both of less government interference in the market process in general and yet of government intervention to increase home-ownership. But since all interventionary policies will have some repercussions on the economy as a whole it surely befits any government espousing both objectives to choose a form of housing policy which is likely to have as small a disruptive effect on the efficiency and growth of productive capacity in the economy as possible. As we have argued, however, the subsidy system chosen in Britain is less compatible than most alternatives with the objective of encouraging new productive entrepreneurial activity.

6. Implications and conclusions

If we accept that the governments of most western countries are committed to the creation of 'property-owning democracies', the rationales for the particular subsidy systems they choose are still open to question. Any system will have implications for the supply of productive entrepreneurial effort to the economy: some, as we saw in section 4, have less far-reaching effects than others. We have attempted to address the questions: What is wrong with the current British system, and how could it be improved?

There are two reasons for stressing the effects of housing subsidies on entrepreneurship. Firstly a large and unpredictable subsidy system offers potential for capital gain, and to the extent that individuals in Britain do possess entrepreneurial ability in the Austrian sense we must assume that they will have acted so as to actualise this potential. Secondly we have stressed that entrepreneurship is not in unlimited supply, even though its market price is zero, since effort takes time, and time and the agility to use it effectively are limited. The British subsidy system drains effort into unproductive uses, and we have argued that this diversion of entrepreneurial abilities has been a major cause of slow small business formation and the consequent slow rate of economic growth.

We have seen that tax relief on variable interest rates for loans, as seen in the USA and Ireland as well as the UK, are at the heart of the problem. They encourage trading-up: the main vehicle of speculation. They also present governments with political problems which induce them to keep interest rates down. This appears to have been a very important influence on monetary policy in a number of countries in the 1970s. There are advantages to a fixed rate or bond system such as those still in use in Denmark and Italy, but they also have drawbacks. A fixed rate loan will discourage reborrowing just at the moment when any interest rate subsidy would be at its highest; when interest rates reach their peak. It thus militates against trading-up at this point, unlike the flexible rate system which encourages it most at the interest rate (or inflation) peak. Despite this advantage the fixed rate system may still induce entrepreneurial effort in housing: the financial burden of high interest payments seems to frighten governments, and they tend to intervene to hold housing rates down at their peaks, thus leaving the possibility of speculative gains for the alert individual.

What tool is available besides interest rate subsidies? We could have building subsidies, such as exist in several European countries. These can act to expand the supply of housing and so reduce its cost, thus stimulating ownership. Of course the supply can only expand if enough housing land is made available, either by rezoning or allowing densities to rise. British governments have seemed loath to employ these policies, but a building subsidy system without them is just a transfer to the owners of the land. Individual subsidies have become more common in Europe (they are employed in France and the Netherlands). These have a number of advantages. The real size of the subsidy can be fixed in advance, as in France, and the number of times it is received can be controlled. This removes the possibility of speculative gain during a mortgage and also can remove the inducement for trading-up.

Individual rather than interest rate subsidies seem to be the way to free entrepreneurship from its unproductive involvement in housing. First-time buyers could be offered lump sums proportional to either their savings or their incomes (both methods are used in France). The size of the subsidy for house purchase could be determined in relation to the costs of the current system. Alternatively all buyers could be offered a subsidy in proportion to their incomes. Although this would encourage wasteful trading-up this would not involve entrepreneurial effort. Individuals could only increase the subsidy per move by increasing their incomes; a desirable incentive in the eyes of most governments. These schemes may seem inequitable, but they are less so than the current British system, and they would at least not be the 'real deterrent to initiative and enterprise'[12] in the productive sector, which we believe the current housing subsidy system to be.

NOTES

1 For striking evidence of the British Government's intellectual attachments one need look no further than the now famous reading list Sir Keith Joseph prepared for his civil servants, which featured works by Schumpeter and Frank Knight, along with those of such latter-day Austrians as Professors Littlechild and Cheung, both writers for the Institute of Economic Affairs, in whose publication lists they have kept company with Hayek in recent years.
2 There is a significant difference between the views of entrepreneurship of Schumpeter and of modern Austrian writers such as Kirzner. Kirzner (1973, 79ff) points out that Schumpeter's characterisation of the entrepreneurial role is an essentially disequilibrium one. For Schumpeter the entrepreneur is a person who makes the economy lurch out of static equilibrium by introducing technological innovations. He was still tainted by the static equilibrism of the classical economists, whereas for modern Austrians, economic equilibrium, to the extent they find it a useful concept at all, is dynamic. Kirzner does not stress the other major difference between himself and Schumpeter; the relative spread of entrepreneurial ability. Schumpeter sees it as essentially unusual, located in only a few individuals, whereas Kirzner and von Mises believe that 'knee jerk' entrepreneurship is *the* distinguishing feature of human action. It is characterised as an all-pervasive attribute.
3 See Kay and King (1978) for further evidence.
4 As Armen Alchian (1950) has argued, those that fail to do so will go out of business in a competitive environment anyway.
5 It would be possible to design an equitable non-front-loaded scheme; for instance a repayment of 6 per cent of the nominal value of the house each year for twenty years. The most efficient way to calculate the nominal value would be to use an index such as the GDP deflator. This would involve approximately 3 per cent real return to the lender. The government could then decide to tax or subsidise this interest payment if it wished. Building societies would probably not object to the reforms proposed. They are not, and were not, set up as profit maximisers. They obviously maximise 'managerial goals', if they maximise anything. Variables such as total size, number of branches, degree of decision making in the hands of managers etc., will enter their 'objective function'. The current market structure inevitably means nearly continuous mortgage rationing and shortage of funds, which induce a lot of managerial stress and remove managerial discretion. A new system would allow societies more flexibility.
6 Of course not all redemptions result from sales: in 1973 22 per cent of redemptions were for other reasons (*Housing Policy Technical Volume*, Part II, HMSO, 1977), and it is believed that these were largely financed by inheritances.
7 The date of moving is of course itself an entrepreneurial decision, and so is really an endogenous variable. We do not want to claim that all home-owners act entrepreneurially, but it is interesting to note that 27 per cent of mortgages taken out in 1975 had been redeemed by 1978 (*Building Societies Association Bulletin*, 1981).

8 Detailed calculations are available.
9 This is partly because of the asymmetry of treatment of mortgages. Businesses receive interest relief on loans as well, but since the removal of Schedule A Assessment for houses in 1963 a difference has appeared. Businesses pay tax on returns and capital gains – householders do not (see Kay and King, 1978, chapter 4).
10 According to Kay and King (1978) houses, like other liquid assets, 'are well suited to people who have conventional intentions and predictable career prospects, but not to those who have no settled plans, who wish to take risks, or who have uncertain incomes. [They cannot] be readily realised in an emergency, to tide over the period between jobs, to start a business, or to buy or expand one.'
11 'The accumulation of property has the effect which it has always had upon thrifty men, it makes them steady, sober and diligent. It weans them from revolutionary notions, and makes them conservative' (Samuel Smiles in 1864, quoted in Pawley, 1978, 34).
12 This was Mrs Thatcher's description of capital transfer tax (Thatcher, 1979).

REFERENCES

Alchian, A. (1950) Uncertainty, evolution and economic theory, *Journal of Political Economy*, 58, 211–21.
Bannock, G. (1981) *The Economics of Small Firms*. Oxford: Basil Blackwell.
Coddington, A. (1975) Creaking semaphore and beyond: a consideration of Shackle's 'Epistemics and economics', *British Journal for the Philosophy of Science*, 26, 151–63.
Cmnd 4811 (1971) *Report of Committee of Inquiry on Small Firms* (The Bolton Report). London: HMSO.
Cmnd 7503 (1979) *The Financing of Small Firms* (The Wilson Committee Interim Report). London: HMSO.
Dolan, E. (ed.) (1976) *The Foundations of Modern Austrian Economics*. Kansas: Sheed and Ward.
Downs, A. (1980). Too much capital for housing?, *Brookings Bulletin* 17 (1), 1–5.
Housing Policy Review, Technical Volume II (1977). London: HMSO.
Kay, J. and M. King (1978) *The British Tax System*. Oxford: Oxford University Press.
Kirzner, I. (1973) *Competition and Entrepreneurship*. Chicago: University of Chicago Press.
von Mises, L. (1949) *Human Action*. London: Hodge.
von Mises, L. (1978) *The Ultimate Foundation of Economic Science*. Sheed, Andrews and McMeel.
Pawley, M. (1978) *Home Ownership*. London: Architectural Press.
Robinson, R. (1978) *Economic Journal*, 88, 182.
Schumpeter, J. (1942) *Capitalism, Socialism and Democracy*. London: Allen and Unwin.
Smith, A. (1976) *The Wealth of Nations* (ed. Edwin Cannan). Chicago: University of Chicago Press.
Spadaro, L. (ed.) (1978) *New Directions in Austrian Economics*. Sheed, Andrews and McMeel.
Thatcher, M. (1979) Debate on the Queen's Speech, *House of Commons Debates*, 1138.

Energy Policy

Energy policy over the past decade can be described as having been on a nonstop roller coaster. The upturns, nosedives, and stalls have all been part of the policy process. The nation has been through oil boycotts, Project Independence, 55-mile-per-hour speed limits, and an accident at the Three Mile Island nuclear power plant. At present, the Reagan administration is committed to eliminating the Department of Energy and fracturing energy policy among several remaining executive agencies and departments. Evident in the actions and reactions of the federal energy policy apparatus is that no political consensus—indeed, no will—exists to establish and sustain a coherent and unified approach to the use, conservation, and creation of energy. The articles in this section address each of these three aspects of energy policy.

The role of nuclear fuel in industrial societies is a flash point of political conflict. The spectrum of views on this subject ranges from the political far right to the far left, from all-out production and increased reliance to outright rejection and shutdown of those plants now operating. The nuclear fuel issue has implications for strategic military policy, for domestic energy needs, for storage of ever-accumulating nuclear waste, and for the physical health and survival of people everywhere.

What has complicated the policy process is that some aspects of nuclear technology are far advanced over others; for example, the creation of nuclear weapons versus their control or the creation of nuclear fuel versus the storage of the waste, some of which has a potential half-life of more than 100,000 years. La Porte addresses the policy issues inherent in developing a strategy to manage nuclear waste. Rydell assesses the capability of nuclear suppliers to ensure an ongoing supply of the fuel to various users, while at the same time discouraging the proliferation of nuclear weapons. His chapter presents a striking analysis of the international linkages and interdependencies involved in the nuclear question that make it difficult if not impossible for any one supplier country individually to solve either the supply or control problem.

Finally, Morell explores the public policy (or lack thereof) with respect to energy conservation. His analysis of the policy process in this area suggests: (1) that certain assumptions about the continued availability of energy are congruent with "basic American myths," while arguments for conservation run contrary to these myths; (2) that the structure of American energy companies and government bureaucracies is oriented toward continued emphasis on supply strategies, not toward conservation; and (3) that continuing to emphasize consumption requires efforts of only a few persons, whereas countervailing conservation activities involve the participation of large numbers of persons in the society. The conclusion to be drawn from these factors is that the future of energy policy in the United States rests on political and economic considerations, not on technological development.

38

MANAGING NUCLEAR WASTE

Todd R. La Porte

Since the dawn of the nuclear age in the early 1940s, there has been a slow accretion of radioactive garbage resulting from the production of nuclear weapons and, more recently, from the fabrication and burning of nuclear fuel in electric power generators. Until the early 1970s, it was assumed that the problems of putting these radioactive wastes out of harm's way were strictly technical ones of limited policy significance. Increasingly in the past several years, environmentalists and scientists, concerned respectively about the long-term damage to the biosphere and the threat of further proliferation of nuclear weapons, have called this assumption into question. Considerable public debate has ensued and waste management is now one of the most troubling aspects of widespread deployment of nuclear power reactors. The policy debate about waste management, however, has emphasized the long-term physical isolation of nuclear wastes, ignoring the problems associated with a fully deployed U.S. waste management system operating as part of a mature nuclear economy. This emphasis has resulted in neglecting shorter-term social and institutional challenges of waste disposal systems and focusing primarily on small-scale demonstration of disposal techniques.

The problem of radioactive waste management challenges us, as a society, to take as much care for present and succeeding generations as for those in the distant future. That challenge derives as much from the extraordinary institutional (and perhaps technical) design problems of dealing with large quantities of radioactive materials *before* their ultimate burial as from the scientific and technical puzzles of sequestering these materials deep under the ground for well over 100,000 years. The properties of radioactive materials and wastes, the way society is coming to view them, and the size and complexity of industrial operations reduce the utility of trial-and-error learning as a basis for improving policy and waste-management systems, as well as create the extraordinary tasks of developing nearly error-free operational systems for handling radioactive materials and wastes and nearly escape-proof burial grounds for them. These are remarkable demands upon a society and an intellectual community which have deeply embedded within their institutions and workways a short-time perspective, confidence in incremental, pragmatic processes of policy and substantive improvement, and an aversion to comprehensive, synoptic plans productive of constraining, inflexible programs. Thus, the social properties of a large-scale nuclear waste management system present unprecedented theoretical and methodological challenges not only for the policy community, but especially for the social science community.

While these dilemmas take an extreme form in the area of radioactive waste management, they are not unique to it. An increasing number of problems—such as pesticides, food additives, air and water pollution, air traffic control, the operation of the international monetary system, and global warfare—are coming to take on many of the same properties. Futhermore, similar problems attach not only to waste disposal, but to the handling of radioactive materials throughout the nuclear fuel cycle.

Analytical Challenges

Much of the policy debate about the disposal of radioactive wastes has been dominated by concerns for the distant future—for the safety of generations thousands of years hence who might be harmed by releases of radioactive materials from deep geological repositories. This is not surprising, for some of these materials remain potentially hazardous for well over 100,000 years. Add to this the fact that a well-developed nuclear economy based on today's Light Water Reactors (LWR) and reprocessing could be expected to last over 200 years, during which all of the nation's, indeed, the world's, nuclear wastes that *could* be produced *would* be produced.

Published by permission of Transaction, Inc. from SOCIETY, Vol. 18, No. 5, Copyright © 1981 by Transaction, Inc.

(If the breeder reactor, LMFBR, were introduced, nuclear power could be produced for about 2,000 years.) Thus, after the close of the nuclear age, sometime around the year 2200 A.D. (or 4200 A.D.), the storage of radioactive wastes would have to be effective for something like 100,000 years—until around 102,000 A.D. In effect, the benefits of energy for the world's economy would have been derived in about 1/500 (or 1/50) the time-span during which nuclear wastes are hazardous to health and possibly to genetic development.

The technical elements of the debate on nuclear wastes have emphasized development of techniques to immobilize the wastes in such a way that they will stay where they are put for a very long time. The heart of this challenge is to design waste forms, containers, and other manmade barriers and to select geological environments for repositories such that the chemical transformations of the wastes and the migration of radionuclides through the ground will take so long that, if there is a release into the biosphere, the effects will be negligible. The emphasis is upon keeping wastes in place once they are buried. This

> Problems attach not only to waste disposal, but to the handling of radioactive material throughout the nuclear fuel cycle.

is primarily a scientific and technical challenge, albeit an unprecedented one, because it demands assured knowledge of the physical properties of waste forms and their interactions with various geological media.

The social/political elements of the debate, consistently subordinated to its technical elements, have turned on different preferences for the process that should be employed and the factors that should be considered to legitimate the decisions about the safety of the repositories and their location. Often termed "the problem of public acceptance" by the technical community, these elements have emerged at both state and federal levels and are a continued source of frustration to the energy community.

In neither technical nor institutional considerations has there been more than perfunctory attention paid to the problems of preparing and getting nuclear wastes to and into repositories during the next 200-2000 years in a way that will avoid untoward health and/or social consequences. From the nearly exclusive emphasis on the scientific and technical problems of assuring perpetual isolation of radioactive wastes from the biosphere, it could be inferred that these issues do not require special concern. Implicitly, the safety of humanity over the next several hundreds of years seems to be viewed by planners as relatively assured. But is this preoccupation with the potential hazards to distant generations justified?

Such a long-term view is unique in bureaucratic perspectives. Is this a rare case of bureaucratic *fore*sightedness, commendable in its focusing on a problem in the distant future and avoiding the usual myopia of large organizations? Or is this perhaps the first instance of bureaucratic *far*sightedness, hyperopically seeing the forest but missing the trees?

Two questions point to conditions that, if not avoided, would suggest we have mistaken farsightedness for foresightedness: (1) How do radioactive materials compare with other toxic substances in their unhealthy effects, especially cancer, and their mutagenic effects that could be passed on to succeeding generations? (2) Could we be in jeopardy of accidentally releasing in the near future as much or more radioactive hazard than would likely be released "by design" from geological repositories in the distant future?

The first consideration is fundamental to our fear of nuclear wastes and of the whole nuclear fuel cycle. It is the sense that radioactive hazards may be potentially greater than those from other toxic materials. There is no question about the general carcinogenic properties of radioactivity. Allowing much radioactive material into the biosphere could add a great burden of sickness and death to an increasingly cancer-ridden planet. Reluctance to export such a burden into the distant future is one reason great care is taken in the design and establishment of nuclear wastes repositories. But if increased likelihood of cancer or other somatic effects were the only hazard associated with nuclear wastes, the public's response to the problem would probably be less agitated.

Radioactive materials—it could be argued—would not be viewed much differently from other carcinogenic substances were it not for the possibility that exposure to radiation might also increase the risk of transmissible genetic damage and/or changes. If cumulative genetic effects were definitely not possible, we would probably continue to treat radioactive materials like other toxic substances. That is, some classes of people would be encouraged to handle them—as needed for industrial and national defense purposes—in reasonable though not absolute safety—and thereby risk a somewhat earlier death. We have for at least a century allowed the uneducated and untrained, and/or the economically disadvantaged, to expose themselves more than the members of society-at-large to a variety of risks, usually in exchange for modest sums of money.

Whether radiation could, in fact, produce a genetically cumulative effect is a matter of some debate. It seems clear that radiation can injure genetic materials, sometimes inducing genetic changes. However, it is not obvious that transmissible change would occur in human beings, nor is it clear what level of radiation a population or person would have to sustain to begin such transmissible effects. It seems that such an untoward consequence is a low-probability risk. Nonetheless, at present there appears to be at least a theoretical basis for not rejecting the plausibility that cumulative genetic damage may be done. From a public-policy perspective, this property of radioactive materials puts them in a toxic class nearly by themselves. While radiation may or may not result in transmissible genetic damage, *if it does*, and as a result of nuclear waste management practices the chances are appreciably increased, the consequences are very troubling indeed. If we are unwilling to export such consequences into the future, we must act as if there were a definite correlation between radiation and mutation.

Settling these matters of radiation safety will consume many years, so many that we are not likely to wait for answers before making plans to deal with present wastes and those to be generated in the near future. There is already a large store of wastes to be put away, and the nuclear industry insists that a long delay—one sufficient to assure a credible resolution of the radioactivity/genetic relationship—would destroy our capacity to build and deploy nuclear power reactors. Thus a great deal of effort is being devoted to developing waste handling, as well as storage, regimes so that further deployment of nuclear energy may proceed.

The need to develop methods for handling nuclear wastes leads into the second central question, which contrasts the hazard likely to be exported to the distant future, due to leakages of dissolved wastes from repositories, with the accidental releases of radioactivity, of a fresher, more dangerous sort, during the operational phases of waste handling, reprocessing, solidification, transport, and emplacement. Such a contrast suggests that at least as much care should be taken with the present and succeeding generations as with those far in the future. This implies an operational goal for the performance of waste management systems (and the rest of the fuel cycle): that no more radiological hazard should be released into the biosphere during active preparation and handling of radioactive materials and wastes over the lifetime of a nuclear economy, say 200 years, than would be released from wastes stored in well-designed repositories throughout their effective lifetimes. To get a clearer sense of how stringent this requirement is, answers to the following questions should be sought from the relevant agencies and industries. (1) What is the estimate of the total amount of the world's wastes that will be stored in repositories at the end of the nuclear fuel economy? (While estimates vary greatly, doubling the estimated 4.2 million tons of U.S. uranium reserves gives some idea of magnitude.) (2) What are the likely release rates of radiological materials per ton of these wastes as they rest in repositories through the long holding times? (If there were the unlikely high cumulative release rate of one percent, some 84,000 tons of materials would escape.)

Such analyses would establish an upper boundary for the magnitude of the management problem (i.e., get it *all* in the ground and keep nearly all of it there). That is the challenge—*if* all goes perfectly in the next several hundred years as we prepare and emplace a growing volume of nuclear wastes. But if we are not so clever as we need to be and all does not go perfectly, then we have a rough guide for the level of performance that should be expected in the management of waste-processing systems throughout their lifetimes. That is, we would have estimated the total likely release from the systems intended to keep wastes isolated from the biosphere. As an operational goal, then, this repository release (hazard) figure should not be exceeded by releases (hazards) experienced during the process of preparing and getting wastes into the repositories.

For this performance standard to be useful, an additional calculation is required: given the character of waste forms likely to be produced in the near future from LWRs and LMFBRs, what volume of materials and amounts of radioactivity, if released accidentally during preparation and handling operations, would equal or exceed the level of radiological hazard resulting from the long-term release of the world's well-stored wastes? A great deal of time and effort is being devoted to the design of waste forms, cannisters, emplacement beds, etc., to assure the integrity of nuclear wastes once they are put to rest. It is plausible that, if given sufficient time and money, nuclear wastes can be so engineered that they will be quite isolated from the environment for many thousands of years. Therefore, when all the calculations are completed, it is likely that, even with an accumulation of all the radioactive wastes from a completed world nuclear energy economy stowed away in repositories, the amount of radiological hazard exported into the distant future as releases from those repositories will be rather small. Thus in the development of U.S. radioactive waste management policy, the distant future is being provided remarkable protection, *and* a very stringent level of performance is being established as a goal for operating nuclear fuel production and waste-handling systems.

If nearly escape-proof burial systems are developed in pursuit of safety for the distant future, it would be ironic if, through insufficient attention to the design of the operational systems needed, we were inadvertently to allow more radiological hazard to foul our present society than is bequeathed to generations many thousands of years from now. If our society holds to the notion that we should be as fair with ourselves as with the future, then we face the challenge of assuring nearly error-free operational management, as well as nearly escape-proof burial, of radioactive wastes.

Management Challenges

These challenges are due in part to the character of error. Radioactive materials have very long lifetimes; most of the releases of wastes produced during the nuclear age will contribute cumulatively to the burden borne by the distant future. Therefore, an error must be defined as any release (escape) of radioactive materials from the operational system such that recapture is either impossible or too costly to effect. There are two major types of situations in which such errors would occur: (1) the up-take of radioactive substances, especially plutonium by human beings involved in the handling of nuclear materials; and (2) spills and emissions of such materials outside the barriers designed to contain and recapture accidental and/or intentional escapes from the processing, transport, and emplacement systems. There have been some instances of both types of escape.

In late 1967, there was an unfortunate instance at the Nuclear Fuel Service Corporation (NFS), West Valley, New York, in which a young man inhaled a large dose of plutonium as he emerged from a decontaminating room in which he was working. No one knew how much he inhaled initially, but several days after the incident he registered 7800 counts per minute, 40 to 50 times the maximum permissible lung burden. Another instructive situation was the practice of using "transient workers" in these and other facilities to do particularly radiation-prone jobs. Radiation standards are cumulative as a function of time; if a worker's exposure nears them in a period shorter than the standards allow, he is prohibited from entering a radiation-prone area until the required time period has elapsed. Rather than subjecting trained

---

Much of the debate about the disposal of radioactive wastes has been dominated by concerns for the distant future.

---

personnel at the facility to quick bursts of radiation that approach permissible monthly or annual doses, thereby necessitating that they stay away from the facility, NFS and other nuclear materials handling facilities would hire transient, unemployed workers, paying them a day's wages for often less than ten minutes work—ten minutes in which they would receive the allowable monthly radiation dose. The obvious problem with this practice is that necessary safety training for such workers may not be sustained, and sufficient information about the hazard may not be given them.

An example of the second type of error comes from the now familiar Rocky Flats facility near Denver, Colorado, where radioactive materials have been discovered in the soil surrounding the main buildings. Even though this contaminated soil has been dug up and is now treated as radioactive waste, there is evidence that sufficient contamination remains to make the facility a public nuisance, if not a serious hazard.

Obviously, we have learned some things that will help prevent such errors in the future. But the nuclear waste management system likely to be necessary to accommodate a mature, large-scale nuclear economy may be such that lessons learned from our early experience will have only limited utility when applied to the fully deployed operational system. Some of the properties that would greatly increase the challenge of nearly error-free management are the degree to which: (1) trial-and-error learning as a mode of system improvement is drastically limited or unacceptable; (2) the system is very large in scale, and (3) internally complex; and (4) its task structure is routinized.

The first, most important, factor is that the public appears to be sufficiently fearful of the consequences of *any* significant error that we seem likely to forego the possibility of learning systematically from trial-and-error. By an essentially tacit agreement, the policy community, perhaps in response to strong pressures from environmental intervenors, seems to be saying that *any* error resulting in significant releases of radioactivity might occasion such untoward, potentially ruinous consequences that committing an error is unacceptable in the first instance. This is an extraordinary situation, i.e., it demands decision making without feedback. When coupled with the requirement for highly reliable, nearly error-free operations in systems which are large, highly complex and routinized, it presents one of the most rigorous challenges faced by social science today.

Decisions without Feedback

For the past three decades, a slowly maturing science of decision making has evolved, based increasingly on a combination of the information sciences, a refined understanding of the social psychology of decision makers, and the limitations of organizational behavior. When faced with increasingly complex situations, the most effective, least error-prone strategy in decision making is employment of an incremental, essentially trial-and-error, method of policy development. Its primary feature is to continue developing in the manner of recent past policies, awaiting confirming or dissenting signals from those most affected, while remaining ready to alter existing policies to rectify errors due to miscalculation or ignorance. This is at root a pragmatic approach trusting to the efficacy of error correction through feedback from customers and from a pluralistic, representative political system; an approach contrasted to the alternative of comprehensively analyzed plans which are impossible to attain.

The incremental approach is tailored best to situations that change slowly, in which errors can be quickly identified by those affected and those responsible, and in which the consequences of errors can be either remedied or repaired at reasonable cost or accepted as a cost against obviously greater benefits. As these conditions become difficult to meet, the utility of the incremental approach diminishes. When relatively rapid change is believed to be necessary, when actual errors take a long time to be recognized, and when the consequences of error are believed to be so ruinous and irreversible that they are too costly to countenance, our established processes of policy development falter as a means of arriving at decisions that can win the support of those groups in society necessary to legitimate and implement them.

The problem of disposing of radioactive wastes challenges us on each count. Demands for rapid resolution of the problem are pressed on the government by those who believe that continued deployment of nuclear energy reactors is necessary now to avoid an unacceptable energy shortage in the near future. In view of substantial uncertainties about the physical properties of wastes stored in the ground, some view these demands as radical and dangerously hasty. Due to uncertainties about the cumulative effects of radioactivity and the long duration of the waste's toxicity and necessary storage period, errors of several kinds, if they occur, could not be detected for many years (and then might not be understood by those threatened). Finally, the consequences of significant error to future generations are seen as so irreversible and so dreadful that we cannot imagine how trial-and-error learning about the overall performance of the system can be used to improve it. When mistakes are made, they will be discovered so far in the future that those responsible for them will be gone and the properties of the wastes will make remedy of the error nearly impossible. In essence, when an error is observed on the basis of the first trial, it is already too late.

Such a construction of the radioactive waste problem poses extraordinary political and analytical problems. Processes of public involvement, agency coordination, and regulatory procedures are designed to evoke opinion and may well aggregate interests and identify people who believe themselves to be jeopardized as well as bene-

> There is no question about the general carcinogenic properties of radioactivity.

fited. But in the face of uncertain consequences, magnitudes of harm, and fear of any significant errors, what is missing is the information necessary to reassure those who fear injury or to moderate the enthusiasms of those concerned only with short-term benefits. The process we now use becomes mainly a vehicle for mobilizing opposing factions. Confidence in our procedures of policy review is rooted in the assumption that the participation of many promoting and affected groups will reveal missing information about effects and inspire solutions to unexpected problems before they occur. It also assumes that if significant errors do occur in implementing policies so derived, their consequences will not be so egregious as to seem grievous to those affected. Our now familiar hearing processes bring people together for the airing of complaints and support. They make visible to all the range of potential problems and maldistribution of benefits possibly associated with particular policies. If the questions so raised appear to be quite serious and to require sophisticated informaton for resolution, and that information is unknown, this visibility has the effect of intensifying opposition and may result in paralysis. Such an outcome does little to enhance the legitimacy of agency decision making.

When a society has chosen to forego learning by trial-and-error in a particular area, the usual processes of pol-

icy implementation are wanting. Other methods of reducing uncertainty are required. This means paying much greater attention to improving the basic understanding of the phenomenon in question before action is taken; that is, approximating more nearly a comprehensively analyzed plan. The scope of such planning would require coverage of economic, social, and political phenomena, as well as the usually recognized technical elements. But this strategy is increasingly maligned and recognized as difficult, if not impossible, to effect with high degrees of completeness. Nonetheless, this is the approach now being followed increasingly to provide the detailed analysis necessary to assure the escape-proof burial of nuclear wastes. Thus far, it has not been applied to the processes of preparing and getting wastes to the repositories.

When we turn to the matter of processing and emplacing wastes so effectively that few, if any, errors occur, we are required to take the measure of actual operational demands as against the requisites for highly reliable, nearly error-free performance of large-scale organizations. Before we turn to these requisites, let us explore briefly something of the scale of the U.S. waste management challenge.

Whether or not there is further deployment of nuclear reactors in this country, a significant radioactive waste management problem already exists. At a minimum, it will be necessary to process and dispose of the high-level, transuranic, and low-level wastes that exist already in the form of spent fuel, as well as the wastes to be produced by the LWRs likely to be put into operation within the next few years. If the Interagency Review Group on

> Whether radiation could, in fact, produce a genetically cumulative effect is a matter of some debate.

Nuclear Waste Management (IRG) convened by President Carter can be considered authoritative, by about 1990 some 150 plants will be in operation, each one estimated to produce 1000 megawatts or 1 gigawatt of electrical energy. To these wastes must be added those likely to be "imported" from foreign producers into the United States, estimated to be something like ten percent of the wastes generated by foreign, free-world countries. Based on the IRG report figures, this would represent about twenty percent of the total annual burden upon U.S. capabilities by 1990. This assumes that the United States will seek to reduce the risk of nuclear proliferation through agreements to "buy-back" wastes from nations whose nuclear development we have encouraged and who are dependent upon U.S. suppliers for fresh nuclear fuel.

The following estimated extent of the minimum challenge assumes that no wastes will be reprocessed and that nuclear energy development will be limited to the 150 plants now projected. By late 1980, 17 million cubic feet of transuranic and nearly 9.5 million cubic feet of high-level wastes awaited some sort of disposition. In all, some 66.5 million cubic feet of low-level wastes have already been buried. By the end of the century, an additional 120 million cubic feet of low-level wastes will require burial, and over 6.7 million cubic feet of transuranic wastes and 1.2 million cubic feet of spent fuel will have accumulated for disposal. Perpetual storage of this material will require something like 2,650 acres, or 4 square miles. By the time the approximately 150 reactors generating power have completed their useful lifetimes—30 to 40 years—some 355 to 430 million cubic feet of wastes would require handling, of which some 110,000 to 150,000 metric tons (MT) would be very radioactive spent fuel. Add to these figures the 75 million cubic feet of wastes associated with decommissioning these 150 reactors. This represents an expansion by the year 2000 of annual waste handling capacity to some 3.2 million cubic feet per year, which includes something like 3800 MT per year of heavy metal embedded in spent fuel. The safe transportation of this material alone will pose a substantial operational challege. Thus, the nuclear waste management problem "on hand" is already considerable. It represents an irrevocable commitment to deal with radioactive waste until about 2040; i.e., after the 40-year active life of the "last" nuclear reactor has ended and some 10 to 15 additional years of handling time necessary to dispose of the "last" bits of wastes from spent fuel and the decommissioned reactors themselves have elapsed. In operational and institutional terms, this is already a stiff challenge to put before producing and regulating organizations.

As a rough upper boundary of estimated demand, if upper-level estimates consistent with the national plan announced by former President Carter in April 1977 were followed past the year 2000 and extended to about 2040, we would have expanded the number of nuclear plants to about 1000, adding 850 plants to those 150 likely to be on-line in 1990; i.e., at the rate of about 17 new plants a year over a 50-year period. If all these plants were LWRs (this is not likely—perhaps a third would be breeders) estimated annual waste flows would involve 25,000 MT of heavy metals and 20 million cubic feet of low-level wastes, not including the wastes from decommissioning. If the effective lifetimes of each plant facility were extended to about 40 years, an additional 12.5 cubic feet of low-level wastes would issue from complete decommissioning operations, though such extensive removal each year might not be necessary.

In the process of scaling-up from the 1990s level of 150 power plants to a 1000 plant system in 2040, over 29,000 reactor years of operation would have been added to the approximately 1100 projected until 1990. This represents an 8400 percent increase in power plant operations over the approxixmately 365 plant years (for reactors of 400 megawatt capacity or more) we have experienced thus far. This plan would obviously require considerable investment in reprocessing facilities and involve relatively large annual volumes of high-level wastes from the extraction of uranium and plutonium to be recycled for further use. This system would enable us, if we could accept the social and political requirements, to provide electric energy for some 2000 years and would afford generous opportunity for management error.

Because of the potential magnitude of the annual "throughput" of hazardous materials, we can expect strong pressures to achieve nearly error-free operations. To attempt this, it will be necessary to achieve the following conditions for the design and operation of a highly reliable, large-scale organizational system:

- Unambiguous, nearly complete causal knowledge about the necessary functioning of the system to assure expected outcomes.
- Nearly error-free performance from both personnel and machines that do not deviate from these activities/functions necessary to assure the consistent operation of the system.
- Error-detecting regimes designed to identify very small deviations from the operational norm for each component of the system and for behavior necessary to assure reliable functioning.
- Redundant "channels" of operation and error-absorbing/rectifying regimes that would (1) carry on activities in the face of inoperative components or miscalculations of human performance and (2) repair or eliminate the sources of errors in the system.

Three additional conditions are necessary in the event that the technology has not developed into a large-scale system but exists only at a small-scale demonstration phase, and that the consequences of error are such as sharply to limit the utility of trial-and-error learning.

- Systems to contain the consequences of error of sufficient effectiveness that, if potentially serious errors do occur, their consequences do not affect those outside the system.
- A well-developed, tested, and credible science of analogical learning and simulation of large-scale systems.
- Considerable caution in inferring that what has been learned in the small-scale, experimental phases will be nearly adequate for the design of highly reliable large-scale systems, especially if they are likely to be internally complex and composed of many routinized tasks.

These requisites are very rigorous for any type of technical or organizational system. They are especially stringent when applied to the management of radioactive wastes. Knowledge of the behavior of various waste forms in different types of geological media, both in the short- and long-term, is uncertain. Information about the requirements for the processing necessary to transform spent fuel into various waste forms is equally uncertain. And there is a near absence of knowledge about the scale and dynamics of a complete radioactive waste transforming and disposal system that would take into account the means for handling and transporting wastes necessary to produce highly consistent, nearly error-free performances from the people and machines associated with the process. Furthermore, the design of error-detecting, absorbing, and containing systems, or the requirements for redundancies within such systems, have not been applied rigorously to waste management in toto. This is especially true when considering the large volumes of wastes likely to be produced in a mature nuclear economy. Finally, one cannot put much confidence in our present understanding of analogous learning and simulation technology as a substitute for trial-and-error learning. Experience with waste management systems of any respectable scale must await future development; therefore, knowledge about such systems and their organizational operations can only be derived from analogous systems, i.e., those that are similar but not identical to waste systems yet to be developed. Armed with this inexact information, simulation techniques could be used, though they have not reached more than a modest level of complexity and have rarely been tested against very large-scale, complex organizations.

The fact that our past experience with radioactive waste handling is exclusively at the experimental, early demonstration level simply exacerbates the problem. We cannot confidently suppose that simply scaling-up from

---

Because settling matters of radiation safety will consume many years, we are not likely to wait for answers before making plans to deal with present waste.

---

existing systems will suffice. It seems clear that a radioactive waste management system, as it moves from a demonstration phase to a fully deployed, mature system, will take on quite different properties.

Such a system is likely to be very large and quite complex internally, with a variety of technical and management activities that will encourage attempts to routinize many of them. To the degree this is so, it confounds our abilities to devise and operate coordinative processes over which executives have a sure sense of control and which minimize errors and their consequences. Thus, the properties of scale, complexity, and routinization reduce the utility of experience based on experimental, smaller-scale demonstrations and immeasurably complicate the

analytical and operations problems involved. It is the combination of these three properties that confounds the development of policies and operations. In situations where only one increases—with the others held constant—problems are interesting and tractable. But in programs employing relatively sophisticated technologies, the properties of scale, complexity, and routinization are likely to increase together.

For systems based significantly on sophisticated knowledge and involving a relatively complicated series of technical processes, an increase in the scale of operations means an increase in internal technical and managerial complexity as well. It is obvious that nuclear waste processing systems meet the first condition. The requirement to process different forms of wastes issuing from military operations and both light water and fast breeder reactors results in the second condition. In-

---

At least as much care should be taken with the present and succeeding generations as with those far in the future.

---

creased volume of activities, as the waste processing systems expand in overall capacity, require that more people be employed. If sophisticated technical operations are involved, increased differentiation of specialists and technical groups is likely to occur. This is followed, with some lag, by the spread of both formal and informal means of coordinating these specialists and groups, resulting in the growth of internal interdependencies. As the scale of operations grows to meet the demands of a large number of nuclear reactors, multiple waste facilities and transport links between them are required, further increasing the complexities of operation.

If the consequences of error are believed to be very serious, as is the case here, we could expect an emphasis on means for anticipating and/or reducing errors; an emphasis which would further increase both formal and informal interdependencies. It is also likely that internal operations, as well as the links between facilities, will be influenced strongly by externally imposed standards of safety, enforced by agencies monitoring the adequacy of both technological and human performances. The increases of internal and network complexity confront managers with a situation that becomes increasingly problematic and difficult to comprehend fully.

The sense of integrated organizational coordination is apt to decline, and measures would then be taken to reduce managerial uncertainty in an attempt, in part, to prevent surprises and untoward errors. At least two measures are likely to be intensified, each intended to increase the predictability of operations: the use of management information control systems (often utilizing computerized monitoring procedures) and the routine standardization of specialized tasks. The elaboration of control systems would increase reliability insofar as they are based on complete, accurate information concerning the operation of the system to be controlled. Routinizing tasks reduces costs and usually increases the predictability of performance. Both these measures may be satisfactory if the consequences of errors are limited. If they are not, additional efforts are required.

If significant error must be avoided and effective reliability achieved, workers must be attentive to the demands of the task, however uninteresting they become. More importantly, workers must remain watchful for surprises and accommodate to circumstances not usually "programmed" into their routines. As the size and complexity of operations increase, the adequacy of the knowledge base declines and job "programming" necessarily is less complete. The need for both reliable and adaptive behavior from the people involved in waste handling, therefore, remains high, even as they are confronted with routinized, automated systems. This challenges management to provide incentive and training to compensate for the inherently error-inducing conditions of routine, familiarity, and continual success. Boredom and familiarity often result in inattentiveness to early signs of error and, combined with continual success (especially during the first several work generations), erode the experiential basis necessary to motivate subsequent generations to be watchful and to retain the ability to adapt to the unexpected (for it so rarely occurs). The burden on training and incentives is heavy: to so motivate reasonably able people that they will remember (through 7 to 8 work generations or more, covering some 250 years—and possibly a good deal longer) why they should be watchful over a system that seems not to fail, is so routinized and automated as to evoke ennui, yet demands the ability to recognize instantly the first signs of error onset, accommodate to such warnings and, if necessary, endanger one's life to mitigate the consequences of error.

Finally, we do not have (nor can we have) a relatively large-scale waste processing system from which to learn the particular technical and operational difficulties of scaling-up to handle and dispose of nuclear wastes at the volumes likely to be produced annually in the future.

Present and Future Threats

In the development of widely deployed nuclear waste handling systems, we risk increasing the possibilities for incurring error both in the design and in the operation of the system: errors that we do not want to make and from which remedial learning is of dubious value. Moreover, scaling-up and increasing the complexity of, say, a U.S. Nuclear Waste Management Service will increase the likelihood of errors and, implicitly, the economic and social costs of the system. The solution to the design and operation, and very likely the regulation, of radioactive waste disposal systems may not be as straightforward as for other large-scale engineering and regulating systems. The properties of the phenomenon confound established approaches and pose strong challenges for both technical and social science perspectives.

In the past, the Department of Energy (and its predecessors), the Nuclear Regulatory Commission, and the nuclear industry—those party to the deployment and regulation of nuclear power and its wastes—have not seen the need to treat radioactive waste disposal much differently from other technical systems. Rather they have behaved as if (1) the costs of waste management systems are likely to be so small a portion of the benefits of nuclear energy as to be unworthy of clear specification, and (2) the problems of scale-up and increasing complexity can be met without extraordinary efforts, perhaps with near perfect performance (or alternately, the consequences of potential errors are essentially insig-

> Whether or not there is further deployment of nuclear reactors in this country, a significant radioactive waste management problem already exists.

nificant and/or bearable in view of the benefits). Consequently, a precise specification of the actual scale, internal complexity, and routinized character of the projected system has not been made; and the character and costs of training programs required are uncertain. As a result, the data upon which to base estimates of the consequences of error, the costs of remedy, and the likelihood of error are not available.

The behavior of the agencies reflects a large measure of faith that the technical community will be able to devise relatively inexpensive, nearly error-free technosocial systems able to handle and sequester a large volume of very dangerous materials. Technical experts have acted as if there were highly reliable, large-scale, and only moderately expensive systems in other areas from which to derive analytical insight and/or there were available from simulations the high-quality design information needed for the development of such organizations. But there is neither actual experience nor credible causal knowledge to draw upon. It is warranted, therefore, that policy makers and citizens insist upon careful analytical treatment of the design and the socioeconomic questions involved. For the technical and regulatory communities to ignore these matters is now tantamount to intensifying the political conflict about nuclear energy. But when these matters are taken up seriously and attempts are made to improve the precision of social analysis, severe limitations in current social science conceptions are revealed.

These limitations stem in part from the onset of conditions only recently associated with organizational capacities; hence they have not confronted policy makers or social analysts before. The limitations include:

- the perception of potentially ruinous consequences should the preferred policy option turn out to be only partially successful;
- the realization that remedying the consequences of error, should it occur, would be extraordinarily costly, if not impossible altogether;
- the fact that indications of a significant error would occur so far in the future as to limit drastically the possibility of improvement;
- the sense that onset of error, however ruinous, may be quite unlikely;
- the probability that, in our concern to protect the distant future, error and significant shorter-term harm will be increased by the development of large-scale, internally complex, and routinized operational (and regulatory) organizations.

As these factors vary in intensity, so do the challenges of organizational design and the character of organizational regulatory politics. A careful review of social science theorizing and analysis reveals scant systematic development in our understanding of: the analysis of decision/policy situations in which incremental, trial-and-error learning has diminished utility, especially in providing schemes of error analysis, detection, and remedy regarding the internal operations of organizations as well as the outcomes of overall performance; the social design of highly reliable, large-scale organizations, with particular attention to various socialization processes and their fiscal and human costs; the effects upon the reliability and costs of the system of increasing scale of operations and tightening patterns of interdependence within and among organizational units; and finally, the dynamics of dissent and conditions of increased consensus within political systems of varied socioeconomic and ideological characteristics as they confront a growing range of low-probability, high-risk policies. Thus, the emerging and increasingly troubling challenge of radioactive wastes management, indeed of the whole nuclear fuel cycle, poses very substantial general theoretical and analytical problems for the social sciences, as well as enormous practical problems for the society.□

READINGS SUGGESTED BY THE AUTHOR:
La Porte, Todd R. "Nuclear Wastes: Increasing Scale and Sociopolitical Impacts." *Science* 191 (July 1978): 22-29.
Office of Technology Assessment. *Commercial High-Level Radioactive Waste Management.* Washington, D.C.: Government Printing Office, 1981.
Willrich, M., and Lester, R.K. *Radioactive Waste: Management and Regulation.* New York: The Free Press, 1977.

Todd R. La Porte is professor of political science and associate director of the Institute of Government Studies at the University of California at Berkeley.

APPROACHES TO NUCLEAR FUEL ASSURANCE
Balancing Nonproliferation with Energy Security

Randy J. Rydell

Nuclear fuel assurances are the formal promises that international suppliers extend to consumers of nuclear fuel for the twin purpose of meeting energy security needs and discouraging the proliferation of nuclear weapons. This article examines various international perspectives on the implementation of fuel assurances and suggests that a supplier's unilateral ability to solve either problem may be far more limited than is commonly believed. The relevance of fuel assurances in future international regimes for nuclear energy will be dependent upon the future structure of the nuclear market and the political linkages that are made between energy security and nonproliferation commitments.

The author is with the Lawrence Livermore Laboratory, University of California, PO Box 808, CA 94550, USA.

The views expressed in this article are solely those of the author and he wishes to thank J. Mullins, F. Mackie, G. Blair and S. Aoki for their criticisms and suggestions.

Countries that operate nuclear reactors, whether for research or power generation, are sensitive to the possibility that the fuel for these reactors might one day be cut off or interrupted by foreign suppliers. One way an importer might deal with this problem is by seeking an independent ability to supply this fuel through the development of national facilities for reprocessing, enriching and breeding nuclear fuel. Yet as these technologies are enormously expensive and produce fissile material suitable for the manufacture of nuclear weapons, most importers have to rely on formal promises from suppliers that fuel will be provided on a timely, reliable and economic basis. These promises, called nuclear fuel assurances, constitute a major element of ongoing international efforts to pursue the twin goals of energy security and nonproliferation.

This article will identify five regimes now under international discussion for the provision and disposition of nuclear fuel and will specify the likely effects of these arrangements on nuclear nonproliferation and energy security. It will discuss the emerging international consensus on the potential of nuclear fuel assurances to solve these problems and will argue that this consensus is based on some dubious assumptions about the impact such measures can have in either area. To the extent that fuel assurances will play an important role in any of the five regimes, this role will most probably be limited to certain special circumstances as discussed below.

An emerging consensus on fuel assurances

Recent discussions in several diplomatic arenas are revealing a growing international consensus, shared by nuclear suppliers and consumers alike, on the pivotal role that nuclear fuel assurances will play in the regime to govern future international commerce in nuclear technology. The most visible institutional expression of this consensus is the International Atomic Energy Agency's (IAEA) Committee on Assurances of Supply, which met in Vienna in September 1980. Nuclear fuel assurances were also key topics at recent conferences of the nuclear industry (Amsterdam,

London and Mexico City in autumn 1980), meetings of international research groups such as the Rockefeller Foundation's International Consultative Group on Nuclear Energy, NASAP and INFCE,[1] the Second Review Conference of the Nonproliferation Treaty (NPT) in August 1980;[2] and recent conferences of Heads of State of Non-Aligned Countries (eg Havana, September 1979). Specific US initiatives emphasizing fuel assurances are contained in Title I of the Nonproliferation Act of 1978.[3] Further illustrations of the wide international importance attached to fuel assurances are provided in the statements cited in Appendix 1.

The basic idea of fuel assurances as a tool of nonproliferation policy was formally enunciated in the US Atomic Energy Act of 1954, but has been subsequently used by suppliers to encourage adherence to the NPT and restraint in developing sensitive technologies such as enrichment, reprocessing, heavy water facilities and breeder reactors. According to a former US State Department spokesman for nonproliferation,

no principle was recognized earlier and was more important to the development of the current nonproliferation regime than the need to provide dependable fuel supply assurances to other countries.[4]

The linkage between fuel assurances and energy security is based on a variety of political and technical considerations concerning the operation of the international market for nuclear technology. Developing countries, which will have an estimated installed nuclear capacity of 27 GWe by 1990,[5] are increasingly aware of the importance of secure sources of supply. The industrialized world is also concerned, especially in light of a projected 150-250 GWe nuclear capacity for OECD countries by the same year.[6] The USA alone now has 298 contracts for enrichment services with domestic and foreign utilities, most of which extend into the next century, with a present value of $75 billion.[7] Thus, for a combination of economic and security-related reasons, both importers and exporters of nuclear fuel see fuel assurances as an attractive means of reinforcing energy security while discouraging proliferation.

Five international regimes

It is one thing for countries to agree on the centrality of fuel assurances in the wider international regime for nuclear power, but quite another to build a consensus on the policies required to implement the notion. A brief survey of recent literature on nonproliferation reveals no less than 16 different measures currently being advanced under the rubric of nuclear fuel assurance (see Appendix 2). Ranging from renegotiated bilateral guarantees to allocative schemes involving a global authority, all of these measures attempt to strike a balance between energy security and nonproliferation. The diplomatic challenge thus lies more in reconciling different national interpretations about where this balance should lie than in the establishment of fuel assurances in the nonproliferation regime. In various combinations, these separate measures form the bases of five regimes for the international market in nuclear fuels, with each regime differing in terms of the amount of central international coordination required.

Centralist regimes

In the early days of nuclear power (1946), the USA, the UK and Canada

---

[1] The International Nuclear Fuel Cycle Evaluation (INFCE) was a two year international assessment of the dangers of proliferation posed by various nuclear fuel cycles. It was proposed by President Carter in his nuclear energy policy address of 7 April 1977 and took place between October 1977 and February 1980. The American input into this review was supported by the Nonproliferation Alternative Systems Assessment Program (NASAP).
[2] See Marsha M. McGraw, 'The NPT review conference', *Arms Control Today II*, February 1981.
[3] Text available in US Congressional Research Service, *Nuclear Proliferation Factbook*, 96th Congress, 2nd Session, Government Printing Office, Washington, DC, September 1980, pp 71-84.
[4] Myron B. Kratzer, Testimony before the US House of Representatives Committee on Science and Technology, Subcommittee on Energy Research and Production, 5 June 1980.
[5] Thomas J. Connolly et al, *World Nuclear Energy Paths*, Rockefeller Foundation, New York, 1979, p 40. (A GWe, or gigawatt, is a billion watts of electric power).
[6] Chauncey Starr and Chaim Braun, *Supply of Uranium and Enrichment Services*, paper presented to ANS/ENS/AIF Conference, Washington, DC, 18 November 1980, Electric Power Research Institute, Palo Alto, 1980, p 3.
[7] Ruth M. Davis, *Commercial Enrichment Services and Supply Assurance*, paper presented at Atomic Industrial Forum/ Dutch Atomic Forum, Conference on the Nuclear Fuel Cycle, Amsterdam, The Netherlands, 15 September 1980, p 10.

favoured the creation of an International Atomic Development Authority (IADA) with the highly centralized tasks of owning and operating all sensitive steps of the fuel cycle. The monopolistic role of the IADA has been echoed in supranational provisions of the EURATOM Treaty and, most recently, the American proposal for an International Nuclear Fuel Authority (INFA). At the opposite extreme, a far more decentralized approach is embodied in the free market commercialism of the 'Atoms for Peace' period, and more recently, with the liberal nuclear trading positions taken by would-be nuclear suppliers in the developing world, such as India, Argentina and Brazil.

The most centralist regime in effect replaces the fuel 'market' with a centrally directed arrangement linked with the idea of 'global resource management'. In this view, uranium (like many other scarce minerals) is too sensitive strategically and too valuable economically to be allocated on the basis of *ad hoc* transactions. Resources should be mined, brought to central processing centers, organized on a regional or global basis and then distributed to customers depending on a variety of conditions. These conditions would include the country's economic need and its international reputation *vis-à-vis* nonproliferation. The proposal for INFA has been supported in the US Congress by Representative Jonathan Bingham and Senator Charles Percy, who is now chairman of the Foreign Relations Committee.

The mercantilist regime

As states are reluctant to sacrifice national sovereignty over their resources, a second means of allocating fuel supplies has evolved. In accordance with principles deeply embedded in European economic history, a mercantilist market structure was developed during the postwar breakdown of Anglo–Canadian–American nuclear cooperation and subsequent scramble for uranium. Mercantilism prevails when key consuming states cultivate exclusive trade relationships with specific producing states, often ex-colonies, involving the exchange of finance and technology for raw materials. A clear illustration of this pattern is seen in the economic ties between France and its former African colonies, especially Niger and Gabon.

The two-tiered regime

Another means of assuring nuclear fuel supplies is found in the US Nuclear Nonproliferation Act (NNPA) of 1978. This scheme departs from the bilateral or regional arrangements associated with mercantilism and sets forth a two-tiered market structure permitting some nuclear fuel activities (eg reprocessing, breeding, enrichment and plutonium storage) in some countries while denying them to other countries. The act attempts to discourage the national development of sensitive nuclear technologies in non-weapons states, and prefers international control or concentration of these activities in weapons states. Several features characterize this system: a predominant leadership role for the USA; the formalization of technological discrimination between non-weapons or 'proliferation-sensitive' states and nuclear weapons states; the continued financial and technological dependence of less developed states on the advanced states; and the continuing horizontal dependence of the latter on American leadership. Title I of the NNPA thus promises fuel assurances only to 'those nations and groups of nations which adhere to policies designed to prevent proliferation'.

The modified two-tiered regime

Amid international discussion of this approach following the conclusion of INFCE, a modified two-tiered scheme for fuel supply has been favoured by spokesmen of nonproliferation policy in the Carter administration and the UK Atomic Energy Authority. Like the preceding scheme, this approach reserves certain sensitive nuclear activities to states that satisfy the twin requirements (as set by the advanced nuclear states) of demonstrable economic need and assured peaceful use. A central feature of this approach is its purported 'evolutionary' nature: virtually all states can become eligible for inclusion in the upper tier, but only after they have reached a high level of economic and technological development while also maintaining good nonproliferation credentials. Until these importing states attain this level of development, however, they must continue to rely upon fuel assurances extended by existing suppliers.

The three-tiered regime

Finally, a three-tiered market structure has emerged from recent meetings of non-aligned nations that hope to acquire the ability to supply advanced nuclear technology and fuel services. As conceptualized by Argentina, Brazil and India, a small group of less developed but technologically independent countries will abandon the two-tiered market and deal directly with new nuclear customers.

The prime motivation of countries supporting this arrangement is to escape what many states perceive as discriminatory elements of the two-tiered scheme and unilateralism in the establishment of the rules of the nuclear fuel game. The three-tiered market structure has been advanced in recent meetings of the 'Group of Non-Aligned Coordinating Countries on Peaceful Uses of Nuclear Energy' held in Belgrade in December 1978, Havana in 1979 and in Buenos Aires in summer 1980. As stated in one of their communiques, the group stresses:

... the need for extensive cooperation among the nonaligned and other developing countries with the aim of achieving self-sufficiency in all respects of the nuclear fuel cycle for peaceful purposes.*

The five approaches to nuclear fuel assurances are listed in Table 1.

Nonproliferation and energy security

*Final Document of the Preparatory Meeting of the Group of Non-Aligned Coordinating Countries on Peaceful Uses of Nuclear Energy, Belgrade, Yugoslavia, 4-6 December 1978, p 2.

A central premise links all of the regimes outlined above: that fuel assurances can contribute to nonproliferation by reducing national economic incentives to acquire sensitive nuclear facilities. By this reasoning, the availability of credible fuel assurances makes it more difficult for

Table 1. Five approaches to nuclear fuel assurances.

Approach	Major advocate	Distinguishing features
Centralist	USA (1946) (1977)	Planned allocation of fuel on a global basis.
Mercantilist	France (1960 +)	Bilateral arrangements of exclusive character.
Two-tiered	USA (1978)	Creation of an exclusive international service sector for sensitive steps of the fuel cycle.
Modified two-tiered	UK and USA (1979)	As before, but with wider membership and emphasis on continued research and development on breeders and reprocessing.
Three-tiered	Argentina (1980)	Decentralization of the international market for nuclear technologies, services and fuel.

a country to use economic arguments as a pretext for a political decision to acquire the means of building a nuclear weapon. Yet fuel assurances *per se* can only address part of the problem of nonproliferation and energy security. As INFCE pointed out, proliferation is mainly a political problem and is not always susceptible to technical or economic solutions. Furthermore, the long-term problems of national energy security confronting most nations are related far more to the price and availability of fossil fuels than to the economics of the nuclear fuel cycle. There are some particular circumstances, however, in which nuclear fuel assurances are more likely to contribute to the solution of both problems.

Status of the global market in nuclear fuels

The scarcer the world supply of uranium and enrichment services, the greater will be the potential role for fuel assurances as an instrument for pursuing energy security and nonproliferation. The key here is perceived availability rather than statistical estimation. If consuming nations have at their disposal a variety of suppliers to choose from, and abundant fuel supplies are reliably available, the leverage that specific suppliers will have over consumer policies will decline. In contrast, supplier influence will grow when consumers cannot find alternative supply arrangements. Both of these propositions follow from the basic idea that dependence buys influence.

The present fuel market is not encouraging with respect to the role fuel assurances can reasonably be expected to play as an instrument of nonproliferation policy wielded by suppliers over consumers. First, uranium is now cheap (\$25.00/lb as of 31 May 1981)[9] and uranium reserve estimates and inventories of yellowcake are growing steadily. In light of reduced growth estimates for nuclear power, it is clear that uranium supply will exceed demand internationally to the year 2000 and possibly well beyond.[10] Second, with the entrance of URENCO, Eurodif and the USSR during the 1970s as major suppliers of enrichment services, the present oversupply of such services will probably continue until at least the early 1990s. The net result of these trends will be to reduce both the economic incentives for prematurely closing the nuclear fuel cycle and to reduce the dependence (and vulnerability) of consumers on fuel assurances from single suppliers. With this reduced dependence, once-privileged suppliers will be less able to shape the energy policies of consumers *via* the threat of interrupted supplies. In a soft fuel market, such threats would be neither credible nor effective.

Economic and political circumstances of specific countries

Fuel assurances will have greatest influence on the energy policies of countries anticipating a relatively large percentage of electricity generated by nuclear power, limited domestic nuclear resources, high external dependence on foreign technology and materials, and good prospects for economic growth. Brazil, South Korea, Taiwan and Spain are examples of countries in this category. Short of closing the nuclear fuel cycle (which perhaps only India can accomplish soon in the Third World), these countries must continue to rely extensively on foreign supplies of nuclear fuel and services. However, the leverage of single suppliers over the energy and security policies of consumer nations will be tempered by the multiplicity of suppliers on the market.

Although fuel assurances may, in the cases above, marginally affect the economics of alternative fuel cycles, it is not clear that economics deter-

[9] NUEXCO exchange value, May 1981. This compares with a peak exchange value of \$43.50 in summer 1978.
[10] See Thomas L. Neff and Henry D. Jacoby, *Nuclear Fuel Assurance: Origins, Trends and Policy Issues*, MIT Energy Laboratory Report No MIT-EL 79-003, MIT, Cambridge, MA, February 1979. Also *idem*, *The International Uranium Market*, MIT Energy Laboratory Report No MIT-EL 80-014, December 1980.

mine national decisions to reprocess, enrich or breed nuclear fuel. In many countries (including Brazil, Argentina, Pakistan, India, Israel and South Africa), political factors weigh heavily in such decisions. Thus when the desire for autonomy, national prestige or a potential nuclear weapons option are driving local nuclear policy decisions, fuel assurances lose their value as an instrument of nonproliferation. The high economic cost of nationally closed fuel cycles is seen in these countries as more acceptable than the political and economic uncertainties that lie in continued dependence on foreign fuels and services. In such situations, cost comparisons of alternative fuel cycles appear rather irrelevant, because the basis of choice is not always economic merit but the pursuit of national economic and political autonomy.

For selected instances, where fuel assurances may serve as a useful tool of nonproliferation, the success of these measures depends upon the amount of confidence that consumer countries have in the reliability of the fuel market. There can be little confidence in a market in which suppliers apply retroactive conditions to fuel supply arrangements or disagree about the terms governing commerce in nuclear fuels. Confidence is increased when nuclear suppliers act predictably and in accordance with universally known criteria. In the words of the INFCE working group on fuel assurances,

commercial markets for nuclear supply . . . have generally worked satisfactorily in recent years in terms of assurance of supply and they could probably do so in the future. Where cases of interruption or threatened interruption of nuclear exports have occurred in the past, they have . . . been in the context of governmental intervention in furtherance of economic and nonproliferation objectives. Such interruptions have caused delay and expense rather than damage to power production.[11]

Opportunities for unilateral governmental intervention arise from two political circumstances. First, domestic politics in supplier states can jeopardize fuel shipments by means of the nuclear export process. Examples of this include changes in Canadian nuclear export policy after the May 1974 nuclear explosion in India, and the opposition of the US Congress to the sale of fuel for India's Tarapur reactors. Second, consumers see undue intervention when certain suppliers (eg Canada, Australia and the USA) require full-scope safeguards and prior consent over the disposition of spent fuel, while other suppliers (eg France, the UK and West Germany) require no such conditions. The development of an international consensus on the conditions of trade would go far toward restoring the confidence of consumer countries in the fuel market, as would the development of a domestic consensus in supplier states on the contribution that fuel assurances can make to controlling proliferation.

Conclusions

The effectiveness and relevance of nuclear fuel assurances as instruments of nonproliferation policy vary with the status of the international market in uranium and nuclear fuel services and the special economic and political circumstances of consumer nations. Fuel assurances contribute to nonproliferation to the limited extent that they can influence local economic calculations about alternative nuclear fuel cycles.

To a nation determined to acquire nuclear weapons, however, nuclear fuel assurances will fail to address the fundamental political and military demands which motivate interest in a weapons capability. The margin of

INFCE, Draft Final Report of Working Group 3, INFCE/WG 3/41, International Atomic Energy Agency, Vienna, 11 June 1979, p 11.

influence that suppliers will have over these nations is very low and will be limited to measures that affect the political environment giving rise to demands for nuclear weapons; such measures would include military assistance, alliance commitments, energy security arrangements and nuclear arms control agreements. As Thomas Schelling once said,

it would be a ... mistake to think that 'nonproliferation policies' are the most important policies for dealing with proliferation.[12]

There is at present very little international agreement on the structure of the market for nuclear fuel and services. A coherent international regime for fuel assurances will have to be based on a consensus of both suppliers and consumers about the degrees of uniformity and segmentation that will characterize the international market. Will there be a uniform code of conduct as illustrated in the 'centralist' scheme, or will the market be parcelled out on the basis of some political or economic formula as suggested in the other schemes? The most likely outcome will be the modified two-tiered scheme, coupled with continued international support for the rudimentary principles of nuclear commerce as set forth in NPT and IAEA guidelines. Movement toward a more uniform international code of conduct, perhaps combined with an international uranium commodity agreement, will have to await the development of a stronger international consensus on the relationship between fuel assurances and the energy security needs of consumers.

Another issue requiring further international discussion is the clarification of who will be subjects of the new fuel assurance regime. Nuclear fuel assurances are currently provided in one form or another by a variety of participants ranging from corporate, national and joint-venture, to international. Public utilities are now becoming active participants in uranium exploration and fuel 'swapping' which, without appropriate nonproliferation commitments, could have major impacts on the nonproliferation regime. Without the resolution of the problem of 'who is bound?' by international agreements, there cannot be a stable or effective regime.

Taken together, these steps constitute only a beginning. The ultimate relationship between future nuclear fuel assurances and nonproliferation will evolve from hard bargaining over the difficult political problems of who will get what from which regime. Nonetheless, given the alternative of an international *sauve-qui-peut* for sensitive fuels and technologies, the effort to build a global consensus on these issues is well worthwhile.

[12]Thomas C. Schelling, Statement before US Senate Committee on Governmental Affairs, Subcommittee on Energy, Nuclear Proliferation and Federal Services, 4 April 1977, p 44.

40

ENERGY CONSERVATION AND PUBLIC POLICY
If It's Such a Good Idea, Why Don't We Do More of It?

David Morell

Many observers of America's growing energy problem during the 1970s have emphasized the critical role of more efficient use of available energy supplies. Yet conservation has been neglected in formulation and implementation of national energy policies, as policies to achieve supply increases—especially through electrification—remain dominant. Political and social factors help explain this anomaly. Supply-oriented policies are compatible with basic American myths; conservation is seen as antithetical. Energy users are reluctant to take action alone, preferring instead to wait for leadership on what they see as a national problem. Many feel that technology introduced by others will solve the problem for them, without any need for difficult personal efforts. Energy companies and government bureaucracies both have vested interests in continued pursuit of supply strategies; to them, conservation is a diversion from their fundamental institutional rationale. While response to increased prices has been evident, it has been modest even in 1980. Personal comfort, convenience, and safety have all taken precedence over individuals' energy-conserving behavior.

To succeed, energy conservation policies must eliminate or neutralize several significant institutional and regulatory impediments. This phenomenon is explored through examination of the importance of rate base considerations to electric and gas utilities, and of cogeneration of electricity with industrial process steam. In the broader political context, energy conservation is seen as a challenge to the American political system. While energy supply increases seem to require decisions by only a few corporate or government officials, pursuit of this approach eventually will lead to greater polarization and conflict between organized groups, economic sectors, and geographic regions. Coping with the energy crisis will require the effective involvement of the millions of individual decision-makers who are citizens as well as energy users.

From David Morell, "Energy Conservation and Public Policy: If It's Such a Good Idea, Why Don't We Do More of It?" 37(2) *Journal of Social Issues* 8-30 (1981). Copyright 1981 by the Society for the Psychological Study of Social Issues. Reprinted by permission of Plenum Publishing Corporation.

Syn fuels, nuclear power, offshore oil and gas, biomass. . . . Since 1973, national energy policy has focused on possibilities such as these, designed to increase the supplies of energy available to American consumers. From the Project Independence days of Presidents Richard Nixon and Gerald Ford to the National Energy Plan of President Jimmy Carter, with its emphasis on an $88 billion federal subsidy for development of synthetic fuel technologies, energy conservation, as opposed to the development of energy supplies, has consistently been relegated to a subordinate position.

The need for conservation is clear. Though constituting only about six percent of the world's population, Americans consume about 33 percent of the world's energy used each month. America's automobiles alone use about one of every nine barrels of petroleum consumed throughout the world. As a result, U.S. oil imports increase. Indeed, "while the declared aim of American policy is to reduce the use of imported oil, the United States is in fact becoming more and more dependent upon it" (Stobaugh & Yergin, 1979, p. 4).

Conservation remains fundamentally rhetorical, not real, even though it is increasingly evident that this is the principal basis of a sensible energy policy, from both economic and environmental perspectives. Conservation relies primarily, though not entirely, on technology and energy efficiency, rather than on energy abstinence and life-style change. Stobaugh and Yergin (1979) put it as follows:

> "Conservation—not coal or nuclear energy—is the major alternative to imported oil. It could perhaps 'supply' up to 40 percent of America's current energy usage, . . . Moreover, the evidence suggests that there is much greater flexibility between energy use and economic growth than is generally assumed, and that a conservation strategy could actually spur growth" (pp. 11-12).

Similarly, Ross and Williams (1979) have noted that, with respect to homes:

> "A goal to reduce fuel consumption for space heating 50 percent or more in existing residences by the mid to late 1980's is technologically, economically and institutionally feasible. This goal is far greater than the 4 percent savings potential estimated by the Department of Energy" (p. 2.).

Yet conservation is still neglected, as policies to achieve supply increases remain the order of the day.

The reasons for this ironic, and serious, gap between the results of analysis and the realities of American public policy on energy conservation may be understood best from social and political perspectives. Why, since energy conservation is such a marvelous idea, is the United States still pursuing an ineffective energy supply strategy? Are there political reasons and psychological constraints behind America's anti-conservation mentality? And what social science and public policy research would be appropriate to increase our understanding of attitudes toward energy conservation, both individual and institutional?

NATIONAL ENERGY POLICY: THE PAUCITY OF SERIOUS ENERGY CONSERVATION

The Carter administration's policy statements on energy certainly have included plenty of verbiage about the need for conservation. Yet if one looks underneath the immediate rhetoric at actual policies and programs, it is evident that the United States is still basically pursuing a fuels supply policy, not one focused on energy conservation.

Ever since 1973, a principal national goal has been to lessen America's reliance on imported oil. This objective has taken precedence over all others. Imported oil is increasingly expensive and its supply is ever more unreliable. Dependence on this fuel has contributed to rampant inflation at home, a weakened dollar abroad, a constrained foreign policy stance around the world, and the ever-present possibility of massive supply interruptions with the consequence of gasoline lines, cold homes, and a panicked, angry citizenry.

The government's strategy to achieve this goal has not been energy conservation, nor even increased domestic production of oil (or natural gas), though both of these objectives receive encouraging words and some policy support. By far the main thrust of the government's energy program has been a two-for-two fuel switch. The idea is to transfer as much of the nation's energy use as possible from oil and gas to coal and nuclear fission, and therefore predominantly to electricity generation, even though electricity is the least efficient of all the various energy supply systems (in terms of energy lost through waste heat).

Because of the importance of this national strategy, more social science research ought to be directed toward electricity: its uses and misuses, people's attitudes toward power plant siting and electricity generation and transmission, and the characteristics of the principal private and governmental institutions involved in providing electricity. Second, popular attitudes toward the environmental and safety implications of coal and nuclear energy deserve greater attention, since these forms of energy production are receiving national policy attention. Much needs to be done regarding attitudes toward nuclear energy in particular, especially the relationship of these attitudes to ethics, values and American political culture. Hohenemser, Kasperson and Kates (1977) have explored reasons for people's widespread distrust of nuclear power; Otway and Fishbein (1976) and Maderthaner, Pahner, Guttman and Otway (1976) examined attitudes of people living near nuclear power plants, especially the prevalence of "cognitive dissonance." In general, disaggregating energy-related research by fuel categories seems imperative as long as energy efficiency goals are being subordinated to fuels policy objectives.

To date, relatively few studies have examined the electricity sector. In contrast, Big Oil—The Seven Sisters—has consumed the attention of academics and journalists (see Bradford, 1975; Engler, 1961; Sampson, 1975; and, much earlier, Lloyd, 1894). Where are the similar studies of decision making in the major utilities (e.g. Commonwealth Edison, Pacific Gas and Electric); in the public power agencies (Tennessee Valley Authority, Bonneville Power Authority); in rural electric cooperatives; in municipal utilities; and in the regulatory structure encompassing electricity (state public utility commissions and the Federal Energy Regulatory Commission, formerly the Federal Power Commission)? For two such studies of the electric utility industry, see Berlin, Cicchetti and Gillen (1974), and Cicchetti, Gillen and Smolensky (1977). Messing, Friesema and Morell (1979), Novick (1976), and Rodgers (1972) give useful overviews of the industry. Nevertheless, the literature's overall emphasis on Big Oil, rather than on the electric utility industry, remains striking. Perhaps the main reason for this lack of attention to institutional factors in the electricity sector is that utilities, as regulated monopolies, are rather boring topics for study when compared to the Seven Sisters.

It is odd that, while federal fuels policy has encouraged electrification, federal regulatory actions have concentrated primarily on oil and natural gas (see Willrich, 1976). Prices of oil and gas have dominated the debate in Congress and the White House. It is true that reform of rate structures (to modify or eliminate declining block incentives toward greater consumption, for example) and other pro-conservation actions were addressed in the Public Utility Regulatory Policies Act of 1978 (PURPA—Public Law 95-617); and that several state public utility commissions have experimented with conservation-oriented policies regarding electricity. Nevertheless, the fundamental strategy of the White House and the U.S. Department of Energy—and the Congress—has stressed oil over electricity, and fuel supplies over conservation.

Various factors explain this national preference for a fuels policy over a conservation-oriented energy policy. It is easier politically to talk about greater supplies—growth—than to address what is commonly thought of as less: conservation. Supply-oriented policies are compatible with basic American myths and values, while conservation it seen as antithetical (see Miles, 1977; Ophuls 1977). Coal is plentiful in the United States and thus provides a vehicle for continuing the dialogue of "energy independence"; the same is true of nuclear power. Neither supply option requires the nation to deal with the politics of reducing energy demand. Synthetic fuels are seen as the answer for the transportation sector and for industrial uses, both symbols of growth and America's strength. Yet Gorman and Heitner (1980) conclude that a number of automotive technology options for conserving energy exist whose cost is much less than the cost of synthetic fuels. This difference is on the order of $40 billion over the next 10 years. The basic national strategy is oriented toward minimizing the need for new decisions and actions by the millions of individual energy users, who see electricity as convenient, clean, immensely flexible—the perfect, almost magical energy form.

The ample profits associated with a supply-oriented approach to energy are of overriding importance. From John D. Rockefeller and the Standard Oil Trust in the late nineteenth century (see Lloyd, 1894) to the huge oil company profits reported for 1979 and 1980, the potential for corporate profits in fuels supply has been evident. In contrast, the investment community and the energy industry have had no experience in making substantial profits from conservation. The motivation of the large oil companies constrains the United States from the aggressive pursuit of energy conservation or decentralized use of renewable energy sources. Through their subsidiaries, the oil companies now own or hold leases on a large proportion of the country's resources of coal, uranium, and oil shale. Neither they nor the major corporations involved in nuclear power have a significant financial stake in energy conservation. One is not surprised, therefore, to find these enormously powerful corporate entities, and the financial institutions with which they are intertwined, lobbying successfully in both the Administration and the Congress in favor of particular supply policies rather than for effective conservation (and of course, lobbying against taxes on windfall profits). (See Kolko, 1963, for a model of a possible future study of corporate power in the energy industry.)

ENERGY TECHNOLOGY AND SOCIAL SCIENCE RESEARCH

In large measure, energy conservation involves improved energy efficiency rather than altered attitudes, behavior, or lifestyles. This is certainly the theme of many of conservation's strongest supporters (Ross & Williams, 1981; Stobaugh & Yergin, 1979). In devising their research agendas, social scientists need to be sensitive to this fact, and to relate their research to those areas of energy conservation where a new technology purports to be the answer. The studies using "feedback" of information in conjunction with set-back thermostats to affect conservation in the residential sector, reported in Becker, Seligman and Darley (1979), illustrate the potential for cooperative interaction between social and physical scientists. This will require that social scientists become aware of the research emphases of engineers and other energy conservation technicians, and that technical specialists become aware of the research possibilities of social scientists.

In other cases, changes in attitudes, life styles, institutions, and other non-technical aspects of energy use will be critical to creating and sustaining a true conservation ethic (see Miles, 1977; Ophuls, 1977; Sansom, 1976). Indeed, the belief that we can rely on technical fixes alone is naive. Surveys of consumer attitudes toward the energy shortage taken by National Opinion Research Center at the University of Chicago in 1973-1974 showed that most U.S. consumers were aware of the energy crisis but few believed it was a major, long-lasting problem (Erskine, 1977). Most consumers believed that the federal government, the oil companies, and OPEC were responsible for the energy crisis (Rosen & Salmore, Note 1) and, in addition, that the crisis had been contrived to boost profits. Few expected to experience major changes in lifestyle due to energy shortages. There were few significant relationships between energy attitudes, conservation behavior, and demographic variables such as education, income, and region of residence (Cunningham & Lopreato, 1977). Generally, all age groups and all socioeconomic groups throughout the U.S. were skeptical about the energy problem and seemed to be minimally affected by it (Murray, Minor, Bradburn, Cotterman, Frankel & Pisarski, 1974). Rosen and Salmore (Note 1) reach the following conclusion: "Energy conservation is not related to the public's perception of the seriousness of our energy problems. Those who are cynical and disbelieving are as likely to take steps to save energy as those convinced of the gravity of our present problems" (p. 17).

Drawing on the results of a September 1978 public opinion survey of 1,006 New Jersey residents conducted by the Eagleton Institute of Politics at Rutgers University for the New Jersey Department of Energy, Rosen found that: "The public apparently does not share the sense of urgency about energy problems which is prevalent in some quarters in Washington and Trenton. Energy is seen as an important issue, but is not among the top priority concerns of the people. Energy problems achieve high prominence only when they have a direct and immediate impact on the population. This tends to produce erratic fluctuations in public concern about energy. . . . Americans are far more likely to view energy as a national rather than state or local issue . . . people will turn to Washington, rather than their state houses or city halls, for solutions . . . the complexity and long-term implications of energy issues are best understood by those with more education" (Rosen, Note 2, pp. 3, 4, 5).

When people believe that technology will provide an alternative energy source and that pollution control devices will clean up the damage already done, they do not feel they have to make any efforts themselves toward solving the problem. Thus, they become caught in a trap known as the "technological fix" (Tichenor, Donohue, Oben & Bowers, 1971; Rosen & Salmore, Note 1). In order for new technology to have a real impact on the nation's energy use, the general public must be willing to adopt these new energy efficient mechanical devices. Researchers should pay attention to constraints on market penetration, and to techniques to accelerate the adoption of new technologies.

Gas-efficient automobiles that remain on the drawing boards of Detroit and Tokyo or in dealer showrooms in Akron and Peoria simply will not contribute to reducing America's dependence on imported oil. Americans have begun to buy small cars now, to the apparent chagrin of some executives of the fiscally-strapped Chrysler and Ford companies. Even with gasoline priced over $1 per gallon, however, it simply does not pay an individual to trade in an older (but still operative) 14 mpg car; the savings in gas are nearly always less than the interest cost of the new-car loan. In addition, the energy costs and environmental implications of making automobiles are not trivial; U.S. policy needs to be cautious about the speed with which usable products are simply thrown away. It is important to remember that the energy savings from both a national and an individual perspective are negated if gas-efficient cars are simply driven more miles. Sinden (Note 3) has calculated that the complete energy savings from a proposed new office building using the most advanced techniques of conservation and solar energy could well be offset by the consumption of gasoline in the automobiles of this building's employees, assuming typical patterns of commuting to work. Again, attitudes and patterns of living—suburban sprawl or urban revitalization, for example—are interwoven with use of energy efficient technologies.

The transportation sector is replete with opportunities for innovative social science research associated with conservation. Why have the comfort and convenience of large automobiles been so important to the American consumer (though patterns of new auto purchases have begun to change in 1979-80)? How important an influence has advertising been in this regard? Will technology allow our national love affair with the automobile, and the patterns of land development and life style dependent on private cars, to be maintained in an era of energy scarcity? Or is the automobile itself an endangered species, to be replaced—reluctantly but inexorably—by mass transit, denser patterns of housing, greater compatibility between employment and residential locations, and so on? Americans will probably resist such changes in lifestyle (Sansom, 1976). During the 1979 gasoline shortage there were some shifts in commuting patterns. In New Jersey, for example, the number of people driving to work alone decreased substantially (63.2 percent in the summer of 1979 versus 73.3 percent a year earlier); most (5.5 percent) shifted to car pools, some to walking and mass transit. However, "with the end of gasoline lines, most commuters returned to their pre-shortage patterns." The percentage driving to work alone was 70.6 in the summer of 1980 (Rosen & Salmore, Note 1, pp. 9-10). As long as the maxim "mini-cars mean mini profits" continues to prevail, can one expect the Big Three auto companies to move aggressively toward truly fuel-efficient machines? Or is it essential that the federal government play a role, one much greater than seen to date in the 27.5 mpg corporate average fuel economy (CAFE) standard for 1985? This standard is calculated for each automobile maker on the basis of its total car production for that model year. Moreover, EPA estimates that actual mileage from these autos will be substantially less than the stipulated average. Sound national energy policy requires us to know much more about Americans' attitudes toward transportation.

Energy Prices and Conservation

Normally one assumes that demand for energy, or any other commodity, will fluctuate as a function of price; the higher the price, the lower the demand. This is basic to contemporary economics, and central to the position of many energy experts. For example, Landsberg (1979) leaves no question about this issue:

> "The central message of the present report is that energy—expensive today—is likely to be more expensive tomorrow and that society as a whole will gain from a resolute effort to make the price that the user pays for energy, and for saving energy, reflect its true value" (p. xvii).

The study directed by Schurr (1979) also endorses a market-oriented price elasticity response to energy.

However, elasticity in demand for motor gasoline has been strikingly weak in the U.S., calling into question conventional economic predictions of the market forces relevant to energy demand. Certainly energy is price-elastic, like everything else, at least to *some* degree. What needs to be determined is the magnitude of the elasticity, its time lags, and the differences in elasticity between various energy forms (electricity, gasoline, and home heating oil, for example). Econometricians tend to look at past responses to price changes, projecting these patterns into the future. Instead, it might be more instructive to look at a range of possible future responses to higher energy prices (buy a smaller car, use the bus more often, move closer to work, etc.) and then project the elasticity and lags for each.

Some relationships between income and conservation efforts seem to exist (Boulding, 1974; Cunningham & Lopreato, 1977; Hass, Bagley & Rogers, 1975; Hummel, Levitt & Loomis, 1978; Pallack & Cummings, 1976). Middle income households are not only more likely to believe in the reality of the energy crisis and thus reduce their consumption but also, of all income groups, seem to have the greatest knowledge about energy use. In contrast, upper income households have increased their consumption and have consumed at their desired level regardless of price. Morrison and Gladhart (1968) found family income to be the single best predictor of energy consumption. Housing factors, floor space, type, age, and quality of construction, interior layout, utilities, location of residence, appliance saturation and types of heating and cooling units, as well as single-versus multi-family arrangement, were all directly related to income, and thus strongly related to consumption. Rosen and Salmore (Note 1) found a paradox between income levels and energy conserving behavior.

> "Those with the greatest economic incentive to save because they are most adversely affected by rising energy prices—lower income groups—are the least able to take effective actions.... Upper income residents who have the knowledge and financial resources to take effective action have less economic incentive to do so, ... We will probably see the largest increases in conserving actions from the middle income group that has both the economic incentives and the financial ability to act" (pp. 17-18).

Conservation incentives accepted by the public have leaned overwhelmingly to those policies that require the least personal sacrifice and change in lifestyle. In a 1974 study, all income groups cited price as the major reason for conservation (Cunningham & Lopreato, 1977, p. 18). Rosen's (Note 2) analysis of 1978 survey data shows that

> "support for energy policy options varies with the perception of the direct costs they will be required to bear. They tend to support measures whose costs are minor, indirect, or distant, and oppose those policies which necessitate tangible sacrifices" (p. 9).

Safety, convenience, and comfort are three main factors that inhibit response to energy prices and thus stand directly in the path of consumer adoption of energy-efficient technologies and patterns of action. In large measure, energy is not seen as an item one purchases by choice, but rather as an unavoidable expense. As the cost of energy has increased, many people have simply spent a higher proportion of their disposable incomes on it. This has been especially hard on the poor and those with fixed incomes. There are limits to such a pattern, obviously; but in the meantime the nation's dependence on imported oil grows daily. Identification of the factors that contribute to relatively inelastic response to energy prices and an understanding of their bases in tradition, attitudes, and value preferences are priority tasks for social science researchers concerned with energy conservation.

Safety as a Constraint on Response to Energy Prices

The desire for safety is one principal factor inhibiting a change of life-style that would result in energy conservation. If subways and bus stops are perceived as dangerous places, the haunts of muggers, thieves and rapists, people will continue to drive their private autos, regardless of the price of gasoline or the need to wait in line to buy it (and regardless of the fact that 50,000 deaths per year occur as a result of automobile accidents). As long as urban residential areas are felt to be dangerous, and city schools are seen as unhealthly for their children, people will continue to prefer suburban housing, even if this entails a long commuting trip to their jobs. When downtown shopping areas are believed to be dangerous, especially after dark, people will drive distances to regional shopping malls in the suburbs. If lighter sub-compact cars are seen as death traps in a possible collision, people will feel safer in a giant V-8, and many will continue to buy them, even as gasoline reaches $1.50 or perhaps even $2.00 per gallon.

"Security" has an additional meaning with respect to energy policy. People feel insecure with change, secure in pursuing the traditional patterns of the past: large autos, single-family homes far out in the suburbs. Corporations feel secure in making incremental, gradual changes in their policies, altering this pattern only under government pressure. Kraft (1980) addressed this point in his essay on decision making in the automobile industry:

> "In the past, when G.M. followed the market, and only the market, it used to make decisions slowly, almost inch by inch. Innovations . . . were introduced over a long period of time. . . . But government-mandated actions don't allow for decisions on a slow curve, . . . When Congress enacts a law, the new standards apply to all models, and they must be put into effect by a certain date" (p. 159).

Convenience and Conservation

Convenience means different things to different people, but its pursuit often leads people—consciously or not—to reject energy conserving actions. Perhaps mass transit could take you where you're going. But if this means waiting for the bus (in the cold wind), or walking a block, or transferring from one bus to another (with another wait), then you drive instead. Certain kinds of appliances may offer convenience at the price of higher energy use: frost-free refrigerators, self-cleaning ovens, plate-warming dishwashers, cuisinarts, hair dryers, and so on. People know that they can insulate their homes better, or turn down their thermostats when they go away for the weekend, but many simply do not bother. Car pools might be a feasible alternative for many people to use less energy in getting to and from their jobs; but since it is inconvenient to coordinate one's schedules with others', most people still drive alone. In fact, low-income people who own automobiles evince the same commuting patterns as those of higher-income groups. Variations in use of mass transit versus autos to commute to work are explainable almost entirely by relative rates of automobile ownership; "when people own automobiles they will use them to get to work" (Rosen, Note 2, p. 19). In sum, for many Americans convenience continues to overwhelm energy costs. Economists view convenience as a price on one's time; in those terms, most Americans see their time as a very valuable commodity indeed.

Comfort and Use of Energy

Comfort is a third key factor undercutting the elasticity of demand for energy in the U.S. Though central air conditioning really is not a necessity, many consumers demand it in a new home. It is simply more comfortable to ride in a 5,000 lb., powerful American sedan than a 3,000 lb. European subcompact; and millions of Americans are still prepared to pay the energy cost differential to obtain this added pleasure. Becker, Seligman and Darley (1979) identified comfort as the critical variable in energy conservation in residential dwellings:

> "By far the best predictor (and the only consistent predictor) of actual energy consumption . . . is the residents' attitude about thermal comfort. The more that one feels that being comfortable in the summer depends on a cool house, the more electricity (for air conditioning) is used. The more one feels that being comfortable in the winter depends on a warm house, the more natural gas (for space heating) is used" (p. iii).

From the perspective of American energy policy, several additional comments on price elasticity of demand seem in order. First, even with all the price increases, energy has remained a relative bargain in the U.S. when compared to other countries and to the prices of many other goods and services in the U.S. economy. In 1976, according to Federal Energy Administration data, gasoline at the pump was cheaper than it had been in 1960 when adjusted for overall price inflation. Gasoline cost less per gallon in 1976 than did milk or spring water. Measured in 1975 dollars, prices in 1976 had decreased to 55.8 cents from 57.6 cents a gallon in 1960 (U.S. Federal Energy Administration, 1977). Although this was no longer true in early 1980, with regular gasoline in many areas priced at about $1.25 per gallon (current dollars), energy in general remained relatively inexpensive in the U.S. (largely because of price controls). Natural gas for home heating is still cheap for many homeowners when compared to the expense of installing storm windows. Inflation, and a somewhat increased demand, have affected the cost of storm windows, insulation and smaller autos, too, of course. As a result, many people have continued to postpone such energy-conserving investments.

Time lags are another important influence on price elasticity of demand for energy. Most energy is consumed in long-lasting capital stock: homes, office buildings, industrial boilers, automobiles. Energy is only one among many costs of daily use; and when replacement of a still-usable building or car is being considered, interest rates for borrowed capital—a home mortgage, for example—may often overwhelm calculations of energy costs. Also, energy costs occur in a cumulative pattern over a long period of time, whereas many energy-conserving investments (insulation, for example) must be paid for in advance. Builders anxious to hold down first-costs to enhance sales potential are unlikely voluntarily to emphasize conservation investments. As long as such long-term costs are not incorporated directly into traditional financial instruments (home mortgages, for example), conservation efforts will remain constrained.

Social status is another potentially important variable. As long as higher status is associated with energy-wasteful products such as large automobiles, certain people will buy them whatever the price of energy.

In general, energy conservation researchers and policy makers might study the degree to which higher prices for energy—direct and indirect—would stimulate conservation. Are there any dollar-per-BTU thresholds for attitude change in this regard? And if so, what are they? How important is the rate of change in energy prices? Gradual price increases, for example, may have a very different impact than sudden, sharp increases.

BARRIERS AND IMPEDIMENTS TO CONSERVATION

To succeed, energy conservation policies must eliminate or neutralize several significant institutional and regulatory impediments. Life-cycle energy costs may be lower for a house with better insulation, but initial costs will be higher. What attitudes toward this issue prevail among home buyers, builders and developers, bankers? What institutional changes might reduce this barrier to conservation? Industries are concerned that, if they cogenerate electricity with their process steam, they will come to be treated as a regulated entity (like the utility company to which they would sell their excess electricity). Utility executives express concern over possible dependence on "unreliable" industrial sources of cogenerated electricity. To what extent are such attitudes subject to change over time, or to sensitive new public policies? The following sections illustrate two institutional barriers to conservation: utility reliance on rate base calculations, and the use of cogeneration.

Institutional Impediments to Conservation: Utilities and the Rate Base

Institutional barriers to energy conservation are evident in the decisions that electric and gas utilities make about investing their money, prestige, and management attention in supply increases rather than conservation. Specifically, to what degree have the utilities supported the actions identified by Socolow (1978), among others, to achieve greater energy efficiencies in the residential sector? Is conservation antithetical to the utilities' corporate interests? Should public policies encourage—or even compel—the utilities to move more aggressively in this direction?

The energy needed to heat and cool our homes can be reduced by a number of measures: weather stripping, insulation, and similar actions designed by "house doctors" (Socolow, 1978). Since many individuals cannot or will not spend the money required to accomplish these long-term energy savings, several proposals call for utilities to include these investments in their "rate base." The rate base is the amount of capital investment, including such equipment as turbines, generators, power plants, and cooling towers on which utilities are allowed guaranteed rates of return (i.e., profits). The rates charged to customers reflect this profit formula, as well as actual operation and maintenance costs of service including fuel, personnel, and other expenses. These latter costs are included in the rates, but without any profit to the utility (Messing, Friesema & Morell, 1979; Novick, 1976).

Therefore, in pursuit of maximum profits—within the obvious constraint of providing "safe, adequate and reliable service"—utilities naturally want to maximize the capital intensity of their activities. That is, the proportion of their total expenses accounted for by capital investments (the rate base) should be as high as possible. Large, base-load central station power plants, especially nuclear reactors, are ideally suited to this criterion; investments in residential energy conservation are not, for even when materials (insulation, caulk, and so on) are allowed into their rate base, ancillary, non-profitable activities associated with conservation normally are not. In a conservation effort, labor costs are high; transportation of workers and materials to homes is expensive; and the administrative and management tasks involved in operating a large conservation program all militate against typical utility preferences.

Moreover, two other factors exacerbate the gap between the utilities' vested interests and the national interest in residential energy conservation. First, a large proportion of home heating is done by fuel oil, not natural gas or electricity. Of about 70 million homes in the country, some 16 million are heated by oil. Fuel oil is supplied by private firms, not by regulated utilities. Any conservation program focusing on the utilities would have to be supplemented to reach the millions of homes heated by oil, the primary energy commodity from the national perspective.

Second, the utilities' operational philosophy has emphasized continual growth, not demand reduction and supply stability. Capital investments in the rate base are funded in large measure with money raised through issuing utility bonds; ownership of the company, of course, is evidenced through shares of equity stock. The basic concept, simply stated, is to achieve growth in the rate base, paying for these capital investments through increased bonded indebtedness while minimizing stock issuance. As a result, the increasing profits are divided among a constant (or more slowly expanding) number of stockholders. From this perspective, risk-averse institutions like utility companies prefer construction of new power plants to investment in energy conservation.

Nevertheless, some utilities have decided to become involved in conservation. Pacific Power and Light Company, for example, obtained permission from the Oregon and Washington state regulatory commissions to include residential energy efficiency investments in its rate base. The 1978 National Energy Conservation Policy Act (Public Law 95-619) required utilities to inform their customers about energy conservation methods, offer home audits, and suggest energy saving strategies. So that the utilities would not overwhelm small local contractors, this act specifically precluded utilities from becoming involved in conservation installation and financing. This suggests a number of worthwhile issues for the energy research agenda. Given their institutional structure as regulated monopolies, their reliance on rate base calculations, their traditional dominance over the decisions of state public utility commissions, their preference for large-scale facilities (Messing, Friesema & Morell, 1979), and their already enormous size and power, should utilities be the principal agencies relied upon in national policy on residential energy conservation? Instead, alternative forms of financing (federal loans through banks and savings and loan institutions on the model of national direct college student loans would be one example) and of program implementation (state or county energy conservation agencies, for example) might be preferable.

Consumer attitudes toward energy conservation investments in their own homes also deserve intensive examination. Why has there been so little response to utilities' offers of home audits? How can the energy use decisions of millions of individual consumers be made more compatible with national policy objectives? What mix of public policies (taxes, loans, regulations), price incentives, and psychological messages is needed to increase adoption of life-cycle costing as the framework for such decisions?

Institutional Impediments to Conservation: Industrial Cogeneration

Cogeneration of electricity with process steam at industrial facilities offers intriguing possibilities for energy efficiency. The technology is available, with short construction lead times; it is economical; and it can produce electricity and process steam together for approximately half of the fuel requirements of separate central station electric power plants and industrial steam boilers. Industry generated about 60 percent of America's electricity in 1900, and 30 percent in 1925; in 1977 it generated only a miniscule proportion of the total (Messing, Friesema & Morell, 1979, p. 59). The principal reasons that this technology is not being widely adopted today are institutional and regulatory; thus cogeneration presents an excellent example of institutional impediments to energy conservation.

In cogeneration systems, electricity is generated at industrial sites as a by-product of process steam production. With cogeneration systems scaled to steam capacity rather than the industry's own on-site electricity requirements, the units can function as small, decentralized base-load power plants, linked directly into the overall utility grid (Williams, 1978). Though this is common practice today in Europe, U.S. utilities have resisted using cogeneration in this way, preferring their own separate power plants. (Indeed, when they refer to "cogeneration" they normally mean sale of steam from their own power plants, not generation of electricity at industrial sites.) If the generating unit is owned by the industry, it will not count toward the utility's rate base; if it is owned by the utility, PUC regulatory restrictions might be imposed on the nonregulated industrial partner.

How electricity exchanged in the cogeneration arrangement would be priced is a crucial question too. Will the utility pay for electricity from base load cogeneration systems at a rate equivalent to that generated at its other base load power plants, or at some lower rate? And what rate will be charged the industry for the electricity which it buys when needed from the utility? Utilities also express concern over the reliability of industrial cogeneration systems; "will the electricity be available when we need it?" they ask. How would national fuels policy be affected? Most of today's cogeneration systems burn fuel oil or natural gas, not coal; thus adoption of this fuel-efficient electricity technology would run counter to the national two-for-two fuel switching policy. Policy makers must decide whether we have an energy crisis—requiring efficiency—or a fuels crisis, requiring switching away from oil.

With cooperation among utilities, industrial managers and state regulatory agencies, these problems could be resolved. This is evidenced in the few cases where cogeneration does exist today, as in the cooperative arrangement between the Weyerhauser Company and the Eugene (Oregon) Water and Electric Board (Messing, Friesema & Morell, 1979, pp. 139-140). This issue arises for wind-generated electricity as well as cogeneration. Rates for backup power and sales of excess electricity to the utility grid were major issues requiring litigation between Consolidated Edison Company of New York and a windmill installed on a tenement on East 11th Street in Manhattan (Messing, Friesema & Morell, 1979, pp. 136-138). Sensitive analyses of existing attitudes toward cogeneration, and of possible policies to accelerate adoption of this technology across the country, deserve a position of prominence on the energy conservation research agenda.

Energy Conservation and Political Authority

The American political system's continuing strong preference for energy supply policies rather than conservation is seen in the exercise of political authority at federal and state levels. Centralized power is the dominant mode not only in the scale of electricity generating systems but in politics as well.

President Carter's proposed Energy Mobilization Board, a version of which passed both houses of Congress in 1980 in different versions (it then failed to survive critique in the Senate-House conference committee), would have had authority to make decisions in lieu of normal federal, state, and local agencies—and perhaps to override national environmental laws—in order to accelerate siting of priority energy projects: synthetic fuels production facilities, power plants, refineries, and so on. Where is an equivalent Energy Conservation Mobilization Board? It simply does not exist. Analogous strong regulatory and tax measures to induce conservation—including gasoline rationing—have time and again been deemed "politically unacceptable." We are willing to tolerate use of federal preemption to locate a liquified natural gas facility, power plant, pipeline, or storage depot in a community that does not want it. Yet we are not willing to require strict national energy efficiency standards for all new housing or all new appliances, nor to provide meaningful incentives to insulate existing houses, nor to require Detroit to develop and sell really fuel-efficient autos (beyond the modest 27.5 mpg average by 1985).

Of course, it is possible that economic incentives alone will suffice to induce energy conservation, obviating the need for mandatory (non-fiscal) actions by government. As noted earlier in this paper, however, careful study of price elasticity issues is of vital concern. Based on the evidence available to date, economic incentives alone do not seem adequate in the face of institutional and political barriers to conservation. However, the implications of mandatory conservation for individual freedoms deserve special attention. Experience in attempting to implement land use and transportation controls under Section 110 of the Clean Air Act Amendments of 1970 (see Hagevik, 1974; Krier & Ursin, 1977; Sansom, 1976) may have important lessons for the politics of energy conservation.

Several states have adopted preemptive approaches to energy facility siting similar to the Energy Mobilization Board, ensuring that "needed" projects will be located where industry and state agencies want them, even in the face of opposition from the local community. State exercise of political authority to induce conservation is, once again, far less prevalent. In sum, the imbalance between the use of excessive power and authority to site new energy facilities and the continuing confusion and inertia over mandatory versus voluntary conservation is a direct reflection of the nation's overall emphasis on supply increases.

Looking to the Future: Conflict or Coherence in Energy Policy?

Formulating effective public policies to cope with the energy crisis in the last two decades of the twentieth century will challenge the very core of the American political system. To date, "business as usual" attitudes have prevailed. Labeling the cause the "moral equivalent of war" has not created better energy policies, any more than wearing "whip inflation now" buttons brought double digit inflation under control.

The battle over energy policy has the potential to polarize American society as has no other issue except racial prejudice. Following the present period of confusion and inaction, conflict rather than consensus may well characterize the eighties. Without policies to bring energy demand into consonance with available supply, international vulnerability could combine with internal disagreements to tear the U.S. polity asunder. Overall, it is not a very rosy political picture. Yet conservation continues to be a myth when compared to the reality of national energy policy.

America's inability to adopt an energy conservation program is a classic example of the "failures of discourse" identified by Socolow (1976) as characteristic of many environmental conflicts. Young v. old; poor v. rich; scientists v. citizens; oil companies and electric utilities v. consumers; energy producing areas v. energy deficient ones—each arena of discord reflects a profound failure to communicate, to achieve a coalescence of individual, institutional and national values.

Most people simply think of "energy" as an end in itself rather than a medium of exchange, or stored-up work. Their perceptions are couched in terms of fuel categories, and their images of energy conservation encompass cold houses, people out of work, and cars idled by a lack of gasoline. In contrast, energy specialists see energy as a means to accomplish physical tasks, and energy conservation as a way of accomplishing those same tasks with less energy inputs (that is, with greater efficiency in energy use). With deprivation the focal idea on one side, and technical fixes the main thrust of the other, it is no wonder that there is a failure in the conservation dialogue.

The various technical and utility examples set forth in this paper all illustrate the ways energy problems challenge scientists to understand the relation between public and private institutional decision centers in the U.S., and the individual and group actions needed to implement energy conservation. Research is required to understand more fully the relation between national energy conservation policies (or supply policies) and the institutions that influence development of these policies: oil companies, auto companies, banks, and utilities, for example. Research is needed on what factors actually induce people to act in certain ways: suggestions from a utility's "house doctor," a presidential appeal on television, higher prices, or tax incentives. Some of the difficulty in individual reactions to the energy crisis may come from the immense distance between users of energy and those who appear to have the power to influence its availability or price: Arab sheiks, oil company presidents, heads of automobile companies, the Secretary of Energy. In the face of such a gap, the motivations to act individually, to take personal risks and suffer direct costs, may be greatly inhibited. People await clear, coherent, trustworthy leadership on energy: words matched by deeds.

Contrasts between the economic behavior of those who can afford to conserve energy and those who cannot is another area worthy of sensitive new research. Equity concerns dominate the discourse about energy pricing (deregulation of natural gas, gasoline taxes, subsidies of various kinds), but such equity considerations normally remain unstated in the conservation debates.

Because the energy situation is so complex, it is easy to blame some culprit (Arabs, OPEC, oil companies, utilities, government) or to place unquestioning faith in some technical fix (fusion, solar, breeder reactors). This makes it possible to avoid confronting today's energy realities. As Rosen (Note 2) concludes:

> "It is far more pleasant to believe that energy problems can be resolved through reforms of someone else's . . . behavior or the wonders of science, than to face real and tangible personal sacrifices. Disabusing the public of easy answers and forging a constituency for difficult energy solutions will provide a test of the capacity and responsibility of American political leadership" (p. 24).

Cheap energy and abundant land and materials typified America's frontier era, greatly influencing the nation's political culture and patterns of development (Miles, 1977; Turner, 1920). Now that the "frontier" of cheap oil is gone forever, however, the wasteful patterns of energy usage must disappear as well. It is difficult to meld the actions of millions of individual decision makers— home owners and automobile drivers—in ways compatible with a national conservation effort. Energy supply increases, in contrast, seem to require decisions by only a few corporate or government actors, and thus appear easier to accomplish. This view is an illusion, however, since in the end pursuit of the supply rather than the demand side of the problem will only lead to greater polarization and conflict. The energy crisis is fundamentally political and economic (pressures by the vested interests of major corporations) rather than technical. In a democratic society, the millions of individual decision makers are not only energy users but citizens. Their involvement is as vital as it is inescapable.

As Pogo the possum once said in his cartoon strip: "We has met the enemy and they is 'us'."

REFERENCE NOTES

1. Rosen, D. J., & Salmore, S. A. *A prospective and retrospective view of public attitudes about energy problems in New Jersey.* Paper presented at the New Jersey State Economic Conference, New Brunswick, New Jersey, April 1980.
2. Rosen, D. J. *Public attitudes and alternative energy systems: The end-user perspective.* Paper presented at the 1979 Annual Meeting of the American Society for Public Administration, Baltimore, Maryland, April 2, 1979.
3. Sinden, F. Personal communication with the author, September 1980.

REFERENCES

Becker, L. J., Seligman, C., & Darley, J. M. *Psychological strategies to reduce energy consumption: Project summary report.* Princeton, NJ: Princeton University, Center for Energy and Environmental Studies, Report No. 90, 1979.

Boulding, K. The social system and the energy crisis. *Science,* 1974 (April), *184,* 255-257.

Bradford, P. *Fragile structures.* New York: Harper & Row, 1975.

Berlin, E., Cicchetti, C., & Gillen, W. J. *Perspective on power: A study of the regulation and pricing of electric power.* Cambridge, MA: Ballinger, 1974.

Cicchetti, C., Gillen, W. J., & Smolensky, P. *The marginal cost and pricing of electricity: An applied approach.* Cambridge, MA: Ballinger, 1977.

Cunningham, H., & Lopreato, S. C. *Energy use and conservation incentives: A study of the southwestern U.S.* New York: Praeger, 1977.

Engler, R. *The politics of oil.* Chicago, IL: University of Chicago Press, 1961.

Erskine, H. The polls: Pollution and its costs. *Public Opinion Quarterly,* 1977, *36,* 120-135.

Gorman, R., & Heitner, K. L. A comparison of costs for automobile energy conservation vs. synthetic fuel production. U.S. Department of Energy, *Conference preprint: Fifth international symposium on automotive propulsion systems* (Conf.-800419, April 1980), 513-540.

Hagevik, G. *Air quality management and land use planning.* New York: Praeger, 1974.

Hass, J. W., Bagley, G. G., & Rogers, R. W. Coping with the energy crisis: effects of fear, appeals upon attitudes toward energy consumption. *Journal of Applied Psychology,* 1975, *60,* 754-756.

Hohenemser, C., Kasperson, R., & Kates, R. The distrust of nuclear power. *Science,* April 1, 1977, 25-34.

Hummel, C. F., Levitt, L., & Loomis, R. J. Perceptions of the energy crisis: Who is blamed and how do citizens react to environment lifestyle trade-offs. *Environment and Behavior,* March 1978, *10,* 37-88.

Kolko, G. *The triumph of conservatism: A reinterpretation of American history, 1900-1916.* New York: Free Press of Glencoe, 1963.

Kraft, J. Annals of industry: The downsizing decision. *The New Yorker,* May 5, 1980, 134-162.

Krier, K., & Ursin, E. *Pollution and policy.* Berkeley, CA: University of California Press, 1977.
Landsberg, H. H. (Study Group Chairman). *Energy: The next twenty years.* Cambridge, MA: Ballinger, 1979.
Lloyd, H. D. *Wealth against commonwealth.* New York: Harper, 1894.
Maderthaner, R., Pahner, P., Guttmann, G. & Otway, H. J. *Perception of technological risks: The effect of confrontation.* Vienna: International Institute of Applied Systems Analysis, RM-76-53, June 1976.
Messing, M., Friesema, H. P., & Morell, D. *Centralized power: The politics of scale in electricity generation.* Cambridge, MA: Oelgeschlager, Gunn & Hain, 1979.
Miles, R. E. Jr. *Awakening from the American dream: The social and political limits to growth.* London: M. Boyers, 1977.
Morrison, B., & Gladhart, P. M. Energy and families: The crisis and the response. *Journal of Home Economics,* January 1968, 15-18.
Murray, J. R., Minor, M. J., Bradburn, N. M., Cotterman, R. F., Frankel, M., & Pisarski, A. E. Evolution of public response to the energy crisis. *Science,* 1974, *184*(4134), 257-263.
Novick, S. *The electric power war: The fight over nuclear power.* San Francisco, CA: Sierra Club Books, 1976.
Ophuls, W. *Ecology and the politics of scarcity.* San Francisco, CA: W. H. Freeman & Co., 1977.
Otway, H. J., & Fishbein, M. *The determinants of attitude formation: An application to nuclear power.* Vienna: International Institute of Applied Systems Analysis, RM-76-80, December 1976.
Pallack, M. S., & Cummings, W. Commitment and voluntary energy conservation. *Personality and Social Psychology,* 1976, *2,* 27-30.
Rodgers, W. *Brown-out: The power crisis in America.* New York: Stein & Day, 1972.
Ross, M., & Williams, R. *Drilling for oil and gas in our buildings.* Report No. 87. Princeton, NJ: Princeton University, Center for Energy and Environmental Studies, July, 1979.
Ross, M., & Williams, R. *Our energy: Regaining control.* New York: McGraw-Hill, 1981.
Sampson, A. *Seven sisters.* New York: Viking, 1975.
Sansom, R. *The new American dream machine: Toward a simpler lifestyle in an environmental age.* Garden City, NY: Anchor/Doubleday, 1976.
Schurr, S. (Project Director). *Energy in America's future: The choices before us.* Baltimore, MD: Johns Hopkins University Press, 1979.
Socolow, R. Failures of discourse. In L. Tribe (ed.), *When values conflict.* Cambridge, MA: Ballinger, 1976, 1-33.
Socolow, R. (Ed.). *Saving energy in the home.* Cambridge, MA: Ballinger, 1978.
Stobaugh, R., & Yergin, D. (Eds.). *Energy future.* New York: Random House, 1979.
Tichenor, P. J., Donohue, C. N., Oben, C. N., & Bowers, J. K. Environment and public opinion. *Journal of Environmental Education,* 1971, *2*(4), 38-42.
Turner, F. J. *The frontier in American history.* New York: H. Holt & Co., 1920.

U.S. Federal Energy Administration. *Energy Reporter*, June 1977, 1.
Williams, R. H. Industrial cogeneration. *Annual Reviews of Energy*, 1978, *3*, 313-356.
Willrich, M. *Administration of energy shortages: Natural gas and petroleum.* Cambridge, MA: Ballinger, 1976.

ABOUT THE EDITOR

RAY C. RIST is currently the Deputy Associate Director, Institute for Program Evaluation, United States General Accounting Office. He has also served as the Associate Director of the National Institute of Education and as a Senior Fulbright Fellow at the Max Planck Institute for Educational Research in Berlin (West), Federal Republic of Germany. Rist has served as a consultant to numerous national and international organizations and has lectured in more than twenty countries. He was a Professor at Cornell University from 1977 to 1981 and now is an Adjunct Professor with the College of Education and Human Development, The George Washington University.

Ray Rist is the author or editor of eleven books and has written more than one hundred articles. His areas of specialization include program evaluation, qualitative research methods, youth unemployment, and migrant groups in Western Europe. Among his most recent books are *Guestworkers in Germany* (1978), *The Invisible Children* (1979), *Confronting Youth Unemployment* (1980), and *Earning and Learning: Youth Employment Policies and Programs* (1981).